Resort Development Handbook

ULI Development Handbook Series

Urban Land Institute

About ULI–the Urban Land Institute

ULI–the Urban Land Institute is a nonprofit education and research institute that is supported and directed by its members. Its mission is to provide responsible leadership in the use of land in order to enhance the total environment.

ULI sponsors educational programs and forums to encourage an open international exchange of ideas and sharing of experience; initiates research that anticipates emerging land use trends and issues and proposes creative solutions based on this research; provides advisory services; and publishes a wide variety of materials to disseminate information on land use and development.

Established in 1936, the Institute today has more than 13,000 members and associates from over 50 countries representing the entire spectrum of the land use and development disciplines. They include developers, builders, property owners, investors, architects, public officials, planners, real estate brokers, appraisers, attorneys, engineers, financiers, academics, students, and librarians. ULI members contribute to higher standards of land use by sharing their knowledge and experience. The Institute has long been recognized as one of America's most respected and widely quoted sources of objective information on urban planning, growth, and development.

Richard M. Rosan
Executive Vice President

For more information about ULI and the resources that it offers related to resort development and a variety of other real estate and urban development issues, visit ULI's Web site at www.uli.org.

Project Staff

Rachelle L. Levitt
Senior Vice President for Research, Education, and Publications

Frank H. Spink, Jr.
Vice President/Publisher

Dean Schwanke
General Editor and
Project Director

D. Scott Middleton
Initial Project Director

Nancy H. Stewart
Managing Editor

Carol E. Soble
Manuscript Editor

Garruba Dennis Konetzka
Designer of Book Series

**Helene Redmond/
HYR Graphics**
Book Design/Layout

Janice Olson
Book Layout, Chapter 6

Kim Rusch
Artist

**Maria-Rose Cain
Joanne Nanez**
Word Processing

Diann Stanley-Austin
Production Manager

Recommended bibliographic listing:

Schwanke, Dean, et al. *Resort Development Handbook*. Washington, D.C.: ULI–the Urban Land Institute, 1997.

ULI Catalog Number: R33
International Standard Book Number: 0-87420-784-3
Library of Congress Catalog Card Number: 97-60271

Copyright ©1997 by ULI–the Urban Land Institute
1025 Thomas Jefferson Street, N.W.
Suite 500 West
Washington, D.C. 20007-5201

**Books in previous series,
Community Builders Handbook Series:**
Business and Industrial Park Development Handbook, 1988
Downtown Development Handbook, Second Edition, 1992
Mixed-Use Development Handbook, 1987
Office Development Handbook, 1982
Residential Development Handbook, Second Edition, 1990
Shopping Center Development Handbook, Second Edition, 1985

Authors

Principal Author and Project Director

Dean Schwanke
ULI–the Urban Land Institute,
Washington, D.C.

**Primary Contributing Author and
Initial Project Director**

D. Scott Middleton
Land Use and Conservation Consultant,
Washington, D.C.

Contributing Authors

Wayne S. Hyatt and **Jo Anne P. Stubblefield**
Hyatt & Stubblefield, P.C.,
Atlanta, Georgia

J. Richard McElyea, Robert Chickering, and
Gene Krekorian
Economics Research Associates,
San Francisco, California

M. Chase Burritt and **Dexter Tom**
E&Y Kenneth Leventhal Real Estate Group,
Coral Gables, Florida

Christine Kaufman
PK Realty Advisors,
Rockville, Maryland

Eric Smart
Bolan Smart Associates, Inc.,
Vienna, Virginia

Patrick Phillips
Economics Research Associates,
Washington, D.C.

Paul O'Mara
CMA Management Consultants,
Vienna, Virginia

Christopher Chaffin and **Kenneth S. Braverman**
ULI–the Urban Land Institute,
Washington, D.C.

Diana B. Permar
Permar & Ravenel, Inc.,
Kiawah Island, South Carolina

Donald W. Y. Goo
Wimberly Allison Tong & Goo,
Honolulu, Hawaii

ULI Advisory Committee

Acknowledgments

The Urban Land Foundation (ULF), as part of its commitment to support ULI's core research program, is providing major funding for the new and revised editions of the ULI Development Handbook Series being published during the last half of this decade. The *Resort Development Handbook* was funded in part by grants from ULF, for which the Urban Land Institute is very grateful.

The preparation of this book involved the time, effort, and cooperation of a great many individuals over the course of many years. Although it is impossible to mention everyone who participated in the project, a number of individuals deserve special thanks.

Acknowledgments are due first to the many contributing authors who gave their expertise in writing sections of the text. D. Scott Middleton, while a director of research for ULI, prepared the history section of Chapter 1 and most of Chapter 7 on trends, and contributed portions of many other sections. He also served as project director for the book during its inception and early stages of development.

Wayne Hyatt and Jo Anne P. Stubblefield of Hyatt & Stubblefield in Atlanta contributed the major sections in Chapter 5 on community management and operation and on club management and operation. J. Richard McElyea, Robert Chickering, and Gene Krekorian of Economics Research Associates in San Francisco contributed the section on financial analysis in Chapter 3, including the detailed spread sheets that are presented there. M. Chase Burritt and Dexter Tom of E&Y Kenneth Leventhal Real Estate Group in Coral Gables, Florida, provided material for the section in Chapter 2 on hotel and guest markets as well as for the section in Chapter 4 on hotel products and design.

Christine Kaufman with PK Realty Advisors in Rockville, Maryland, prepared the initial drafts for many of the case studies as well as a number of the feature boxes throughout the text. Paul O'Mara with CMA Management Consultants in Vienna, Virginia, conducted interviews and wrote drafts for the "Profile and Comments" feature boxes that appear throughout the text, presenting the views of key players in the resort development field.

Eric Smart of Bolan Smart Associates in Washington, D.C., contributed sections on commercial and retail uses in Chapters 2 and 3, and wrote the case study on the Little Nell Hotel. While a senior associate for ULI, he also served as the principal author of ULI's *Recreational Development Handbook*, from which some material has been incorporated into this new book. Patrick Phillips of Economics Research Associates in Washington, D.C., contributed material for the discussion of amenities in Chapter 4. While a senior associate with ULI, he wrote a book for ULI entitled *Developing with Recreational Amenities: Golf, Tennis, Skiing, and Marinas*, which this text draws from in part.

Christopher Chaffin, while a research assistant with ULI, prepared portions of the timeshare sections and the land use planning section, and also acquired many of the photo illustratrations. Kenneth Braverman, while a research associate with ULI, developed several of the project profiles in the text as well as two of the case studies. Finally, Libby Howland, as a consultant to ULI, worked on the various sections of Chapter 4 that cover amenities.

Diana B. Permar of Permar & Ravenel, Inc., in Kiawah Island, South Carolina, contributed material for the section on residential market segments for Chapter 2. Donald W. Y. Goo of the firm Wimberly Allison Tong & Goo in Honolulu, Hawaii, contributed material that serves as the basis for much of the discussion in Chapter 6 on renovation, repositioning, and revitalization.

The text also incorporates materials that were previously published in *Urban Land* magazine or other sources; these sources and authors are cited where appropriate throughout the text.

In addition to the authors, many others contributed to the book in a variety of ways. Special thanks are due to the many development companies providing data and background information for the projects profiled in Chapter 6. These companies are listed at the end of each of the case studies in that chapter. Many others too numerous to mention also provided information on various other projects highlighted throughout the book.

Several architecture and design firms were very helpful in providing photographs, including Design Workshop Inc. in Denver, Colorado; Wimberly Allison Tong & Goo in Honolulu, Hawaii; and Edward D. Stone & Associates in Fort Lauderdale, Florida. Many other developers and architects, too numerous to list, also provided photographs for specific projects.

In addition, several ULI staff and staff consultants were instrumental in getting the book published. Thomas Black and Rachelle Levitt provided the management support necessary to keep the book moving through a long development process. Frank Spink and Nancy Stewart coordinated the editing and production of the book. Carol Soble edited the manuscript. Helene Redmond implemented the book design and prepared the layout. Janice Olson prepared the layout and graphics for Chapter 6. Kim Rusch reworked several site plans for use within the book. Maria-Rose Cain and Joanne Nanez provided word processing support. Ronnie Van Alstyne assisted with administrative and correspondence tasks. Diann Stanley-Austin coordinated the printing and binding with outside firms.

The overall book design guidelines were prepared by Garruba Dennis Konetzka of Washington, D.C., with special credit going to Michael Dennis and Christine Barrera. Christine also did the layout of most of the tables that appear in the book.

Finally, thanks go to the members of the ULI Advisory Committee (listed on page iv) who spearheaded the book's development over many years and provided general guidance as well as insightful reviews that both shaped and enhanced the final product.

Dean Schwanke
Principal Author and Project Director
Resort Development Handbook

Contents

Foreword

This handbook is the first in the completely redesigned ULI Development Handbook Series, a series that traces its roots back to 1947 when ULI published the first edition of the *Community Builders Handbook*. This first ULI handbook was revised and updated several times over the next 25 years, and in 1975 the Community Builders Handbook Series was initiated. This series included a number of titles—beginning with the *Industrial Development Handbook*—published over a period of years on industrial, residential, shopping center, office, mixed-use, downtown, and recreational development. Also included was the *Recreational Development Handbook*, the predecessor of the *Resort Development Handbook*; it has been renamed to reflect its new and narrower focus.

Resort development is a complex field spanning a wide range of real estate products, settings, and recreational activities. It is part and parcel of one of the world's largest industries—travel and tourism. Understanding the complexities and nuances of such a diverse business is a daunting undertaking.

The objective of this handbook, as with all of the handbooks in the ULI Development Handbook Series, is to provide a broad overview of the land use and real estate sector under discussion as well as a guide to the development process. As such, this book presents a comprehensive and lengthy discourse on resort development, including discussions of different resort types, the history of resorts, resort markets and market analysis, feasibility analysis and financing, land use planning and product design, operations and management, and trends and outlook.

Among the strengths of the book is its reliance on a variety of examples and real-world situations. The case study chapter fully documents 13 profiles of resort projects, including multiuse resorts, second-home communities, hotel resorts, and timeshare resorts. Numerous other examples are cited throughout the text or appear in feature boxes. The book also includes profiles of and insights from a variety of industry leaders.

Successful resort development requires expertise in market analysis, human psychology, finance, design, construction, recreation, management, and a host of other fields. Risks often run high, and fortunes have been won and lost. The development process works best when the developer's "dream" is the same dream held by a defined and viable marketplace. Resort developers who build their own untested idea of a wonderful resort often miss the mark. The risks are especially high for large-scale projects and for pioneering projects in remote locations.

Resort development, probably more than most other types of development, can be a highly enjoyable business, as it involves building and developing places in which people will, above all else, enjoy themselves. Creating such a place requires imagination, and succeeding can be rewarding both financially and emotionally. It is hoped this book will help the reader better understand the business and achieve such rewards.

Dean Schwanke
General Editor
ULI Development Handbook Series

Resort Development Handbook

1. Introduction and Background

The topic of resorts and second-home communities encompasses such a wide range of property types, recreational amenities, and natural settings that it makes a general overview necessarily broad. Many of the issues involved in developing a ski resort in Colorado, for example, differ markedly from those involved in planning a second-home golf course community in South Carolina or an oceanfront resort hotel in Hawaii. What resorts and second-home communities have in common, however, is that they serve a common market demand created by three fundamental human desires—the desire for a change of pace, to get away from a familiar environment; the desire to pursue recreational interests and to be stimulated and entertained in the process; and the desire to travel to interesting or attractive places and unusual settings. Different resorts have different appeals as related to these desires, and the priority that individuals and families attach to these desires is the primary determinant in their choice of a resort experience.

Thus, while the various projects discussed in this book encompass widely differing resort concepts and products, they are all similar in that they are direct competitors for vacation and leisure dollars. People can choose to ski one week, play golf the next, and visit the ocean on another occasion, and their choice of accommodations

Amelia Island Plantation in Florida is both an ocean resort and a golf resort, and includes over 2,000 residential units on 1,250 acres of land.

can range from a hotel to a condominium rental to a timeshare to a second home. Upper-income individuals and families often have multiple timeshares and/or leisure homes in a variety of locations; timeshares are frequently exchanged as well, affording the timeshare owner a wide choice of resort and vacation experiences.

Successful resort development requires an understanding of the variety of recreational and resort options available to the consumer. Only by focusing on the big picture can a resort be effectively positioned to tap the market for specific resort products and experiences. Planning, programming, and building the various real estate products that make a specific resort location attractive to a competitive marketplace begins with an understanding of the dynamics of the leisure market and how a particular resort site can position itself to serve that market.

This book provides an overview of the resort marketplace while discussing the processes and strategies—with examples—for developing successful resorts. It focuses on for-profit resort and second-home community development in the United States and, to a lesser extent, in Canada, Mexico, and the Caribbean. It deals primarily with the following types of real estate development projects: resort hotels, timeshare resorts, second-home developments, and multiuse resort communities. To provide as much information as possible about these types of resort projects, the book does not deal specifically with the following types of projects: commercial recreation projects (including theme parks, amusement parks, and miniature golf courses), campgrounds and recreational vehicle parks, not-for-profit projects, and projects located in parts of the world not mentioned above.

The book is intended to function as both a general introduction to resort and second-home development and a general reference. Chapter 1 provides general definitions, historical background, and an overview of the resort development process. Chapter 2 presents a detailed review of resort real estate markets and market analysis. Chapter 3 examines resort programming, feasibility analysis, and financing. Chapter 4 discusses land use planning and product design, and Chapter 5 reviews management and marketing issues. Chapter 6 presents detailed profiles of 13 illustrative resort and second-home development projects while Chapter 7 concludes the book with a summary of the general issues and trends that are likely to affect the development of resort and second-home developments in the near-term future.

The principal purpose of this book is to promote high standards of land use in resort and second-home developments. As such, the book addresses four general groups of readers, each of which has an important role in making land use decisions:

- Developers and Investors—those who make financial and business decisions about the location, design, and operation of resort real estate ventures;

Carambola, St. Croix, United States Virgin Islands, is a destination resort located on an isolated site with a dramatic coastline. The resort draws visitors from great distances because of its spectacular setting and ideal climate.

- Development Consultants—those who provide consulting services to resort developers or owners. Such consultants include planners, architects, landscape architects, golf course architects, engineers, attorneys, amenity operators, and feasibility, marketing, and management advisers;
- Public Sector—legislators and public officials, including representatives of planning, economic development, and redevelopment agencies, who set and carry out local, state, and national land use and development policies; and
- The Public—citizens' groups and individuals concerned about growth and development in their communities and the effects of growth on the environment.

Definitions and Resort Types

The word "resort" is used widely and diversely and often means different things to different people. For some, an entire city—such as Aspen, Colorado; Naples, Florida; or Ocean City, Maryland—is a resort. For others, a resort is a second-home golf course community in South Carolina, a hotel on the beach in Hawaii, or a ski facility in Utah. Resorts as discussed in this book encompass many of these meanings, but a more precise definition is required. Resorts as discussed in this book reflect three primary characteristics as follows:

- They are real estate developments that have been developed and planned and are currently operated by a private business enterprise.
- They offer proximity and easy access to significant natural, scenic, recreational, and/or cultural amenities that make them attractive places to visit.
- They include lodging accommodations, timeshare ownerships, and/or residences used largely by tourists, vacationers, weekend travelers, seasonal residents, and/or owners or users of second homes.

Resorts can be categorized along three major dimensions: by their proximity to their primary markets, by their setting and primary amenities, and by their mix of residential and lodging products. In general, resorts often do not fall discretely into any one category, but for discussion purposes, the book treats them as relatively discrete.

Resorts can also be classified by their quality, pricing structure, and overall appeal to different income groups; according to this system, there are budget resorts, mid-priced resorts, and luxury resorts as well as a host of products in between. These quality and pricing distinctions are not treated separately here but rather are discussed within the schema outlined below.

Resort Types by Proximity to Primary Market

Some resorts are described as "destination resorts." While nearly all resorts are located at a "destination"

The Governor's Land at Two Rivers in Williamsburg, Virginia, is a 1,444-acre recreational community set at the confluence of two rivers—the James and the Chickahominy. The community features a golf course and a marina.

some distance from the primary residence of the resort user, five significant characteristics distinguish "destination" from "nondestination" resorts: the proximity of the resort to its primary market, the means by which the resort user reaches the resort, the frequency with which a user patronizes the resort, the typical length of stay, and the quality of the resort setting.

In short, destination resorts tend to be a considerable distance from their primary markets, usually several hundred miles or more. Users travel to destination resorts by air rather than by car and tend to visit infrequently, usually once a year or less and often only once. Users tend to book relatively long stays, often for one- or two-week vacation visits. Destinations tend to be located in dramatic or particularly attractive locations—places that can lure the resort user to make an extra effort to get there. Many resorts in Hawaii (see case study on page 296), Mexico, and the Caribbean are typically referred to as destination resorts.

Nondestination or regional resorts, on the other hand, are often located within a two- to three-hour trip of their primary market and are not positioned or marketed to attract visitors from farther away. Users generally travel to nondestination resorts by car, although some may rely on commuter air services. Users visit the same resort frequently, as many as 15 to 20 times per year or more. Nondestination resorts often book short stays, frequently for weekend users and the four-day vacation market. Many resorts within a three-hour drive of major metropolitan areas in the Northeast and Midwest (see case studies on pages 304 and 312) provide examples of regional resorts.

The byproduct of these distinctions is that destination resorts generally tend to have a higher ratio of hotel rooms to second homes, whereas the reverse is true for regional resorts. Destination resorts also tend to be more upscale and expensive than regional resorts.

With these distinctions, it is important to keep in mind that several resorts cater somewhat equally to both destination and regional markets. Ski resorts near Denver and Salt Lake City, for example, draw heavily on drive-in visitors from these metropolitan areas as well as on visitors who fly in to use the resorts. The better golf resorts in northern California cater even more equally to both local markets and destination resort markets. Moreover, many destination resort areas, such as southeast Florida, Palm Springs, Scottsdale, and Las Vegas, also claim a substantial in-place retirement population that distinguishes them from other more purely destination resorts, such as those in the Caribbean.

Resort Types by Setting/Amenity Mix

Resorts and resort communities are usually thought of by resort users—the market—in terms of their setting and the primary recreational amenities they provide. Resort names often reflect the sites' natural features (bay, beach, creek, desert, forest, grove, island, lake, mountain, ranch, river, spring, valley, etc.) and/or their primary recreational amenities (club, golf, spa, tennis, trails, etc.). Since people are typically motivated to visit and purchase real estate in resort and second-home communities by a desire to find opportunities for rest, relaxation, recreation, and social interaction, the character and quality of the natural environment and the recreational amenities offered by the facility are an important factor for the resort's success in the marketplace. In terms of the setting/amenity mix, there are four primary resort categories—ocean resorts, lake/river resorts, mountain/ski resorts, and golf resorts—and several secondary categories, all of which are outlined below.

Ocean Resorts. The nature of an ocean resort can vary considerably depending on the nature of the oceanfront location and the variety of other amenities provided. To varying degrees, ocean resorts rely on the quality and

Vail is a ski and mountain resort in Colorado that has helped pioneer the four-season resort concept.

extent of their beaches, the quality of the views, the quality of the climate, and the watersports activities that the ocean affords. These are all affected by the nature of the ocean/land interface, which can be characterized as a bay, barrier island, isolated ocean island, inland waterway fed by the ocean, gulf, etc. Ocean resorts in areas such as Florida, the Caribbean, and Hawaii are frequently positioned as destination resorts reached by air, as they appeal to seasonal visitors who may be located some distance from the ocean, often in colder climates. Ocean resorts in the northeastern United States cater more to weekend users and the second-home market.

Lake/River Resorts. Lake/river resorts are similar to ocean resorts in that they are water-oriented, but they often rely more on the recreational activities associated with water, especially boating and fishing, and less on beaches and views. They are frequently positioned as second-home communities, often within a three-hour drive of a major city, rather than as destination resorts reached by air. They are usually more modest in scale and quality than ocean resorts.

Mountain/Ski Resorts. While skiing has traditionally been the primary draw for these resorts, mountain resorts have increasingly been capitalizing on their setting and are now at the forefront in pioneering the four-season resort concept. More and more, they are diversifying their amenity package to attract visitors throughout the year. In fact, many mountain resorts were founded as spas, drawing on their setting and surrounding springs to establish themselves as places to foster good health or help cure the ailing. Mountain resorts in the western United States tend to be destination resorts while those in the Northeast and Midwest are generally more regional in orientation.

Golf Resorts. While golf is an important component of many resort types, including those already mentioned, some golf resorts rely primarily on golf as a recreational amenity to attract visitors. With the dramatic increase in demand for golf and golf courses of all types over the last decade, the number of golf resorts has grown substantially. The use of golf as the primary amenity in a resort is a function of this growth, but it also reflects the fact that waterfront sites available for new resort development, the generally preferred location for a resort, are increasingly hard to find. As a result, golf resorts and second-home golf communities have been a major force in states such as Florida, North Carolina, and South Carolina, which have largely exhausted their supply of suitable oceanfront property for new resort development and must therefore use inland areas for continued growth (see feature box on page 158). Golf resorts and communities are also highly popular in desert settings in Arizona, Las Vegas, and the Palm Springs area of California, which have little water for resort development and instead rely on scenery, climate, and golf to draw resort users.

Some resorts are primarily golf resorts even though they occupy waterfront locations. Pebble Beach and the adjacent Spanish Bay Resort are both well-known golf resorts and are top international destinations for golfers, but they are ocean resorts as well. In these examples, beaches are not the draw because of rocky coastlines and generally frigid water temperatures. Instead, golf courses have been sited along the coastline to create a dramatic setting for the golf experience.

Other Setting/Amenity Mixes. Other popular mixes of settings/amenities and themes are numerous, including those with active recreation and health orientations and those with entertainment, cultural, and amusement orientations. Tennis resorts cater primarily to tennis players and may offer extensive instruction programs. Most tennis facilities in resorts are combined with other amenities, but some resorts cater primarily to tennis players. Equestrian communities attract primary- and second-home owners who wish to board horses or enjoy horseback riding. Ranch resorts provide vacation experiences for those who wish to ride horses and/or experience Old West traditions. Health resorts and spas offer health-related services and invigorating programs to help visitors lose weight, relieve ailments, develop healthful habits, or simply pamper themselves. Natural-attraction resorts provide accommodations for visitors wishing to experience nearby landscapes and attractions such as national parks, waterfalls, unique rock formations, etc. Sporting expedition lodges—specializing in activities such as fishing, hunting, diving, climbing, etc.—provide accommodations and/or outfitter/guide services for a variety of specialized, nature-based recreational activities.

Entertainment, cultural, and amusement-oriented resorts come in several varieties. Theme park resorts provide vacation and resort experiences related to theme and amusement parks (e.g., the various Disney resort products around Disney World). Historic attraction and heritage resorts provide resort services that focus on historic sites and towns or landscapes with a unique heritage; examples include resort hotels and communities surrounding the Williamsburg and Jamestown areas of Virginia, where colonial history and culture is the attraction; around Santa Fe, New Mexico, where western and Native American history and culture is the attraction; and in the Napa Valley of California, where wineries and agriculture are the attraction. Cultural and music-oriented resorts provide access to cultural and music attractions; the tremendous growth in resort products around Branson, Missouri, and its country music venues is a prime example of this phenomenon. Casino resorts provide not only casinos for gaming enthusiasts but also live music and other entertainment and amusement opportunities. Urban resorts provide vacation accommodations for those seeking urban vacation experiences usually associated with nearby cultural, entertainment, and shopping facilities.

Many of these specialized resorts involve amenities that are not part of the resort property. As such, many resorts are simply lodging facilities that cater to vacationers visiting the surrounding attractions; in fact, some of the above resort types can be noticeably small. Nonetheless, they are resort products that compete for dollars spent for vacation experiences and thus must be kept in mind when assessing the resort market and the dollars available for tourism and leisure.

Resort Types by Residential/Lodging Types and Mixes

From a real estate point of view, resorts are often categorized in terms of the type, extent, and mix of the residential and lodging facilities they offer. From a de-

veloper's perspective, the extent and mix of the housing and lodging on a property is critical for three reasons. First, housing and lodging accommodations are the major sources of revenue for the property. Second, planning for the development of accommodations consumes most of the developer's time. Third, housing and lodging are essential to defining the nature and positioning of the resort.

Based on this approach, three major real estate product types are marketed in resort properties. Generally, the products can be distinguished by the level of financial commitment required from the guest or user. Hotels require only a relatively modest financial commitment, usually from $50 to $400 per night. Timeshares and other vacation ownership products require a modest investment, usually a one-time cash investment of $5,000 to $100,000 depending on the value of the property and the use rights assigned to the share. Second homes require a major financial investment similar to a primary home, anywhere from $50,000 to $500,000 or more.

Each of these three products can be a freestanding resort property in itself or combined in some fashion to create a fourth type of resort—a multiuse resort community. Thus, reliance on the residential/lodging type and mix approach gives rise to four major types of resorts—the resort hotel, the timeshare resort, the second-home community, and the multiuse resort community; each is discussed in greater detail below. Much

Kingsmill Resort and Conference Center, a 2,900-acre residential and resort community in Virginia, is sited close to the historic sites around Williamsburg and Busch Gardens. The resort was developed by Busch Properties.

of this book focuses on the development of multiuse resort communities, as they encompass all of the development issues involved in the development of the various resort components as well as a variety of larger issues that make multiuse resorts an exceedingly complex development type.

Resort Hotels. Resort hotels are by far the most common type of resort property. The accommodations in these facilities range from very modest and/or rustic facilities, such as tent cabins, to luxury resort suites with all the comforts of home and more.

The differences between a resort hotel and a traditional, or commercial, hotel can be described in terms of the guests' purpose in staying at the facility. The guest at a resort hotel typically visits for relaxation or recreation, whereas the guest at the commercial hotel typically visits to satisfy a need for convenience. Increasingly, however, resort hotels are catering to commercial guests, especially conferees during off-season periods, while traditional hotels are catering to leisure travelers, particularly during weekends and holiday periods.

Resort hotels and lodging facilities generally differ dramatically from most commercial hotels in terms of their setting and level of amenities. Whereas a typical commercial hotel is set on a fairly small site in a downtown or along a suburban highway, a resort hotel or lodge is often located on a fairly large site away from unrelated commercial activity and highways; room accommodations in resort hotels are often carefully positioned within attractive settings, frequently offering exceptional views of and/or access to the natural surroundings.

Traditional hotel amenities are typically limited to an exercise room, a small pool, and the concierge's ability to arrange off-site activities. Resort hotels and lodges often include extensive on-site amenities, including large swimming pools, tennis courts, boating and watersports facilities, equestrian facilities, gardens and landscaped courtyards, golf courses, and a wide range of other amenities, including the hotels' own ski slopes. Golf, in particular, accounts for the success of resorts in attracting business meetings, an increasingly important source of revenue. Resort hotels are often set within larger resort communities, allowing them to offer access to a range of amenities included in the community, such as beaches, parks, amusement facilities, retail services, etc.

Resort hotels can be classified in several ways. One broad classification divides them into two categories: hotel resorts—large, often self-sufficient hotel properties that include major on-site amenities such as tennis courts, golf course(s), large swimming pools, retail operations, and numerous restaurants; and resort lodging facilities—smaller hotels that do not include major amenities but are located near off-site amenities and attractions. The former category—hotel resorts—often includes projects that begin to take on the characteristics of multiuse resorts. For example, the Spanish Bay Resort is known primarily for its resort hotel—the Inn at Spanish Bay—and its golf course, but the resort plan also includes 80 condominium units, of which more

than 40 have been built (see case study on page 352). Similarly, the Arizona Biltmore includes plans for 78 condominium units, of which over 40 have been built (see case study on page 346). In both cases, the units are generally available as rentals (managed by the hotel) when they are not occupied by their owners.

Hotel resorts and resort lodging facilities can also be classified as destination and regional facilities and in accordance with setting and amenity mix, all described in previous sections. Moreover, like commercial hotels, facilities are also frequently classified as economy, mid-priced, or luxury properties and by their overall quality—which is assessed by travel services such as Mobil and the American Automobile Association (AAA) that assign star or diamond ratings on a five-point scale. Invariably, the quality ratings are directly reflected in room rates and the overall pricing of resort services. In addition, facilities can be classified as conference- and nonconference-oriented hotels.

This section of the book generally refers to hotel resorts and resort lodging facilities as hospitality facilities, but the numerous names given to such facilities need to be understood as well, including terms and types such as resort motels, guesthouses, bed and breakfasts, lodges, boutique resort hotels, and megaresort hotels. These are explained below.

Perhaps the simplest way to classify and think about hotel resorts and lodging facilities is by their size. Hospitality facilities can range in size from less than five rooms to 1,500 rooms or more. The small end of the spectrum—hospitality facilities under 25 rooms—accounts for lodging types such as guesthouses, bed and breakfasts (B&Bs), country inns, guest ranches, fishing and hunting cabin rentals, and small motels. Resort motels are usually small, low-amenity facilities that cater to low-budget automobile travelers. Guesthouses, B&Bs, and country inns are usually located in rural areas and cater to the weekend traveler and short-stay guests. They are often older facilities, sometimes converted mansions or farmhouses.

These small lodging facilities are usually independently owned and operated, often by families, and are not a major concern of large resort developers and operators. In some cases, however, these types of facilities can be a part of a larger resort property. For example, the Wintergreen resort in Virginia includes a bed-and-breakfast lodging facility for those who prefer this type of accommodation. Some second-home communities also provide a small, often temporary lodging facility on site to accommodate prospective buyers.

Hospitality facilities in the 25- to 125-room range can include some of the previously mentioned types but may also include small specialty hotels in resort markets. Resort lodges, for example, often fall into this size range; lodges are typically rustically designed hospitality facilities in a mountain or rural setting that include restaurant services as well as an extensive lobby and comfortable sitting areas where guests can congregate. Lodges often cater to skiers, hunters, and hikers. While the term

Marriott's Desert Springs Resort and Spa is a large resort hotel that includes 884 guest rooms, 51 suites, 36 holes of golf, five swimming pools, 20 tennis courts, a 30,000-square-foot spa, and 51,000 square feet of meeting space.

Photo courtesy of Marriott Creative Services

"lodge" is used loosely to name hotels that do not necessarily fit this description, the concept remains useful.

Several market observers have noted the relatively recent emergence of boutique resort hotels, a special category of small resort hotel that focuses on service, quality, and privacy for a select type of highly discriminating guest, typically upscale individual travelers and attendees of small business meetings. Examples include the Ventana Inn in Big Sur, California; Robert Redford's Sundance Lodge in Utah; Jumby Bay on Antigua; and the Salish Lodge in Washington state (see feature box on page 192). This type of resort hotel usually has between 50 and 100 rooms, provides limited shopping and dining facilities, does not usually provide access to a golf course, and is generally not part of a multiuse resort community, although it certainly can be accommodated in such a community (see case study on page 362). Boutique resort hotels do not try to provide "everything to everyone" but rather promote a mystique and market niche.[1] The facilities are often located in extraordinary but sensitive settings that are not suitable for larger hotels. The 59-room Ventana Inn in Big Sur, for example, is located in a setting that provides exquisite views of the California coastline, but it took six years for the developer to obtain the permits required to expand the existing 24-room facility to 59 rooms on this high-profile site. Health spa resorts are also typically sized in this range.

Resort hotels in the 125- to 400-room range are usually chain-affiliated hotels located in major resort areas. They range from low- to mid- to high-rise facilities that offer restaurant services, conference facilities, and their own recreational amenities. While these facilities are sometimes similar in construction to commercial hotels, their design is usually markedly different. Mid- and high-rise resort hotels invariably include balconies, for example, and rooms are often larger and incorporate more room amenities, reflecting the fact that guests in these hotels represent a higher percentage of couples and

families that frequently stay longer and spend more time in their room than guests in commercial hotels. These resort hotels, even when they use concrete or steel-frame construction, are generally designed to be more horizontal than vertical. They are also often made up of several buildings, including low-rise structures with walkout units. This allows the hotel to offer a variety of room options that appeal to a range of guests seeking different experiences. A honeymooning couple, a conference attendee, and a family require different room types and settings, which a large resort hotel tries to provide. The Spanish Bay Resort, with 270 rooms, is an example of a luxury hotel that fits into this category (see case study on page 352).

Resort hotels with more than 400 rooms are generally found only in prime resort locations that offer major amenity attractions, such as prime beach frontage (as in Florida, the Caribbean, and Hawaii), prime ski facilities (as in Colorado or Utah), a major theme park or parks (such as those around Orlando), major gaming facilities (such as those in Las Vegas), or a prime golf course (as in Arizona or Palm Springs). Among the case studies in this book, the Arizona Biltmore provides a useful example of a large resort hotel (see case study on page 346). The Boca Raton Resort & Club is an even larger example with 963 rooms; however, it was much smaller when it opened in the 1920s and has grown over time to become a major hotel resort (see case study on page 340). Another early example of a large resort hotel is the Fontainbleau in Miami Beach, which includes over 1,600 rooms.

Some of the more recent versions of these hotel resorts, which became popular in the mid-1980s, are referred to as megaresorts or fantasy hotels. Generally in the 800- to 2,000-room range, these large-scale hotel resorts combine lodging, meeting facilities, and an extensive array of amenities and activities, many with fantasy themes. Examples include the Hyatt Regency Waikoloa and Kauai Lagoons resorts in Hawaii and the Walt Disney

Disney's Vero Beach Resort, Florida, is one of four Disney vacation ownership projects—offered in the Disney Vacation Club—that are interchangeable. The resort features a 115-room inn and 60 vacation villas. Disney Vacation Club members can also exchange points with Interval International and the Buena Vista Trading Company to have access to over 100 locations around the world.

Photo courtesy of Walt Disney Co.

World Dolphin and Swan Hotels and the Grand Cypress Hotel in Orlando, Florida.

Capital and operating costs are extremely high for these hotels, which not surprisingly require high room rates and occupancies throughout the year. While the Orlando resorts have tapped a strong year-round market, those in Hawaii have not been as successful of late. Despite their attraction, the long-range viability of the more elaborate of these resorts is in question.[2] Typically, this type of resort hotel is not incorporated into a multi-use resort community.

Timeshare and Vacation Ownership Resorts. Timeshare and vacation ownership resorts provide accommodations that share features with both resort hotels and resort condominium properties but differ significantly from both in terms of their design and their buyer/user profile. Timesharing is a type of shared ownership in which the buyer purchases the right to use a residential dwelling unit for a portion of the year. Traditionally, the timeshare has been sold as a specific time period—typically equivalent to a specified one- or two-week period per year—in a specific unit, but more flexible programs are now much more prevalent in the industry. Timeshares may also include longer time periods known as fractionals that vary from one month to one-quarter of a year.

Timeshare resorts closely resemble resort hotels in that they require extensive daily on-site management, including regular maintenance and cleaning services, as visitors to the properties generally book short stays. Timeshare resorts also usually include extensive on-site amenities—such as swimming pools, golf courses, and/ or tennis facilities—similar to a resort hotel. Timeshares are like resort condominiums in that the units usually include multiple rooms—typically living, kitchen, and bedroom areas—and thus are generally larger than hotel rooms. Timeshare projects can be configured in a variety of physical layouts, from a single high-rise structure to multiple low-rise buildings.

The primary marketing advantage of timeshares as compared to more traditional second homes is affordability. With timeshares, owners enjoy the benefits of a unit that is similar to a resort condominium, though without the financial burden of purchasing the unit. Prices for new timeshares may range from $5,000 to over $100,000, although the average price for a short interval in a two-bedroom unit is roughly $10,000.

A second major marketing advantage of a timeshare is the trade-in service. A timeshare owner of an interval in South Carolina can exchange his or her interval for a similar interval in France or Mexico, thus allowing the timeshare owner to change or vary his or her vacation experience without selling his or her property. In the United States, 870 timeshare projects (with more than five units) are affiliated with one of the two major timeshare exchange companies—Resort Condominiums International (RCI), based in Indianapolis, and Interval International (II), based in Miami. Sharing over 45,633 units with an average of 52 units per project, RCI and II facilitate trade-in services, which permit members of an affiliated timeshare to trade their rights for another timeshare of equivalent value at another location for an annual membership assessment of about $70. The time purchased has averaged about 1.4 weeks.

The timeshare industry has evolved in the past 20 years to create a myriad of timeshare product strategies. Timesharing and vacation ownership programs range from traditional structures, where owners are limited to the use of the same unit for exactly the same period each year, to highly flexible point-based structures, where owners can select from a range of unit types, time periods or lengths of time, and other travel/vacation opportunities.

Even the timeshare name itself has undergone change. At this writing, industry leaders are still struggling to reach consensus on industry terminology, using both "timesharing" and "vacation ownership." The latter has been gaining ground in recent years, though this book uses the terms "timesharing" and "vacation ownership" interchangeably. More specific terms used to describe various alternative types of timeshare products include club ownership, interval ownership, fractional ownership (including monthly, tenth shares, and quarter shares), right-to-use, nonequity clubs, shared ownership, deeded ownership, nonproprietary clubs, undivided interest clubs (UDIs), vacation point clubs, and vacation clubs. Most of these timeshare products may be considered examples of either the fee-simple timeshare or "right to use" vacation ownership product. The differences between the two systems—and the various timeshare products mentioned here—are clarified in the history of the timeshare industry and explored further in Chapter 4.

Vacation clubs and the concept of selling vacation points has grown tremendously in recent years, and many industry leaders acknowledge that it is the most significant emerging trend in the timeshare industry. The vacation owner uses points like currency to design a vacation according to length of stay, size of unit, season, and even types of services desired. In general, the timeshare industry is moving toward more flexible programs that allow purchasers to vary their vacation by time of year, length of stay, and location.

Second-Home Developments. A second-home development is a special type of resort project that is substantially made up of second homes but does not include a

Forest Highlands, outside Flagstaff, Arizona, is a medium-sized, golf-oriented second-home community that is planned for 655 single-family homes on a 657-acre site.

resort hotel. Technically, a second home is defined as a home that is owned fee simple by an individual or family that also owns or rents another home as a primary residence. A second home may in fact be a third or fourth home, one of many "second" homes that an individual or family may own. Second homes are sometimes also referred to as seasonal homes, weekend homes, or vacation homes, depending on how they are used by the owner.

In reality, some individuals—especially retirees, independent executives, and those with independent means—often use two or more homes equally; they may reside in several homes, none of which is necessarily primary. Thus, another way to define a second home more broadly is a home owned by an individual or family that resides in the home as well as in at least one other home for substantial parts of the year.

Second homes need not be located in resort areas, but most second-home *developments* are. Many second homes are located in major urban areas—such as New York, Los Angeles, San Francisco, and Paris—but seldom is a project developed principally for second-home owners in these locations (although there are now examples of timeshare projects under development in urban areas).

Second-home developments may consist of or include detached, attached, and/or multifamily properties. Wherever they are located, attached and multifamily resort units are more likely to be marketed and sold as second homes with income potential and thus tend to be placed in a rental pool operation. Single-family detached homes are more likely to be sold to second-home users who do not expect to rent extensively, although many detached-home communities may include homes available for rent through real estate agents or rental agencies.

Primary and/or retirement homes may be incorporated into second-home developments as well, and some are actually hybrids that include primary homes, second homes, and retirement homes. A large number of hybrid

The Resort at Semiahmoo, Washington, is a destination resort offering second homes to a Pacific Rim international market. While enjoying the prestige of a destination resort, Semiahmoo also is less than two hours from Seattle and Vancouver, making it an ideal location for weekend homes.

communities are located within or near major metropolitan areas in states that are well-established retirement-
home and second-home locations, such as the Miami
region in Florida, the Phoenix region in Arizona, and
the Palm Springs region in California. Second-home
communities may also shift their mix and status over
time. For example, a community might start out as a
second-home community and later evolve into a retirement community; some second-home communities
near major urban areas have evolved into primary-
home communities.

Four basic types of second-home developments predominate. The first type is the resort condominium, such
as the high-rise residential buildings typically found in
oceanfront areas such as Miami Beach or Ocean City,
Maryland. The second type is the small, low-density residential community that relies on an adjacent or nearby
amenity such as a beach or lake to draw its market. Seaside, located on the ocean in the panhandle of Florida,
as it is built out today is an example of this type of resort, although a hotel is planned (see case study on
page 334). Dewees Island in South Carolina is another
example (see case study on page 320). The third type
is a single-family development that incorporates a golf
course and/or country club. Forest Highlands in Flagstaff, Arizona, for example, is a mid-sized golf-oriented
second-home community that is planned for 655 single-
family homes on a 657-acre site (see case study on page
328). And fourth is a large planned community that incorporates a variety of housing types with several major
amenities, usually including a golf course; Harbour
Ridge in Florida is an 885-acre second-home community that offers both single-family homes and garden
apartments as well as two golf courses, all located on
an oceanfront site.

The site size of second-home development projects
may range from several acres to several hundred acres
and from a handful of units to many thousand. The size
of the second-home case study developments in this book
ranges from 80 acres (Seaside) to 1,205 acres (Dewees
Island) and from 137 residential units (Dewees
Island) to 642 units (Forest Highlands). Densities can also vary
greatly. Dewees Island is developed at a gross density of
0.1 units per acre while Seaside is developed at a gross
density of about nine units per acre. Moreover, projects
may involve either a land developer who also builds
homes or a master developer who sells lots to homebuyers and/or homebuilders.

Even though developers of second homes and second-
home communities do not reinvent the wheel when it
comes to homebuilding and residential development,
housing units developed in second-home developments
and housing units developed in primary-home communities evidence significant differences. While Chapter 4
outlines these differences in great detail, suffice it to say
that the design of second homes generally differs in the
following ways: homes place greater emphasis on outdoor living areas, they are often developed at lower
gross and net densities than primary homes, and their
architecture tends to be less formal than that associated
with primary homes. Housing styles vary greatly, however, depending on region of the country, target market, and developer and designer preferences.

Revenues in second-home projects can be derived from
the sale and/or operation of a wide variety of residential
products, recreational amenities, and club memberships.
While the residential products are the most important
source of revenue for a second-home community, the
right to use a community's recreational amenities, such
as a golf course, is often sold separately from the residential real estate products either through equity or
nonequity club memberships or fees. The amenity may
also be sold to a separate amenity operator.

Second-home communities can also be distinguished
from resort hotels, timeshare resorts, and multiuse resort communities through their long-term management
arrangements. A community association rather than a
developer or resort operator invariably assumes management responsibility for a second-home community.
Nonetheless, either the developer or a resort operator
may be involved in the management of certain elements
of the community, such as a golf course or marina, but
in many cases the developer's interest in the property
ceases entirely once the project is built and sold out. In
such cases, community associations can undertake the
management of the amenity program, although a club
structure may also be put in place to do so. These issues
are discussed in greater detail in Chapter 5, which deals
with management issues.

Multiuse Resort Communities. A multiuse resort community is a special type of resort that combines several
of the resort property types already discussed. In addition to offering numerous amenities, a multiuse resort
community is positioned to offer a mix and range of
both ownership and transient housing facilities.

Multiuse resort communities can range widely in both
size and mix of residential and lodging facilities, but the
classic examples are large-scale projects on sites of 500
acres or more that include a full range of housing types
and hotel accommodations. For example, of the five
multiuse resort case studies featured in this book, the
sites range from 514 acres at the Homestead in Michigan to 10,000 acres at Kiawah Island in South Carolina.
In terms of offering a full range of real estate products,
perhaps the singularly classic example among the case
studies is Beaver Creek in Colorado, a large-scale, 2,777-
acre mountain resort community that is planned to include 204 detached homes, 1,187 condominiums/town-
houses, 221 timeshare units, and 471 hotel rooms (see
case study on page 286). Sea Pines, a pioneering multiuse resort in South Carolina, is another example of a
diversified multiuse resort (see feature box on page 15).

Multiuse resort communities also vary greatly in terms
of the nature and density of their residential and lodging facilities. Some may incorporate predominantly
mid- and high-rise housing and lodging facilities as with
Beaver Creek; others largely feature low-rise facilities
as with Kapalua (see case study on page 296). More fre-

The Peninsula, located on Lake Norman, North Carolina, is a country club community with golf, tennis, and water facilities and a 35,000-square-foot clubhouse.

Beaver Creek is a multiuse mountain resort community that includes 471 hotel rooms, 221 timeshare units, 1,187 condominiums and townhouses, and 204 single-family homes.

Jane Lidz

In the last decade, the term "mixed-use" or "multiuse resort" has entered the vocabulary of an increasing number of resort developers. Where vacation resort properties once tended to emerge as single-purpose entities developed with one exclusive form of ownership or use, many developers now appeal to a broad range of potential visitors and owners by building multiuse resorts that accommodate all types of vacation properties within the confines of a large resort. In their wake, the giants of the vacation resort property industry have created exciting new opportunities as well as equally challenging difficulties for the companies involved in designing, building, managing, and marketing these megadevelopments.

"The essential advantage of the multiuse resort is ultimately in having a whole that is greater than the sum of the parts," explains Richard Hulbert, principal architect and planner for the Vancouver, British Columbia-based Hulbert Group International, Inc. A veteran of multiuse development projects in North America, Asia, Europe, and Australia, Hulbert says that when done right, multiuse developments offer great opportunity. Where a lot of developers have gone wrong in the past is in failing to understand that for this approach to work, each part of the development must stand on its own, Hulbert remarks. "Too often, it's assumed that a use that will not succeed on its own will suddenly work in a mixed-use resort."

In Hulbert's view, the increasing sophistication of resort goers drives the need for more sophisticated resort properties offering a wide range of vacation amenities and ownership opportunities. Indeed, developers of multiuse projects can make more money than developers of single-use resorts. But a larger, more complicated resort can just as easily misfunction and leave developers worse off than if they had concentrated on creating smaller, single-use projects that are more easily built, managed, and marketed.

From a developer's standpoint, building a multiuse project poses daunting challenges. By definition, these developments tend to be much larger than single-purpose resorts. Accordingly, they require more upfront capital for planning, land acquisition, infrastructure, and property construction expenses. One solution, says Bill Byrne, president of the Byrne Corporation in Big Canoe, Georgia, and developer of properties there and in Hilton Head, South Carolina, is to start with a small mixed-use or single-purpose facility and expand as the demand for additional properties allows.

Byrne argues, "It's only logical to start with one or two product offerings that you are comfortable with and then, as they mature and you see that you're on the right track, you branch out more and add others as time goes on. Not many developers have pockets deep enough to manage developing all these different uses at once."

Deciding which path a new resort should follow is always difficult. Multiuse properties offer customer diversity, deeper market penetration, and some marketing advantages and economies of scale in their operation, but these benefits must be balanced against higher upfront development costs and enormous management challenges. Some developers with broad experience in the field see industry trends swinging away from large, complex projects and back to single-purpose resorts.

One primary factor is cost. While it is still possible to buy the thousands of acres needed to build a comprehensive, multiuse resort in more remote, underdeveloped areas, it is virtually impossible to afford that much land in an existing destination resort area. Building in a remote area means marketing aggressively to attract visitors to the area, thereby adding another cost to an already expensive proposition. Building smaller projects, which can still include either timeshare and other short-term residency properties or fractionals as well as full-ownership homesites, "offers a better return on investment," according to Paul Masarrachio, former corporate vice president of marketing for Fairfield Communities, Inc., a firm based in Little Rock, Arkansas, that owns and manages 14 resorts, including several multiuse developments.

Source: Adapted from David McCarty, "Mixed-Use Resorts: Opportunities and Challenges," *Urban Land*, August 1995, pp. 30–33, 80.

Aerial Ventures Incorporated

Pelican Bay is a 2,104-acre multiuse resort community in Naples, Florida, that has been approved for 600 single-family and 8,000 multifamily residential units, 1,336 hotel rooms, and 1.1 million square feet of office/commercial space.

A surprisingly large number of today's planning and marketing ideas in recreational development can be traced directly to Sea Pines. If these ideas were not invented by Sea Pines, they were popularized by it while the evolving resort was nurturing many of today's resort developers.

In 1957, a young Charles Fraser, fresh out of Yale Law School with a headful of rash ideas, acquired from his father 5,200 acres of oceanfront forest on subtropical Hilton Head Island, South Carolina. Fraser immediately commissioned a land plan by Hideo Sasaki. The revolutionary land plan was the first such effort to win a coveted American Institute of Architects award. And the rest is history.

The list of innovations arising out of Sea Pines would fill a book. A few of the development's notable contributions to the art of resort development follow:

- siting the main access road in the interior parallel to the ocean, with feeder roads connected to homesite-lined culs-de-sac leading toward the ocean; placing 50-foot-wide walkways on both sides of each subdivision to permit residents to walk to the beach without crossing a street and to provide view, breeze, and underground power/water easements;
- requiring approval to cut down any tree more than six inches in diameter; establishing a forest preserve in the middle of the development; and preserving and enhancing ruins such as the 2,000-year-old Native American shell artifacts found at Sea Pines and an 1805 plantation house;
- setting aside one-quarter of the 5,200 acres as a nature preserve, complete with interpretive trails and observation areas;
- giving roads a rural feel by not installing curbs or gutters;
- establishing extensive architectural restrictions and covenants down to such details as no visible clotheslines or garbage cans, encouraging the architectural use of wood and brick, and setting a building height limit not to exceed the tree line (about 40 feet high along the ocean);
- using wood for signage to blend into the surroundings;
- relying more on public relations than on advertising. At Sea Pines, a low-key sales firm featured the area's natural attributes and history; sales materials highlighted publicity quotes; and outdoor displays featured panels showing the site's history and planning. Daily history/nature tours introduced prospects to the real estate, and the developer hosted parties to mix residents with prospects; and
- using resort rather than real estate advertising to draw prospects. Sea Pines was used as a marketing tool. Sports and cultural events were held to draw

The Harbour Town area of Sea Pines.

potential buyers to Hilton Head Island. As the resort matured, major televised sports events—such as the Heritage Classic golf tournament and *Family Circle* tennis tournament—promoted the island and Sea Pines to a national audience.

Following the success of Sea Pines, Fraser extended the concept of the nature- and family-oriented, amenity-rich resort and club community to many other resort projects. Moreover, Fraser's original Yale Law School development team of John McGrath and Theron L. "Pete" Caudle went on to fame in other resort developments, as did architects John Wade and Richard McGinty, creators of the Sea Pines look. An impressive number of resort, club, and residential developers working around the world today cut their teeth at Sea Pines.

The resort was sold to its property owners and members a few years ago. Its careful planning and development still make it a required visit for anyone thinking of developing a resort community.

Source: Adapted from David Pearson, "It Started at Sea Pines," *Urban Land*, August 1994, p. 22.

Charles E. Fraser
President
Charles E. Fraser Co. LLC
Hilton Head, South Carolina

Fraser was founder and chair of the Sea Pines Company, the principal resort community builder on Hilton Head Island, South Carolina, from 1956 to 1982. In 1956, Fraser completed his six-year research program and began building the eight-square-mile Sea Pines community on Hilton Head. It was the island's first large-scale planned community and the site of its first golf and tennis facilities. Fraser initiated what at that time was an innovative policy of deeding property subject to land use covenants that specified aesthetic design requirements for all buildings. The success of Sea Pines inspired others to use similar covenants.

Under Fraser's leadership, the Sea Pines Company was responsible for planning and developing several recreational and resort communities, including Hilton Head Plantation on Hilton Head, Amelia Island Plantation in Florida, Kiawah Island and River Hills Plantation in South Carolina, Brandermill in Virginia, and Palmas del Mar in Puerto Rico.

Since 1983, Fraser has served as senior strategic planning consultant to public and private corporations for resort projects in Florida, Hawaii, Mississippi, Belize, and France.

Fraser was born in 1929 and received a law degree from Yale University in 1953.

New resorts and second-home retirement communities have a far greater chance of success if their sites are located 30 minutes or less from established medical services and one hour or less from scheduled airlines. New starts ideally should be in areas that already have achieved significant regional or national identity as choice vacation areas and that are abundantly endowed with existing attractions.

A large percentage of projects that pioneer new geographic areas have generated a loss of part of the capital invested by the initial developer. The first developer finds that there is inadequate transportation, inadequate civic services, inadequate schools and that he cannot succeed until those things change. The new developer begins to tackle those things, and, once the issues have been resolved, a favorable environment is created for others to come in. It is fairly rare that the investors who financed the initial pioneering development in an area lacking key facilities recover their money. A developer pioneering an area needs to have deep pockets or negotiate a program with the governmental entity that, as a development begins to impact the tax base, a portion of the tax proceeds are poured back to help the development, much like a tax increment financing district for redevelopment projects.

New vacation resorts work best if the climate of the area encourages in-migration by new year-round residents, whether retirees, professionals, resort workers, or "modem cowboys" riding the Internet with their laptop computers. Also, resort communities work best when they are not 100 percent resort but have a mix of full- and part-time residents. Full-time residents provide customers for the doctors, the lawyers, and the restaurants year round. It enables the community to provide a myriad of services that would not be possible with just seasonal residents.

It is unwise for anyone to conclude that an area is ripe for a major, new second-home development without living on or near the site for a year to see all the seasonal changes in climate, insects, and tempo of life. By living there, prospective developers can read every issue of the local paper and gather informal intelligence from those who are not as biased as legal, real estate, and architectural advisers by the prospect of directly profiting from the initial expenditures on development services. The failure rate of brand new resort starts is very high while the failure rate of, say, the 14th residential subdivision in town is less than 5 percent. Developers get busy with so many projects that they don't take the proper precautions of locality analysis when they get interested in a new territory.

Even in a good climate, heavy infestation of biting insects in the prime season can make life miserable, so insect analysis and control is a first priority in starting up a new development.

Where land costs exceed more than five to six times the land's pure agricultural or pure forestry land prices, it becomes a large financial burden to acquire more than 500 to 800 acres for residential or other building uses. Purchasing more than 800 acres typically involves an "off the shelf" asset that is unlikely to be converted into revenue for many years. The interest costs for carrying land that is not likely to generate revenue for seven to ten years can eat up all the profits and produce losses. Extensive acreage worked for Sea Pines on Hilton Head and Del Webb in Arizona because the original land costs were modest and did not impose a financial strain.

Only those developers with both an excellent financial structure and remarkable marketing and development skills are prudent to buy 3,000 to 5,000 acres for a new startup project in the vacation and retirement fields where the "interest meter" immediately begins to tick on all land. Not many people can satisfy these two criteria, however. Only when acquiring land transferred in

Amelia Island, Florida, was one of Fraser's first master-planned communities and incorporates many fundamental features from Hilton Head Island, including an emphasis on nature, beaches, and golf and a mix of residential product to attract a diverse market.

progressive "takedowns" at preestablished prices can large-tract acquisitions be considered prudent.

Whether the land tract is large or small, the first stage of a resort development should have an attractive entrance, excellent directional signage leading from the main highways, a finished look to the initial area, and one or more congregating places for new residents and overnight prospective customers to encourage intimacy and easy introductions. Friendly and interesting neighbors and accessible senior project management already living in a community are strong positive attractions to new buyers. These things need to be done before spending all capital on a new golf course and on the new course's costly maintenance.

Income patterns and executives' confidence in their job positions have undergone dramatic shifts since 1982. During this period, large segments of the former corporate executive, second-home ownership market have lost jobs due to downsizing, and replacement jobs often have been at lower salary levels. Those remaining in executive positions are likely to build up their savings before investing in a second home. Lawyers at large firms have had stable revenue streams, but doctors have seen the income effects of restructuring in the medical and health services world.

Despite this, developer perceptions of the composition of the resort market are highly distorted by the purchasing power of the top one-tenth of 1 percent of the market, which has grown dramatically since 1982. Ultra-high-income people tend to gravitate to the very established top-tier places within the range of their normal geographic movements and pay whatever price is necessary to buy a choice property on resale.

For the first time since 1945, the top 20 percent of Americans suffered a slight decline in average incomes between 1988 and 1992. Optimism for significant income gains in the near future is not rampant. Uncertainty as to once-ensured income streams reduces the demand for second-home purchases and increases interest in high-quality timeshares supported by major hotels like Marriott and Hilton or by Disney.

There has been a 20-year gap in training new resort developers. The opportunities for new graduates to learn and do have been limited. There was a flood of talent that came into the industry between 1968 and 1974. The national skill base rests with those who were recruited young at about five companies in that period and were given an excellent start in the business. This may result in a big problem for the resort development industry in about ten years. ∎

quently, multiuse resorts offer a variety of product types to suit various market segments and settings.

The variety of products in a multiuse resort can be used strategically to maximize the resort's appeal to a variety of users, often allowing the resort to provide a broader and higher-quality selection of amenities. In general, multiuse resorts tend to be larger than the single-use resort described earlier and often include a more extensive amenity package.

Multiuse resorts are more likely to offer two major amenities, such as beaches and golf courses and/or ski slopes and golf courses, and to function as four-season resorts. The variety of products and amenities allows the multiuse resort to cater to the needs of resort users over time as their interests and discretionary income change. From the multiuse developer's perspective, a hotel or other transient guest is a potential timeshare, condominium, or single-family-home purchaser; a time-share owner is a potential condominium or single-family-home purchaser; a condominium owner is a potential single-family-home purchaser; and the owner of an attached single-family home is a potential purchaser of a detached single-family home. Similarly, a downhill skier or a windsurfing buff may over time develop an interest in another recreational pursuit such as golf. The ability to provide the resort user with a wide variety of resort experiences allows the resort to become a dominant player in the market.

The greater diversity inherent in multiuse resorts means that such properties generally require a more sophisticated development and management operation than other resort types. The multiplicity of issues associated with multiuse resorts presents a good model for the organization of the remainder of this book. Thus, while the book is designed as a guide for the development of all the resort types discussed above, it is targeted to a large degree to the development of multiuse resorts. The developer of a multiuse resort must consider not only all of the issues involved in the development of the various product types already discussed, but also how to program, develop, and operate them so that they work together to create a properly integrated and well-balanced resort environment. The book therefore focuses more on the big picture and must necessarily leave some of the details of resort development—for example, the specifics of resort hotel operation, the details of a point-based timeshare program, and the technical aspects of ski facility planning—for other texts to address.

Historical Background

Throughout history, people have traveled to mountaintops, coastlines, hot springs, and other special places in search of physical relaxation and spiritual renewal. Over the centuries, the establishment and growth of resorts has been largely linked to the availability of convenient modes and routes of travel; in fact, advances in transportation have helped popularize resorts in once-remote locations. Resorts, however, have generally been the province of the wealthy and the aristocracy. For the most part, the resort "industry" is a 20th-century phenomenon whose growth has paralleled the emergence of the affluent society in the United States and the industrialized nations.

In North America, the earliest examples of second homes and resorts can be traced to the colonial aristocracy—which continued the European tradition of maintaining both country homes and townhouses—and the modest resorts that grew up around hot springs in the Appalachian Mountains. The Homestead in Hot Springs, Virginia, dates to 1766, when a bathing pavilion and an

The Homestead in Hot Springs, Virginia, dates back to 1766, when a bathing pavilion and an inn were built around mountain hot springs.

To encourage ridership on a newly developed railroad line between San Francisco and Los Angeles, in 1879 the Pacific Improvement Company, led by Charles Crocker, purchased 5,300 acres of the Monterey Peninsula, located 120 miles south of San Francisco. The initial plan called for development of a destination resort hotel between California's two population centers. The company initially built the Hotel Del Monte, whose amenities included a bathing pavilion, racetrack, polo grounds, and golf course as well as a 17-mile scenic coastal road along the Monterey Peninsula.

As the hotel gained popularity over the years, the Pacific Improvement Company recognized that a growing number of people had come to appreciate the beauty and climate of the area. As a result, the company began selling homesites to the general public. By 1909, the heirs of the Pacific Improvement Company had turned the Monterey operation into a full-fledged real estate development, focusing their business efforts on land sales, particularly along the 17-mile scenic drive.

In a few short years, the ill-planned real estate development operation began to have an adverse effect on the once-thriving resort property. In 1915, the grandson of Charles Crocker hired Samuel F.B. Morse to oversee liquidation of the Monterey holdings. Morse, understanding the complexities of resort community development, was able to convince the Pacific Improvement Company to upgrade the rundown resort while reducing residential development, thus preserving valuable land resources for the development of community and recreational facilities. Morse abandoned plans to sell homesites on a coastal plateau known as Pebble Beach, where he instead laid out one of the nation's most distinguished golf courses. Morse's development plan also included a resort lodge built with the primary intention of attracting prospective homebuyers to other areas along the scenic peninsula. With confidence in his plans, Morse acquired the site in 1919 and subsequently formed the Del Monte Properties Company.

From the beginning, Morse envisioned that his resort community would be developed around "spheres of influence." He planned to cluster homes around the lodge and other resort and recreational amenities. Tolls collected on the scenic drive helped offset the costs of developing and maintaining roads and infrastructure within the development's private and gated residential community, which was known as Del Monte Forest.

World events, including the Great Depression and World War II, affected Morse's ability to implement his plan fully. Nevertheless, the area continued to grow and prosper by capitalizing on the fame of its legendary golf course. During World War II, the Del Monte Properties Company sold the Hotel Del Monte to the U.S. Navy, which now uses the building to house an educational program. The last plan Morse developed, in 1966, called for a final buildout of 8,515 homesites dispersed accross the 5,300-acre site.

Today, the resort is generally known as Pebble Beach and is owned and operated by the Pebble Beach Company, which operates two hotels on the site: the Lodge at Pebble Beach and the Inn at Spanish Bay (see case study on page 352). Pebble Beach is known internationally for its high-quality golf facilities; in fact, the Pebble Beach Company currently operates four championship courses on the site: the Old Del Monte Course, the Pebble Beach Golf Links, the Spyglass Hill Golf Course, and the Links at Spanish Bay.

In recent years, a variety of entities have owned the Pebble Beach Company. In 1990, the Japanese investor Minoru Isutani acquired the company for an unprecedented $840 million. To support this exorbitant acquisition price, Isutani proposed selling Pebble Beach club memberships for over $100,000 apiece. "When California regulators squashed the plan, Isutani sold Pebble Beach to another Japanese buyer, Lone Cypress Co., for a reported $500 million."[1]

Real estate development continues to be one of the Pebble Beach Company's primary interests. A land use plan prepared in the 1980s provides for the development of up to 899 homesites around Del Monte Forest; however, the Pebble Beach Company has recently been involved in revising the plan to reduce the number of planned homesites to 350 and to develop additional golf facilities. If approved, the final residential buildout will total 3,108 homesites, approximately one-third of Morse's 1966 plan.

The renowned golf course and the golf tournaments it has attracted have afforded the resort extraordinary television exposure, which has been a major marketing benefit. The resort hosted the U.S. Open in 1972, 1982, and 1992.

Note
1. Thomas Jaffe, "Forbes Informer," *Forbes*, June 7, 1993, p. 20.

Source: Neil Hoteling, Golf Administration Department, Pebble Beach Company, Pebble Beach, Calif.

■

inn were built around some mountain hot springs. The Greenbrier near White Sulphur Springs, West Virginia, dates to 1779, when a lodge was built to house tourists.

As in Europe, resort development in North America began to proliferate with the advent of pleasure travel by coach, steamship, and rail. New opportunities later emerged with the introduction of automobile and airline travel and the rapid growth of the middle and upper-middle classes.

Late 19th Century

By the middle of the 19th century, popularly priced resort communities flourished at the seashore and in the mountains. Cape May, New Jersey, was the foremost resort of the mid-1800s, with tourists flocking there at first by steamboat and later by rail. Many of the emerging seasonal resort communities for the growing middle classes had a religious or cultural orientation. Accommodations were modest—rustic tent cabins or cottages with few amenities, often densely built around lakes or at the shore. The Wesleyan Grove retreat at Oak Bluffs on the island of Martha's Vineyard off Cape Cod, Massachusetts, started in 1835 and survives as an early example of this type of vacation-home development. Later examples include Ocean Grove on the New Jersey shore and Pacific Grove on California's Monterey Peninsula.

1870s. The 1870s saw the founding of Chautauqua, a summer community started by a Methodist minister as a two-week retreat for Sunday school teachers at Chautauqua Lake in northwestern New York state near Jamestown. This first Chautauqua started a movement that spawned as many as 200 other similar summer communities throughout North America.[3] Now interdenominational, the original Chautauqua Institution currently attracts an average of 7,500 people each week during its nine-week summer season of educational and cultural events for all ages.

The 1870s also saw Newport, Rhode Island—which before the Civil War had been a popular summer destination for wealthy plantation owners from the South—transformed by the construction of grand summer homes built primarily for wealthy New Yorkers. In the years following the Civil War, General Lee spent many summers in White Sulphur Springs, West Virginia, at the genteel resort known as the Old White, which later became part of the Greenbrier when the latter was established in the early 1900s. The 1870s also marked the beginning of Pebble Beach (see feature box on page 19).

1880s. The 1880s brought a surge of recreational development that catered to both the rich and the not-so-rich. For the general public, rail transportation opened up new areas close to home while city trolley companies often developed picnic groves and amusement parks at the end of their trolley lines to encourage weekend trips. Coney Island was the prototype of American amusement parks. Its development between 1860 and 1890 included huge resort hotels, ballrooms, beer gardens, bathing piers, and rides and games that attracted thousands and, later, millions of New Yorkers. Like many recreational ventures, the exotic Margate Hotel on Coney Island, built in 1881 in the shape of an elephant, was designed as an attraction for a land sales promotion.

For the wealthy, railroads provided access to new geographic areas and sparked the development of a number of large resort hotels, often built by or with the financial support of railroad companies. The Ponce de Leon in St. Augustine, Florida, the most lavish and expensive resort hotel of its kind built during the period, opened in 1888 and contributed to Florida's growing reputation as a tourist destination. Other grand resort hotels that opened in the 1880s included the Sagamore Hotel on Lake George, New York (1883; see feature box on page 21); the Grand Hotel on Mackinac Island, Michigan (1887); the Banff Springs Hotel in Alberta, Canada (1888); Hotel Del Monte on the Monterey Peninsula in California; and the Hotel del Coronado in San Diego (1888). Most of these hotels were closely associated with land sales operations for resort and recreational real estate development. And in 1889, Macy's department store owner Jerome B. Wheeler opened the Hotel Jerome in Aspen. Society from around the globe attended the hotel's grand opening.

Railroads also facilitated the creation of early planned recreational communities. Tuxedo Park, New York, a prototypical private residential recreational community, was started in 1885 when Pierre Lorillard, heir to a vast tobacco fortune, purchased 7,000 acres of land about an hour's train journey from New York City in the Ramapo Mountains of southern New York state. Lorillard's vision was to create an exclusive but informal summer community whose plan and architecture would respect both the land and the character of the site. Lorillard disdained the excessively scaled houses in Newport and intentionally specified a more modest style for the original clubhouse and the first homes, although a 140-foot-high barbed-wire fence completely enclosed the compound. Membership in the 400-member Tuxedo Club was required for property ownership. Outside the gates, Lorillard constructed a village to house the 200 artisans and merchants required to maintain the preserve and its life.[4]

1890s. During the 1890s, the Jekyll Island Club was established on Jekyll Island, Georgia, as a private winter community for the Morgans, Rockefellers, Vanderbilts, and many of the families that summered in Newport. They built giant "cottages" and a fabulous clubhouse where they convened for ten-course evening meals. The club remained in private use until World War II and is now operated as a resort hotel.[5]

The Pinehurst Resort and Club was established in 1898 in North Carolina by soda-fountain magnate James Tufts. Although the first golf course in the United States is generally acknowledged to be the St. Andrew's course in Westchester County, New York, established in 1888, the first golf course significantly linked to a real estate project was designed for Pinehurst (see feature box on page 22).

Over 100 years ago when hotel operator Myron O. Brown sought to build an exclusive resort community on a 72-acre island in Lake George in New York state's Adirondacks, he looked to four Philadelphia millionaires who were summer residents of the area: E. Burgess Warren, William B. Bement, Robert Glendenning, and George Burnham. Together, they bought Green Island for a hotel site and formed the Green Island Improvement Company. They were later joined by investor John Boulton Simpson of New York City, who became the company's president.

The Sagamore opened in 1883 with luxurious and spacious accommodations that attracted a select international clientele. Twice damaged by fire—in 1893 and 1914—the Sagamore was fully reconstructed in 1930 through the concerted efforts of Dr. William G. Beckers of New York City, one of the hotel's early stockholders, and William H. Bixby, a St. Louis industrialist. They financed the cost despite the bleak economic climate of the period. Donald Ross designed the hotel's nearby 18-hole, par-70 golf course and, in 1928, supervised its construction.

Throughout its history, the Sagamore provided a social center for the wealthy residents of the mansions—known as Millionaires Row—located along Lake George's western shore. As a planned community, the Sagamore was designed for limited development to preserve the ecological integrity of the area and to maintain its investment potential.

In the 1950s, the Sagamore demonstrated a strong ability to attract convention business; in 1954, the hotel hosted the annual Governor's Conference. Nonetheless, age finally took its toll on the grande dame of Adirondack resorts, and in 1981, the Sagamore closed its doors. In 1983, however, 100 years after construction of the Sagamore began, builder and real estate developer Norman Wolgin purchased the hotel and restored it to its former grandeur. With Kennington Properties, Inc., of Los Angeles, Wolgin formed a partnership under the name of Green Island Associates to bring about the restoration. The resort is now known as the Sagamore, an Omni Classic Resort, and includes 100 rooms in the main hotel and 240 rooms in lakeside lodges. It continues to undergo renovations, some of which are financed through fundraising efforts undertaken by the Sagamore Board of Directors.

The Sagamore is listed on the National Register of Historic Places.

Source: Adapted from marketing materials and brochures. ∎

The Sagamore, which opened in 1883, has maintained its charm and prestige as the grande dame of the Adirondacks.

North Carolina's Pinehurst Resort and Country Club is among the best-known and most famous golf resorts in the United States. Its eight championship golf courses are complemented by a wide variety of recreational amenities and hotel facilities as well as by the small village of Pinehurst. Pinehurst's resort and recreational resources were the vision of the resort's founder, James Walker Tufts.

In 1895, Tufts, a Boston businessman and philanthropist, purchased 5,500 acres of North Carolina timberland for approximately $1 per acre with the goal of building a resort. Tufts believed that Pinehurst's mild winters would provide the ideal setting for a winter health retreat. With this vision, Tufts secured the services of world-renowned landscape designer Frederick Law Olmsted to complete the resort's site planning and design. Tufts actively solicited referrals to the health resort/retreat through brochures mailed directly to doctors.

Originally, Pinehurst offered tennis as its primary recreational activity along with riding, hunting, lawn bowling, and archery. In 1898, the first rudimentary nine-hole golf course was laid out at Pinehurst and quickly became the resort's central attraction. Scotland-born golf course designer Donald Ross came to Pinehurst in 1900 and, over a 48-year period, redesigned and created four legendary courses. Pinehurst's Victorian-style hotel, often referred to as the White House of Golf, opened its doors

The Pinehurst Resort and Country Club is a golf and tennis resort with a rich history dating back to 1895.

on New Year's Day 1901 and today remains the center of the Pinehurst Resort and Country Club.

Ownership of the Pinehurst resort eventually passed from family hands when the Diamondhead Corporation purchased the property in 1970. ClubCorp, the resort's current owner, acquired the property in 1984. The U.S. Department of the Interior recently designated the Pinehurst resort and village a National Historic Landmark. ∎

Early 20th Century

1900 to 1920. The Pocono region of Pennsylvania experienced a boom in popularity during the early part of the 20th century with the establishment of Buck Hill Falls (1900); Pocono Manor (1902), which was built by the Quakers as a hotel and retreat; and the Shawnee Inn (1912). These resorts and others located farther north in the Catskills and Berkshires of New York state and Massachusetts initially were open only during summer months and catered to guests from nearby metropolitan areas. Other summer resort areas that gained popularity during this period included Lake Geneva, Wisconsin; the Great Lakes coastal areas of Michigan; and Hot Springs, Arkansas.

Most of the great camps of the Adirondacks had their heyday between the early 1900s and the 1930s. During this time, visiting and living in wilderness settings became popular as a retreat from the congestion of newly industrialized cities. Sagamore Lodge, the Vanderbilts' great camp near Raquette Lake, is considered by many to be the prototypical great camp. It was one of the first to use a rustic architectural style that incorporated indigenous materials and handcrafted details. This style

eventually served as a model for public buildings in many national parks.

By the early years of the 20th century, the exclusive resort communities of the wealthy sported summer "cottages" that rivaled their European predecessors in grandeur and opulence. Newport, Bar Harbor (Maine), the Hamptons (Long Island, New York), the Adirondacks, and Palm Beach are all renowned today for splendid seasonal homes built primarily during the late 1800s and early 1900s.

Palm Beach began its life in 1894 as a winter resort spurred by Henry Morrison Flagler's development of the East Coast Railway and the subsequent opening of two hotels: the Royal Poinciana Hotel, destroyed by a hurricane in 1934, and the Breakers, which, twice destroyed by fire but completely rebuilt after the second fire in 1925, remains open today.[6] In 1917, Paris E. Singer, heir to the sewing machine fortune, visited Palm Beach and decided to develop a community that would become the winter counterpart to Newport, where families would move for the season. When World War I effectively put an end to transatlantic travel, Singer's self-taught architect, Addison Mizner, responded by synthesizing Mediterranean motifs to create an architectural style that evoked a strong sense of place and soon came to symbolize Florida architecture in the popular imagination. With his completion of a private clubhouse known as the Everglades Club and a retail area on Worth Avenue dubbed the Via Mizner, Mizner was besieged with residential commissions.[7]

1920s. As the automobile became a popular means of transportation, the pattern of American recreational activity underwent a dramatic change. No longer limited to stagecoach, trolley, rail, and steamer routes, Americans began to look farther from home for a diversity of recreational experiences. A growing awareness of the physical wonders of the country and the expanding naturalist movement stimulated interest in the outdoors. The National Park Service, established in 1916 to manage and protect the nation's scenic wonders, built large, rustic hotels such as the Awahnee at Yosemite National Park (1927) and the Old Faithful Lodge at Yellowstone National Park. These hotels attracted travelers in small numbers arriving, first, by stagecoach and, later, in increasing numbers, by car.

This same period saw the beginning of the first recreational land booms, most notably in Florida and California. The Florida land boom reached full swing between 1921 and 1926. As development moved down the state's east coast, several new grand resort hotels opened, including Henry Flagler's Royal Palm Hotel in downtown Miami, the Cloister Inn (now the Boca Raton Hotel) in Boca Raton (1926), and the Biltmore in Coral Gables (1926). Coral Gables, founded in 1921 by George Merrick, was planned from the start as a recreational real estate venture. Buildings and landscape elements generally followed a Spanish/Mediterranean architectural style, but several other styles, including Chinese, South African, and French, distinguished some neighborhoods. A system of canals allowed Merrick to advertise more than 40 miles of waterfront. A spectacular public swimming hole known as the Venetian Pool and created from an abandoned gravel pit also helped create publicity for the community.[8]

New grand winter resort hotels opening in California in the 1920s included La Valencia in La Jolla (1926), La Quinta near Palm Springs (1926), and the Biltmore in Santa Barbara (1927). The Arizona Biltmore in Phoenix (1929), designed in part by Frank Lloyd Wright, helped establish the Arizona desert as a winter resort. Over time, these hotels and others like them helped attract both seasonal and permanent residents to their surrounding areas.

Sea Island, Georgia, was another major addition during this period. The property was purchased in 1926 by the former chief engineer of the Hudson Motor Company, Howard Coffin, who, with his cousin Alfred W. Jones, created a "cottage" colony with a "friendly little hotel" where people could stay while selecting lots. The hotel, named the Cloister and designed by Addison Mizner, opened in 1928. In the years to come, more rooms were built in guesthouses and in three beach houses. Today, the Sea Island Company, a family-run business, owns the club and operates the hotel. The

364-key hotel and a vacation colony of 300 private homes share four nine-hole golf courses, 18 tennis courts, and two swimming pools.[9]

1930s. The growth of private leisure home and resort developments ended abruptly in 1929 with the Great Depression. The depression also took its toll on small commercial/recreational entrepreneurs, forcing many businesses to close as people could no longer afford leisure time or leisure activities. The depression affected the national parks as well, but in favorable ways, as the Civilian Conservation Corps and other federal work projects brought in crews to develop recreational areas within the parks. Not until after World War II did the recreational and second-home market begin to revive.

The 1930s did, however, witness the establishment of two high-profile winter resorts: Lake Placid, New York, which hosted the Olympic Winter Games (1932), and Sun Valley Lodge in Idaho (1936). Sun Valley was the vision of Averell Harriman, who at the time ran the Union Pacific Railroad and saw the ski resort as a way to get people to ride trains to the site. The resort has maintained an exclusive aura throughout the years due to its out-of-the-way location, spectacular scenery, sensational skiing, and deluxe accommodations.[10]

Mid-20th Century

1940s and 1950s. The 1940s and 1950s marked an unprecedented boom in family travel by automobile. The touring trip became the most popular type of family vacation, giving rise to the widespread growth of highway-oriented lodging, including auto courts and motels.

The burgeoning "upper-middle" professional class was growing more affluent, mobile, and—with the post–World War II baby boom—more family-oriented. Walt Disney captured the imagination of this new market and in 1955 brought to life at Disneyland the fantasies that were pictured on television and in films. Bowling alleys, drive-in movie theaters, swim clubs, go-cart tracks, public golf courses and driving ranges, and other types of

America's first destination ski resort was born with the opening of the Sun Valley Lodge in 1936, now a historic landmark. Today, many guests return for summer activities.

commercial recreation facilities and attractions sprouted in suburban areas in response to the demand for close-to-home family-oriented recreation and entertainment. Country clubs also found their way into new suburban areas, cultivating and capitalizing on an increasing interest in tennis and golf. Many new marinas and yacht clubs opened near metropolitan areas along the coasts and the Great Lakes.

With an increase in recreation and vacation travel, skiing became popular. The old mining town of Aspen, Colorado, experienced a major reorientation to skiing during this period. Aspen had fallen on hard times with the collapse of the silver market, but Chicago industrialist Walter Paepcke set out to revitalize the community in the late 1940s. His vision was to build a ski resort as well as a retreat and mecca for thinkers and outdoor lovers alike. He started the Aspen Institute for the Humanities and the Music Associates of Aspen, institutions that today have earned international reputations.[11]

Aspen is one of the world's top ski destinations, although people visit it for the "Aspen experience," as well. Festivals, such as the Winterskol carnival, are one of many features that create an exciting experience and a unique sense of place.

Photo courtesy of Design Workshop Inc.

Many other new ski areas and resorts took root in the Northeast and West during this period. The 1950s also saw the opening of the Desert Inn in Las Vegas, planting the seed for the renowned "strip" of large, self-contained casino-based resort hotels that quickly became a popular vacation destination, particularly as air travel became more available and affordable.

1960s. A major boom in recreational real estate development coincided with the 1960s and early 1970s. Land speculation and the strong demand for recreation spurred developers into action as the market accelerated. Second-home projects and recreational lot subdivisions proliferated. A lack of regulation in most rural areas allowed developments to grow unchecked, however. Large corporations participated in the land sales boom, subdividing and marketing huge tracts of land. High-pressure salespeople sold thousands of acres to eager but naive investors.

As complaints about misrepresentation and fraud concerning "dirt" sales began to surface, consumer and environmental groups took issue with irresponsible development practices. Environmentalists were especially influential in changing development practices. Soil erosion, inadequate sanitary disposal, and insensitive intrusions into scenic areas caused by certain recreational projects helped focus public attention on environmental concerns associated with irresponsible development. Nonetheless, local forces often had little control over or simply assumed a low profile with respect to issues raised by the thousands of recreational subdivisions undertaken during the boom of the 1960s. Many local governments lacked zoning or other regulations during this time, particularly in rural areas where land use controls have traditionally been weakest.

The response to both consumer fraud and environmental abuses was increased regulation. In 1969, the U.S. Department of Housing and Urban Development established the Office of Interstate Land Sales Registration (OILSR). The OILSR requires all developments of 50 lots or more to register a prospectus with the department if they intend to use interstate commerce to market their properties. From 1971 to 1977, the OILSR received an average of 3,000 consumer complaints a year. Over this time, the office initiated indictments against a number of companies and suspended sales at hundreds of developments pending OILSR review. Most of the fraudulent activity was centered in Florida, Arizona, Colorado, and California.

A further federal effort to offer protection from irresponsible development practices came with the 1969 enactment of the National Environmental Policy Act (NEPA). The law established the format of the environmental impact statement (EIS) for all development projects involving federal lands or funding. Most state and local governments subsequently followed suit by establishing environmental regulations and review processes for development activities in environmentally sensitive areas and for projects of a certain size.[12] By some accounts, however, the lack of implementation

Opening in 1962, Vail Village was the first ski resort involving a planned unit development (PUD) approach. The village was designed after Austrian and Swiss ski villages.

Photo courtesy of EDSA

The Carambola Beach Resort on St. Croix is one of many boutique resort hotels that Rockresorts built in an effort to capture a highly affluent market.

and enforcement of the regulations meant little change in many land development practices.[13] But public reaction to the publicity surrounding these activities produced a strong and pervasive negative image of recreational land sales.

Another movement afoot during this period looked for ways to establish higher standards for resort development. During the late 1950s and early 1960s, several major destination resort and second-home communities started in Florida, California, Colorado, New England, South Carolina, Hawaii, and many other parts of the country set new standards for resort planning, design, and development. These efforts captured the attention and imagination of many others whose projects were then in the startup phase. Notable large-scale resort and recreational community projects undertaken during this period include Sea Pines Plantation on Hilton Head Island, South Carolina (1960); Vail, Colorado (1962; see feature box on page 241); and New Seabury,

Cape Cod, Massachusetts (1962). In many ways, these projects were the resort counterparts to the large-scale suburban new towns also started during this period, including Reston, Virginia; Columbia, Maryland; and Irvine, California.

A number of smaller resort and recreational development projects started in the 1960s demonstrated the merits of environmentally sensitive land use planning and design and thus had a major educational impact on consumers and the development industry. These included two resort and second-home communities on the West Coast—Sea Ranch in northern California (1964) and Salishan in Oregon (1965)—and the deluxe resort hotels built by Rockresorts (headed by Laurence Rockefeller) in the Caribbean and Hawaii, namely, Caneel Bay on St. John; Carambola Beach Resort on St. Croix; Little Dix Bay on Virgin Gorda; Dorado Beach in Puerto Rico; and Mauna Kea in Hawaii.

Late 20th Century

1970s. As demand for recreational real estate continued to grow in the 1970s, it was clearly moving away from recreational lot sales toward high-amenity, second-home and resort condominium communities. The late 1960s and early 1970s witnessed a significant increase in the sales of condominiums to be used for recreational purposes. New resort and recreational development communities and projects initiated during this period included Northstar at Tahoe in Truckee, California (1970); Keystone, Colorado; Waikoloa, Hawaii (1974); and Amelia Island Plantation near Jacksonville, Florida (1974).

The OPEC oil embargo from 1973 to 1974 and the recession of 1974 and 1975, however, proved disastrous for many resorts and resort communities. Consumers by necessity cut back on "luxury" purchases while some developers were left holding large inventories. During the mid-1970s, interest and carrying costs ate up profits, forcing a number of developers into default. Some of the nation's most prestigious financial institutions were also caught in the recession's real estate debacle when resort homeowners and developers alike defaulted on their loans (see feature box on page 26).

Also during the 1970s, timesharing made its initial appearance on a large scale in the United States, in part as a marketing response to high inventories and poor sales of vacation condominiums in 1974 and 1975. Conversion of failing projects into timeshare units could not, however, turn poor projects into good ones. The overall upgrading of the timeshare product and its management since 1976 is in large part the result of units and resort operations increasingly designed and built expressly for timeshare use.

The late 1970s saw the initiation of many large-scale resort communities, including Kiawah Island in South Carolina (1976); Kapalua on Maui in Hawaii (1978); Carmel Valley Ranch near Carmel, California (1977); Pelican Bay in Naples, Florida (1978); Palm Beach Polo and Country Club in Florida (1978); and Palmas del

Mar in Puerto Rico (1978). Many of these projects were undertaken by professionals who had, in a sense, cut their teeth on one of the major resort community projects started in the early 1960s. The Sea Pines Company, for example, was involved in several projects during the 1970s, including Amelia Island, Kiawah Island, and Palmas del Mar.

1980s and 1990s. The 1980s and early 1990s have been a period of major growth and change for resorts and resort communities. This recent history has been significantly influenced by changing economic conditions, shifting demographic and psychographic profiles, and advances in communication and information technology.

The early and mid-1980s was generally a time of optimism for real estate development, and resort development was no exception. Resort communities initiated during this period included Beaver Creek, Colorado (1980); Grand Traverse Resort, Michigan (1980); Deer Valley, Utah (1981); Seaside, Florida (1982); Harbour Ridge, Florida (1984); Gainey Ranch, Arizona (1984); and Semiahmoo, Washington (1985). These and other projects started in the 1980s generally required longer startup periods for planning and permitting than projects initiated in the 1970s and earlier. The reason was the broader scope of environmental regulations coupled with increased environmental awareness and concerns about environmental impacts.

The tax law changes of 1986, the stock market crash of 1987, and the subsequent 1990 recession marked the beginning of a slow period for resort and recreational community development. Further exacerbating the slowdown was the limited availability of financing for real estate projects, which resulted from the failure of many financial institutions. Congress created the Resolution Trust Corporation (RTC) in August 1989 to deal with this situation. In the following four years, 740 institutions with assets in the neighborhood of $442 billion were assigned to the RTC. Since a significant number of these institutions held assets associated with resort and recreational communities, subsequent disposal of the assets at "cents-on-the-dollar" substantially influenced the course of development for many resort projects. One of the largest dispositions involved the assets of the Landmark Land Company, whose portfolio included the Palm Beach Polo and Country Club in Florida; Carmel Valley Ranch, PGA West, and Mission Hills in California; and portions of Kiawah Island in South Carolina.

Resort and recreational community projects started in the late 1980s and early 1990s include Fisher Island, Florida; Spring Island, South Carolina; and Indian Ridge Country Club, California. These and many other high-profile communities initiated during this period were targeted to a rarefied market of those at the top 1 percent of the income range. Differences between these

The 1970s Resort Condominium Market in Ocean City, Maryland

Ocean City, Maryland, illustrates the difficulties experienced by many resort and recreational communities during the mid-1970s. Because of rapidly increasing land and construction costs and pent-up demand for condominiums, unit prices escalated dramatically in 1970, 1971, and 1972. Annual increases of 25 to 30 percent were not uncommon. So great was the opportunity to realize an extraordinary gain that the market was soon swarming with speculators. In fact, in late 1972 and early 1973, speculators accounted for 50 to 90 percent of all deposits.

Developers reacted as expected to the speculative demand and increased construction accordingly, just as the speculators began to retreat from the market. The result was severe overbuilding, which left 5,100 units on the market in Ocean City at the end of 1974, at which time the settlement rate dropped to only 500 units per year. The primary lesson to be learned by the private real estate sector from Ocean City's resort condominium experience is that developers and their financial backers must distinguish between final-use demand and intermediate-speculative demand.

In 1974, estimates projected that it would take four to ten years to sell Ocean City's complete inventory of re-

sort condominiums. By 1979, the glut had been absorbed and new development was continuing, although cautiously. This pattern was repeated in other areas affected by the 1974–1975 recession. Gradually, the recreational development industry recovered and returned to a healthy, if not exuberant, state.

While second-home sales in Ocean City in 1977 were down by one-third from their 1973 levels, the demand for recreation of all types continued to increase, with vacation-home development remaining an important part of that market. The 1980 recession found recreational developers much better prepared to weather the market. Inventories had been kept lower with more presales and fewer speculative units while development had generally proceeded more conservatively. Real estate investors had recalled and applied the lessons of the recent past.

Source: Adapted in part from Jim Haimes and Marvin Rose, "The Second-Home Condominium Boom in Ocean City, Maryland," *Urban Land*, December 1974, p. 14.

Several projects started in the late 1980s and early 1990s, such as the Indian Ridge Country Club in Palm Desert, California, have been successful in targeting the very high-end resort and second-home market. Indian Ridge Country Club is a classic example of a resort community that uses golf not only for sport and recreation but also as a landscape amenity for the community.

communities reflect the diversity of values and lifestyles even within this narrow market segment.

The late 1980s and early 1990s was also a time of Japanese investment in resort and recreational community development projects.[14] The most highly publicized of these was Minori Isutani's purchase of the Pebble Beach Company in 1990. Japanese investors played a significant role in the startup and refinancing of many other projects during this period until the Japanese financial market's crash in the early 1990s effectively halted Japanese investment activities.

The resort hotel industry also experienced much growth and change during the 1980s and early 1990s. The construction of megaresort hotels, including Kauai Lagoons and the Hyatt Regency Waikoloa in Hawaii and Las Vegas casino hotels such as the Mirage, Treasure Island, and the Luxor, exemplify the increasing role of entertainment in resort lodging facilities. This period also saw the sensitive restoration of a number of vintage resort hotels, including La Quinta in California (1980–1984) and the Sagamore in New York.

The timeshare industry was also substantially reborn during the late 1980s and early 1990s as major corporations such as Marriott, Hilton, and Disney entered the market. Between 1980 and 1990, the number of timeshare resorts quadrupled to nearly 2,400 worldwide, of which 1,200 were located in the United States. During the same period, the number of timeshare owners increased by more than a factor of 11 to approximately

1.8 million worldwide, nearly 1.2 million of whom were residents of the United States.[15] As the timesharing industry has grown, it has seen fewer and larger companies dominate while gaining increased respectability (see feature box on page 28). Chapter 7 discusses many other trends for the 1990s and beyond.

Overview of the Development Process

As with the development process for other types of real estate, resorts and resort communities depend on a complex, iterative, and multidisciplinary development process. The process is not a simple series of steps; instead, it calls for many interrelated activities that require simultaneous review and constant adjustment. These activities involve many areas of expertise. The process demands increasing levels of refinement in which all elements must be weighed and pass the test of economic feasibility.

This section provides an overview of the major activities involved in the development process for resorts and resort communities (see figure 1-2). Chapters 2 through 5, which cover specific aspects of the process, provide further detail.

The Development Team

In general, the developer's role in a resort project is to orchestrate the development process and bring a project to fruition (see Figure 1-1). Depending on the type of resort, the developer may also be the resort manager and must therefore assume responsibility for the on-going operation of the resort and its various components. In large multiuse resort developments, which frequently require several decades for completion, developers often change over time such that several developers play a major role in a community's creation, maturation, and evolution. Moreover, large multiuse resort communities may involve various levels of developers, such as a master developer, who usually programs the resort concept and develops the infrastructure, and various subdevelopers —such as hotel developers, housing developers, timeshare developers, and golf course developers—who develop specific properties within the resort.

Since the process of developing a resort is complex, experts from various disciplines must necessarily participate in all aspects of decision making. An individual

developer can never expect to be an expert in all disciplines. Even for small-scale projects, a team of experts is required.

The developer functions as the team leader throughout the development process. In most development companies, an individual in the company is designated as the project manager and assigned the responsibility for day-to-day decision making. As the project changes direction or proceeds from one stage to the next, it may be appropriate for different individuals to fill the role of project manager. Throughout the development process, however, owners and investors retain ultimate decision-making responsibility for determining how to proceed in accordance with the realities of the marketplace. Their decisions must be based on qualified input from all members of the development team.

Competent, experienced team members can help maximize the site's potential for development, decrease

History of Timesharing/Vacation Ownership

The history of the timeshare industry may be divided into three slightly overlapping phases that began in 1964 with the Superdolovy Resort in the French Alps. The Club Hotel, also located in France, adapted the concept for application to other resorts in 1968. Timesharing made its debut in the United States as an alternative to poor sales of vacation condominiums and a temporary marketing strategy to survive the 1973–1975 housing slump.[1] During this period, most timeshares took the form of condominium conversions. Between 1976 and 1979, sales doubled annually; in 1980, sales exceeded $1 billion.

Many of the early conversions from condominiums to timeshares were undercapitalized, poorly organized, and reflected a poor understanding of the hospitality environment. Not surprisingly, timesharing gained an

unsavory reputation during this period, primarily as a result of the practices of unregulated, opportunistic developers who engaged in questionable or unethical marketing and sales techniques. And yet the timeshare concept prospered; by 1980, about 155,000 households in the United States owned timeshare intervals in about 500 resorts.

The timeshare industry entered its second phase during the early 1980s as sales expanded and came to represent a legitimate investment opportunity. Improved brokerage and financing support helped boost the reputation, popularity, and profits of timesharing and timeshare units. The following factors also contributed to the second-phase growth of the industry:

- regulation of marketing and sales practices;
- required disclosure and product offering;
- well-managed regional developers and management companies;
- improved quality of product; and
- increased sales volume.

As market conditions improved, many timeshare projects began constructing buildings designed specifically for timeshare use. In 1984, Marriott entered the timeshare business, purchasing the assets of the most successful timeshare developer of its time—American Resorts Corporation, which was founded by Ed McMullen in 1977. Among the assets purchased by Marriott was the highly successful Monarch at Sea Pines in Hilton Head, South Carolina. Foreshadowing future events, the Marriott acquisition of American Resorts Corporation marked the beginning of two trends that have continued into the 1990s: the consolidation of the vacation ownership industry and the entry of major hospitality companies.

Monarch at Sea Pines on Hilton Head Island in South Carolina was the most successful timeshare during the early 1980s and was later acquired by Marriott as a key element in its entry into the timeshare industry.

construction and maintenance costs, and add immeasurably to the project's appeal and marketability. Since successful developers take the attitude that sound advice makes money rather than costs money, they are willing to request professional advice whenever necessary.

Depending on the project, assistance from the following types of professionals (and others not listed) may be required: architects, attorneys, construction managers, engineers, environmental scientists, financial analysts, financiers, landscape architects, management advisers, market analysts, marketing advisers, planners, public relations advisers, real estate agents, resort operations professionals, sales managers, and various specialists who understand the many property types and recreational elements in the development. For discussion and organization purposes, team members can be generally grouped into five disciplines: legal, financial, management, marketing, and planning/design (see figure 1-1).

Effective organization and management of the development team is fundamental to project success. Part of the developer's responsibility as team manager is to ensure good communication among the various members of the team. Team review and coordination meetings are essential in optimizing efficiency and making sure that the overall effort is on the right track.

Even though a development company may, depending on in-house expertise, be able to perform all or most of the required functions, expert help will eventually be needed. Most developers, even large diversified development companies, do not retain a staff with all the technical talents needed by the development team. Instead, they hire consultants. One advantage of relying on consultants is that the experts can be tapped only when needed. Individual consultants and multifaceted consulting firms can provide consulting services pertaining to every issue associated with resort development.

Disney has played an important role in improving the timeshare name by providing a reliable product of quality through the Disney Vacation Club. Pictured is Disney's Hilton Head Island Resort.

The third phase began in the early 1990s when major changes resulted from the entry of several other large hospitality companies into the timeshare business, especially Disney and Hilton but also Hyatt, Westin, Radisson, and others that followed Marriott's lead. These companies brought credibility and innovations; Disney's entry into the business in 1991, for example, provided a strong boost to the vacation club and point system. The creation of the Hilton Grand Vacations Company in 1992, which offered a vacation club as well, gave further credibility to the point system, as did the conversion to a point system by Fairfield Communities—a major player in the timeshare industry for many years. The participation of hospitality companies has brought much-needed clout to the vacation ownership industry by irrevocably influencing management and bringing to the industry a new standard of quality and consistency.

Other important trends that have defined vacation ownership in the 1990s include

- increasing flexibility for timeshare purchasers;
- a greater variety of types of timeshares offered;
- development of larger projects that offer a more complete amenity package;
- a growing number of multisite timeshare programs;
- more professional resort management;
- globalization of the industry; and
- continued expansion of annual sales.[2]

During the past few years, timesharing has been one of the fastest-growing vacation and real estate industries in the country and in the world. It is estimated that over 2.5 million households own a timeshare interval in over 4,145 resorts, 800 percent more than in 1980.[3] Sales approached an estimated $4 billion in worldwide timeshare sales volume in 1994.[4] About 560,000 timeshare intervals were sold in 1994 (roughly 460 percent more than in 1980). In addition, timeshare ownership has grown at an average compound rate of 16 percent annually over the last eight years.[5]

Notes

1. David M. Disick and George W. Van der Ploeg, "Vacation Ownership Clubs: Planning, Financing, and Development," *The Real Estate Finance Journal*, Spring 1994.
2. Personal communication with Edwin McMullen, chair, Hilton Grand Vacations Company, 1994.
3. Ragatz Associates, Inc., *The 1995 Worldwide Resort Timeshare Industry* (Washington, D.C.: American Resort Development Association, Alliance for Timeshare Excellence, 1995).
4. Ragatz Associates, Inc., *The Resort Timeshare Industry in the United States* (Eugene, Ore.: Ragatz Associates, Inc., 1995).
5. Ragatz Associates, Inc., *The 1995 Worldwide Resort Timeshare Industry.* ■

figure 1-1

Development Team Organization

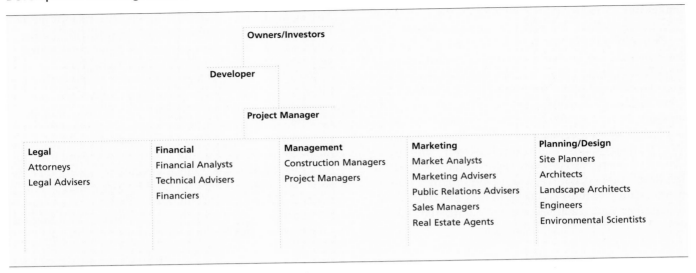

In seeking consultants, developers should inspect other projects in which prospective consultants have participated and review their qualifications and experience with other developers. Developers must also be certain that the most competent members of the consultant's staff are assigned to their projects. Before retaining a consulting firm, developers should meet with key members of the firm's staff to gauge each individual's as well as the firm's qualifications.

The development team should also include individuals with extensive local experience in and knowledge of the relevant regulatory processes and a demonstrated ability to anticipate potential public concerns. Developers should avoid the pitfall of assembling a team of consultants who are experienced in designing and constructing the type of project planned but lack a full understanding of the local environment. An appropriate mix of national and local talent is generally more successful in getting the job done.

Stages of the Development Process

The development process for resort and resort communities consists of three general stages: feasibility analysis and planning (including permitting and financing), construction, and operations/management. Because the development of a resort community is often undertaken as a number of separate but interrelated development projects, each with its own development time line and development team, the general stages often overlap during the creation, maturation, and evolution of a specific resort or resort community.

Feasibility Analysis and Planning. The feasibility analysis and planning for a resort or resort community begins when a developer becomes interested in responding to market demand in a specific geographic area. During

this stage, the developer evaluates market demand, identifies a development site, formulates a development concept, considers options, refines the project concept, determines whether the concept is feasible, prepares plans, obtains the necessary approvals, and arranges the needed financing (see Figure 1-2).

In some cases, the developer begins with a determination of the best use for a specific site. In other cases, the developer begins with knowledge about a potential market and initiates a search for the best available site. Experience has shown that the latter approach stands a better chance of success for new development. Too frequently, problems stem from attempts to force a project on a particular site simply because the developer already owns or controls the site and not because the desired use or site is appropriate. Much resort development today, however, involves the repositioning of existing resort properties, which must necessarily begin with a specific site. Nevertheless, while the initiating factors differ from one case to another, the development practices required to plan a project and ensure its success demonstrate many similarities.

Essentially, creating a project concept calls for identifying the nature of the proposed development or its desired image. Determining project image or ambience in turn influences decisions about the type of required facilities, their arrangement and quality, operational needs, marketing techniques, and many other details.

As will be reiterated throughout this book, piloting a project through the development process to maturity involves the constant thinking and rethinking of the project concept as well as the continuous reevaluation of available information and refinement of projections, especially in the case of large-scale, long-term multiuse resort projects. The ongoing effort requires reconnais-

figure 1-2

Feasibility Analysis and Planning Process

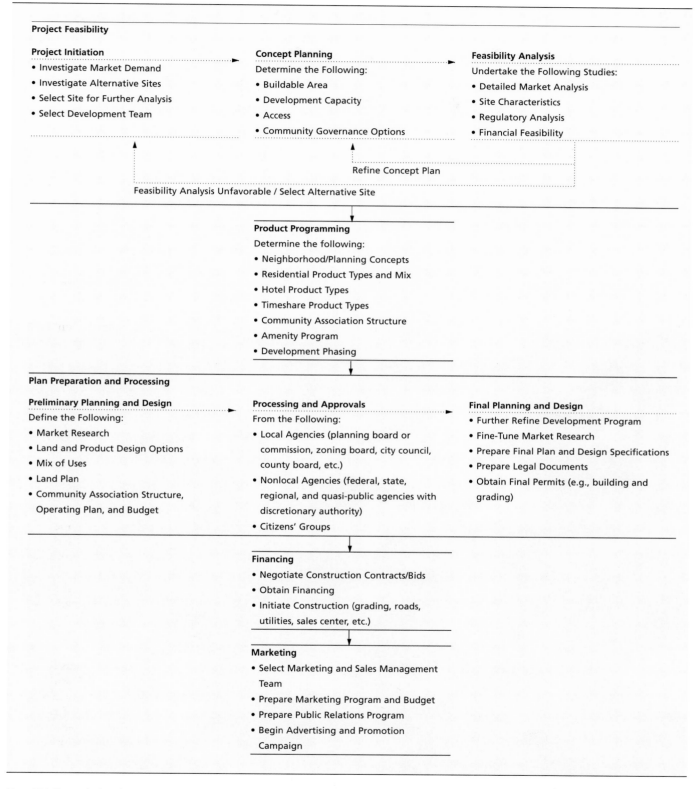

Project Feasibility

Project Initiation
- Investigate Market Demand
- Investigate Alternative Sites
- Select Site for Further Analysis
- Select Development Team

Concept Planning
Determine the Following:
- Buildable Area
- Development Capacity
- Access
- Community Governance Options

Feasibility Analysis
Undertake the Following Studies:
- Detailed Market Analysis
- Site Characteristics
- Regulatory Analysis
- Financial Feasibility

Refine Concept Plan

Feasibility Analysis Unfavorable / Select Alternative Site

Product Programming
Determine the following:
- Neighborhood/Planning Concepts
- Residential Product Types and Mix
- Hotel Product Types
- Timeshare Product Types
- Community Association Structure
- Amenity Program
- Development Phasing

Plan Preparation and Processing

Preliminary Planning and Design
Define the Following:
- Market Research
- Land and Product Design Options
- Mix of Uses
- Land Plan
- Community Association Structure, Operating Plan, and Budget

Processing and Approvals
From the Following:
- Local Agencies (planning board or commission, zoning board, city council, county board, etc.)
- Nonlocal Agencies (federal, state, regional, and quasi-public agencies with discretionary authority)
- Citizens' Groups

Final Planning and Design
- Further Refine Development Program
- Fine-Tune Market Research
- Prepare Final Plan and Design Specifications
- Prepare Legal Documents
- Obtain Final Permits (e.g., building and grading)

Financing
- Negotiate Construction Contracts/Bids
- Obtain Financing
- Initiate Construction (grading, roads, utilities, sales center, etc.)

Marketing
- Select Marketing and Sales Management Team
- Prepare Marketing Program and Budget
- Prepare Public Relations Program
- Begin Advertising and Promotion Campaign

Note: This figure depicts the general sequence of activities typical for resort development projects; however, there are many variations. The figure emphasizes planning and design factors; many other items that are part of the development process are not shown. Resort development is an iterative process, and it may be necessary to return to and repeat some steps in the process several times.

William Bone
Chair of the Board
Sunrise Company
Palm Desert, California

William Bone founded the Sunrise Company in 1963 and is chair of the board and chief executive officer. The Sunrise Company develops recreational and residential communities in southern California and Mexico. It is currently developing Indian Ridge Country Club, a private community located in Palm Desert, California. This $500 million community, with 1,300 homes planned around two 18-hole Arnold Palmer golf courses, broke ground in 1992. Sunrise recently ventured into Mexico with the development of two golf resort communities, Sunrise at Bajamar and Cabo San Lucas Country Club, both in Baja California.

The Sunrise Company has built approximately 10,000 homes; in fact, the Los Angeles Times *annually lists the Sunrise Company as one of the largest residential builders in southern*

California. In addition to Indian Ridge, the company has developed the following golf course-oriented recreational communities in or near Palm Springs: Sunrise Country Club, Rancho Las Palmas Country Club, Monterey Country Club, Lakes Country Club, Palm Valley Country Club, PGA West, Rancho Las Palmas Marriott Resort, and the Desert Springs Marriott Resort. In addition, the Sunrise Company was a partner in the development of Eastlake Country Club near San Diego. Eastlake Country Club is a golf course-oriented, primary-home master-planned community with 3,200 residences.

Born in 1942, Bone received a BA in economics from Stanford University in 1963 and an MBA from the Harvard University Graduate School of Business Administration in 1965.

Starting large-scale, multiphased developments toward the end of a business cycle can be very risky. It is preferable to start early in an economic recovery since most large projects experience at least one economic down-

The Lakes in Riverside County, California, has transformed a barren desert landscape into a golf oasis with 23 lakes and over 1,000 shade trees. The 902 homes all have lakeside or golf course views.

turn before they are completed. It is best if the downturn is in a project's later years when debt is lower than in earlier years, which is when debt is at its greatest. Nonetheless, a developer must have sufficient debt and equity resources to carry a project through to fruition.

Staying power is the first requirement for success; without it, projects that might have been successful fail. And, it is important to calculate the break-even point before committing to a project. A higher break-even point—that is, a higher sales rate—means that the project is riskier. Develop a pro forma (both cash flow and profit and loss) to the actual sellout of the last phase of multi-phased projects. Interim accounting can be deceiving as to how the project actually is doing.

It's easy to make money in the good times; the key is to survive the bad times. The only thing for sure is that when business is really good, it will get worse and vice versa. A developer needs to build up strong liquidity in the good times to survive and take advantage of the opportunities in the bad times.

Avoid personal guarantees on land acquisition and development loans. The failure to heed this advice has broken more developers than anything else. If more equity is needed to avoid the need for a guarantee, then by all means put it in or find a partner.

Since experience is the best insurance against making expensive mistakes, a developer needs to make sure he can keep an experienced management team.

Drive-to resorts (those within a two- to three-hour drive) have a tendency to be less cyclical than fly-to resorts.

It is important to identify an unfulfilled demand for a specific product in a specific location. A developer must be able to describe the housing product in sufficient detail for an architect to design the product. A developer needs to select the best possible location for the project in comparison to the existing and future competition. Be sure that everyone else is at a competitive disadvantage to you.

The most common mistake is not having a superior land plan, including the appropriate recreational and other amenities. The objective is to maximize the residential lot values in the process by creating the maximum lot premium potential. In addition, the developer must create a superior housing product, not only the internal function of the house, but also the architectural and landscape architectural appeal. Moreover, the design features of a pure vacation home are different from the design features of a preretirement second home, and customer preferences regarding product design, quality,

amenities, price points, and security are constantly changing. A constant updating of consumer research is critical.

It is necessary to establish sales prices so that the consumer receives the best value in relation to the competition. The consumer will weigh the tradeoff between quality and price. The maximum market penetration is typically not achieved by delivering either the highest quality or the lowest price, but it is a delicate balance somewhere in between.

Build the project on schedule and within budget; merchandise and market the project aggressively to maximize sales in a short time frame; and service the customer after the sale professionally and expeditiously. Customer satisfaction is paramount, not only to minimize future problems but also to maximize referrals. Fifty percent of master-planned community home sales typically come from referrals by happy homeowners. Moreover, it is necessary to watch the housing resale market. The resale market must be healthy for the new home housing market to be healthy.

A resort operating company is in the fantasy fulfillment business. It is necessary to cultivate a hands-on, management-intensive business rather than sitting back and expecting that the business will be successful.

■

sance of the prospective market at the same time that product types and densities, amenities, facilities, and buildout periods are conceptualized and potential development constraints evaluated. All these items require a preliminary investigation. Thereafter, as each step of the feasibility analysis is completed and used in further refining the project, more detailed steps must be pursued. Without provision for the careful coordination and consideration of all these factors, the development process will be flawed from the start.

Construction. The construction stage for a resort or resort community not only marks the beginning of construction, but also triggers the continuation of planning and the initiation of the marketing and sales program. The planning stage typically extends into the construction stage, with changes made to the development concept, development program, and development plans in response to new information about market demand, site conditions, competition, and other factors.

Cordillera, a mountain resort in Colorado.

The Mahogany Run Golf Course, St. Thomas, United States Virgin Islands, offers striking views of the ocean and surrounding hills, making it a choice location for a resort.

During the construction stage of the development process, the developer is exposed to many uncertainties, all of them potentially expensive. Unlike the planning stage, where an option on the land may have kept the cash contributions to a minimum, major amounts of cash and human effort are now committed. Even when developers have nonrecourse financing and receive substantial fees upfront, their reputations—and usually a lot more—are on the line. The developer must be able to manage the construction activities—ensuring that all players complete their jobs on time and within budget —in an environment characterized by a high degree of uncertainty.

In most large resort development projects, the developer acts as the general contractor and subcontracts most of the construction. For smaller projects, a general contractor is often hired to oversee construction. In either case, the developer plays a vital role in coordinating all the players during the construction process. The developer must also make sure that construction and marketing occur within budget and with long-term management in mind, especially in complex multiphase developments that involve several builders, many different users and markets, and many opportunities for public involvement. The construction phase may begin and end many times in the life of the project as different elements are started and completed.

Operations/Management. The operations/management stage begins when the first element of the resort is ready for use. This project element may be a hotel or lodging facility, a housing product, or a recreational facility or program. The operations/management stage of the development process extends for the life of the community, even after the original developer may no longer be involved. Revitalization, renovation, and repositioning of the community or of specific elements of the community can be an integral part of this stage of development.

The management of the residential component of resort communities differs from that of primary-home residential communities in that owners often reside in their units only periodically. This often necessitates more extensive professional property management services, especially for landscape maintenance. Where properties are available for rent, a much more intensive property management system similar to a hotel operation is required. Resort communities and facilities can be owned and managed as commercial for-profit enterprises or as part of a not-for-profit community association of the property owners.

Developers often plan for the eventual transfer of community management functions to community associations. When a community association is to be empowered, the particulars of control should be clearly disclosed in consistent documents covering land covenants, bylaws, sales literature, sales contracts, and property reports. The period of developer ownership and support should be precisely defined with an appropriate transitional phase and legal documentation of the

Deering Bay is a 220-acre resort community located south of Miami on Biscayne Bay. It comprises 286 condominiums, townhouses, and single-family detached residences, an 18-hole golf course, three marinas, beaches, and a tennis center. One of the unexpected challenges Deering Bay faced in its early stages of development was the natural disaster caused by Hurricane Andrew in 1992, which tore through the property leaving only royal palm trees standing. The development went through four months of cleanup and replanting that involved the replacement of the mangrove barrier and 3,000 trees.

specific terms and conditions. The access rights of non-property owners to facilities (through club ownerships, for example) must be clearly defined.

Specialized contracted management can be particularly useful when commercial ownership or community association expertise is not available or is uneconomical. This strategy requires careful negotiation of a management services contract that specifies the level of management involvement and financial objectives. The use of specialized management is particularly attractive in the case of a substantial resort community operation. Good communication between owners and operators is important to ensure the proper level of management.

Notes

1. J. Richard McElyea and Gregory L. Cory, "Resort Investment and Development: An Overview of an Evolving Market," in *Property* (Mellon/McMahan Real Estate Advisors, Inc., Summer 1992), pp. 3–6.

2. Ibid.

3. Amy Willard Cross, *The Summer House: A Tradition of Leisure* (Toronto: HarperCollins Publishers, Ltd., 1992), p. 105.

4. Robert A.M. Stern, ed. *The Anglo American Suburb (issue of Architectural Design Profile)* (New York: St. Martin's Press, 1981), p. 68.

5. *Fodor's Selected Resorts and Hotels of the U.S.* (New York: Random House, 1988), p. 140.

6. Andrea Chambers, *Dream Resorts: 25 Exclusive and Unique American Hotels, Inns, Lodges and Spas* (New York: Clarkson N. Potter, Inc., 1983), p. 36.

7. Stern, *The Anglo American Suburb*, p. 69.

8. Ibid., p. 73.

9. Chambers, *Dream Resorts*, pp. 42–48.

10. *Fodor's*, p. 212.

11. John Bowermaster, "Aspen: The Call of the Wild," *New York Times Magazine*, January 21, 1990.

12. Robert Burchell, and David Listokin, *The Environmental Impact Handbook* (New Brunswick, N.J.: Center for Urban Policy Research, 1975), p. 8.

13. Morton C. Paulson, *The Great Land Hustle* (Chicago: Henry Regnery Co., 1972), p. 213.

14. Jonathan Tisch, president, Loews Hotel Corporation, speech at ULI Seminar "Trends and Issues in Resort Development," Tucson, Ariz., 1991.

15. Ragatz Associates, Inc., *The Worldwide Resort Timesharing Industry* (Eugene, Ore.: Ragatz Associates, Inc., 1990).

2. Resort Market Analysis

A well-conceived resort project *must* begin with a thorough understanding of its prospective market. The process may start with either a formal exercise or the results of years of familiarity with the market under consideration. Market analysis is fundamental to a development project's financial feasibility and success. No matter how attractive a project's physical plan or how resourceful its financial plan, the numbers will not work unless the project appeals to targeted market segments.

Market analysis must start with an understanding of the broad demographic and psychographic trends that are taking place nationally and internationally and that drive opportunities for resort development. It must then follow up with careful research into the competitive situation for a specific concept and location—including both demand and supply factors—to guide the identification of a strategic insight and a development opportunity. Depending on the objectives and the nature of the site, the market analysis may involve several types of markets, including recreational user markets, residential markets, timeshare markets, hotel and guest markets, and commercial real estate markets.

Native trees, indigenous grasses, and exposed lava outcroppings are part of the landscape design at the Gold Course at Wailea on Maui.

Overall Resort Market Analysis

Although appropriate market research is important in the planning of any real estate project, it is particularly important in the case of resort and second-home development projects because of both demand-timing issues (the decision to take a vacation or purchase a second home is discretionary and can be postponed or accelerated) and location issues (vacationers and second-home buyers can choose to travel or locate to any one of a number of areas across the country or around the world). Given that resort vacations and second homes are not absolute necessities, estimating the quantity and quality of demand does not rely solely on population or household growth. This characteristic necessitates a close examination of the quality of potential demand. Moreover, resort demand is guided by economic activities at locations away from the site of the resort—the feeder markets. As a result, the analyst must determine from where the demand for second homes and room reservations is likely to emanate —from the immediate state, from a multistate area, from completely different sections of the country, or from international locations. As an example, California is a primary feeder market for resorts in Hawaii, Baja Mexico, the desert Southwest, and the Pacific Northwest. Therefore, the demand for resort properties in these locations is in part a function of the California economy.

Most resorts compete over a much wider geographic area than most commercial hotels and/or traditional

Sports such as windsurfing and sailing are popular recreational pursuits that can provide additional activities for resorts at relatively low costs.

primary-home residential communities. Resort hotels in Hawaii draw from the entire United States as well as from Japan, other Pacific Rim nations, Europe, and South America—essentially the entire globe. Even regional resorts draw from a relatively broad geographic market. For example, the Semiahmoo Resort in Blaine, Washington, draws approximately one-third of its second-home buyers from Washington state; one-third from outside the state, particularly from California; and one-third from Canada (particularly recent Asian immigrants).

Understanding Demographics and Psychographics[1]

In general, current demographic and psychographic trends suggest that the market should favor resort and recreation development in the latter part of the 1990s and into the next century. The baby boomers began turning 50 in 1996, and 78 million of them began to enter the period of highest earnings and greatest discre-

tionary dollars. Notes James Chaffin, president of the Spring Island Company in Spring Island, South Carolina, "Remember, ours is not a need business, ours is a want business. Our markets do have increasing discretionary time and money, but they are increasingly sophisticated consumers demanding higher quality in real value, more services, and more conveniences. We must first find out what people want, and then find out if we can figure out a way to give it to them."

It is clear that targeted marketing will be the watchword for the remainder of the 1990s. It is always true that, looking backward, it is easy to see enormous changes that have taken place and that are still unfolding. But what is more important is the prospective changes that we need to understand. The immediate task is to look at the demand profile ahead and build for that. The people who will reside, work, and spend their leisure hours in our real estate over the next 20 years can be counted today. We know their ages and ethnicity and, for the most part, their household composition and educational attainment. From these basic data, we can predict a broad range of consumer wants and needs.

In general, demographic trends suggest that the near future will see slower growth in population, households, and the labor force. Instead, increased diversity by household type, income distribution, ethnicity, and geography will characterize the nation's population. An increasingly segmented marketplace will require careful targeting of product types.

The overriding issue is the importance of the baby boomers. Through the decade of the 1990s, the number of people in their 40s will have expanded by 11 million and the number of people in their 50s by almost 1 million. The result is progressively mature consumers into the first decade of the 21st century, at which time the greatest numeric growth will occur among people in their 50s and 60s. In other words, demand for recreational property is likely to continue grow for the next

Fishing at the Homestead in Hot Springs, Virginia. Fishing remains one of the most popular recreational pursuits in North America.

Many market analysts and researchers recognize that demographic measures such as age, race, or income are not the only sources of data for predicting consumer demand and behavior. Understanding a consumer's attitudes and values—*psychographics*—has become an increasingly important market analysis tool within the real estate industry.

Marketers use psychographic segmentation systems to predict consumer purchase behavior by segmenting consumers according to key psychological attributes. A commonly used psychographic tool in today's market is SRI International's Values and Lifestyles Program (VALS™ 2). The basic premise of VALS psychographic marketing is that people buy products and services that fit easily into their lifestyle or that remind them of themselves. VALS and other psychographic segmentation systems enable marketers to identify and match the characteristics of the target consumer with the characteristics of the product they want to sell.

The VALS program contains an eight-part consumer segmentation system that is based on two dimensions: self-orientation and resources. Research shows that consumers are motivated by one or more of three basic self-orientations: principle, status, and action. Principle-oriented consumers are guided by an internal set of values, morals, or idealized criteria that they believe to be good and true. Status-oriented consumers are driven to purchase products and services that demonstrate their success to other people, especially those within their peer group. Action-oriented consumers are guided by a desire to make either an emotional or physical impact. A consumer's resources include health, energy level, self-confidence, and eagerness to buy, along with age, education, and income.

Psychographic segmentation systems can be an important resource in the merchandising, marketing, and sales of real estate products. Understanding the consumer's values, beliefs, and motivations can enable design and development professionals to create a product image that successfully reflects consumer demand. When applied to advertising campaigns, psychographic segmentation/classification allows for more precise market penetration and product positioning. In addition, properly trained sales representatives can use psychographic classification techniques to identify elements of importance to prospective buyers.

■

20 years. Other key demographic trends of importance to resort developers are outlined below.

Household Structure. Over the last 20 years, the United States has moved inexorably away from the traditional household model of a married couple with children at home. Today, only about 25 percent of all households account for married couples with children at home. About 30 percent of households are married couples without children at home, 10 percent single parents with children, 25 percent singles, and 10 percent other types of family and nonfamily households. Homebuyers, shoppers, and workers consist of the full range of household types.

Twenty years ago, 70 percent of all households included a married couple. By 1990, the proportion fell to 55 percent. In the 2000 Census, households with and without married couples are expected to be about equal. In the 1950s, 70 percent of American families consisted of a sole wage-earner father, a stay-at-home mother, and a couple of baby boomer kids. Today, less than 12 percent of all households fit that mold, a fact that is extremely important for marketing. For example, the percentage of single timeshare owners rose from 7.4 percent in 1978 to 13.7 percent in 1990 and can go higher. Further, singles, especially single women, are increasingly interested in second homes.

Income. The last couple of years have focused considerable attention on the degree to which America's rich are getting richer as the poor account for a larger percentage of the population and the middle class shrinks. While there is some basis to each of these contentions, the various income trends deserve more detailed examination. For example, households headed by people between 45 and 54 years of age registered the highest median income in the 1990 Census at about $42,000 a year, followed by $38,600 for households aged 35 to 44 years. The numbers fail to reflect that middle-income households experienced real income increases in the 1980s, as did 65- to 74-year-olds, even though all other age categories experienced real income declines. The significant point for the 1990s is the sharp income growth that will occur in the 35- to 54-year-old population, which is typically the highest-income group. So the prospects for the resort industry are quite favorable from an income perspective.

Employed persons generally achieve their highest earnings during their late 40s, with discretionary spending power greatest for people in their 50s. Accordingly, the aging baby boomers command the wherewithal for high levels of consumer spending over the next 20 years. Moreover, the roughly 65 million Americans who are now over age 50 control two-thirds of the nation's net wealth, account for 80 percent of luxury travel, buy 48 percent of luxury cars, and own 46 percent of all timeshares—and 78 million baby boomers are now moving through their 50s.

But developers must keep in mind that discretionary income does not have to be spent; it can be invested.

figure 2-1

Sports and Recreation Participation Rates—Participated More Than Once

In Millions/Seven Years of Age and Older

	1991	1992	1993	1994	1995
1. Exercise Walking	69.6	67.8	64.4	70.8	70.3
2. Swimming	66.2	63.1	61.4	60.3	61.5
3. Bicycle Riding	54.0	54.6	47.9	49.8	56.3
4. Exercising with Equipment	39.2	39.4	34.9	43.8	44.3
5. Fishing	47.0	47.6	51.2	45.7	44.2
6. Camping	47.1	47.3	42.7	42.9	42.8
7. Bowling	40.4	42.5	41.3	37.4	41.9
8. Billiards/Pool	29.6	29.3	29.4	34.0	31.1
9. Basketball	26.2	28.2	29.6	28.2	30.1
10. Hiking	22.7	21.6	19.5	25.3	25.0
11. Boating—Motor/Power	22.4	22.3	20.7	26.4	25.0
12. Golf	24.7	24.0	22.6	24.6	24.0
13. Roller Skating—In-Line	7.3	9.7	12.4	19.5	23.9
14. Aerobic Exercising	25.9	27.8	24.9	23.2	23.1
15. Running/Jogging	22.5	21.9	20.3	20.6	20.6
16. Dart Throwing	17.0	18.8	19.2	21.2	19.4
17. Volleyball	22.6	22.1	20.5	17.4	18.0
18. Softball	19.6	19.2	17.9	18.1	17.6
19. Hunting with Firearms	17.1	17.8	18.5	16.4	16.3
20. Baseball	16.5	15.1	16.7	15.1	15.7
21. Roller Skating	18.6	16.8	15.3	14.0	13.6
22. Tennis	16.7	17.3	14.2	11.6	12.6
23. Football (Touch)	NA	NA	NA	NA	12.1
24. Soccer	10.0	10.6	10.3	12.5	12.0
25. Step Aerobics	6.8	9.2	10.6	11.5	11.4
26. Target Shooting	11.5	12.3	12.8	12.2	11.2
27. Mountain Biking—On-Road	NA	NA	10.5	9.0	10.5

Note: NA = not available.

Source: National Sporting Goods Association, Mt. Prospect., IL , 1996.

And savings rates typically rise as people age. To the extent that the baby boomers view second homes as investments, developers can benefit from consumer interest in investing rather than spending. With half the population over age 35, most people do not have to buy and furnish a first or a second home or acquire other essentials. Therefore, most consumer spending is discretionary by about the time a person reaches age 35. As a result, people buy largely because they want to upgrade, and only when they feel feel comfortable about job security and their economic well-being.

Another important issue is the huge inheritances that baby boomers can expect to receive. Their parents are the wealthiest generation in American history. According to David Stewart at the University of Southern California, persons over age 60 have a net worth of $6.8 trillion. Stewart projects that between 2002 and 2006 the transfer of funds from parents to heirs could reach 6.5 per-

cent of the gross domestic product and represent a potentially immense source of capital for baby boomers.

Ethnicity. One of the most significant demographic shifts in the United States is the population's growing ethnic diversity. Non–Hispanic whites represented 75 percent of the 1990 population, African Americans 12 percent, Hispanics 9 percent, Asians 3 percent, and Native Americans almost 1 percent. A dynamic change is occurring among the various populations. Approximately 80 percent of all population growth for the next 20 years is expected to come from the African American, Hispanic, and Asian communities. Minorities now represent about a quarter of the population; by 2010, they will represent about a third.

Immigration totaled approximately 8 million people in the 1980s, 75 percent legal and 25 percent illegal, and will probably remain at the same level throughout the 1990s. The Bureau of the Census estimates that

	1991	1992	1993	1994	1995
28. Backpacking	10.4	9.7	9.2	9.8	10.2
29. Skiing (Alpine)	10.4	10.8	10.5	10.6	9.3
30. Calisthenics	12.3	11.5	10.8	8.5	9.3
31. Table Tennis	NA	9.5	NA	7.8	9.3
32. Football (Tackle)	NA	NA	NA	NA	8.3
33. Canoeing	8.7	7.2	6.5	8.5	7.2
34. Ice/Figure Skating	7.9	6.7	6.9	7.8	7.1
35. Water Skiing	9.0	7.9	8.1	7.4	6.9
36. Badminton	NA	7.0	NA	5.4	5.8
37. Mountain Biking—Off-Road	NA	NA	4.6	5.7	5.7
38. Snorkeling	5.4	4.8	4.9	5.9	5.7
39. Archery (Target)	NA	NA	NA	NA	4.8
40. Racquetball	6.3	6.6	5.4	5.3	4.7
41. Martial Arts	3.2	NA	3.6	NA	4.5
42. Skate Boarding	8.0	5.5	5.6	4.9	4.3
43. Climbing—Mountain/Rock	NA	4.3	NA	3.4	4.0
44. Sailing	4.1	3.5	3.8	4.1	3.7
45. Skiing (Cross-Country)	4.4	3.5	3.7	3.6	3.4
46. Hockey (Roller)	NA	NA	1.5	2.2	3.2
47. Cheerleading	NA	NA	NA	NA	2.9
48. Hockey (Ice)	1.8	1.6	1.7	1.9	2.5
49. Kayaking/Rafting	2.0	NA	2.1	NA	2.5
50. Scuba (Open Water)	2.0	2.2	2.4	2.2	2.4
51. Snowboarding	1.6	1.2	1.8	2.1	2.3
52. Boxing	NA	0.7	NA	NA	1.4
53. Snowshoeing	NA	0.4	NA	NA	0.6
54. Windsurfing	0.8	0.8	0.6	0.7	0.5

51 percent of African Americans and 55 percent of Hispanics reported middle-level incomes in 1989. In other words, middle-class America is rapidly becoming as diverse as the country as a whole. Yet, the real estate marketplace has not sufficiently recognized ethnic diversity. Specialized demand is strongest for residential and retail projects, but more inclusive marketing could benefit most land uses, particularly for second homes, resorts, and timeshares.

Psychographics and Recreational/Leisure Preferences. In a resort, demand needs to be approached in terms of the demand for the enjoyment of a particular amenity and/or lifestyle that is to be offered and marketed to the visitor or buyer. The analysis must consider the psychographics of the market as well as its economics and demographics (see feature box on page 39). It must determine what recreational and leisure pursuits interest specific market segments as defined by geographic area

and income level. It is for these reasons that demand analysis must go beyond the methods of demographic and/or economic analysis often associated with primary-home communities and commercial hotels and inevitably involve some original research and surveys. Specifically, the analysis must determine what combination of leisure pursuits, settings, and residential accommodations are underserved in the market.

From a broad perspective, it is critical to gather and evaluate data on recreation and sports participation rates to understand what the potential market prefers in leisure activities and whether the market encompasses underserved segments. Each year, the National Sporting Goods Association conducts a national survey to determine the recreation and sports participation rates for 54 separate recreation/sports activities (see figure 2-1 above). The data can be used to identify emerging trends in recreational patterns. For example, in-line skating

Ernest M. Miller, Jr.
Chair
Miller Financial Enterprises
Boca Raton, Florida

Ernest M. "Bud" Miller is chair of Miller Financial Enterprises, a firm he founded in April 1996 to pursue various real estate investment opportunities. Before founding his own firm, Miller served as chair of the Arvida Company, which currently has 20 primary- and second-home communities under development in five states. Of these, seven are golf course communities.

Miller joined Arvida in January 1980 and served as vice president for finance and administration until February 1984. At that time, he cofounded Wilson Miller Capital Corporation, a real estate and investment banking firm, and served as its chair until April 1987. He rejoined Arvida in April 1987 as executive vice president and chief financial officer and, in March 1989, was named president and, in 1992, chief executive. Miller stepped down as CEO in March 1995 and became chair.

Before 1980, Miller was a vice president at Penn Central Corporation and director of business analysis and planning at the Pennsylvania Company. He also served in other positions, including director of acquisitions and vice president of the financial service group at Sperry & Hutchinson Company.

Miller was born in 1942. He received a BS in psychology from Tufts University in 1964, served for four years in the U.S. Marine Corps, and received an MBA from the Harvard University Graduate School of Business Administration in 1970.

Note: Mr. Miller made the following observations during an interview that took place while he was still chair of Arvida. Many of his comments relate to Arvida's business practices rather than to those of Miller Financial Enterprises.

In prior years, in our industry as well as other industries, market research too often consisted of several execu-

Longboat Key Club, one of many projects developed by Arvida, is a 1,100-acre resort, private club, and residential community located on the gulf coast of Florida.

tives sitting in a room discussing what customers wanted based on "our years of experience."

In the early 1990s, Arvida started a more disciplined approach to market research. We wanted to base our decisions on facts, not beliefs. We instituted programs to obtain demographic data on our specific markets: the size of the population base; growth trends; age groups; income groups; and major employers and trends among these employers. We also did surveys to determine what the various market segments wanted to find in a community and housing product. We then used focus groups to help us refine product design and floorplans. We gathered hard data on the competition to determine what was selling, where it was selling, and at what price it was selling.

As a result, Arvida knows who its customer is, how many there are, what they want, and what they are willing to pay. This enables the firm to design a better product, and our sales and profit margins have increased significantly.

Market research does not stop once a community is started but is an ongoing process. We instituted a system at Arvida that gathers data on everyone who comes into our sales centers. Arvida can track people who did not buy and find out why. Arvida can track who bought and build up profiles of who is buying and why. The firm will continue to survey customers at sale, at closing, three to four months after closing, and then annually. This enables us to remain in touch with our customers. We do not want to wait until we have a problem before we address what needs to be changed. In addition, Arvida has a great base to assist us with new product design. The market today is shifting faster than ever before. Resort developers need to stay on top of the market to be able to refine products so as to meet ever-changing customer demands.

Market research also helps us in designing amenities for our communities. By using detailed information on what our customers want and what they are willing to pay for, we are building amenities that are more suited for our target markets. As a result, we are able to get a "bigger bang" for our amenity dollars while often being able to lower our expenditures for amenities because of our sharper focus.

Some of Arvida's new communities will continue to include golf courses. The design of the courses will be targeted to our customers, e.g., if customers have mid-teen handicaps, we avoid building a course for low-handicap players. The membership structure needs to reflect the target market, i.e., a high-end second-home community probably should have an equity membership, whereas a

moderately priced community might need a semiprivate or daily-fee structure.

A resort developer's organization must change to meet the challenges of the 1990s. As many others had done, Arvida had built up a bureaucracy in the 1970s and 1980s, and it was not appropriate for the 1990s. We restructured our company, pushed decisions to those closest to the customers, and removed several layers of management. To accomplish this, we had to ensure that we all had a common understanding of the company's vision, direction, and values.

Arvida has also been trying to integrate functions and have employees think and act as a team. If there is a problem, we do not want the answer to be "It isn't my job to fix it." It is everyone's job to fix it. If a customer has a problem, everyone should be able to deal with the issue. This team approach requires rethinking compensation philosophy. Arvida historically has had an incentive-driven compensation program. What we are changing is that the incentive will be tied more to the results of the team rather than to the individual.

There are and will be great opportunities for resort developers, but to capitalize on these opportunities developers must be flexible and willingly embrace new concepts while maintaining core values. Customers will reward developers who are customer-oriented and provide products with quality and value.

Typical homebuyers at Harbour Ridge—an 814-acre primary- and second-home community in Stuart, Florida— are couples from the Northeast and Midwest in their early 50s to early 60s who will make the community their second home until they retire.

showed a dramatic increase in participation rates from 1991 to 1995, rising from 7.3 percent to 23.9 percent.

Most activities in the survey can be accommodated both within and outside a resort, but resorts can offer especially attractive environments for many of the activities. Swimming, the second-ranking activity, is a perfect example of a recreational activity that can be more attractively offered in a resort than in most urban areas. Many activities are poorly suited to urban areas but lend themselves well to a recreational or resort setting. These include fishing, camping, hiking, hunting, mountain biking, backpacking, Alpine skiing, canoeing, snorkeling, climbing, kayaking/rafting, and scuba diving. Other activities such as bicycle riding, boating, golf, and tennis can be accommodated attractively in both urban and resort environments.

A resort must carefully assess how it can differentiate its recreational offerings to attract a market with access to the same offerings in an urban setting. Usually, the setting itself is the primary means of differentiation, but other design and programming features should be considered when assessing market potential.

Surprisingly, resorts often fail to accommodate some of the simplest activities in an appealing fashion. For example, exercise walking—the top-ranking activity in the survey—merely requires an aesthetically pleasing pathway or trail. Yet, it is striking how many resorts do not provide attractive walking facilities.

Conducting Overall Resort Market Studies

For sizable resort ventures that can accommodate a variety of resort uses, detailed market studies should be conducted to indicate the potential revenues and absorption associated with

- residential properties in terms of price, rental rates, ownership types, lots versus units, single-family versus multifamily units, and owner-occupancy versus vacation use;

- hotel rooms in terms of quality classification, facilities, and average room rates;
- timeshare properties in terms of price, ownership types, and unit sizes;
- potential revenue-producing recreational facilities such as tennis, golf, skiing, marinas, etc.;
- retail commercial areas in terms of tenant mix, supportable square footage, and obtainable lease rates; and
- other types of development opportunities such as recreational vehicle parks.

The market analysis should include, but not necessarily be limited to, the following tasks:

- defining a primary market region from which buyers and tourists could be expected to be drawn. Market area definitions should be based on such factors as time-distance relationships, comparable travel costs, the information available at competitive projects, and tourist origin and destination data.
- estimating the potential demand for various types of development within the defined market. Demand estimates should be based on past preferences of different income groups as reflected in the purchase of recreational lots and homes and modified to reflect current and projected economic conditions and buyer attitudes toward recreational properties. Estimates should be linked to product type and price range and further reflect the regional buyer's ability to purchase. Notes Diana Permar of Permar and Ravenel in Kiawah Island, South Carolina, "Estimates should also be 'reality tested.' Often market estimates exceed any number that any development has ever achieved."[2]
- identifying and surveying related competitive projects in the primary market region. Projects should be surveyed in terms of such factors as physical features, recreational orientation and facilities, locational char-

acteristics and access to market, and real estate products. The intent of the survey is not only to develop a profile of competitive projects but also to synthesize from recent project histories relevant trends in products and markets and to determine the success of such projects in the current market.

Figure 2-2 below provides an organizational framework that describes the type of data and information necessary for a market analysis.

A thorough evaluation of supply and demand characteristics should indicate the product type, price, and size that would maximize market opportunities for new resort development. An analysis of the effect of various recreational development programs and facilities on potential sales and prices should suggest a suitable recreational amenity package. Based on the projected increase in visitors, potential demand for various types of retail and commercial recreational facilities can be estimated. The market study findings provide physical and economic planners and market analysts with guidance for jointly developing a realistic plan for land use allocations for the various development components.

The quality of the market analysis is of paramount importance. Michael Rubin of MRA International notes, "There are two ways to test the market—the soft or 'dumb way' and the hard or 'smart way.' In a rapidly expanding market, the dumb way may suffice . . . in a competitive market, it does not." He differentiates between the dumb and smart approaches in the feature box on page 47 and maintains that dependence on soft market analysis has contributed to disasters. "You do not achieve competitive advantage by reading the same 'play book' as the competition."

figure 2-2

Information for a Resort Market Analysis

Economic Trends
In Resort Area
In Market Area
Labor Force/Unemployment
Income

Population Trends
In Resort Area
In Market Area
Magnitude
Composition (age, income, family type)

Tourist Attractions
Outdoor Recreation
Scenic Features
Cultural/Historic Features
Business/Shopping Opportunities
Conferences/Conventions
Regional/Destination
Climate
Image and Reputation

Tourism Trends
Number
Origin
Seasonality
Composition (age, income, family type)
Expenditure Patterns
Repeat Visits
Length of Stay

The Site
Attractiveness/Views
Access
Proximity to Airport
Quality of Air Service
Surrounding Uses
Utilities and Services
Drive-By Traffic

Competition
Resort Lodging
Hotels/Motels
Resort Condominiums
Vacation Homes
Timeshares/Vacation Ownership Options
Camp Resorts
Costs/Rates
Quality
Absorption Rates
Occupancy Rates
Existing and Proposed
Image and Reputation

Market Area
Location/Delineation
Size
Existing Penetration
Remaining Potential
Composition
Access (distance and costs)

Local Government Climate
Public Regulations
Decision-Making Process
Reaction to Change

Survey of Potential Consumers
Awareness
Likelihood of Purchase
Composition
Desired Product
- Type
- Season
- Price
- Size
- Access
- Amenities
- Services

James J. Chaffin, Jr.
President
Spring Island Company
Spring Island, South Carolina

James J. Chaffin, Jr., is the cofounder (with James W. Light) and president of Chaffin/Light Associates. He has over 27 years of experience in recreational community development. Since 1978, Chaffin and Light have developed Snowmass, Colorado; Semiahmoo near Blaine, Washington; Lake Arrowhead, California; and Callawassie Island and Spring Island near Hilton Head, South Carolina.

Before 1978 and as senior vice president of the Sea Pines Company, Chaffin was involved in several major community developments, including Sea Pines Plantation and Hilton Head Plantation in Hilton Head, South Carolina; Brandermill in Richmond, Virginia; Amelia Island Plantation in Florida; Palmas Del Mar in Puerto Rico; Kiawah Island in Charleston, South Carolina; Wintergreen in Virginia; Big Canoe in Atlanta; and River Hills Plantation in South Carolina.

Chaffin is a graduate of the University of Virginia and holds an MBA from Georgia State University.

Our company is very research-oriented, particularly on the front end of a project. With the technology available today, it is not too difficult to build shelter, and certainly there aren't many new marketing techniques available. Therefore, I believe that the development business is really a process of market identification and product definition. What do people want, do they have a propensity to buy it, is it feasible to provide it, is anyone else currently providing that product, and, if they are, are they doing it well? The rest is just the execution of the idea. Sometimes developers don't take the time to research

Spring Island, near Beaufort, South Carolina, is a 500-member private community on a 3,000-acre island that emphasizes the natural environment.

their markets and go into a project on gut feel alone. Often they fail to capitalize their projects well, relying much more on the potential upside than the possible downside. In addition, many developers change their project focus too quickly. Sometimes they are more focused on a project during the embryonic stages than in the later stages, when it is equally important.

New pioneering developments will probably take the form of attractions—perhaps related to entertainment—that we haven't imagined yet. In addition, a poll in 1991 reported that 60 percent of Americans thought of themselves as environmentalists. While the numbers may not actually be that high, it does point out a second trend: people want to think of themselves that way. People are more interested in how they spend their time rather than how they spend their money. Quality of life is important, particularly to the baby boomers. They want things that are real, that are family-oriented. They don't really want to be on the edge, but they want to feel as if they have been on the edge. Bigger is not better. Glitzy is not nicer. People are looking now for what Hilton Head was 20 years ago. Our project at Spring Island is an embodiment of that new attitude. It is a project that could not have been done ten years ago, and ten years from now perhaps it could be done without the golf and tennis. A third trend is a desire for seclusion.

People are willing to travel to an attraction, if only for a few days, to be entertained. When people are looking for quality of life or "to live the life they have imagined," however, they are more interested in some place that's genuine—to be in touch with things that are real.

Over the next ten years, access will become very important—successful second-home projects will typically be located within a three-hour drive of the primary home. Consequently, a second home is becoming more of an extension of the first home. Communities that offer not only recreational activities but also strong cultural and educational activities will be successful. While America is graying, people nonetheless are expected to live longer, and they are making plans to meet that expectation.

To meet these new opportunities, it is important for a developer to have vision (to see what others don't see), creativity, persistence (development is not an exact science), courage (have a good attitude toward risk), a sense of humor, discipline, integrity (developers have a responsibility for the environment, both natural and built), and humility (90 percent of the development business has more to do with humility, i.e., experience, than it does intelligence).

■

figure 2-3

Strategic Positioning by Using Hard and Soft Market Assessments

---

Strategic Positioning: Hard Market Assessments

Hard or strategic market analysis is more realistic because it is based on

- shifts in tourist demand;
- context-based patterns of growth/decline and strengths/weaknesses;
- specific segmented/clustered sources of demand;
- specific consumer intelligence;
- specific competitor intelligence;
- a dynamic link to operating alternatives; and
- positioning tactics.

Strategic Positioning: Soft Market Assessments

Soft market analysis is typically unrealistic because it is based on

- historical tourist data (often inaccurate);
- generalized patterns of growth/decline;
- extremely broad demand segments;
- little intelligence on consumer patterns;
- no real competitive analysis;
- undeveloped operating assumptions; and
- comparables (even when none exists).

Market Tests

There are two ways to test the market: the soft or "dumb way" and the hard or "smart way." In a rapidly expanding market, the dumb way may suffice . . . in a competitive market, it does not.

The Resort as a Destination Based on Dumb Comparables

- Collect available tourist demand data from tourism bureaus, U.S. Department of Commerce, tracking sources.
- Evaluate standard performance data, including average length of stay, average daily rate, seasonality of demand, growth.
- Assume market capture/penetration of existing demand commensurate with performance data.
- Compare to "comparables."
- Adjust capture expectation to reflect comfort zone in assuming risk.

The Resort as a Product Offering Based on Informed Differentiation

- Identify core segments of demand through customized market analysis.
- Evaluate sources of current and future competition for desired market segments.
- Calibrate market capture/penetration by assessing competitive weaknesses and opportunities.
- Benchmark against best-in-class competitors.
- Elevate performance above expectation and reduce risk through customization of offering.

Source: MRA International, Philadelphia, Penn.

Residential Markets

Successful resort community developers understand that different motivations and factors influence the purchase decision of the various segments that make up the residential resort market. Less successful or unsophisticated developers often emulate the physical plan, amenities, and real estate products of existing resort communities without understanding the market segmentation of the buyers attracted to those communities. While market segments may appear demographically similar, specific segments embody varied push and pull factors. Understanding these factors is critical to the successful planning and marketing of a resort community.

Market analysis for a residential development in a metropolitan area oriented to primary-home residences involves a fairly straightforward market analysis process. Demand for houses is driven by local employment, population, per capita income, and other key variables. For a resort community, however, several different components of housing demand might exist, including second-home investment and second-home, preretirement-, retirement-, and primary-home use, each of which is explained below.

In assessing the market for resort home sales, a few key facts culled from a 1995 study by Ragatz Associates can help set the stage. First, while second homes can be found in nearly every state in the United States, the top six states, in order of preference, are Florida, California, Colorado, North Carolina, Texas, and Arizona. Second, Americans prefer the beach for recreational property ownership, followed by lake settings and the mountains. Other types of locations—such as the tropics, golf course areas, attraction areas, ski areas, and the desert—are significantly less popular.[3]

Residential Market Segments

Each resort community is oriented to different market segments. While some communities are completely dominated by a single principal market segment, others appeal to a range of market segments and differ by the proportion of the targeted segments. For example, at Spring Island in Beaufort, South Carolina, approximately 30 percent of the buyers are expected to become residents of the community (many of them are retirees) and 40 percent seasonal residents, with the rest using their property as a second home for vacations or weekend visits. As illustrated in the matrix in Figure 2-4 (developed for resort communities in the Hilton Head area), the

figure 2-4

Market Segmentation Matrix for Recreational Communities on Hilton Head Island

	Second-Home Investors	Timeshare Buyers	Second-Home Users
Estimated Percentage of Sales	23%	2%	15%
Definition	Investment/vacation use Rent property	Vacation only	Vacation only Seasonal home Does not rent
Profile Age Household Income Net Worth	 35–55 $150,000+ $1.5 million	 35–55 $75,000+ $500,000+	 40–55 $150,000+ $2.5 million
Existing Residence Local Regional National	 5% 30% 65%	 0% 40% 60%	 0% 40% 60%
Product Preferences	Condominiums Cottages	Condominiums	Condominiums Cottages Single-family dwellings Lots
Decision Influences	Variety of experience Use and cash flow Appreciation Access to amenities Ease of ownership Views	Variety of experience Use Access to amenities Ease of ownership Convenience of experience	Use Value and quality Near water Access to amenities Ease of ownership Convenience of experience

Source: Permar & Ravenel, Inc., Kiawah Island, S.C., February 1994.

potential market is generally made up of six principal market segments. Each market segment can obviously be subdivided into submarkets, but this discussion is limited to the principal market segments. While market segments are by definition mutually exclusive, resort communities and individual products within the communities can be designed to appeal to a range of market segments.

Second-Home Investors. These buyers are generally attracted to an area by a wide variety of resort experiences. Most such buyers prefer primary resort locations dominated by natural amenities—the ocean, mountains, lakes—and are most likely to purchase properties in communities with an active resort component and an excellent rental occupancy history. These buyers, like other second-home buyers, are attracted to the idea of owning a second home for their own or business use but either cannot afford or cannot rationalize the purchase without rental income to offset the cost of ownership. Beyond the natural assets of the area, second-home investors are interested in the same kinds of amenities that attract resort guests to an area—a wide variety of recreational amenities and experiences, shopping opportunities, restaurants, entertainment venues, and an emotionally satisfying lifestyle.

Since second-home buyers by definition want to rent their unit when not occupying it, the ease of ownership, availability of high-quality property management services, quality of the community's marketing effort, and history of rental occupancy become influencing factors. Further, with the second-home tax benefits eliminated by the Tax Reform Act of 1986, second-home buyers are now principally interested in a property's cash flow and appreciation expectations.

The second-home market is typically made up families whose household heads are in their 40s and early 50s with incomes in the top 10 percent of all households. Buyers are drawn from large metropolitan areas where the stress of everyday life is an additional motivation to own property in a completely different environment. Although the type of product preferred by the second-home market segment differs among communities, the

Preretirees	Retirees	Primary-Home Users
25%	25%	10%
Vacation now, retirement later	Permanent or seasonal home	Permanent home
Investment now, retirement later	Household head retired	Household head employed
50–60	60+	35–55
$75,000+	$50,000+	$75,000+
$1.5 million	$1.2 million	$0.7 million
10%	10%	50%
40%	40%	20%
50%	50%	30%
Lots	Single-family dwellings	Single-family dwellings
Single-family dwellings	Model homes	Model homes
Model homes	Lots	Lots
Appreciation	Medical facilities	Schools
Community	Convenient shopping	Employment location
Social fabric	Convenient services	Convenient shopping
Amenities	Access to water	Convenient services
Medical facilities	Amenities	
Convenient shopping	Security	
Convenient services	Permanence (no change)	
Access to water	Privacy	

market generally favors condominiums or small detached cabins or cottages, with landscaping and exterior maintenance managed by a condominium regime or homeowners' association. In general, those units that rent best to transient guests are in greatest demand. Therefore, the community's guest market orientation has a considerable impact on the buyer's product preferences. For example, in areas dominated by conference guests, a one-bedroom condominium may rent well and therefore have strong buyer appeal; in areas dominated by family vacationers, two- and three-bedroom cottages or condominiums may be the preferred rental product and thus the product demanded by the second-home investor.

Timeshare Buyers. Like second-home investors, timeshare buyers are generally attracted to an area as a result of their vacation experiences. Yet, they usually purchase a "fixed-price" vacation rather than a real estate asset. In addition to all the factors that motivate second-home investors and second-home users, timeshare buyers are attracted by the flexibility inherent in a timeshare program and the quality of other resorts or locations that

are part of any exchange program in which the property participates.

Timeshare buyers tend to be younger and less affluent than second-home buyers but represent a rapidly growing and potentially huge segment of today's second-home market. The section on timeshare/vacation ownership markets describes timeshare buyers in greater detail.

Second-Home Users. Second-home users or owners are differentiated from second-home investors principally by their financial independence. Given that these owners do not require rental income to support their investment economically or emotionally, they can select from many more alternatives. They may purchase in an active resort community or a low-key residential community depending on family needs and personal preferences.

The most affluent buyers in this segment are multiple-home owners who may own three or four homes. The segment includes international buyers as well as Americans who may own additional homes outside the United States. The options are limitless for this group and therefore the competition difficult to define.

Hidden Valley Resort, Pennsylvania, offers a product mix of townhomes, condominiums, and luxury detached housing. Located within 200 miles of the District of Columbia and major cities in Ohio, Maryland, New York, and Pennsylvania, the resort enjoys a broad regional draw for weekend homeowners.

A beach cottage at Windsor, a 412-acre community in Vero Beach, Florida.

Since second-home buyers by definition do not rent their property to others and instead maintain their units for personal and business use, access to the property is a major influencing factor. At the high end of the market, access by air and even the availability of small airports serving private aircraft are important considerations. For most of the market, however, driving time from the owner's primary residence is an important, if not pivotal, consideration.

People buy second homes to get away, to retreat from their everyday life, to relax and recharge. They also buy second homes to escape harsh climates at certain times of the year. Northeasterners and Midwesterners want to escape harsh winters while south Floridians and Arizonans want to escape hot summers. The locations that appeal to most buyers offer high lifestyle and activity contrasts as compared to the location characteristics of the owners' primary home.

The three major types of second-home users are weekend-home users, seasonal-home users, and vacation-home users. Weekend homes are generally located within a two- to three-hour drive of the owner's primary residence. Owners generally occupy their units on weekends and holidays regularly throughout the year for a total of more than four to five weeks over a year. Seasonal homes are often located beyond a two- to three-hour drive of the owners' primary residence. Owners typically occupy the units full-time for more than four to five weeks during all or part of a specific season. Owners of vacation homes generally occupy their units for less than four to five weeks during a year, typically over school vacations.[4]

While some second-home buyers prefer or choose condominium ownership, most prefer a detached product—single-family homes, cottages, or cabins. In addition, a portion of this market buys a lot in anticipation of building a second home sometime in the future. Some lot buyers are attracted by the quality of a golf course and associated club facilities or other amenities in a private community and purchase property primarily to secure access to private club facilities. Many of these buyers never build.

Preretirement- and Retirement-Home Buyers. The preretiree purchases property with the intent of eventually using it as a retirement home. Typically, the buyer is still working and is five to seven years away from retirement. The preretiree may use the property as a second home until retirement, thus making it difficult to distinguish the preretiree purchaser from the second-home purchaser. Even after retirement, many buyers think of their property as a second home if they continue to maintain a home in their place of origin. The mindset of a preretiree, however, differs significantly from that of other market segments discussed.

Preretirees are attracted by a community's recreational amenities but are also concerned about its social fabric. For preretirees, privacy and security issues assume greater importance in view of the likelihood of their establishing permanent residence in the community. As a result,

Timber Pines, Spring Hill, Florida, is a country club community created for today's active retirees. The community features 54 holes of golf, one championship and two executive courses, two country clubs with heated pools and spas, six lighted tennis courts, shuffleboard and bocci courts, a fitness and walking trail, and a variety of club activities and cultural events.

preretirees are more likely than other segments to buy property in a private community. In addition, while preretirees are more likely to buy in a less established community, they are still interested in climate, the quality of the area's medical facilities, convenience shopping and services, cultural opportunities, the cost of living, and learning opportunities.

In resort communities that sell lots to individuals, preretirees typically purchase lots, although they may also buy a single-family detached home. Preretirees buy an attached product only if driven to that product by price considerations or plans to maintain their existing home and divide their time between the new home and their place of origin.

Some recreational communities position themselves as "adult" communities and partially target to the preretirement market. Heritage Hills in Somers, New York, for example, is an 1,100-acre recreational community that started out as a community for "active adults." Purchasers were required to include at least one owner over age 40, with children under age 18 not permitted to maintain full-time residence. In the mid-1980s, changes in federal

Sun City Las Vegas, located in the master-planned community of Summerlin near Las Vegas, is a recreational retirement community for an active lifestyle. Modeled after developer Del Webb's first major retirement community—Sun City Phoenix—Sun City Las Vegas was the first development of its kind in southern Nevada, with the concept adapted and honed to meet contemporary needs.

Del Webb's tremendously successful retirement community concept began in Phoenix in 1959 with an effort to convert a cotton field into a new community, complete with a golf course, recreation center, shopping center, and five model homes. Del Webb hoped that 10,000 visitors would attend the New Year's Day opening; instead, 100,000 people toured the property over that three-day weekend.

Today, more than ten similar communities have resulted from this not-so-modest beginning. Sun City Las Vegas is one of those successor communities. Del Webb Corporation, which went public in 1963, posted net earnings of $17 million for fiscal year 1994.

The Market and Concept

In 1987, market research identified Las Vegas as an ideal location for a Sun City community. The warm climate, low cost of living, lack of state income and inheritance taxes, immediate availability of world-class entertainment, and high level of senior citizen migration were all factors involved in site selection.

Sun City Las Vegas, located in the master-planned community of Summerlin near Las Vegas, is a recreational retirement community offering residents an active lifestyle.

Recent trends have borne out the accuracy of the research. Of the more than 65,000 people who moved to Las Vegas over 1993–1994, 35 percent were age 55 or older. In 1994, *Money* magazine ranked Las Vegas as the fourth best place in the country for retirement living, capitalizing on a low crime rate, mild weather, affordable housing, a strong economic outlook, and excellent health care. As the popularity of Las Vegas as a retirement community continued to grow, so has the population of Sun City Las Vegas.

The first residents moved to Sun City Las Vegas in November 1988 upon the opening of the community's first phase. Sun City Las Vegas is built on what is currently a 2,373-acre parcel carved out of the Summerlin community. Sun City's 1,900-acre first phase was Summerlin's first land sale.

On its initial 1,900 acres, Sun City originally planned a total of 5,600 residential units at buildout, with approximately 4,000 single-family residential units and 1,600 attached units. The original development plan also called for 84 acres of commercial land, which was sold to independent developers for the construction of houses of worship, shopping centers, and service centers in accordance with Sun City's development standards. Sun City has since acquired additional land and is currently home to 8,500 residents with 14,000 expected at buildout. It has already seen construction of 5,000 homes with a total of 7,700 units now planned, many located on the 842 contiguous acres optioned in 1991. A new expansion is also under serious consideration in response to the greater-than-expected pace of sales.

According to the Del Webb Corporation, the average resident in the early 1990s was 62 years old, had a net worth of $400,000 and an average household income of $40,000, had about $50,000 on deposit with a local bank, and spent an average $18,000 per year on retail purchases. Only about 25 percent of the residents worked full- or part-time.

Homebuyers can choose from 15 Southwestern-style home models, including single-family, duplex, and garden villa homes, with a variety of options, floorplans, and amenities. Prices in 1995 ranged from $95,675 to $271,000.

The community currently features two 18-hole golf courses, with an executive par-60 course on the way. The team of Billy Casper and Greg Nash designed the courses. Golf fees vary with the season. The two par-72 courses are championship courses but are designed to accommodate golfers of all skill levels, from the novice to the professional. The second of the courses was also designed to accommodate seniors.

Evaluating the Experience

The Del Webb Corporation has relied on extensive research to hone its concept of creative retirement communities. It spends over $1 million each year to research such issues as senior migration patterns and attitudes about health, housing, and recreation. Telephone and written surveys and focus groups provide the basis for analyzing, segmenting, and targeting markets.

The research is particularly useful in identifying the active lifestyle facilities and programs demanded by the retirement market in the various Sun City locations. Extending well beyond simply offering a golf or country club lifestyle, activities provide residents with instant community, something they seek as they pull up roots from the areas where they raised their families. Clearly, the Sun City Corporation sells more than housing units; it sells an active adult lifestyle in a controlled environment with covenants, conditions, and restrictions, the most significant of which is the age restriction. That restriction requires every dwelling to be occupied by at least one person not less than 55 years of age.

Sun City also offers seniors the certainty of a quality environment and the track record that is the Del Webb tradition. Buyers are confident that anything that goes wrong in their new residence will be rectified and that the grounds and common areas will be professionally maintained, all for reasonable rates.

The final important factor is that Sun City has consistently offered affordable living to a wide range of income levels. Although generally affluent, retirees are cost-conscious and concerned about supporting themselves through their lifetime. By separating golf fees from association dues, Sun City ensures that those who do not care to play golf or cannot afford the dues do not have to subsidize their neighbors.

Sun City and Summerlin greenbelts for stormwater runoff are distributed into eight separate channels that convey local stormflows in drainage courses; they also serve as golf course fairways, regional parks, and enhanced natural washes.

As part of the active retirement lifestyle fostered at Sun City Las Vegas, residents may participate in some 50 volunteer, recreational, and social clubs.

and state age and housing discrimination laws permitted 55- and-older age restrictions only. Heritage Hills did not plan to be a retirement community and did not change its positioning strategy as a result of the new laws; instead, the community has retained its active adult composition as a result of its early establishment as an adult community and the types of amenities and units provided, which are not designed for families. Currently, the typical buyer is an "empty nester" over age 50. As of 1995, the composition of the community was roughly 10 percent second-home owners, 10 percent investment owners, and 80 percent primary owners. Less than half the residents (45 percent) are retired.

Retiree households are looking for a place for immediate occupancy. While they may buy a lot and build a custom home, they are typically concerned about the ultimate cost of the home and are drawn to built-for-sale single-family detached homes, model-home products, and resale single-family homes.

Primary-Home Buyers. Primary-home buyers are distinguished from other market segments in that they are either currently employed in the area or planning a move to the area. Most of these households include school-age children and therefore prefer to buy single-family detached homes. Primary-home buyers often make up a large percentage of the buyers in second-home communities.

Residential Market Analysis

Resort-home purchases are generally discretionary purchases. As a result, it is more difficult to determine demand for resort homes than for primary homes. For example, a particular household that fits a certain demographic profile almost certainly occupies a primary home that fits its profile; this same household will not necessarily buy a second home even if its profile points to the household's financial ability to do so. A primary residence is a necessity, but a second home is a luxury that competes with many other discretionary purchases.

Boca West in Boca Raton, Florida, is a 1,436-acre community of 4,500 homes, featuring condominium homes for both primary- and second-home buyers.

For this reason, original survey research is a necessary component of resort market analysis and the basis for understanding the psychographics of the target market.

Research must determine the potenial size of the market, the composition of the market, and the kind of product demanded by the market. Only careful consumer research can disclose consumer preferences. In Palm Springs, for example, it is difficult to sell a non-golf course home or a two-story home. Ideally, then, market research should design the resort-home product.

In addition, while resort-home markets generally track closely with the economic cycle, their swings are often more severe, creating significant hazards for the resort homebuilder. Recent data gathered by Ragatz Associates, for example, indicate that 60.3 percent of households in a 1995 survey felt they had a chance of purchasing a recreational property in the next ten years as compared with only 25.5 percent in the 1990 survey and 43.8 percent in the 1993 survey. Even though other factors may be involved, the 1990 recession and the recovery that followed it are clearly factors in increasingly favorable market attitudes.[5]

A case study illustrates the process of market research for residential uses in a resort or retirement community. The example involves a 1,000-acre parcel of land with ocean access across a river in the southeastern United States.[6] For convenience, let us refer to the parcels as the Riverfront property.

The owners of Riverfront had envisioned the creation of some deepwater lots that would sell for more than $200,000 as well as some interior lots that would sell for much less and appeal to retirees and families with more modest incomes. However, the owners had not decided exactly what type of development to undertake on the parcel. The analysis therefore involved a market study to determine the demand for a variety of residential uses, not a marketability study focusing on an already well-developed plan.

Particularly on the demand side, a market study for a resort or retirement development differs significantly from a traditional market study. The basic steps for the resort community's demand analysis follow:

- Arrange in matrix form the demand components and the relevant geographic areas for each component (see Figure 2-5).
- Insert any available data or estimate the percentage allocation of demand for each cell. In making the allocation as to sources of demand, consider the function of the resort community as compared to its competition. The best data source for such analysis is buyer data from competing projects.
- Consider which cells may be combined to simplify the market analysis risk. In most cases, it is easier to combine cells across geographic areas than across demand components, but even calculating cross-area combinations of geographic areas can be a major task. (Depending on the individual project, Step 3 might be more properly completed before Step 2.)

figure 2-5

Demand Matrix For Riverfront Property[1]

Demand Component	Southeast	Middle Atlantic	New England	Midwest	Other	Total
Retirement	5%	5%	0%	5%	0%	15%
Preretirement	20	10	5	10	4	49
Second Home	10	3	0	0	0	13
Primary Home	13	0	0	0	0	13
Investor	0	5	0	5	0	10
Total	48%	23%	5%	20%	4%	100%

[1]Percent allocation of demand.

Source: Robert H. Pittman, Henry O. Pollakowski, and Maury Seldin, "Market Research for Resort/Retirement Planned Communities," *Urban Land*, November 1992, pp. 35–39.

- Decide what type of demand research to conduct for each cell or combination of cells. The demand research could involve simply gathering basic data and market information for each cell or could require a more sophisticated approach such as a spreadsheet analysis or even an econometric modeling procedure.
- Follow through with the analysis determined in Step 4.

Figure 2-5 presents the demand component/geography matrix for Riverfront. The data to construct this demand matrix came from a local real estate research and brokerage firm that had collected lot purchase data for comparable communities in the area for several years. Even with the available data, a good deal of discretionary judgment informed the estimates in some cells. The matrix was tremendously useful in developing an understanding of the demand components for Riverfront. The row totals show clearly that the demand components in order of priority call for preretirement-, retirement-, second-home, local primary-home, and investor units. It should also be noted that the matrix is informative for marketing purposes. For example, it provides the developer with data on the precise market segments and geographic areas to be targeted in an advertising campaign.

In practice, a demand matrix is usually reduced to make the market analysis more tractable. In the case of Riverfront, the analysts reduced the demand components by combining retirement and preretirement demand and focusing their detailed analyses solely on retirement- and local primary-housing demand. The analysts did not consider the second-home component important for future lot sales and concluded that the investor market in the area had significantly declined with the 1986 federal tax law change.

The analysts were fortunate to obtain from a local real estate research firm a fairly good database on lot sales volume. By using the available data, which covered six years, the analysts constructed an econometric model that statistically related annual retirement and preretirement lot sales to key explanatory variables, including per capita income in the eastern United States and a housing price index that measured the average annual percentage change in housing prices in seven northern cities.

The model found a striking relationship between retirement and preretirement lot sales volume in the Riverfront area and housing price change in the northern cities. An obvious interpretation is that people are encouraged to purchase retirement or preretirement property as they sell their primary houses in strong markets or when they just feel wealthier. Conversely, in weak markets, people do not sell their primary homes (or feel poorer) and do not purchase retirement properties. The model also disclosed a clear relationship between per capita income in the south Atlantic region and retirement/preretirement lot sales volume in the Riverfront market area.

Determining the statistical relationship between the volume of retirement/preretirement lot sales and key explanatory variables allows for the development of alternative forecasts for total sales volume in the market area based on alternative scenarios for housing prices in northern cities and per capita income in the East. Figure 2-6 presents the results of this alternative-scenario exercise. Projecting lot sales under alternative growth scenarios is a critical part of an overall market analysis. Since no one can be expected to forecast a market and absorption with 100 percent accuracy, it is useful to plot alternative scenarios such as those shown in Figure 2-6. The alternatives give decision makers some useful information about the likely range of sales volume and help developers assess the risk involved in a project. Some developers are sitting on a gold mine of data in their own files that could be used in this type of analysis.

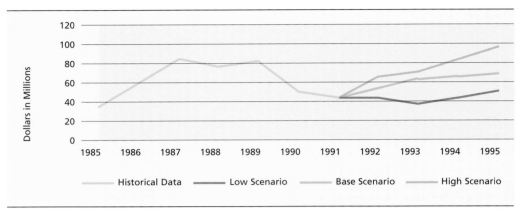

figure 2-6

Riverfront Resort/Retirement Community Sales Volume—Historically and Forecast

Source: Pittman, Pollakowski, Seldin Analyses, 1991.

Compared to the demand analysis for the Riverfront project, the supply analysis was fairly simple. It involved the usual steps of identifying the relevant market area, analyzing past supply trends, performing a pipeline analysis, and focusing on future supply constraints.

Basic economics tells us that demand is one blade of the scissors and supply the other. To see the whole picture, however, demand and supply must be analyzed together. In the case of a real estate market analysis focusing on absorption, demand is generally what drives the absorption forecast; supply plays a lesser role. When, however, constraints such as land availability, zoning problems, or growth management determine absorption, supply drives the absorption forecast. By comparing future demand projections with future supply projections, the analyst can determine which side of the equation is the constraint or which side may generate an imbalance. If no perceived supply constraint would limit absorption to a level below that projected by demand, demand projections become the absorption projections. In the case of a projected demand/supply imbalance, significant price adjustments would likely result.

A market study may also indicate that the timing for development is not quite right. The study may reveal that the market is adequately supplied and that many months or years must elapse before demand will be sufficiently strong to support additional supply. Dividing an already small pie among participants is a frequent but unprofitable approach. A market study might also indicate that investment in a particular development would yield a higher payoff if postponed to a period when the projected demand and supply balance is more favorable. The decision to postpone development involves weighing carrying costs against the present value of future higher revenue streams.

In these cases, a monitoring system can be useful in determining shifts in optimum development timing. A monitoring system focuses on the key variables identified by the market study as driving the demand for a product in an area. In the case of Riverfront, two key variables were housing market activity in northern cities and per capita income in the eastern United States. Gathering data on a regular basis and comparing them with projections to identify the stage of the market cycle and to forecast imminent turning points in the market should be an integral part of an overall market study and development plan. It can prevent disaster and help a developer secure maximum return from an investment.

In summary, understanding and selecting the market analysis technique best suited to a resort community is important because resort projects can involve higher risks and more complicated market research challenges than in the case of primary-home developments. In particular, a developer cannot simply rely on a cursory analysis of the history of comparable developments in the market area. To do so invites potential disaster by possibly overlooking major market turning points. In addition, the market analysis must identify different demand components and geographic areas for each component. Many of the cells in the matrix perform differently and thus require a full understanding. Finally, it is important to develop the demand component/geography matrix even if the analyst does not plan to conduct a sophisticated market research and data-gathering exercise for each cell. The matrix helps the developer in both understanding the market and making the appropriate decision as to what type of development is appropriate. It also helps in marketing and advertising the development.

Developing a resort or retirement community without first performing the type of market research outlined here is tantamount to playing Russian roulette. In the 1980s, many projects succeeded solely on the strength of the market. In today's market, however, many are not succeeding. Market fundamentals have changed significantly. Research is critical, particularly for such niche products as upscale resort and retirement communities.

John W. Temple
President and Chief Executive Officer
Temple Development Company
Boca Raton, Florida

John W. Temple is president and chief executive officer of Temple Development Company (TDC), a real estate development and management firm. Major TDC projects in and around Boca Raton include Presidential Place, a 42-unit, $75 million oceanfront condominium project; Florida Atlantic University Research and Development Park; Towne Park, a 1,400-acre planned community; and a 55-acre community on the ocean at Key Biscayne, Florida, for development into 585 luxury condominiums and a 475-room hotel. TDC is also involved in projects in South Miami Beach and Fort Lauderdale and in Telluride, Colorado. Temple Management Company, a subsidiary of TDC, retains 20 percent of the voting control in the Boca Raton Resort & Club.

Before starting TDC, Temple was president of the Arvida Corporation and Arvida/Disney. Under his leadership as president, Arvida set the standard of excellence for comprehensively planned communities throughout Florida, Georgia, and California. In 1983, Temple and a small number of his associates along with the Bass brothers of Fort Worth, Texas, purchased Arvida in a leveraged buyout. In 1984, Arvida merged with the Walt Disney Company; Temple assumed additional responsibility as president of Arvida/Disney. In this capacity, Temple helped Disney organize its real estate development plan.

Before Arvida and Arvida/Disney, Temple spent eight years with Kaiser Aluminum and its affiliated real estate development activities. He received a BA in mathematics from the University of Washington, served for four years as a naval officer, and received an MBA from the Stanford University Graduate School of Business.

Development is still an entrepreneurial business, whether one is working for a large company like Arvida or is out on one's own. The way the business is run is not any different. When it comes to hotels, most will have some sort of chain affiliation. Yet, there is a market for an independently owned and operated hotel such as the 963-room Boca Raton Hotel. When it comes to planned communities, though, there really aren't any national or international planned community companies.

In recent years, I have seen a trend where business executives have bought large second homes in golf course communities and luxury condominiums near the ocean, and because of transportation and advanced communication technology, these people can now run their businesses for part of the time from these second homes, without actually being in their office. Boca Raton is growing with CEOs whose businesses are somewhere else and who are running their businesses out of their second

home, which is now their second, third, or fourth primary home. They have several homes and don't differentiate between what is a primary home and what is a second home. Clearly, ten years ago, they were second homes; now they are just homes.

Another trend is that these people do not want to be bothered; therefore, the condominium form of ownership is appealing to them. My latest project, a 42-unit project on the Boca Raton Hotel property, where each unit contains an average of 5,000 square feet of living space, epitomizes that trend. It has 24-hour valet service, security guards, and room service and maid service from the Boca Raton Hotel. Yet, residents can walk away and lock the door.

Second-home developers have always done some primary-home development as well. The Sea Pines Company started out as a second-home company, but it built primary homes too. So did Arvida. It has not changed. You hear more about the resort business because it is more glamorous, and you have a much broader marketing area. It is still planned community development whether it is a primary home or second home.

Whether it is a primary-home community or a recreational second-home community, I see more market segmentation. I see smaller communities (200 to 300 acres) as the norm rather than more of the 1,000-acre communities, which are difficult to finance and develop.

Despite increased globalization of the development business, U.S. companies are typically not developing much of an international presence—in part, because they do not have the cash. Rather, international companies are often either recruiting senior talent from U.S. development companies to manage their own international projects or entering into management agreements with U.S. developers.

Timeshare/Vacation Ownership Markets

The vacation ownership market has grown dramatically over the past decade, with recent surveys indicating that the market will continue to expand and deepen into the next century. An unprecedented number of Americans will be financial and psychographic contenders for timeshare purchases. Furthermore, as recently developed, high-quality timeshares help dispel the questionable image of the timeshare industry, timeshares will remain the fastest-growing type of resort accommodation in the industry.

The aging baby boom generation is an especially important population segment for the timeshare industry. Analysts concur that timesharing will benefit immensely from the baby boom generation's desire for a higher quality of life today. Unlike their parents, baby boomers are not prepared to make sacrifices today for tomorrow. Yet, with most baby boomers unable to afford a second home, they recognize that timeshares offer a similar product at a fraction of the cost.

Baby boomers command the discretionary income to afford vacation ownership units and are growing more disposed to buy. As already noted, a 1995 survey indicated that 60.3 percent of responding households believed they had some chance of buying a recreational property in the next ten years as compared with 25.5 percent in a 1990 survey.[7] Financially speaking, a vacation ownership unit is the most realistic option for the vast proportion of the baby boom market.

Not only is the market psychologically and financially able to purchase timeshare intervals, in many ways it prefers the benefits of timesharing over other real estate options. Indeed, resort and recreational markets have responded favorably to the flexibility offered by vacation ownership. Over 80 percent of today's timeshare owners purchased in response to a desire for flexibility in their vacations.[8] Hotel/vacation companies such as Hilton, Marriott, and Disney are seeking to emphasize flexibility in the use of their timeshare resorts through vacation point systems and other options.

Today's Timeshare Buyer[9]

Who are today's timeshare owners, and what do they have in common with other consumers around the world? *RCI Perspective*, a timeshare industry magazine, sums up their diversity. "Today's timeshare customer is a dual-income married couple with two children. It's a retired couple who bring along their three grandchildren. It's a thirty-something married couple without any children. And it could be a single woman who prefers to travel alone."[10] Although the timeshare consumer may seem to defy description, research helps us compile a profile.

A 1995 Ragatz Associates report entitled *Timeshare Purchasers: Who They Are, Why They Buy* indicates that major changes have occurred since the first survey of resort timeshare owners in the United States 17 years ago. The 1995 study, based on almost 2,400 responses from a random sample of timeshare owners throughout the United States, provides the following data:

- In 1978, the average household income of timeshare owners was about $23,000; today, it is more than $63,000.
- The average age of timeshare owners is 51; however, it is only 46 years for persons who purchased in 1993 or 1994. Among recent buyers, 45.9 percent are between 40 and 54 years of age.
- Couples account for 86.5 percent of all timeshare owners, but the percentage of singles has increased from only 7.4 percent in 1978 to 13.5 percent today.
- Only 44.2 percent of owners have children younger than age 18.
- Timeshare owners are highly educated; some 55.7 percent have earned at least a bachelor's degree and

The Hilton Grand Vacations Club at Sea World International Center in Orlando. Orlando is one of the world's leading timeshare markets.

- Timeshare owners are highly educated; some 55.7 percent have earned at least a bachelor's degree and 26.8 percent a graduate degree.
- Compared to all households in the United States, timeshare owners have higher incomes (69.5 percent have incomes of more than $50,000 as compared to 31.1 percent of the general population); are older (67.5 percent are at least 45 years of age as compared to 51.3 percent); and have attained higher levels of formal education (55.7 percent have earned at least a bachelor's degree as compared to 23.7 percent).
- Finally, 82 percent cite the exchange opportunity as an important motivation for purchasing a timeshare, followed by the ability to save money on future vacation costs (61 percent) and simply liking the timeshare resort and its amenities (54.4 percent).

In 1995, Simmons Market Research Bureau surveyed 2,000 of the 1 million subscribers to *Endless Vacation* magazine and discovered similar demographics. The Simmons study fixes the average age of *Endless Vacation* readers (all of whom are timeshare owners) at 50.1 years (the median was 49.9 years) and the average total household income at $73,920 (the median was $63,480).

How do these owners feel about the product? As in past surveys, the 1995 Simmons study on timeshare purchasers indicates a high level of satisfaction. The vast majority (77.5 percent) report that their timeshare purchase has "matched or exceeded their original expectations." Almost two-thirds believe that ownership has saved them money on vacations. In fact, current owners have been so satisfied, the study shows, that 41.2 percent have purchased more than one interval while 24.2 percent own timeshares at more than one resort. Among the benefits listed by well more than half of the surveyed owners are an increase in their "looking forward to vacation"; the opportunity to stay in higher-quality resorts; and a wider range of vacation experiences and more vacation destinations.

Despite timeshare's steady growth and high approval rating among timeshare purchasers, owners constitute only 1.72 percent of all U.S. households (the percentage increases with higher levels of income). The industry is still battling image problems fostered by the sales and marketing abuses of the 1970s, but the picture is brightening. Information obtained by Ragatz Associates in 1992 from 16 focus groups conducted with timeshare buyers and nonbuyers suggests that the image of resort timesharing has improved dramatically during the past ten years. Few focus group participants expressed concerns about the concept itself, and even fewer questioned the quality of the timeshare resorts with which they were acquainted. Focus group participants with negative perceptions of timesharing generally cited two types of sales and marketing abuses: hard-close sales tactics and irrational, last-minute drops in sales prices, with statements from the salesperson that "this discount applies only to you" and "only if you buy today."

The Marriott Harbour Club on Hilton Head is a vacation ownership resort comprising 39 two-bedroom, 1,400-square-foot villas.

Interestingly, in the 1992 Ragatz study and another one in 1995, participants who had attended a sales presentation had more favorable impressions of timesharing than those who had received mail or telephone solicitations but had not attended a presentation. The findings suggest that direct exposure to the product in a pressure-free setting helps overcome negative stereotypes. And the fact that the majority of nonbuyers remained interested after attending a presentation challenges the industry to develop so-called "be-back" programs to follow up with prospects. Today's sophisticated consumers rightly insist on adequate time to make up their minds about major purchases.

Several important niche segments require special consideration in today's market, including seniors/mature adults, families with young children, singles, and the international market. Each is discussed below.

Seniors/Mature Adults

As noted above, the average age of timeshare owners is 51, which means that approximately half of the owners fall into that generation and demographic group just ahead of the baby boom generation. The Lawrence Welk Resort Group (LWR), which counts 230,000 timeshare owners in Escondido and Cathedral City, California, and Maui, Hawaii, reports that at least 50 percent of its owners are over age 50. LWR exemplifies a vacation ownership corporation that has successfully tapped into a solid market niche by developing an understanding of niche interests and delivering a consistently high-quality product. And LWR's attention to the mature adult market is well justified considering that people over 60 have the highest discretionary income in this country. Typically, the over-60 set does not spend a lot of money on material goods regardless of affluence. When seniors do spend, however, they place a higher priority on value rather than price. In general, seniors are in the process of divesting themselves of material possessions they no longer need or use. They are more interested in convenience and a low-maintenance lifestyle. Timeshare products fit well with this demographic and psychographic profile.

Families with Young Children[11]

The 1995 Ragatz survey found that 44.2 percent of timeshare owners have children younger than age 18. While this is a sizable group, families with young children have not traditionally represented the strength of the timeshare market; however, some projects are now targeting the family segment by developing more affordable products. Resort Development International, a Florida-based development company, is pursuing this younger, less affluent group in its projects. Many of its resorts feature a homey atmosphere and high-quality service at affordable prices in such locations as Daytona and the Wisconsin Dells, affordable destinations where its buyers have traditionally vacationed and felt at home.

Families with children are the bread and butter of the Village at Smugglers' Notch resort in rural Vermont. Positioning itself as America's family resort, Smugglers' Notch relies on massive direct-mail targeting of families with incomes of $75,000 or more and two children under age 12. The resort guarantees a good time for each family member and backs up its promise with a refund program for those few customers it fails to please.

Singles

As already noted, singles are a growing niche for timeshare developers. Vacation ownership marketers are realizing that singles are now often older and more affluent than in the past. Further, singles place a strong emphasis on comfortable homes and high-quality vacations. Many vacation ownership corporations are experiencing a growing percentage of timeshare purchases by singles. Dr. Simon Crawford-Welch, director of marketing for the International Resort Group, predicts that the singles market will grow from 14 percent of vacation

In the early 1980s, Marriott entered the vacation ownership industry with the acquisition of Monarch at Sea Pines on Hilton Head in South Carolina and other resort properties developed by American Resorts. Since the entry of Marriott and other hospitality companies, the industry has enjoyed an improving image with higher-quality "brand" products.

ownership owners to 20 percent by the turn of the century. Trendwest Resorts in Kirkland, Washington, reports that singles account for nearly 25 percent of sales at its 15 resorts. Marketing to this amorphous group presents challenges (discussed in Chapter 5), but the numbers point to an important niche. Single adults now constitute one in four households as compared to one in ten 30 years ago. And, according to *American Demographics*, the number of single households is expected to grow by 28 percent between now and 2010.[12]

International Market

With growth in the vacation ownership market strong in the Unites States, it is even stronger and more impressive at the global scale. International vacation ownership owners fall into one of two categories: "on-shore" owners, those who own a timeshare within their home country; and "off-shore" owners, those who own a timeshare outside their home country. Developers generally prefer on-shore buyers because they visit more often and constitute a more consistent market. However, current market analysts perceive that the major timeshare opportunities of the future will be worldwide, not domestic. Current vacation ownership market polls concur.

Even though some of its timeshare developments have struggled, Europe is the strongest region within the international timeshare market. The number of resort timeshare owners residing in Europe, according to Ragatz Associates, increased from 254,000 in 1990 to 669,000 in 1994 (see Figure 2-7) for a 163 percent rate of growth. A dramatic increase also occurred with on-shore timeshare owners. While 257,000 resort timeshare purchasers owned in Europe in 1990, that number grew to 658,000 by 1994 for an increase of over 150 percent.[13] In 1994, of all timeshare owners, Europeans accounted for 20.9 percent of "owners owning in the area" and 21.3 percent of "owners residing in the area."

A look at the increase of new owners owning in the area shows that, by far, the two leading areas were the United States and Europe. Growth rates in these two areas were 22.3 percent and 54.2 percent, respectively, from 1990 to 1994. While absolute gains were considerably less, South America and Canada experienced large relative gains at 336.9 percent and 50.5 percent, respectively.

The vacation ownership industry extends primarily to 15 countries. About 52 percent of worldwide vacation ownership owners reside in the United States, although the U.S. share is decreasing as the international market expands. The United Kingdom ranks second with 286,259 owners or 9.1 percent of the total. Three countries account for over 100,000 owners: Mexico (171,900), South Africa (162,339), and Canada (127,050). Other countries in the top 15 include Germany (80,024), Venezuela (70,671), Japan (59,435), Italy (56,980), Australia (56,967), France (54,259), Spain (51,214), Argentina (46,049), Portugal (28,481), and New Zealand (26,890). The rest of the world accounts for 216,922 owners or 6.9 percent.

figure 2-7

Resort Timeshare Market by Area of World, December 31, 1994

Area	Resort Timeshare Projects		Resort Timeshare Owners Owning in Area		Resort Timeshare Owners Residing in Area	
	Number	Percent of Total	Number	Percent of Total	Number	Percent of Total
United States	1,546	37.3	1,538,000	48.9	1,648,000	52.4
Europe	1,888	28.7	658,000	20.9	669,000	21.3
Mexico	291	7.0	319,000	10.1	172,000	5.5
South America	276	6.7	104,000	3.3	138,000	4.4
Caribbean	202	4.9	139,000	4.4	9,000	0.3
Southeast Asia/Japan	160	3.9	39,000	1.2	82,000	2.7
South Africa	142	3.4	161,000	5.1	162,000	5.2
Australasia	117	2.8	84,000	2.7	84,000	2.7
Canada	93	2.2	57,000	1.8	127,000	4.0
Other	130	3.1	45,000	1.4	53,000	1.7
Total	4,145	100.0	3,144,000	100.0	3,144,000	100.0

Source: Ragatz Associates, Inc., *The 1995 Worldwide Resort Timeshare Industry* (Washington, D.C.: American Resort Development Association, Alliance for Timeshare Excellence, 1995).

Of late, South America appears to be the most impressive emerging market. South American vacation ownership analysts point to at least two reasons for the burgeoning numbers. First, developers have only just recently tapped the market and did not anticipate the overwhelmingly positive response. Second, countries such as Argentina, Brazil, Chile, Colombia, and Venezuela are all experiencing a growing middle class. With their discretionary income, the newly affluent want to enjoy the fruits of their prosperity. However, analysts are still looking to the South Pacific as the next surging region. As the numbers indicate, the vacation ownership industry is growing extremely fast and reaching all areas of the globe.

Hotel and Guest Markets

The success of a resort hotel and guest rental program depends on the developer's and operator's understanding of the dynamics of each segment of market demand. Equally important is an understanding of consumer trends such as geographic origin and the demographics and values that influence demand within each market segment.

Due to climatic conditions, lodging demand in many resort areas exhibits distinctive seasonality patterns as reflected in peak and off-peak periods. Peak periods are generally characterized by maximum published room rates and occupancy levels. In contrast, off-peak periods are characterized by lower published room rates and generally reduced occupancy levels. In certain market areas, intermediate periods marked by moderate demand are referred to as shoulder seasons and characterized by published room rates and occupancy levels that fall below peak periods but exceed off-peak periods.

Given that some groups prefer to take advantage of the cost savings associated with off-peak periods, the growth of the group and convention market segment has helped balance seasonal variations in many resort markets. In addition, a growing number of South American visitors prefer to visit during the South American winter months, helping boost summer occupancies in many North American destination resorts.

Hotel and Guest Market Segments

Traditionally, several major market segments generate resort market demand. In general, market segments are defined in terms of purpose of trip, seasonality, length of stay, price sensitivity, the nature of the facilities and amenities required, and the number of rooms required. Market segments include the free independent traveler (FIT) market, the group market, the wholesale market, and the commercial market. Each is discussed below.

FIT Market. The FIT market segment consists of destination tourists and other transient travelers. Destination tourists represent visitors who have selected a resort market area as their primary vacation destination and arrange for their accommodations either directly with the hotel or through a travel agent. Because individuals book their own accommodations, little or no discounting is available.

A range of on-premises recreational amenities and facilities such as beach frontage, casino gaming, swimming pool(s), tennis courts, and/or an 18-hole championship golf course attracts the FIT segment. In addition, a strategic location near such recreational and entertainment centers as theme parks, world-class golf courses, snow skiing areas, watersports venues, shopping opportunities, cultural activities, and/or spectator sports facilities can be an important factor in effectively marketing to the FIT segment. Typically, the FIT segment is not price-sensitive. Peak seasons and weekends account for significant FIT demand.

The FIT market encompasses many demographic subsegments, including singles, couples, and families—all in a variety of price ranges. Condominium and second-home rental programs are particularly appealing to these travelers. Specifically, families and extended families often look for accommodations larger than a single hotel room.

Wholesale Market. The wholesale market segment extends to tourists who purchase discount packages that include any combination of hotel, airfare, food and beverage, automobile rental, tours, and/or discounts at

Profile and Comments: Edwin H. McMullen, Sr.

Edwin H. McMullen, Sr.
Chair
Hilton Grand Vacations Company
Orlando, Florida

Edwin H. "Ed" McMullen, Sr., is chair of Hilton Grand Vacations Company. He has been involved in the vacation ownership industry since 1977 when he founded American Resorts Corporation. American Resorts merged with the Marriott Corporation in 1984 to form Marriott Ownership Resorts, Inc. (MORI). As executive vice president of MORI from 1984 until 1991, McMullen was responsible for strategic planning, product development, and marketing and sales, during which time MORI emerged as the world's leader in vacation ownership sales.

McMullen resigned from MORI in 1991 to form Hilton Grand Vacations Company, a joint venture with Hilton Hotels Corporation, American Resorts, and the Mariner Group. The company operates 15 vacation ownership resorts in Florida and Las Vegas. It was formed to develop a system of vacation ownership resorts under the Hilton name both nationally and internationally.

The resort vacation ownership industry began in the United States in the early 1970s and has grown into a significant component of the larger travel and leisure industries. Annual sales in 1983 exceeded $5 billion and are expected to reach $20 billion by the turn of the century. There are now over 3,500 vacation ownership resorts worldwide with over 3 million families involved in the concept. The rapid growth of the industry has been fueled by the vacation ownership products fitting well within the major consumer trends of evolving vacation and leisure expectations, travel patterns, work habits, taxation, and leisure economics.

Over the past 20 years, the industry has evolved through four distinct phases. The first phase that lasted from the early 1970s to the early 1980s was a troubled time for both developers and the consumer. Vacation ownership or timesharing, as it was called during this period, was a niche industry started for the most part by small entrepreneurial real estate developers who were poorly financed and had little or no hospitality experience.

There was little regulatory control, poor product quality, and sales and marketing largely relied on the high-pressure land sales techniques of the 1970s.

The second phase began in the early 1980s. As the industry began to expand, product quality improved with the introduction of purpose-built resorts. Increased consumer acceptance of the fractional ownership concept and improved state and federal regulation provided a solid base for rapid growth.

The third phase began in the mid-1980s with the entry into the market of larger, well-capitalized hospitality companies such as Marriott, Disney, and Hilton. High-quality projects often developed in conjunction with large mixed-use destination resorts, and offering well-balanced amenity packages began to be the norm. Professional resort management techniques were perfected, and the industry became truly global with projects located in over 60 countries worldwide.

The fourth phase that began in the early 1990s will be known as the "maturity phase." The industry has now matured into a well-organized international business and will have an expanding role in the future. Large hospitality companies and experienced regional developers will continue to enter the industry in expanding international markets. Consumer acceptance and demand for vacation ownership products will grow with the development of innovative "system product" concepts and "one-stop shopping" services that use vacation clubs and highly flexible point-based systems.

The consumer of the future will demand a wide variety of vacation and leisure services not generally available today. As the vacation ownership products and services are expanded and integrated into a wider product definition, the industry will evolve from its basic "service provider" role into the broader role of "vacation experience" management provider. The industry is well positioned for continued growth and has a very bright future.

■

retail outlets. Travel agents and tour operators, the primary vendors of discount packages, typically negotiate room rates with a range of resort properties on an annual basis. The negotiations specify the number of rooms booked and the time of year that the rooms are available. Accordingly, room rates are generally much lower relative to other demand segments.

Discount packages are popular, particularly among European tourists, because of the assurance that travelers' full range of needs will be addressed without unexpected expenses. Some consumers purchase discount packages based on the price/value relationship while others like the convenience of making a single purchase for all their vacation needs. Wholesale travelers are generally extremely price-sensitive and therefore tend to travel during off-peak seasons. As with the FIT market segment, the wholesale market segment looks for the availability of a range of on-premises recreational amenities and facilities coupled with a strategic location near recreational and entertainment centers.

Group Market. The group market segment generally includes three primary subsegments: corporate group meetings, association groups, and special interest groups. Due to the nature of the clientele and the source of business, room rates for this segment are negotiated and specify the number of rooms booked and the time of year that the rooms are available.

One of the most significant trends in the operation of resort hotels over the past 20 years has been the marked shift to conference business as one of the major contributors, if not the major contributor, to resort occupancy. Although a limited number of resort hotels rely almost entirely on occupancy by free independent travelers, most have mounted major efforts to attract conferences and business meetings as an economic necessity. For most large resort hotels, between 45 and 70 percent of occupancy now takes the form of group business.[14] Some recently developed resort hotels, such as the Lansdowne Conference Resort in Loudoun County, Virginia, targeted this market as a primary source of business. The Desert Springs Marriott in Palm Desert, California —which includes over 900 rooms—is capable together with surrounding hotels of attracting major conventions to the Palm Springs area.

The corporate group subsegment consists of groups such as individual companies and professional organizations that select a resort as a meeting location. The purposes of the subsegment's meetings are generally twofold: to accomplish the business of the organization and to provide an opportunity for members of the group to socialize. In addition, incentive travelers—travelers who take advantage of travel programs sponsored by a company or a corporation as a reward for employee service or achievement of a particular objective or goal— are included in this category. The subsegment generally requires audiovisual equipment, banquet facilities, and professional support in technical and meeting planning. Golf is a particularly important amenity for this subsegment.

The Hyatt Regency at Beaver Creek, as with many large resort hotels, caters to both the group market and the free independent traveler.

Association groups are defined as professional or fraternal groups in excess of 75 members that meet to discuss new developments or issues affecting their area of expertise or concern. The subsegment also includes trade associations as well as industry and trade exhibitions. The association group market generally exhibits price sensitivity and prefers to schedule events during off-peak periods.

Special interest groups are made up of individuals who travel to a resort to partake of a specific activity. The category includes social organizations and/or individuals who share a common set of interests, goals, and/or objectives. Meeting purposes include varied forms of information dissemination, sales, or training. The subsegment also includes professional seminars designed primarily for presenting and discussing specialized information. Professional seminars may be hosted by companies that provide topic-specific seminars or by business organizations that provide seminars on a recurring basis. The latter subsegment is similar to the association subsegment, but the groups are often less formally organized and do not necessarily meet on a regular schedule. In addition, gatherings of special interest groups are often smaller than association gatherings.

The 350-room Hapuna Beach Prince Hotel, set within the Mauna Kea Resort on the big island of Hawaii, is a destination resort hotel that was opened in 1994 to complement and expand on the market success of its adjacent sister hotel, the Mauna Kea Beach Hotel, which was developed by Laurence Rockefeller in the 1960s. The latter was closed for reconstruction immediately following the opening of the Hapuna Beach Prince Hotel.

Commercial Market. The commercial market segment, made up of both domestic and international business travelers, typically represents a minor source of demand for resorts. Business travelers include managers at all levels, sales representatives, official trainees, and recruits. A crucial criterion in the selection of lodging facilities is location. Primary locational considerations include proximity to centers of business activity and ease of access to and from airports. The typical length of stay is approximately one to two days while seasonality and price sensitivity are limited concerns. Commercial market demand is typically concentrated on Monday through Thursday nights. In many resort markets, however, some commercial visitors extend their stay through the weekend to enjoy the resort and its amenities.

Hotel Market Analysis[15]

An accurate hotel market analysis calls for a close look at several interrelated circumstances, including location of the subject site with regard to market demand generators, the sources and strengths of transient travel, location of competitive properties and their physical and operational characteristics, current and future travel patterns, economic growth within the market area, and special local conditions and trends.

The project initiator or hotel market analyst must collect the quantitative data for compilation into a database that will form the basis for future development decisions. The database provides a reference point for making project recommendations and guiding comparisons of the subject property's projected performance with actual results obtained at similar existing properties.

The market area for a lodging facility is the geographic region embodying the facility's major sources of demand. To determine the boundaries of the market area, the market analysis needs to evaluate the location of competitive hotels and the segmentation and origination of the facilities' major sources of business; the travel patterns and trends of vacation, commercial, and convention visitors to the proposed site; the distance between the proposed site and major recreational centers (theme parks, public parks, ski slopes, oceans or lakes, golf courses, tennis facilities, and the like); expenditure patterns of area visitors; and existing socioeconomic boundaries.

Lodging Demand. The process of assessing market support for a lodging facility usually begins while the delineation of the market area is still underway. The sources of demand for a resort lodging facility may be segmented into three major categories, which, in descending order of importance, include vacation or pleasure travelers, convention travelers, and commercial travelers. The following methodology is useful in identifying and assessing the sources of lodging:

- Interview representatives from the local tourist and convention bureaus and chambers of commerce to identify the number, length of stay, expenditure patterns, typical group size, lodging demand, and seasonality of tourists and convention delegates. (Note that these agencies sometimes overstate tourist statistics. In addition, they frequently do not maintain a research program that adequately quantifies travel patterns.)
- Interview officials from major ground transportation firms (automobile rental agencies and bus companies, for example) to determine the source, seasonality, and profile of their principal users.
- Interview corporate travel officers, meeting planners, association executives, wholesale tour operators, travel agents, brokers specializing in group or corporate travel, incentive-travel organizers, and spokespersons for travel clubs in feeder cities. Determine their clients' lodging needs, perception of the area, frequency of visits to the area, primary reasons for visiting, typical group size, and seasonality of travel plans. Find out how their clients view the competitive strengths and weaknesses of existing properties in the subject area and other market areas; what services and amenities they seek; the magnitude of their typical lodging budgets; their future travel plans; and client perceptions of the need for additional local lodging facilities. Interviews with major air and ground carriers and consultations with local operators can aid in the identification of feeder cities.
- Identify and speak with officials of comparable hotels to determine their properties' number of guest rooms, average annual occupancy, average annual room rate, market mix of guests, and type and class of facilities. If no comparable properties exist in the market area, locate similar facilities in nearby market areas and then adjust the associated data for the subject location.
- Assess existing capacity and arrival/departure patterns at the major airport within the market area and then determine the mix, seasonality, and growth rate in the number of airport passengers.

The Hapuna Beach Prince Hotel.

- List the major tourist attractions, community special events, regional and state fairs or expositions, athletic contests, and the like and determine their typical needs for lodging facilities. Interview attraction or event organizers, hotel operators, tourist bureaus, and others.

Lodging Supply. An inventory of the existing and proposed competitive lodging supply in the market area helps predict the likely impact of a new lodging facility on the operating performance of that supply. For each existing and proposed lodging facility that, because of its location, size, and room rate, will compete with the subject hotel, the initiator should quantify size (number of rooms), location, affiliation (chain or independent), orientation (convention delegates, business travelers, vacationers, etc.), amenities, room rate (average annual), occupancy (average annual), and competitive strengths and weaknesses.

Proposed hotels should be scrutinized to determine what innovations they are bringing to the market. In Las Vegas, for example, several major theme resort hotels built in the early 1990s have created new competitive standards for hotels in that city. These properties include the MGM Grand's 5,000-plus-room hotel and theme park, Mirage Resorts's 3,000-room Treasure Island, and Circus Circus Enterprises's 2,500-room Luxor. Caesar's Palace has also added an innovative retail component—the Forum Shops—to its hotel. To

Laurence S. Geller
Chair
Geller & Company
Chicago, Illinois

Laurence Geller is chair and founder of Geller & Company, a Chicago-based international real estate and financial advisory firm founded in 1989. Geller has over 30 years of experience in hospitality industry-oriented real estate development and hotel operations. His firm specializes in the lodging, tourism, leisure, gaming, and related industries.

Before establishing Geller & Company, Geller was chief operating officer and executive vice president of Hyatt Development Corporation, where he was responsible for all development and real estate activities associated with the lodging and related industries. Previously, Geller was a managing partner of Safari Management, Inc., an owner and operator of 18 Holiday Inn hotels. In addition, he was a founding partner of Berins & Co., one of the nation's foremost lodging consultancy firms, and served as a consultant to the Marriott Corporation, Hyatt Corporation, and Holiday Inns, Inc. Geller also served as senior vice president in charge of development and franchising for Holiday Inns, Inc., and was responsible for the company's international interests. Before joining Holiday Inns, he oversaw all development activities for the U.K.-based Grand Metropolitan Hotels.

Geller is a graduate of the Ealing (U.K.) Hotel School with a national diploma in hotel management and catering.

A notable trend in the resort industry is the movement toward packaged vacations of shorter duration. The United States is leading this trend, followed by Japan. Europeans, however, still take the longest trips. Look at the success of cruise ships. First, there were two-week cruises, then one-week, then three days. Some cruises are just overnight. It is often cheaper to go to London for a weekend at the last minute than it is to go to Chicago at the last minute.

Megaresorts are a thing of the past, except for casino-oriented destination resorts. For the most part, their success was exaggerated based on the expectation of incredible cap rates and room rates, which couldn't be achieved. They were a distinctly American phenomenon. The mass market is now more price-sensitive. At one time, megaresorts may have been successful, but it was a different economic time. They also have to be very foreign travel-oriented. It was a thin part of the recreation market, and it is now even thinner.

Many megaresorts were "environmental terrorists." A developer could plop them down anywhere. There may be large resort hotels built, but they won't have all the "toys" and nonsense of a megaresort. The resort busi-

ness is not theater. The overall cost of maintenance of a single megaresort is unbelievable.

Conversely, another trend is toward smaller (200 to 300 rooms) service-oriented resorts that are developed worldwide with less emphasis on the physical product. They are easier to build. Also, more remote and unusual locations will become developed globally. These resorts will be simple and elegant with fewer amenities but with a major emphasis on service. Understated not overstated—"barefoot" elegance. There is more emphasis on service and quality, not capital expenditure. People have become more cynical so the resorts have to be genuine. You cannot fake it. When the consumer wants it to be fake, he goes to Las Vegas.

All of these resorts will pencil out on a cash flow basis rather than some hoped-for residual value and some mystical future buyer. Other than casinos, hotels have gone back to being hotels rather than show business.

Within the global arena, several constraints work against the success of worldwide resorts. The first is the simple fluctuation in airline schedules. Second are geopolitical issues. Third, some areas in the world are environmentally unsafe. Fourth is the availability of discretionary dollars, and resorts compete for global discretionary dollars. Fifth is the ability to find local partners who can help protect the developer.

A hotel itself might not be able to pay for all of a resort's infrastructure, say, a golf course. Therefore, condominiums and timeshare units may be built to complement the hotel and pay for some of the infrastructure. Financial institutions are beginning to understand that this mix may be necessary.

It may be easier to finance a resort outside the United States than inside. Several public agencies in other countries are involved in promoting economic development and creating jobs and therefore may be interested in financing a resort. Also, a developer might be able to get World Bank financing for a resort.

While there may be conflicts among the needs of owners versus hotel guests, the conflicts are more manageable if the resort is master planned as a whole from the start rather than permitted to grow merely by accretion.

As an amenity in a master-planned resort development, golf will become even more popular in the future, particularly in areas such as Europe and South America where there is a shortage of golf courses. Golf now has a global following. One of the mistakes of the 1980s, however, was that developers built golf courses that may not have been playable by all the guests. ■

remain competitive, any proposed hotel in Las Vegas must respect these innovations and anticipate those of tomorrow. In recent years, Las Vegas in general has made a serious effort to reposition itself as a theme park destination suited to families; such shifts can create important development opportunities.

The ultimate result of the market analysis process is the identification of an opportunity, i.e., currently underserved market demand. Sometimes hotel owners/operators already in the market can easily identify the underserved market. For example, at the Pebble Beach Resort in Monterey, California, the resort's owners became acutely aware that they could not adequately serve the conference business with one small hotel in a high-demand golf resort setting. To tap this demand, they developed the Spanish Bay Resort on an adjacent site; the resort's hotel was positioned as a group meeting hotel while the Pebble Beach Lodge was positioned as a hotel for the free independent traveler, although both properties can be used jointly for larger meetings. In this case, the market analysis process was simplified by the fact that supply was severely restricted in an environmentally sensitive, world-class resort location.

Commercial Real Estate Markets

Commercial components associated with recreational destination projects can, if included at all, range from a simple camp store to sophisticated niche boutiques and from varied eating and entertainment venues to mass market retail, service, and office complexes. The purpose of these facilities can extend from providing essential household supplies and traditional souvenirs to offering alternative leisure activities, elaborate home and lifestyle support services, and, increasingly, business support services for the rapidly growing telecommuting (full-time and part-time) workforce. The role and potential for com-

mercial facilities as part of the recreational or vacation-related experience is considerable and growing.

Conventional retail market analysis can offer some clues as to the level of demand for some commercial products and services, such as simple grocery products, while general patterns of expenditures can be tracked for impulse clothing shopping and other traditional vacation-related acquisitions. The demand for other types of goods and services is, however, more difficult to predict.

The developer or operator contemplating a typical recreational-based commercial business needs to approach the initial market analysis by relating the concept under consideration to specific examples for the type of environment defined by the envisioned project. For more unusual concepts, such as a duck-carving operation, the market potential is not likely to be quantified in conventional terms and will instead rely on common sense and the power (and luck) of the operator to succeed.

The size, location, and nature of ancillary commercial elements in resort or recreational projects is derived from three principal influences: purpose and character of the subject resort, the size and character of the market, and the availability and type of existing off-site facilities. These commercial components may be subsidized in some form by a master developer, operated as free-standing profit centers, or owned and managed by independent operators.

Type of Resort

Many different project types have been outlined elsewhere in this book, each with its own unique needs, features, and demand for commercial facilities. For example, a remote seasonal hotel destination may feature specialized sports clothing and equipment shops, whereas a new large-scale retirement community may require a full complement of seemingly conventional retail and professional service facilities. Whether a second-home community is reachable primarily by car for weekend

The Spanish Bay Resort, directly adjacent to and affiliated with the famed Pebble Beach Resort, was developed in part to serve the group market at Pebble Beach. The original Pebble Beach Lodge remains as a hotel primarily for free independent travelers.

use or by air for longer stays is another example of the myriad factors that begin to define the relative importance of locally available commercial operations.

With the exception of some hotel-anchored destinations, most successful recreational projects will not succeed without proximity to a minimum of essential retail services. In their most highly refined form, commercial facilities can become a major attraction in and of themselves. For example, some popular resort destinations such as Harbour Town at Sea Pines Plantation on Hilton Head Island and Snowmass Village near Aspen enjoy the synergy generated by commercial components and core recreation-based businesses. The growth of outlet centers in many resort areas is further evidence of this synergy.

A major factor in evaluating the need for commercial facilities (which, unfortunately, is not synonymous with substantiated demand) is an understanding of what facilities and services can be profitable and, if not directly profitable, critical in helping expand or maintain the overall project's user base. Commercial facilities can offer five broad types of goods and services as follows:

- essential provisions, equipment, etc.;
- alternative leisure activities for persons not engaged in the primary recreational or business purpose of the visit to the overall project;
- collectibles not necessarily available at the visitor's place of origin;
- medical and other professional or trade services; and
- essential dining and entertainment services.

Market Size and Characteristics

The challenge of programming commercial facilities for recreation-anchored projects—already complicated

The local gathering spot at Disney's Old Key West Resort in Orlando, Florida, is the Turtle Krawl boardwalk, lined with a restaurant, snack bar, general store, game room, and community hall.

by the discretionary nature of spending on recreational activities—is compounded by issues of seasonality and peak demand. Many commercial establishments might be economically viable if the total potential business volume in any one year could be stretched relatively evenly throughout the year, which invariably is not possible in a recreation-anchored location. Unlike their metropolitan brethren with a more consistent business base, most businesses located in recreation-anchored locations cannot justify the space, inventory, and experienced staff needed to serve the infrequent days of highest-volume sales potential. The situation becomes even more uncertain given the risks of unfavorable weather, restricted travel considerations, or other factors that can literally wash away the biggest potential sales days of the year.

An important factor for consideration is sources of demand surrounding the subject development. The critical mass sufficient to support a collection of commercial establishments may already exist but remain underserved because of a perceived lack of appropriate locations, conservative local business practices (including approaches to financing), and a general slowness in defining or recognizing the magnitude of recreation-based demographic and economic change. Obviously, great care needs to be applied in estimating demand potential within the area surrounding a given project, with critical distinctions made between the indigenous population and visitors.

Finally, a significant determinant of the prospects for operating local commercial establishments relates to the possible interest, depth of talent, and financial resources represented within the visitor population to a resort community. A base of skilled people and capital sources with an interest in setting up shop in recreational environments—for reasons ranging from practical to romantic to "I'm bored"—can provide an important source of entrepreneurs and labor.

Competitive Context

In the case of spearheading a new recreational project, commercial operations can take advantage of an established destination setting with commercial infrastructure already in place. Not only do existing facilities provide convenience for the visitor to the new project, but the presence of such operations allows a new development to pick and choose what it feels might make the sensible addition. At the other extreme and by far the most common situation, many well-positioned recreational locations are rendered unmarketable because of the total lack of reasonably convenient or appropriately targeted supporting services.

Distance to commonly needed facilities, such as a limited-choice grocery store, video rental outlet, service station, and restaurant, should not generally exceed 15 to 20 minutes by car. Specialty needs such as hardware and building supplies, medical facilities, etc., can range farther, but one-way distances beyond 30 minutes begin to stretch the comfort limit.

In the instance where the existing commercial offerings may be underserving a market, the decision to construct additional facilities can be attractive. The potential benefits may include both direct economic returns and significant indirect marketing and image-related bonuses.

When studying the role of existing commercial facilities—in particular, retail operations—it is valuable to remember that retail centers and operators typically come and go, especially at recreation-anchored destinations. The dynamics of retailing therefore can allow a new entrant with a superior location or product the possibility of successfully realigning a market that may already seem oversupplied. Going a step further, many successful retailing operations actually grow out of creating a market where none was apparent before.

Notes

1. Adapted from Leanne Lachman, Presentation at ULI Seminar "Trends and Issues in Resort Development," Pebble Beach, Calif., June 21–22, 1993.

2. Personal communication with Diana Permar, Permar and Ravenal, August 1996.

3. Ragatz Associates, Inc., *The American Recreational Property Survey: 1995* (Washington, D.C.: International Timeshare Foundation, 1995).

4. Personal communication with James W. Light, chair, Snowmass Corporation/Chaffin Light Associates, Snowmass Village, Col., April 29, 1994.

5. Ragatz Associates, *Property Survey.*

6. Adapted from Robert H. Pittman, Henry O. Pollakowski, and Maury Seldin, "Market Research for Resort/Retirement Planned Communities," *Urban Land*, November 1992, pp. 35–39.

7. Ragatz Associates, *Property Survey.*

8. Ragatz Associates, Inc., *Timeshare Purchasers: Who They Are, Why They Buy* (Washington, D.C.: Alliance for Timeshare Excellence, 1995).

9. Adapted from Richard L. Ragatz and Carol A. McInnis, "Timesharing: Keeping Pace with the Times," *Urban Land*, August 1996, pp. 43–46.

10. *RCI Perspective*, January/February 1995.

11. Ragatz and McInnis, "Timesharing."

12. Patricia Braus, "Sex and the Single Splendor," *American Demographics*, November 1993, pp. 28–34.

13. Scott Burlingame, "Worldwide Annual Vacation Ownership Growth Averaged 16% Over Last Eight Years," *Resort Development and Operation*, June 1995, pp. 29–30.

14. J. Richard McElyea and Gregory L. Cory, "Resort Investment and Development: An Overview of an Evolving Market" (San Francisco: Mellon/McMahan Real Estate Advisors, Inc., 1992).

15. Adapted from David E. Arnold et al., *Hotel/Motel Development* (Washington, D.C.: ULI–the Urban Land Institute, 1984), pp. 59–63.

3. Feasibility Analysis and Financing

Feasibility analysis and programming is the process of defining and testing a project concept and program for a specific site. It includes the preparation of a detailed financial model and a financing plan. The feasibility analysis and programming process varies with the situation and the developer's objectives. Projects sometimes begin with sites, but more often with concepts and ideas, or perceived opportunities. Ultimately, the process analyzes the opportunities associated with a particular site. Through market analysis and feasibility analysis and programming, the developer analyzes development opportunities and develops, tests, and refines the physical and programmatic elements of a project. Continuous reevaluation of project feasibility and the program is required during all stages of the development process.

The feasibility analysis seeks to determine whether the economic, legal, political, physical, financial, and marketing environments favor implementation of the proposed project. Simply put, the feasibility analysis and programming process is intended to identify an optimum development program that will succeed financially. The process usually tests several different concepts to determine if any is viable and/or optimum.

The feasibility analysis must provide for sudden and unforeseen changes in circumstances. Even the best-conceived development plans can be undermined by

Woodrun Place is a resort condominium in Snowmass, Colorado, that offers convenient access to the slopes.

delays in obtaining government approvals, unexpected construction delays and cost overruns, slower-than-forecast housing sales or hotel revenues, lower-than-projected revenue from other components, higher-than-expected interest rates, and a host of other problems. The more complex the project and the longer the time required to complete it, the more uncertain is its financial feasibility.

Given the element of unpredictability in any project, feasibility analysis operates in the realm of probability. It can be used to make reasonable estimates of a project's financial feasibility. While it cannot ensure a project's success, it is an invaluable tool in helping developers decide whether to proceed with a project and helping lenders or investors decide whether to finance a project.

This chapter reviews the several issues involved in feasibility analysis and financing by first discussing the development program and its many possible elements. The second section covers the site selection and analysis process. The third section presents a detailed hypothetical financial model for a multiuse resort, and the fourth section discusses the financing of a resort property.

Development Program

Establishing the right program for a successful resort is a challenging undertaking. The programmatic elements of a resort or resort community can include, among others, recreational facilities and programs, housing units,

Deer Valley in Utah, like many resorts, has introduced mountain biking during the summer months to create a two- or three-season resort. Bikers can take ski lifts to the top of the mountain, allowing them to use a greater number of trails.

hotel and conference facilities, commercial facilities, community infrastructure and services, club membership structures, and community governance structures. The development program typically describes the location, size, number, and character of these elements. Phasing, which describes how the facilities and programs will be staged over time, is central to the product programming process.

The development program and amenity program are determined early in the process and adjusted and refined continuously throughout the planning, construction, and operations phases. Flexibility is essential. The more latitude that can be built into the development program upfront, the easier it will be to adjust to changes in the market and other sectors.

A resort developer embarking on a development process should first consider a range of options and identify a general project concept. Many variables in combination determine the appropriate development concept. The developer might begin with a certain site whose best use is readily apparent, though not automatically assumed to be appropriate. In another instance, the developer might be interested in tapping a potential market and therefore would need to identify an appropriate site. Experience has shown that the latter approach stands a better chance of success. Too frequently, problems stem from attempts to force a project on a particular site simply because the developer owns or controls the land, not because the site is necessarily appropriate. Nevertheless, while the initiating factors differ from one case to another, the development process that guides a project to success exhibits general similarities across circumstances and project type.

MRA International, a development advisory firm, has developed a strategic process for positioning a resort (see Figure 3-1). MRA uses a matrix to identify nine basic stratagems that are a function of the state of the market and the developer's positioning objectives/options. Markets are defined in a hierarchy as follows:

virgin, emergent, defined, mature, dense, and saturated. Positioning strategies call for dominating or positioning for cost/scale leadership, penetrating and focusing, or differentiating and creating product distinctiveness. A clear understanding of where a proposed resort fits into the matrix can help define a positioning strategy and the resort's place in the market.

Essential to a calculated resort development process is the constant thinking and rethinking of the development concept, the continuous reevaluation of available information, and the subsequent refinement of projections. This approach requires the developer to survey the prospective market while simultaneously conceptualizing the product type, project densities, and buildout periods for evaluation against the real estate development constraints projected over the development period. All these considerations require preliminary investigation. Yet, as each element of feasibility is addressed and used in further refining the development concept, more detailed steps are essential. Without the careful coordination of development considerations, a resort project may easily be flawed from the start. One mistake often made in this process is to contract with an outside firm for a one-time market and feasibility analysis at the outset of a project without bringing the consultant back to review, update, and refine the development concept when conditions change.

Fundamental to creating a development concept is establishing the nature of the development or its desired image. Establishing a psychological goal helps determine a project's image or intended ambience, which in turn influences decisions on facility types, facility arrangement and quality, operational needs, marketing techniques, and many other details. Chapter 4 discusses the myriad product and design choices to be considered in planning a resort property.

The importance of developing a long-range concept of resort development early in the planning process cannot be overstated. Certainly, small projects will experience fewer complications, but in any situation that involves phased development, the initial actions must support the long-term goal, which points to the importance of establishing development standards. To this end, the developer must answer a plethora of detailed questions. In fact, building resort communities is not unlike building new communities in general. The resort developer needs to consider the roles he or she will play throughout the development of the project—from its beginning to its maturity. Those roles may include an involvement in hotel and recreational facility operations, home construction, new home sales, real estate resales, rental programs, retail management, golf course management, etc. Chapter 5 addresses issues associated with resort operations and management.

The initial steps in the feasibility and programming process must address several basic categories of programs—the amenity program, the residential and lodging program, and the commercial program—and the phasing and timing of the development.

The Amenity Program and Strategy

As a first step in programming the resort, the developer must consider what amenities to include in the project. That decision should draw on the market studies already completed. At the outset, the developer should identify the natural amenities, such as beaches, wetlands, hillsides, woodlands, vistas, etc., to be protected and then determine how those amenities can be enhanced—for example, a beach can be created on an already existing lake, or a woodland can be made more accessible with trails for hiking, cross-country skiing, or mountain biking. An existing facility such as a ranch, historic building, or ski facility may also serve as an attraction.

Following this assessment, the developer should consider the creation of additional primary amenities. If golfing, skiing, boating, or tennis are to be primary attractions, they demand an early and obvious commitment. The following four major questions should guide determination of the amenity package:

- How does the amenity fit into the total project—physically, economically, and thematically?
- What quantity of the amenity should be provided?
- What should be the timing for construction?
- Is the cost justified?

In general, created amenities should be planned and constructed well or not at all. Since the purpose of a resort is to offer a pleasant and substantive experience, inferior facilities that disappoint or frustrate the user are worse than no facilities at all.

The selection and quantity of amenities depends on the type of consumer, the significance of other attractions, and the project's lodging type(s). Added amenities can provide an alternative to heavy use of other

figure 3-1

Basic Stratagems in Resort Development—Preferred Positioning Option

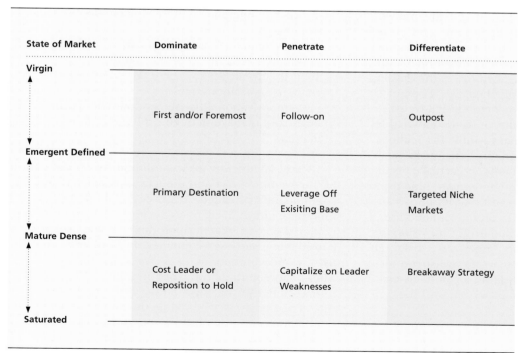

State of Market	Dominate	Penetrate	Differentiate
Virgin			
	First and/or Foremost	Follow-on	Outpost
Emergent Defined			
	Primary Destination	Leverage Off Exisiting Base	Targeted Niche Markets
Mature Dense			
	Cost Leader or Reposition to Hold	Capitalize on Leader Weaknesses	Breakaway Strategy
Saturated			

Source: MRA International, Philadelphia, Penn.

Designed by golf course architect P.B. Dye, the Links at Fisher Island in Miami, Florida, as well as being a popular recreational amenity, also enhances the prestigious island by providing vistas of landscaped open spaces.

recreational facilities, but only if they reflect consumer interest. To some degree, amenities can be added or extended as demand grows. The amenity strategy must also formulate an operational plan that delineates who will develop, own, and operate the facilities and for how long as well as who will use the facilities on what terms.

The challenge is to plan a specific mix of recreational facilities and programs that best reinforces the development's real estate and operating objectives. Potential guests and real estate buyers look closely at a resort's range of activities and the quality of its recreational facilities. As a result, two sometimes conflicting realities drive amenity planning: the amenity benchmark established by competitive developments and actual consumer amenity use patterns. Even though demographic trends and participation rates may suggest that tennis is waning or that community pools attract only limited use, departures from the market standard for inclusion of tennis courts and swimming pools may prove risky. On the other hand, no developer wants to overspend on amenities that remain unused. Thus, a careful assessment of the costs and benefits associated with the amenity is essential.

A successful strategy for determining the mix of recreational amenities should

- match the mix, quantity, and quality of amenities to the project's market concept;

- set clear priorities for the expected roles of the amenities over the project's life;
- balance the timing and magnitude of capital expenditures for amenities against the benefits derived from them;
- ensure adequate developer control over the operations and management of the amenities;
- allow the developer sufficient flexibility to react to changing conditions; and
- provide for rational transfers of ownership, use privileges, and management control as the project matures.

Clearly, an amenity package should reflect the nature of the overall project and the type of residence or accommodation provided. A conventional hotel room or timeshare unit is likely to create more demand for recreational services than a single-family home, which is considerably more self-contained and less intensively used. Condominiums available for rental fall somewhere between these two types of accommodation in terms of intensity of use and their associated demand for recreational facilities. While the nature of the residential uses may not matter to the short-run investor, from the perspective of the master developer, residential types, user habits, and satisfaction with the quantity and quality of demanded and provided recreational amenities may affect future land values and potential profits from overall operations.

In addition, the developer must relate the amenity package not only to resort visitors and guests, but also to the surrounding community. This relationship is particularly important when facilities such as ski resorts depend on an operating cash flow to support themselves and must at times rely on off-site consumers for a substantial part of their revenue. In some cases, however, the amenity package is designed for the exclusive use of owners and guests—as with a private country club— such that off-site support is not an issue.

Making a profit from or at least breaking even on commercial recreational operations should be a development objective. However, when recreational development is slated for an isolated location without a threshold community population, the developer is sometimes well advised to subsidize certain facilities or activities, such as limited-version golf, swimming, restaurant dining, and special convenience services. In the case of a large community, facilities ultimately should pay for themselves directly.

The sizing of the amenity is an important component of the programming process. For example, to be feasible, golf courses require a certain number of users and private country clubs a minimum number of members, which in turn depends in part on the size of the proposed resort community. Recent research from Economics Research Associates, for example, reveals that 40 to 80 percent of households in golf-oriented resort or second-home communities buy golf memberships at the community's country club. In retirement communities, 25 to 50 percent of households purchase memberships while only 20 to 30 percent of primary-home community households do likewise.[1]

Other research has suggested that in resorts (or retirement areas) favored with good weather and residents with considerable leisure time, a population as small as 2,500 can support a regulation 18-hole golf course. But this type of golf amenity may remain subordinate to the marketing concept for the whole project if it is simply assumed that the target market will also demand a golf course.

A primary obligation of the resort developer is to maintain expected standards of quality in all recreational facilities. For example, where golf is promoted as the chief amenity and facility usage exceeds capacity, the developer must provide another recreational facility within or beyond the confines of the development. Otherwise, users will grow dissatisfied as the project is built out.

Tennis, however, is a simpler amenity to add and/or expand than a golf course. A golf course consumes over 25 times as much land as a tennis facility capable of handling a comparable number of users. Golfing areas, though, offer substantial aesthetic, environmental, and other values that may more than justify their expense. Other facilities for consideration include those for watersports, walking trails, outdoor cooking areas, equestrian operations, and a host of others discussed in Chapter 4.

In working up an amenity package, the recreational planner must undertake the same careful demand evaluations and apply the same types of standards that drive the overall resort development process. To some extent, the developer is in a position to influence demand through the amenities provided but cannot guarantee that such amenities will contribute effectively to the development. The case studies in Chapter 6 describe how individual projects have dealt with different amenity concerns.

Residential and Lodging Program and Strategy

The market analysis discussed earlier suggests the appropriate mix of hotel, condominium, timeshare, and single-family products, along with some indications of size, style, ownership types, and price range. While amenities may be the primary drawing card for a resort, programming an appropriate mix of residential, hotel, and timeshare products is the bread and butter of profitable resort development. The sale and/or operation of these properties is the source of most project revenues.

Among the numerous real estate strategies for developing resort homes and accommodations, each has its own set of advantages and disadvantages. While most strategies involve land development, they diverge when it comes to the real estate product offered and the developer's level of long-term involvement. The strategies may range from lot sales to homebuilding (both single- and multifamily) to timeshare development to hotel operation. Multiuse resorts might offer all of these product types, in which case additional issues pertain to which product will be developed first and who will manage the development over the short and long terms.

Lot sales have historically represented a profitable type of resort development in that they require less capital investment and less managerial skill than other development alternatives. Depending on the improvements made to the land, land sales transfer most of the carrying costs and construction and operational responsibility to others. If, however, the quality of the overall resort environment is to be maintained, the developer must establish and enforce design guidelines as part of any lot sales program. Indeed, the responsible resort developer usually has a long-term stake in the project. As a result, the developer may be willing to assume the burden of building extensive amenities, roads, and utilities as part of the lot sales package. Such an undertaking, though, is not without risk. Competitors can enter into lot sales development relatively easily in rural areas, particularly given the frontier appeal and low utility of undeveloped parcels.

In addition to selling individual lots, many developers of large resort communities sell parcels to builders/ developers on a controlled and phased basis. Carefully timed and coordinated land sales that release different tracts of land for purchase under specific restrictions and covenants can help maximize returns by allowing land values to increase in advance of sales.

Hotel and/or timeshare properties can also be developed through land sales strategies. Given that these are specialized operations that demand particular expertise, they might require the involvement of outside entities. In some cases, the resort developer might enter into a joint venture with such an entity.

More recently, a popular strategy for resort residential uses has been the development and marketing of a complete resort home product, including interior furnishings and housewares. Under this approach, the resort developer has the opportunity to profit not only from land sales but also from constructing and marketing the product. Building the units provides the developer with additional control over the product as well as with the flexibility to plan for open space and unit density, which would not be possible under many lot sales programs. When a resort community is located in an isolated setting with no suitably equipped local home-building industry to develop a project, the developer may have no choice but to initiate a building program. Although the construction of units can increase gross profits, it also increases capital needs and risk. In an economic downturn, the developer/builder may have to carry the land as well as the buildings. At any rate, the combined land development and building approach requires additional construction, managerial, and marketing skills.

A strategy that involves an even greater long-term commitment and added risk is the operation of the resort's residential and hotel facilities—whether that means managing a hotel, operating a unit rental pool program, or providing maintenance services or a resales program. This strategy provides the ultimate degree of developer control over project destiny along with such benefits as long-term profits, the potential for continued cash flow when the project is completed and/or real estate sales slow, influence over and capture of land values as a result of a successful resort operation, and an increased ability to maintain project standards (perhaps through subsidization). Again, a successful operations program depends on extensive management expertise and financial backing and is usually combined with the long-term operation of other elements such as amenities and commercial uses.

Many multiuse resorts now employ all of the above strategies, thereby allowing the astute resort developer to benefit from a flexible business plan that builds on the strengths of the individual strategies. Occasional land sales may help generate funds for debt service or new capital expenditures. Joint ventures that involve partners in ownership and operations can reduce risk as well as management requirements. A building program can create momentum during a lull in land sales and help generate sales that increase the market for existing amenities and facilities. Owning and operating the resort over the long term can yield attractive profits once the project matures. The developer assumes fewer risks by spreading the investment over the many business aspects of a resort/residential development. As further

The Semiahmoo Company brought in Hyatt to handle the operation of the hotel at the Semiahmoo Resort in Blaine, Washington. This strategy minimized the risks involved with hotel management and introduced a name that visitors would associate with a high level of service.

Peter Timmermans

Pelican Bay, a large-scale resort community in Naples, Florida, contains 1.1 million square feet of commercial space, including both retail and office.

incentive, the developer may realize certain tax benefits from balancing profits and losses across the various facets of resort recreational development.

Programming Commercial Uses

Under normal circumstances, the best measure of potential for a given commercial operation in a resort property is the level of interest demonstrated by third parties in investing in and operating commercial facilities and services. Such feasibility testing presumes a typically motivated economic interest, which cannot be assumed in the context of many recreational developments. Instead, many resort locations are often too small, too immature, too seasonal, or otherwise lacking a major attribute to justify independent commercial operations.

Assuming for the moment that the maturity or size of a resort community is as yet inadequate to support a desired amount of retail services, a motivated developer must look for ways to close the gap between insufficient economic feasibility and the importance of the service to the overall success of the development program. Strategies might take the form of free or subsidized rent, assistance in financing startup costs, or other cost-covering devices. Two important opportunities for the developer interested in promoting commercial services is leveraging customer expectations of high prices and, as mentioned earlier, capitalizing on the available owner/staffing labor pool that may be willing to accept lower earnings in exchange for the benefit of residing near the recreational environment.

The following simple rules can guide development planning for commercial elements in a recreation-based project:

- Determine the significance of a given service to the project's broader development purpose, including tolerable or appropriate consumer inconvenience thresholds.

- Consider a range of options and activities to stimulate commercial activity, including creation of a partnership that operates on- or off-site establishments, shoring up or repositioning an existing operation, or entering into a joint venture with perceived competitors to help kick-start the requisite commercial facilities.

- To the extent possible, conduct feasibility analyses that use conventional norms in their marketing and operating assumptions for commercial facilities. Far too often, commercial commitments in recreational environments are subjected to little, if any, market and operational feasibility analysis. Even worse, they are forced to function in totally inappropriate settings and thus are virtually condemned to failure.

- Explore opportunities to piggyback commercial operations with other building uses or operational activities. Examples include shared staffing, encouragement of coordinated off-site vendor deliveries, or inclusion of provision-stocking services in conjunction with house-cleaning services.

- Investigate ways for the real estate or resort component to capitalize on and promote its identity by licensing the use of its logo on clothing, equipment, and novelties offered for sale locally.

- Prepare for changes as the resort community evolves and matures. Allow for a range of possible on-site commercial facilities or, if appropriate, secure off-site locations. If projections call for increased full-time residential occupancy, the development plan should provide ground for commercial facilities, though well into the future. By allowing for lifestyle changes and going so far as to dedicate ground for seniors' housing, the initial developer may be able to achieve the desired marketing impact while retaining flexibility and avoiding any material commitments.

- Conduct an initial screening and undertake subsequent monitoring of commercial operations and watch out for excessively optimistic or inexperienced operators who may leave a trail of oversupply, vacancies, and generally negative impacts. Furthermore, in most instances, the priority of maintaining and enhancing the desired image of the larger development points to the importance of targeting the right service niche.

- Link up with experienced third-party owners and operators of commercial establishments in resort locations with opposite seasonality.

- Keep to the core recreational business, especially in the early stages of a project. If the feasibility of a particular resort investment depends on seeding and sustaining independent commercial operations, then these operations must be viewed as part and parcel of the core business. When the need for a range of commercial operations is less clear, caution is in order.

Profile and Comments: James W. Light

James W. Light
Chair
Chaffin/Light Associates
Snowmass Village, Colorado

Since 1978, Jim Light has led Chaffin/Light Associates from its first development at Snowmass Village, Colorado—a single venture in a 3,000-acre ski resort community—into several recreational community development ventures in Washington state, Florida, and South Carolina. From 1978 through 1994, the firm's gross sales volume of new residential products exceeded $250 million.

As a young man, Light was put in charge of the planning and execution of Harbour Town at Sea Pines Plantation on Hilton Head Island, the most ambitious private harbor development ever built on the East Coast. In 1975, he was named president of the Sea Pines Company.

Light was born in 1943. He received a BA from the University of North Carolina and an MBA from the Harvard University Graduate School of Business Administration.

There have been a few companies that have attempted to be national developers. We, however, are more focused on recreational community development on the local level. We have been opportunistic in the projects we have undertaken, which may account for the fact that we operate in several markets. But we are not a big national company. We are national by opportunity rather than by design. When one stays in a regional economy solely, though, a developer's timing or structure needs to be right in order to deal with all the changes in that regional economy. By comparison, our projects are regionally diversified.

There is no retail business in America, except the development business, that would purchase a ten-year inventory and hope it was right in that purchase decision. A developer needs to try to break projects into more manageable parts, to make the project cycle a little shorter. It may be buying less land initially or bringing in a partner. Also, it could involve properly capitalizing a project

for the long haul. Essentially, we have financed land with equity, and we have financed the operating properties—golf, tennis, etc.—with debt. A developer may project lower returns because of the amount of equity involved, but it is safer.

A developer should first define what business he is in. Then he can look for other businesses and services that complement his original business strategy. A question a developer should ask is, Who are my most profitable customers and what other services can I provide them? A developer can define what business he is in and either export that one business to a variety of markets or stay in one market and look for a series of complementary services to his prime business. That latter strategy, however, may subject the developer to more risk by being more dependent on one regional economy, as noted above.

A developer must be crystal clear on what type of project he is developing and commit to it. That is not to say that a community cannot evolve. But consumers today are so sophisticated and the development choices so great that not having a clear concept can be detrimental to the marketing of a project. The customers are less trusting of the developer because they have seen projects that have not worked.

I think a growing issue for developers is the political risks involved in undertaking a project. A developer needs to prepare a strategy to deal with those risks, allow adequate time and money to address the concerns, and participate with both constituents and potential opponents. It's an issue that cannot be understated.

Community institutions, such as music and cultural events, are critical to the success of real communities, in shaping the personality of a place. Churches are also important institutions. All add a richness and diversity to a community, often without providing real estate. In Aspen, I can cite the Aspen Institute, the Aspen Music Festival, the ballet, and a wine and cheese event as examples of community institutions that have become asso-

Phasing and Timing

Phasing and timing are principal dilemmas in resort development. Adequate infrastructure, recreational amenities, and commercial facilities should be provided at the outset of project development to draw and satisfy customers in sufficient numbers and thus meet the developer's growth needs. Yet, recreational amenities in particular require heavy front-end financing, first, for construction and, second, to cover high initial operating losses. Until the number of visitors or residents and the concomitant revenues begin to support the facilities' operating costs, the front-end capital costs and early operating losses remain sizable, causing the initial returns on the total investment to remain unsatisfactorily low for long periods.

Balancing Upfront Costs and Benefits. The amount of existing recreational consumer traffic in the area of a new project is an important consideration in sizing

Snowmass, a 3,000-acre ski community in Colorado, is one of several resort community projects being undertaken by Chaffin/ Light Associates.

ciated with Aspen. The golf, tennis, and skiing are only threads of the community mosaic that is being created. It is in the best interest of the community developer to make sure that these community institutions become independent and self-sufficient.

Compared with companies like Sea Pines Plantation that invested heavily in the education and development of its staff, there hasn't been the same investment by today's firms in training raw talent to be developers. New forms of joint ventures may serve as a training ground. These include joint ventures between well-capitalized, seasoned developers and local developers. They also include joint ventures between seasoned developers and large paper companies, railroads, or other such firms.

■

Before the first home was built in 1989 at Sun City Las Vegas—a retirement-/second-home recreational community —approximately $50 million was invested in the development of amenities and other community infrastructure. Featuring an 18-hole championship golf course designed by Greg Nash and PGA Hall of Fame member Billy Casper, the community also built the $6 million, 38,000-square-foot Mountain Shadows Recreation Center.

Tony Scodwell

the initial amenities. For example, a resort community located amid a well-established and substantial user market can select from several options. On the one hand, the project might start with a sizable amenity package and tap existing demand, thus helping ensure that facilities do not operate at a loss from the outset. On the other hand, the project might forgo initial upfront amenity development and instead rely on the area's existing amenities. Another possibility is to establish cooperative use agreements with other projects, allowing the residents of one development to use the facilities of another.

In the absence of consumer traffic in the project's general or immediate vicinity, the developer can still choose from a range of phasing strategies. Rather than start with a full complement of amenities, the developer may rely on the area's existing natural amenities while concentrating on the construction of accommodations. A portion of the targeted market will be drawn to the development simply because of its attractive natural surroundings. As the number of accommodations increases, the community will establish a sufficiently broad base to justify the installation of such operating amenities as a golf course. With the addition of amenities, the developer can step up the promotion campaign and growth rate so that the revenue-producing amenities will break even as soon as possible.

In addition to the above approaches, developers can use various strategies to postpone the development of some recreational amenities, to pass along the costs of amenity development, or to accelerate the revenues produced by amenities built upfront. To develop a golf course at the outset of project development, for example, developers can donate land to a golf course operator who then constructs the course. The developer avoids the front-end cost but retains the land premiums from golf course frontage. In adopting this strategy, the developer must specify in agreement provisions that course design, construction, and operation will meet project standards.

Another strategy is to open recreational facilities to nonresidents, either as member or nonmember users. Ideally, this strategy offers two advantages: it attracts potential real estate prospects by exposing the project to a wide audience and provides dues and/or fee revenues. For projects marketed as "exclusive," however, residents may perceive the opening of facilities to outsiders as compromising the value of the amenity and the community.

For major projects, the upfront development of at least one high-profile amenity is critical in establishing the resort as a new destination. When a property is large and the developer properly capitalized, building extensive and high-quality amenities upfront is often the best strategy. At Sun City Las Vegas, a retirement-/second-home recreational community in Nevada, Del Webb invested approximately $50 million in the development of amenities and other community infrastructure even before building the first house. The community not only features a championship 18-hole golf course designed by Greg Nash and PGA Hall of Famer Billy Casper, it also is home to the $6 million, 38,000-square-foot Mountain Shadows Recreation Center. These major upfront investments paid off by helping accelerate the community's rate of sales—over 1,000 sales in the first year alone, more than twice the number that the Del Webb Corporation had projected. As a result, the entire community has developed at an accelerated pace.

While controlling the costs of upfront amenity development is a legitimate developer concern, developers need to exercise care in not undersizing or phasing an amenity in such a way that the market views it as unacceptable or unmarketable as compared to similar amenities in other projects. For example, at Sandpines, a second-home community in Florence, Oregon, the developers learned that they should have built the entire golf course in one stage rather than phasing it nine holes at a time. In today's golf market, a nine-hole course is generally not an acceptable or marketable amenity. It should be noted that *Golf Digest* magazine recently rated the 18-hole course at Sandpines the number one public golf course in the country.

Operational Control and the Exit Strategy. That the developer needs to retain control over recreational facilities and the property as a whole for a substantial portion of the buildout period is one of the most widely accepted principles in amenity-oriented development. "Control" means the ability to ensure that the construction, operation, and maintenance of facilities remain at a level commensurate with the project's overall image and objectives. In most cases, operational control also extends to the assumption of operational expenses and risks. But relinquishing control to an independent operator to avoid these expenses and risks gives rise to another risk: that the facilities may be improperly operated or maintained. Such a result can tarnish the project's image.

The recommended period of developer control over major amenities in resort communities usually lasts until the project is 80 to 90 percent sold out, but a variety of factors, including lender requirements, may cut it short. Whatever the length of the period, the developer must continuously allay residents' concerns about the operation and long-term viability of the amenities. Many developers have learned that an advisory committee or board made up of club members or community residents is a useful vehicle for improving developer/community relations and easing the later disposition or transfer of amenities.

A developer normally separates from a resort community development in accordance with a carefully planned exit strategy that involves the orderly sale and disposition of real estate property, recreational facilities and programs, and other assets as well as the orderly transfer of management responsibilities. An exit strategy must include contingency plans for dealing with sudden and unforeseen changes in circumstances—economic downturns, financial problems, shifts in government policy, or unexpected turns in the market.

In certain projects with capital-intensive, profit-oriented amenities—such as most ski resorts—amenity disposition is not generally an issue. The developer of a ski resort usually plans to retain—either directly or through a subsidiary corporation—operational control and ownership of the ski facilities. For many second-home community projects, on the other hand, amenity disposition is usually a central issue that demands resolution early in the development process. These projects usually transfer (essentially give away) or sell recreational facilities to residents, club members, or a third party, which is often a company specializing in club operations.

Developers dispose of project amenities for economic reasons. In cases where the amenities primarily add real estate value (as opposed to operating profits), the economic value of the amenities package to the developer declines with the sale of each parcel of land or housing unit. Accordingly, when the project is substantially sold out, the economic value of the amenities to the developer is exhausted—unless the amenities are profit centers within themselves. Therefore, the developer no longer has an incentive to retain control or responsibility. Increasingly, however, resort community developers are programming recreational amenities as ongoing, profit-making centers to be retained or sold at a profit. Chapter 5 provides a detailed discussion of various strategies involved in managing and exiting from a resort development.

Site Selection and Analysis

In general, the least justifiable reason for developing a parcel is because "I already own it." Only in rare instances should developers design a project around a piece of raw land they already own (see case study on page 296). Instead, developers should identify a concept they wish to carry out (based on the findings of a thorough market analysis) and then locate a site with the appropriate characteristics. The primary rule is to match a concept to a site. The only good site is one that is marketable, competitive, and capable of making the development concept succeed. The chief criteria for selecting a site for a major resort or resort community relate to setting, access, physical constraints, the regulatory environment, and price.

While the standards and practices for assessing a site's physical and environmental constraints are growing increasingly sophisticated, the difficulty of locating suitable sites for development has increased markedly. Because of escalating land costs in prime locations, sites previously considered undevelopable have emerged as candidates for development. On the other hand, environmental standards and constraints have complicated site selection in desirable locations; often the most desirable resort sites are located in environmentally sensitive areas. Therefore, careful analysis is necessary early on to determine accurately a site's developability.

The frequent requirement for an early environmental impact assessment for private development (whether mandated legally or merely part of good practice) has brought with it the necessity of accurately measuring any environmental constraints—constraints that must be recognized before the purchase of the site is negotiated—that might dictate the ultimate use of the land. This early environmental assessment further requires some preliminary indications of development size, grading and drainage needs, alternative site uses, projected traffic generation, and mitigation actions.

Much of the conceptualization underlying project design must be generated during this initial site evaluation of project feasibility. The increased front-end costs involved in employing specialists in zoning, land planning, geology, civil and traffic engineering, and the social and biological sciences are justifiable as a protective investment for the developer. In the end, such an investment can significantly shorten the time required for project planning and approvals. Without an early

While remote, the setting for Kananaskis Village in Alberta, Canada, provides a compelling reason to visit the resort, which is located 20 miles east of Banff.

evaluation, a developer could purchase land with physical, social, or political constraints that could prove insurmountable. Further, the early study phase provides the developer with the opportunity to seek an option on the property and thereby limit long-term financial exposure. Most letters of intent allow for a "free look" period before the developer must commit to purchasing the property.

The Setting

The starting point for any successful resort is a compelling natural environment, a salubrious climate, or an attractive social and cultural setting. It is within such a setting that recreational facilities supplement and provide a focus for resident/guest activity; the amenities rarely supplant the setting. The determinants of setting include aesthetic and climatic attributes, cultural attractions, recreational opportunities related to the setting, the character and compatibility of nearby and surrounding uses, and the availability of services. These factors should be evaluated for their consistency with the proposed development's image.

A distinctive natural or cultural setting defines a resort or recreational community. Virtually all successful resorts and recreational communities—and particularly those such as Sea Pines Plantation that significantly advanced the state of the art—have been planned to conserve and enhance the best of their natural and social settings. Some of a setting's valuable attributes may be obvious, such as mountain views or a seashore. Others are more subtle, such as wildlife or vegetation, evidence of past settlements, or even local place names.

When considering sites, a developer should first look at how the setting affects the requirements for recreational facilities. If protected and enhanced, the natural qualities of some sites can serve the same value-creation function as built amenities. Thus, the need for additional recreational amenities may be minimal, especially in the case of smaller projects. The Preserve, a 25-acre second-

home community in Bethany Beach, Delaware, abuts an oceanfront beach, which is its primary amenity. The developer provided only a swimming pool, a single tennis court, and a small clubhouse. In larger projects, it may be possible to create value through site planning strategies that maximize views rather than by adding a golf course. Moreover, if accessible and high-quality recreational facilities—such as a public golf course or tennis courts or a park *or* open space that can be used for cross-country skiing or hiking—are located nearby, a developer may not have to provide similar amenities on site.

Finally, assessing the ecology of a site and its setting is an important consideration; significant natural amenities can be parlayed into important amenities. By accommodating a bald eagle nest in its site plan, for example, Harbour Ridge in Stuart, Florida, earned publicity-generating conservation awards, as did Kiawah Island, a South Carolina beach resort, which won recognition for its sea turtle hatchery program.

Location

Several major factors should be considered in evaluating a resort location: the maturity of the location as a resort destination, access to the location, land costs, and development costs. The location for a resort project can range from undeveloped to fully established or, as MRA International outlined earlier, can take the form of one of six general location types: virgin, emergent, defined, mature, dense, and saturated. Traditionally, most successful resort projects have been developed around established resort areas. Pioneering a new area presents far greater risk than making a new offering in an established area. Public recognition and acceptance of an area as a vacation destination have been important factors in the marketability of most resorts. Further, established resorts offer the built-in entertainment and physical amenities desired by consumers.

In some cases, developers have succeeded in creating new resort destinations—in essence, they have opened

Photos courtesy of Design Workshop Inc.

up new areas. New destination developments are typically large-scale operations that expand on an already existing natural feature—such as a body of water or a mountain—with the construction of golf, tennis, skiing, boating, or swimming facilities in some combination to create a wide range of recreational alternatives. This project type is extremely expensive to develop in that it requires the developer to construct all the amenities and undertake a substantial marketing effort to promote the property. However, the land for such a development can often be acquired at lower cost than land in an existing destination, and the potential to create value once the location is established is tremendous. The problem is to stay the course long enough for value to be created and captured—a most challenging task that requires exceptional financial and organizational resources on the part of the developer.

The recreational development in the area around Orlando, Florida, is a case in point. Before the construction of Disney World, land values in Orlando's outlying areas were fairly low, and recreation was not an important factor in the local economy. But the theme park and its satellite developments have come to represent a critical mass of recreational alternatives that have created a new destination and now attract hundreds of thousands of visitors every year. Less dramatic examples can be found in Hawaii, where resorts have established strong destination locations where none previously existed.

The character and marketability of any resort project depends on such factors as distance from population and employment centers and the types of available transportation services, which are measured in terms of frequency, quality, and cost. An inaccessible resort community location will experience difficulty in maintaining adequate occupancy and real estate sales volume. As a result, access issues often become determining factors in programming the resort. For example, an emerging but relatively inaccessible location may be suitable only for modestly sized facilities targeted to adventure travelers or ecotourists. On the other hand, a resort location that enjoys good air access but is remote from its primary markets must rely on its setting and range of offerings to compensate for the distance or inconvenience involved in getting there.

Improving the major means of transportation to a resort or resort community is usually beyond the resources of the developer. Clearly, the development of transportation access involves extremely long lead times and heavy capital investment. Further, establishing service stations, rental car services, airfields, and commercial air service is a formidable task. In other words, the community should be positioned to take advantage of already operating transportation facilities, which, if not adequate, could be upgraded. The larger the contemplated resort or recreational community, the more important is the existing availability of high-volume commercial transportation in the area.

Finally, the remoteness of a location has an impact on land, development, and operating costs. While the benefits of a remote location on land costs have already been noted, it may be difficult to bring in construction materials and labor. A remote location may also involve higher operating costs related to management training and the increased risk of ineffective management.

Physical Analysis

Once the developer has identified a potential site, closer physical scrutiny of the tract is in order. The developer must collect all existing base data for the site as well as identify future information needs. Physical analysis studies should address

- topography and slope;
- hydrology—major and minor drainage and water source features and resources, including flood hazards and erosion;

A beachfront setting allowed the developer of the Preserve—in Bethany Beach, Delaware—to minimize expenditures for manmade amenities. Other than the beach, the 25-acre community includes a swimming pool, a tennis court, and a small clubhouse.

- geology—surface and subsurface conditions;
- oceanography—shoreline, littoral drift, soundings, and wave action (where applicable);
- vegetation—major vegetative covers, forests, and agriculture;
- wildlife;
- meteorology—wind, temperature, humidity, rainfall, and sun angles;
- other ecological and environmental factors—views, sounds, and special conditions;
- utilities—power, water, sewage, and communication services;
- circulation and related infrastructure—highways and roads, railways, airports and air routes, ports and harbors, and bridges and dams;
- natural resources;

Recreational Development and the U.S. Forest Service

The U.S. Forest Service (USFS), an agency of the U.S. Department of Agriculture, has historically played a major role in recreational development throughout the United States. Created in 1905, the Forest Service was established to manage and administer the nation's forest reserves, which were later renamed national forests. The newly created agency operated under many of the same rules and regulations that had previously guided grants of permission for the use of public forestlands for the development and operation of hotels, summer homes, and sanitariums. In 1915, the Term Occupancy Act established the legislative framework that permits the private use and development of public forestlands for terms of up to 30 years by persons or organizations proposing to erect hotels and other resort facilities.

Today, numerous resorts, hotels, ski areas, marinas, and similar recreational facilities occupy USFS lands. Developed under special use permits, these properties follow strict government guidelines. The permits can be perceived as licenses rather than as leaseholds; they convey limited rights for the use of public lands. Permit issuance is based on a proposed project's compliance with a Comprehensive Forest Management Plan, which the USFS prepares and issues. If a proposed use is deemed compatible with the Comprehensive Forest Management Plan, the USFS conducts an investigation to identify any competitive interests. If none is found, the USFS issues a permit. In the case of identified competitive interests, the USFS issues a prospectus to solicit applications. Before the grant of final approval, the USFS relies on the procedures of the National Environmental Policy Act (NEPA) to evaluate and analyze the environmental impacts of an application's development and operating plans.

The USFS imposes a unique fee system on its special use permit holders. The Graduated Rate Fee System (GRFS), based on a variation of a percentage of rent, uses a rate schedule that progresses with sales after achievement of a break-even point. The brackets for the rates are based on the magnitude of the permit holder's capital investment in facilities. When operation occurs over an area of mixed ownership of private and USFS land, the final fee depends on the percentage of sales generated on USFS lands. For ski areas operating on mixed-ownership land, the fee is calculated as a function of ski-lift capacity.

Over the years, the GRFS has had its share of critics. Permit holders commonly raise concerns regarding the fee system's complexity and failure to assess true market values fairly. In the face of mounting criticism, the Forest Service is developing an alternative fee system for ski areas, which currently generate 90 percent of the fees collected under the GRFS. In 1990 alone, the USFS issued over 200 special use permits to ski areas, which sent over $200 million to the U.S. Treasury.

Use of Forest Service lands for recreational development has frequently spurred public controversy and debate. As early as 1921, conflict surrounded the plans to develop a privately financed resort and tramway on Mt. Hood within the Mt. Hood National Forest in Oregon. A private developer submitted plans to the Forest Service to develop a lodge at Mt. Hood's timberline. At the same time, another private developer submitted plans for a hotel and a tramway to the top of Mt. Hood. After years of controversy and public debate, the USFS issued a special use permit in 1930 to the company whose proposal included the tramway. Due to financial shortfalls, however, the developer never began construction. In 1937, the USFS resurrected the plans when financing became available from the Public Works Administration. Ownership and administration of the facilities was then transferred to the Forest Service. Today, a concessionaire operates and maintains the Timberline Lodge and lift(s) under a special use permit.

- historic sites and landmarks;
- existing land uses and proposed future changes or developments; and
- permitting process and legal restrictions—zoning, building codes, and applicable restrictions (including proposed changes); certainty of approvals over time; and easements and deed restrictions (covered more thoroughly in the following section).

Information from the above studies should be synthesized into a series of analysis drawings and reports that provide a factual basis for the proposed project's ongoing planning, engineering, and design efforts. At the same time, the developer must continue to refine development areas and concepts and identify areas of high construction cost and environmental sensitivity as well as areas possessing special physical characteristics and the potential for high-priority recreational attractions, which in turn deserve more concentrated study.

Once the site is deemed generally suitable for the proposed concept, it is time to develop and evaluate one or more concept designs to determine how a proposed program or programs might fit on the site. The data and studies developed during the physical analysis form the basis for preliminary programs for facility types and attractions. Based on these studies, the developer's economists and planners along with other team members can evaluate various development areas and make recommendations for the specific area or areas with the greatest development potential. The team's work should include

- conceptual diagrams;
- ideal functional relationship diagrams;
- site-related functional diagrams, with special attention to land particularly well suited to resort development;
- preliminary land use diagrams;
- capacity studies of gross areas available for development and of probable areas for preservation;
- suitability studies of various alternative land uses;
- alternative density and yield evaluations;
- other illustrations and perspective drawings that may be required to show more fully any special project features or characteristics; and
- preliminary project staging plans.

Regulatory Analysis

Some of the early measures to take in preparing a development program and plan call for identifying and cataloging the relevant public agencies charged with development approval responsibility, preparing to meet with public officials in proper sequence, and crafting a plan for negotiating the needed public approvals. In addition to the approval requirements mandated for typical urban development, a resort development may have to overcome serious environmental hurdles (because of such a development's natural affinity for unique natural areas) as well as address such issues as the public service demands associated with the impact of a large project

By accommodating a bald eagle nest in its site plan, Harbour Ridge in Stuart, Florida, won publicity-generating conservation awards. The community's programmed sensitivity toward the environment has proven to be an important draw for prospective homeowners.

in a rural area and local officials' lack of familiarity with planning for resort development.

As part of the approval process, a developer must meet certain requirements as a condition of securing the government permits and community approvals needed to undertake and complete a project. The development approval process is extremely important to the developer. Denial of a permit or approval could kill or indefinitely delay a project and lead to financial disaster. Even when the project proposal represents the best land use practices, addresses all environmental concerns, and meets all stipulated regulatory requirements, it is not guaranteed either a timely approval or any approval at all. To obtain permits and approvals in the shortest time, the developer should at the earliest possible stage prepare a regulatory analysis and a plan of action. That analysis should identify all the factors, conditions, and forces, both favorable and unfavorable, that could influence the decisions and actions of public officials, community leaders, and special interest groups. The analysis should present a thorough and fair assessment of the project's predicted impact on the community. In the face of any rapid changes in social, political, and regulatory conditions, the developer is obligated to update the regulatory analysis.

The analysis should include as much relevant information as possible about potential issues of public concern and the individuals likely to be involved in the approval process. Specifically, the developer should determine the likely position of public officials and interest group leaders with regard to the project. Obviously, these persons may wield significant influence in controlling the permits and approvals required for development. Chapter 4 provides further detail on regulatory issues and the approval process.

---

figure 3-2
Sample Site Analysis Checklist

Mapping
- Boundary survey/acreage
- Legal description
- Patterns of ownership
- Easements (by type and location)
- Rights-of-way
- Topography
- Aerial photography
- Regional/site location

Topography
- Slopes (mapped by percentage categories)
- Elevations (high and low points)
- Ridges
- Drainageways
- Special features (e.g., rock outcroppings)
- Views (on- and off-site)

Soils
- Types and characteristics
- Depth of topsoil
- Subsoil conditions
- Potential "borrow" sites for construction materials
- Depth to bedrock/groundwater

Drainage
- Surface drainage features
- Groundwater table
- Floodplain boundaries
- Wetlands/marshes
- Locations of wells
- Depth to groundwater
- Sources of on- and off-site pollution
- Tide data

Vegetation
- Species present on site
- Woodlands/fence rows/vegetative masses
- Locations/sizes of specimen trees
- Special features/habitats

Land Use
- Existing on-site uses (structures and activities)
- Historical site uses (potential for disturbance)
- Surrounding uses (any objectionable uses or activities)
- Adjacent plats
- Open space/vacant land
- Qualitative assessment of neighborhood
- Growth/development patterns in area

Regulations
- Government authorities (city, county, school district, park district, utility districts, other)
- Master/general plan policies
- Existing zoning (for site and adjacent parcels)
- Subdivision ordinance
- Applicable development/impact fees
- Special assessments
- Other applicable municipal, regional, and state regulations

Transportation/Circulation
- Existing traffic patterns
- Access points/entries
- Proximity to regional transportation system
- Planned/proposed transportation system improvements
- Trails/paths (existing and planned)
- Access to transit

Utilities
For each, describe location, design, purveyor, availability, tie-in distance from site, costs borne by utility company, and developer fee structures. Note any potential for moratoriums or other factors that could delay or prohibit development.
- Sanitary sewer
- Water
- Stormwater
- Electricity
- Natural gas
- Cable television
- Telephone

Public Services/Conveniences
- Schools
  - Location/proximity to site
  - Capacity
  - Reputation of school district
- Parks and recreational services
- Emergency services
  - Fire
  - Police
  - Ambulance/paramedic
- Public transportation/transit
- Commercial services/shopping
- Employment services

Other Features
- Prevailing wind direction
- Climatic conditions
- Archaeological sites
- Wildlife (special and habitats)
- Sources of noise
- Aesthetic quality of site and environs

Financial Analysis

Essential to the successful development of resort projects are analyses that evaluate the financial feasibility of the proposed program, guide revisions to the recommended composition and phasing of the development to maximize financial returns consistent with development goals, and provide a database and convenient means of monitoring and maintaining financial control throughout the implementation phase.

The Financial Model

The ultimate purpose of the financial analysis is to model and define a proposed project's expected profitability and rate of return and to determine whether the proposal represents the optimum program and meets the financial objectives established by the developer. Central to the financial analysis is the preparation of the project's pro forma cash flow statement, which contains an estimate of the project's revenues, costs, and net cash flow before and after debt service. The exercise is most effectively completed by evaluating several development alternatives to determine the preferred alternative. The program, phasing, and financial analysis must yield a result that can work financially over both the short and long terms. As noted earlier, the optimum program may change over time, thus underscoring the importance to the developer of a flexible position.

The following procedures are recommended in developing the financial analysis:

- Develop input parameters not otherwise generated in the market analysis. Examples include infrastructure costs for roads, sewers, drainage, utilities, etc.; hotel construction and furnishing costs; residential site development and construction costs; development costs for such amenities as golf courses, swimming pools, bicycle paths, tennis courts, and the like; and assumptions regarding such items as depreciation rates, the capitalization of development costs, financing costs, engineering and consultant fees, real estate taxes, promotion and advertising expenses, project management and overhead costs, and expenses for maintenance and utilities.
- Analyze the effects of inflation on project costs and revenues and calculate the necessary inflation adjustment for inclusion in the financial modeling of the project.
- Prepare a pro forma annual balance sheet, income statement, cash flow statement, and profitability analysis by detailed land use components. The pro forma statements should be provided for as long a period as necessary to reflect the full buildout and absorption of the property or at least to that point at which a positive and continuing cash flow is established after financing charges are deducted.
- Revise the proposed development plan in accordance with a review of the financial analysis and discussions

held between the developer and the physical planning consultants.
- Interpret the results of the financial analysis and its recommendations concerning the feasibility of the development's timing, phasing, strategy, marketing program, and potential for joint venture or bulk sales.

The cash flow statement measures cash flow over a period of time, usually the length of the project. For example, a statement may show cash flow annually over a ten-year project. The statement can be structured to show pretax cash flow, cash flow after taxes, and cash flow before and after debt service. In a large-scale, long-term project, the cash flow in the later years may be highly speculative but should nonetheless be included to determine a potential cash flow scenario.

In determining project return, developers often use discounted cash flow analysis to account for the time value of money. This analysis recognizes that tomorrow's cash is worth less than today's cash and applies an appropriate discount to the cash to be received in the future. Various methods of discounted cash flow analysis are available, including net present value and internal rate of return (IRR) analyses. An IRR analysis should always be balanced against the expected gross profit margin that the project is expected to generate.

The financial model of the project is used throughout the planning and implementation period to test various alternatives and to evaluate financial sensitivity. Sensitivity analysis measures the impact of changed financial and operating assumptions on the project's profitability and financial returns. Often, a developer bases the financial model of the project on different scenarios— pessimistic case, base case, optimistic case—to generate a likely range of financial returns.

A primary assumption in any analysis involving the sale of homes or timeshares—one that must be both carefully estimated and managed—is the sales rate. If the sales rate proves to be significantly lower than that assumed in the pro forma, carrying costs and other soft costs will increase and possibly lead to serious cost overruns. William Bone of the Sunrise Company in Palm Desert, California, notes that incorrectly estimating and/ or managing the sales rate is a far more likely cause of serious cost overruns than construction problems. Referring to many of his projects, Bone comments, "We can save $5 million in soft costs if we can move the sales rate up by one year. If the sellout date slips by a year, it can cost the project an additional $5 million. A key question that must be addressed is, How many units do you need to sell over what period to break even?"

The remainder of this section presents a hypothetical example of a financial analysis for a multiuse resort. Robert Chickering, Gene Krekorian, and Richard McElyea of the San Francisco office of Economics Research Associates prepared the example.

Hypothetical Example

The sample analysis (on pages 91 through 101) is based on a hypothetical multiuse resort community concept. The project encompasses a mix of residential real estate, resort leisure amenities, lodging facilities, and related commercial activities. While the example sets forth valid analytic approaches, the figures do not necessarily represent typical numbers. The projections are expressed in constant 1996 dollars and are net of taxes, depreciation, and debt service. Core components of the sample concept are itemized below.

- Residential real estate
  - Residential homesites
  - Golf villas
  - Clustered townhouses and apartments
  - Timeshare village
- Resort hotel
- Semiprivate resort golf course
- Retail center

In addition to the facilities listed above, the site will be distinguished by high-quality landscaping and leisure facilities within each development parcel. Amenities include tennis courts and walking and jogging trails.

Land and Infrastructure Costs. Figure 3-3 details land and infrastructure costs. Land value could be based on recent purchase price, the owner group's internal valuation, or a recent appraisal. The example has assigned a land value of $10 million. Infrastructure costs include all projectwide infrastructure such as primary arterials, utility trunk lines, entry treatment, landscaping, off-site costs, and other similar costs. The example estimates these costs at $5 million subject to 20 percent for soft costs and a 5 percent contingency.

Consolidated Cash Flow. Figure 3-4 sets out a consolidated cash flow expressed in constant 1996 dollars and presented before development financing. Land acquisition and site development commence in year one. Land and projectwide infrastructure costs are deducted from the net cash flow contribution of the various project components. For a project developed by multiple developers, it is often useful to allocate land and infrastructure costs to each land use or each profit center so that the investment return calculations for each land use include real costs. Regardless of how many different entities are involved in the project, however, the nonallocated approach is used to determine the feasibility of the overall project.

Residential Homesites. Figure 3-5 presents cash flow projections for residential homesite development with absorption projections and pricing based on market analysis. The model shows that homesites are placed on the market in four phases, with phase I commencing in year three.

Total lots: 200
Average lot size: 45,000 square feet

Selling price per lot	
Phase I	$120,000
Phase II	$130,000
Phase III	$140,000
Phase IV	$150,000

Absorption period: 4 years
Average annual absorption: 50 units

Commissions: 8%
Closing: 3%
Marketing: 4%
Site improvement costs: $20,000 per homesite

Development costs include all in-tract costs such as roads and all in-tract amenities such as playgrounds, landscaping, utility infrastructure, and site preparation. Soft costs are estimated at 20 percent and contingency at 5 percent. Marketing and improvement costs lead sales by one year.

Detached Golf Villas. Figure 3-6 shows the cash flow projections for the detached golf villas. The value of these units would be greatly enhanced if they were developed around the golf course. Once again, pricing and absorption rates must be based on market analysis. Villas will be sold in three annual phases commencing in year three.

Total units: 150
Average villa size: 2,500 square feet

Selling price per unit	
Phase I	$340,000
Phase II	$360,000
Phase III	$380,000

Absorption period: 3 years
Average annual absorption: 50 units

Commissions: 5%
Closing: 2%
Marketing: 3%

Construction cost has been estimated at $65 per square foot or $195,000 per unit. In addition, in-tract site improvements are estimated at $15,000 per unit and are subject to an additional 20 percent soft cost and 5 percent contingency allowance.

Clustered Units. Figure 3-7 shows the cash flow analysis for clustered units, which consist of a series of low-rise attached townhouses and apartments developed in clusters. It is assumed that units will be sold in four annual phases commencing in year three.

Total units: 200
Average unit size: 1,800 square feet

Selling price per unit
Phase I $200,000
Phase II $210,000
Phase III $220,000
Phase IV $230,000

Absorption period: 4 years
Average annual absorption: 50 units

Commissions: 5%
Closing: 2%
Marketing: 3%

Preliminary construction cost estimates have been set at $60 per square foot or $108,000 per unit. In-tract site improvement costs are estimated at $8,000 per unit. Soft costs have been estimated at 20 percent and contingency at 5 percent.

Timeshare Village. Figure 3-8 analyzes the timeshare village. Standalone timeshare developments of good quality in an attractive environment can succeed but require assertive marketing over a longer absorption period, as is reflected in the financial analysis set out in Figure 3-8.

The following specifications are assumed for the timeshare village:

- The standard, quality, and design of the complex will be high.
- The units will be developed into a village-style cluster served by leisure amenities (pool, tennis courts, children's play area).
- The development will be professionally marketed; however, we do not assume that the village will be a product of a major hotel or entertainment organization.
- Seven-day shares will be sold (weekly intervals).

Additional assumptions pertaining to the timeshare village are detailed below.

Total units: 50
Total shares: 2,500
Average unit size: 1,200 square feet
Absorption period: 4 years
Average annual absorption: 625 shares

The high-quality golf and country club facilities will create an attractive resort environment. We have assumed the sale of 50 weekly shares per year for each unit. While share prices generally vary depending on season or other variables, the model uses an average price of $10,000.

The norm for timeshare cost of sales (other than for major hotel and entertainment organizations such as Disney, Marriott, Hyatt, and others) is 35 to 50 percent. The model uses 35 percent; 10 percent for commissions, 5 percent for closing, and 20 percent for marketing. The high cost of sales reflects high marketing costs typically required to sell the high number of available shares. The construction cost is estimated at $75 per square foot or $90,000 per unit. In addition, furniture, fixture, and equipment costs are estimated at $15,000 per unit and site improvement costs at $8,500 per unit. Construction costs include timeshare-specific leisure facilities. We have assumed 20 percent soft costs and a 5 percent contingency.

Golf and Country Club Operations. Figures 3-9, 3-10, and 3-11 show inputs and analyses for the golf and country club facilities. The golf and country club operation is analyzed differently than the straight real estate cash flows. Since the golf and country club is an operating entity, it is necessary to project a budgeted operating statement for the facilities. The net operating income generated from the facilities is then shown as one of the primary sources of funds in the cash flow analysis along with membership sales proceeds.

The provision of high-quality recreational facilities in a club environment is one of the key strengths of a resort, particularly with regard to selling real estate at premium prices. It is thus necessary to include sufficient amenities such as food and beverage facilities in the clubhouse and to budget for ancillary facility costs, especially if the goal is to sell memberships as well as to provide high-quality amenities to resort guests. Accordingly, the golf and country club encompasses the following facilities:

- an 18-hole resort golf course;
- a driving range;
- eight tennis courts;
- children's playground;
- outdoor leisure pool;
- poolside bar;
- members' bar and dining room;
- informal food and beverage operation; and
- formal food and beverage operation.

The golf and country club commences operation in year three. It is important to initiate the golf operations as soon as possible to stimulate real estate sales and hotel room occupancy. Golf and country club memberships will be sold optionally to property owners and offer free access except for carts, priority tee-off times, and other benefits. Initiation fees will increase annually as the project approaches buildout. The operating assumptions are listed below.

Initiation fee (nonequity): $12,000–$17,000
Monthly dues: $250

Projected golf rounds

Members	60 rounds per year
Members' guests	30 rounds per member per year
Hotel guests	0.2 rounds per room night
Timeshare residents	0.3 rounds per occupancy unit night
Daily-fee rounds	5,000 per year

Greens fees (including carts)

Members/resort guests	$40
Daily fee	$60

Other revenues

Member cart per member round	$10
Food and beverage revenues per round	$5
Merchandise per round	$10
Driving range per round	$2
Club rental/miscellaneous per round	$1

Cost of sales

Food and beverage	35%
Merchandise	65%
Club rental/miscellaneou	40%

Operating expenses

Course maintenance	$650,000
Golf operations (pro shop, carts, range)	$350,000
Food and beverage (45% of sales)	$209,000
Undistributed clubhouse	$100,000
General and administrative	$525,000
Replacement reserve (3% gross)	$132,000
Total	$1,966,000

Resort Hotel. Figures 3-12 and 3-13 show a budgeted operating statement and cash flow projections for a 150-room resort hotel. High-specification rooms and public areas are assumed.

The projected annual occupancy for a stabilized year (estimated to be year three) is 70 percent. Occupancy builds from 55 to 70 percent over the first three years.

It is assumed that the published rate for a standard double room is $160 to $200. It will be necessary to offer discounts to certain market sectors such as inclusive tour groups, the off-season short-break market, and conference groups. The model uses an average achieved room rate of approximately $140. Other operating assumptions are listed below.

Department	Revenues per room night
Rooms	$140 (60%)
Food and beverage	$80 (35%)
Telephone	$4 (2%)
Other	$6 (3%)
Total	$230 (100%)

As mentioned above, the ratio of department costs to department revenues includes spending by hotel guests and function groups.

Department expenses

Rooms	22%
Food and beverage	75%
Telephone	90%
Other	50%

Undistributed operating expenses

General and administrative	7.5%
Management fee	4.0%
Marketing	5.5%
Property operations and maintainence	4.0%
Utilities	3.5%

Fixed charges

Insurance	0.4%
Property taxes	1.5%
Capital reserves	1.0%

Net operating income is set out in Figure 3-13 and has been projected before depreciation and debt service.

Development costs for the hotel include furniture, fixtures, and equipment. Soft costs and contingency have been estimated at 20 percent and 5 percent, respectively.

Commercial Complex. Figure 3-14 shows projections of both operations and cash flow for a small retail center that primarily supports the residential component. Country club visitors and resort guests would also use the center, which would incorporate a mix of retail, restaurant, and entertainment facilities.

Leasable area: 10,000 square feet
Stabilized occupancy: 95%

Average rent per square foot (NNN)

Phase I	$15.00
Phase II	$17.50
Phase III	$20.00

Operating expenses: 10% of lease revenues

Assuming a construction cost of $55 per square foot of gross leasable space, the model has used a development cost estimate of $550,000. Soft costs and contingency have been estimated at 20 percent and 5 percent, respectively.

figure 3-3

Sample Resort Complex Pro Forma Model—Land and Infrastructure Costs

Thousands of 1996 Constant Dollars

Land Costs	
Total Land Cost	$10,000.0
Total Number of Acres	500
Land Cost per Acre	$20.0
Infrastructure and Common Area Costs	
Roads	$2,000.0
Utilities/Landscaping	$3,000.0
Subtotal Hard Infrastructure Costs	**$5,000.0**
Soft Costs @ 20%	$1,000.0
Contingency @ 5%	$250.0
Total Infrastructure and Common Area Costs	**$6,250.0**

Source: Economics Research Associates, San Francisco, Calif.

figure 3-4

Sample Resort Complex Pro Forma Cash Flow Model—Consolidated Cash Flow

Thousands of Dollars/Inflation 0%

	Total	Year 1	Year 2	Year 3	Year 4	Year 5	Year 6	Year 7	Year 8	Year 9	Year I0
Product Contribution— Net Cash Flow											
Commercial Complex	$1,859.5	$0.0	$0.0	$0.0	($687.5)	$87.8	$108.0	$149.6	$149.6	$171.0	$1,881.0
Resort Hotel	$24,718.9	$0.0	$0.0	($9,375.0)	($9,375.0)	$2,033.2	$2,492.9	$2,781.6	$2,781.6	$2,781.6	$30,597.9
Golf and Country Club	$28,194.1	$0.0	($4,062.5)	($3,733.1)	$2,720.3	$3,798.8	$3,506.5	$1,854.6	$1,854.6	$1,854.6	$20,400.3
Timeshare Village	$9,450.0	$0.0	$0.0	($1,440.0)	$1,960.0	$2,640.0	$3,400.0	$2,890.0	$0.0	$0.0	$0.0
Clustered Units	$10,100.0	$0.0	($7,450.0)	$1,835.0	$2,285.0	$2,735.0	$10,695.0	$0.0	$0.0	$0.0	$0.0
Golf Villas	$9,787.5	$0.0	($13,447.5)	$2,332.5	$3,232.5	$17,670.0	$0.0	$0.0	$0.0	$0.0	$0.0
Residential Homesites	$17,950.0	$0.0	($1,490.0)	$3,830.0	$4,255.0	$4,680.0	$6,675.0	$0.0	$0.0	$0.0	$0.0
Cash Flow before Projectwide Costs	**$102,060.0**	**$0.0**	**($26,450.0)**	**($6,550.6)**	**$4,390.3**	**$33,644.8**	**$26,877.4**	**$7,675.8**	**$4,785.8**	**$4,807.2**	**$52,879.2**
Land Cost	($10,000.0)	($10,000.0)									
Infrastructure Costs	($6,250.0)	($3,125.0)	($3,125.0)	$0.0	$0.0	$0.0	$0.0	$0.0	$0.0	$0.0	$0.0
Net Cash Flow	**$85,810.0**	**($13,125.0)**	**($29,575.0)**	**($6,550.6)**	**$4,390.3**	**$33,644.8**	**$26,877.4**	**$7,675.8**	**$4,785.8**	**$4,807.2**	**$52,879.2**
Cumulative Cash Flow	—	($13,125.0)	($42,700.0)	($49,250.6)	($44,860.3)	($11,215.5)	$15,661.8	$23,337.7	$28,123.5	$32,930.7	$85,810.0

Internal Rate of Return 21.5%

Net Present Value @ 12% $19,703.9

Source: Economics Research Associates, San Francisco, Calif.

figure 3-5

Sample Resort Complex Pro Forma Cash Flow Model—Residential Homesites

Thousands of Dollars/Inflation: 0%

	Total	Year 1	Year 2	Year 3	Year 4	Year 5	Year 6	Year 7	Year 8	Year 9	Year 10
Revenue Assumptions											
Projected Absorption	200	0	0	50	50	50	50	0	0	0	0
Average Price per Unit (000s of constant $)		$0.0	$0.0	$120.0	$130.0	$140.0	$150.0	$0.0	$0.0	$0.0	$0.0
Sales Proceeds											
Gross Sales	$27,000.0	$0.0	$0.0	$6,000.0	$6,500.0	$7,000.0	$7,500.0	$0.0	$0.0	$0.0	$0.0
Less Commissions @ 8%	$2,160.0	$0.0	$0.0	$480.0	$520.0	$560.0	$600.0	$0.0	$0.0	$0.0	$0.0
Less Closing @ 3%	$810.0	$0.0	$0.0	$180.0	$195.0	$210.0	$225.0	$0.0	$0.0	$0.0	$0.0
Less Marketing @ 4%	$1,080.0	$0.0	$240.0	$260.0	$280.0	$300.0	$0.0	$0.0	$0.0	$0.0	$0.0
Net Proceeds from Sales	$22,950.0	$0.0	($240.0)	$5,080.0	$5,505.0	$5,930.0	$6,675.0	$0.0	$0.0	$0.0	$0.0
Development Costs (per site)											
In-Tract Improvements $20.0	$4,000.0	$0.0	$1,000.0	$1,000.0	$1,000.0	$1,000.0	$0.0	$0.0	$0.0	$0.0	$0.0
Soft Costs @ 20%	$800.0	$0.0	$200.0	$200.0	$200.0	$200.0	$0.0	$0.0	$0.0	$0.0	$0.0
Contingency @ 5%	$200.0	$0.0	$50.0	$50.0	$50.0	$50.0	$0.0	$0.0	$0.0	$0.0	$0.0
Total Development Costs	$5,000.0	$0.0	$1,250.0	$1,250.0	$1,250.0	$1,250.0	$0.0	$0.0	$0.0	$0.0	$0.0
Net Cash Flow	$17,950.0	$0.0	($1,490.0)	$3,830.0	$4,255.0	$4,680.0	$6,675.0	$0.0	$0.0	$0.0	$0.0
Cumulative Cash Flow	—	$0.0	($1,490.0)	$2,340.0	$6,595.0	$11,275.0	$17,950.0	$17,950.0	$17,950.0	$17,950.0	$17,950.0

Net Present Value @ 12% $10,279.7

Source: Economics Research Associates, San Francisco, Calif.

figure 3-6

Sample Resort Complex Pro Forma Cash Flow Model—Detached Golf Villas

Thousands of Dollars/Inflation: 0%

	Total	Year 1	Year 2	Year 3	Year 4	Year 5	Year 6	Year 7	Year 8	Year 9	Year 10
Revenue Assumptions											
Projected Absorption	150	0	0	50	50	50	0	0	0	0	0
Price per Unit (000s of constant $)		$0.0	$0.0	$340.0	$360.0	$380.0	$0.0	$0.0	$0.0	$0.0	$0.0
Sales Proceeds											
Gross Sales	$54,000.0	$0.0	$0.0	$17,000.0	$18,000.0	$19,000.0	$0.0	$0.0	$0.0	$0.0	$0.0
Less Commissions @ 5%	$2,700.0	$0.0	$0.0	$850.0	$900.0	$950.0	$0.0	$0.0	$0.0	$0.0	$0.0
Less Closing @ 2%	$1,080.0	$0.0	$0.0	$340.0	$360.0	$380.0	$0.0	$0.0	$0.0	$0.0	$0.0
Less Marketing @ 3%	$1,620.0	$0.0	$510.0	$540.0	$570.0	$0.0	$0.0	$0.0	$0.0	$0.0	$0.0
Net Proceeds from Sales	$48,600.0	$0.0	($510.0)	$15,270.0	$16,170.0	$17,670.0	$0.0	$0.0	$0.0	$0.0	$0.0
Development Costs (per unit)											
Construction Costs $195.0	$29,250.0	$0.0	$9,750.0	$9,750.0	$9,750.0	$0.0	$0.0	$0.0	$0.0	$0.0	$0.0
In-Tract Improvements $15.0	$2,250.0	$0.0	$750.0	$750.0	$750.0	$0.0	$0.0	$0.0	$0.0	$0.0	$0.0
Soft Costs @ 20%	$5,850.0	$0.0	$1,950.0	$1,950.0	$1,950.0	$0.0	$0.0	$0.0	$0.0	$0.0	$0.0
Contingency @ 5%	$1,462.5	$0.0	$487.5	$487.5	$487.5	$0.0	$0.0	$0.0	$0.0	$0.0	$0.0
Total Development Costs	$38,812.5	$0.0	$12,937.5	$12,937.5	$12,937.5	$0.0	$0.0	$0.0	$0.0	$0.0	$0.0
Net Cash Flow	$9,787.5	$0.0	($13,447.5)	$2,332.5	$3,232.5	$17,670.0	$0.0	$0.0	$0.0	$0.0	$0.0
Cumulative Cash Flow	—	$0.0	($13,447.5)	($11,115.0)	($7,882.5)	$9,787.5	$9,787.5	$9,787.5	$9,787.5	$9,787.5	$9,787.5

Net Present Value @ 12% $3,020.7

Source: Economics Research Associates, San Francisco, Calif.

figure 3-7

Sample Resort Complex Pro Forma Cash Flow Model—Clustered Units

Thousands of Dollars/Inflation: 0%

	Total	Year 1	Year 2	Year 3	Year 4	Year 5	Year 6	Year 7	Year 8	Year 9	Year 10
Revenue Assumptions											
Projected Absorption	200	0	0	50	50	50	50	0	0	0	0
Price per Unit (000s of constant $)		$0.0	$0.0	$200.0	$210.0	$220.0	$230.0	$0.0	$0.0	$0.0	$0.0
Sales Proceeds											
Gross Sales	$43,000.0	$0.0	$0.0	$10,000.0	$10,500.0	$11,000.0	$11,500.0	$0.0	$0.0	$0	$0.0
Less Commissions @ 5%	$2,150.0	$0.0	$0.0	$500.0	$525.0	$550.0	$575.0	$0.0	$0.0	$0.0	$0.0
Less Closing @ 2%	$860.0	$0.0	$0.0	$200.0	$210.0	$220.0	$230.0	$0.0	$0.0	$0.0	$0.0
Less Marketing @ 3%	$1,290.0	$0.0	$300.0	$315.0	$330.0	$345.0	$0.0	$0.0	$0.0	$0.0	$0.0
Net Proceeds from Sales	$38,700.0	$0.0	($300.0)	$8,985.0	$9,435.0	$9,885.0	$10,695.0	$0.0	$0.0	$0.0	$0.0
Development Costs (per unit)											
Construction Costs $108.0	$21,600.0	$0.0	$5,400.0	$5,400.0	$5,400.0	$5,400.0	$0.0	$0.0	$0.0	$0.0	$0.0
In-Tract Improvements $8.0	$1,600.0	$0.0	$400.0	$400.0	$400.0	$400.0	$0.0	$0.0	$0.0	$0.0	$0.0
Soft Costs @ 20%	$4,320.0	$0.0	$1,080.0	$1,080.0	$1,080.0	$1,080.0	$0.0	$0.0	$0.0	$0.0	$0.0
Contingency @ 5%	$1,080.0	$0.0	$270.0	$270.0	$270.0	$270.0	$0.0	$0.0	$0.0	$0.0	$0.0
Total Development Costs	$28,600.0	$0.0	$7,150.0	$7,150.0	$7,150.0	$7,150.0	$0.0	$0.0	$0.0	$0.0	$0.0
Net Cash Flow	$10,100.0	$0.0	($7,450.0)	$1,835.0	$2,285.0	$2,735.0	$10,695.0	$0.0	$0.0	$0.0	$0.0
Cumulative Cash Flow		$0.0	($7,450.0)	($5,615.0)	($3,330.0)	($595.0)	$10,100.0	$10,100.0	$10,100.0	$10,100.0	$10,100.0

Net Present Value @ 12% $3,789.5

Source: Economics Research Associates, San Francisco, Calif.

figure 3-8

Sample Resort Complex Pro Forma Cash Flow Model—Timeshare Village

Thousands of Dollars/Inflation: 0%

	Total	Year 1	Year 2	Year 3	Year 4	Year 5	Year 6	Year 7	Year 8	Year 9	Year 10
Revenue Assumptions											
Units Built	50	0	0	0	20	15	15	0	0	0	0
Projected Absorption of Shares	2,500	0	0	0	720	720	720	340	0	0	0
Cumulative Units		0	0	0	14	29	43	50	50	50	50
Price per Unit (000s of constant $)		$0.0	$0.0	$10.0	$10.0	$10.0	$10.0	$10.0	$0.0	$0.0	$0.0
Sales Proceeds											
Gross Sales	$25,000.0	$0.0	$0.0	$0.0	$7,200.0	$7,200.0	$7,200.0	$3,400.0	$0.0	$0.0	$0.0
Less Commissions @ 10%	$2,500.0	$0.0	$0.0	$0.0	$720.0	$720.0	$720.0	$340.0	$0.0	$0.0	$0.0
Less Closing @ 5%	$1,250.0	$0.0	$0.0	$0.0	$360.0	$360.0	$360.0	$170.0	$0.0	$0.0	$0.0
Less Marketing @ 20%	$5,000.0	$0.0	$0.0	$1,440.0	$1,440.0	$1,440.0	$680.0	$0.0	$0.0	$0.0	$0.0
Net Proceeds from Sales	$16,250.0	$0.0	$0.0	($1,440.0)	$4,680.0	$4,680.0	$5,440.0	$2,890.0	$0.0	$0.0	$0.0
Development Costs (per unit)											
Construction Costs $90.0	$4,500.0	$0.0	$0.0	$0.0	$1,800.0	$1,350.0	$1,350.0	$0.0	$0.0	$0.0	$0.0
Furniture, Fixtures, and Equipment $15.0	$750.0	$0.0	$0.0	$0.0	$300.0	$225.0	$225.0	$0.0	$0.0	$0.0	$0.0
In-Tract Improvements $8.5	$425.0	$0.0	$0.0	$0.0	$170.0	$127.5	$127.5	$0.0	$0.0	$0.0	$0.0
Soft Costs @ 20%	$900.0	$0.0	$0.0	$0.0	$360.0	$270.0	$270.0	$0.0	$0.0	$0.0	$0.0
Contingency @ 5%	$225.0	$0.0	$0.0	$0.0	$90.0	$67.5	$67.5	$0.0	$0.0	$0.0	$0.0
Total Development Costs	$6,800.0	$0.0	$0.0	$0.0	$2,720.0	$2,040.0	$2,040.0	$0.0	$0.0	$0.0	$0.0
Net Cash Flow	$9,450.0	$0.0	$0.0	($1,440.0)	$1,960.0	$2,640.0	$3,400.0	$2,890.0	$0.0	$0.0	$0.0
Cumulative Cash Flow	—	$0.0	$0.0	($1,440.0)	$520.0	$3,160.0	$6,560.0	$9,450.0	$9,450.0	$9,450.0	$9,450.0

Net Present Value @ 2% $4,748.5

Source: Economics Research Associates, San Francisco, Calif.

figure 3-9

Sample Resort Complex Pro Forma Cash Flow Model—Golf and Country Club Operating Assumptions

Inflation: 0%

	Total	Year 1	Year 2	Year 3	Year 4	Year 5	Year 6	Year 7	Year 8	Year 9	Year 10
Revenue Assumptions (constant dollars)											
Membership Sales											
Country Club Memberships	550	0	0	150	150	150	100	0	0	0	0
Cumulative Memberships		0	0	150	300	450	550	550	550	550	550
Initiation Fee (constant values, not thousands)		$0	$0	$10,000	$12,000	$15,000	$17,000	$0	$0	$0	$0
Membership Sales Proceeds[1]	**$7,250.0**	**$0.0**	**$0.0**	**$1,500.0**	**$1,800.0**	**$2,250.0**	**$1,700.0**	**$0.0**	**$0.0**	**$0.0**	**$0.0**
Monthly Dues (constant values, not thousands)		$0	$0	$250	$250	$250	$250	$250	$250	$250	$250
Projected Golf Rounds											
Membership Rounds @ 60		0	0	9,000	18,000	27,000	33,000	33,000	33,000	33,000	33,000
Guest Rounds @ 20		0	0	3,000	6,000	9,000	11,000	11,000	11,000	11,000	11,000
Hotel Guests @ 0.2 room nights		0	0	0	0	6,023	7,118	7,665	7,665	7,665	7,665
Timeshare 70% Occupancy @ 0.3 unit nights		0	0	0	1,104	2,208	3,311	3,833	3,833	3,833	3,833
Daily Fee @ 5,000		0	0	20,000	15,000	10,000	5,000	5,000	5,000	5,000	5,000
Total Projected Rounds		0	0	32,000	40,104	54,230	59,429	60,498	60,498	60,498	60,498
Greens Fee Revenues[1]											
Member Guest Fees @ $40.00	$2,920.0	$0.0	$0.0	$120.0	$240.0	$360.0	$440.0	$440.0	$440.0	$440.0	$440.0
Hotel Guest Fees @ $40.00	$1,752.0	$0.0	$0.0	$0.0	$0.0	$240.9	$284.7	$306.6	$306.6	$306.6	$306.6
Timeshare @ $40.00	$878.1	$0.0	$0.0	$0.0	$44.2	$88.3	$132.5	$153.3	$153.3	$153.3	$153.3
Daily Fee @ $60.00	$4,200.0	$0.0	$0.0	$1,200.0	$900.0	$600.0	$300.0	$300.0	$300.0	$300.0	$300.0
Total Greens Fees	**$9,750.1**	**$0.0**	**$0.0**	**$1,320.0**	**$1,184.2**	**$1,289.2**	**$1,157.2**	**$1,199.9**	**$1,199.9**	**$1,199.9**	**$1,199.9**
Other Revenues											
Member Cart Revenue per Member Round		$0	$0	$10	$10	$10	$10	$10	$10	$10	$10
Food and Beverge Revenues per Round		$0	$0	$5	$5	$5	$5	$5	$5	$5	$5
Merchandise Revenues per Round		$0	$0	$10	$10	$10	$10	$10	$10	$10	$10
Driving Range Sales per Round		$0	$0	$2	$2	$2	$2	$2	$2	$2	$2
Club Rental/Misc. Revenues per Round		$0	$0	$1	$1	$1	$1	$1	$1	$1	$1

Net Present Value @ 12% $10,279.7

[1]Thousands of dollars.

Source: Economics Research Associates, San Francisco, Calif.

figure 3-10

Sample Resort Complex Pro Forma Cash Flow Model—Golf and Country Club Budgeted Operating Statement

Thousands of Dollars/Inflation: 0%

	Total	Year 1	Year 2	Year 3	Year 4	Year 5	Year 6	Year 7	Year 8	Year 9	Year 10
Operating Revenues											
Annual Dues	$10,950.0	$0.0	$0.0	$450.0	$900.0	$1,350.0	$1,650.0	$1,650.0	$1,650.0	$1,650.0	$1,650.0
Greens Fees	$9,750.1	$0.0	$0.0	$1,320.0	$1,184.2	$1,289.2	$1,157.2	$1,199.9	$1,199.9	$1,199.9	$1,199.9
Member Cart Fees	$2,190.0	$0.0	$0.0	$90.0	$180.0	$270.0	$330.0	$330.0	$330.0	$330.0	$330.0
Food and Beverage	$3,203.7	$0.0	$0.0	$201.1	$282.6	$403.4	$458.4	$464.5	$464.5	$464.5	$464.5
Merchandise	$4,277.5	$0.0	$0.0	$320.0	$401.0	$542.3	$594.3	$605.0	$605.0	$605.0	$605.0
Driving Range	$641.6	$0.0	$0.0	$48.0	$60.2	$81.3	$89.1	$90.7	$90.7	$90.7	$90.7
Club Rental/Misc.	$427.8	$0.0	$0.0	$32.0	$40.1	$54.2	$59.4	$60.5	$60.5	$60.5	$60.5
Gross Operating Revenues	$31,440.7	$0.0	$0.0	$2,461.1	$3,048.1	$3,990.4	$4,338.4	$4,400.7	$4,400.7	$4,400.7	$4,400.7
Less: Cost of Goods Sold											
Food and Beverage Sales @ 35%	$1,121.3	$0.0	$0.0	$70.4	$98.9	$141.2	$160.4	$162.6	$162.6	$162.6	$162.6
Merchandise Sales @ 65%	$2,780.4	$0.0	$0.0	$208.0	$260.7	$352.5	$386.3	$393.2	$393.2	$393.2	$393.2
Club Rentals/Misc. @ 40%	$171.1	$0.0	$0.0	$12.8	$16.0	$21.7	$23.8	$24.2	$24.2	$24.2	$24.2
Net Operating Revenues	$27,367.9	$0.0	$0.0	$2,169.9	$2,672.4	$3,475.1	$3,767.9	$3,820.6	$3,820.6	$3,820.6	$3,820.6
Operating Expenses											
Course Maintenance	$5,200.0	$0.0	$0.0	$650.0	$650.0	$650.0	$650.0	$650.0	$650.0	$650.0	$650.0
Golf Operations (pro shop, carts, range)	$2,800.0	$0.0	$0.0	$350.0	$350.0	$350.0	$350.0	$350.0	$350.0	$350.0	$350.0
Food and Beverage (45% of sales)	$1,441.6	$0.0	$0.0	$90.5	$127.2	$181.5	$206.3	$209.0	$209.0	$209.0	$209.0
Undistributed Clubhouse	$800.0	$0.0	$0.0	$100.0	$100.0	$100.0	$100.0	$100.0	$100.0	$100.0	$100.0
General and Administrative	$4,200.0	$0.0	$0.0	$525.0	$525.0	$525.0	$525.0	$525.0	$525.0	$525.0	$525.0
Replacement Reserve @ 3%	$777.9	$0.0	$0.0	$0.0	$0.0	$119.7	$130.2	$132.0	$132.0	$132.0	$132.0
Total Operating Expenses	$15,219.6	$0.0	$0.0	$1,715.5	$1,752.2	$1,926.2	$1,961.4	$1,966.1	$1,966.1	$1,966.1	$1,966.1
Net Operating Income	$12,148.3	$0.0	$0.0	$454.4	$920.3	$1,548.8	$1,806.5	$1,854.6	$1,854.6	$1,854.6	$1,854.6

Net Present Value @ 12% $10,279.7

Source: Economics Research Associates, San Francisco, Calif.

figure 3-11

Sample Resort Complex Pro Forma Cash Flow Model—Golf and Country Club Cash Flow

Thousands of Dollars/Inflation: 0%

	Total	Year 1	Year 2	Year 3	Year 4	Year 5	Year 6	Year 7	Year 8	Year 9	Year 10
Sources of Funds											
Net Operating Income	$12,148.3	$0.0	$0.0	$454.4	$920.3	$1,548.8	$1,806.5	$1,854.6	$1,854.6	$1,854.6	$1,854.6
Asset Value @[1] 10%	$18,545.8										$18.545.8
Membership Sales Proceeds	$7,250.0	$0.0	$0.0	$1,500.0	$1,800.0	$2,250.0	$1,700.0	$0.0	$0.0	$0.0	$0.0
Total Sources of Funds	$37,944.1	$0.0	$0.0	$1,954.4	$2,720.3	$3,798.8	$3,506.5	$1,854.6	$1,854.6	$1,854.6	$20,400.3
Uses of Funds											
Development Costs											
Golf Course Construction $5,000.0	$5,000.0	$0.0	$2,500.0	$2,500.0	$0.0	$0.0	$0.0	$0.0	$0.0	$0.0	$0.0
Maintenance/Equipment/ Grow-In $1,300.0	$1,300.0			$1,300.0							
Clubhouse and Amenities $1,500.0	$1,500.0	$0.0	$750.0	$750.0	$0.0	$0.0	$0.0	$0.0	$0.0	$0.0	$0.0
Soft Costs @ 20%	$1,560.0	$0.0	$650.0	$910.0	$0.0	$0.0	$0.0	$0.0	$0.0	$0.0	$0.0
Contingency @ 5%	$390.0	$0.0	$162.5	$227.5	$0.0	$0.0	$0.0	$0.0	$0.0	$0.0	$0.0
Total Uses of Funds	$9,750.0	$0.0	$4,062.5	$5,687.5	$0.0	$0.0	$0.0	$0.0	$0.0	$0.0	$0.0
Net Cash Flow	$28,194.1	$0.0	($4,062.5)	($3,733.1)	$2,720.3	$3,798.8	$3,506.5	$1,854.6	$1,854.6	$1,854.6	$20,400.3
Cumulative Cash Flow		$0.0	($4,062.5)	($7,795.6)	($5,075.3)	($1,276.5)	$2,230.0	$4,084.6	$5,939.2	$7,793.7	$28,194.1

Net Present Value @ 12% $8,590.2

[1] Assumes asset sale in year 10.

Source: Economics Research Associates, San Francisco, Calif.

figure 3-12

Sample Resort Complex Pro Forma Cash Flow Model—Resort Hotel Operating Statement

Thousands of Dollars/Inflation: 0%

	Total	Year 1	Year 2	Year 3	Year 4	Year 5	Year 6	Year 7	Year 8	Year 9	Year 10
Operating Assumptions											
Number of Rooms		0	0	0	0	150	150	150	150	150	150
Average Annual Occupancy Rate		0%	0%	0%	0%	55%	65%	70%	70%	70%	70%
Projected Room Nights		0	0	0	0	30,113	35,588	38,325	38,325	38,325	38,325
Average Daily Room Rate (constant values)		$0	$0	$0	$0	$130	$135	$140	$140	$140	$140
Operating Revenues											
Gross Room Revenues	$30,180.9	$0.0	$0.0	$0.0	$0.0	$3,914.6	$4,804.3	$5,365.5	$5,365.5	$5,365.5	$5,365.5
Food and Beverage per Room Night @ $80	$17,520.0	$0.0	$0.0	$0.0	$0.0	$2,409.0	$2,847.0	$3,066.0	$3,066.0	$3,066.0	$3,066.0
Telephone per Room Night @ $4	$876.0	$0.0	$0.0	$0.0	$0.0	$120.5	$142.4	$153.3	$153.3	$153.3	$153.3
Other Depts. (% room) $6	$1,314.0	$0.0	$0.0	$0.0	$0.0	$180.7	$213.5	$230.0	$230.0	$230.0	$230.0
Gross Operating Revenues	$49,890.9	$0.0	$0.0	$0.0	$0.0	$6,624.8	$8,007.2	$8,814.8	$8,814.8	$8,814.8	$8,814.8
Operating Expenses											
Departmental Expenses (% of revenues)											
Rooms 22%	$6,639.8	$0.0	$0.0	$0.0	$0.0	$861.2	$1,056.9	$1,180.4	$1,180.4	$1,180.4	$1,180.4
Food and Beverage 75%	$13,140.0	$0.0	$0.0	$0.0	$0.0	$1,806.8	$2,135.3	$2,299.5	$2,299.5	$2,299.5	$2,299.5
Telephone 90%	$788.4	$0.0	$0.0	$0.0	$0.0	$108.4	$128.1	$138.0	$138.0	$138.0	$138.0
Other 50%	$657.0	$0.0	$0.0	$0.0	$0.0	$90.3	$106.8	$115.0	$115.0	$115.0	$115.0
Total Departmental Expenses	$20,568.2	$0.0	$0.0	$0.0	$0.0	$2,776.4	$3,320.3	$3,617.9	$3,617.9	$3,617.9	$3,617.9
Undistributed Operating Expenses											
General/Administration 7.5%	$3,741.8	$0.0	$0.0	$0.0	$0.0	$496.9	$600.5	$661.1	$661.1	$661.1	$661.1
Management Fee 4%	$1,995.6	$0.0	$0.0	$0.0	$0.0	$265.0	$320.3	$352.6	$352.6	$352.6	$352.6
Marketing 5.5%	$2,744.0	$0.0	$0.0	$0.0	$0.0	$364.4	$440.4	$484.8	$484.8	$484.8	$484.8
Property Operations and Maintenance 4%	$1,995.6	$0.0	$0.0	$0.0	$0.0	$265.0	$320.3	$352.6	$352.6	$352.6	$352.6
Utilities 3.5%	$1,746.2	$0.0	$0.0	$0.0	$0.0	$231.9	$280.3	$308.5	$308.5	$308.5	$308.5
Total Undistributed Operating Expenses	$12,223.3	$0.0	$0.0	$0.0	$0.0	$1,623.1	$1,961.8	$2,159.6	$2,159.6	$2,159.6	$2,159.6
Fixed Charges											
Insurance 0.4%	$199.6	$0.0	$0.0	$0.0	$0.0	$26.5	$32.0	$35.3	$35.3	$35.3	$35.3
Property Taxes 1.5%	$748.4	$0.0	$0.0	$0.0	$0.0	$99.4	$120.1	$132.2	$132.2	$132.2	$132.2
Capital Reserve 1.0%	$498.9	$0.0	$0.0	$0.0	$0.0	$66.2	$80.1	$88.1	$88.1	$88.1	$88.1
Total Fixed Charges	$1,446.8	$0.0	$0.0	$0.0	$0.0	$192.1	$232.2	$255.6	$255.6	$255.6	$255.6
Total Operating Expenses	$34,238.3	$0.0	$0.0	$0.0	$0.0	$4,591.6	$5,514.3	$6,033.1	$6,033.1	$6,033.1	$6,033.1
Net Operation Income	$15,652.6	$0.0	$0.0	$0.0	$0.0	$2,033.2	$2,492.9	$2,781.6	$2,781.6	$2,781.6	$2,781.6

Source: Economics Research Associates, San Francisco, Calif.

figure 3-13

Sample Resort Complex Pro Forma Cash Flow Model—Resort Hotel Cash Flow

Thousands of Dollars/Inflation: 0%

	Total	Year 1	Year 2	Year 3	Year 4	Year 5	Year 6	Year 7	Year 8	Year 9	Year 10
Sources of Funds											
Net Operating Income	$15,652.6	$0.0	$0.0	$0.0	$0.0	$2,033.2	$2,492.9	$2,781.6	$2,781.6	$2,781.6	$2,781.6
Asset Value @[1] 10%	$27,816.3										$27,816.3
Total Sources of Funds	$43,468.9	$0.0	$0.0	$0.0	$0.0	$2,033.2	$2,492.9	$2,781.6	$2,781.6	$ 2,781.6	$30,597.9
Uses of Funds											
Development Costs											
Construction $15,000.0	$15,000.0	$0.0	$0.0	$7,500.0	$7,500.0	$0.0	$0.0	$0.0	$0.0	$0.0	$0.0
Soft Costs @ 20%	$3,000.0	$0.0	$0.0	$1,500.0	$1,500.0	$0.0	$0.0	$0.0	$0.0	$0.0	$0.0
Contingency @ 5%	$750.0	$0.0	$0.0	$375.0	$375.0	$0.0	$0.0	$0.0	$0.0	$0.0	$0.0
Total Uses of Funds	$18,750.0	$0.0	$0.0	$9,375.0	$9,375.0	$0.0	$0.0	$0.0	$0.0	$0.0	$0.0
Net Cash Flow	$24,718.9	$0.0	$0.0	($9,375.0)	($9,375.0)	$2,033.2	$2,492.9	$2,781.6	$2,781.6	$2,781.6	$30,597.9
Cumulative Cash Flow		$0.0	$0.0	($9,375.0)	($18,750.0)	($16,716.8)	($14,223.9)	($11,442.3)	($8,660.6)	($5,879.0)	$24,718.9

Net Present Value @ 12% $3,022.3

[1] Assumes asset sale in year 10.

Source: Economics Research Associates, San Francisco, Calif.

figure 3-14

Sample Resort Complex Pro Forma Cash Flow Model—Commercial Complex Cash Flow

Thousands of Dollars/Inflation: 0%

	Total	Year 1	Year 2	Year 3	Year 4	Year 5	Year 6	Year 7	Year 8	Year 9	Year 10
Revenue Assumptions											
Gross Leasable Area		0	0	0	0	10,000	10,000	10,000	10,000	10,000	10,000
Average Annual Occupancy Rate		0%	0%	0%	0%	65%	80%	95%	95%	95%	95%
Average Rent per Square Foot (constant values)		$0.00	$0.00	$0.00	$0.00	$15.00	$15.00	$17.50	$17.50	$20.00	$20.00
Lease Revenue	$930.0	$0.0	$0.0	$0.0	$0.0	$97.5	$120.0	$166.3	$166.3	$190.0	$190.0
Operating Expenses											
Operations and Maintenance @ 5%	$46.5	$0.0	$0.0	$0.0	$0.0	$4.9	$6.0	$8.3	$8.3	$9.5	$9.5
General/Administration @ 5%	$46.5	$0.0	$0.0	$0.0	$0.0	$4.9	$6.0	$8.3	$8.3	$9.5	$9.5
Total Operating Expenses	$93.0	$0.0	$0.0	$0.0	$0.0	$9.8	$12.0	$16.6	$16.6	$19.0	$19.0
Net Operating Income	$837.0	$0.0	$0.0	$0.0	$0.0	$87.8	$108.0	$149.6	$149.6	$171.0	$171.0
Sources of Funds											
Net Operating Income	$837.0	$0.0	$0.0	$0.0	$0.0	$87.8	$108.0	$149.6	$149.6	$171.0	$171.0
Asset Value @[1] 10%	$1,710.0										$1,710.0
Total Sources of Funds	$2,547.0	$0.0	$0.0	$0.0	$0.0	$87.8	$108.0	$149.6	$149.6	$171.0	$1,881.0
Uses of Funds											
Development Costs											
Construction $550.0	$550.0	$0.0	$0.0	$0.0	$550.0	$0.0	$0.0	$0.0	$0.0	$0.0	$0.0
Soft Costs @ 20%	$110.0	$0.0	$0.0	$0.0	$110.0	$0.0	$0.0	$0.0	$0.0	$0.0	$0.0
Contingency @ 5%	$27.5	$0.0	$0.0	$0.0	$27.5	$0.0	$0.0	$0.0	$0.0	$0.0	$0.0
Total Uses of Funds	$687.5	$0.0	$0.0	$0.0	$687.5	$0.0	$0.0	$0.0	$0.0	$0.0	$0.0
Net Cash Flow	$1,859.5	$0.0	$0.0	$0.0	($687.5)	$87.8	$108.0	$149.6	$149.6	$171.0	$1,881.0
Cumulative Cash Flow	—	$0.0	$00	$00	($687.5)	($599.8)	($491.8)	($342.1)	($192.5)	($21.5)	$1,859.5

Net Present Value @ 12% $463.0

[1] Assumes asset sale in year 10.

Source: Economics Research Associates, San Francisco, Calif.

Harry H. Frampton III
President
East West Partners–Western Division
Beaver Creek, Colorado

Harry H. Frampton III is currently a senior partner of East West Partners for the western United States. Specializing in real estate development, East West Partners is currently developing resort properties in Vail and Beaver Creek, Colorado, as well as several communities in Washington state.

Frampton began his real estate career with the Sea Pines Company at Hilton Head, South Carolina. He served in various capacities and ultimately reached the position of executive vice president and member of the board of directors. In 1976, he became president and majority stockholder of the Brandermill Group in Richmond, Virginia, a position he held until 1982. From 1982 to 1986, he served as president of Vail Associates, the creators and operators of the Vail and Beaver Creek mountain resorts in Colorado.

Frampton is a graduate of Clemson University with a degree in economics. He has also undertaken graduate studies in business administration at Georgia State University and is a graduate of Harvard University's Small Company Executive Management Program.

There are no absolutes in the resort business. Nonetheless, resort real estate projects that work well tend to have a clearly definable market niche. Projects that attempt to appeal to multiple market segments are generally not as successful financially as those that appeal to a single market. The complexity of multiple markets is just too much to handle. Each segment has different needs and, as communities mature, there are conflicts among groups.

A developer should spend more time preparing for the downside of a project rather than just the feasibility on the upside. Most people do just the opposite. In this business, if it can go wrong, it will. If a developer is prepared for problems, he usually can develop a business plan that will allow him to succeed in spite of the problems. All of us as developers have spent too much time early in the development process talking about how the project will work. What a developer needs to create are business strategies that recognize that there will be times when some of those unthinkable things in a project will go wrong. The companies that win will be those that, as a result, do not have disastrous projects.

Many developers run their sensitivity analyses only on the upside. A developer needs to do just as many on the downside. When a developer thinks about the possible downside problems beforehand, there are ways of dealing with them. A developer gets in trouble when he

hasn't thought about them and by then it is usually too late.

Projects that take 15 to 20 years to pay off never will. When it takes 15 to 20 years, too many things change. Large-scale projects have never worked very well and are not going to work in the future. I'll bet that less than 5 percent have produced meaningful returns to the developer. Sea Pines is probably one of the few large-scale projects that did make money. If a developer does a large-scale project, it makes more sense to break it down into a series of smaller discrete projects with relatively short time frames. But a developer still needs to have the financial staying power to hold the undeveloped parcels until they are ready for development. Our company looks for real estate projects that will completely pay off the debt in two to four years, preferably two.

Developers should test their product in the early stages of design development. Too many of us design the product for ourselves. A developer should present the initial concept drawings both to customers who meet the basic market criteria and to the salespeople who will be selling the product. It is especially important to listen carefully and not confuse their ideas with your goals.

Successful resort developers are those who not only deliver the initial product but also set up the systems, programs, and organizations that make the vacation experience a superb one once the product is purchased. The goal is to take the hassle out of the vacation experience, whether the vacationer is a resort guest or a second-home owner.

It is imperative to recognize that it is the quality of the resort that is most important in the sales process and not the real estate product. A condominium is only as valuable as the overall quality of the entire resort experience. And that has not necessarily been the case in the past. It's been more of a real estate mentality. The business people who will win in the future, however, will be those who recognize that distinction and do a good job at delivering on it.

Financing

There is no single formula for financing resort development. Each project is distinguished by various characteristics of ownership, development needs, and market conditions and therefore requires different financing arrangements. The unique financial package that is the life blood of a given resort development is determined by, among other considerations, the merit of the particular proposal, the business reputation and development experience of the developer (applicant), the applicant's equity and collateral, the type of financing institution involved, the attitude of the lender, the general economic prospects of the times, and the currently available financial instruments.

Resort development financing has its counterpart in many other types of real estate development, from small-scale land sales that may be financed entirely with equity and short-term construction loans to large-scale new communities that require direct long-term ties with numerous money sources. In general, the financing needs typical of real estate development extend to

- early planning, in which developer/owner equity investment is essential;
- land acquisition, possibly first through land options with purchase by a mortgage, seller's note, or other traditional method;
- site improvements commercially financed through presales or other means with the land as collateral;
- construction financing in the form of a short-term funding proposition requiring guarantees to satisfy the risks to lending institutions; and
- permanent financing, in which evidence of market viability permits long-term mortgage repayment of interest and principal on the full development, if necessary.

The sources of funds are many and relate to the type of financing. Money may be obtained from individuals, banks, insurance companies, pension funds, foreign investors, government programs, savings institutions, public bonds, and others and might be structured in a variety of ways such as conventional mortgages, loans with equity kickers, loans with options to acquire ownership, and joint ventures. Depending on the nature, size, and organization of the real estate project, financial sources more typical of commercial businesses might be available, such as unsecured lines of credit, inventory and receivables loans, and preferred stock, though the last example is unusual.

In some situations, public financing may be available, particularly in the Caribbean and Mexico, where some governments have a strong interest in using resorts to spur economic development. In Puerto Rico, for example, several entities and programs have been established to provide financial assistance to and to engage in joint ventures with resort developers (see feature box on page 104). Cancun, a major resort area in Mexico,

Ski resorts are considered risky ventures because of their seasonal limitations and remoteness. However, because of its outstanding setting and quality skiing and service, Blackcomb in British Columbia was able to minimize the risk to become a successful destination resort.

evolved largely in response to the efforts of the Mexican government.

With the above forms of financing fairly common in the real estate industry, this book does not address them in detail. Rather, the discussion focuses on the unique financing requirements, problems, and opportunities associated with resort development, especially large-scale resort communities and multiuse resorts.

Special Resort Financing Problems

One reason that the financing of resort development is different and difficult is that resorts involve, to varying degrees, specialized facilities, services, activities, and amenities not normally associated with other types of real estate development. In particular, the economics and long-term financial implications of providing specialized facilities have not been the subject of careful study. Therefore, it is little surprise that would-be lenders or investors are not inclined to finance a development type that is perceived as risky and remains largely unknown. To complicate matters, resorts are frequently seasonal operations that rely on good weather for part of their success, making them inherently more risky undertakings for both investors and lenders over the short term. A three-month period of relatively inclement weather during the peak season can ruin a whole year, especially in the case of beach resorts and ski operations.

It is also important to recognize that resort home sales typically involve a slow-paced sales program that may take many more years to complete than in the case of a similarly sized primary-home community. For resort project sales versus typical residential project sales, the time required to pay off the construction loan and provide equity returns is considerably longer, thereby exposing both the investor and the lender to more cycles of economic risk.

Financing the Westin Rio Mar Beach Resort and Country Club

The Westin Rio Mar Beach Resort and Country Club in Puerto Rico is a recent example of a multiuse resort that involves a variety of financing sources and development partners. The project, located 16 miles from San Juan, opened in 1996. It consists of a 600-room luxury hotel, a 6,000-square-foot casino, over one mile of beachfront, a country club with a Greg Norman–designed 18-hole golf course, an upgraded Tom Fazio–designed golf course, tennis courts, and a clubhouse. The development partnership—Rio Mar Associates L.P, S.E.—includes comanaging general partner Tishman, which is responsible for the hotel component; comanaging general partner Willowbend, which is responsible primarily for the country club component; and general partner Hotel Development

Corporation, a subsidiary of the Puerto Rico Tourism Company, which is a financial partner and committed to the growth of Puerto Rico's hospitality industry.

The financial structure for the $178.5 million project includes $59 million in equity, of which $24 million came from the general partners and $35 million from the limited partners, who are generally Puerto Rico residents and corporations. The $35 million limited-partner equity offering includes substantial tax incentives, such as

- Tourism Development Act Tax Credits
  - A front-end incentive in the form of an investment tax credit equal to 50 percent of the initial investment.

The Westin Rio Mar Beach Resort and Country Club in Puerto Rico includes a 600-room luxury hotel, a 6,000-square-foot casino, over one mile of beachfront, and golf courses designed by both Greg Norman and Tom Fazio.

Attempts at analyzing the economics and financial needs of a given project are likewise complicated by the typically long-term nature of resort land development and the related susceptibility of a project to wide swings in the economy, market attitudes and tastes, inflation, interest rates, availability of credit, labor supply, and more. For example, during the real estate recession of the early 1990s, many resort properties ended up in the

• Back-end protection in the form of a loss tax credit equal to up to 50 percent of any net loss realized upon sale or other disposition, including liquidation.
• Tax Loss Deductions
  • Limited-partner receipt of 100 percent of tax losses during construction and 100 percent of any potential losses thereafter.
• Tax Exemptions (also available to developer)
  • 90 percent exemption on income from hotel and golf operations.
  • 90 percent exemption on capital gains derived from sale of limited-partner unit.

One of the problems with the limited-partner equity offering is that it is a Securities and Exchange Commission-registered offering, which has meant excessive legal and administrative expenses and an ongoing intensive management effort by the developer.

The government of Puerto Rico—through its Hotel Development Corporation—provided a direct equity investment of $8.5 million, with the remainder of the $24 million in general-partner equity covered by Tishman and Willowbend. In addition to the equity and tax incentives, the government acts as a development facilitator that coordinates with regulatory and infrastructure agencies.

Debt financing took the form of a $116 million bond offering through a commonwealth of Puerto Rico tax-exempt financing authority. The bond includes total interest costs of 7.2 percent (before guarantee fee). It is made up of serial, capital appreciation, and term bonds; offers a last maturity date of September 2004; and includes interest only through the first six years of the loan term. The Puerto Rico Tourism Development Fund guarantees the debt financing—both principal and interest; the guarantee fee is 1.5 percent per year.

hands of the Resolution Trust Corporation (RTC). In August 1993, the *RTC Investor* reported that six premier golf course and resort properties were purchased from the RTC for bids totaling $404.2 million at auction. By contrast, most real estate developments, with the exception of large land developments, are relatively short-term projects that permit the developer to identify and remain relatively certain of such economic considerations as construction costs, interest rates tied to permanent financing, and revenues associated with presales or preleasing. Finally, other factors compounding the difficulties associated with long-term resort development are the often-required heavy front-end costs during the period of negative cash flow and the fact that in many cases investments can be recovered and profits realized only in the final phases of development.

General Resort Financing Guidelines

In part because of the special issues and problems associated with financing a resort development, the financial community has not developed a good understanding of long-term resort community development. Certainly, short-term development and land loans (provided in some cases by real estate investment trusts) are not the answer. As a result, the resort developer may have to make do with financing techniques and approaches intended for quite different undertakings.

Because of the considerable financial risks involved, a resort developer should use prudent financing strategies and devise a contingency plan to deal with sudden and unforeseen changes in circumstances. Such contingencies might call for maintaining reserve equity, investigating refinancing options, accelerating land sales, halting construction, or even selling out. On the extreme downside, a developer may require a complete strategic and functional overhaul, which usually occurs when the existing owner(s)—or, more probably, the project's creditors—lose confidence in the project. An overhaul may accompany a foreclosure, further funding, or an outright creditor takeover. Whatever the circumstances, a development in such a precarious financial position must be turned around if investors are to recover their outlay.

Perhaps the best advice is to rely heavily on equity in the early stages of resort community development. "The sound financing of any project," notes Robert J. Lowe, president of Lowe Enterprises, Inc., in Los Angeles, "is based on having adequate equity capital that understands the cyclical nature of the real estate business and has the patience to accept the slower times in anticipation of boom times. Similarly, debt should be structured to adequately accommodate the conservatively projected revenue stream for each part of a project."[2]

The heavy-equity approach to an inherently risky, long-term venture will likely require creative partnership arrangements with equity partners willing to sacrifice short-term returns for long-term values. The alternative solution is for the resort developer simply to revise, modify, and tailor the development program to fit the avail-

Bank financing was used at PGA National in Palm Beach Gardens, Florida, to acquire the property and develop the infrastructure. In this case, Manufacturers Hanover Bank provided the funds. The site acquisition cost was $10.5 million and site improvement costs were $26.6 million, resulting in a total initial development cost of $37.1 million.

able financing—or abandon the development proposal altogether.

The circumstances can be optimized by making the financial proposal as attractive as possible. The applicant's proven skills and the project's physical appeal alone will not impress the lender. Thus, a sophisticated and well-presented feasibility analysis is an indispensable tool in soliciting financing support. Pro forma statements are essential in making the "go/no-go" decision and obtaining a financial commitment.

A strong managerial commitment is also necessary. The mixed success of large diversified corporations in real estate development during the last two decades attests to the need for specialized managerial skills in the development process. In particular, an experienced financial intermediary with personal contacts, knowledge of markets, and a demonstrated ability to structure deals can be an invaluable asset to the development team by seeking out funds in what is generally an imperfect capital market.

In many instances, the developer goes ahead with the project with whatever financing can be obtained, however inadequate or unrealistic it may be. This approach accounts in some measure for the high failure rate of resort properties and the belief that a resort project must go through much hardship and two or three owners before it can succeed. While it is not true that resort community development is necessarily unprofitable, it is clear that few people genuinely understand the complex long-term economics of such developments. Too often, projects are financed in a way that dooms them to failure, except under the most favorable circumstances.

Land Acquisition Financing

A developer can finance the acquisition of land for development in many ways, the most common of which are discussed below. Generally, lenders make land acquisition loans only to their strongest customers and only if developers have secured the necessary entitlements

to develop the land and can demonstrate the ability to repay the loans from sources other than the sale or development of the land. At Forest Highlands (see case study on page 328), for example, bank financing was used to acquire the land. The project was conceived by Jim Bartlett and Dick Bailey, who formed a general partnership in 1986 expressly for the project; the partnership included several financial partners who advanced working capital until financing for land acquisition could be obtained from an Arizona bank. Subsequently, a limited partnership was formed; a regional savings and loan took a 49 percent limited-partner position.

PGA National in Palm Beach Gardens, Florida, used bank financing for acquisition and infrastructure development; in this case, Manufacturers Hanover Bank provided the financing. The site acquisition cost totaled $10.5 million and site improvement costs $26.6 million, resulting in a total initial development cost of $37.1 million. The initial land carrying cost was greatly reduced, however, when the PGA purchased 625 acres, about a quarter of the site, and leased all but five acres back to the developer for the construction of four golf courses. Since its inception, PGA National has seen more than $500 million in residential retail sales such that cash flow from lot sales rapidly reduced the original acquisition/ development loan. The sale-and-leaseback arrangement with PGA of America for the golf course land was an important element of the initial financial structure. In addition, the project used special district bonds to finance drainage systems and roads.

Other factors also contributed to the development's financial success. First, the project was able to attract a strong equity partner and to acquire the land at a reasonable cost. Second, the Kemper Insurance Companies, which provided the development financing and has now been repaid, continues as a partner in PGA National Venture, Ltd. Debt-free ownership of the land and the owners' retention of the last prime parcels illustrate the strong financial planning that has gone into the project over the years.

Developing a strategy to lower the immediate cost of carrying the land is always prudent. Notes Gary Fenchuk of East West Partners in Midlothian, Virginia, "We employ risk management. We try to be selective and prudent in our original purchase of the land and do as much pre-selling to spec builders as possible before we undertake the project. We try to sell retail lots at the front end, which tends to reduce the risk. We capitalize well or find a joint venture partner and keep the time horizon short. We don't want to be too vulnerable."[3]

Optioning the Land. An option on land allows developers to buy time by obtaining control of a property for a short period while retaining the option to buy the parcel later for a specified price. Developers usually make a small cash payment to the landowner and may pay some of the property's carrying costs (interest charges, overhead, inflation, property taxes) during the option period.

Options permit developers to explore the need for a rezoning, determine whether the land has environmental problems, and secure a commitment from a lender or investor to finance development—all before deciding to purchase the land. At the end of the option period, they give up the option, negotiate its renewal, or exercise it and buy the land. The price paid for the land may be contingent on the density of the development permitted. Developers can develop contiguous land parcels incrementally through a so-called rolling option, which covers a number of tracts. The developer buys and develops the initial tract and, if the development succeeds, exercises the option to buy the next tract and so on.

Financing by the Seller. The seller can help finance the acquisition of the land by taking seller carryback financing or a purchase money mortgage from the developer in lieu of cash (see feature box on page 108).

Historically, one incentive for the seller to agree to finance the sale was the sale's structure as an installment sale. In this case, the gain on the sale could be reported over the period during which the installment note was collected, depending on the downpayment received, the liabilities assumed by the buyer, and the level of the seller's liabilities. As a result of the Revenue Act of 1987, the installment method is no longer available to *dealers* in real property, although *investors* in real property can still use the installment method with certain restrictions on the amount receivable in any one year. Consequently, the availability of financing by the seller may depend on whether the seller is a dealer in real property.

Agreements with Landowners. If the landowner is unwilling to take back a purchase mortgage and the developer cannot obtain a land acquisition loan from a lender, the landowner and developer may enter into a contract for the developer to acquire the land at a specified time. Alternatively, the landowner and developer might enter into a joint venture, usually in the form of a partnership, to develop the land. The landowner might contribute the land in return for an equity interest equivalent to the agreed-upon value of the land, together with a profit interest in the development. The owner is paid out of the initial development proceeds. The developer contributes the equity capital and arranges financing for the project.

Construction Financing

Site Improvements and Infrastructure. To prepare land for the construction of homes and other accommodations, developers typically need to grade the land, build roads, construct drainage and flood control facilities, and install sewer, water, and other utilities. If a major amenity is planned as a primary attraction—such as a golf course and clubhouse—it is often developed early in the process as well. For a project to be economically

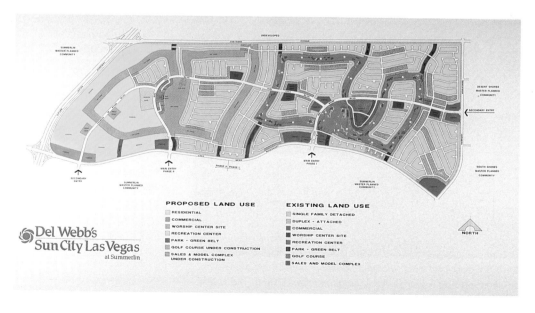

Infrastructure financing for Sun City Las Vegas was provided by the city of Las Vegas, which declared it a special improvement district. The city issued bonds to finance the infrastructure, which was defined broadly to include water and sewer, parks, trails, and landscaping—and, most important, a major four-lane, limited-access parkway that connected the property to U.S. 95 and brought it within minutes of downtown Las Vegas.

feasible, developers must seek out the least costly source to fund expensive upfront site improvements.

Site improvements and infrastructure can be financed with the acquisition of land as part of the construction loan, with a standby or construction/miniperm loan as part of the permanent project financing, or through various public/private financing alternatives. The principal alternatives for public/private financing are assess-ment districts, special districts or taxing authorities, tax increment financing, and federal and state grant and loan programs.

The major source of public financing for land development is municipal bonds. Counties, cities, and local government agencies issue municipal bonds for a variety of purposes, including construction of highways, roads, bridges, sewer systems, parks, and

Financial Strategy for Spring Island in South Carolina

Spring Island is a 3,000-acre private club community, with a maximum of 500 homesites, located on an island in South Carolina's Low Country. Amenities include a highly acclaimed 18-hole golf course, tennis courts, swimming pool, marina, equestrian facility, family sports garden, working nature laboratory, two dining facilities, and approximately 30 miles of hiking, biking, and bridle trails. The development strategy involves sales of undeveloped homesites.

The land was optioned in January 1989. During the option period, the developer secured the master plan and bridge permit approvals and closed 36 "founding member" presales for a total of $10.8 million. The founding members invested $300,000 each, for which they received at closing a five-acre homesite, a golf membership, and other financial considerations. The presales gave the project much-needed equity capital, created a level of credibility needed for traditional bank debt financing, and provided 36 "sales ambassadors" to give early momentum to the referred-sales process. In addition, the general partners of Spring Island Company contributed $1 million in equity.

The $17 million land purchase was consummated in March 1990. The purchase price was financed with $6 million in equity and $11 million in seller carryback financing from the landowner. In early 1991, traditional

bank acquisition and development debt was arranged as well as equity from a Japanese investment firm, thereby retiring all but $1.5 million of the seller carryback financing. NationsBank provided a classic debt acquisition and development loan with a 45 percent sales receipt "release" provision (to retire the loan, 45 percent of homesite sales revenues went to the bank each time a lot was sold). Nippon Landic, the real estate investment and management arm of a major Japanese bank, provided an additional $16 million in equity financing to ensure the timely completion of first-phase infrastructure and amenities.

Early retirement of all but $1.5 million of the seller financing gave the developer greater flexibility in balancing inventory and amenity development. The final $1.5 million for the land will be paid off gradually from sales revenues. Future lot sales will retire the remainder of the debt and provide capital for infrastructure and operating costs.

Financial Structure
1989–1990
- $1 million in equity from Spring Island Company
- $10.8 million in presales

1990
- $11 million in "seller carryback" financing with land purchase

1991
- $9.5 million NationsBank loan retires most of "seller" financing
- $1.5 million of "seller financing" remains
- $16 million equity investment from Nippon Landic

Financial Snapshot
- $50 million for acquisition, amenities, and infrastructure
- $50 million for general and administrative expenses, interest, and operating losses
- $150 million for anticipated real estate sales revenues

Spring Island's creative financial strategy incorporated presales to 36 "founding members" and seller carryback financing from the landowner.

other infrastructure improvements. Increasingly, large-scale developments are relying on municipal bond financing, not only for its tax and marketing advantages but also because such financing may be more accessible than large-scale financing from financial institutions. Another advantage of hard financing is that developers do not have to increase the price of the lots or houses to cover the costs of the infrastructure and other facilities. Rather, the costs are passed along to homeowners in the form of higher property taxes or an annual assessment for bond repayment. As such, bond financing of improvements might dampen housing sales in districts where property taxes and housing costs are already relatively high.

The city of Las Vegas provided infrastructure financing for Sun City Las Vegas by declaring the community a special district and issuing bonds for infrastructure, which the developer defined broadly to include water and sewer systems, parks, trails, and landscaping—and, most important, a major four-lane limited-access parkway that connects the property to U.S. 95 and brought it within minutes of downtown Las Vegas.

Building Construction. Construction of buildings on land acquired and prepared for development by the developer is ususally financed with a construction loan and the developer's equity. The loan may also cover some or all of the costs of site development. The greatest risk with a construction loan is that the community may not be completed on schedule and within budget, which could cause problems for the project. For example, delays in construction could result from labor strikes, material shortages, inclement weather, poor workmanship, or other problems. Another risk is that the housing units may not sell or rent as rapidly as expected or for the projected price. Meanwhile, the carrying costs mount, resulting in cost overruns that may require the developer to raise additional equity or return to the lender to request an increase in the amount of the construction loan.

A construction loan is a short-term loan that runs from six months to two years. For a hotel or other income-producing project, the loan is repaid from the long-term (permanent) mortgage when construction is completed and cash flow established; for a for-sale residential project, the loan is repaid from the proceeds of house sales. The construction loan is secured by a mortgage that gives the lender a first lien on the land and improvements. The lien is removed from each house when the house is sold and the loan paid down by a specified amount.

Heritage Hills in Somers, New York, a community of primarily attached condominiums and recreational amenities, provides an example of a rolling construction loan and the problems that can arise when the economy takes a downturn. The project, begun in the 1970s, had a front-end cost of approximately $25 million, including acquisition and site improvements. A $15 million rolling line of credit was put in place for construction. As the condominium units sold, the line was made available for the next section. When the mar-

ket slowed during the recession of 1990–1991 and banks pulled back on their lending activities, the lender called the line. As was typical at the time, the lender would not renew the line and stopped issuing new lines. Subsequently, each new section required its own financing. The most recent condominium section, which began construction in 1995 with projected sales revenues of approximately $25 million, required a loan of approximately $19 million.

Workouts

The term "workout" refers to piloting a financially distressed project through a strategic and functional overhaul with the hope of turning losses into profits or at least minimizing further losses. As with most other types of real estate development, workouts are common in resort community development and are a consequence of the high risks often associated with the development business.

The typical workout strategy is to overhaul the development program and operation aggressively. The sale of the most marketable assets helps regain financial stability and maximizes immediate returns. Thus, if a project can sell for a price greater than the outstanding debt, it should be sold.

A workout is not just about economics; it is also a political process. Therefore, the relationship between developer and lender is critical during a workout. The developer needs to be effective in managing negotiations with the lender in order to avert an unnecessary bankruptcy. At the same time, developer and lender should realize that through their interdependent involvement in a large real estate development, they may eventually become active partners. However, the developer who wishes to continue managing the project in question must present a variety of feasible alternatives to the lender. He or she must convince the lender that he or she is as good or better than any other management choice. If the lender rejects the developer's restructuring proposals, the developer should offer further alternatives even up to the moment of foreclosure; continuing attempts to negotiate are essential.

Workout programs often call for diversifying a project's market appeal and product line. For example, a resort rental program may be used to help carry the operation and introduce potential buyers to the property. Lowering prices is not always a good practice unless the product was initially overpriced. Price cuts can seriously undermine the true value of a project.

Notes
1. Desmond Muirhead and Guy L. Rando, *Golf Course Development and Real Estate* (Washington, D.C.: ULI–the Urban Land Institute, 1994), p. 24.
2. Personal communication with Robert J. Lowe, president, Lowe Enterprises, Inc., Los Angeles, Calif., 1995.
3. Personal communication with Gary Fenchuk, East West Partners of Virginia, Midlothian, Va., 1995.

4. Land Use Planning and Product Design

From a planning standpoint, a resort is made up of an interrelated set of physical and programmatic elements. The elements may include any or all of the following: recreational facilities and programs, housing, hotels and conference facilities, commercial facilities, community infrastructure and facilities, and open space. Once a developer decides on a proposed resort's development program, he or she must oversee the formulation of a master plan that both incorporates all the specified elements and guides the design and construction of the basic infrastructure and individual project elements.

This chapter provides an inventory and assessment of the major types of land use and physical elements currently incorporated into resort development projects as well as an overview of planning and design issues and processes associated with these various uses. Since the elements are in a constant state of evolution and are closely tied to specific markets, a successful developer must remain flexible with respect to the selection, definition, and creation of each project element for the duration of the development process. This is especially true for large-scale projects developed over a long time frame.

The resort at Squaw Creek in California is a four-season resort near Lake Tahoe that offers a variety of recreational amenities including golf, swimming, and skiing facilities.

Site Planning Issues

Site plans differ widely according to project site and environment. Different settings and environments require different analyses of the physical limitations and opportunities presented by the site. The site characteristics of a mountain resort community, for example, differ greatly from those of a desert or ocean setting. Site planning for a resort involves weaving various land uses into the natural environment to create a high-quality setting that will attract visitors and homebuyers. While the physical attributes of the setting define the project, the quality of the buildings and how they are integrated with the setting are critical in determining the overall character of the resort environment.

Creating a Sense of Place

One of the primary objectives of resort planning and design is to create a sense of place. The effort begins with the setting. Planning and design are essential in shaping the setting, visitors' or residents' perception of it, and, ultimately, the sense of place conveyed by the resort in the context of its natural surroundings.

There are many approaches and many considerations to take into account when creating a sense of place. In the end, however, the process calls for creating a style or theme—a vision of what the resort should be. The process requires the developer to observe the surrounding area and to visit and learn from other successful

Brays Island Plantation, a 5,800-acre island for 325 homesites, includes the Barony House, once the original plantation house and now an inn. Brays Island Plantation sees itself as a model by which the South can develop plantation lands while still preserving the environment and endangered historic treasures. The property includes 3,500 acres of open space.

resorts or tourist destinations distinguished by their own unique styles. Charles Fraser of the Charles E. Fraser Company in Hilton Head notes

> For the most part, the architectural community and developers both have failed themselves and their customers by not developing something unique and distinctive, something that builds on what has made well-planned resorts successful over time. I have now reached the opinion that no one should start buying land or planning the use for land until they first buy a camera and go out on field trips or tear pictures out of books and magazines and plaster pictures on a wall of places and designs that form a starting point, a vision for what will be developed. The uniqueness of a good resort is not odd, never-seen-before buildings, but the integration of appropriate, appealing buildings into the natural environment of the site. Until you have evolved in your mind an image of a new or old style or theme that fits a particular area and a particular target market, don't start, don't buy the land, don't go out searching for land. First, look for cost-effective activities and amenities that your guests and residents can enjoy at your future resort, and then search for visual images of what you are going to build and what you envision the place to be like in the future.[1]

Fraser goes on to remark, "As we think new, we also need to think old. The places that have the huge flow of people today are often places that are rich in culture. For example, Charleston, South Carolina . . . attracts four or five times as many vacation visitors as Hilton Head Island, with its beaches and 20 golf courses."[2] Charleston is a brilliant example of American architecture at its best in the early 1800s. It includes a wonderful array of restaurants, shops, and interesting places. Moreover, some of the finest resorts today—such as the Boca Raton Resort & Club, the Homestead, Pinehurst Resort and Country Club, and the Sagamore—are old, established resorts that are still operating because of the quality and historic nature of their original buildings and site design.

Many resort sites feature historic buildings and sites that can be used to create a sense of place. Old farm, plantation, or ranch buildings—as well as historic mansions—can add character to a resort site. Both Brays Island Plantation in South Carolina and Silverado Country Club and Resort in California, for example, incorporate historic mansions as key elements; one mansion serves as an inn (Brays Island Plantation) while the other functions as a clubhouse (Silverado Country Club and Resort).

In some cases, historic sites can be redeveloped or enhanced to create an attractive resort setting. The Woodstock Inn and Resort in Woodstock, Vermont, is a venerable resort hotel that traces its history back 200 years. Laurence Rockefeller redeveloped the inn in the 1960s—after the existing historic inn burned—to create a first-class hotel at the center of the historic town of Woodstock, one of the most attractive villages in New England. The town features a village green, covered bridge, and four church bells cast by Paul Revere. The resort includes both a golf course and skiing facilities on nearby sites. The setting is unusual for a resort in that it combines recreational amenities with a historic town setting.

Archaeological sites can also be important assets. While many developers would consider archaeological findings such as Native American settlements or burial mounds an impediment to development, archaeological features can help create a sense of place. Today, developers must allow a state archaeological team to conduct tests to identify potential sites where artifacts might be found. If such sites are identified, the developer can either leave the site as a greenway or open space or fund a shovel test to assess any significant features. Spring Island, an environmentally responsible second-home community in South Carolina, has transformed its archaeological treasures—sites of Native American communities and artifacts—into an asset. Spring Island invites archaeology graduate students to participate in deciphering the mysterious existence of the Calawassie

Indians, offers local grade schools hands-on learning opportunities, and donates artifacts to local and state archives. Residents of Spring Island can even participate in archaeological explorations. The historic sites provide an attractive amenity, lend themselves well to study in Spring Island's "curriculum," and enrich the community's history and sense of place.

While modern resorts cannot create truly historic buildings or settings (at least not over the short run), they can create distinctively designed places and settings that either reflect the best of regional/local architecture or create the historic architecture of tomorrow. Perhaps the best example of how neotraditional architecture and design can be used to create a sense of place is Seaside, a beach community in Florida developed by Robert Davis and designed by Andres Duany and Elizabeth Plater-Zyberk. This second-home community is located on the Florida panhandle—not the state's most sought-after resort area. Yet, Seaside has earned acclaim largely because of the charming small-town image it has achieved through rigorous town planning principles, strong architectural guidelines, and the creative design work of more than a dozen good to great architects.

On the other hand, in some cases a resort can successfully pioneer its own modern and unique style that is skillfully developed to suit unusual site conditions. Among the best examples is Sea Ranch, a second-home community started in the mid-1960s on the California coast. Sea Ranch evolved a distinctive style by relying on many of the leading planners and architects of its day, including Lawrence Halprin, Charles Moore, Joseph Esherick, and William Turnbull. Notes *Progressive Architecture* magazine, "The original Sea Ranch condominium is perhaps the most influential American building of the 1960s."[3] The project includes both single-family homes and condominiums, but the two housing types "employed a remarkably similar vocabulary: shed roofs to deflect the wind, no eaves or overhangs, large windows punched

through walls of natural redwood boards. These became the principal ingredients of the Sea Ranch style through both regulation and emulation. . . . The original buildings were ubiquitous in the international architectural press, and design awards became routine. They were emulated far beyond the site."[4]

Whatever image or style is sought, contextual design and sensitivity to the surrounding area is an important consideration in creating the appropriate sense of place. "A movement is underway in resort design," notes John Cottle of Cottle Graybeal Yaw Architects in Aspen, Colorado. "Its emergence demands that developers, planners, and architects focus on regional specificity. In return, resorts will realize greater success. This movement studies a resort in terms of its site-specific and regionally unique qualities; its history, culture, climate; and reflects those in concept, amenities, land use, and design. The inherent site qualities form the basis of a design philosophy."[5]

The Wailea Resort on Maui in Hawaii, for example, is located in a larger community characterized by a distinctive local culture and the absence of a large urban center. Clearly, the resort was designed with its environment in mind. Design guidelines and the master plan prohibit high-density development and restrict building heights in order to preserve views and the low skyline typical of the area. Hawaii's regional architecture and indigenous landscaping are strongly encouraged. Similarly, the Koll Interests are appropriately using traditional Mexican architecture in developing their Baja resorts while the Marriott Kaui Resort in Hawaii has recently renovated its property to replace a European design theme with an indigenous Hawaiian theme.

Environmental Preservation

Perhaps more than with any other type of development planning, resort planning gives rise to environmental issues of paramount importance. After all, it is the resort's environment that draws the customer. Thus, resort planning must carefully consider the advantages and disadvantages of development versus environmental preservation and discriminate between areas to be maintained for their environmental integrity and areas more suited to development.

Environmental law has grown increasingly stringent in the past two decades, dramatically influencing the design of resorts. The National Environmental Policy Act (NEPA), the Clean Water Act, and the Endangered Species Act have been the most influential federal laws affecting resort and recreational communities. NEPA was the springboard that propelled the federal recognition of an environmental ethic into statehouses and city halls. Because resort development typically takes place in environmentally sensitive areas, often on "green" or previously undeveloped sites, developers frequently experience the most direct effects of the myriad environmental laws enacted at all levels of government.

Moreover, it is not just environmental regulations per se that affect resort developers. The strong environmen-

Wachesaw Plantation in South Carolina requires design guidelines for new construction that emphasize historic styles.

tal ethic of resort users and homebuyers also influences site planning. Polls indicate that a high proportion of Americans now claim that they are environmentally sensitive. As a result, particularly in second-home communities, citizen concern over the preservation of surrounding areas or open spaces is on the increase. And second-home owners are generally more environmentally sensitive at second-home locations than at their primary-home locations.

One project that was especially influential in furthering environmental values in resort planning is Sea Pines on Hilton Head Island, South Carolina. The resort, started during the 1950s, marked a new type of resort in terms of purpose, architecture, design, and environmental sensitivity. The success of Sea Pines is largely attributable to extensive planning efforts aimed at ensuring that the community would engender a unique sense of place with minimal disruption to the natural environment. The environmental planning hallmarks included restrictions on cutting trees more than six inches in diameter, establishing a forest preserve, preserving and enhancing Native American ruins on the site, restricting building heights, and preserving the community's sand dunes. Environmental sensitivity was both a product of extensive planning and a pervasive influence on the design of Sea Pines. Numerous resorts in a variety of settings—ocean, mountain, and desert—such as Kiawah Island, South Carolina; Amelia Island, Florida; Beaver Creek, Colorado; Semiahmoo, Washington; and the Boulders, Arizona, reflect the values that distinguish Sea Pines.

Another early and influential resort community that made environmental sensitivity a hallmark of its plan was Sea Ranch. Before preparing the plan, Lawrence Halprin carefully studied the ecology of the coastal site —its wooded hills to the east and meadows to the west and its rows of trees that divide the meadows and protect against strong winds. Notes Halprin, "We understood that we were confronting an austere, windswept, and often foggy landscape of great power and presence."[6] The Halprin plan tucks houses into the woods and along the windrows, leaving the meadows as open space. Moreover, studies of wind erosion as it affected the cypress trees on the site—and how they were shaped into specific slopes and pitches—provided sound information and models for establishing building designs and roof slopes that could best stand up to the winds.[7]

More recently, many Florida projects have also contributed to environmental planning efforts, especially as related to wetlands. At the 2,340-acre PGA National, started in the 1980s, land planning and engineering design methods ensured preservation and restoration of wetlands and maintenance of water quality. The project created over 100 acres of new wetlands and restored to their natural state over 270 acres of existing wetlands, most of which were located along the community's western border. The western wetlands preserve treats runoff from the golf courses and residential uses before it enters a nearby canal. By relying on natural processes

to meet water quality standards, the project did not have to implement more expensive structural solutions. This sophisticated water retention and purification system established PGA's reputation as a leader in environmental protection.

Today, ecological considerations are central in resort planning as resort developers recognize that environmental assets are the primary amenities that attract visitors and homebuyers. Among the more significant recent examples is Dewees Island in South Carolina (see case study on page 320), which uses setting and environmental preservation as its primary amenity. Planning any new resort must begin with the recognition that preserving and enhancing the environment is an integral part of the resort concept and plan.

Positioning Uses

A major challenge in planning the layout of a resort community is to position residences, hotel rooms, and other accommodations in a way that provides each use with a high-quality view or access to an amenity while creating rational relationships among uses. The price differential commanded by a prime-location unit is considerable, often ranging from 20 to 100 percent or more. Therefore, it is to the developer's advantage to maximize the orientation of each unit toward any amenities.

Yet, other community design principles must be considered if the resort is to succeed. Notes Larry E. Helber of Helber Hastert & Fee, Planners, Inc., in Honolulu, "Plans that spread and intersperse low-rise development with major open spaces to preserve a natural, rural character run the risk of producing lifeless resort settings. Concentration is important in site planning to produce social nodes or 'positive congestion,' along with placement of activities/attractions that enhance user convenience."[8]

Each resort community has its own hierarchy of preferred locations based on views and proximity to amenities. In a beach resort, the prime location is the waterfront; in a ski area, it is next to a ski run. The next preferred location might be frontage on or a view of some other amenity such as a lake, open space, or golf course. The third ranking location is what might be called an "overview." An overview permits views of an overall amenity such as the ocean, golf course, or ski slope from a distance and across other properties. Lesser locations prevail next to less important amenities and views.

Pelican Bay in Naples, Florida, provides an interesting example of how various buildings and uses were sited to maximize the overall value of the property. With three miles of beach along the Gulf of Mexico, the site offered an enormously attractive natural recreational amenity that the developer wanted to use to best advantage; however, the beach was largely cut off from developable inland areas by a mangrove estuary system. In earlier decades, the mangrove area might have been filled and developed. The plan that evolved for Pelican Bay pre-

The Wailea Resort on Maui in Hawaii is set within a larger community characterized by a distinctive local culture and the absence of a large urban center. The resort was designed with this environment in mind.

Sand Dunes

Sand dunes are a necessary element in preserving vegetation along the sea coast. Walking on the dunes will damage the sea oats and destroy the dunes.

Please use the boardwalk.

Marriott's Harbor Beach in Fort Lauderdale, Florida. In exchange for re-creating the primary dune, the developer was allowed to build underground parking seaward of the coastal construction set-back. A full mix of amenities is integrated on a small site, including a tennis club, pool, beach club, and cabanas.

The Pelican Bay site plan. The higher buildings are arranged along the western portion of the uplands, providing dramatic views for many of the units.

served over one-quarter of the property (570 acres) in the form of sensitive coastal wetlands and mangrove forests and set the acreage aside as a conservation area that is protected in perpetuity. Most of the developed areas are concentrated upland toward the interior of the site and are connected to the beach by two elevated boardwalks through the conservation area.

The residential areas are positioned to take advantage of views and site amenities; the higher-density housing is configured in a long strip at the center of the site running parallel to the gulf. Clustered villas, mid-rise structures, and multistory buildings are arranged progressively, with the mid-rise buildings positioned along the golf course on the inland side and the higher multistory structures bordering the conservation area on the gulf side. Single-family homes are sited at the easternmost edge of the property. By arranging the taller buildings along the western portion of the uplands, the site plan provides dramatic views—of the Gulf of Mexico and the conservation area to the west and of the golf course to the east—for the maximum number of units.

The land plan at the 1,493-acre Wailea Resort in Hawaii follows a different approach that is more typical of Hawaiian resort planning. Developed on oceanfront land that rises quickly and sometimes steeply from the beach, Wailea devoted its beachfront property primarily to the resort hotels, which could benefit most by their proximity to the ocean, and sited parcels for homes farther away from the beaches at higher, sloped elevations with spectacular mountain and ocean vistas. These parcels are ideally suited to residential projects whose property values tend to increase with the availability of views and proximity to the various amenities, especially golf, that serve the resort.

At PGA National in Palm Beach Gardens, Florida, the master plan called for a unified, planned resort community that would provide a variety of product types within a coherent framework and offer golf as the community's primary feature. A central planning issue was how best

to integrate the project's resort elements with the wide variety of residential neighborhoods. The solution was to create a "resort core" at the community's hub. The resort, which consists of a four-star hotel with 334 rooms and 25,000 square feet of convention space, a private members' club for residents, and a health and racquet club, is clustered on about 38 acres near the project's main entrance. Short-term visitors are concentrated in the hotel and the nearby condominiums. The circulation pattern provides resort guests with direct access to the resort facilities without infringing on residents' privacy.

The residential neighborhoods' attached units are located at the site's interior adjacent to the resort core, with lower-density detached homesites grouped around the perimeter. The primary residential sites lie toward the edges. A broad range of housing types at varying densities (two dwelling units per acre up to 15 dwelling units per acre) has been developed.

Individual neighborhoods within PGA National reflect a specific housing type and architectural style. While there is diversity throughout the entire project, each neighborhood presents a unified appearance. The mix of residential types aims to achieve a variety of lifestyles. Products do not compete with each other directly but rather overlap in some of the price ranges. Sites at the edges of the project, less suitable for residential development, are allocated to parks, open space, offices, or light industrial uses. Of PGA's 2,340 acres, less than 1,000 are devoted to residential use; more than 1,000 acres are dedicated to wetlands, lakes, parks, and recreation.

Often the most efficient method for maximizing residential lots while preserving open space is to cluster units. The arrangement of structures in closely related groups, often in accordance with the provisions of a planned unit development (PUD) ordinance, is based on the concept of concentrating density in physically suitable locations and preserving natural features and open space. For example, at Heritage Hills, an 1,100-acre adult recreational community in Somers, New York, cluster planning techniques preserved the site's abundant hills, streams, rocks, and woodlands and minimized the removal of earth, trees, and vegetation. Nearly one-third of the land was retained as open space with housing located in small clusters. The street plan, which allowed various widths, grades, and setbacks, limited disruption to the terrain. The combination of clustered development and large areas of open space provided the solution to the dilemma of providing high-density housing with a rural character in an area typified by low-density housing. Had the project been forced to develop within the town's then-existing land use requirements, it would have been deprived of much of its natural beauty.

A more recent example of clustering can be found at Spanish Bay, near Pebble Beach, California. Spanish Bay uses clustered housing to maintain open spaces and enhance the project's ambience. Townhomes near the inn are concentrated on terraced lots to provide maximum views of the ocean, dunes, forest, and fairways while allowing a significant portion of the site to remain in its natural state.

Special Considerations for Mountain Sites

Mountains create an environment that evokes the power and raw beauty of nature. Their appeal is not merely aesthetic. They beckon respect, interaction, and awe. Thus, there is perhaps no greater challenge than creating a high-quality community on a mountainside while simultaneously respecting a mountain's splendor. Because the natural topography of the mountains so dominates the possibilities of the site plan, a successful plan requires a thorough understanding of the mountain environment, its geologic processes and rhythms, its ecology, and its values.

The several physical factors to consider in planning a mountain resort or recreational community vary by the type of mountain environment. Older and more inactive geologic mountain ranges such as the Appalachians and the Adirondacks are more stable and thus more predictable. Younger and more active geologic formations such as those found in the Rocky Mountains hide potentially dangerous geologic hazards.

Mountain planning requires a greater degree of analysis than that demanded of most other geographic locations. Mountain topography is a complex web whose many variables challenge the feasibility of building. The following factors must be considered:

- steep slopes, unstable slopes, and rockfall zones (in general, slopes exceeding 30 percent are not suitable for building);
- (heavy) snowfall;
- avalanches;
- microclimate conditions such as wind hazards;
- watersheds and wetlands;
- flooding and unstable surface water flows;

At PGA National in Palm Beach Gardens, Florida, the master plan for the community was conceived to produce a unified planned resort community that would offer a variety of product types within a coherent overall framework.

- air quality conditions due to inversions;
- vistas; and
- sun orientation and shadows.

In addition, mountain resorts are often four-season resorts. As a result, planning must carefully consider the implications of seasonal changes on the resort's activity patterns. Moreover, with modern construction technology, it is possible to construct buildings previously considered unbuildable. Accordingly, a more complex analysis of environmental concerns is necessary to determine just how much risk is reasonable. Yet, the issue of planning around slopes is the overriding consideration. Snowmass Village, Colorado, is an example of a prominent ski resort that has experienced growth pains as a result of initially building on a steep gradient. The unpredicted implications of growth, coupled with a limiting environment, have forced Snowmass Village into a less-than-ideal situation.

At the outset in the early 1970s, the objective at Snowmass Village was to provide a village or series of small villages similar to those in the Alps. For developers Bill Janss, then the owner of Sun Valley, and D.R.C. Brown, a former owner of the Aspen Skiing Company, the most important planning determinant was proximity to the ski slopes. While the village could have been sited on the valley floor, such an arrangement would have compromised access to the ski slopes and limited the ski-in-ski-out alternatives. Instead, the developers wanted to unite the ski slope and village experience; thus, they sited the village on a relatively steep slope (10 to 15 percent) along the side of the mountain.

Except for the arterial road that runs through the center of the village (a 14 percent slope that requires electric heating in winter), the village street system is limited to a series of finger roads perpendicular to the arterial road and the ski slope. The village itself consists of a series of pedestrian malls and lodges placed along contour lines; the main pedestrian mall is lined with retail stores and provides access to transportation services. While the mall has been recently renovated to reflect updated architecture, the resort still does not convey a sense of community like neighboring Aspen. Indeed, the resort plan resulted in a disjointed series of pedestrian malls and lodges. Yet, once the town configuration had been established, town councilmembers and planners dogmatically refused to authorize the modifications necessary to create a more coherent town center. In retrospect, if the village had been sited at the base of the mountain, the community could have achieved a better sense of place, thereby making a smoother transition from a ski resort to a conventional community.

It should be stressed that environmental sensitivity has become a crucial aspect of recreational mountain planning not only for environmental protection reasons but for marketing purposes as well. The Divide, located in Snowmass Village, Colorado, provides a good example. The Divide is a neighborhood of 40 single-family homesites planned for minimal environmental disturbance while offering spectacular views of the remote East Snowmass Valley and providing a ski-in-ski-out amenity. Roads and driveways were designed to fit the topography, and planners did not draw lot lines until they had determined optimum homesites. These considerations produced a community whose houses nestle into the edges of Alpine meadows and aspen forests and capitalize on outstanding views. The community does not dominate the environment but rather coexists within it. The Divide's sensitivity to the environment immediately increased its perceived value. Clearly, the community parlayed the limitations of the property into an asset through sensitive planning and an appreciation for the environment. This method of development is extremely costly and thus can be undertaken only where the market can support expensive homes.

The Divide at Snowmass Village, Colorado, illustrates how critical environmental planning is to the success of mountain projects. The Divide is a neighborhood of 40 single-family homesites planned to disturb the environment as little as possible while offering spectacular views of the remote East Snowmass Valley. Roads and driveways follow the topography to minimize soil erosion.

Special Considerations for Coastal Sites

For the most part, the coasts of the United States have been either preserved as open space or thoroughly developed, with only a few concentrations of developable land remaining. As the interface between two ecologic environments, the coast supports a rich web of life that can be easily stressed by development. Consequently, today's coastal developers face increasingly stringent environmental protection laws and major hurdles to any type of beachfront development. New coastal development stands little chance of gaining approval unless it reflects extreme sensitivity to the environment.

Spanish Bay, a resort golf community on the famed 17-mile drive near Pebble Beach, California, is an example of a resort project that simplified the planning process by becoming proactive in addressing environmental concerns. The developers of Spanish Bay came to the community armed with an array of studies that addressed a range of impacts—favorable and unfavorable—on the environment. By illustrating their concern for the site, the developers earned the support and confidence of the community, which helped ensure the success of the project. In the end, Spanish Bay transformed an abandoned quarry into a golf course and planted sea grasses to refurbish depleted sand dunes.

Shoreline and beach erosion is the single greatest problem faced by developers of coastal resorts. Beach erosion is an inevitable process and must be respected. Many older resort communities and towns—Atlantic City, New Jersey; Fort Lauderdale, Florida; and Ocean City, Maryland—have suffered from erosion as a result of buildings placed at the ocean's edge in defiance of natural processes. Destruction of the dune systems has necessitated restoration, which is continuous and costly and compromises beach quality. Not surprisingly, stringent laws have redefined development along the coast such that building envelopes and setbacks from the beach are deep (often 180 to 240 feet) and densities typically low. In addition, the laws require primary and secondary dune preservation for erosion control and other ecological purposes.

Dewees Island, a private-home recreational community near Charleston, South Carolina, has addressed erosion problems by planting indigenous sea grasses to buffer the primary and secondary dunes, thereby creating more stable beaches (see case study on page 320) and inviting a more diverse wildlife habitat consistent with the island's mission statement—"A private oceanfront island retreat dedicated to environmental preservation." Unlike many resort communities, Dewees Island leaves untouched the beached flotsam of storms, allowing it to help anchor sand against the grinding of the surf. In some areas, the island has actually experienced an accretion of its beaches, which is partly the result of favorable tidal currents. Similarly, at Kiawah Island, South Carolina, the developer set the building line far back from the ocean edge, even though recent local history had pointed to beach sand accretion rather than erosion.

Dewees Island, a private-home recreational community near Charleston, South Carolina, has planted indigenous sea grasses to buffer its primary and secondary dunes and prevent erosion. Houses are constructed with environmentally sensitive products, and builders are carefully monitored to ensure that they do not disturb surrounding areas during the construction process.

Over 25 percent of its 5,000 acres is in wetlands at Brays Island, a hunting and second-home community in South Carolina. The land is used as an open space amenity and for recreational purposes, including hunting game fowl.

Wetlands are potentially a major development deterrent in coastal areas, particularly along the southeastern coasts of Florida, Georgia, and South Carolina. In such lowland areas, inner-coastal islands and the mainland are characterized by large expanses of wetlands. Over 25 percent of the 5,000 acres of land at Brays Island, a hunting and second-home community in South Carolina, has been deemed wetlands. The community's planners, however, have been able to transform the wetlands into an amenity by using the area for hunting and preserving it as natural open space.

Pelican Bay in Naples, Florida, parlayed 500 acres of mangrove forests and sensitive coastal wetlands into an environmental asset. Instead of attempting to secure permits to fill the wetlands that separated the beach from higher land, Pelican Bay installed a series of wooden walkways that permit residents and visitors to enjoy the experience of walking to the beach through pristine wetlands. Pelican Bay is another example of a develop-

Lyle H. Anderson
President
The Lyle Anderson Company, Inc.
Scottsdale, Arizona

Lyle Anderson has been involved in real estate investment for more than 25 years. His current investment and development activities are centered in Arizona, Washington state, New Mexico, Nevada, Hawaii, and Scotland. Beginning in 1982 as one of three principals of the Highlands Development Company, Anderson developed Desert Highlands, a luxury residential golf community in Scottsdale, Arizona, in partnership with the Bass brothers of Fort Worth, Texas. The community's golf course, site of the first two Skins Games, was designed by Jack Nicklaus and was ranked 25th in the United States by Golf Digest *magazine in its first year of eligibility.*

In 1984, Anderson began developing Desert Mountain, an 8,000-acre multiuse project in Scottsdale. It features three Nicklaus-designed golf courses with a fourth under construction and a fifth in the planning stages. In 1989, Anderson entered into a joint venture with a company owned by Mobil Land Development Corporation to run and develop Desert Mountain. As host of the Tradition, founded by Anderson, Desert Mountain is linked with one of the four major events on the Senior PGA Tour.

Anderson is currently involved in a partnership that is developing Las Campanas, a 5,000-acre golf, residential, and mixed-use project with two Nicklaus-designed golf courses in Santa Fe, New Mexico, and in other partnerships that are planning to develop two residential golf projects with approximately four miles of oceanfront on Hawaii's Kona coast. He also owns the Loch Lomond Golf Club in Scotland in partnership with a privately held investment company.

Anderson graduated from the University of Washington with a degree in electrical engineering.

At our projects, we have placed great emphasis on consistent quality at all levels of development—from the beauty of the land, to quality infrastructure, to high-quality golf courses and other recreational amenities. We believe this appeals to the high-end market, and we believe it helps establish a reputation that can overcome cycles in the market. A developer loses his competitive edge if he wavers on the issue of quality. Quality always sells. There are no geniuses in the development business; I think that too many developers try to time the market perfectly. Build your business plan based on not having perfect market timing. The real key is being positioned with consistent quality when an up cycle hits.

We have emphasized conceptualizing a long-term need so people who can afford it can live in a great place. Our projects have tended to be in geographic locations offering fine primary-home community living as well as attractions for those who live in a number of places throughout the year. We are in the large-lot, custom-home business with strict architectural controls. We structure our amenities a little differently than the developer who is focused entirely on building a finished product. For our type of buyer, the level of our amenities is such that no one can come in and outdo us. Our strategy has a lot to do with market positioning for the long term. For us, this is a national market and in some ways an international market. At each project, we have endeavored to position ourselves uniquely so as to minimize or eliminate competition. Our goal is to develop projects that do not have equals in our market.

It is our goal to blend marketing and development with a long-term, realistic sense of costs and profits. Long-term profits must far outpace development costs if there is to be adequate insurance against cyclical economic conditions.

We seek to become involved with sizable pieces of property. This enables us to capitalize to the greatest extent on upfront amenity and infrastructure costs and to benefit from development over a longer period of time, which often includes several market fluctuations. We look at a project to see how soon we can get our land and amenity costs back. The real value of a big project is that one can build all the amenities and still have a significant amount of land left over. We want to be competitive throughout the life of a project.

Because we are developing one-of-a-kind communities, there really isn't any market research that can be done because there are no communities with which to compare us. And we are not comfortable with research that covers a 20-year time frame. It is really a "now" decision for us. Rather than market research, we engage in market sensitivity. We are intuitive and entrepreneurial and try to induce a market rather than capture one that exists. To use the *Field of Dreams* analogy, "Build it and they will come." We try to introduce a totally new product to a market, not just another old one.

■

Desert developments like the Boulders Resort and Ventana Canyon Resort have assumed roles as land stewards and are seriously committed to the inherent values of the desert. This ethic has played an integral role in the success of these communities.

ment that transformed a potential problem into a marketing advantage.

Other potential development problems in coastal areas include water availability; water quality in adjacent rivers, lakes, streams, or the ocean; and hurricane evacuation.

Special Considerations for Desert Sites

The elemental harshness and solitude of the Southwest desert landscape presents a formidable challenge for resort developers. In particular, water, a limited resource throughout much of the western United States, is costly and often must be pumped from great distances. Further, the acquisition of water rights is a difficult process.

In addition to water availability and access issues, the desert landscape raises concerns about drainage. Deserts are not simply flat wastelands that lend themselves to development. The desert floor is made up of intricate networks of drainage beds that may remain dry for months but become pathways for flash floods after a rainfall or mountain snowmelt. The desert's parched soils are easily saturated with rain and shed large proportions of groundwater along the paths of least resistance, the seemingly innocuous dry river beds. Thus, a proposed desert development plan requires careful analysis of natural drainage systems. At Sun City Las Vegas, for example, the steeply sloped desert site was traversed by numerous ephemeral desert washes with a combined stormwater runoff in excess of 6,100 cubic feet per second. Through extensive planning with local agencies and negotiation with adjoining landowners, the developer made provision to distribute the stormflow into eight separate channels that convey local and regional stormflows into drainage courses that double as golf course fairways, regional parks, greenbelts, and enhanced natural washes. The drainage system encompasses only one hardscape channel.

The need for a golf course in today's desert resorts is nearly a given, even with limited water availability. While strategically angled fairways might minimize water con-

sumption, golf course operation costs are considerably higher in desert environments due to limited water resources. Desert Highlands, an environmentally sensitive golf community outside Scottsdale, Arizona, solved its water problem by building a sewage treatment plant on community land and donating the facility to the city of Scottsdale (see feature box on page 123). In return, Scottsdale granted Desert Highlands the effluent rights to the facility, including rights for any future develop-

The Lakes Country Club in Palm Desert California. The Sunrise Company has developed a series of undulating lakes that creates the atmosphere of an oasis in the desert.

ments. These rights will become increasingly valuable over time. To be certain, the transaction has created a solid relationship between the city of Scottsdale and Desert Highlands.

Closely related to water availability is the desert's plant ecology. The landscape plans for desert resorts can follow one of several approaches ranging from careful preservation of the existing desert ecosystem to complete transformation of the landscape into an oasis in the desert. For example, indigenous plants require significantly less water than nonindigenous species while native species are durable, require less attention, and stabilize soils against erosion. In addition, xeriscaping (using indigenous species in landscaping) is a landscaping approach that reinforces the natural equilibrium of the ecological system. Of late, xeriscaping has become an integral aspect of highly successful developments that focus on the uniqueness of the desert, particularly its "moonscape," harsh vistas, and diverse ecology. Developments such as Desert Highlands, the Boulders, Ventana Canyon Resort, and Sun City Las Vegas have all assumed roles as land stewards seriously committed to the inherent values of the desert. In particular, by providing housing designs that complement the desert environment and selecting high-quality desert landscaping in common areas, Sun City Las Vegas has encouraged low-water-consuming residential development that requires only 50.7 percent of the local per dwelling unit water demand. A majority of residents at Sun City have installed desert landscaping on a totally voluntary basis.

Coupled with the importance of environmentally responsible development is the role of design integrity. Because the topography of the desert suggests a reduced-height profile, developments generally should deemphasize structures. For example, Ventana Canyon Resort, a resort and recreational community outside Scottsdale, reflects the values and proportions of the surrounding hills. The resort's low-rise hotel at the base of the rugged Sonoran foothills affords views of the saguaro cactus for-

ests and surrounding mountains without competing for attention. The visual mass of the hotel is tamed by the alternating setbacks of the top-story rooms while ribbed, vertical columns displace the structure's bulk. The facade's local aggregates blend with the soft hues and rugged texture of the surrounding foothills and desert.

The Boulders, near Scottsdale, followed a plan that disturbed as few significant plants and land features as possible. In fact, the designer who sited the casitas—which are located for optimum views of the desert and genuine privacy—lived for months in a tent in the desert to develop a sense for the local environment and its landforms. The use of natural colors and textures in the casitas helps integrate the buildings with the desert. As a result, the resort is positioned as a peaceful and unspoiled hideaway.

While xeriscaping and indigenous landscaping represent important approaches to desert resort planning, many desert resorts completely transform the desert landscape. Clearly, any resort that includes a golf course must necessarily take steps to make the golf course viable, but many resorts go beyond simple accommodation of an amenity to create a seemingly magical oasis that includes lakes, green open spaces, 72-hole golf courses, luxurious country clubs, and elegant homes with green lawns. And many of these projects have been extremely successful. Projects such as the Vintage Club and the Lakes Country Club, near Palm Desert, California, feature verdant, expansive golf courses and open spaces, acres of linked lakes separated by spill falls, and magnificent clubhouses. Built in the mid-1980s, the Lakes successfully tapped a high-end market in the Palm Desert/ Indian Wells resort area, which is home to over 60 country club complexes. Single- and multifamily houses sold at a premium that covered costly operational expenses (now transferred to the homeowners' association). Instead of capitalizing on the values of the desert, these projects have created a perceived paradise in the form of an idyllic landscape for a high-end niche market.

Desert Highlands in Scottsdale, Arizona, is an upscale, gated golf course community developed by Highlands Development Company, whose principals were Lyle Anderson, Richard Bailey, and James Bartlett. The community was the first of its type in Arizona and, as of the early 1980s, one of only a few such developments in the Southwest. Widely known and respected in the recreational development community for its high quality, Jack Nicklaus-designed golf course, and ecologically sensitive development of a steeply sloped desert site, Desert Highlands was also the first project to be developed under the city of Scottsdale's hillside development ordinance. The project has created a standard of quality and respect for the natural environment that has become the prototype for subsequent projects in desert hillside settings.

The development started with a clear concept and a site perfectly suited to the marketing opportunity identified by the developers. Located in affluent north Scottsdale, the south slope of Pinnacle Peak is one of the most prominent and picturesque formations in the Sonora Desert's McDowell Mountains. Before its development, the site was characterized by lush desert vegetation interspersed with meandering sand washes and dramatic rock formations. Views from the mountain look westward to the setting sun and the lights of Scottsdale and Phoenix.

Originally conceived as an 860-acre planned residential recreational community that would accommodate 860 units, Desert Highlands counts about 600 dwellings. An 18-hole golf course and six amenity areas are carefully integrated into the project. The amenity areas include a series of neighborhood parks and gardens and four tennis court sites that feature hard courts, clay courts, and grass courts. To create valuable nonfairway frontage

Desert Highlands in Scottsdale, Arizona, is an upscale, gated golf community widely known for its ecologically sensitive development and success as a recreational community. The Jack Nicklaus golf course preserves the natural features of the desert landscape by including rock formations, limiting grassed areas, and providing for flash-flood streambeds. By working closely with the city of Scottsdale, the owners constructed a wastewater treatment plant on site and donated it to the city; the city in turn promised future effluent rights to the project, including effluent created by adjoining projects in the future.

A specialist in clubhouse architecture, William Zmistowsky designed a top-quality clubhouse at a modest size of around 20,000 square feet. A decision was made to invest in a relatively small, environmentally sensitive clubhouse design that seemed to evolve organically from existing rock formations, rather than in a more typically sized clubhouse of 45,000 square feet. The decision reduced upfront infrastructure costs while still achieving a high-quality building and amenity.

lots, the plan scattered the amenity areas throughout the neighborhoods.

Planning and Design

To build with minimal impact on the fragile desert ecology, the design team, which included Gage Davis Associates, Taliesin Associates, and William Zmistowski & Associates, undertook detailed environmental studies and mapping. In compliance with the hillside ordinance, the team developed vegetation, geology, soils, slope, and drainage overlays to determine the least intrusive and least costly methods of siting building parcels, circulation systems, the golf corridor, and amenity locations.

The design team's plan allowed over 50 percent of the property to be retained in natural open space, thus protecting existing plant communities and animal habitats. In addition, the plan aligned with the topography and around natural features; provided stringent siting, architectural, and landscape architectural design guidelines; and defined highly specific building envelopes for each residence. The building envelope was defined as an area not exceeding 50 percent of the lot as determined mutually by the owner and the design review committee. No more than half the building envelope could be altered in connection with building. In addition, the plan called for the preservation and provision of native desert vegetation. A projectwide transplant program succeeded in reestablishing over 1,700 saguaros, hundreds of palo verdes, and thousands of smaller cacti and desert shrubs.

Desert Highlands provides an innovative design solution to the Southwest's ever-present water usage problem. First, by working closely with the city of Scottsdale, the developer ensured annexation of the community and thereby a water supply but also agreed to water usage monitoring, especially in view of the needs of the 18-hole golf course. Second and more important, the development constructed an on-site wastewater treatment plant and donated it to the city of Scottsdale; the city in turn promised future effluent rights to the project, including rights to effluent created by adjoining projects. The agreement ensured an adequate supply of water to irrigate the golf course and amenity areas for the foreseeable future.

In keeping with water conservation goals, homeowners at Desert Highlands received a list of plants approved for the Sonora Desert environment. This list outlawed high-water-consuming plants, encouraged arid land plantings, and discouraged grass. An important by-product of the plant list was the discouragement of fast-growing, pollen-producing plants and grasses, providing relief to allergy sufferers.

The golf course and club were carefully sited and developed so as to preserve as much of the natural desert landscape as possible. The golf course, one of the first courses designed by Jack Nicklaus, was innovative for its time in that it incorporated desert plants and rock formations, limited the extent of grassed areas, used revegetation techniques, and kept the number of irrigated acres to 85. The course's grading plan allows irrigation water to remain within the fairways without producing an adverse impact on adjacent desert flora. The few water features are located only where water naturally accumulates in wet seasons.

William Zmistowsky, a specialist in clubhouse architecture, designed a top-quality clubhouse at a modest 20,000 square feet. The intentionally small, environmentally sensitive design seemed to evolve organically from the existing rock formations and stands in sharp contrast to a typically sized clubhouse (45,000 square feet). The clubhouse design reduced upfront infrastructure costs while still achieving a high-quality building and amenity.

Project Sales/Financial Results

The Desert Highlands project was conceived by its developers in 1980, with the Bass brothers of Fort Worth, Texas, as a financial partner. The developers invested approximately $50 million in land, infrastructure, amenities (including the 18-hole golf course and clubhouse), and all soft costs (including the initial planning studies). Residential building sites became available to prospective buyers in spring 1983 at prices ranging from $125,000 to $250,000 for a one-half- to one-acre site.

In the first few years, the first 468 lots sold out, with prices by 1985 exceeding $625,000 per lot. At the close of the first year alone, land sales accounted for approximately $39 million, making Desert Highlands one of the most financially successful land developments of its time. Although prices dropped during the recession at the end of the 1980s, they have since recovered strongly.

Most lots sold on terms secured with notes. To accelerate the pace of lot sales, buyers had the option of borrowing through the project. They signed a note that required them to pay for the lot over a specific term, normally ten years, at a specific interest rate. The notes receivable, together with improved inventory, provided the security for the refinancing of the project in spring 1994.

The first phases of the project consisted primarily of single-family houses, with approximately 200 homes built on the 468 lots sold as of 1995. In addition, Desert Highlands sold four remaining development parcels to separate entities. Except for one parcel, which was originally zoned for 59 units and is undergoing subdivision for low-density single-family units, the other parcels were developed by both an entity related to the developer and a nonrelated entity. Although the original plan for these other parcels called for a product mix of between 125 and 150 higher-density villas and attached and detached condominiums, the parcels have been subdivided at almost half the originally planned density.

Lessons Learned

Desert Highlands is a trendsetter for sensitive environmental planning on a steeply sloped desert site. The community provides an excellent example of how fragile desert ecosystems can be protected by strict development standards that limit the area available for residences and regulate the native desert vegetation that owners can plant.

The sensitive treatment of the desert environment has paid off handsomely. From the clubhouse to the golf course to the controls on lot siting, it is the high quality of Desert Highlands that has been largely responsible for the project's financial success. Buyers and owners responded favorably to the various design principles and restrictions. They understood that sensitive treatment of the environment and high-quality design can enhance the value of both their property and the community as a whole. After the initial sales of lots began exceeding projections, the developers increased their investment to provide even higher-quality amenities, such as the clay and grass tennis courts.

The developers have learned that one of the greatest contributions to value in an upscale development is lower density. While the project's advantageous timing cannot be overlooked, the developers firmly believe that they and the homeowners have benefited from a lower-density community environment; if a comparable return can be made on fewer units, risk may be reduced with the need for fewer sales. The homeowner also benefits from the likely appreciation in value that accrues to buyers over the long run.

Regulatory Issues

Before physical planning can begin, the developer needs to evaluate the relevant regulations that might constrain the proposed development. With the benefit of basic community regulatory and political information, the developer should prepare a plan of action for negotiating the development approval process—particularly as relates to the individuals to be dealt with and the issues to be addressed. The plan should identify all the formal permits required by the project—from each of the various federal, state, and local agencies—as well as the estimated time and work needed to obtain each. If well conceived, the developer's strategy can help avoid unpleasant and costly surprises and identify tools to be used in overcoming anticipated opposition. Early on, the developer should undertake studies that specify strategies for mitigating adverse environmental impacts, document beneficial economic and fiscal effects, and accomplish whatever else may be required to address each particular issue and concern.

Public Policy Issues

Although local and state government regulations affecting resort development are generally growing more and more restrictive, communities still evidence considerable variation in their level of regulatory control. Nonetheless, given that much resort development takes place in nonurban locations, both state and local governments are often ill-equipped to regulate new development in a responsible manner. Where planning and zoning controls do not exist, it may become incumbent on the developer to educate the local community about responsible land use practices.

Yet, several state governments are remarkably advanced in their recognition of the benefits of statewide programs for land preservation and economic development involving resort development. For example, Florida's ambitious Preservation 2000 program targets the preservation of sensitive environmental resources through land acquisition and other protection strategies. The state of Washington has facilitated the creation of new resorts in economically disadvantaged regions such as the Columbia River Gorge. Puerto Rico offers a tax incentive program to encourage investment in the development of new and existing resorts. Other precedents abound for an increased state role in guiding and controlling land use in rural areas that offer resort development opportunities.

Several federal government regulations currently affect resort development both directly and indirectly. The deductibility of second-home mortgage interest from federal income taxes (see feature box on page 399), interstate land sales laws (see feature box on page 216), and environmental protection regulations that govern wetlands, endangered species, floodplains, and coastal areas are but a few examples. As a landowner, the federal government also has a potentially significant role to play in the future development and redevelopment of resort real estate. The management of national parks, the relationship between national parks and surrounding communities, and the use of U.S. Forest Service land for recreational pursuits suggest a range of significant opportunities and constraints for future resort development. The federal government is in a unique position to provide guidance and oversight in these areas.

Managing the Approval Process

After completing the regulatory analysis, the developer or developer representative should meet with the appropriate elected and appointed officials to brief them on the proposed project concept and learn first-

At PGA National in Palm Beach Gardens, Florida, the development team worked with the city of Palm Beach Gardens to draft a new zoning district (a planned community district) (PCD) that would allow large-scale projects. To facilitate the approval of individual parcels as detailed plans were completed, PCDs were excepted from future public hearings. All other provisions of planned unit development (PUD) plans were required. This flexibility has allowed for great variation in land planning development regulations, customized to each of the residential neighborhoods.

Development of the Carmel Valley Ranch in Carmel Valley, California, involved a long process. The resort community includes 340 primary and secondary homes, a 100-room resort hotel, an 18-hole golf course, and a 12-court tennis club. Five years of discussion—ranging from community forums to hearings before the county board of supervisors—gave the community an opportunity to influence the nature and intensity of the development. During these meetings, the developer—Landmark Land Company—had to address a variety of important concerns, including the availability of water in a drought-prone area, the impact of additional traffic, and viewshed protection. Landmark agreed to set aside approximately 70 percent of the property as a scenic easement.

hand of their concerns. With this meeting arranged before the project is presented to the community and special interest groups, officials will have an opportunity to express their opinions on the proposal and suggest any revisions. Conceptual approval might be possible at this point, thus justifying more detailed planning.

At PGA National in Palm Beach Gardens, Florida, the development team worked at the outset with the city of Palm Beach Gardens to draft provisions for a new zoning district (a planned community district, or PCD) that would allow for the approval of large-scale projects. To facilitate the approval of individual parcels as detailed plans were completed, the city exempted PCDs from future public hearings but continued to enforce all other provisions of the planned unit development (PUD) ordinance. Palm Beach Gardens's flexible approach to regulation has allowed the city to tailor its land planning development regulations to the needs of individual neighborhoods.

During the PGA National permitting process, the developer dealt with no fewer than 34 local, regional, state, and national agencies with jurisdiction over the project. Indeed, PGA National was the first large-scale community planned and permitted in south Florida following implementation in the mid-1970s of new environmental legislation, including Florida's Local Government Comprehensive Planning Act and Environmental Land Management Act and the federal government's Section 404 of the Clean Water Act. Under

Florida law, PGA was deemed a development of regional impact and, at the same time, became the first Florida development supervised by the Corp of Engineers under federal wetlands protection regulations. By adopting a cooperative approach, the developer was able to secure all required approvals within an unprecedented nine-month period, saving many millions of dollars in potential carrying costs.

Despite a developer's best efforts, a comprehensive resort development proposal may be subject to years of exhaustive study, negotiation, and waiting and require what may often seem an endless process of duplicate steps. The developer must anticipate delays and, in trying to expedite the process, remain respectful of the various participants. The developer should encourage cooperation and take care not to assume an adversarial role. When, however, the developer has exhausted all channels of reasonableness, it might be time to take legal action. Litigation or the threat of it may be required to ensure the exercise of a developer's rights.

Flexibility Concerns

Developing a workable plan and successfully negotiating the potential pitfalls that characterize the approval process requires a precarious balance between short-term objectives and long-range needs.[9] "The word that is most important, from the developer's perspective, is flexibility," says W. Michael Clowdus, a partner in the Denver law firm of Bearman Talesnick & Clowdus Professional Corporation. "Flexibility is important in two ways. First, although the marketing people may say otherwise, no one can know what consumer demand will be next year, much less in ten years. So you need to maintain the flexibility to build and sell what people want to buy. Second, you need flexibility because of the economic climate. There were many projects started in the 1980s with limits on how long the developer would retain control over the project. These developers thought they would reach buildout in six years, but many have barely started to reach that stage even today. So you can have problems in your legal documents with artificial time limits on how fast development will occur."

In addition to ensuring adequate flexibility to deal with ever-changing consumer demand and economic forces, Clowdus says that developers must carefully

---

Ten Ways to Expedite Project Review and Approval

1. *Know what approvals you will need.* Rules and procedures vary widely from one municipality to another and may change frequently. To avoid unpleasant surprises, get the most recent version of every applicable regulation and require the development team to become completely familiar with the appropriate regulations. A further caution is in order. Some permits may depend on others. A planning commission may not be willing to sign off on your project until the local traffic or utilities commission approves it. Plan your schedule and lead times accordingly.

2. *Know the agency's procedures.* How much notice is required for hearings and inspections? How much documentation is required? Some agencies are satisfied with plans and specifications; others require full details, including structural calculations, analyses of traffic capacity, survey notes, and logs of test borings.

3. *Inform yourself about local issues.* Elected officials and published regulations are only part of the story. Hidden agendas—concerns over land development, traffic generation, aesthetics, water quality, requirements for open space, school capacity, or other issues—might affect how the public perceives and evaluates your project.

4. *Make sure every application is as complete as possible before you submit it.* If changes—even negligible changes—are necessary later in the approval process, you should provide detailed, specific information as quickly as possible. Approval boards can become highly suspicious when they learn of changes secondhand.

5. *Make your presentation as comprehensible as possible without compromising technical accuracy.* This requirement may be harder than it sounds. An accurate discussion of air quality, for example, may lead into a discussion of methods for predicting concentrations of pollutants and various models of emissions and dispersion. Your audience is probably unprepared to follow such a technical argument. Revise and rehearse your presentation until you are sure your message is comprehensible.

6. *Whenever possible, use graphics to make your points.* You may have an inch-thick stack of tables and analyses to prove that your contingency traffic plans will protect local motorists during construction, but the review board may never consult the information. Presenting the same data on a large map with clear overlays can make the information instantly and easily understandable.

7. *Disarm mistrust by cultivating a reputation for openness.* Be candid and answer questions honestly—even if the answers mean "bad news" for the approval board. Members will get the information anyway, and you will benefit over the long run if you are the source.

8. *Consider the regulators' point of view.* Members of review boards and regulatory agencies have their own orientation and mandate, which determine how they regard your project and plan. By understanding an agency's position and rationale, you may be able to avoid unnecessary confrontations.

9. *Before making any formal submission, speak informally with those involved in the review.* Make a point of letting them know what you are doing, and learn everything you can about their concerns and what they expect. They will appreciate this courtesy and be much more disposed to viewing your project favorably if they have a chance to discuss it with you informally beforehand.

10. *Finally, get whatever expert help you need.* Seek out the professional experts—engineers, planners, construction managers, environmental specialists, and lawyers—who understand what you are trying to do and can put your project in the best possible light. Include on your team experienced and credible local spokespersons who know the local authorities and understand the local political dynamics.

Source: Peter Salwen, "Shepherding Large Projects through Reviews," *Urban Land*, July 1988, p. 13.

■

examine the legal issues surrounding the resort's relationship with its local government and its approach to private covenants with property owners. Both areas, he explains, can pose problems for unwary multiuse resort developers. "When you're dealing with government, you must go through zoning and subdivision approval. Typically, you get what's commonly called planned unit development, which is a topic that's gigantic in and of itself," he advises. Approval to develop and operate a particular type of resort property usually boils down to a political decision that depends on the shifting political climate of a community, Clowdus argues. For example, he represented a small timeshare development that successfully opened in Aspen, Colorado, in 1984. "If I were to go in there now with the same proposal, I imagine they wouldn't be able to stop laughing," he says. The pitfall facing the developer revolves around the crucial point of obtaining long-range approval to develop future properties that will meet the resort's needs years after the initial development proposal is approved.

"The developer must have a vested right to go forth with the project," Clowdus contends. "Governments usually want to know how a development fits in with everything else in the community, so there's pressure on the developer to be more specific than you want to be about your plans for the future." Failing to lock in a certain level of flexibility at the project's inception can inhibit profitable development years in the future.

Uniform Common Interest Ownership Act

Another potential problem pertains to how states regulate the application of covenants and other owners' rights issues.[10] Colorado, along with about a dozen other states, has adopted the Uniform Common Interest Ownership Act, known among attorneys as the UCIOA, to establish a more universal set of rules for private covenants. "In UCIOA states, there are some difficult problems for large, multiuse projects," Clowdus reports. Under the UCIOA, developers must state the total number of units to be built in the resort community and establish recorded declarations of any restrictions on use or occupancy. "There's no rational reason to have those restrictions in one set of recorded documents, so that's a problem," Clowdus asserts.

Under the UCIOA, the developer must also set forth in detail future development rights. This requirement poses obvious problems for developers unable to predict growth patterns and other factors influencing future decisions on what property type(s) to build: timeshare units, residential homes, townhouses, hotel rooms, or other vacation properties. "You must reserve these rights before you know what problems you will be addressing," Clowdus cautions. For example, the UCIOA requires the original developer to set specific limits on where sales and marketing offices may be located within the development. Yet, plans may call for bringing in six or more subdevelopers to buy land for multiuse developments around the resort's common golf course. "Each developer will want his own sales office, so how will you

know ahead of time where they will go?" Clowdus asks.

When Vail Associates in Colorado was considering a new development near the existing Beaver Creek resort, the firm realized that the UCIOA restrictions Clowdus finds objectionable would render their project unworkable. Fortunately, Clowdus reports, "They were able to get exemptions for larger projects, which are clearly for mixed use. That needs to be the trend, because the UCIOA is too restrictive for projects with a mix of uses . . . where varied uses need to evolve, and units must be built over several years."

To John McCabe, legal counsel and legislative director of the National Conference of Commissioners on Uniform State Laws, which promulgated the UCIOA in 1982 and works for its passage by state legislators, the act would, if adopted by all 50 states, benefit national developers by imposing a single set of restrictions. Under the current legal system, mixed-use resort projects are subject to a nearly endless range of legal requirements imposed by both states and individual municipalities. "UCIOA essentially is a single act under which you can organize any common-interest community," McCabe explains. Its scope extends to creation, management, and termination of such a community and point-of-sale consumer protection, including warranties, recision rights, and conversion rights.

To McCabe, "Even in mixed-use resorts, the availability of comprehensive legislation is a boon. If you're doing a mixed-use operation, you want to do different things to different parts of a complex of real estate and the more problems you have creating the project. Relying on the skill of your lawyers to correctly and accurately divide property into its proper forms and make sure it carries forward is a daunting task. The better law you have, the better off you are."

Site Planning Process

Site planning and design involves a process that transforms the project from concept to reality. The process typically involves a methodical sequence that is usually divided into three incremental stages: the concept plan, the preliminary plan, and the final plan. Each stage produces a master plan that becomes an evolving foundation as the project develops. Limiting parameters—whether environmental, legislative, political, or otherwise—are often major forces that influence the design and development process. For this reason, the stages are organized in a way that allows considerations from different disciplines to be synthesized in an appropriate sequence.

The developer and planner of a resort community should examine a variety of alternative primary layout schemes to ascertain which options will produce the best and most productive plan. Edward D. Stone, Jr., president of the planning firm Edward D. Stone, Jr., and Associates (EDSA), suggests the formulation and analysis of at least three serious site plan alternatives.

Haig Point, Daufuskie, South Carolina. To preserve the culture and history of the Low Country, the Haig Point Lighthouse was restored and now serves as an intimate guesthouse and private dining room. The lighthouse was recently listed on the National Register of Historic Places.

Photo courtesy of EDSA

Planning the project layout is an ongoing process that requires the synthesis of many variables and calls for a large measure of flexibility. The three-stage process (concept, preliminary, and final plan stages) involves the collection and analysis of detailed information about the site, the identification and evaluation of alternatives based on programming and feasibility analysis, and the selection and refinement of a preferred alternative among the several alternatives studied in the initial stages. Highly interdependent, these activities are normally undertaken in several cycles during each stage.

It is important to note, however, that because each project is unique, the planning process must be tailored to site-specific needs. Variations occur according to the environmental risks involved, political issues, phasing considerations, and other issues. A well-drained and relatively flat project site, for example, does not require the same level of attention as a mountainside that needs to be analyzed to determine what, if anything, can be built on it. Moreover, for some project proposals, portions of the proposal might be in the concept stage while another portion of the proposal is in the final stage. Finally, the terms "concept plan," "preliminary plan," and "final plan" are not universal to all developers but rather are general terms that many developers and planners use.

Concept Planning

Concept planning involves collecting and evaluating information about the site to guide an understanding of the site's development potential for a particular resort type. It deals with site-specific issues at the broadest possible level. Often conducted before committing to purchase a site, concept planning explores opportunities as well as constraints. The product of concept planning is a diagram of the site—or concept plan—that schematically depicts generalized land use areas and major road alignments.

Resort and recreational communities generally place substantial emphasis on the conceptual planning stage as a means of properly analyzing risk. One reason is that resort and recreational communities tend to be built in environmentally sensitive areas. Furthermore, the rules and procedures associated with the permitting process have become increasingly stringent. As a result, developers must invest substantial upfront capital during the concept plan stage for information and analysis of site-specific risks, especially environmental conditions—such as an endangered species habitat—that may make development extremely difficult or even infeasible. For instance, determining during the conceptual planning stage whether the geology and slope of a mountain is suitable for building can dramatically affect the value of the land as well as the project's potential profit margin.

A detailed concept plan should include the following:

- a written program that conveys the vision of the project. The program should outline architectural themes, seasonal uses of amenities, and recreational activities.
- a graphic depiction of the project's general land uses. Often "bubble" diagrams identify locations for different land uses and include a rough estimate of the number and size of housing or lodging units.
- an analysis of land resources based on a written explanation of the land's assets and liabilities.
- a market analysis that indicates demographic, psychographic, and sociographic trends.
- an economic analysis that outlines rough costs and expenses as well as a financing strategy.

It is essential that the sponsors of the proposed project identify all local, state, and federal regulatory agencies and their particular requirements for submissions and reviews. Regulations that directly affect the project's schedule can often be an important consideration in evaluating alternatives.

A comprehensive database of physical land constraints should be completed by the end of the concept plan stage. The project team should always seek existing data from local sources before engaging teams to produce site-specific geophysical and other data for the property. Often, information about the site is available from municipal agencies, public libraries, planning staffs, public works and building departments, utility companies, state highway departments, county offices, and local engineering firms. A data search should generally yield the following: topographic maps, soil surveys, soil borings, percolation tests, and environmental assessments for other projects in the area.

Tax assessment offices and recorded deeds are sources of information on easements, rights-of-way, and covenants. The telephone company or the electric utility may contract periodically with a major engineering firm for controlled aerial photographs. Identifying existing

data that cover the target site and its surroundings can be a great time and money saver. In general, a planning/engineering firm that has extensive experience in the jurisdiction can greatly facilitate the data-gathering process.

Concept planning presents the developer with the first opportunity to test several specific development programs for the site under consideration. By the end of the concept planning stage, the development team should articulate the optimum plan for the site based on an understanding of the market, regulatory constraints and requirements, and a determination of project feasibility. The plan should include information about the type and use of amenities, the character of the project, residential and nonresidential land uses to be accommodated on the site, and functional relationships among the site's various land uses. Clearly, the plan should define the developer's values and intentions. Because sev-

An artist's rendering of the basic plan for Windsor, a 412-acre community in Vero Beach, Florida, that features an ocean-front setting, an 18-hole golf course, two polo fields, and a neotraditional village design.

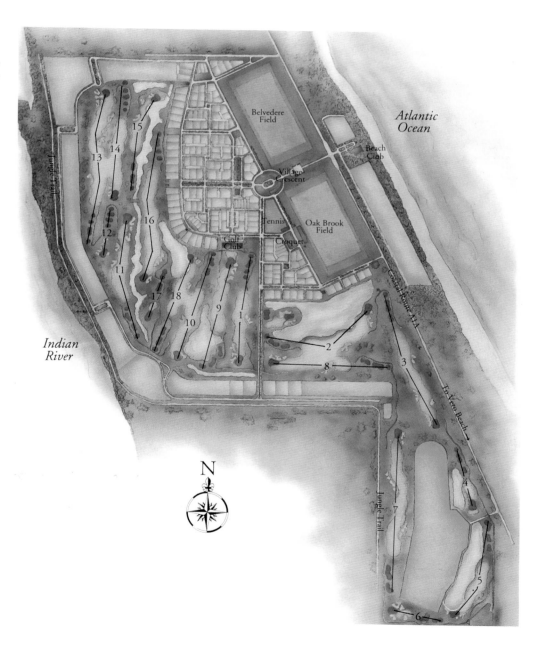

eral alternative development programs often need to be considered, several concept plans should be tested to determine whether the program can be effectively accommodated on the land.

Although there is no formal requirement for such a step, a preapplication conference with local officials during the concept planning phase is generally a prudent move. Successful developers typically meet with selected local officials as early as possible to establish a working dialogue so that they can keep surprises to a minimum. In addition, developers should generally review a range of development options for the site during a town meeting to develop a sense of the community's receptivity to various alternatives. Importantly, the developer gains insight into what type of community resistance may arise and how to respond to it.

Profile and Comments: James R. Bartlett

James R. Bartlett
President
Highlands Management Group
Scottsdale, Arizona

Since 1985, Jim Bartlett has been involved in the development and management of Forest Highlands, a 657-acre residential community near Flagstaff, Arizona. The project's centerpiece, an 18-hole championship golf course designed by Tom Weiskopf and Jay Morrish, opened in July 1988 and, during the past four years, has been ranked among the nation's top 50 golf courses in Golf Digest's *biennial ranking. In 1992, Bartlett joined with investor Richard Rainwater to acquire Mira Vista, a golf course community in Fort Worth, Texas. Since 1994, Bartlett has been involved in the development of the Highlands, a 1,200-acre single-family residential community in Breckenridge, Colorado. Bartlett's partner in all of these projects has been Nick J. Hackstock. Bartlett and Hackstock do business as the Highlands Management Group.*

Jim Bartlett began his career as a management consultant for Touche, Ross and Company in Denver, Colorado. In 1970, he joined Vail Associates, owner/operator of the Vail Mountain Resort in Colorado, where he served first as vice president of finance and subsequently executive vice president of operations. During his tenure, he was closely involved in the acquisition and planning of the Beaver Creek Resort.

After leaving Vail Associates in 1977, Bartlett became an investment adviser to Bass Brothers Enterprises of Fort Worth, Texas. He oversaw the finance, marketing, and administration of the development of the Singletree Golf Club and Resort community near Vail. In 1981, Bartlett became managing partner of the Highlands Development Company, the developer of Desert Highlands in Scottsdale, Arizona. Bartlett is a graduate of DePauw University and the Stanford University Graduate School of Business.

Success in community development, like success in other areas of real estate development, generally requires a clear concept for the development at the outset. Projects with "fuzzy" concepts frequently don't make it except under the very strongest market conditions. Successful developers in virtually every real estate segment generally start with a clear concept of what they want to do. They may make revisions or refinements as the project evolves, but more often than not, the concept survives intact throughout the development process and provides a framework for decision making along the way.

Too often, I have seen developers try to jump into the business and "catch a wave" without any real knowledge of the business. They get into the business with a fuzzy concept for a "smorgasbord" product offering that inevitably fails in all but the very strongest market. There are too many people in the real estate business who don't have the fundamentals at heart. They are in the business less to create than they are to make fees and "be a player." These folks pay less attention to the fundamentals, frequently working off a less-than-clear concept. They are looking for a project for which they get financing, because it allows them to "play the game." They are not as concerned with the ultimate success of the project as was the generation of management that was spawned at such projects as Vail or Sea Pines.

There is no single development template that works for community development, however. Each community has to be strongly adapted to its particular market circumstance. It has a lot to do with matching the right piece of property in the right location to a clearly identified market opportunity in the first place.

There is a fine line between building too much and building too little. Incomparable project elements can become either so costly that they exceed the market's ability to pay for them initially or over time, or the sheer combination of the elements becomes excessive. There are problems with doing this. One is that you squander capital. If you try to force real estate fundamentals with the application of investment capital, you can be made to look very foolish and lose a heck of a lot of money. The word that comes to mind is contrive. You can take a development so far that you are literally trying to contrive something. It either doesn't fit in with what is already there, or there is just so much of something that it overwhelms. The result can be a real "mish mash" or, worse, simply a "mess."

Successful developers are the ones who pay the most attention to getting their projects sold out. We have found in the last three or four years that we have been

Typically, the concept plan stage moves into the preliminary planning stage when the physical planning database is complete. The concept plan stage's master plan should include a schematic presentation of land uses. A complete concept plan should allow the developer and planner to determine if the site merits further investment. If so, the developer and planner can then move to the next stage of creating a strategy for phased implementation.

Preliminary Planning

Once the concept plan is established, the project planning team is in a position to identify additional information that must be collected and analyzed. As new information about the site becomes available and alternative preliminary plans are evaluated, the preliminary master plan begins to evolve. By this stage, the project planning team should be able to identify prototypical building footprints for the various land uses under consideration for the site. These building footprints may be refined later as the study of alternative preliminary plans progresses.

During this stage, the planning team

- prepares the preliminary cost estimates for all facilities for review and refinement by the marketing/economic planners;
- updates and refines facility designs with the marketing/economic planners;
- prepares detailed plans of land use areas to allow for continuous physical refinement and financial analysis;
- refines capacity studies of gross acres of developable land and facilities;
- prepares interim projections portraying development alternatives for financial evaluation by the economic planners; and
- prepares preliminary project design guidelines.

Upon completion of these tasks, which evaluate all aspects of site planning, physical design, engineering, architecture, and market and financial conditions, the physical planners proceed with preparation of the preliminary master plan.

Requirements for submission of the preliminary plan for public review vary but often include written documents, site plans, and other graphic information. The list of required documents may include but is not limited to the following:

- a legal description of the site, including ownership;
- a statement of planning objectives for the project;
- a construction schedule;
- quantitative information, including number of housing units, lot sizes, lot coverage and densities, and total amenities and nonresidential construction; and
- any additional market, feasibility, or other studies required by the review body.

Required graphic information may include the following:

- site plans showing existing site conditions;
- proposed lot lines and plot designs;
- maps showing the location and size of all existing and proposed structures and improvements;

Forest Highlands is a golf-oriented second-home community located in a forested highland near Flagstaff, Arizona. The 657-acre project offers 655 single-family lots, including 515 lots that are approximately one-half acre in size and distributed around the golf course, plus 140 cottage lots that are clustered around the clubouse near the center of the site.

more cautious about pricing so that we can keep our absorption rates up. Over the years, we have tended to underestimate the importance of absorption—how many lots you sell versus price. If we try to charge too much for lots, it inevitably comes at the expense of absorption, a concept we all learned in Econ 101.

The analogy I have used from time to time is that of flying an airplane. Absorption is like flight speed. You feel a lot more comfortable if you can keep the speed up than if you are going slowly and trimming the treetops. This is most evident in projects that are fundamentally unsound, where the numbers don't make sense, and the only way that they do make sense is to push the price. The further you push up the price, the lower the absorption. To continue the analogy further, ultimately you have a stalled airplane that crashes into a mountain. ∎

- maps showing the location and size of all areas to be reserved as common open space, developed as recreational facilities, or allocated to other uses;
- a general landscape plan, which may include the proposed treatment of the development's perimeter; and
- any additional information regarding adjacent areas that might assist in the evaluation of the proposed project's impact.

Typically, local officials do not require specific building information until submission of the final site plans or building plans. Developers who submit detailed building information before it is required run the risk of limiting their flexibility to alter plans and adapt to changing market conditions.

The local planning commission normally reviews the preliminary plan, often under a time limit imposed by ordinance. During this period, staff members may confer with the developer to clarify matters or to request additional material.

The developer has an opportunity to make a formal presentation about the project at a hearing before the planning commission. If a development is to be phased, as most resort projects are, the developer should submit a preliminary development plan for the first phase. As a part of the hearing, the public is entitled to make comments—both favorable and unfavorable—about the project. The commission then approves, approves with conditions, or denies the development plan. More often than not, it grants conditional approval and requires the applicant to change or modify the proposal before granting final approval. In the case of a denial, the applicant usually has the right to appeal the decision.

Deering Bay south of Miami on Biscayne Bay is surrounded on three sides by "protected" land and bay. The developers were faced with the challenge of integrating the natural features of the bayfront with a luxurious golf and condominium community. With only 220 acres to work with and strict building and density restrictions set forth by Dade County, the project was designed as a village, with the majority of the residences and amenities clustered together, giving residents access to all areas either on foot or by golf cart.

After the preliminary development plan is approved, the developer must submit a final development plan within a specified period. If the developer fails to meet the deadline, the planning commission usually revokes its preliminary approval. In fact, if within a specified time a developer has not moved toward completion of the final development plan for the phase under consideration, the planning commission can in some cases nullify and void all previous approvals. In addition, in the case of a zoning variance, it too can be withdrawn, causing the zoning to revert to the original class.

Final Planning

The major difference between preliminary and final plans is the required level of detail. Drawings that might have been presented in schematic form in the preliminary submission must be engineered for the final master plan. Site plans must be sufficiently detailed for legal recording, and any other graphic information, such as landscape plans, must also be submitted in final form. Legal documents required for establishing a community association or dedicating public land may also be required.

The final plan is normally submitted to the planning commission, which may issue another staff report documenting compliance with the preliminary plan and any conditions of preliminary approval. Because approval of the final plan usually requires legislative action related to acceptance of dedicated properties or approval and recording of site plans, responsibility for the grant of final approval typically rests with the city council or other local legislative body. Following approval of the final plan, the developer must obtain any other necessary administrative approvals. With the issuance of building

The plan for Horseshoe Bay Resort in Texas, a 4,500-acre multiuse resort community.

In 1993, recognition of the need for better movement systems in resort communities prompted ULI members William R. Eager of TDA Associates in Seattle and Adam Krivatsy of International Tourism and Resort Advisors (INTRA) to undertake a survey of developers and operators of 65 major destination resort communities in the United States. Many of the resorts were 20 to 30 years old. Survey results indicated that the average length of stay at destination resorts is 5.42 days, with stays at ski resorts averaging nearly a day longer. The average resort hosts 7,031 guests and relies on 1,087 employees, representing an average daytime population of 8,118.

The study also found that resort guests spend 39 percent of their waking hours moving about. More than one-third of this time is devoted to sightseeing (on foot). Guests divide the rest of their time equally between browsing (on foot) and taking tours to nearby attractions (by vehicle, vessel, bicycle, or horseback). On average, guests spend more than 3.5 hours each day walking about and 1.7 hours enjoying excursions. The figures point to a 20 percent increase over the past two decades in time spent in these activities.

As the stationary mode of vacation gives way to more mobile stays, the number of person trips increases, and the need for transportation becomes more pronounced. The most frequent transportation problems cited by resort operators, along with the most successful solutions, are listed below.

Common Problems
- The resort was not planned to accommodate transportation.
- The road system suffers from inadequate capacity.
- Service/delivery traffic causes bottlenecks.
- Transportation services provided by concessionaires are not sufficiently controlled.
- Public utilities commission regulations limit options for devising the most desirable transportation.
- The disincentives to driving are inefficient.
- Guests do not understand the transportation options that are available to them.
- Resorts do not provide off-site employee parking.
- The cost of shuttle service to off-site parking is high.

Popular Solutions
- Introduce a flexible, personalized transport system.
- Discourage use of private cars and provide an internal transport system.
- Regulate deliveries; provide "service alleys."
- Initiate customer surveys; adjust service accordingly.
- Lobby for amendment of regulations on the basis of survey data.
- Introduce appropriate parking policy (fees).
- Provide maps and handouts in the rooms and in an early orientation at the check-in counter.
- Provide off-site parking or arrange for vanpools.

The Caribbean Beach Resort, Lake Buena Vista, Florida, uses an extensive trail system as a primary amenity and to connect its 2,000 rooms.

- Subsidize the cost of service through on-site parking fees.

In response to visitors' growing interest in walking, most resorts have expanded their trail systems. Three-quarters of the surveyed resorts have developed walking trails while 80 percent offer bicycle trails and 78 percent offer bicycle rentals.

Although one-third of the surveyed resorts offer some form of transportation system within the resort, only one-quarter of the systems provide free transportation. (Another 8 percent offer free transportation to senior citizens.) More than three-quarters of the resorts offer excursions to regional visitor destinations at some cost.

The best internal resort transportation systems provide highly personalized transportation and reliable schedules. Such systems can reduce traffic congestion and increase safety within a resort. Experience has shown that all-weather vehicles staffed by trained, hospitable drivers make for good public relations.

Parking is a land-eating monster and an environmental liability at many resorts. The survey found that, to accommodate full occupancy, most operators must provide 100 to 120 parking spaces for each 100 rooms in the resort. (The figures include parking for overnight guests, day visitors, and employees.) Accommodated on the surface, such a large volume of parking can disrupt both the resort operation and the resort environment. At higher development intensities, extensive surface parking wastes valuable land resources.

Clearly, parking must be planned as an integrated system for maximum efficiency and must be consciously managed as a function of land values. Few successful resort developers can afford to devote extensive acreage to surface parking. As land values escalate, however, the construction of strategically located parking structures becomes increasingly feasible.

Resort managers caution their peers: "Don't involve the community in running transportation services! Such involvement can be costly." (The needs of community residents differ from those of resort guests.) Other golden nuggets include the following:

- Provide opportunities for walking, bicycling, and cross-country skiing in a pleasant environment.
- Offer modes of transportation that differ from those that guests use at home and that enhance the character of the resort.
- Whenever possible, build on-site parking structures rather than off-site lots served by a shuttle service.
- Integrate car rental facilities into the resort layout and operation and make hourly rentals available to guests.
- Whenever possible, plan for an internal shuttle system that serves all lodging facilities and attractions within the resort.
- Ensure that the transportation system has an appropriate identity and character.

Resort developers, owners, and managers should stay abreast of guests' needs at all times. They need to strive for sufficient flexibility to accommodate peak loads and cut back as needed. In addition, they should monitor parking as both an important part of the transportation system and a land use within the context of prudent real estate management and regularly review facilities requirements.

Source: Adapted from Adam Krivatsy, "Transportation at Resort Communities," *Urban Land*, August 1994, pp. 12–15. ■

permits, construction can begin. Failure to undertake construction within a specified period normally results in revocation of the approval.

Developers should keep in mind that the approval process can often take several years. Therefore, the first phase should be scaled to coincide with market demand at the time construction is likely to proceed. The longer the processing time, the more difficult it is to achieve market objectives.

Often, the developer finds it necessary to change the master plan in response to market shifts or other factors. Sometimes the limits of permitted deviations from the plan are specified; other times they are left to the discretion of public officials. While minor changes usually do not affect the overall integrity of the development and are easily addressed, major changes may force the developer back through the preliminary plan approval process. Developers need to be aware of the local agency's parameters for allowing amendments to the master plan. Unless a change is absolutely necessary, applicants should not deviate from the approved plan.

Transportation Facilities and Utilities

Developers of large multiuse resorts and second-home communities must invariably consider the development of community facilities and infrastructure. It is these elements that support and permit the development of other uses such as homes and hotels. The larger and more complex the resort, the greater are its infrastructure requirements. A community's primary infrastructure elements include transportation and utilities. Civic and institutional facilities such as schools and libraries and services such as police protection and emergency rescue operations may also be required. The need to provide sites for these buildings depends on the availability of such services off site and any existing plans for their future provision. The developer should determine appropriate locations for public buildings within a resort or recreational community during the overall site planning and design process.

Transportation Infrastructure and Services
Resort developers and operators need to ensure ease of access and mobility. They must pay attention to how residents and visitors get to and about the resort and to nearby natural attractions. In addition, they need to design facilities and services that meet peak demand without overspending. The results of a 1993 survey by ULI members William R. Eager and Adam Krivatsy highlight some of the key transportation problems faced by resorts (see feature box on page 136).

Roads and Streets. The internal road and street system is the basic element in any resort transportation plan, and its design often differs from that in primary-home communities in terms of the composition of the streets, layout patterns, street widths, and even the modes of permitted transportation.

Island resorts often offer unusual transportation facilities. Melrose on Daufuskie Island, South Carolina, has a fleet of sleek passenger ferries to transport members from nearby Hilton Head Island. Neighboring Haig Point, on the same island, restricts auto traffic and encourages golf carts and horse-drawn carriages.

For example, at Brays Island Plantation in South Carolina, except for the asphalt entrance road that leads to the sales office, all new roads are unpaved, much like those found on traditional plantations. For Brays Island, the unpaved roads provide an environmental and aesthetic asset that would be unacceptable in most primary-home communities. The project manager spent considerable time in the field to site each mile of the 26 miles of new roads. Civil engineers then surveyed the field stake-out and plotted the roads onto the base map. Before construction, the roads were engineered and staked in the field. The land planners then walked each mile to make final adjustments before clearing began. All utilities are placed underground within the shoulders of the road. Dewees Island, also in South Carolina, goes one step further by using sand-based roads with crushed oyster shells and allowing electric golf carts as the only vehicle type on the island, thereby reducing infrastructure costs and enhancing environmental preservation.

At Sun City Las Vegas, the city of Las Vegas agreed to accept narrower street widths in recognition of the reduced traffic and parking requirements of the community's retirees and active adults. A modification to Nevada's motor vehicle regulations also permitted the use of golf carts for intracommunity transportation in accordance with Sun City's transportation planning requirements. Residents enjoy cart access to all areas of the community without leaving the internal community street system. Specially designed community entrances reduce the speed of vehicles entering the community, and the design of the internal street system discourages use by regional traffic not accustomed to golf carts. In addition, residential garages (two-and-one-half-car capacity) and commercial and recreational facilities are designed to accommodate cart parking.

Resort communities have also pioneered the rediscovery and use of traditional grid street design patterns, as evidenced by the tremendous popularity of Seaside in the panhandle of Florida (see case study on page xx). In this case, the street system creates a pedestrian-friendly environment, a much sought-after but not always successfully achieved quality in many resort settings.

In some cases, portions of the transportation and street network may be public. At Wailea Resort on Maui in Hawaii, the county of Maui owns the main thoroughfares and beach access roads, including paved parking along with the restrooms and beach showers near the beaches. Wailea Resort, however, privately maintains these facilities for use by the public. The arrangement ensures public access to the resort's amenities as well as a consistent standard of maintenance within the resort. Wailea also provides an internal shuttle system that serves its five hotels and all major amenities.

Special Transportation Facilities/Services. Resorts are often on the cutting edge of providing innovative private transportation services. The monorail system at Disney World is especially notable, but examples of more modest systems and services abound. At the Grand Cypress

At the Grand Cypress Resort in Orlando, a turn-of-the-century electric trolley system is used to transport guests throughout the resort.

During the planning process at Sun City Las Vegas, the city of Las Vegas was persuaded to accept narrower streets because of the reduced traffic and parking requirements of retirees and active adults in the community. Pictured is the entry feature to the community.

Resort in Orlando, adjacent to Disney World, the 1,500-acre resort's elongated configuration, which includes extensive hotel and attached/multifamily properties, inspired the developers to create a turn-of-the-century electric trolley system that transports guests throughout the property. Charm is often an important consideration in providing transit services. Beaver Creek and several other winter resorts rely on horse-drawn sleighs for transportation as well as for recreation.

Many resorts also provide special transportation systems for reaching the resort. Dewees Island and Daufuskie Island in South Carolina use passenger ferries to transport visitors to the properties. Spring Island in South Carolina paid for a bridge. And some resorts even provide their own on-site airfields. At Horseshoe Bay Resort in Texas, a lighted airport provides landing aids and complete fuel facilities, 24-hour propeller and jet plane maintenance and service, and hangar facilities. A 6,000-foot runway on a hill overlooking the resort

can handle DC-9s and features one of the more attractive and functional private terminals in the nation. In addition, an on-site people mover serves the airpark. The 3,300-acre Sunriver Lodge and Resort in Sunriver, Oregon, includes a 5,500-foot-long lighted runway. Casa de Campo in the Dominican Republic also includes an airstrip, as do many other resorts.

Utilities

Resort and recreational community developers often face unique challenges in the provision of basic utility services and infrastructure. The principal challenge relates to resort communities' typical siting in areas where municipal water and wastewater systems do not usually exist. In particular, a resort's remote location often makes it infeasible to connect with public water and sewer systems. Therefore, the early planning stages must identify the community's infrastructure requirements and determine how various systems will be accommodated. At the same time, the developer should make every effort to obtain accurate cost estimates.

Water. Water provision is typically the responsibility of a municipality or a special district. Particularly in the West, where long-term availability of water is a politically charged issue, developers must often assist the municipality or special water district in identifying potential water sources. Sometimes suitable sources of groundwater or surface water are available on site. Even then, obtaining the right to use the water may prove difficult. If an off-site source of water is available, the developer may need to subsidize the construction of infrastructure needed to tap the source and transport the water to the site. The associated infrastructure can include wells, reservoirs, storage tanks, and treatment facilities. Particularly if water availability is an issue, the developer will find it advantageous to incorporate water conservation measures into development plans, thereby minimizing long-term water needs.

A central water supply is always preferable to individual wells. As areas develop, however, the water supply and water quality of wells may become undependable. Two or more wells placed near each other can interfere with one another, and saltwater intrusion of wells is a common problem in coastal areas. Small private water companies can often deliver satisfactory service when larger municipal water services are not available; they can also be cost-effective and become profit centers as the community reaches maturity.

When considering extensions of water mains, developers must be aware not only of who pays but also of the legality of the extensions. In general terms, the obligation of a private water company to extend its lines within its franchised territory is undeniable. With nonfranchised companies or those operating outside their franchised territory, however, the obligation is based on the extent of their profession of service. A company denied an application for extension can appeal to the state public utilities commission and, ultimately, to the courts.

Some cases require unusual solutions, and even relatively small resort projects can face daunting challenges when it comes to providing water service. During the 26-room expansion of the Ventana Inn in Big Sur, California, for example, the developers experienced a major challenge in providing water services. One of the unique solutions to developing the inn's environmentally sensitive site was a comprehensive water management and water monitoring program that evolved over a several-year period. The plan provides for conjunctive use from several sources, including wells, streams, and springs, with limits on water quantities that can be drawn from each. A detailed monitoring program measures all major sources and uses of water and requires the compilation of an annual report for submission to the California Coastal Commission.

Wastewater. Two basic alternatives are available for disposing of domestic waterborne wastes: piping the wastes off site to a municipal sewage treatment system or treating and disposing of the wastes on site. From the developer's perspective, public sewer systems are preferable but not always available. The developer's next choice is an on-site, small-scale community system rather than individual on-lot disposal. Such systems mandate a state permit for any discharge of sewage effluents into streams and rivers, and effluents must meet standards for the receiving body of water. In most cases, secondary treatment is a requirement.

At Horseshoe Bay Resort, a 4,500-acre resort community 50 miles west of Austin, Texas, the developers formed a municipal utility district and installed one of the first tertiary sewage treatment plants in Texas as well as one of the first major pressurized sewage collection systems in the United States. The sewage effluent is used to irrigate the resort's golf courses.

At the Grand Cypress Resort in Orlando, the resort donated land for a potable water plant and a county

At Wailea Resort on Maui in Hawaii, the main thoroughfares and beach access roads are owned by the county of Maui, including paved parking, restrooms, and showers near beaches. These facilities, however, are privately maintained by Wailea Resort for use by the public; this arrangement ensures public access to the resort's amenities as well as a consistent standard of maintenance within the resort.

wastewater treatment plant, which were constructed at the developer's expense. The water treatment facility serves not only the resort but other developments in the vicinity as well. The treatment plant's effluent is used for irrigating the resort's 45-hole golf course. The arrangement reflects the resort's respect for local communities' water conservation concerns and provides a safe means of disposing of wastewater.

Sewage disposal by septic tanks and tile fields is generally the least preferable alternative. If, however, the densities are sufficiently low and soils appropriate, individual septic systems may be the most cost-effective choice. Individual on-lot disposal requires a sufficiently large parcel of land for an adequately sized disposal field. The disposal field must slope away from the house and be kept free of trees and shrubbery to permit needed

Horseshoe Bay Resort near Austin, Texas, formed a municipal utility district and installed one of the first tertiary sewage treatment plants in Texas. The 4,500-acre resort includes its own on-site airfield and operates much like a small city.

Stan Kearl

Pirate's Cove is a distinctive residential-marina-resort community located on the Outer Banks of North Carolina. It is one of the largest boating communities in North Carolina offering homesites on deep-water canals and sounds. Although the entire project was designed around an existing canal system and marina foundation, approval was difficult. To develop sensitive land, Pirate's Cove was required to obtain approval from 13 state and federal environmental agencies.

sunlight action. The soil and subsoil types affect both the amount of area needed and the possibility of polluting nearby surface water or wells.

If developers are considering individual septic tanks, they should notify the state board of health and be prepared to conduct percolation tests to determine the final required dimensions of the lots. They should also bear in mind that disposal fields might have to be abandoned after some years, as reconstruction of septic tanks is seldom practical or satisfactory. In any case, proper design and construction are absolutely essential.

Water Amenities and Boating Facilities

Water views and waterfront locations, water-moderated climates, and various shore and water activities appeal to a large number of people, making water amenities critical assets for many resort communities. A site's waterfront and land/water interface can be programmed for a variety of low- to high-intensity uses, including the following:

- Natural Beaches—For natural beaches, the most passive and easily accommodated waterfront uses are sunbathing, swimming, and beachcombing. Natural beaches are a highly marketable amenity for a resort and can be left largely undeveloped, although many require some modification and may carry substantial maintenance requirements. Bath houses and food facilities can be added where appropriate. Complementary activities include snorkeling and scuba diving.
- Open Space/Trails—In areas without natural beaches, such as around many lakes or wetlands, waterfront areas can provide attractive open space for trails and bicycle paths as well as appealing sites for fishing or camping. The trend toward ecotourism makes open space/trails increasingly popular. They can incorporate waterfront environments for observing wildlife and waterfront ecosystems. The Grand Cypress Resort in Orlando created a series of interconnected lakes that emulate the regional geography while retaining runoff, enhancing the visual experience, and allowing for a variety of recreational uses.
- Golf Courses—In some situations, golf courses can be an attractive and sensitive use for waterfront areas. The Pebble Beach Resort and Spanish Bay Resort in Monterey, California, for example, have established themselves among the premier resorts in the United States due in large part to the outstanding oceanfront setting of their world-class golf courses (see case study on page 352). Both Casa de Campo in the Dominican Republic and Kiawah Island in South Carolina are additional examples of resorts with oceanfront golf courses, the latter including ten holes that stretch along the ocean.
- Marinas and Boating Activity—Providing facilities for boating and other marine activities often requires substantial waterfront development, such as the cre-

ation of marinas, although sailboat and windsurfing rentals can often be accommodated with little development. Taken together, boating activities are one of the most popular forms of recreation, and resort environments often offer the best opportunities for boating. (See next section for an extended discussion of marina development.)
- Residential Development—Sensitive residential development of waterfronts generally provides the best balance between ecological preservation and economic return. Waterfront homesites command significant premiums over nonwaterfront sites. Given that residential development can range from high-rise condominiums to single-family homes, the degree of ecological balance varies from project to project.
- Commercial Development—Commercial development makes the most intensive use of a resort's waterfront areas, usually for hotels, retail establishments, and/or restaurants. Many waterfronts are ecologically or otherwise unsuitable for intense commercial development.

Waterfront Design

In water-oriented resort communities, residents and guests want to be near the water and to use it for a variety of recreational activities. At the same time, they demand preservation of the waterfront's beauty and natural qualities to the greatest degree possible. Not surprisingly, use and preservation demands conflict, requiring developers to find adequate solutions. Finding a solution is easier for sites with extensive waterfront areas that afford the opportunity to develop some areas while leaving others untouched.

Two developments—Pelican Bay in Naples, Florida, and Horseshoe Bay Resort in Texas—illustrate two contemporary approaches to two markedly different types of water amenities. Pelican Bay, located directly on the Gulf of Mexico, exemplifies the sensitive use of oceanfront areas. Approximately two-thirds of the development's three-mile beach has been left undeveloped, as have the mangrove estuaries that lie directly inland of the beach. Two boardwalks cross the estuaries to provide access to a portion of the beach for community residents. Beachfront uses include sundecks, lockers and restrooms, and a casual cocktail and dining facility. Sensitively developed multifamily housing and watersports facilities characterize the northern one-third of the beachfront area. While Pelican Bay does not offer a marina, canoe launching sites in the mangrove estuary allow for quiet exploration of this natural amenity and its wildlife.

A lake is the primary water amenity at Horseshoe Bay. Because the developers hold title to the 700 acres of lake bottom fronting the development, they can build up to and into it. With the water in the lake controlled and maintained at a constant level, waterfront residents enjoy their own private boat docks or slips. The resort includes a marina with 300 covered slips, a ship store,

A lake is the primary water amenity at Horseshoe Bay Resort in Texas. The resort includes a 300-slip marina.

and a 28,000-square-foot yacht club with pool, spa, and private beach.

Many resorts offer a variety of waterfront settings. The 2,000-acre Palmetto Dunes on Hilton Head Island in South Carolina, for example, includes three miles of white sand beach along the ocean, a 200-slip marina, and ten miles of navigable lagoons ideal for canoeing, rowing, or fishing.

Types of Boating Facilities

Patterns of watersports and boating activity—fishing, water skiing, sail boarding, canoeing, kayaking, power-boat cruising, sailing, and racing—vary widely with the body of water and its geographic region, climatic differences, and the influence (or absence) of boating traditions. As a result, the type of boating support facility also varies and may accommodate sailboats, windsurfers, canoes, or personal motorized watercraft rented at the beach or stored in dry dock; simple boat launching facilities for small watercraft; small docks for individual homes; touring or sightseeing boats; and/or small to large marinas. For example, at the Sagamore on Lake George in upstate New York, the *Morgan*—the resort's touring vessel—offers sightseeing and dinner cruises. The resort also provides motor-boat rentals, fishing guides, sailboat charters, snorkeling trips, water skiing, and parasailing.

From a resort developer's point of view, the marina is the most challenging type of boating facility to develop. In recent years, amenity-oriented developments have greatly advanced the concept of marinas, which have evolved from typically ramshackle boatyards to luxurious waterfront complexes that can serve as a pivotal recreational amenity in a second-home community or the principal organizing element for an entire resort area. Marinas have become the central features of some well-known resorts, including Harbour Town at Sea Pines on Hilton Head Island, South Carolina.

Marina Site Requirements

Including a marina in a project can greatly complicate the site selection process. While most developers know a good deal about the requirements of land development, they are far less familiar with the special needs of marinas and the complexity of offshore conditions. Accordingly, developers need to recognize that money spent on rigorous analyses of alternative marina sites will probably pay off by preventing crippling problems later in the development process. In particular, a poorly sited facility can complicate the development approval process, result in added development and maintenance costs, and, ultimately, prove unpopular with boaters.

The one site requirement that most clearly separates a marina from other uses is that the facility must offer safe access to a usable body of water. What constitutes "usable water," of course, depends on the anticipated market characteristics and local use patterns. The water access requirements for deep-sea fishing, for example, differ sharply from those for small sailboats, although some marina sites can accommodate a range of boating uses. The St. Lucie River in Stuart, Florida, at the site of Harbour Ridge, for example, is about a mile wide and about an hour away under power from the open ocean; thus, it is suitable for cruising and deep-sea fishing craft as well as for small sailboats and freshwater fishing boats.

Physical site selection variables for a marina can be conveniently divided into two categories: onshore characteristics and offshore characteristics. The basic onshore requirement for a marina is adequate space. The land area should be roughly equal to the water area regardless of facility size. An acre of water can generally be expected to handle from 25 to 65 boats, depending on facility layout and boat size.[11]

If at all possible, the land to accommodate onshore facilities should lie above the floodplain and demonstrate adequate bearing capacity to support construction. Particularly in areas of recent fill, soil characteristics demand careful examination. Where fill operations are proposed, the developer must check the quality of the source material. The developer should also pay careful attention to shoreline conditions. Marina development can exacerbate erosion or sedimentation potential unless the shoreline is stabilized with bulkheads, revetments, or other measures.

Onshore factors for successful marinas do not differ significantly from site factors for any development activity: appropriate access, sufficient space, adequate soil properties, and so on. Most developers, however, are not acquainted with offshore factors and therefore should, upon site selection, solicit the advice of an experienced civil engineer. In fact, the wise developer should consult with such an expert early in the site selection process.

Two key offshore factors to be considered in marina development are water depth and water-level fluctuation. An ideal minimum depth for a marina site is eight feet below the low-water datum. If an offshore site is too shallow, the marina will be unable to accommodate a wide range of craft. Admittedly, basins can be dredged, but the cost of dredging depends largely on the physical and chemical makeup of the bottom material. Extremely deep basins, on the other hand, may not provide adequate protection from wave action or may inhibit proper water circulation. They also limit pier design alternatives.

The variable water levels associated with tides, storm surges, wind and wave action, precipitation, and, in reservoirs, periodic drawdowns clearly pose a threat to marina facilities and equipment. Therefore, feasibility considerations as well as later design and engineering considerations need to account for seasonal wave and wind action; ice's seasonality, thickness, and movements; and various other climatic and topographic factors that could push water levels to extremes. In severe climates, marinas are often designed so that virtually everything can be removed from the water. Finally, a marina needs adequate water flows, without which it will likely face a number of water-quality problems such as stagnation, pollution from runoff or fueling operations, and the accumulation of floating debris.

Planning the Water and Boating Component of a Marina

Boating facilities must relate to the characteristics of the water to which they provide access. The water's extent, connections, recreational value, and other basic traits largely determine potential boat traffic. At the same time, activity at the marina is a function of the character of and access to the facility's landside facilities.

Any successful marina development must carefully mesh water- and land-based program elements. The design criteria should reflect the program's demands as well as the site's capabilities. Based on an analysis of the market, the program should include preliminary determinations of

- expected boat size (length, beam, and draft);
- percentage of sail- and power boats;
- transient slip demand;
- required services;
- cruising versus racing orientation;
- shoreside amenities; and
- seasonal variation in use.

The heart of the marina design problem lies at the land/water interface. Although a marina's basic configuration is usually a function of the site's geography, some sites can accommodate a number of configurations. Adie classifies marinas as offshore, recessed, built-in, and landlocked.[12]

Besides geography, the factors that influence marina configuration are permit requirements, cost, environmental protection, navigational safety, and water circulation. In most jurisdictions, permit requirements increase in direct proportion to the amount of needed dredging and filling. Built-in and landlocked marinas require the most dredging and filling, making them also generally

The marina at Semiahmoo in Blaine, Washington, is located on the spit tip portion of this 800-acre resort. An offshore marina was appropriate for this protected site just off of Semiahmoo Bay on Drayton Harbor. The 296-slip marina is a favorite among cruisers because of the Inn at Semiahmoo, quality dining, and resort facilities. The marina can be expanded to 800 slips.

the most expensive configuration, although the breakwater and special deepwater pier anchorage system requirements for some offshore marinas can be extremely expensive. Where bottom conditions are unsuitable for an offshore configuration, recessed marinas offer the principal advantage of allowing for an economical balance of dredge and fill. Material inland of the original shoreline is dredged and deposited offshore to raise the

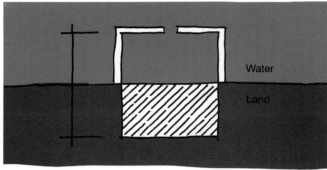

Offshore Marina

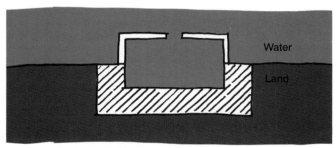

Recessed Marina

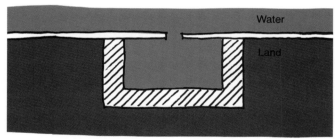

Built-In Marina

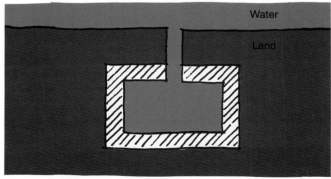

Land-Locked Marina

Basic marina types.

bottom to a suitable level. Alternatively, material dredged beyond the bulkhead line is used to fill and stabilize the upland area for building sites.

On rivers and estuaries, protruding marinas (offshore and recessed) may pose navigational hazards. Built-in and landlocked marinas offer the greatest protection against weather and wave action but may be prone to water stagnation problems. Nonetheless, they provide the best opportunities for locating real estate frontage on moorings while retaining open views to the larger body of water.

Mooring layout is clearly a function not only of the site's constraints and opportunities but also of the expected market. Within the limits of the basin's shape and the marina's market, a number of criteria should govern layout decisions. At the outset, laying out mooring space is similar to designing a parking lot or subdividing land into building lots. In many instances, especially for small or relatively simple marinas, considerations of maximum efficiency govern most design decisions for the water area. But as in parking lot design and subdivision planning, the developer must often couple efficiency with other considerations. Except for perhaps the saltiest boating enthusiasts, endless rows of boats are only marginally more attractive than unrelieved rows of parked cars or identical tract houses.

One of the most important decisions in marina planning—a decision that has implications for mooring layout, use patterns, cost, and maintenance—is the choice between floating or fixed piers. Fixed piers are generally easier and less costly to maintain and are stronger and more stable. Floating piers, on the other hand, are safer in areas with marked water-level fluctuations and permit easier expansion and modification. The appropriate pier type depends primarily on the expected water-level fluctuation at the marina site, the marina budget, and concerns about safety and convenience—which largely relate to user characteristics. Some marinas effectively use a combination of floating and fixed piers.

The major structural elements of a marina—bulkheads, breakwaters, and piles—form the basic framework for piers, slips, and other service facilities. Along with dredging and sometimes locks, these features also account for the major costs in marina construction and operations. Although the design and engineering of structural items is best left to experienced marina engineers, a developer considering a marina as an amenity should have a grasp of the basic issues associated with these critically important elements.

The placement of breakwaters (used to protect a marina from wave action), channel entrances, bulkheads (used to prevent erosion of the shoreline and to provide safe and convenient access to the waterborne parts of the marina), and other marina structures can have significant impacts on existing natural patterns of siltation and erosion. For example, by modifying the existing bottom profile and hydraulic regime, dredging often exacerbates siltation problems. Excessive siltation can prevent needed marina expansion. Maintenance

dredging and disposal to alleviate siltation problems is expensive and inconvenient. Erosion can pose a threat to piles, bulkheads, and other marina structures. Bulkheading can preclude development of a beach area, which, even when small, remains an extremely popular marina amenity. Revetments—bank protections usually made of concrete or riprap that lie at the shoreline's natural angle of repose—are much less expensive than bulkheads and provide superior wave attenuation and a more congenial environment for fish habitat. Thorough analysis of natural hydraulic patterns can help avoid siltation, erosion, and water-quality deterioration. The developer who hires an experienced coastal engineer for this analysis is spending his or her money wisely.

Planning the Land Portion of a Marina

In a resort setting, marinas must be planned to serve more than boaters' needs. Resort marinas often include such facilities as restaurants, a beach, or shops that support other project elements. Marinas that resemble fishing villages more than boatyards—that is, those planned to establish a close relationship between the project's real estate, boats, and the water—are likely to create considerable real estate value. But the greater the diversity of land uses within and around a marina and the closer the relationship between the marina and the residential and lodging elements of a resort, the greater are the potential conflicts between the recreational and industrial aspects of the marina—heavy equipment, paint shops, and service yards that use flammable, toxic, or foul-smelling materials.

The potential conflict between the social and industrial aspects of a marina also affect the layout of roadways, parking areas, and pedestrian circulation ways. Marinas that offer a wide range of service and repair facilities attract and therefore must be able to accommodate a wide range of vehicles. The process of locating a marina parking lot highlights the tradeoff between convenience and real estate economics. In other words,

car storage may not be the best use for valuable waterfront land.

Marina clubhouse design is not unlike clubhouse design for golf or tennis amenities. And boaters, like tennis players, are less likely than other resort facility users to expect a luxurious setting and a high standard of personal service in their recreational facilities. But, as noted, resort marinas often include support facilities that are not necessarily targeted to boaters. A general rule is that 10,000 to 15,000 square feet of clubhouse floor space is required to support 500 slips, depending on the number and extent of clubhouse facilities.[13]

Mountain Amenities and Ski Facilities

Mountain settings provide dramatically different environments for resorts. While ski slopes and related facilities may be the key amenity at a ski resort, many ski resorts are expanding their Nordic facilities while others are seeking to broaden their appeal by offering snowmobile or dogsled rides that take advantage of such nearby attractions as ghost towns and the West's backcountry and wilderness areas. Moreover, spas and health-related facilities are important amenities that have a long history in mountain resorts, especially those associated with natural springs.

Ski resorts in particular can include a relatively large number of collateral development opportunities: resort hotels, second-home communities, vacation condominiums, timeshare projects, and a wide range of supporting retail and entertainment uses. In the late 1960s and early 1970s, whole-unit condominiums were by far the predominant form of ski-area development. Now, standard one-week timeshares or quartershares and other forms of segmented ownership products have expanded many ski resort markets. With proximity to the slopes an important consideration, higher-density housing is common in ski resorts.

Ski Incline at Lake Tahoe offers a dramatic view of the lake and surrounding mountains.

Photo courtesy of Design Workshop Inc.

Given the economics of resort operation, many resorts now offer activities that attract people year round. For example, cross-country ski trails or snowmobile trails make attractive hiking, backpacking, or mountain biking trails in the warm months. Golf courses and tennis courts can also increase the year-round appeal of ski resorts and augment the core skier market.

The aptly named Whitetail Ski Resort and Mountain Biking Center demonstrates the importance of off-season mountain biking to a resort. The resort began in 1991 as a ski facility with few other uses in place, although plans called for eventual golf course and residential development. With the need to generate revenues from its recreational operations, the resort promotes mountain biking as a main draw during the summer. The chairlift service operates on weekends during the summer to transport bikers—and hikers—up the mountain. Whitetail offers numerous events and training programs as well, including a mountain biking summer camp for 12 to 16 year olds. With over 26 miles of dedicated trails on the resort's 1,600 acres, the facility encompasses terrain for novices as well as challenging technical trails for expert riders.

The creation of a mountain bike trail system might at first seem an expensive and daunting undertaking, but a careful review of the terrain may reveal otherwise. Winter Park, Colorado, for example, offers over 500 miles of mountain bike trails that were for the most part already in place. The trails are generally old logging trails, mining trails, and railroad rights-of-way. The resort simply mapped the trails, marked them with signs, and promoted them.

One point to consider with mountain biking, however, is the need to avoid conflict between bikers and hikers. Trails dedicated to one or the other can prevent problems.

Types of Mountain/Ski Resorts

Because of the high costs of developing Alpine skiing facilities, ski areas are much more likely than other re-

sort amenities to be conceived and developed as profit-making ventures that may engage secondarily in real estate development. The real estate in ski-oriented developments may exist as much to support the recreation as the recreation exists to support the real estate, although in recent years skiing has been nearly inseparable from development, especially at larger areas. In 1993–1994, only 36 percent of all North American ski areas engaged in land development.[14] The low average is attributable to the large number of small ski areas targeted to weekend skiers. Larger ski areas, however, are more likely than smaller areas to engage in land development.

Ski-area planner James Branch has developed a typology of ski areas that is useful in considering real estate development issues.[15]

- A Type I resort is a true international destination facility associated with a superb mountain or mountains. It offers a broad array of lodging and real estate options and appeals to a wide range of potential real estate investors, including foreign and corporate investors.
- A Type II resort is similar in scope to a Type I resort but is less established in the marketplace and offers fewer social and cultural opportunities and less diversity. It appeals to a more limited market and tends to cater to ski clubs and other groups.
- A Type III area is a facility that features high-quality skiing but, for a variety of reasons (including insufficient space), offers little in the way of on-site real estate development. It may operate only on weekends or otherwise not cater to destination or overnight skiers. It may aspire to Type II status and thus offer substantial development opportunities.
- A very small ski operation is often operationally marginal and usually operates only on weekends.

Most ski resort-related real estate development occurs in Type I or Type II areas, which generally offer expensive real estate that appeals more to users than to investors. Buyers at Type I resorts tend to be older, more loyal to the area, more family-oriented, and less inclined to rent out their units. The probable buyers at Type II resorts are more likely to be interested in the investment potential of their real estate. Because they are younger and more likely to be single or divorced, Type II buyers usually ski more often and at more areas.

For large ski resort projects, the major impediment to development is cost. Furthermore, the long lead time for ski resort development—which ranges from seven to ten years for typical western resorts—and sizable soft costs for planning, engineering, and securing the necessary approvals can exacerbate the already high capital cost. In the case of most Rocky Mountain and western ski facilities, which are usually developed on public land, the approval process can be especially difficult.

Given the entry barriers for large projects and a skier market characterized by many dual-earner households with tight schedules if not budgets, small ski areas located close to metropolitan areas could become one of the most promising ski-related development opportunities. Success will hinge on tailoring the associated real estate to an increasingly segmented local market. An excellent example of such a resort is Whitetail (mentioned earlier) in Mercersburg, Pennsylvania, within a one-and-one-half-hour drive of both Washington, D.C., and Baltimore, and three hours from Pittsburgh and Philadelphia.

Many observers expect demand to grow for well-developed and carefully maintained areas specifically designed to serve the cross-country skier. New Alpine areas are recognizing the complementary cross-country market and understand that they can offer a relatively unique cross-country experience by locating cross-country trails high up on the mountain—accessible by lifts—to take advantage of dramatic views. At Beaver

Snowmass Mountain, Colorado, recently expanded its ski terrain and access with the Twin Creeks quad lift to maintain a competitive edge on other mountains. Two other lifts were upgraded to high-speed capacity to enhance the quality of the ski experience. Continual expansion or upgrading of a mountain ski area improves an amenity and stimulates press coverage, which in turn attracts interested skiers.

Creek Resort in Colorado, for example, cross-country ski trails sited at the top of the mountain offer breathtaking vistas. Moreover, snowboarding has added new life to many ski resorts, which are transforming special trails and runs into snowboarding facilities.

Ski Site Considerations

What constitutes a large enough site for a ski amenity clearly depends on a project's market and overall concept. In the United States, ski areas range from less than 100 acres to several thousand acres. Many potential sites are constrained by inadequate room at the base to accommodate all the necessary support facilities, especially parking. The mountains that operate most efficiently disperse skiers throughout the area via a lift system that radiates from one or more central points at the base. Therefore, a site should be wide enough at the mountain's base to permit a similar lift pattern.

The amount of vertical drop is one relatively simple way of measuring a ski area. Aspen Mountain in Colorado offers about 3,000 feet of vertical drop, but an adequate ski hill can provide far less. A small, one-lift hill provided as a residential amenity could offer as little as 150 feet of drop. Most ski areas in the East range between 500 and 1,500 feet of vertical drop.

A wide variety of gradients is the mark of a potential Alpine ski area. Ideally, the distribution of terrain types—low, medium, and high gradients—should match the distribution of the market's skiing ability levels—novice, intermediate, advanced. A mountain with a predominance of expert terrain—gradients between 45 and 75 percent—would not be financially feasible in most markets. In other words, each market/mountain matchup requires individual analysis. For example, novices may make up 15 percent of the market, but novice slopes can account for less than 15 percent of total slopes because an acre of slope can accommodate more novices than experts.

One of the most important considerations in ski-area development is that a given area of ski slope supports fewer and fewer skiers as their ability level increases. In addition, as skiers improve, they become more expensive to accommodate. For example, expert skiers demand many more vertical feet of skiing per day than novices. And because they demand more vertical drop per day, they ride the lifts more often. Further, experts tend to ski at the top of a mountain, where construction and maintenance costs are greater. Finally, fewer accomplished skiers can be accommodated on a trail because they ski faster. Given that novice and intermediate skiers tend to generate the most revenues per skier visit, a ski area cannot remain financially feasible by catering solely to advanced skiers.

Beyond the ability level of a ski development's patrons, the resort's ability to retain snow is almost as important as its snowfall. Slopes should face predominantly north or northeast to avoid long exposure to the sun. But in some cases, modern snowmaking and grooming technology permits the development of trails on sites with

Aspen Highlands, Colorado, is redesigning its base village to create a small village community that will complement Aspen's character and improve services. Instead of developing a resort from raw land, many developers have found it more cost-effective and logistically more efficient to refurbish a preexisting ski facility.

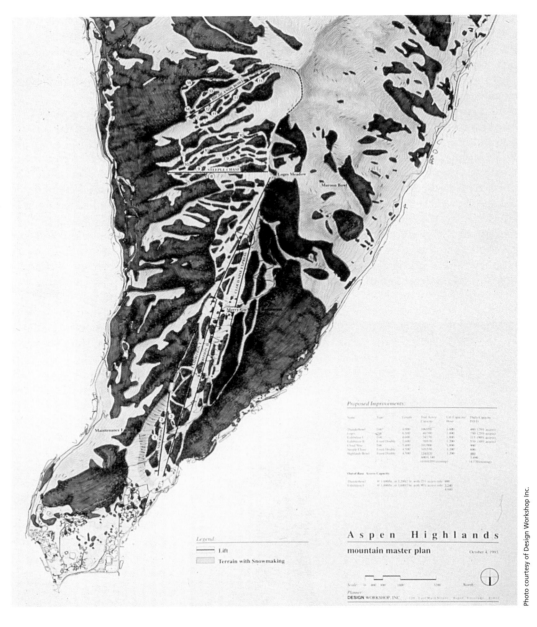

other orientations. Nonetheless, wind can be more destructive than sun, stripping exposed sites bare in hours. For obvious reasons, wind is also unpopular with skiers. In areas of heavy snowfall, avalanches may also be a concern.

Before snowmaking technology made it possible to build successful facilities in relatively snow-barren locations, a prospective ski-area site needed at least 100 inches of natural snowfall annually to be considered feasible for development. However, technology has made it possible to build facilities in locations where, without snowmaking, the ski season would last less than a week. In most regions, though, a ski area needs a combination of natural and artificial snow that permits about 80 to 100 days of skiing. For snowmaking, this requirement translates into about 800 to 1,000 hours of temperatures below 28 degrees Fahrenheit.

Snowmaking, along with several other ski-area functions, requires a dependable, high-quality water supply,

sufficient room for a reservoir, and adequate access to utilities. In remote areas in particular, utilities might not be available at reasonable cost. For its first seven years, Vail operated on a central propane system after the developers discovered that the nearest natural gas service was 30 miles away.

Soil types are another critical factor in ski resort development. Soil erosion, which can be particularly severe with certain soil types, is one of the greatest environmental challenges in ski-area construction and usually requires carefully designed mitigation measures. Similarly, groundwater runoff from subsurface springs can cause problems such as snowmelts or icing on slopes. Prevention may require expensive tile systems, culverts, and piping.

Vegetation as the element that defines the edge of a ski trail, frames vistas, and shelters skiers from harsh winds is another important concern. Often vegetation must be cleared from trails. For ski developments on federal land, the U.S. Forest Service evaluates the site's ability to "absorb" the development visually, which depends in large measure on the diversity of existing vegetation.

Cross-country facilities encounter many fewer site constraints. Given that a much broader range of terrain types is suitable for cross-country skiing, facilities can be located closer to the market. In addition, cross-country facilities involve much lower capital and operating costs in that lifts are unnecessary and trails are relatively narrow. And, because they are much less disruptive to the environment, cross-country areas are unlikely to face substantial regulatory hurdles. Further, because of lower fixed and variable costs, a developer can break even on a cross-country facility with a season of only 40 to 80 days.

Base Area Planning and Design

A characteristic Type I or Type II ski resort follows planning principles similar to those for any planned community. The base area, the principal activity focus, is usually surrounded by high-density, expensive real estate products—often hotels or other accommodations whose occupants stay a relatively short time.

Frequently located farther away from the core area are medium-density vacation condominiums or time-share products of a similar design. Units with direct access to the slopes command premium prices. Single-family homesites are generally located away from the activity core, but perhaps on surrounding slopes with desirable views.

Retail development is usually arranged to serve the resort's various user groups, with specialty shops, restaurants, and ski shops and services located close in; convenience retail establishments located in a middle zone; and various services and larger stores set farther out. Satellite development—which may involve lower-priced hotels or condominiums developed indepen-

Wintergreen offers night skiing to attract skiers after work from nearby Charlottesville, Virginia. For a minimal cost for improvements, a ski resort can increase its operation time and serve a broader market of skiers.

dently of (or sometimes in cooperation with) the ski-area operator—often spring up still farther from the ski area. Many such projects offer transportation service to the mountain.

Most of the basic planning and design criteria related to base facilities, from ski storage racks to remote parking, depend on the number and types of skiers accommodated on the slopes, although some project elements—retail, lodging, second homes—may be planned independently of the ski facility. From a purely physical standpoint, the most problematic part of base area planning is mitigating the potential conflicts between vehicles, pedestrians, and skiers. Many large ski areas such as Beaver Creek in the Colorado Rockies, Park Creek in Utah, and Loon Mountain in New Hampshire have located much of the parking underground, thereby reserving the surface for real estate development. This solution, although expensive, helps create a safer, more

Vail Village offers a base area village modeled after the European Alpine village, including narrow streets designed in proportion to three- to four-story buildings, uniform building materials, a Tyrolean architectural style, an irregular street pattern, a mix of retail and residential uses, and prominently located public plazas.

The Blackcomb/Whistler ski resort in British Columbia offers top-quality skiing; with its ideal snow conditions and fine service, the area has been consistently recognized as one of the top three ski areas by ski magazines.

pleasant pedestrian environment and a cohesive resort village core.

Ski lodges vary tremendously in their design and in the facilities they offer. Most are designed with between ten and 14 net square feet per unit of skier capacity. They need not be located only at the base. Mid-mountain lodges, though posing tricky operations problems because of their limited vehicular access, provide a highly attractive, away-from-it-all atmosphere.

Even the simplest ski lodge incorporates space for equipment rental, a ski shop, a first-aid station and ski patrol office, a ski school with adequate gathering room outside, and food and beverage service areas with areas for eating and warming up. The trend in recent years has been to offer a spectrum of high-quality food and beverage services, which can help carry the lodge through the warm weather months as well.

Trail Planning

The trails are the heart of the ski area. Designing them is an art that requires great sensitivity to both a mountain's natural features and skiers' perceptions. Poorly designed ski trails can be irritating at best and a threat to life and limb at worst.

Trail planners begin by identifying the fall lines (the paths of natural descent from one point on a slope to another) and then looking for logical lift locations. Major cut-and-fill can be minimized by tucking trails into natural hollows and depressions. Following the fall line as much as possible produces the most efficient and highest-quality trails.

Natural clearings can be incorporated into trails and thereby lessen the need for tree removal. For appearance and wind control, the edges of cleared trails should be feathered and uneven, with trees left at varying heights and distances from the trail's centerline. Islands of trees can channel traffic, separate skiers by ability level, and create visual interest. Of special concern in managing existing vegetation on the mountain is the degree to which clearing operations expose weak or shallow-rooted trees to damaging winds. Islands of conifers, for example, may be blown down easily without the protection of a surrounding forest.

Trails should be oriented primarily north/northeast to reduce the erosive effects of the sun and the prevailing westerly winds. Trails should generally widen as they become steeper, increasing from a minimum of about 80 feet up to 250 feet. Staging areas at the top of lifts should be sheltered from the wind. Knobs and ridges should generally be avoided. Bailout positions and stopping points should be provided on novice and intermediate trails.

Designers must balance the uphill capacity of the lifts with the downhill capacity of the trails. Otherwise, the tops and bottoms of trails will become unacceptably crowded during peak periods. To ease congestion further, the tops and bottoms of trails should be sufficiently wide.

Perhaps most important, the ski trail should be considered as a series of experiences that add up to a unified, memorable whole. The designer should strive for a variety of speeds, views, and perceptions. Skiers entering the trail at the top of a mountain should be able to see enough of the run to determine its general character, but they should also encounter some surprises on the way down.

Trail planning should consider the special needs of cross-country skiing, snowboarding, snowshoeing, and other snowsports enthusiasts. Cross-country skiing and snowshoeing require their own dedicated trail networks. Golf courses, unused during the winter months, are ideal for cross-country trails while nature trails can double as snowshoeing trails during the snow season. In some areas, snowshoers also enjoy hiking up the ski slope. The fast-growing snowboarding segment can also benefit from specially designed trails.

Golf Amenities

For resort developers, a golf amenity can be the primary amenity or one of several primary amenities. It can help support the marketing effort, raise project land values, and evolve into a profit center in its own right. In addition, golf course land often qualifies as open space under regulations that require a prescribed amount of open space in development projects. The golf course can also serve as a means of organizing a site plan by clarifying circulation, defining neighborhoods or subareas, and providing the project with a clear identity.

Despite a golf amenity's potential contributions to a resort development, developers should and do approach golf course development cautiously. The chief reason, of course, is cost: high construction and operation costs as well as the opportunity cost of devoting a substantial amount of buildable land to golf. Golf's high costs pose key strategic challenges to developers.

Site Considerations

The most crucial site requirement for a golf course is adequate land. According to Desmond Muirhead and Guy Rando, developers often underestimate the amount of land required for a golf course. Physical conditions—topography, drainage, configuration, soils, and the presence of sensitive habitat—as well as a project's overall development program affect the amount of land required. When golf-oriented real estate is involved as well, the question of how much land is needed for golf becomes even more complex. While 120 to 130 acres might be sufficient for a regulation 18-hole course with modest facilities on a flat, unconstrained site, the same course on difficult terrain might require 150 acres or more.[16]

The shape of the property is also important. Long, narrow sites may restrict layout options. Other limitations such as an inordinate number of road crossings compromise site suitability. Orientation can also affect a course. A long, narrow site oriented northwest/southeast, for example, means that holes face the morning or afternoon sun, which can make play difficult. For individual holes, a north/south orientation is best.

For course architects and players, the most important site characteristic is topography. The site should offer a combination of sloping and flat areas where tees, greens, and fairways (or landing areas) can be fitted to the land's contours. Steep, continuous grades can make a site unsuitable. If flatter terraces can be graded (an expensive undertaking), however, a steep site can be made workable. In any event, steep slopes generally increase the acreage required for a golf course. Flat sites, on the other hand, may offer the player little interest, although careful design of individual holes can overcome the limitations of undifferentiated terrain. Most courses include excavated lakes and ponds, and the dug material is often suitable as fill to create topographic relief. Topography is also a critical factor for the golf/real estate connection. Sites offering expansive views of the course command premium prices.

Topography, of course, is inexorably linked to drainage, another common site limitation. Various types of land not usable for development, such as wetlands, floodplains, drainage channels, and dry streambeds, can make suitable golf course sites. In Scottsdale, Arizona, one of the nine-hole circuits at Gainey Ranch has been dubbed the Arroyo Course after the seasonally dry watercourses that lace its fairways. Similarly, the course at Harbour Ridge in Stuart, Florida, is skillfully integrated among wetlands, not only to make more efficient use of the site but also to add visual interest.

In each of these cases, however, course construction costs have been proportionately higher. Among the features required on low sites or in areas with a high drainage table are drainage swales, crowned fairways that shed runoff, and drainage structures such as headwalls, drop inlets, and subsurface tile systems.

Over the long run, however, inadequate attention to drainage can cost a developer even more. For example, chronically wet conditions can reduce the rounds played on a course and translate into a corresponding drop in revenues and generally detract from the course, making it less enjoyable to play on and more expensive to maintain. For real estate courses, the drainage system needs to be scaled to accommodate runoff from future development near the course. At the same time, though, stormwater management for the real estate component can take advantage of golf course water features for biologic filtering.

Vegetation ranks second only to slope in its influence on overall course character. Vegetated areas, including woods, can be put to good use in enhancing the course's visual (and ecological) appeal, separating fairways, and providing locations for other recreational uses such as walking, cross-country skiing, or bicycling. The principal disadvantage of a heavily wooded site is the high cost of clearing the land and, in some areas, disposing of the cleared material.

Amelia Island, near Jacksonville, Florida, offers a truly diverse golfing experience with 27 holes of Pete Dye–designed golf that are true links on sand dunes overlooking the sea, and 18 Tom Fazio holes winding through marshes, forests, and oceanfront dunes.

The golf course at the Boulders, Carefree, Arizona, is built into the desert and flows with the terrain so that each hole provides its own scenic setting. Players can tee off from massive boulders, look out over fairways framed by ancient saguaros, and enjoy a challenging course that blends with its dramatic setting.

If vegetation serves an important wildlife habitat function, the associated land may not be developable or may require costly mitigation. Further, the potential for golf course development and operations to be an environmental liability—as they affect wetlands and other habitat degradation, soil erosion, contamination of water and the surroundings with fertilizers and pesticides, and/or high water use—can make golf course development on many environmentally sensitive sites a difficult proposition. In many locations, the only way to obtain development permission is to make the course an environmental asset through design and operating methods; doing so, however, can be expensive.

Already clear sites, such as a desert area or farmland, offer the advantage of lower site preparation costs and, usually, fewer environmental restrictions. But these sav-

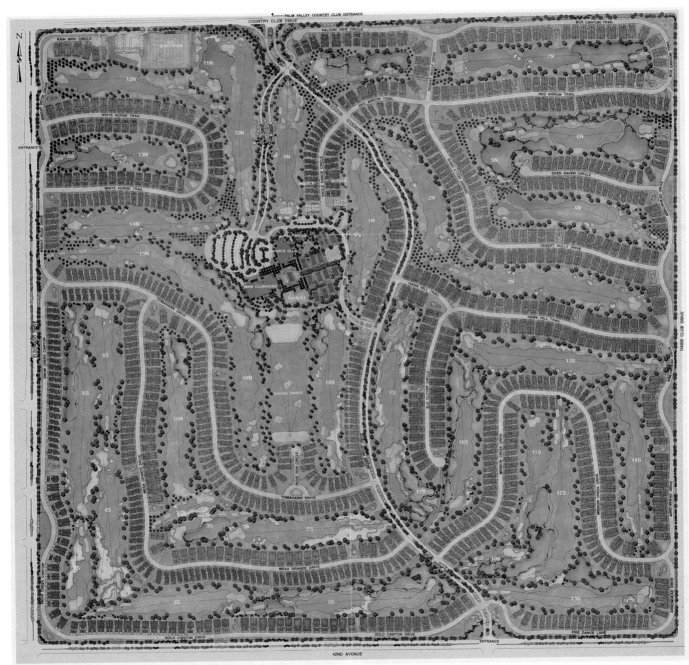

The golf course at Indian Ridge Country Club in Palm Desert, California, is designed to maximize the number of lots that can front on it. All of the 1,300 homes planned for the community will front on the golf course.

ings are offset at least partially by higher landscaping costs. In addition, courses on such sites generally look unfinished and new for several years.

A golf course can never have too much topsoil, a key factor in providing and maintaining vigorous, healthy turf at reasonable cost. During grading, developers should take great care to conserve as much topsoil as possible by stripping and stockpiling it. Well-drained, sandy loam soils are most conducive to course construction and maintenance. Alluvial soils in coastal areas can make for particularly cost-effective development. Easy-to-work soils can help minimize costs for earth moving and stockpiling and for the construction of drainage structures and irrigation systems. On the other hand, peat and muck soils, which are unstable and high in organic content, can severely constrain course development. Clay soils make the construction of ponds less costly but can be problematic if percolation rates are insufficient to provide adequate drainage. At the same time, high percolation rates can increase irrigation and fertilizer needs. Courses on rocky soils are usually more expensive to develop even though rock outcroppings and boulders can present unusual design opportunities. Gravel beds have to be covered with an adequate layer of topsoil.

An ample supply of water is essential. From the standpoint of permitting, the lack of irrigation water in many locations poses a major hurdle to golf course development. A regulation 18-hole course needs between 1.5 and 3.5 million gallons of water per week depending on the amount and type of turf, the irrigation system, and the climate. The quality of the water is also important; in particular, the concentration of soluble salts should be less than 2,000 parts per million if grass is to survive and flourish. Irrigation water can come from a variety of sources, including wells, existing watercourses, built or natural lakes, or canals. Treated wastewater offers an increasingly acceptable source. Irrigation water may be purchased but can be extremely costly.

Climate, as it affects season length and maintenance needs, is a primary revenue and cost consideration for the golf course developer. While a course in a moderate climate may accommodate more than twice as many rounds per year as its northern counterpart, the northern course incurs sharply lower expenses for maintenance and operations in the cold season. The moderate-climate course, although it too experiences an off season, continues to incur relatively high costs for maintenance year round. In the Palm Springs desert, for example, the greatest need for costly irrigation coincides with the off season.

Planning and Design

A developer should undertake the golf course design and planning process with a clear understanding of the course's strategic role within the overall project. Where real estate value ranks as the primary concern, the developer needs to site buildings to take advantage of views, plan water elements as both scenic amenities and golf

hazards, and reserve the most valuable land—ocean-front, for example—for uses other than golf.

If image (or accelerated marketing) is the main goal, the developer should construct the course early in the development process, design it to support tournament play, and plan it for memorable, photogenic holes that take advantage of spectacular site features. Such an image-conscious course is substantially more expensive to build and maintain than the average course.

If the main goal is to provide a high-quality amenity to the targeted real estate market, which is likely to include mostly average golfers, golf course design must emphasize playability and course integrity. Thus, with less focus on premium fairway frontage, the course might be built in phases or concurrently with the residential real estate.

The golf/real estate connection offers great opportunities but can also pose serious and costly problems. One of the most notable problems is safety in the golf corridor. A well-hit golf ball, report Muirhead and Rando, can travel faster and longer than a bullet from a shotgun. The temptation to gain frontage or economize on the golf course by encroaching on the safety perimeter is, they say, considerable.[17]

In recent years, golf's ecological impact has become an important design consideration. In fact, ecocentric design is now a prerequisite for public approval. Today, designers are striving to reduce golf's adverse impacts and accentuate its environmentally positive features—to satisfy both permitting requirements and the growing environmental consciousness of homebuyers and golfers. The most common issues in this regard are preservation of wetlands, conservation of other habitat, protection of groundwater supplies, and designs that allow control and minimal use of chemical turf nutrients and pesticides.[18] To assess a site's environmental conditions and help determine design elements, construction needs, and management practices, developers should include ecologists and environmental scientists on the design team at the outset.[19]

Basic Course Types

Over the past 30 years, the regulation course has emerged as the standard golf facility. Generally speaking, a regulation course has 18 holes and plays to a par of between 69 and 73 strokes, with par 72 considered the ideal. The standard length for such a course averages between 6,300 and 6,700 yards from the middle tees. Assuming three sets of tees, a standard regulation course could effectively be played from 5,200 to 7,200 yards long.

- Regulation course layouts are based on one or a combination of five basic models, with the type of real estate planned for development largely determining the optimum course layout.[20]
- In the core course, the holes are clustered together and arranged either in a continuous sequence with one starting hole and one finishing hole at the club-

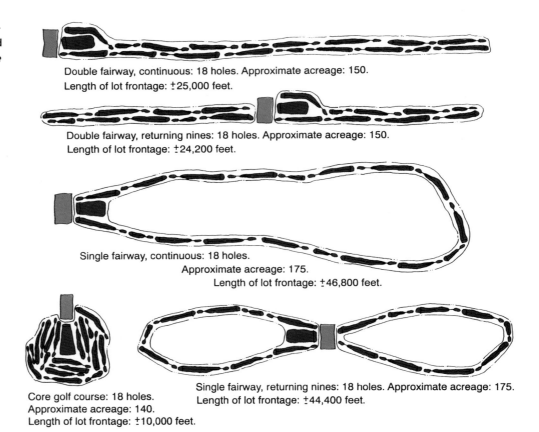

Possible configurations for a golf corridor. (Drawings reproduced from Desmond Muirhead and Guy L. Rando, *Golf Course Development and Real Estate*, (Washington, D.C.: ULI–the Urban Land Institute, 1994), pp. 45–46.)

Double fairway, continuous: 18 holes. Approximate acreage: 150. Length of lot frontage: ±25,000 feet.

Double fairway, returning nines: 18 holes. Approximate acreage: 150. Length of lot frontage: ±24,200 feet.

Single fairway, continuous: 18 holes. Approximate acreage: 175. Length of lot frontage: ±46,800 feet.

Core golf course: 18 holes. Approximate acreage: 140. Length of lot frontage: ±10,000 feet.

Single fairway, returning nines: 18 holes. Approximate acreage: 175. Length of lot frontage: ±44,400 feet.

house or in returning nines with two starting holes and two finishing holes at the clubhouse. This arrangement uses approximately 140 acres and offers about 10,000 feet of lot frontage; its compactness increases the speed of play and reduces maintenance needs; golfers like its integrity.

- The single-fairway, continuous course takes the form of an open loop that starts from and returns to the clubhouse. It requires about 175 acres and provides about 46,800 feet of lot frontage. With only one starting hole, flexibility of play is limited; with widely spaced tees and greens, maintenance requirements can be high. The layout is not suitable for golfers who want to play only nine holes.

- The single-fairway, returning-nines course has two loops of returning nines with the clubhouse located in the center. The layout needs about 175 acres and offers about 44,000 feet of lot frontage; two starting holes provide playing flexibility. Maintenance costs can be high because of the dispersed pattern of tees and greens.

- The double-fairway, continuous course features a single loop of adjacent, parallel fairways with one starting hole and one finishing hole at the clubhouse. The layout needs about 150 acres and provides about 25,000 feet of lot frontage. The single starting hole reduces playing flexibility; compared to a single-fairway layout, maintenance costs should be lower.

- The double-fairway, returning-nines course uses two circuits of nine holes each with adjacent parallel fairways. It requires 150 acres of land and offers about 24,200 feet of lot frontage; playing flexibility is enhanced by two starting holes. Maintenance is easier than on a single-fairway layout.

Each design option has particular implications for the amount and type of land, the development potential along the frontage, real estate development flexibility, the integrity of the golf experience (the degree to which golfers perceive that surrounding land uses visually or physically impinge on their game), the speed of play, and the cost of golf course maintenance. Muirhead and Rando note that a combination of configurations is often dictated by the site characteristics of or objectives for the golf course or the objectives for the golf-oriented real estate. It is not unusual for real estate courses to incorporate a single fairway on one part of the facility and a double fairway on another, for example.

Should an 18-hole regulation course be infeasible, developers should consider alternative course types. A decision to build a nonregulation facility, however, demands careful analysis of golf's role in the overall project. If a shortage of land or money suggests a less extensive or expensive alternative, the developer may decide to build a nine-hole regulation course (with or without the intention of adding another nine holes later), an executive course, or a par-3 course. If, by contrast, the issue is ample land and a generous budget in conjunction with a strong golf market, the developer may choose to plan a 27- or 36-hole layout or an even more extensive facility.

Larger-than-regulation golf amenities usually take the form of a 27- or 36-hole layout, although some resorts may offer 72 holes or more. Laying out 27 or more holes with as many starting and finishing holes as possible—three returning nines rather than one continuous 18 and one returning nine, for example, for 27 holes—provides for the fastest and most flexible play. With careful planning, a 27-hole layout can offer almost as much overall playing capacity as a 36-hole course. Sometimes one segment of the golf course can be geared to novices and high-handicap players, although the concern in resorts is that lower-skilled players will shun the easier course.

At PGA National in Palm Beach Gardens, Florida (see feature box on page 158), a 2,340-acre community, each of the four 18-hole courses responds to different development objectives. The flagship course is a core course and a world-class tournament facility fronted by only four development sites. A second course, planned to create high property values for relatively large, single-family lots, is a continuous, single-fairway course. In an area of smaller single-family lots, a third course uses a mix of single and parallel fairways for its two returning nines. The fourth course is designed with parallel fairways to complement a number of multifamily projects. At Pinehurst, five of the seven 18-hole courses are played out of a central clubhouse. The courses radiate from the clubhouse like the spokes of a wheel, forming a golf complex with few rivals.

Design for the Market

Four important market considerations in golf course design are the relationship within the project between golf and real estate, the ability levels and diversity of players, the overall level of demand for the course, and the frequency of play by the same group of users. At one end of the spectrum are courses in second-home communities. These courses are likely to be designed with single fairways to create maximum fairway frontage. At the other end of the spectrum are resort hotel courses built to attract serious and accomplished players; to protect the integrity of such courses, the facilities are more likely to be designed as a core layout or with parallel fairways.

Between these two extremes lie any number of hybrids and variations. A golf course as the principal amenity in a project with primary homes, second homes, a resort hotel and conference center, and investor-owned time-share units needs to cater to an enormously wide range of players. The best solution might be to develop multiple courses, each serving a different group of users.

At resorts without many repeat players, an important consideration is visibility of the green and all hazards from the tee. The best holes drop in elevation from tee to landing area and from landing area to green. On courses with many repeat players, visibility is less important. The design of golf courses in second-home communities, which serve both frequent and infrequent players, should provide good tee-to-green visibility, tees that accommodate various skill levels, relatively smooth greens surfaces, and fairly generous fairways.

In a destination resort featuring golf, the golfer market expects premier facilities. The golf course must be more of an attraction in its own right rather than a feature designed primarily to enhance the value of adjacent real estate. Luxury resort courses should be challenging, spacious, memorable, and beautiful. To serve image/marketing purposes, they should include dramatic and unusual signature holes. Many resort golfers play often, though within a limited time frame. For this reason, courses should offer a fair amount of variety, with multiple tees and fairly large greens.

At Pinehurst, five of the seven 18-hole courses are played out of a central clubhouse. The courses radiate out like the spokes of a wheel, forming a golf complex with few rivals.

PGA National is a 2,340-acre planned resort/recreational community in Palm Beach Gardens, Florida, that features golf like few other resorts can. E. Llwyd Ecclestone's initial vision called for creating a large, resort-oriented, planned residential community, including a resort hotel, that would be moderately priced and attract a broad range of buyers. To turn visitors into residential purchasers, the project's initial concept specified the development of high-quality, outstanding amenities.

In 1976, the developer scored a coup for the project when he negotiated to bring the Professional Golfers Association of America (PGA) headquarters to the proj-

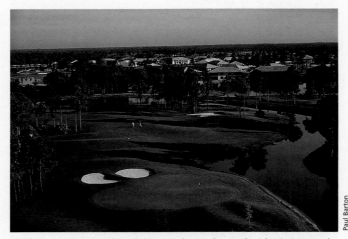

Golf at PGA National in Palm Beach Gardens, Florida, is integral to the resort's success. The community is the home of the PGA of America headquarters (top photo), and includes four very different golf courses that are used effectively to further numerous objectives: to provide a variety of golf experiences for different markets—tournament play, resort play, member play; to enhance real estate values for a variety of housing types; and to provide strategic open space buffers.

ect. The PGA purchased 625 acres of the site for its corporate home and leased all but five acres back to the developers for the construction of four golf courses. The PGA presence is a key factor in the project's overall development concept and market image, not to mention that it provides the project with a unique and highly marketable name.

PGA National's site offers several benefits: access to the Palm Beach International Airport, proximity to Florida's Turnpike and Interstate 95, convenient east/west access, and a single landowner. However, the PGA National site, located about seven miles from the Atlantic Ocean, lacks beach access in a resort region noted for its oceanfront orientation. Without beach proximity, the developer recognized the importance of creating compelling amenities. The PGA and the four 18-hole championship golf courses provided the initial draw.

The golf courses, named Champion, Haig, Squire, and General, were built over a five-year period. Each course has been designed to help stitch the overall project together by acting as a buffer and spatial organizer for neighborhoods and by providing fine competitive experiences for a range of ability levels. The Haig was the first course to open, in 1980, but the Champion, which opened in 1981, is the course intended to establish PGA National's golfing reputation. It covers just over 7,000 yards and boasts 19 water hazards. It was designed by George and Tom Fazio as a true championship course, predominantly in a core configuration with returning nines. Despite some development frontage on its fairways, the course design was dictated by the needs of tournament golf. To this end, the course is exceptionally spacious, with special "gallery mounds" and other areas for spectator viewing and media coverage.

The 6,900-yard Haig relates more closely to the residential products that line its fairways. On the front nine, the course follows a largely single-fairway configuration. The adjacent single-family homesites average about 15,000 square feet. The back nine, which starts from the clubhouse, is distinguished by detached and attached housing that fronts on parallel fairways. The third course, the Squire, is a 6,550-yard continuous course that winds through detached single-family residential areas and a small amount of attached residential frontage. Virtually all of the Squire's holes lie in a single-fairway arrangement, with only four holes parallel to another hole. The newest course is the General, designed by Arnold Palmer. It is a 6,900-yard continuous course with mostly parallel fairways lined with attached residential products.

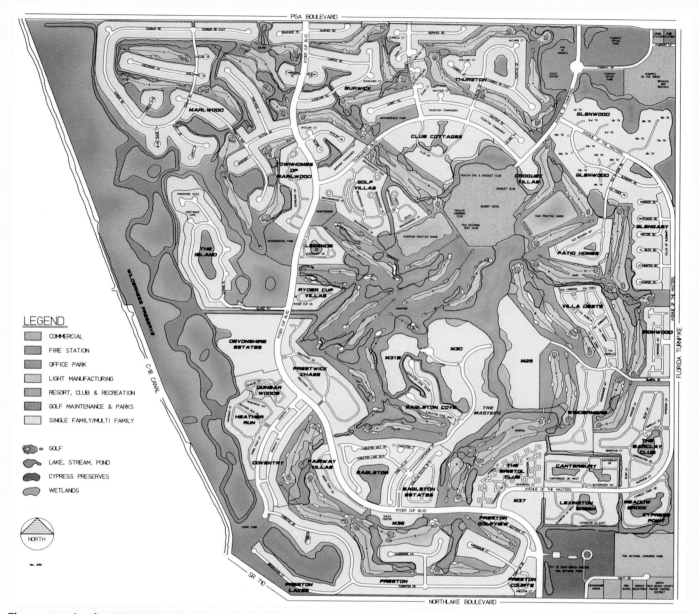

The master plan for PGA National in Palm Beach Gardens, Florida.

Golf at PGA National, while neither the only amenity nor the sole reason for the resort's success, is the project's single most important defining element. The four markedly different courses are used effectively to further numerous objectives: providing a variety of golf experiences for different markets—tournament play, resort play, member play; enhancing real estate values for a variety of housing types; providing strategic open space buffers; and so on. The golf amenity added significantly to PGA National's lot values; about 80 percent of the single-family lots and 60 percent of the attached units feature golf course frontage. In addition, the presence of the PGA of America was a critical element in the project's early success. The project's association with the PGA and its ability to draw crowds for many golf championships—as well as for tennis and croquet matches—has created numerous promotional advantages for the resort community.

Wachesaw Plantation, Murrells Inlet, South Carolina. Designed in traditional style, the Wachesaw clubhouse is part of a trend toward smaller facilities.

Photo courtesy of EDSA

Adios in Deerfield Beach, Florida. This exclusive golf club uses an old Florida theme for its design.

Photo courtesy of EDSA

In resorts located on spectacular sites, the most desirable land may be given over to golf. To ensure a high-quality course, the overall plan might even preclude development along the course frontage. When high lot values or other site requirements dictate development close to the fairways, as at Beaver Creek in Colorado and Harbour Town at Hilton Head Island, South Carolina, carefully devised architectural controls can encourage compatible development.

Clubhouses

Golf-course-associated clubhouses have become highly complex and often lavish structures that serve many needs in addition to golfers' needs. Often, they are central elements in project marketing. As multiple-function facilities, clubhouses can pose complicated programming and design problems. A developer should carefully balance the resources committed to a clubhouse against the expected returns—both direct and indirect. The

biggest mistake commonly cited by golf course developers and owners is a clubhouse that is too large for its membership and thus too expensive to operate for the income it generates.[21]

In a resort project where hotels cater to guests' non-golf recreational needs, a relatively small clubhouse of approximately 4,000 square feet focused on a pro shop and lockers may be adequate. Similarly, second-home communities in most markets usually feature relatively modest clubhouse facilities compared to the heavily used, programmatically complex clubhouses often built in golf-oriented primary-home communities. But, depending on the number of members, clubhouses in second-home communities can be fairly large. They tend to include flexible, multifunction spaces that can be adapted to seasonal demands.

Clubhouses are often located on highly visible, centrally located sites. In general, they should be near the first and tenth tees and ninth and 18th greens, the practice green, and the driving range. On many hilly sites, the clubhouse may be best located roughly between the highest and lowest points to avoid grueling climbs up the back nine on continuous courses. Other factors to consider in clubhouse siting are pedestrian and vehicular circulation, the location of maintenance facilities and storage areas, and the relationship between the course and various real estate products. Developers are advised to involve the clubhouse architect early in the planning process.

When designing the clubhouse, a developer must have a firm understanding of the composition of the user group, both at the project's early stages and at buildout. One of the most complex issues in clubhouse design is separating or buffering various groups of users. A club that caters to homeowners, resort guests, and nonresident members is likely to face some conflicts, some of which can be addressed by careful planning and design. Even within broad groups of users, other categories of clubhouse users—tennis players, children using the pool, community groups, and so on—might have different needs.

Two strategies can help mitigate conflicts between user groups. The first strategy is to isolate groups spatially by providing, for example, separate locker rooms for golfers and tennis players or a members-only dining room closed to resort guests. The second strategy is to manage access to the facilities by user group. For example, some daily-fee courses associated with real estate projects give project residents preference for golf starting times and advance reservations.

Phasing and expansion in relation to changing needs should be important considerations in clubhouse planning. An active, bustling clubhouse can be a strong marketing tool, but it takes time to create the resident base that can make the facility bustle. To generate clubhouse activity (and revenues), some developers open membership to outsiders in the early stages of development. Another tactic is to design the clubhouse to grow along with the project's population or to start with a small (reusable) facility to be superseded by a more elaborate clubhouse as membership grows.

Most new golf clubhouses include a set of practice facilities that are sometimes remarkably elaborate. A typical practice area occupies four to six acres (twice the area of the average hole) and includes a driving range (which should not be oriented directly east/west), putting greens, target greens for practicing short shots, and practice bunkers. In general, practice areas should be located close to the pro shop and the starting holes. Some measure of buffering between the practice range and other clubhouse areas is advisable.

Developers might also consider including a golf academy, which is a facility for a full-range golf teaching curriculum.[22] Golf academies are suited to sites ranging from 16 to 65 acres. A 16-acre site can accommodate a double-ended driving range with target greens and chipping greens, a putting course, and a clubhouse with video teaching facilities. A larger site would allow the

addition of a par-3, executive, or regulation nine-hole course. Night lighting and covered tee stations for the driving range can maximize the academy's use.

Other Recreational Amenities

A wide variety of other recreational amenities can be incorporated into a resort plan, including racquet, swimming, fitness, and health spa facilities; equestrian amenities; open space and nature-based recreation; skating facilities; and lawn/field sports. Each has its own design and development requirements that go beyond the scope of this text, but a cursory examination of how these amenities can play a role in the overall resort program and land use plan is in order.

Tennis, Swimming, and Health Spa/Fitness Facilities

Facilities for such recreational activities as tennis, swimming, fitness training, and personal body care can be and often are sited in proximity to each other and positioned as a single multipurpose amenity. Such facilities make relatively modest demands on land and site requirements, as compared to boating, skiing, and golf amenities. A complex that includes tennis courts, swimming pools, a spa, and fitness facilities can be as small or as extensive as the market warrants and may be associated with a club or a hotel or simply provided as an

Photo courtesy of EDSA

The Grand Cypress Resort in Florida features a half-acre pool with a dozen waterfalls and a 45-foot waterslide.

amenity for homeowners. Relatively economical to build and tremendously flexible in terms of details, a tennis, swimming, or spa amenity can be an important aspect of the marketing program for a resort's residential, lodging, and conference center elements. Such a facility can also help add balance to a recreational program.

Tennis and Racquet Facilities. Resorts that include tennis facilities generally fall into two categories: tennis

The tennis facility at Pinehurst in North Carolina.

An important amenity at the English Turn Golf & Country Club, the English Turn Tennis Center in New Orleans, Louisiana, features six Rubico tennis courts. Facilities housed in the pavilion include separate locker rooms, a snack area, and a lounge. A second-level covered observation deck tops the tennis pro shop.

resorts and, more frequently, resorts that offer tennis. Tennis-focused resorts tend to be relatively small, highly service-oriented operations located in established markets. First-class food and lodging, superb service, highly developed instructional programs, and a low player-to-court ratio are important elements. The Naples Bath and Tennis Club in Naples, Florida, provides a good example. The project includes 32 tennis courts, a 30,000-square-foot clubhouse, 430 condominium units and 93 single-family homes, and several lakes, all on 160 acres.

For the most part, tennis is usually offered together with other amenities; indeed, it enjoys a strong complementary relationship with numerous other recreational activities, including golf and skiing. To broaden the project's market appeal, the golf-oriented PGA National near Palm Beach, Florida, added the Health and Racquet Club, a 19,000-square-foot structure surrounded by 19 tennis courts (one of which can be converted to a 4,500-seat stadium court); a world-class spa; and the United States Croquet Association national headquarters. The Women's Tennis Association (WTA) is also headquartered at the project. Its facility is a stop on the women's professional tennis tour.

Many ski resorts have developed tennis and fitness complexes to bolster summer and off-season occupancy. To extend its season, Colorado's Snowmass, for example, added the Snowmass Club, a luxurious 76-room hotel that offers a comprehensive health and fitness package, including tennis.

Although a decline in the popularity of tennis since its rapid growth in the 1970s and 1980s has left a lot of underused tennis courts in its wake, most resort projects still include tennis. In fact, the capital costs of and maintenance requirements for tennis facilities are relatively low. The National Sporting Goods Association recently found that 12.7 percent of the population played tennis in 1995, down from 18.8 in 1989. The sport ranks 22d out of 54 sports in terms of participation rates. Moreover, tennis players tend to come from households with relatively high discretionary incomes, making them an attractive market for a resort.

Swimming Pools. Of the various sporting/health activities and facilities, swimming pools are almost mandatory in a resort and are often sited as freestanding amenities. In fact, resort hotels are often designed around swimming pools, which can provide an attractive visual amenity. In large resort hotels, in particular, swimming pools are often enormous and elaborately designed. The Westin Maui in the Kaanapali Beach Resort in Maui, Hawaii, provides a good example. It incorporates a series of interconnected pools surrounded by lush landscaping, palm trees, decks, walkways, and cabanas. The Kauai Marriott Resort and Beach Club boasts a 26,000-square-foot pool, the largest in Hawaii, rimmed by waterfalls and complemented by five whirlpools. At the Grand Cypress Resort in Orlando, the half-acre swimming pool features a 45-foot waterslide and a dozen waterfalls that cascade into the swimming area. Tall palms and hot tubs line the pool's perimeter;

an ice cream bar can be reached by swimming through a series of caverns.

The Hyatt Regency Cerromar Beach in Puerto Rico offers a truly extravagant pool, reportedly the longest pool in the world at 1,776 feet. "The $3 million aquatic amusement is a series of five connected free-form pools spread over four acres between the hotel and the ocean. A swift current propels bathers past waterfalls, waterslides, flumes, ersatz grottos, peripheral Jacuzzis, and a swim-up bar where the pina coladas are nonpareil. The pool's landscaping—30,000 tropical plants and hundreds of palm trees—is exceptional. Assuming no stops are made along the way, it takes 15 minutes to travel from the top of the river pool to its main basin."[23]

Pools are usually a requirement—whether a resort is located on the beach or in the mountains and whether a hotel is involved or not. Mountain pools understandably take on a much less opulent and lush character, involving far less landscaping and often incorporating some type of indoor facility. The Hyatt Regency at Beaver Creek includes a heated outdoor pool used throughout the year while the Homestead, a mountain resort in Hot Springs, Virginia, offers an indoor pool. In second-home communities, swimming pools can be provided as part of club facilities or may simply be an amenity available to residents.

Health Spas and Fitness Facilities. Modest fitness facilities are also nearly mandatory for resort hotels, and more extensive health and fitness facilities such as health spas have become increasingly important amenities in resorts in recent years. Spas can be the major amenity at a resort—the spa resort—or one of many amenities in a diversified package of amenities.

Health spas provide specialized facilities and services "that have one or more specific functions relating to mind, body, and spirit, such as fitness, weight loss, behavior modification, beauty, pampering, or holistic approaches to health."[24] Spas are "a retreat for men and/or women who have been abusing their minds, bodies, and spirits." Set programs may extend from several days to several weeks.

Canyon Ranch in the Berkshires in Lenox, Massachusetts, provides a good example. The resort is made up of an interconnected facility that includes a historic mansion that houses a library, dining rooms, and the medical, behavioral health, and movement therapy departments; a three-level, 100,000-square-foot spa; and a two-story inn with 120 rooms. The spa features exercise and weight training rooms; indoor tennis, racquetball, and squash courts; an indoor swimming pool and jogging track; herbal and massage rooms; and skin care and beauty salons. Additional facilities include saunas, steam rooms, whirlpool baths, lockers and showers, and an outdoor swimming pool and tennis courts. The facility is billed as the only major coed health and fitness vacation resort open year round in the northeastern United States.

A relatively new twist on the spa concept is wellness clinics. Amelia Island Plantation's Baker International

The pool at Cordillera, a mountain resort in Colorado, is a modest-sized facility that features a hot tub.

The Spa Internazionale at Fisher Island has received international acclaim as a top-of-the-line facility. Beauty treatments, fitness programs, and cuisine programs are all part of the spa experience, which is limited to 20 guests per week.

Wellness Clinic exemplifies the recent trend in wellness centers that specialize in preventive medicine and the promotion of good health. The clinic, a joint venture between the resort and a top U.S. cardiology team, offers a six-day program targeted to corporate executives. The program blends a comprehensive medical diagnostic evaluation with traditional health spa activities and includes biofeedback, stress reduction, tailored exercise regimens, diet analyses, and wellness education. A sports medicine program addresses sports-related injuries and problems.

Moreover, the inclusion of health care facilities in large resorts is growing increasingly important. Given that a large portion of the homeowners and visitors in any resort and second-home community are seniors—both retirees and preretirees—the availability of quality

Racquet Park at Amelia Island Plantation in Florida features tennis, racquetball, a swimming pool with a retractable dome, a health and fitness center, and the Racquet Park Conference Center.

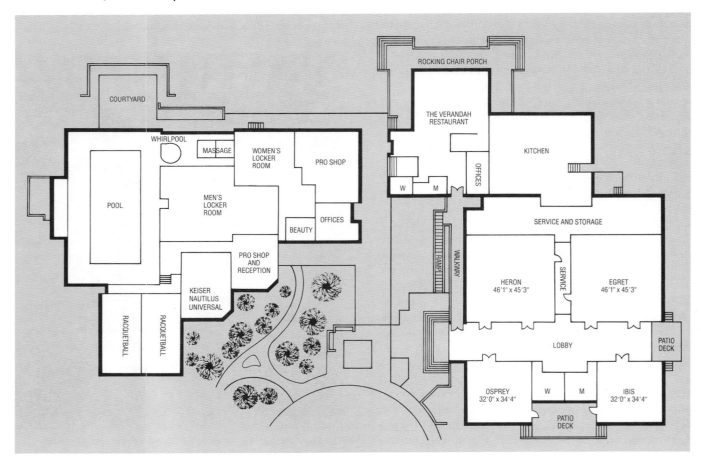

medical care is of critical importance. Many resorts market their proximity to high-quality health care facilities; some even include their own on-site clinics and other facilities. If a resort is large enough, it might identify an appropriate site for such a facility.

Multipurpose Recreational Facilities. Where tennis, swimming, fitness, and spa facilities are combined into a multipurpose facility, they can create a synergy that becomes a major draw for a resort. The Amelia Island Plantation recreational package, for example, supplements the resort's 45 holes of golf and four miles of beaches with 14 swimming pools and an eight-acre recreational complex called the Racquet Park, which features 23 tennis courts (19 Har-Tru, two Deco-Turf, and two Omni courts), two racquetball courts, a 60-foot indoor-outdoor heated lap pool with whirlpools under a retractable dome, a weight room, beauty services, locker rooms, a tennis pro shop, and the state-of-the-art health and fitness center mentioned earlier.

An executive conference center with a restaurant and more than 3,000 square feet of meeting space is located next door. The neighboring Courtside Village at Racquet Park provides hotel rooms and suites for conference goers. The overall package is marketed to groups seeking to incorporate a fitness and health element into executive meeting programs. The tennis program at Amelia Island Plantation includes two professional tournaments: the Bausch & Lomb Women's International Tennis Championships and the annual DuPont All-American Finals.

And at Coto de Caza in southern California, the Coto de Caza Sports Complex offers an Olympic-size pool, aerobic and aquatic classes, a sauna, a Jacuzzi, weight training, volleyball, basketball, racquetball, handball, two lanes of bowling, and tennis. The tennis program's Vic Braden Tennis College draws players-to-be from around the country; in addition to 16 tennis courts, the facility includes 17 Braden geometric teaching lanes with ball machines.

Multipurpose recreational facilities are also important in large-scale second-home and retirement communities. At the 2,373-acre Sun City Las Vegas, for example, the first of the community centers, a 38,000-square-foot complex that opened in 1989, provides tennis courts, racquetball courts, an Olympic-size outdoor pool, an indoor therapy pool, a full-time fitness specialist on staff, an arts and crafts village, a large multipurpose room, a 460-seat social hall, horseshoe pits, a nine-hole miniature golf course surrounded by palms and desert landscaping, an exercise room, a billiards room, bocci ball courts, and a 20-seat spa. These amenities far exceed those found in most golf-oriented resort or retirement communities. A second, more modest 18,000-square-foot facility opened in 1992, and a third community center of 40,000 square feet opened at the end of 1994.

Of those resorts that aspire to offer the best tennis or spa facilities and successfully attain a certain threshold of quality, their market appeal largely depends more on programmatic aspects than on physical characteristics.

Fitness classes, swim-team programs, personal trainers, personal fitness diagnostic services, clean locker facilities, high-quality food service, daycare services, and the like often spell the difference between a productive benefit to the collateral real estate and a drain on project resources.

When it comes to expressing a strong individual character or image, multipurpose recreational facilities do not offer a resort the same marketing opportunity as ski runs or golf courses. Yet, what makes the difference at any tennis, swimming, or spa facility, no matter its size or complexity, are the character and quality of the support facilities and buildings. Shade structures such as pavilions, pergolas, and gazebos; landscaping and walkways; viewing areas; and drinking fountains, benches, and other "furniture" all make recreational activities more pleasant. Especially at major resort swimming pools, landscape features—and the architecture of surrounding buildings—can provide the pool area with a dramatic or inviting setting that conveys a distinctive visual image.

Equestrian Amenities

Resorts and resort communities that provide equestrian amenities can vary widely in their equestrian offerings. Some are equestrian communities that may offer an equestrian center with horse-boarding facilities, horses to ride, trails, indoor arenas, and outdoor rings. Others simply allow owners to keep horses on their own

The Palm Beach Polo and Country Club in Palm Beach, Florida, is one of the most elaborate equestrian communities in the United States and exemplifies the use of an equestrian amenity appealing to a rarefied market. Developed by a leading polo player, this 1,650-acre resort community offers extensive equestrian facilities: 11 polo fields, including championship fields and an international field with a spectator capacity of 15,000; show barns for stabling 2,000 horses; show rings; turnout paddocks; a grand prix jumping ring; schooling facilities; bridle trails; and a circular riding trail around a central green space.

The equestrian center at the Grand Cypress Resort in Orlando, Florida, features a 42-stall stable. The hotel resort boards its own horses and provides space for horses brought by guests.

Photo courtesy of EDSA

lots and perhaps offer a trail network and modest central boarding/riding facilities. And some are vacation-oriented with lodgings but no residences, such as the many dude ranches in the West that offer boarding facilities and an equestrian-based vacation experience. Still others may be horse-back-riding facilities associated with major resort hotels that offer a variety of other amenities.

An equestrian facility can offer important benefits to a resort developer. Certainly, the sight of horses grazing in a pasture is attractive, and offering riding opportunities to resort guests can give a resort a competitive advantage. But equestrian facilities present difficult development problems, too. They are management-intensive; they must be sited and carefully designed so that they do not conflict with other land uses; and they tend to serve a relatively small market.

Equestrian Communities. Equestrian-based communities are generally a high-risk venture. Many equestrian com-

munities begun in the 1980s—many of them primary-home communities—failed for one reason or another. Therefore, developers should carefully weigh the benefits of an equestrian facility against its costs and risks. Usually, such a facility is most likely to succeed where a strong equestrian culture already exists. Most equestrian resort communities flourish only if they can attract a large percentage of homebuyers who are not horse owners.

To operate profitably, equestrian facilities in residential resorts (and other residential communities as well) usually need to market their horse-boarding facilities, lessons, and other services to nonresidents. In general, the best approach for the developer is to work with an equestrian owner/operator in a cooperative venture. The developer may be required in effect to donate the land or even to fund part of the construction cost.

The Palm Beach Polo and Country Club in Palm Beach, Florida, is one of the most elaborate equestrian communities in the United States and exemplifies how an equestrian amenity can appeal to a rarefied market. Developed by a leading polo player, the 1,650-acre resort community offers an extensive equestrian program: 11 polo fields, including championship fields and an international field with spectator capacity of 15,000; show barns for stabling 2,000 horses; show rings; turnout paddocks; a grand prix jumping ring; schooling facilities; bridle trails; and a circular riding trail around a central greenspace.

Polo is a recreational activity that draws a small but exclusive group of participants. As a result, a project that includes polo and its associated facilities as a recreational amenity gains an image of exclusivity—which can add considerable value to lots and homes. Many of the estate homes at the Palm Beach Polo and Country Club, several of which are in the $1 million range, are second, third, or fourth homes for some of the world's best polo players and for polo team sponsors. An image of exclusivity can attract homebuyers who do not ride. However, the number of horse owners or lovers who play polo is noticeably small; thus, polo is not likely to be an important amenity for most equestrian communities. A more modest use of equestrian amenities in a resort community can be found at Spring Island in Beaufort, South Carolina, which simply includes stables (with around 15 to 20 horses as of 1996) and bridle trails.

Guest-Oriented Equestrian Amenities. Equestrian amenities are more frequently included as guest amenities in resort hotels, multiuse resorts, and ranch resorts. Ranch resorts—also known as dude ranches—are a special type of equestrian-oriented resort that are most commonly found in such states as Colorado, Wyoming, Montana, and Idaho. They combine horse-back riding with slice-of-the-Old-West activities like cattle drives and calf roping. Ranch resorts tend to be fairly small operations with modest lodging facilities and are often run by small businesses or families.

Wit's End Guest Ranch and Resort near Durango, Colorado, is one of the larger and more upscale ranch resorts. It can accommodate about 120 guests in log cabins as well as conferences of up to 100 persons. In addition to horse-back riding, Wit's End offers a wide variety of activities, including swimming, boating, tennis, hiking, cross-country skiing, and fishing. Molokai Ranch on the island of Maui in Hawaii offers an annual rodeo that draws visitors from far and wide.

Many resort hotels and multiuse resorts also offer horse-back-riding amenities for guests. The Grand Cypress Resort, a major resort hotel in Orlando, includes a 42-stall stable, covered ring, outdoor jumping ring, regulation dressage ring, exercise track, and paddock. The resort boards its own horses and provides space for horses transported by guests. Black Butte Ranch, an 1,830-acre four-season resort community in Sisters, Oregon, has its own stable of horses. Pony rides for kids as well as hourly, half-day, and all-day rides are available, many of them traveling far into wilderness areas. In many cases, a resort's horse-related amenity may simply be a horse-drawn carriage, sleigh, or haywagon that offers a tour of the property or nearby areas. These low-cost amenities can add considerable charm to a resort.

Bicycling, Skating, and Lawn/Field Sports

Resorts that offer one or more of the big draws—golf, skiing, tennis, and water-related activities—cover a lot of recreational ground. Still, other sports attract their own players or participants, and resorts that provide relatively modest programs and facilities for sports other than golf, skiing, and water-based activities can draw guests. Moreover, numerous activities such as croquet or horseshoes can be provided as pastimes rather than as major draws.

Ice Skating Facilities. Among the sports that offer special marketing opportunities for today's resorts are ice skating. The importance that ice skating can achieve in a resort is best illustrated by the Sun Valley Resort in Idaho, which has developed some of the most advanced ice skating facilities and programs of any U.S. resort. The resort includes a 2,000-seat lighted outdoor arena that has featured performances by some of the world's finest skaters, including Scott Hamilton, Oksana Baiul, Kristi Yamaguchi, Brian Boitano, Katarina Witt, and Nancy Kerrigan. There is also a separate hockey arena. The summer ice carnival is a major draw for the resort, as is the Summer Skating School, which attracts aspiring skaters from around the United States.

Bicycling and In-Line Skating. The new sport of in-line skating can be accommodated easily on existing paved bicycle trails, although such trails are often in short supply in resort areas. Some East Coast ocean resort areas, such as Bethany Beach and Dewey Beach in Delaware, are experiencing an explosion of in-line skating on streets and roadway shoulders, a hazardous situation that points to an opportunity for resorts and resort areas to provide off-road facilities for the sport. Resorts that are near or connected to paved bicycle trails are in a good position to tap the in-line skating market as well as the much larger cycling market.

Sea Pines Plantation on Hilton Head Island, South Carolina, is attracting bicyclists and in-line skaters with its extensive trail system that skaters share with cyclists; Sun Valley in Idaho also offers paved trails that attract in-line skaters; and Sunriver, Oregon, has over 30 miles of bicycle trails. Other trail-rich locations that draw in-line skaters and bicyclists alike include St. Petersburg, Florida; Washington, D.C.; Santa Monica and San Diego, California; Boulder, Colorado; and Minneapolis, Minnesota.

Some resorts are providing specialized in-line skating facilities and services. Stowe Mountain Resort in Vermont, for example, offers an in-line skate park (all-day admission $10 in 1995) that includes a small timed training loop, a hockey rink, a "half pipe" and ramps, a lift-served downhill slalom, and a training program. An extensive public trail system for in-line skating is located five miles away.

Lawn and Field Sports. Lawn and field sports can be important elements in positioning a resort or can serve simply as unusual diversions from other leisure pursuits. In addition to its polo fields, the Palm Beach Polo and Country Club provides two croquet lawns near the tennis center, two stick and ball fields, and a site for a planned soccer field. The Sagamore in New York offers croquet as a lawn sport. And at Spring Island in Beaufort, South Carolina, the second-home community incorporates a family sports garden, which is a multiuse sports and recreational area that includes lawns, fields, and open areas for croquet, ballfields, horseshoes, and picnic and family gatherings as well as a pond, tennis courts, and a swimming pool. The Phoenician Resort in Scottsdale offers several lawn sports, including croquet, sand volleyball, and lawn bowling (bocci). The nearby Wigwam Resort offers shuffleboard, badminton, and croquet.

Other field sports such as archery and trap shooting are also offered by resorts. At Coto de Caza (which literally means preserve of the hunt) in southern California, guests can hunt dove and quail in season, although skeet

The Silver Circle Studio Ice Rink in Aspen provides an important alternative to skiing.

Brays Island in South Carolina includes a 3,500-acre hunting preserve as well as a gun club designed to simulate a traditional hunting lodge. Sport fishing has also gained popularity among members.

and trap shooting have eclipsed hunting's popularity; archery is also popular. The resort offers two pistol ranges for practice and lessons.

Open Space and Nature-Based Recreation

For most resort developments, the setting is the primary attraction. Preserving attractive open space—private, public, or common—is a key amenity planning principle. The type and amount of open space should relate to the expectations of the targeted markets. Open space requirements can be reduced if a government agency or land trust maintains adjacent forests, mountainsides, or waterfront as public open space. As compared to residents of primary-home communities, residents and guests in resort communities are likely to place a higher value on open space left in its natural state.

Gardens and Programmed Open Space. Open space can simply serve as a visual amenity and environmental asset, or it can be carefully programmed for recreational uses. Programming can range from something as modest as a trail to extensive landscaped gardens. At the Phoenician Resort, a 130-acre desert resort in Scottsdale, Arizona, a cactus garden containing 350 varieties of cacti and succulents is located on the site's northern two acres. The Boca Raton Resort & Club boasts 60 acres of botanical gardens and a 30,000-square-foot on-site nursery; its 14,000 feet of formal hedges require weekly shearing and hand pruning. The project received the 1992 Grand Award from the Professional Grounds Maintenance Society (see case study on page 340).

At Callaway Gardens in Pine Mountain, Georgia, 1,700 of the resort's 2,500 developed acres are devoted to regional plant and flower species, following the wishes of the development's founder, who was a gardening en-

thusiast. The project includes numerous woodland trails devoted to specific plant varieties: Azalea Trail (with more than 700 species of azalea), Rhododendron Trail, Holly Trail (the largest public display of holly in the world with nearly 500 varieties), and Wildflower Trail. There is also a seven-acre vegetable garden and a horticultural center, and the Cecil B. Day Butterfly Center is the largest free-flight, glass-enclosed, live-butterfly conservatory in the United States, with more than 1,000 butterflies in residence. The resort also includes 63 holes of golf that are carefully integrated into this garden setting.

Open space may also be used to establish a rural character, as at Quail Lodge Resort & Golf Club in Carmel, California, which includes a working farm—with horses, burros, sheep, Andalusian goats, and unusual long-haired Scottish Highland cattle—as well as a 600-acre nature preserve and a lake stocked with trout.

Trail systems are a particularly effective way to enhance open space and afford nature-based recreational activities for a wide range of markets. Walking for exercise and bicycling are two activities that lead the list of recreational pursuits in which Americans participate. Similarly, running and cross-country skiing are extremely popular activities. Trail systems are a highly flexible amenity that can support all of these pursuits. Like a golf course, a trail system can also be a useful mechanism for organizing and unifying a project's site plan. Trails can buffer adjacent uses, link various project elements to premium amenities, tie a project to adjacent regional amenities, and help reduce vehicular trips and parking requirements at destinations within the project.

Trails do not, however, necessarily impart much or any value to adjacent real estate and may provide only a slight marketing punch. But if well planned and designed, they can become a popular and heavily used resort amenity. Among the attributes of a well-planned trail are clear destinations, appropriate safety measures, a design that accommodates various likely uses, and adequate provision for maintenance needs.

Nature-Based Recreation. Some highly popular recreational pursuits require only the proper natural terrain, climate, and setting (and sometimes specialized equipment). Chief among these are hiking, backpacking, camping, wildlife observation, scuba diving, rock climbing, fishing, and hunting. Brays Island Plantation in South Carolina, for example, includes a 3,500-acre hunting preserve as well as a gun club that offers the ambience of a traditional hunting lodge. Sun Valley Resort in Idaho has long been a mecca for fly fishing enthusiasts. They are drawn to the resort in part because of the surrounding mountains' many rivers and lakes that offer both a variety of trout fishing opportunities and a spectacular setting.

In some cases, natural areas may require some level of continuous investment and management if they are to support recreational activities. For example, both Forest Highlands in Flagstaff, Arizona, and Broken Top in Bend, Oregon, stock their fishing ponds. Even the mountain lakes surrounding Sun Valley, Idaho, require the restocking of trout, which are not a natural inhabitant of the lakes.

Other recreational pursuits that simply require the great outdoors—along with a good launching site and the right climatic and wind conditions—include hang gliding and hot air ballooning. Aspen, Colorado, and Napa Valley, California, for example, have both become established areas for hot air ballooning.

With the proper setting, a resort can maximize its appeal to practitioners of various pursuits by providing modest support services and facilities: equipment rental, sales, and repair; trail maps; guide services and organized outings; and transportation services to off-site venues for various activities. The ecotourism trend that has become popular in many exotic locations internationally is another example of how natural amenities are becoming more important in resort programming.

Cultural, Entertainment, and Retail Amenities

Amenities need not always involve sports and active recreation. Many visitors and buyers are drawn to resorts in part because of their cultural, entertainment, and retail offerings, all of which can add a level of sophisti-

The Philharmonic Center for the Arts—which includes a 1,200-seat main concert hall—is part of the Pelican Bay resort community in Naples, Florida.

cation to a property. These amenities can also fill leisure hours when other recreational pursuits are not feasible, such as in the evening, during rainy weather, or in the off season. In the case of the Las Vegas casino resorts or Disney World, amusement, entertainment, or gaming activities are the primary draw.

Cultural and Entertainment Facilities

Many megaresorts are turning to theme parks, entertainment centers, art collections, live stage shows, cinemas, and performing arts facilities to amuse or attract visitors. Such facilities run the gamut from modest to extremely elaborate. Some resorts, including the Homestead in Hot Springs, Virginia; the Princeville Resort in Kauai; or La Costa Resort & Spa in Carlsbad, California, offer their own cinemas. The Mauna Kea Beach Hotel on the Kohala coast of Hawaii, built by Laurence Rockefeller in the 1960s, features a 1,600-piece collection of folk and tribal objets d'art displayed casually in the hotel lobby and courtyards. Its most prized possession is a pink granite Buddha from seventh-century India. Other modest entertainment uses that may be incorporated into resorts include miniature golf courses and game rooms. On a larger scale, Las Vegas's recently rebuilt MGM Grand, the world's largest hotel at 5,000 rooms, includes a 33-acre theme park. And the newly repositioned Atlantis Resort in the Bahamas includes a quarter-mile water ride, a water slide, and the world's largest outdoor aquarium, including an underwater viewing area (see feature box on page 266).

Music and performing arts are important components in many of the more renowned resorts. Resort community developers have discovered that the inclusion of performing arts facilities can add considerable value to a project. Witness Pelican Bay in Naples, Florida, a

The Aspen Music Tent is one of many summer venues that has established Aspen as a culturally eminent destination resort.

resort and retirement community that, thanks to the developer's contribution of land, is home to the area's Philharmonic Center for the Arts, a 100,000-square-foot facility with a 1,200-seat main concert hall, twin two-story art galleries, sculpture gardens, and a performance pavilion.

Most of the performing arts venues in resort areas are less elaborate, however. At Deer Valley Resort in Utah, music lovers with an affinity for the outdoors can enjoy Utah Symphony Orchestra concerts in the resort's outdoor amphitheater; the venue, located at Snow Park Lodge, provides a casual setting in which concert-goers picnic on manicured lawns and enjoy the cool mountain air. Performances take place most weekends throughout July and August and feature the classics to 1950s rock 'n' roll. And Sun Valley Resort in Idaho offers both classical symphony concerts and a jazz festival during the summer as well as the ice skating performance mentioned earlier. At the Manoir Richelieu in Charlevoix, Quebec, Canada, summer theater productions are staged in a building adjacent to the hotel. And at Callaway Gardens in Pine Mountain, Georgia, Florida State University's Flying High Circus has been performing since 1960 as part of the summer recreational program. The performers also double as teachers, instructing children in simple circus acts and games. Las Vegas casino resorts have long been famous for their entertainers and night shows, and the tremendous growth of Branson, Missouri —a small resort town in the Ozarks that has become one of the largest country music attractions and venues in the country, attracting thousands of visitors annually—also attests to the drawing power of the performing arts.

Many extremely modest entertainment venues are also common, such as nightclubs and other performance venues. At the Balsams in Dixville Notch, New Hampshire, the resort includes a nightclub with cabaret entertainment and dancing, a small lounge with a rock 'n' roll duo, a late-night piano bar, and chamber music recitals on Sunday evenings. Some of these modest offerings can become major attractions in their own right. The Turnberry Isle Resort & Club in north Miami is home to one of the hottest nightclubs in the Miami area.

Retail and Commercial Facilities

Designing and planning for commercial facilities, especially retail operations, is often an integral part of planning other resort-related uses, especially hotels. For example, the Little Nell Hotel in Aspen includes ground-level retail uses that are part of the downtown's retail fabric. In a freestanding hotel, retail uses are likely to be integral to the lobby or a courtyard. In a larger resort community, however, entire shopping centers may be incorporated along major roads to provide services not only to the resort community but to the larger community as well.

Whatever the type of facility, it is important to keep in mind that resort residents and guests come to the re-

sort to find something a little different from what they are used to at home, and this desire and expectation should be reflected in the design and planning of the retail facility. The Forum Shops at Caesar's World in Las Vegas is an extreme example of how to create something unusual in a resort environment; this facility has become an internationally renowned shopping destination in itself, featuring high-end specialty retailers, high-tech entertainment, and an unusual shopping environment that is directly attached to a casino. Another unusual retail center associated with a tourist attraction is Universal City Walk, an "invented street" adjacent to and operated by Universal Studios in Los Angeles. But there are simpler ways to create interesting thematic designs that are refreshingly different.

A unique retail resort setting is to be found at Casa de Campo in the Dominican Republic, a project that features Altos de Chavon, the resort's replica of a 16th-century Spanish colonial village set on a cliff overlooking the Chavon River. "Designed in 1978 by Roberto Copa, set designer for filmmakers Fellini and Visconti, the village was built (and 'aged' to look centuries old) by Dominican stonemasons, iron workers, and carpenters. Visitors are greeted by a massive stone fountain of water-spouting dolphins and other sea creatures poised on coral thrones. Inside the gates of the village, narrow cobblestone streets lead to colorful plazas. Cafés and shops are hidden among the trees and gardens. Art galleries showcase the works of local painters and artisans. The Regional Museum of Archaeology displays pre–Columbian artifacts used by the Taino Indians who once lived along the Chavon River. As a place to stroll after a round of golf, to visit for a cocktail at sunset, or to dine at Casa del Rio high above the river gorge, Altos de Chavon is in a class of its own."[25]

In more sedate second-home environments, retail needs may be more modest, but even in these settings a different design approach is warranted, often involving the creation of a village-style retail environment. Harbour Town in Sea Pines provides a good example of an appealing retail attraction while the resort town of Aspen is an outstanding example of an attractive resort retail environment.

One area of retail development that has not been tapped as much as it could by large multiuse resort owners is the outlet center market. Outlet centers are natural facilities for resorts and have evolved into popular attractions in many resort areas. Yet, most outlet centers are not located within large multiuse resorts themselves. Sawgrass Mills in Florida is one of the larger examples of an outlet center in a resort area, although Kittery, Maine; Rehoboth Beach, Delaware; Lancaster, Pennsylvania; and Las Vegas all feature outlet shopping.

There are no hard rules regarding commercial building type and size except that structures should be sensitive to the needs of the operation (i.e., visibility, convenient parking, etc.) while conveying an image that reinforces the ambience of the larger resort community. One of many issues to resolve is the tradeoff between

The Waterside Shops at Pelican Bay, a 250,000-square-foot upscale retail center in Naples, Florida. The center contains two department stores—including Saks Fifth Avenue's prototype "resort" store—and 47 boutiques.

At well-established resorts and communities such as Vail, Colorado, shopping and dining have become increasingly popular, often surpassing the drawing power of the recreational activities associated with the natural environment. Vail Village, considered the first planned village ski resort, allows visitors to wind through a pedestrian village of shops set between parking and the base of the ski mountain.

Throughout the world, retail plays an integral role in the success of resorts and tourist communities of different types and sizes and at different stages of development. Because of its universal appeal to all demand segments, retail is the glue that holds together mixed-use recreational communities.

Recent U.S. Travel Data Center surveys reveal that as many as 88 percent of international travelers rank shopping as their primary activity. According to the *National Travel Monitor*, shopping has been rated as a more important vacation attribute than "getting exercise" and "staying at the best hotels or resorts." At well-established resorts and communities such as Vail, Colorado, and Whistler, British Columbia, shopping and dining have become increasingly popular, often surpassing traditional recreational activities connected with the natural environment.

Today, Europe attracts nearly 60 percent of the world's foreign visitors because of the way in which its destinations combine natural, historical, cultural, and social resources with such manufactured attractions as retail, recreational, and entertainment facilities. Maintaining the right mix of these elements in a dynamic consumer climate is perhaps the most significant challenge currently facing resort and tourist community developers, planners, and retailers worldwide.

Creating the Right Mix

Recognition of retail's potential contribution to both overall resort profits and the local tax base has prompted major capital investment in many ski areas, resort destinations, and tourist villages. Such investments, however, involve significant uncertainty and risk. Pivotal issues of location, tenant mix, themes, environmental setting, and ambience demand careful analysis. Many retail villages lack the critical mass and magical appeal that entice visitors and residents to purchase goods, dine out, and return time and time again. To create enticing public places, resort and tourist villages must continually reinvent themselves. And developers must understand the difference between resort/tourist retail uses and traditional retail uses and identify the market forces affecting the industry today.

Unlike traditional shopping centers, successful tourist-based retail uses often evidence several characteristics in combination. For example, they

- are heavily geared to visitors and are unable to survive on local traffic alone;
- offer an intimate scale with a distinctive ambience and a strong pedestrian character;
- create an "experience" that increases the community's or resort's lifestyle appeal;

- present a distinctive and consistent architectural design and line of merchandise that convey a unifying theme;
- offer a variety of restaurants, bars, and other entertainment facilities that function as key tenants and help create a social ambience;
- lack traditional anchor tenants;
- may have logo shops and, depending on market profile, higher-end merchandise shops with commemorative or iconic appeal; and
- offer an ongoing program of special events and activities designed to entertain, inform, and amuse.

Tourist villages tend to be more loosely defined than other forms of retail development. Leisure, the outdoors, opportunities for socializing, and entertainment form the basis for an informal environment. Nevertheless, given that tourism and retail are highly susceptible to changing consumer, economic, and social trends, creating the right mix is a task not to be taken lightly.

Principles for Success

The developers, planners, and operators of a prosperous resort retail environment need to identify the services, facilities, and tenants most appropriate to the market. While there is no one formula for creating a successful resort or tourist retail village, six key principles can be identified.

Milieu. Resort and tourist villages depend on the milieu created by the special attributes of their locations. Attributes include spectacular mountain valleys, waterfront settings, and other features such as hot springs or historic associations. The uniqueness of the setting and the way in which the resort or village evolves around the natural environment provide a baseline ambience. In Aspen, Colorado, for example, a small waterway twists its way through the town's pedestrian core. At Mount Tremblant in Quebec, Intrawest Corporation has made the preservation of historic buildings a priority, thus achieving a completely unified Canadian theme that reflects Quebec's heritage, culture, and lifestyle.

Multiactivity Environments. Many resorts and tourist communities striving to become year-round destinations have invested in conference centers, tennis campuses, golf courses, sports institutes, and indoor activity centers, thereby creating multiactivity environments. Wider market appeal enhances the feasibility of more exciting and diverse retail villages.

The market for multiactivity resorts and tourist retail districts is more complicated and less homogeneous than that for traditional shopping centers. Patrons may include overnight visitors such as sightseers, skiers, golfers, or hikers; local residents; regional residents living within a day's drive—day-trippers, resort employees, and corporate, meeting, or conference visitors.

Successful tourist villages cater to the market's current trends and values, particularly the all-important family, mature travel, and educational and business segments. Attracting a wider range of visitors to resorts leads to a synergy that can overcome seasonality by both ensuring higher year-round visitation and creating new retail and business opportunities.

Chamonix, France, has seen significant market diversification. Today, only 50 percent of winter visitors are skiers. Similarly, by providing the right mix of new facilities and amenities—including a conference center and two championship golf courses—Whistler in British Columbia has evolved into a full four-season destination with nonskier visitation now almost matching that of skiers.

Town Center Hub. Clustering town center functions in a central area increases the functions' appeal and drawing power. In addition to retail shops, a town center should offer such services as a visitor information booth, post office, library, medical center, banks, offices, recreation center, and conference or meeting facilities. These services create spinoff traffic for retail shops while building a sense of community. Anchoring major people generators such as lift facilities, skating rinks, and conference centers in the village core, with parking at the perimeter, encourages a pedestrian-oriented atmosphere and helps manage traffic flow. Vail, Whistler, and Chamonix are prime examples of the clustering approach. The Plaza at the Coeur d'Alene Resort in Idaho attracted new patronage by placing a tourist information booth in a strategic location within the shopping area.

Character through Tenant Mix. The single most important attribute of any resort or tourist community is the distinctiveness of its village. While village activities set the stage, a carefully selected mix of tenants well versed in the most up-to-date merchandising techniques creates the ambience that is the community's real attraction. An appropriate mix of retail, restaurant, and entertainment tenants takes into account the needs and interests of each market segment as well as each segment's potential contribution to overall sales. The diverse retail tenant mixes of today's multiactivity resorts move well beyond basic T-shirt, souvenir, and fast-food outlets and instead extend to specialty food and merchandise stores, including cheese and liquor or wines, skin and health care, perfumeries, jewelers, lifestyle apparel, sports and outdoor equipment, novelty gifts, antiques, home accessories, theme restaurants, cultural facilities, and high-tech interactive entertainment.

The Right Retailers. Proactive resorts are developing tenant mixes that capitalize on the tremendous attractiveness of health, wellness, and other services and products designed to make people feel good. It is this emphasis that has made European resorts like Baden-Baden in Germany famous for hundreds of years. Stores such as the Body Shop, Garden Botanika, and Chanel have become popular tenants at mature tourist precincts throughout North America. Spa facilities already exist at Coeur d'Alene and are planned for Whistler and Mount Tremblant.

Gourmet food markets and shops such as Alfalfa's Natural Food Stores in Colorado, Starbucks, Häagen-Dazs, and the Rocky Mountain Chocolate Factory sell high-quality products. The small indulgences offered by these stores are particularly appealing to people on vacation. Other specialty stores enjoying success in the resort environment include outdoor accessory stores such as the Sunglass Hut, which offers top-quality sunglasses; the Right Fit, which sells custom insoles for ski boots; Swatch, which offers novelty and unusual watches; and Roots and Benetton, which feature lifestyle apparel and accessories.

Equally important to the family market is the small-indulgence trend—indulging the children; hence, the popularity of Gap Kids, Gymboree, and Kids Are Worth It!. In the upscale Swiss resort of St. Moritz, Giorgio Armani has established an Armani Kids store alongside an extensive collection of branded fashion stores. The high sales of such retailers as Endangered Species at Kaanapali on Maui demonstrate that families feel a need to learn about and appreciate the environment. Cinemas and comedy club/dinner theaters such as the Cinema Exposition Theater, Family Entertainment Center, and the Alpine Museum in Chamonix, France, respond to family demand for light entertainment. In addition, retailers such as the Warner Bros. Store, the Sharper Image, and F.A.O. Schwarz provide fun and enjoyment for people of all ages.

As tourist villages mature, national and international branded retailers and restaurants increasingly seek tenancy. Recently, the Hard Rock Café, Eddie Bauer, and Guess opened for business in the Whistler Village Center. While some resorts do not allow international fast-food operators into their villages, others control their entry through rigid design requirements.

New technologies are finding a place at Whistler, where Larco Investments, Ltd., and Mountain World Entertainment Corporation are planning to create large interactive entertainment centers. The Larco project, to be situated at one of the central plazas of the old village, is planned as an integrated retail, entertainment, and theme restaurant complex. Mountain World will be located within the existing conference center next to the movie theater and will feature adventures in virtual reality and sports simulators for golf, downhill ski racing, paragliding, and mountain biking.

Design, Merchandising, and Animation. Distinct neighborhoods or merchandising districts with strong themes create a cohesive image for a resort and provide the backdrop for a high level of activity. Design and architectural guidelines further strengthen a resort's identity by ensuring consistency in signage, shopfronts, and individual retailers' merchandising approaches.

Image is enhanced by such features as

- landscaping;
- building volumetrics and massing;
- continuous pedestrian-oriented environments;
- signs and icons, including art, sculpture, water features, and historic points of interest;
- mobile kiosks that sell local crafts, fruits, and seasonal items;

- colorful storefronts and window and vendor displays with inviting entranceways, awnings, umbrellas, banners, and signage; and
- outdoor entertainment and special events such as concerts, street buskers, craftspeople at work, and public or sidewalk markets.

The medieval towns of Germany's "Romantic Road," especially the famous Rothenburg ob der Tauber, provide excellent examples of design, merchandising, and a general liveliness working together to create a unified theme.

Lessons for the Future
Many European resorts provide instructive examples of mature multidimensional tourist villages that successfully incorporate retail uses. In North America, by contrast, the potential for resort retailing has remained largely untapped. With its intimately scaled European fishing village at Harbour Town, Sea Pines at Hilton Head in South Carolina is a North American pioneer. Disney's tourist villages combine animation mastery with main-street, pedestrian-style retailing as in the

The Turtle Krawl is the retail and restaurant center of Disney's Old Key West Resort in Orlando.

replica of small-town America at Celebration in Orlando.

The challenge worldwide is to match tried-and-proven principles to rapidly changing economic forces, values, and retail trends. Planners also must ensure that the retail environment does not come across as too commercial, too glitzy, or too similar to urban shopping experiences. With the right mix of an attractive natural setting, convenience, and creative merchandising, visitors will shop—many even purchasing items that they could but do not buy at home due to lack of time.

The highly competitive field of resort and tourist retailing requires developers and operators to take the following measures:

- Ensure that the scale and tenants of each development phase are realistically matched to market expectations; monitor changing consumer trends on a regular basis.
- Stick to tenant mix principles, generate a commercial plan that creates synergy, and update the plan regularly to ensure that all tenants fit the vision.
- Ensure that the initial tenant mix includes convenience items and integrates value-oriented offerings with lifestyle merchandise.
- Recognize that if the goal is to maintain control of the tenant mix and overall resort experience, the retail and entertainment components may need to be partially subsidized or viewed as a loss leader during the early phases of project development.
- Develop a consistent marketing theme and a story line that fosters a distinctive ambience and sensory impact.
- Add cultural and educational elements to stimulate the discovery experience.
- Work with the resort's tenants to program attractions; rely on such methods as attention-drawing signs and window displays reinforced by animated and interactive in-store merchandising.

Regardless of whether the setting is natural, newly built, or a simulated genuine setting, the resort and tourist experience is capable of drawing large numbers of visitors. But the creators must understand that for that experience to be both enjoyable and memorable, it must be staged with the utmost care and with attention to every detail.

Source: Adapted from Mick Matheusik, "Resort Retailing: Finding the Right Mix," *Urban Land*, August 1996, pp. 68–71.

■

encouraging off-site access to internal commercial facilities and preserving what may be an important sense of community exclusivity.

Casinos

The rapid growth of the gaming industry represents a potentially significant opportunity for the resort industry. As of 1995, 48 states permitted some form of legalized gambling (Utah and Hawaii are the lone holdouts), from horse racing and lotteries to full-fledged casinos.[26] The growth of casinos has taken many forms, including casinos tied to revitalization efforts, riverboat gambling on the Mississippi River, gaming on Indian reservations, and casino megaresorts in Las Vegas. Moreover, gaming is an important draw for many Caribbean resorts as well as for cruise lines serving Caribbean ports and other areas.

Lawmakers who dared propose legalizing or expanding gambling within their state borders have always faced stiff opposition from those who worry that gaming breeds social problems. However, as dwindling state tax revenues and cutbacks in federal aid have filtered down to every municipality in the nation, gaming opponents have lost their persuasive edge. As a result, eager for the tax revenues and hundreds or thousands of jobs that the gaming establishments and their suppliers bring with them, state and local officials have grown more willing to open their doors to casinos, card clubs, and bingo halls. For example, four old mining towns in Colorado have relied on gaming as an economic development tool.

The city of Inglewood, California, has also approached gaming as a revitalization tool. While city officials in Inglewood say they never expected a local construction boom when the new Hollywood Park Casino opened in 1994, the economic benefits of the town's first card club are thus far exceeding initial expectations. With a population of 115,000 mostly low- or moderate-income residents, Inglewood collects $400,000 a month in taxes from its new gambling parlor; that works out to roughly 10 percent of the city's annual operating budget. Equally important, about 800 of the casino's 2,000 employees are Inglewood residents. The 315,000-square-foot casino stands next to Hollywood Park, the fabled racetrack located about 15 miles southwest of downtown Los Angeles and three miles east of Los Angeles International Airport. Since the state still outlaws dice games, the casino can offer only U.S.- and Asian-style poker and California 22, a game similar to Vegas-style 21.

Riverboat gaming is now legal in many states, including Illinois, Indiana, Iowa, Louisiana, Mississippi, Missouri, and Tennessee. While many of the casinos are simply riverboats, larger resort communities are also being planned around these facilities. For example, Grand Casinos, Inc., and the Gaming Corporation of America are planning a 2,000-acre resort community in a rural setting along the Mississippi River south of Memphis. The community will include a 70-acre lake surrounded by 4,200 hotel rooms and timeshare housing, a conference center and theaters, a theme park, a town center, two golf courses, and a large floating casino.

According to real estate academician and gaming consultant Kerry Vandell of the University of Wisconsin, one area of the gaming industry that is just catching its stride and will probably provide substantial opportunity for new real estate development opportunities is tribal gaming.[27] Tribal casinos, permitted by a 1988 federal law affecting reservations and other lands subject to tribe-state compacts, have tended to be located far from population centers. Thus, primary users included locals and vacationers. Over the last several years, however, tribal gaming has moved closer to major population centers; at the same time, the facilities have become much larger and more elaborate.

With more than 1,600 slot machines and 48 blackjack tables, the new 86,000-square-foot Ho-Chunk Casino near Lake Delton, Wisconsin, exemplifies the new breed. The Foxwoods Casino, developed in 1991 by the Mashantucket Pequot tribe in Ledyard, Connecticut, represents perhaps the ultimate potential of tribal gaming near major population centers. With annual gaming revenues of more than $800 million, Foxwoods is one of the most successful casinos in the United States and a major source of revenue for the state of Connecticut. Another is the new Mohegan Sun Casino (see feature box on this page).

Some of the best opportunities for future tribal gaming facilities, according to Vandell, are in California, Florida, New York, Michigan, Arizona, North Carolina, New Mexico, Kansas, and Washington. Developers must, he warns, recognize the uniqueness of the tribal gaming market and its special risks. Following their mixed experience with outside casino managers, the tribes are understandably suspicious of individuals and firms they do not know. At the same time, the tribes are adept at working out franchise and joint venture arrangements that guarantee them a substantial portion of the revenue, low risk, and extensive opportunities for training and employment.

With all of this new competition, it might seem that the future does not look bright for the Las Vegas and Atlantic City casinos. In fact, just the opposite seems to be the case. Casino resort hotels in Las Vegas have proven highly profitable as well as adaptable to a changing market. Many casino hotels in Las Vegas are transforming themselves into megaresort hotels that offer a wide range of amenities attractive to the family market (see feature box on page 180). As a result of growth in its gaming and other tourist attractions, Las Vegas is one of the fastest-growing locations for retirement communities and timeshare projects.

Mohegan Sun: Theme Gaming

Tucked behind rolling hills, trees, and water, Mohegan Sun's natural setting on the banks of the Thames River in southeastern Connecticut provides an attractive location for a gaming facility. From its conception, the facility was intended not only to entertain but also to communicate the heritage and traditions of the Mohegan Indians. With its completion and opening in late 1996, Mohegan Sun, with its Mohegan-themed interior and New England setting, is expected to become a major entertainment venue.

Located in Uncasville, Connecticut, Mohegan Sun is owned by the Mohegan Indians of Connecticut and operated by Trading Cove Associates (TCA). TCA is a 50/50 joint venture that includes Sun International and original TCA partners LMW Investments, RJH Development of Connecticut, and Michigan-based Slavik Suites, Inc.

The 1.4 million-square-foot gaming facility features a 600,000-square-foot casino, including 150,000 square feet of gaming space. It accommodates up to 3,000 slot machines and 180 gaming tables while offering 2,000 seats in four specialty restaurants, in addition to entertainment and shopping.

The project occupies a 240-acre tract that is the former home of nuclear fuel components manufacturer United Nuclear Corporation (UNC). The Mohegan tribe purchased the land and its existing structures in September 1995. The U.S. Department of the Interior then designated the land as the tribe's official reservation. The property is part of 700 acres the tribe may acquire as reservation land.

Before the property was transferred to the federal government (which holds the land in trust for the tribe), UNC conducted a rigorous cleanup of the site under the review of the Nuclear Regulatory Commission and the Connecticut Department of Environmental Protection.

Gaining Recognition

For 188 years, the Mohegan tribe struggled to gain federal recognition. That effort intensified in 1992 when Trading Cove Associates, a group of Connecticut businesses involved in hotel management, land development, and construction, approached the tribe with the idea of entering into a joint venture to develop a casino complex. TCA formed to assist the tribe in obtaining federal recognition, which would pave the way for the tribe to reestablish its reservation and ensure economic well-being and independence.

Throughout 1993, TCA and the tribe worked with various state and federal government agencies to settle centuries-old land disputes. In addition, TCA provided the tribe with the funds needed to obtain the legal support for its efforts to gain federal recognition. By year's end, the tribe had negotiated a compact with the state of Connecticut resolving all land disputes and regulatory issues. On March 7, 1994, the tribe received federal recognition.

Later that year, TCA and the tribe negotiated an agreement with the town of Montville (Uncasville is a district of Montville) to settle any potential tax and town issues related to the development. In December, the town approved all major permits, thereby allowing the Mohegans to begin construction on the site and to expand State Route 2A to four lanes adjacent to the site's access road.

Meanwhile, Sun International entered into a 50 percent ownership agreement with TCA's original partners. Sun International brought to the project considerable experience in resort and casino development (the company operates 11 casinos and resorts in the Bahamas, Comores, Mauritius, and France and is the developer of Sun City and the Lost City at Sun City, South Africa). Sun International was attracted to the Mohegan Sun development in response to the tremendous success of Foxwoods, a casino and resort owned by the Mashantucket Pequot tribe in Ledyard, Connecticut, just ten miles from the Mohegan reservation. In the five years since it opened, Foxwoods has become one of the world's most profitable casinos, reporting slot machine revenues of $541

East entry, Mohegan Sun Casino. Located in Uncasville, Connecticut, Mohegan Sun is a casino owned by the Mohegan Indians of Connecticut that is being developed and operated by Trading Cove Associates. The 1.4 million-square-foot gaming facility will feature a 600,000-square-foot casino, including 150,000 square feet of gaming space, accommodating up to 3,000 slot machines and 180 gaming tables while offering 2,000 seats in four specialty restaurants, in addition to entertainment and shopping.

million for its first 12 months. Market research determined that the demand within New England and the Northeast for gaming entertainment far exceeded what Foxwoods could supply.

Financing

Together, the tribe and its management partners formed the Mohegan Tribal Gaming Authority to oversee development and operation of the new casino. In 1995, in the first deal of its kind, the Mohegans and TCA used the capital market to help fund the casino project. Wall Street investment bankers Bear, Stearns & Company and Donaldson, Lufkin & Jenrette Securities privately placed $175 million in senior notes with institutional investors, guaranteeing a 13.5 percent return on their

investment and a share of the casino's future profits. In addition, Sun International provided the tribe with a $40 million debt investment, allowing the Mohegans to close on their purchase of the former UNC land, as well as with $35 million in equipment financing. The cost of the project, including $29 million for road work and $27 million for property acquisition, totals an estimated $280 million.

The Master Plan

The project's master plan organizes a complex system of roads, buildings, and parking and expands an existing 430,000-square-foot UNC industrial building. The plan also allows for future growth, which will include hotels, recreational, and other entertainment facilities.

View of north pavilion.

Infrastructure work began in late November 1995. A series of road improvements to eliminate congestion were undertaken, beginning with the widening of Route 2A to four lanes, the construction of an overpass into the complex, and the design of a loop traffic pattern around the casino and parking areas. The east and south entrances lead to valet parking in a new, two-level 1,800-car underground parking garage. The north entrance links the casino with a freestanding, five-story, 1,300-car garage and an on-grade parking area that can accommodate 4,500 cars. The west entrance is reserved for bus passengers.

The casino's exterior blends with the topographic contours of southeastern Connecticut. Landscape architects created 15-foot-high earthen berms and extensive landscaping that screen much of the casino structure and help restore the site's natural beauty.

The existing building, which will include a 60-foot-by-60-foot structural grid for maximum planning flexibility, is undergoing total rehabilitation in combination with construction of the new 200,000-square-foot casino. The casino's user-friendly, circular design will make it easy for patrons to navigate through the variety of Mohegan Sun gaming, dining, and entertainment facilities. The perimeter of the casino features ceiling heights of 25 feet, with a 100,000-square-foot central drum structure rising to 45 feet.

The existing L-shaped building is adjacent to the casino's north and west sides. Facing the north side are four restaurants, a coffee shop, and a two-story food court/buffet dining area. A 40,000-square-foot central kitchen serves all food and beverage areas. The remaining portion of the existing structure includes an arcade, a 16,000-square-foot Kids' Quest children's play area and daycare center developed by Minneapolis-based New Horizon Kids' Quest, a bingo hall, a bus passenger waiting area, and other back-of-the-house support services.

Theming

Mohegan Sun's facilities blend with the culture and traditions of the Mohegan Indians, known as the Wolf People. Handmade objects, artisan-created furniture, and the extensive use of timber and water are integrated with the latest sound, lighting, and special effects technology, "transporting" Mohegan Sun customers to a world where yesterday is brought to life today.

Celebrating the tribe's history and traditions, Mohegan Sun's circular design and Indian themes are directly influenced by the tribe's beliefs and culture. The casino is separated into four quadrants, each of which features its own entrance and a seasonal theme—winter, spring, summer, and fall—that highlights the importance of seasonal changes in Mohegan life.

The east (representing spring) entrance has been named the Thunder Moon. A decorative tree gateway with metal springlike flowers, custom ornamental "bud" lamps, and a mural depicting the origin of thunder is accented by handrails that feature decorative metalwork, cherry woods, river rock, and pink granite. The Moon of the Golden Sun, as the south entrance is called, represents summer. The sky is symbolized by an aviary and a mural depicting the legend of Chahameed, the Great Eater and one of the Mohegans' most important ancestors. An overall theme of summer plantings honors the important Mohegan summer festivals.

The west entrance, called the Harvest Moon, is distinguished by an earth carving with inlaid precious stones and a mural describing the Green Corn Festival or Wigwam Festival, the annual fall thanksgiving celebration that has provided America with many of its modern Thanksgiving traditions. The north entrance (the Moon of the First Snow) represents winter as symbolized by fire and the sacred flame contrasted with frost. A mural of winter tales features the story of the Makiawisug, the mysterious little people who live in forests.

At the center of the casino is the dramatic 10,000-square-foot Wolf Bar and Showroom, featuring sculptures of wolves and other animals poised atop giant columns. The bar can be arranged for seating of up to 500 spectators for entertainment and sporting events, including boxing matches. The themed architectural interior is carried over into the restaurants as well. For example, the steak house resembles an Adirondack lodge, and the Italian restaurant a stone grotto. The casino, entertainment, food, and retail facilities are designed to attract and serve 7,000 people daily.

Of the approximately 130 Indian gaming operations in the country, mostly on rural reservations, none compares in size or cost to Mohegan Sun, the first gaming operation financed through Wall Street. The project's Indian theme and single-destination experience promise a distinctive and exciting ambience that will set the complex apart from other North American gaming and entertainment complexes.

Source: Adapted from William Katz, "Mohegan Sun: Theme Gaming," *Urban Land*, August 1996, pp. 32–35.

Gaming properties either under construction or announced keep popping up in Las Vegas and southern Nevada. The list is ever-changing:

- New York-New York, a $350 million joint venture between MGM and Primadonna Resorts, broke ground in March 1995 and was completed in early 1997. Its 20-acre site is located at the corner of Tropicana Avenue and Las Vegas Boulevard South (across from the MGM Grand). The developer is New York-New York Resorts, Inc.; architects are Las Vegans Neal Gaskin and Ilia Bezanski. A 2,000-room hotel will replicate the Big Apple complete with a 150-foot-tall Statue of Liberty and 48-story Empire State Building. A cyclone-style Coney Island roller coaster will transport guests around the property at 65 miles per hour.
- Beau Rivage, at the site of the former Dunes Hotel at Dunes Road and Las Vegas Boulevard, is a $1 billion project exclusive of land, with a 3,000-room, 46-story hotel planned to open in late 1997 or early 1998. The hotel will employ 7,000 people and create an estimated 5,000 construction jobs. Beau Rivage joins other Mirage Resorts, Inc., theme resorts: the Mirage, Treasure Island Hotel and Casino, and the Golden Nugget.
- Bally's Entertainment Corp.'s Paris Casino Resort, a $420 million development, is located on 25 acres at Flamingo Road and Koval Lane with 2,500 rooms in 33 stories. It will include a 50-story replica of the Eiffel Tower and feature its own winery and gondola rides. It will showcase replicas of the Arc de Triomphe, Champs Elysées, and the Seine River. The projected completion date is 1997. The project is expected to add 3,200 jobs to the local economy. The new Paris Casino Resort and Bally's Las Vegas will be linked with the MGM Grand by the MGM Grand–Bally's Monorail.
- The Victoria, developed by Gold Strike Resorts and Mirage Resorts, Inc., will be strategically located on 43 acres between Beau Rivage and New York-New York and will add 3,000 rooms to the Strip. The total cost is projected at $325 million.
- Circus-Circus Enterprises, pushing for a monopoly on the southernmost end of the Strip, is making final plans for a megaresort on the Hacienda property and the land immediately to the south. Circus-Circus plans to rely on people movers to link all of its properties —including the Victoria (scheduled to open in 1997), the Excalibur, and the Luxor—with McCarran International Airport, one-half mile away.
- At the northern end of the Strip, Stratosphere Tower, developed by the Stratosphere Corporation, is a space age $300 million, 135-story high-rise, with a 1,000-room hotel, 310,000-square-foot casino, and 12-story pod enclosing restaurants, rides, and a wedding chapel.

Source: Sydney W. Knott, "Gaming Grows On," *Urban Land*, August 1995, p. 57.

■

Residential Products and Design

The two ways to describe residential products in resort and recreational communities are by type of unit and by type of ownership. Unit types include single-family detached, single-family attached, and multifamily products. Ownership types include fee-simple, condominium, cooperative, and interval or timeshare ownership arrangements. A given community can offer products identical in type of unit and type of ownership or a range of product types and ownership arrangements. At the same time, the physical characteristics of residential products in resort and recreational communities must reflect a combination of factors: the market segment(s) to be served, the physical requirements of a particular site, and financial parameters.

Whatever the direction of individual preferences, the escalating cost of all types of housing and the demand for high-quality living and recreational environments will continue to challenge the imagination of designers and developers. The following discussion surveys the spectrum of specific housing designs available in resort and recreational community settings, ranging from single-family housing—both detached and attached—to apartments in multifamily buildings.

Single-Family Residential

Single-family housing encompasses a wide range of densities and configurations. By definition, a single-family detached house is a freestanding structure that occupies its own lot while single-family attached housing consists of two or more single-family dwelling units constructed with party walls.

Over the past decade, the strong demand for conventional single-family housing coupled with reduced affordability has brought about major changes in the design of single-family units. Overall, single-family lots have become smaller and more complicated in their configuration.

At the Cottages at Flora's Bluff on Bald Head Island in North Carolina, the architecture is based on a romantic image of relaxation and the desire to live in harmony with the environment. The buildings are designed as a kit of small parts, easily fitting within the existing vegetation and dunes. A typical two- or three-bedroom cottage often is grouped with a small one-bedroom guesthouse and a separate garage.

With smaller lots, designers need to consider issues related to privacy, usable yard area, entries, and streetscapes early in project planning. Developers must understand these issues and the potential pitfalls associated with them. In fact, developers must delay the decision about which single-family product(s) to build until they have completed a careful examination of the targeted market, the economics of the project, and the capacity of the land.

Architectural Style. In general, resort homes frequently take on a different character than primary homes. Compared to primary homes, resort homes are often designed to appear more casual and to suggest a relaxed living environment. They also place a much greater emphasis on outdoor living areas; indeed, the home's setting is usually a primary asset of the resort experience. At the Cottages at Flora's Bluff on Bald Head Island in North Carolina, for example, the architecture reflects a romantic image of relaxation and the desire to live in harmony with the environment. The buildings are designed as a kit of small parts that fit easily within the existing vegetation and dunes. A typical two- or three-bedroom cottage is often grouped with a small one-bedroom guesthouse and a separate garage. The collection of buildings, the developer believes, is more sensitive to the natural context and human scale, allowing for the creation of private outdoor spaces and preventing large structures from obstructing crucial ocean views. The standardized components are combined in various permutations to offer a wide variety of forms and spaces within the same project.

Another influential example in resort home design is Seaside (see case study on page 334). This small second-home community on the ocean in Florida's panhandle has pioneered neotraditional planning principles. Other examples of single-family detached products that have been popular since the 1980s are discussed below.

Site Design. The hallmark of resort residential design is the potential of the natural and/or manmade ameni-

ties to enhance real estate values. Yet, achieving the potentials of each landscape requires creative site solutions, particularly in the face of a shrinking number of resort sites and the need to use previously passed-over lands that may have one or more serious physical impediments to development. For example, although they contain an abundance of natural amenities, the heavily wooded sea islands off the southeastern U.S. coast present particularly difficult drainage problems associated with heavy annual rainfall and the land's low elevation.

The Landings on Skidaway Island, Georgia, developed the "hammerhead" street to increase the depth of real estate frontage along golf course fairways and to resolve the engineering costs associated with the drainage systems. The hammerhead is a short, private street that accommodates four to eight one-third-acre lots. The street's 22-foot-wide pavement is designed as an inverted drain without curb or drainage structures. The hammerheads link to collector roads constructed with the standard complement of curb, gutter, and drainage structures. At the Landings in particular, the hammerhead reduced public right-of-way requirements by two-thirds (from the required width of 60 feet to 22 feet) and pavement requirements by over one-third and, with the elimination of curb and drainage structures, largely made the project economically feasible. Moreover, the hammerhead helped preserve the woods and enhance the private, safe, residential character of each small neighborhood.

In response to the obvious potential real estate values associated with an ocean beach, Sea Pines Plantation designed a network of "double-T" residential streets for its ocean frontage. In contrast to the typical coastal road with strip development paralleling the beach, the double-T network is a series of culs-de-sac that lead to the beach from a parallel road deep in the site's interior. The culs-de-sac are crossed twice at the beach end by short intersecting streets to increase the capacity for lots—hence, the term "double T." A pattern of culs-de-sac and paths creates a private and secure residential environment, affords each resident direct and safe passageways to the beach, and dramatically increases the wedge of high-value real estate fronting on the ocean.

Harbour Town at Sea Pines used a "crenelated edge" to triple the frontage real estate around the circular harbor. Townhouses and condominium apartments are sited on landscaped courts that radiate from the harbor edge. The landscaped courts alternate with parking courts to afford each residential unit its required automobile access as well as a direct view of and physical access to the harbor. The project achieved a total linear architectural face of 5,600 feet for a harbor frontage of 2,000 feet.

Conventional-Lot Homes. Conventional lot size in resort and recreational communities varies widely by market depending on land costs and the availability and physical attributes of developable land. The typical conventional lot is square or slightly rectangular and ranges from 6,000 to 12,000 square feet, although half-acre and one-acre lots are also common, especially in high-end second-home communities. Conventional plotting places a single-family detached house somewhere near the center of its lot. Sometimes, however, it is impossible or undesirable to maintain uniform lot shapes and sizes, especially when accommodating irregular site boundaries, natural features, amenity access needs, curvilinear streets, and culs-de-sac.

Two variations of the conventional lot are pie-shaped lots and flag lots. Pie-shaped lots are common around culs-de-sac and streets with sharp turns; they are narrower at the street and wider at the rear of the lot. Flag lots (sometimes referred to as pipestem lots) provide access to what would otherwise be a landlocked parcel; only the access drive of a flag lot fronts the street. Kiawah Island has used flag lots to maximize the number of homes with direct beach access. The design places a row of lots along the beach and a second row of lots directly behind the first row; the second row faces onto a street paralleling the beach. A narrow drive from the street provides access to the homes directly on the beach while the homes on the street parallel to the beach have beach access via a narrow strip of land that runs between the beachfront homes.

Because they often involve custom-built homes, conventional-lot second-home communities usually include strict design guidelines to achieve a desired image or architectural style for the community. The Preserve in Bethany Beach, Delaware, is a small-scale second-home community on the oceanfront that uses a conventional lotting pattern and strict architectural controls. The project consists of 54 conventional single-family lots averaging under 10,000 square feet, together with a small pool and tennis facility.

When the site was acquired, it was one of the last oceanfront tracts available in the mid–Atlantic area; it lies between the ocean and a highway paralleling the ocean and has a single entrance. A single L-shaped dead-end street with three culs-de-sac serve the development. The plan created 16 oceanfront lots and 38 inland lots, all carefully sited to preserve the dunes and inland wetlands while maximizing oceanfront views. Four elevated wooden walkways connect the community to the ocean, minimizing disruption to the dunes. The natural vegetation in the wetlands adjacent to the highway provides a natural buffer.

Central to project success are the Preserve's architectural guidelines—atypical for the area—that assure purchasers a cohesive and harmonious community character. All homes were custom-built but were designed with a remarkably consistent character. The guidelines require understated landscaping of individual properties, thereby allowing the natural vegetation and rolling secondary dunes to remain largely undisturbed. Outdoor living activities are confined to decks and porches; paved patios or lawns are considered unnatural for the site. Houses must be two or three stories and not less than

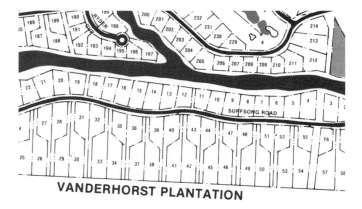

VANDERHORST PLANTATION

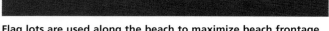

Flag lots are used along the beach to maximize beach frontage at Kiawah Island in South Carolina.

The Preserve in Bethany Beach, Delaware, exemplifies a small-scale second-home community on the oceanfront that uses a conventional lotting pattern and strict architectural controls. The project consists of 54 conventional single-family lots averaging 10,000 square feet, together with a small pool and tennis facility.

The Preserve site plan.

2,500 square feet, exclusive of decks, porches, stairs, garages, etc.

All foundations are required to be constructed of pressure-treated wooden piling, and primary living areas are generally not located at ground level because of the danger of storm flooding. All primary roofs must have a pitch of either 8:12 or 10:12, and all roofing is required to be white cedar shingles, machine split. The rakes of gable roofs are carefully specified, and siding must be wood, either four- or six-inch lap. Six basic colors are carefully specified, typically gray and sandstone, and no primary wall may be windowless. The overall effect is a cohesive and distinctive beach look akin to that found on Cape Cod or in North Carolina.

The Preserve opened in April 1991 and, despite the prevailing market conditions along the Northeast corridor at that time, received an extremely favorable response with 32 sales that same year. The remaining lots sold by February 1993. The sales pace was remarkable for lots generally priced over $250,000.

Zero-Lot-Line and Z-Lot Houses. Zero-lot-line houses were fairly common around the turn of the century and made a strong comeback during the 1960s as an expression of contemporary, higher-density detached housing. The houses are characterized by narrow but deep lots. Instead of providing two sideyards that might each be only five feet wide, for example, the house is located on a side property line to create a more usable ten-foot-wide yard along the other side of the unit. Zero-lot-line houses are typically plotted on lots ranging from 3,000 to 5,000 square feet at densities of about five to seven units per acre.

The "Z" lot emerged in the mid-1980s as a way to overcome some of the design challenges inherent in zero-lot-line houses. The concept derives its name from the staggered sideyard easements that grant each house permanent use of space from each adjoining lot. The frontyard, house, and backyard combine to suggest a "Z" configuration.

A primary advantage of "Z" lots is that, unlike the long windowless wall facing the property line in the typical zero-lot-line house, a home's windows and doors can be placed on both sides of the house. "Z" lots also create more usable yard space by locating the rear side of the house opposite the entry. In most projects, the yard "borrows" space from the adjacent lot through an easement and thus becomes wider and more usable than in the case of zero-lot-line houses.

"Z" lots have been used successfully in a resort community setting at Indian Ridge Country Club in Palm Desert, California—a 640-acre country club community with 1,300 homes planned. The Smoke Tree series of Z-lot homes offers five floorplans that range from approximately 2,392 square feet—for a three-bedroom, three-bath home priced at $330,000 in 1994—to 3,562 square feet for a four-bedroom, 4.5-bath unit priced at $435,000. Lots are long and narrow; the one- and two-story homes include a two-car garage at the front and a patio at the rear that faces onto one of the community's two golf courses. Entry courtyards are located at the front left side of the house and sideyards at the rear right side. Where homes are not directly adjacent, patio walls screen courtyards.

If a resort community is to succeed, small lots and high net densities must be offset by careful design and an appropriate complement of amenities. At Indian Ridge, while the lots are small and homes tightly grouped, the outdoor courtyard areas are private and attractively designed. The rear patio areas convey a sense of spaciousness that is attributable to golf course frontage in every home's backyard. Indeed, Indian Ridge is unusual in that all of the homes in the community enjoy golf course frontage.

Patio Houses. Patio lots are usually square and range from about 2,000 to 3,500 square feet, yielding up to seven units per acre. Patio houses are typically one-level homes built without basements. Each patio house is

Z-lots have been used successfully in a resort community
setting at Indian Ridge Country
Club in Palm Desert, California—a 640-acre country club
community with 1,300 homes
planned. The Smoke Tree
series offers five floorplans,
ranging in size from approximately 2,392 square feet—for
a three-bedroom, three-bath
home priced at $330,000 in
1994—to 3,562 square feet —
for a four-bedroom, 4.5-bath
unit priced at $435,000. The
house pictured is a four-
bedroom home (plan 5 in the
Smoke Tree series) as seen
from the golf course.

Floorplan for plan 5 in the
Smoke Tree series at Indian
Ridge Country Club.

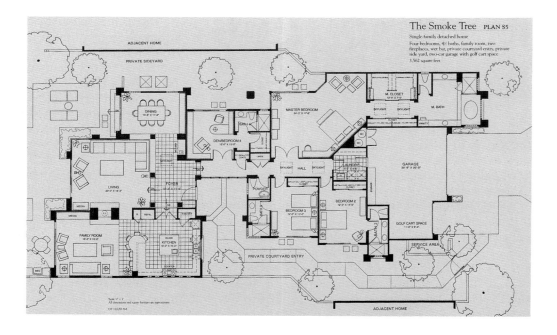

attached to one or more houses yet enjoys adequate privacy. Typically, the available yard areas are consolidated into one or more garden courts either partially or completely bordered by rooms or walls. The outdoor and indoor areas become one secluded space for living.

At Indian Ridge Country Club, one of the primary home series in the community is a patio home product called the Acacia. The series offers nine floorplans, ranging in size from approximately 1,527 square feet—for a two-bedroom, two-bath home priced at $195,000 in 1994—to 2,368 square feet—for a three-bedroom, 3.5-bath unit priced at $265,000. Units are designed in a long, narrow configuration—typically 28 to 32 feet wide—and include a two-car garage at the front and a private landscaped courtyard and/or sideyard. Each unit also features a patio that faces onto one of the community's two golf courses. For the smaller units, the courtyard is located between the house and the freestanding garage; for the larger units, the courtyard is located at the side of the house and the garage is attached. Patio walls screen courtyards from adjacent homes. The units are sold as condominiums; lot size is not an advertised feature of the homes. The typical buyers in the community, as described by the developers, "have worked hard for 25 years, saved their money, invested it wisely, have incomes of more than $250,000 and a net worth in excess of $2 million."[28]

Other Lot Types. Many other lotting patterns can be used. By keeping lots at a more traditional width (55 to 70 feet) but reducing the depth to only about 55 to 70 feet, developers can achieve a density of about seven to eight units per acre. On the other hand, a wide-shallow lot offers the image from the street of a traditional single-family neighborhood. It exposes more of the house's front and orients the front door directly to the street. While wider lots add proportionally to development costs for streets, utilities, and landscaping, many buyers

willingly pay these additional costs in exchange for a more attractive and traditional streetscape.

Alternate-width lots (sometimes called odd lots) combine narrow and wide lots to offer a more varied streetscape. Generally, alternate-width projects do not achieve densities as high as those attainable by using one type of narrow lot, but the versatility of the approach allows for successful applications.

An unusual lot shape is the circular lot used at Brays Island Plantation in South Carolina's Low Country. In an effort to let the land dictate the direction of design, the land planner for the project went into the field and hand selected all homesites. A stake driven in the ground marks the center of a one-acre circular lot. The configuration allows each lot to relate to its specific site conditions rather than to the neighboring circle or homesite.

Townhouses/Attached Homes. Townhouses are single-family attached units, normally two to three stories in height, with common (or party) walls. Narrow lots are the rule in townhouse developments; widths generally range from 22 to 32 feet. The overall density achievable in a townhouse project varies with natural site conditions, the size of the units and building clusters, and parking requirements. Generally, six to 12 units per acre is the norm, but densities can range as high as 20 units per acre when building clusters are closely sited. Designers and developers vary the layout of townhouse units to fit a particular piece of land, its location, and the price range of the market.

Townhouses may be offered for sale or rental, though the method of financing or tenure type (rental, straight sale, cooperative, or condominium) has nothing to do with the unit's classification as a townhouse. Townhouses can offer several advantages over single-family detached houses: lower construction and land development costs, conservation of land and preservation of open space by using less land for a given number of houses, lower long-term maintenance costs, enhanced energy effi-

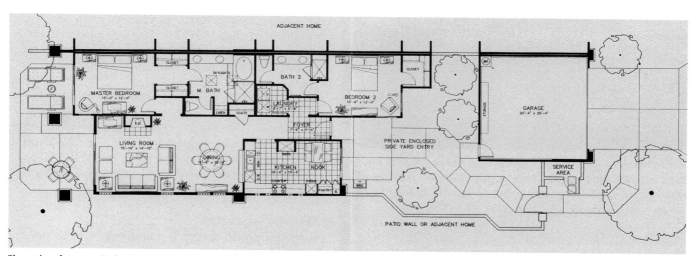

Floorplan for a patio home—part of the Acacia series—at Indian Ridge Country Club in Palm Desert, California.

At Hidden Valley Resort, a ski resort in Hidden Valley, Pennsylvania, the primary product thus far has been a townhouse of about 1,425 square feet that can be purchased fully furnished and placed in a rental program managed by the developer.

The Brittany is a 22-story luxury residential building located on the Gulf of Mexico in Naples, Florida. Three-bedroom and four-bedroom tower and penthouse homes range from 2,500 to 6,000 square feet, and prices range from $695,000 to $2.8 million.

ciency, and increased security for both the house and the neighborhood.

Resorts frequently incorporate townhouses and other attached products because of their affordability and ease of maintenance—both important considerations for a second home. In many cases, attached products sell as condominiums, further reducing the need for maintenance. At Heritage Hills in Somers, New York, for example, an adult recreational community started in the 1970s that continues to develop today, all homes are condominiums. They range in size from 900 to 2,300 square feet; as required by the development permit, about 20 percent are one-bedroom units, 65 percent two-bedroom units, and 15 percent three-bedroom units. During the course of the project, Heritage Hills has offered over 50 different floorplans. Currently 12 different floorplans are constructed, ranging in price from $160,000 to $460,000.

Most homes are attached single-level, "garden"-style units. Buildings of two to at most six units are clustered in several small groups of only two or three structures, thereby conveying a lower-density image. Early on, the project halted construction of interior-unit condominiums, although some corner units incorporate three units on an end. Garages are attached or detached and in some areas follow a motor court configuration. Recently, detached condominiums, some of which are detached townhouses, have been added to the mix, largely in response to the demands of primarily Westchester County residents who are leaving large suburban homes. They want to live in a house with no upkeep but do not like the idea of an attached unit. Approximately one-third of the units in the newer section are detached.

Attached products find application in a variety of settings, including waterfront locations and adjacent to ski slopes or in any other setting that requires a maximum number of housing units near an amenity. Ski resorts, for example, rely on attached products because of the units' requirement for a limited amount of developable land close to the slopes. With ski-in-ski-out units especially popular, townhouse development can maximize the number of available units. Attached products are also popular for resort rental pools, as the rentals can be priced affordably and thus appeal to the broad middle of the market.

At Hidden Valley Resort, a ski resort in Hidden Valley, Pennsylvania (see case study on page 304), the primary product to date has been a townhouse of about 1,425 square feet that can be purchased fully furnished and placed in a rental program managed by the developer. The resort also offers garden apartment condominiums and zero-lot-line single-family homes.

Multifamily Residential

Based purely on design, a multifamily unit is contained within a single multistory building that houses several units. Multifamily buildings can be categorized into three fundamental types based on the size and height of the buildings: two- or three-story low-rise structures (sometimes called garden apartments), four- to six-story mid-rise structures, and high-rise structures.

In resort and recreational communities, low-rise apartment buildings are typically two or three stories without an elevator and house four to ten or more units. They can achieve densities of ten to 25 units per acre. Mid- and high-rise multifamily buildings are generally four stories or more and are equipped with elevators, the number of which is a function of the building's height, number of units, and local building codes.

As a rule, buildings over six floors are constructed of steel frame or reinforced concrete; state and local building codes require buildings over three floors to install a sprinkler system throughout the structure. Because of the cost of sprinkler systems, residential developers contemplating a mid- or high-rise project should investigate applicable building codes before proceeding.

In resorts, multifamily properties are invariably marketed initially as condominiums, although their buyers often place the units in rental pools. Some multifamily properties are also operated as condominium hotels, which are hotels where each room is individually owned; some or all of the rooms are placed in rental pools. The Shoshone Condominium Hotel in Big Sky, Montana, for example, is operated together with the adjacent Huntley Lodge and billed as a property that combines the service of a hotel and the comforts of a condominium. It includes 79 one-bedroom suites suitable for up to four guests and 15 loft units suitable for up to six guests. All units include a full kitchen and a balcony.

Mid- and high-rise buildings vary in shape as well as in height. Most common are the rectangular slab, the tower, and the multiwing building. A trend in the design of these buildings has been to shed the blocklike grid in favor of more articulated building forms. With the rising cost of land, contemporary buildings often incorporate underground parking. Alternatively, parking can

At Amelia Island Plantation, in northeast Florida, mid- to high-rise multifamily housing is used extensively in ocean-front areas but is interspersed with open space and set well back from the beach. The high demand for beach and ocean views at this resort was balanced against the need to maintain the stability and quality of the fragile dune system. The result was generally to limit residential development to the secondary dune. The primary dune and dune trough were preserved for recreational uses and as a protection from storms.

be provided at grade but below a platform that provides space for landscaping or recreational features such as swimming pools or tennis courts.

Mid- and high-rise multifamily housing is especially popular in oceanfront resorts. It allows the developer to site a large number of units in proximity to the beach and thereby take advantage of attractive views. Such housing, however, must be carefully integrated into the beachfront environment lest it detract from this invaluable asset. Creating a wall of high-rise buildings along the beach is not a useful strategy or approach for most resorts. Further, regulators in most locations would not permit such a configuration.

Amelia Island Plantation, an oceanfront resort community in northeast Florida, makes extensive use of mid- to high-rise multifamily housing in oceanfront areas but intersperses the structures with open space. Further, the structures are set well back from the beach. The high demand for beach and ocean views at Amelia Island was balanced against the need to maintain the stability and quality of the fragile dune system. The result is residential development generally limited to the secondary dune, thereby preserving the primary dune and dune trough for storm protection and recreational uses.

Among the more recent multifamily products developed at Amelia Island is Piper Dunes. The new development nestles luxury residences into the tree line a discreet distance behind the community's primary dunes and oceanfront golf holes. The seven-story buildings accommodate only two residences on each floor. Each villa features approximately 2,000 square feet—all on one floor—with three sides welcoming ocean breezes and sunlight. The layout includes a corner living room opening to the dining and kitchen areas, two master bedrooms, a guest bedroom, and optional covered parking. Prices in 1995 started at $393,500.

High-rise multifamily buildings along beachfronts often incorporate design schemes that place all units on the oceanfront side of the building. Such designs may involve "V" shapes, single-loaded corridors for unit access, and a high length-to-depth ratio.

Hotel Products and Design

While an understanding of market dynamics is essential to the success of a hotel development, the attributes and quality of a property's layout, design, and land plan are equally as important. A property's physical attributes influence the overall guest experience as well as potential revenues. Today's resort developers confront both opportunities and challenges in their quest to maximize investment return. In particular, material shifts in consumer demographics and value perception, increasing environmental concerns, and rapid technological advances have redefined the fundamental nature and scope of resort hotel facilities.

Even though resort lodging facilities can vary greatly in type and configuration (see Chapter 1), the typical

resort hotel with 125 to 800 rooms has historically been designed as a self-contained facility, with a range of on-premise facilities and recreational amenities. Its self-contained nature distinguishes the resort hotel from other hotel product segments in that it can readily satisfy most individual or group needs, thereby encouraging guests to remain on the resort hotel's premises.

In addition, due to their orientation toward the vacation and leisure market, most resort hotels experience a much higher average length of stay than typical commercial hotels. As a result, a resort hotel's facility requirements and sizing are generally significantly greater than for other hotel product types as reflected in the following:

- Lobbies are expanded to accommodate live entertainment, retail space, and other services and to serve as a hub that provides access to other areas of the resort. Outdoor courtyards are also more expansive, often including major water features and landscaping.
- Guest rooms are generally large in anticipation of longer average lengths of stay and the possible impact of catering to the family market.
- In markets offering a minimal selection of local restaurants and bars, a resort hotel's food and beverage operations respond to increased capacity. A variety of cuisines accommodates the higher guest retention levels.
- Swimming pool and deck areas as well as other recreational facilities are expanded to satisfy the needs of resort guests, both children and adults. Further, resort hotels generally offer an extensive range of recreational facilities such as a golf course, casino gaming, tennis courts, and/or watersports.

First-generation resort hotels generally consisted of a central hotel structure complete with a selection of food and beverage outlets, meeting facilities, limited

The hotel at the 265-acre El Conquistador in Puerto Rico overlooks the confluence of the Atlantic Ocean and the Caribbean Sea; the topography drops nearly 300 feet to the water.

retail space, and recreational facilities and amenities such as a swimming pool, casino gaming, spa, or fitness center. These resorts also offered a range of on-premise recreational amenities such as beaches, watersports, tennis, and/or golf housed within the resort complex.

In response to an increasingly sophisticated travel market and substantial growth in development costs, resort hotels have evolved into mixed-use resorts that encompass a range of additional land uses strategically located to yield synergistic relationships. In conjunction with market and financial feasibility consultants, land planners and architects have played an integral role in identifying viable land use linkages and successfully implementing transitions in resort facility design. A significant number of the major resorts completed in the 1980s and early 1990s are mixed-use developments in which the hotel structure serves as the center for social activities.

The scope and quality of a resort hotel's facilities and physical plant are expected to continue to evolve. Technological advances and socioeconomic trends will affect virtually every component of resort development, whether new construction or renovation. Furthermore, increased environmental legislation, coupled with continued concern over a resort's ecological impact, is also projected to affect the design of resort hotels. Resort developers and architects are already responding to these changes and environmental concerns by specifying ecologically sound building materials, planning for energy efficiency, and designing properties to incorporate the natural attributes of their given location. In many resorts, interiors reflect the culture of the surrounding area through the use of indigenous materials, local art, and native design styles.

The following sections discuss the various components of a resort hotel's physical plant. Throughout the discussion, it is important to note that the design of resort hotels varies greatly from location to location and by type of facility. A hotel targeted to the resort conference and convention market, for example, differs dramatically from one targeted to the free independent traveler.

Siting and Exterior Design

Whether a resort hotel is freestanding on its own site or sited within a larger resort community, it must be situated in a superior location that provides attractive views and easy access to amenities. Salish Lodge in Snoqualmie, Washington, for example, is a freestanding resort hotel located directly adjacent to Snoqualmie Falls, a 268-foot waterfall in the foothills of the Cascade Mountains (see feature box on page 192). This unique setting gives the hotel an incomparable position in the market.

In a resort community, the hotel should be positioned on the site's most desirable and workable location. After all, the hotel is the resort's primary showpiece. It sets the tone and creates the dominant image for the property. If the hotel is in an oceanfront community, it should be located as close to the ocean as ecologically possible. If

The Sun Valley Lodge and the Sun Valley Inn are two examples of resort hotels that have set important design precedents. The 150-room lodge was built in 1936 by Averell Harriman and is still promoted as a place where you can "rough it in luxury." The 112-room inn was built in 1937 and has the look and feel of a comfortable chalet. Both hotels incorporate rustic design elements and an elegant country French décor.

it is in a mountain location, it should be sited to provide the most dramatic mountain views possible, ensuring that all public areas enjoy attractive vistas. At the Hyatt Regency at Beaver Creek, all public spaces face onto the ski slope. If a resort hotel is located in a golf course community, it should be sited to provide attractive views of the golf course. At PGA National in Florida, for example, the hotel is sited near the center of the resort, affording attractive golf course views in nearly every direction. In some cases, a well-chosen site allows the hotel to take advantage of a variety of attractive views. At Quail Lodge Resort & Golf Club, nearly all 100 rooms in the lodge face onto the golf course, one of the many lakes on the grounds, or the foothills of the Santa Lucia Range.

Clearly, though, practical constraints enter into siting decisions. Large hotel facilities must be set back from oceanfronts and cannot be easily placed at the top or on the side of a mountain. And they cannot always be surrounded by a golf course. Moreover, the hotel must not intrude on sensitive areas and must be designed so that it does not detract from its natural setting. Ultimately, the principal guideline in siting is to provide an impressive visitor experience and to show off the setting to best advantage. It is the setting that draws the guest for return visits. A pleasant hotel experience may also help transform the hotel guest into a timeshare purchaser or a second-home owner in the larger project.

Among the prominent features in a resort hotel, especially in beach and desert areas, swimming pools, water features, and other landscape elements help establish an attractive outdoor setting and amenity. For example, the Maui Prince Hotel at Wakena Resort in Kihei, Hawaii, showcases cascading waterfalls designed by Hideyuki Shibata and a 320,000-gallon koi fish mirror pond, in addition to a large swimming pool. Resort hotels are often designed around a swimming pool or other attractive central space.

The quality of the hotel facility itself is another factor that establishes an image for the project's features. Hotels that can be positioned as the finest of their kind—whether through their franchise affiliation, distinctive architecture and design, or superior service—establish a similarly prestigious image for the resort community as a whole. The Boca Raton Resort & Club, for example, began with a premier hotel facility in the 1920s. Subsequent owners have built a large and exclusive resort community around the facility, drawing successfully on the hotel's high-tone image (see case study on page 340).

It is particularly important that the hotel's architecture also establish an appropriate image. Resort guests, especially at upper income levels, have clear expectations for their ideal resort hotel experience, and a large part of those expectations revolve around architecture. Architectural style should be sensitive to the setting. A hotel in a ski resort, for example, needs to convey the image of a mountain setting, perhaps by incorporating a rustic quality. The Sun Valley Lodge and the Sun Valley Inn have set important design precedents. The 150-room lodge, built in 1936 by Averell Harriman, is still promoted as a place where a guest can "rough it in luxury." The 112-room inn was built in 1937 and conveys the look and feel of a comfortable chalet; both hotels incorporate rustic design elements amid elegant country French décor. Three other day lodges recently added to the mountain turned to similarly rustic styles.

Oceanfront hotels should include balconies that take advantage of ocean and water views and views of other nearby amenities. Large ocean resort properties may encompass several hotels, allowing the resort to provide a variety of hotel settings and experiences at different price points. Pelican Bay, which includes three miles of beachfront, sited two major high-rise resort hotels at opposite ends of the community. Wailea Resort, a 1,493-acre resort on Maui in Hawaii, offers five separate hotels linked together by a beachfront walkway. The U-shaped Wailea Four Seasons Resort Hotel surrounds recreational amenities and a landscaped area, providing interesting views of the amenities, the ocean, and golf courses on the inland side.

To minimize the intrusion into the treeless desert landscape, a hotel in a desert setting might feature a low-profile structure and an organic design. The lodging can be spectacular without overstated architecture. At the Boulders in Carefree, Arizona, the desert setting inspired a design that includes low-profile buildings; the architecture is dominated by the setting, in which manmade elements take second place to natural wonders. Guests stay in 136 private casitas that are nestled into the landmark rock outcroppings that give the property its name. At the Ventana Canyon Resort in Tucson, the 400-room hotel was designed as a low-rise structure to maintain the continuous view of the surrounding mountains and saguaro cactus forest.

On the other hand, a hotel in an area that features a created amenity, such as a theme park, need not be restrained and in fact may be positioned and designed with an image that is distinctive and playful. Disney Development Company is the master of themed hotels, creating a variety of themed hotels within the Disney World resort near Orlando. These hotels have been inspired by national park lodges, New Orleans themes, Polynesian settings, and the grand hotels of the turn of the century such as the Hotel del Coronado. Disney's Dolphin and Swan Hotels, designed by Michael Graves, are pioneering examples of "entertainment architecture"; these two hotels on adjacent sites incorporate large dolphin and swan sculptures into the buildings' architectural profile.

Whatever the style, it is important. Resort hotel architecture should be distinctively different from that associated with a typical commercial hotel. Visitors make a discretionary purchase when they stay at a resort hotel, and they will be less likely to do so if they find the facility ordinary or mundane.

Guest Rooms

Guest rooms in resort hotels have evolved from the standard hotel accommodation of one or more beds, bathroom and vanity area, chair or small sofa, dresser, television, and telephone. Instead, today's resort guests demand many of the comforts they enjoy at home, which may include

- an expanded or oversized guest room or suite;
- a sophisticated telephone system (e.g., two lines, voicemail, in-house autodial);
- smoke-free rooms;
- a writing desk or table;
- cable television;
- an honor bar with a refrigerator;
- an in-room coffee maker;
- increased bathroom amenities (e.g., hair dryer, bathrobe); and
- a large outdoor balcony or patio, including large retractable glass doors that provide views and an easy flow from room to balcony.

At the Boulders in Carefree, Arizona, the desert setting led to a design that includes very low-profile buildings; the architecture is dominated by the setting in which manmade elements take a back seat to natural wonders. Guests stay in 136 private casitas that are nestled in the landmark outcroppings that give the property its name.

Disney's Grand Floridian Beach Resort at Walt Disney World, Florida, re-creates the grandeur of classic Victorian hotels. Distinctive towers, striking redshingle roofs, dormers, cupolas, exposed gable trusses, and a pristine white clapboard exterior are featured in the design. The flavor of the era is carried throughout the project with the use of ceiling fans, gas lamps, intricate latticework, wide verandas, an abundance of wicker, and even attic guest rooms built within the roof structure.

Photo courtesy of Wimberly Allison Tong & Goo Architects

Suitable soundproofing and energy conservation measures are increasingly important in guest room design and material selection. In addition, U.S. hotels must now comply with the Americans with Disabilities Act (ADA) regulations, which mandate numerous previously optional improvements. Among the improvements are wheelchair access and a minimum number of guest rooms designed to accommodate guests with disabilities.

The emergence of the family market as a significant leisure submarket places unique demands on guest rooms. Families generally prefer oversized guest rooms and, in many cases, require a variety of special features. In particular, families with small children expect child-ready guest rooms equipped with safety latches on doors, child-proof safety plugs, and a highchair. In addition, a "lending desk" sometimes offers games and toys. The Hyatt Grand Champions at Indian Wells Golf Resort, for example, is a 336-room all-suite hotel with oversized rooms and private terraces for secluded sunbathing.

The commercial travel and corporate group markets also exhibit needs that influence the design of guest rooms in resort hotels. To conduct business from their guest room, today's business travelers require a functional, well-lighted work area, telephones with multiple lines and voicemail, and/or a facsimile machine/modem hookup.

Food and Meeting Facilities

Historically, hotel restaurants have been noted for their below-average fare. Resort hotel restaurants have likewise suffered from a less-than-stellar reputation. Clearly, though, hotel resorts cannot expect to attract the discretionary guest if they fail to provide good-quality food, particularly given that such hotels are often located in areas with limited restaurant options. In response,

Salish Lodge: A Boutique Resort Hotel

The Salish Lodge, located in Snoqualmie, Washington, about a half-hour drive from Seattle, is a country inn resort in a unique natural setting. It is built at the precipice of a 268-foot waterfall—Snoqualmie Falls—in the foothills of the Cascade Mountains. While the hotel's exterior has the look of a rustic wooden lodge, its interior conveys the image of a sophisticated country inn and features regional arts and crafts. The 91-room resort hotel is also unusual in that its owner, Puget Western, Inc., provided no major on-site amenities, relying instead on the adjacent waterfall park and trails and surrounding golf courses, wineries, and ski areas for the enjoyment of its guests.

Snoqualmie Falls itself drives a hydroelectric plant owned by Puget Power, the parent company of the inn's owner. Built at the turn of the century, the plant earned historic landmark status as the world's first completely underground electric generating facility. With the generators located in solid rock, they do not detract from the serenity of the lodge's setting.

Snoqualmie Falls is one of the largest tourist attractions in Washington state. The original restaurant on the property was well known for its farm breakfasts, elegant dinners, and wedding receptions. In the late 1980s, while seeking a new restaurant operator, Puget Western, Inc., saw a unique opportunity to transform the restaurant into a lodge.

Planning and Design

An initial concern of Puget Western was how to incorporate the restaurant into the new lodge in such a way as to keep the restaurant operating during construction. To accomplish this goal, as well as to provide the best design solutions on what was an extremely tight site, a design team made up of the owner, designers, a hotel consultant, and the contractor facilitated a fast-track construction schedule that met the owner's financial objectives. Even though the team discovered after construction began that the restaurant would have to be rebuilt and could not be merely incorporated into the project in its existing condition, construction proceeded in record time. It began in January 1988 and the grand opening was held just six months later in time for the summer tourist season.

A variety of creative design solutions dealt with the constrained site, which is squeezed between the waterfall and a state highway. Simply put, the 61,132-square-foot building had to be situated on a 1.59-acre site. One solution called for locating additional parking across the highway and connecting it to the inn with an attractive footbridge that would set the stage for a romantic country inn experience. The solution for dealing with the extreme slope was to design an innovative multilevel building that would nestle into the slope adjoining the waterfall without detracting from the aesthetics of the falls. Each section of the rustic yet sophisticated inn has its own peaked roof, providing rooms with spectacular views and masking the mass of the structure.

Erosion concerns at the cliff face and seismic requirements posed additional challenges. An innovative structural system that combined wood framing around a steel-framed seismic core and used a cantilevered foundation with wing walls offered a cost-effective design solution.

Hotel Facilities

The lodge's 91 guest rooms are situated on four levels and include four suites. Each room commands a spec-

resort operators have taken measures in recent years to improve the quality and diversity of their food and beverage offerings. Common solutions include increasing the number of theme restaurants and providing several smaller, more informal restaurants instead of larger, more formal restaurants. Other creative solutions include

- affiliating a food and beverage outlet with a well-recognized concept under a franchise agreement. Food service giants such as Pizza Hut have actively established franchise operations in many U.S. hotels and resorts; and
- leasing one or more food and beverage outlets to a third-party restaurateur recognized for a signature menu theme or celebrity affiliation.

Both of these options allow the resort to enhance the quality and diversity of its food and beverage service while enabling the operator to focus attention on other aspects of the resort. Relinquishing control of food services can, however, pose a major concern for some resort hotel operators. Accordingly, any agreement with a third-party operator should be carefully structured to minimize any potential risks.

The group market segment, expected to continue to represent an important source of market demand for resort hotels, is also influencing food service operations as well as the design of conference facilities. As a result, improvements and renovations to many existing resorts include expansions of or upgrades to banquet and meeting facilities. New resorts are also incorporating a greater range of and larger public facilities as part of their overall development program. Further, to satisfy the growing needs of meeting planners, meeting spaces must be sufficiently flexible and capable of subdivision into a range of configurations. Meeting facilities should also

The Salish Lodge, located in Snoqualmie, Washington, is a country inn resort in a unique natural setting; it is built at the precipice of a 268-foot waterfall—Snoqualmie Falls—in the foothills of the Cascade Mountains.

tacular view and is outfitted with wood-burning fireplaces, whirlpool tubs, goose down comforters, and unique Arts and Crafts Movement furniture and interior design. Some of the rooms feature balconies.

The 10,500-square-foot restaurant overlooks the falls and offers fine cuisine, including one of the largest wine selections in the state of Washington. Other on-site amenities include a library where afternoon tea is served, the Attic Lounge, and a gift shop. The recently added full-scale spa includes a massage room, nail care facilities, locker rooms, exercise lounge, steam room, sauna, and two soaking tubs. Due to lack of land for expansion, the 4,775-square-foot spa occupies two levels atop the loading dock.

Meeting and banquet space were carefully designed but quickly had to be expanded. By 1990, to meet the regional corporate demand for additional meeting space, the owner added 3,132 square feet to the original 3,600 square feet, thereby doubling meeting room capacity. The lodge also provides a full range of business facilities. Meeting facilities include a variety of rooms such as

- the 2,052-square-foot Salish Ballroom whose sliding air wall permits the room to be configured into a variety of seating capacities; between 90 and 180 persons can be seated theater-style and between 60 and 120 reception dinner-style;
- the Potlatch and Falls Terrace Rooms, each about 900 square feet and capable of seating between 20 and 50. The Potlatch Room features a glassed enclosure where Potlatch salmon is grilled over an open flame;

incorporate attractive outdoor areas for receptions, dinners, etc.; these spaces are especially effective in differentiating the resort conference facility from more mundane nonresort conference facilities.

The Lansdowne Conference Resort in Loudoun County, Virginia, for example, was designed and developed specifically as a conference resort. It includes 305 guest rooms, an 18-hole golf course, a 28,000-square-foot health club with swimming and tennis facilities, and 45,000 square feet of meeting space. The conference facility alone incorporates 25 meeting rooms, including 16 breakout rooms located in four clusters and ranging in size from 306 to 456 square feet; six conference rooms ranging from 468 to 2,684 square feet; a wood-paneled board room; a 9,525-square-foot ballroom divisible into four spaces as small as 1,554 square feet; and a 124-seat tiered amphitheater. The prefunction area outside the ballrooms provides attractive views of the golf course.

Timeshare and Vacation Ownership Products

Both physically and strategically, vacation ownership products have evolved dramatically over the past 25 years. As mentioned earlier, most timeshares during the 1970s were conversions of hotels, apartments, and, especially, condominiums that could not sell full ownership. Although many vacation ownership products today are still conversions, roughly 90 percent of all projects are purpose-built.[29] Moreover, vacation ownership products are now much more flexible. Developers can offer buyers the option of designing a vacation annually depending on length of stay, location, size of unit, and season.

Timeshare and vacation ownership products are characterized as much by their ownership structure as by their physical design. Unlike other resort housing

Salish Lodge: A Boutique Resort Hotel *continued*

The lodge's 91 guest rooms are located on four levels and include wood-burning fireplaces and whirlpool tubs. The Salish Lodge illustrates how a small boutique hotel can be successful, even without the on-site amenities typically provided by resort hotels.

- the approximately 400-square-foot Board Room, located adjacent to the Attic Lounge. It offers a balcony and a view of the waterfall as well as executive-style conference table seating for 12. It contains built-in white boards, a pull-down screen, and a wet bar; and
- the Atrium and Vintage Rooms, each about 600 square feet and seating 24 classroom-style, 40 dining-style, and 50 theater-style, with fireplaces. The Atrium Room features a patio and the Vintage Room a wine display.

Evaluating the Experience

The project's total cost of $11.8 million included hard construction costs of $9.2 million; furniture, fixture, and equipment costs of $1.2 million; and soft costs of $1.4 million. Puget Western's parent company had owned the property since the turn of the century and had a land basis of approximately $130,000 in 1987 when project design began. The overall cost structure translates into a per room cost of approximately $130,000. The lodge has been a financial success, enjoying an average occupancy rate at the end of 1993 of 74 percent at an average rate of $150 per night.

The Salish Lodge provides a good example of how a boutique-type hotel can succeed even without the on-site amenities typically provided by resort hotels—provided that the operator pays careful and consistent attention to marketing efforts, operates the hotel as a first-class establishment, and remains flexible enough to cater to the clientele's wishes. Careful building, site, and interior design create a uniqueness that is essential to a resort property of this type. Clearly, the hotel's outstanding site and setting are also fundamental to its success. ∎

figure 4-1

Key Characteristics of Vacation Ownership Products

	Fee Simple and Small Fractions	Undivided Interest	Vacation Clubs	Large Fractions
Proximity to Market				
Regional Resort	100 miles	Varies	Varies	250 miles
Destination Resort	3,000 miles	Varies	Varies	Varies
Length of Stay				
Regional Resort	3–4 days	Varies	3–7 days	7 days+
Destination Resort	7 days	Varies	3–7 days	7 days+
Tourist Profile: Income	$40,000–$70,000	Varies	$75,000+	$75,000+

Source: Ragatz Associates, Eugene, Ore.

products, the nature of the ownership structure—and the flexibility and benefits that go with it—is now the major selling point in the timeshare sector. Figure 4-1 summarizes the characteristics of some timeshare programs.

Fee-Simple versus Right-to-Use Strategies

The fee-simple ownership structure, introduced from France in the 1960s, was the first ownership type. Although it has changed in form since its arrival, it is still the major vacation ownership option in the United States. "Fee simple" is a term used in U.S. law to denote the purchase of all elements of ownership and use of real estate. In other words, the owner holds the deeded right of the real estate and may use the property in whatsoever lawful capacity he or she wishes. A "fee simple timeshare" therefore conveys the same rights *with respect to the period of time the buyer has purchased*.[30] It allows an owner the right to share a homesite for a specifically defined portion of a year in perpetuity.

The right-to-use vacation ownership product has become more popular in recent years. It guarantees the buyer the exclusive use of the designated premises for a designated portion of the year. Right-to-use vacation ownership differs from fee-simple ownership in that it does not involve deeded real estate sales. Often, the developer retains ownership of the land while the vacation ownership buyer holds the right to use the property for a certain period of time. Many vacation club and point-based timeshare programs are right-to-use programs.

Fixed-Interval/Fixed-Unit Programs

The most popular and widely used timeshare is the fixed-interval/fixed-unit interval, often referred to as the one-week interval, although ten-day and two-week intervals are also popular options. Such a timeshare involves either fee-simple ownership or the right to use a specified unit for a specified length of time for a specified time of the year. The average length for short-stay

intervals is 1.4 weeks annually. Fixed-interval programs are sometimes referred to as fee-simple timeshares, but other timeshare forms such as point-based systems may also involve fee-simple ownership of deeded real estate.

Fractional-interest vacation ownership is another version of the fixed-interval/fixed-unit arrangement. It differs from the one- or two-week interval in that fewer owners share the ownership of a unit; as a result, each owner is entitled to spend more time in the unit. Fractional timeshares are usually positioned as quartershares or as one-eighth or one-tenth fractions of the unit, affording the owner, respectively, three months, six weeks, or about 35 days (minus maintenance time) of timeshare use annually. Fractional vacation ownerships are functional for people who want to own a place that feels like a second home while incurring the cost of only a fraction of the product. Fractionals, however, are not a particularly popular form of vacation ownership because they are more difficult to exchange and more costly than other timeshares. Current vacation ownership trends indicate that buyers are interested in shorter stays, greater flexibility, and a lower-cost product.

Undivided-Interest Programs

An undivided-interest (UDI) timeshare creates a membership structure wherein each member shares equal rights to lodging and amenities. UDIs offer high-quality lodging opportunities and amenities in a private club setting. Instead of owning a specific unit, members are deeded a fraction of the entire project. For instance, a member of the Melrose Club in South Carolina becomes a 1/1,550 owner of the facilities (the maximum number of memberships at the club is 1,550). The member is granted a specific number of days of lodging in a rotation that depends on the competition for the reservation. Unlike a vacation club strategy (where members' rights are limited by the length of stay purchased through points), UDI members also have the opportunity to stay at either the 52-room Melrose Inn or one of the UDI

Melrose, South Carolina, is an example of an undivided-interest product. The strategy calls for 1,550 members, and each member becomes a 1/1,550 owner of the facility. The member is granted a specific number of days of lodging in a rotation depending on the competition for the reservation.

The Disney Vacation Club system illustrates the point system. Members can choose their length of stay, unit size, and time of year within a highly variable point system. These points may be transferable to other Disney Vacation Clubs. For example, a member at Disney's Vero Beach Resort (shown at right) may use his or her points at Disney's Old Key West Resort at Walt Disney World Resort.

cottage units for a nominal fee on a space-available basis. Typically, UDIs offer such amenities as tennis, croquet, and other "software" amenities for free while activities such as golf and boat charters might require a nominal fee. Similar in many ways to a country club, UDIs work best if they are easily accessible to their market, thereby ensuring frequent patronage.

UDIs were thought to be the new wave of vacation ownership, but many have struggled. The market has tended to favor vacation clubs (see discussion below), which offer members greater flexibility in tailoring a vacation to their particular needs and preferences. Still, UDIs have established a place for themselves in affluent niche markets. For instance, the Deer Valley Club at Deer Valley, Utah, uses a UDI strategy to offer a traditional timeshare combined with the high-quality service and personal attention a country club might offer. Even though many members of UDIs targeted to niche markets might have the capability to purchase a second

home or a three-bedroom condominium for $600,000, they would rather pay $150,000 for a one-sixth share of a unit and still enjoy the benefits of "software" amenities, such as tuned skis, and the luxury of a high-quality resort. Many resort developers are currently looking to the UDI concept as a strategy to remedy lackluster hotel and condominium projects.

Vacation Clubs and Point Systems

Point systems and vacation clubs provide buyers with the opportunity to design their own vacation. The point value of a vacation is determined by its location, unit size, season, length of stay, amenities, and other unique factors. A buyer purchases an agreement to receive an annual allotment of points for a certain number of years (usually 15).

The Disney Vacation Club (DVC) is a good example of a highly variable point system (see case study on page 370) that permits members to choose their length of stay, unit size, and time of year. To provide further flexibility, members can bank all of their vacation points for one year for application to the following year or borrow up to half of the upcoming year's points.

Other hotel corporations such as Hilton, Hyatt, and Marriott offer similarly flexible point system and club programs. And resorts now offer clubs in both equity and nonequity formats. In some cases, club memberships may provide access to only one resort, but in most cases they offer or plan to offer access to multiple locations. Fairfield Communities, Inc., with the largest timeshare-owner base in the world (132,500 as compared to Marriott's 71,000), has responded to the consumer's need for greater flexibility with an innovative multisite club system called FairShare Plus, which allows owners to purchase points to be exchanged for vacation time at 15 of their resorts around the nation. Some of the club plans offered today include a variety of nonaccommodation benefits such as air travel, golf, car rentals, and other leisure activities. Figure 4-2 outlines some of the pros and cons of point systems and the club ownership concept.

Factors to Consider in Designing a Timeshare Program

Some timeshare industry leaders believe that fixed intervals will succeed in niche markets but that the vast majority of new timeshares will eventually embrace a vacation point system as markets continue to demand maximum flexibility in vacation options. Others, however, have noted that point-based systems are complicated and expensive to manage and that for individual projects not linked to a variety of other properties, fixed-interval and other strategies often perform better, especially those that incorporate flexibility options that mimic point-based timeshares without the complications. Figure 4-3 provides a matrix that can help determine which approach is best for a specific project.

Physical Design Issues

The physical design of timeshare products varies greatly depending on type of program, market, and location. For example, a fractional-share unit (typically a client owns anywhere from a quarter to a tenth of a unit) usually emulates a second home, as evidenced by greater attention to interior design. In contrast, a vacation club program, which is characterized by a higher rate of turnover and owners, offers units that are highly flexible and capable of supporting a multitude of uses. Given the nature of the product, different timeshare programs reflect different priorities.

Although the proportion of residential and hotel properties converted to vacation ownerships has decreased significantly since the 1970s, almost half of today's new timeshares are adapted from preexisting buildings. In terms of unit size and function, a timeshare or vacation ownership unit is configured as a hybrid between a hotel room and a condominium unit. The challenge for developers, then, is to ensure a new sense of spaciousness in the conversion. A hotel conversion should not leave the impression that the residential units were formerly hotel rooms. Generally, a typical hotel bay (standard room) converts into an efficiency, two bays into a one-bedroom unit, and three bays into a two-bedroom lock-off unit.

Innovative design and creative use of space are the hallmark at Club Newport in Miami Beach, Florida. The project used mirrors to enhance the perceived size of

---

figure 4.2

Pros and Cons of Point-Based Vacation Ownership Programs

Pros

Flexibility—as owner's vacation styles change, points allow seasonal and unit size options

Offers new marketing/sales presentation opportunities

Equitable exchange

Daily minimum-use possibility

Split-week options

Low-cost reload

No deliberation over unit size

Easier to sell

Higher percentage of satisfaction among owners

Blend of unit types to meet special customer needs

More flexible development phasing

Focus on program flexibility and buyers' desired vacation experiences rather than on the real estate "investment" abuse that once characterized the industry.

Cons

Developer retention of reserve inventory

Higher maintenance fees

Additional use costs to owner

Need for larger and technically qualified reservation exchange, and MIS staff

Limited availability of special computer software

Regulatory concerns and extended regulatory approval process

Largely unproven track record

Costly transition for developer

No guarantee to owner

No guarantee of reduced point values in low season leading to higher occupancies

Large regional owner bases needed to ensure successful occupancy rates on smaller incremental use

Potential inventory "gridlock"

Possible in-house resales to ensure proper orientation

No recognized uniformity

Source: John F. Sweeney, "Point Systems and Vacation Clubs," in *The ABCs of Vacation Clubs and Point Programs* (Washington, DC: Ingersoll and Bloch, 1994).

figure 4-3

Key Factors Affecting the Success of Vacation Ownership Products

	Fee Simple and Small Fractions	Undivided Interest and Vacation Clubs	Large Fractions
Accessibility to Market	●●●	●●●●	●●●
Tourist Volume	●●●●●	●●●	●●
Repeat Visitation Patterns	●●	●●●●●	●●●●●
Seasonality	●●●●●	●●●●	●●●
Local Market Profile			
Regional Resort	●●●	●●●●●	●●●●
Destination Resort	●	●●●●●	●●●●
Resort Infrastructure	●●●●	●●●	●●●
Extent of Direct Competition	●●●	●	●
Extent of Indirect Competition	●●●●	●●●●	●●●●

●●●●● critical   ●●●● very important   ●●● important   ●● less important   ● not important

Source: Ragatz Associates, Eugene, Ore.

units and, in the project's 364-square-foot units, installed glass shelves to foster a sense of separation between the living and sleeping rooms. The Orange Tree Resort in Phoenix, Arizona, is a timeshare that created a bedroom by using upholstered panels that run along ceiling tracks. When the walls are open, they ensure a sense of spaciousness but otherwise provide privacy for the bedroom. Both of these converted timeshare products reinforce the importance of attending to detail when dealing with limited room size. Even though these creative design solutions have been effective for many timeshare conversions, the most innovative design force in the industry today comes from purpose-built timeshares.

For purpose-built timeshares, the lock-off unit has become an industry standard, offering greater flexibility and a perceived increase in value. The Disney Vacation Club (DVC) in Orlando, Florida, was among the first to adopt the lock-off unit as its core product. At 1,395 square feet, the two-bedroom unit can be divided into a one-bedroom unit and a separate studio unit. The timeshare owner can use the one-bedroom portion of the timeshare unit at a given time in the year and still have the opportunity to use the studio section at another time in the year. Owners can bank the points saved by not occupying the lock-off unit and use the lock-off section at another time. A member can also apply the saved points toward another vacation.

The lock-off is only one of the innovations that has made the DVC one of the most popular vacation ownership products in the business. While an increased emphasis on quality and comfort is typical of many high-quality timeshare resorts today, it represents a dramatic change from timeshares a decade ago. For example, the DVC's standard unit features a king-size bed in the master suite and a queen-size sleep sofa in the living room, washer and dryer, television with VCR in the living room and additional televisions in the bedrooms, whirlpool tub in the master bath, fully equipped kitchen, and private porch. Lock-off studio sections of the unit contain two queen-size beds, color television, wet bar, microwave oven, and coffee maker. Clients want comfort and amenities as part of the experience, not just location.

Without proper attention, interior design treatments can become a financial burden to the developer and owner. Units in continuous need of interior repair and attention are logistically difficult to maintain and lower the owner's perceived quality of both the unit and the vacation experience. Therefore, developers must commit themselves to supplying high-quality, durable products that do not become quickly worn or dated.

Other important considerations for maintaining a durable, high-quality unit call for

- themes and colors that do not show wear or become obsolete;
- lamps with a base lampswitch to prevent unnecessary contact with lampshades;
- carpets that do not mat;
- high-density, all-foam sleeper mattresses that offer durability and comfort;
- a kitchen with complete cooking amenities; and

- designs and materials that respect local climatic factors (such as humidity).

The timeshare product is continually evolving in response to market expectations. Features such as the lock-off design underscore the importance of constant product refinement. With the timeshare product still in its infancy, product innovations are likely in this dynamic segment of the resort industry.

Notes

1. Charles Fraser, Presentation at ULI Seminar "Trends and Issues in Resort Development," Pebble Beach, Calif., June 21–22, 1993.
2. Ibid.
3. Donald Canty, "Sea Ranch," *Progressive Architecture,* February 1993, pp. 86–91.
4. Ibid.
5. John Cottle, "A Regional Approach to Resort Design: Revitalizing Resort Communities," paper presented at ULI Seminar "Revitalizing Resorts: Renewal, Repositioning, and Redevelopment," Lake George, N.Y., June 20–21, 1994.
6. Lawrence Halprin, "Sea Ranch: Halprin's Recollections," *Progressive Architecture,* February 1993, pp. 92–93.
7. Canty, "Sea Ranch," pp. 86–91.
8. Larry E. Helber, "Redeveloping Mature Resorts for New Markets," unpublished paper, 1994.
9. Adapted from David McCarty, "Mixed-Use Resorts: Opportunities and Challenges," *Urban Land,* August 1995, pp. 30–33, 80.
10. Ibid.
11. Donald W. Adie, *Marinas: A Working Guide to Their Development,* 3d ed. (New York: Nichols Publishing Company, 1984), p. 133.
12. Ibid., p. 98.
13. Ibid.
14. C.R. Goeldner, T.A. Buchman, and K.P. Duea, *Economic Analysis of North American Ski Areas* (Boulder: University of Colorado Business Research Division, 1983), p. 13.
15. James Branch, "Classification of Resort Areas by Type," unpublished paper, n.d.
16. Desmond Muirhead and Guy L. Rando, *Golf Course Development and Real Estate* (Washington, D.C.: ULI–the Urban Land Institute, 1994), p. 1.
17. Ibid., pp. 47–53.
18. Miles M. Smart, J. Don Spencer, Ricardo N. Calvo, and Charles H. Peacock, "Working with Nature for Better Golf Developments," *Urban Land,* March 1993, pp. 17–22.
19. Ibid., p. 22.
20. Muirhead and Rando, *Golf Course Development,* pp. 44–47.
21. Ibid, p. 108.
22. Ibid, pp. 58, 61–63.
23. Brian McCallen, *Golf Resorts of the World: The Best Places to Stay and Play* (Harry N. Abrams, 1993), pp. 207–209.
24. Ed and Judy Colbert, *The Spa Guide* (Chester, Conn.: Globe Pequot Press, 1988).
25. McCallen, *Golf Resorts.*
26. David W. Myers, "Gaming Bug Spreads across Country," *Urban Land,* August 1995, p. 55.
27. Kerry D. Vandell, "Tribal Gaming Offers Niche Markets," *Urban Land,* December 1995, p. 40.
28. Personal communication with Edwin McMullen, chair, Hilton Grand Vacations Company, February 9, 1996.
29. Gary A. Terry, "Resort Timesharing and Multiple Ownership Products and Their Benefits to Resort Hotels and the Community," unpublished paper (Washington, D.C.: Jones, Waldo, Holbrook & McDonough, P.C.).
30. Ibid.

5. Operations and Management

The developer's role in the operation and management of a resort community varies greatly depending on the type of development and the stage of the development process. In small, strictly second-home communities, the developer's involvement in ongoing management may be limited and simply terminate with the sale of the last lot; the management system required for such a property could involve merely setting up a community association and planning for its transfer to the homeowners. Where resort communities involve major amenities such as a golf course, specialized management is needed to ensure that the amenity is properly maintained. In this case, management can take several forms and perhaps involve a variety of ownership structures as well. In some large and diverse multiuse resort communities, the management effort is akin to running a small city—and includes a lot of politics.

This chapter focuses on resort operations management and marketing as it relates to multiuse resorts, but it also discusses key operations issues associated with resort residential properties, timeshare/vacation ownership properties, resort hotels, community organization structures, club structures, and major amenities.

The revitalized Hilton Hawaiian Village is the largest hotel complex in Waikiki. Its spacious and villagelike environment has won numerous awards.

General Operations Issues

The operation of a resort property can be an extremely complex and challenging undertaking for several reasons. First, the recreational amenities and products offered by the resort are often diverse, frequently requiring a wide variety of management expertise and intense management effort. Second, the seasonality of many resorts means that management efforts are constantly either gearing up or gearing down; yet, they must be able to deal with peak-season traffic. Third, a resort's location often some distance from major urban areas limits access to both municipal services and a large and diverse employment base. Finally, the targeted market for the resort is dispersed and thus not easy to reach cost effectively. As a result, the property management and marketing functions for a resort property are distinctly different from those required for most other types of real estate.

General Resort Marketing Strategies

Marketing is the process of understanding the market, creating a product to satisfy the market, promoting and selling the product, and satisfying the guest/owner in continued operations. While involving virtually all phases of development, the central elements of marketing include

• market research to define potential markets;

- advertising and promotion to make the product known; and
- presales planning and sales management.

Marketing a resort, as with many other steps in the development process, is an iterative process. It involves creating and fine-tuning the marketing strategy, implementing sales management, and monitoring and measuring market response. Information obtained through this process is not only important to refining the marketing process itself but also crucial to product programming and managing the resort.

The Resort Program as Marketing Tool. The first and most important marketing strategy is to invest dollars in developing income-producing resort facilities that add permanent long-term value to the development. The development of a high-quality resort and amenity program can be well worth the investment. First-rate amenities satisfy visitors and greatly facilitate land and housing sales objectives. In resort marketing, good public relations and word-of-mouth communication is critical. In fact, a high-quality resort often does not need to devote a lot of its budget to advertising and promotion dollars because its reputation speaks for itself.

A good illustration is Semiahmoo in Blaine, Washington. Real estate sales were relatively slow at the resort until the golf course and hotel opened in 1986–1987. In fact, in 1987, *Golf Digest* rated the community as Best

New Resort Course in America, an accolade that greatly enhanced the marketing effort, particularly considering that 60 to 70 percent of the community's real estate buyers expressed an interest in golf. Another marketing lesson learned at Semiahmoo related to naming the project. The name Semiahmoo was taken from the sandspit at the property; because the name is in the public domain, the developers have no control over its use. As a result, other local projects have also adopted the name, creating some confusion in the market.

Ultimately, the primary marketing task is to develop the right product at the right place at the right price and time. Direct selling is only a small part of the overall marketing effort. Accordingly, it is critical that a marketing professional become and remain an integral member of the development planning team.

Preparing a Strategy. Marketing is an enormous up-front budget item that can substantially increase the cost of the product. Indeed, preparation for specific promotional and sales activities should begin well in advance of the release of the product. If a major pre-sales effort is programmed, direct selling can begin almost at project conception. Postconstruction sales require constant monitoring throughout the development phase, although the specific tools may vary when selling commences.

As stressed previously, a critical function in product planning is pursuing the targeted markets. The proj-

At Semiahmoo in Blaine, Washington, real estate sales were relatively slow until the golf course and hotel opened in 1986–1987; the high quality of the golf course especially made a difference in marketing the resort. In 1987, the course was rated the Best New Golf Course in America by *Golf Digest* magazine. This rating boosted the marketing effort, particularly considering that 60 to 70 percent of the real estate buyers expressed an interest in golf.

John Russell

ect's entire image should be carefully presented as a reflection of the interests of the targets. Targets provide a standard by which to maintain and evaluate the project's success and direction. They require the marketing group to maintain the appropriate reputation for the project. Reassessing the targeted markets should be an ongoing activity of the marketing group.

Beyond the basic guidelines, a specific project's marketing strategy depends on the circumstances of each situation. Regardless of circumstances, however, the strategy must always relate to the identified market. It should be comprehensive and flexible and generally encompass a variety of activities, including merchandising, promotion, and advertising. It is imperative to evaluate each marketing program for its cost-to-sales effectiveness. Such an evaluation requires a systematic and rigorous analysis of customer characteristics and responses with respect to the targeted market. Significant benefits can be realized by scrapping high-cost/low-return programs and reallocating expenditures to more productive approaches.

By using market research compiled early in the development process, the marketing team should develop a comprehensive strategy for promoting and advertising the proposed resort. The strategy should carefully spell out the resort's overall concept, identify the appropriate targeted markets and the best strategies for reaching them, provide for advertising and promotion, and determine the budget and timetable for implementation. The marketing strategy should also delineate the timing of the various marketing programs in coordination with the development program, allowing for a reasonable presales period. Timing considerations should also extend to the marketing of prime sites.

Promotion. Designing the promotional material and public relations program is a critical element in marketing the resort property. The overall promotional effort should seek to create an awareness of the development and a favorable public image. For resorts that draw primarily from a single metropolitan area or several nearby markets, public relations and promotional efforts must be continuous and include community involvement such as working with civic groups and maintaining a positive relationship with the press. Where resort projects are part of larger resort areas, developer participation in joint promotional programs can be cost-effective.

For destination resorts that draw from a much broader market, promotion is more difficult and may in fact involve both a good deal of promotion to intermediary groups and joint promotional programs. Promoting the resort to travel agents or agencies, for example, is one strategy. Another strategy is to create joint package deals with airlines. Resorts must also ensure that they are listed and/or discussed favorably in the various travel and vacation newsletters, magazines, and guidebooks that are released annually by a variety of publishers, including Mobil, Fodor's, etc. These publications are of major importance in the promotion of vacation destinations.

High-quality brochures or videotapes should be created from the outset, even during the presales or preleasing period. The printed or graphic materials should incorporate the logo and feature the design theme that characterizes the resort. Developers pioneering a new concept should include appropriate explanations in their brochures and other printed material.

Specific material and programs should include the following:

- Collateral materials required for resort operation. The materials include resort brochures and videotapes for both consumers and travel agents, package brochures and rates for tour operators and airlines, folders with maps for guests, service directories, lists of on- and off-site activities, cards/questionnaires for evaluating services, direct-mail pieces with letters to previous guests, and other items needed to maintain amenities such as menus, room cards that promote facilities, golf course scorecards, napkins, placemats, matches, and so forth.
- News releases concurrent with the advertising program —accompanied by photographs wherever possible— for distribution to editors of magazines and various sections of newspapers in all market areas. First-hand stories are preferable and should relate to all facets of the resort and the developers themselves. Editors should be invited to visit the project.
- Special programs or events for individuals and groups to enhance the resort's activity level. Various types of ongoing promotions such as buffets and on-site parties should be planned to attract different groups. Further suggestions for promoting the resort's image and enhancing its activity level include arranging major on-site activities (possibly for charity) such as golf and tennis tournaments and outings that provide maximum exposure via the media and spectators; engaging a celebrity to host an event; and inviting residents, local officials, prospective purchasers, and others to appropriate social and promotional activities.

Advertising. Because resort community developments typically sell a particular lifestyle, advertising materials must clearly and accurately convey the project's strengths and appeal. The advertising campaign should focus on a central theme that is established early and extends throughout the various stages of development.

The developer's in-house staff should have a general working knowledge of the fundamentals of advertising, although common practice calls for hiring an advertising agency to develop a fresh approach for each new project. An agency typically develops a long-range strategy, plans individual programs, selects the best media outlets for various presentations, prepares copy and designs layouts, and evaluates the results of the promotional campaign. The advertising budget varies with project size, proximity to primary markets, the number of targeted markets, and the degree to which the proj-

Grand Harbor is an 893-acre development in Vero Beach, Florida, that features two golf courses, tennis courts, a deep-water marina, and a beach club. In August 1991, Grand Harbor Associates acquired the amenities, developable land, and title to 125 existing multifamily, golf-oriented units. The immediate marketing challenge was to sell these units. A two-year media and database marketing program was put into effect with 60 percent of the budget allocated to mass media marketing and 40 percent to database marketing to a buyer profile based on 800 current owners in the development. According to Charles Tallman, a partner with Cunningham, Tallman, Pennington in Savannah, Georgia, which helped market the property, in the first year—in a tough real estate market—79 villas were sold. Database marketing generated 2,578 leads; mass media generated another 3,867. The leads from both sources resulted in 686 property tours and 57 sales, at a tour-to-sale closing ratio of 12:1. The remaining 20 sales came from outside real estate agents and miscellaneous sources. Database marketing was responsible for half the year's sales. Pictured are the golf course and the beach club.

ect introduces new concepts to the market. Advertising is an expense incurred during all stages of development—during presales or preleasing, before the project's grand opening, and after operations begin. The expense, however, is proportionately higher during the earlier phases.

Among the more exciting developments in resort advertising are the cost-effective possibilities offered by the Internet and the World Wide Web. These new media allow any resort to advertise and provide users with promotional materials on demand at low cost (see feature box on page 227).

Educational and Activity Programming

One of the most important resort management functions involves programming activities for resort residents and guests. Usually, a special staff manages the various programs, which may extend to such on- and off-site activities as concerts, plays, arts and crafts festivals, and other forms of entertainment and amusement; tours of nearby sites; exploration and adventure excursions; educational programs; sports instruction programs and tournaments; and wellness/spa programs.

Entertainment and cultural events are among today's more common offerings in resort settings and are growing increasingly popular. Concerts, plays, arts and crafts festivals, music festivals, holiday festivals, and special themed events are popular ways to attract visitors. These events can be especially useful in shoulder seasons; for example, many East Coast beach resorts sponsor jazz festivals in the fall to attract visitors following the peak summer season. Sun Valley Resort in Idaho offers a fall jazz festival in addition to a summer arts and crafts festival, an antique show, a summer symphony, live theater, and ice shows.

Exploration and adventure programs and excursions are also popular offerings. For example, notes J. Richard McElyea and Gregory L. Cory of Economics Research Associates in San Francisco, "Many new and larger resorts have begun to provide a variety of off-site excursions for guests who want more adventure and fantasy than traditional resort activities offer. These 'soft' adventures—white water rafting, three-day hikes, wild-game hunting—typically require guides and provisions and include some element of thrill."[1]

One example of a soft adventure program can be found at the Hilton Waikoloa on the island of Hawaii. It offers its guests such recreational variety as wild boar hunting in the wilds of the Hawaiian rainforests, learning to drive a race car under the tutelage of an Indy 500 driver, working for a day as a cowboy at the Parker Ranch, or frolicking with dolphins in a special dolphin pool. Waikoloa calls its programming service Vacations by Design. The resort activities director can develop a personalized schedule of activities for each guest. Examples of activities at other resorts include white water rafting, two- to three-day hiking excursions with meals and accommodations, bare boat charters, or hot air balloon rides. Soft adventures are particularly appealing to the

Hot air ballooning is a soft adventure available at some resorts, including Snowmass in Colorado.

The 53,000-acre Molokai Ranch, located on the island of Molokai in Hawaii, is adopting environmental tourism as an integral part of its operations, which also include agribusiness and community development.

25-to-45-year-old age group and represent a reaction to the sedentary urban lifestyle experienced by many. Today, many people want their vacation to be more than just a trip to the beach or mountains.

The soft adventures scheduled by a resort add considerable opportunity for publicity and recognition, often without substantial investment. For the most part, developing partnerships with concessionaires and other service providers eager to organize soft adventures can greatly enhance a resort's amenity offerings. For example, in its marketing materials, the Kauai Marriott Resort and Beach Club promotes scenic helicopter tours of the island provided by a separate company; the club also promotes catamaran sailing tours. Particularly with repeat guests, it makes sense to add new places to go and things to see that have a different twist.

Base camping is a related and growing resort trend that is capitalizing on the soft adventure trend. In simple terms, a resort can serve as a base point for a variety

Maho Bay in the U.S. Virgin Islands offers a combination of "soft" adventures and an ambience that is attracting a growing market of vacationers interested in alternative sports and committed to protecting the environment. Maho Bay uses "ecotents" made out of recyclable material; power is generated from solar panels. Its sports include sea kayaking, wind surfing, hiking, and snorkeling.

At Dewees Island, a 1,205-acre second-home community in South Carolina, two full-time professionals conduct extensive environmental education and research initiatives and provide residents with the opportunity to learn about and play an active role in the island's stewardship.

of adventures away from the resort, including soft adventures, more rugged adventures, and ecotourism. Base camping is particularly well suited to a resort location that is not characterized by either beach access or proximity to a major tourist attraction but is relatively close to a wide variety of activities to which guests can be transported.

In addition, many resorts offer instruction in various sports, including the standards such as golf, skiing, and tennis but also up-and-coming sports such as mountain biking and in-line skating. Instructional programs are offered both as an ongoing service provided on a daily basis and as part of one- or two-week instructional sessions.

Wellness and health spa programs are also increasingly popular. While such programs are amenities, they depend as much on the services they offer as on the facilities themselves. Thus, management is a critical element in establishing and maintaining the quality of the programs.

Even though activity programming is common at major resort hotels and multiuse resorts, it is becoming more common in second-home communities. For example, at Broken Top, an 866-unit second-home community in Bend, Oregon, a full-time activities director is responsible for organizing community ski trips, outings, father/son weekend camping trips, white water rafting tours, etc. Critical to Broken Top's success is the programming of activities and the resort's packaging as a family environment, which is marketed as Camp Broken Top.

Educational programs are also popular in all types of resorts, including many second-home communities. Clearly, the Disney Institute in Orlando is a leader in providing education within a resort environment. The institute offers more than 80 hands-on programs, ranging from animation and topiary gardening to rock climbing and wilderness exploration. Guests customize their vacation experience as they pursue current interests and explore new ones. At any given time, creative individuals, musicians, dancers, chefs, writers, filmmakers, and others are present at the Disney Institute, taking part in programs, holding workshops, and creating new work. Guests interact with these individuals, observe the creative process, and see new works presented in the resort's performance areas. Evenings are highlighted by live performances and lectures on a broad spectrum of topics.

There are two ways to choose programs. First, preselected program packages are grouped by area of interest and include a range of programs that might relate to nature, animation or culinary arts. "Dabbler" packages allow guests to sample activities from many areas of interest. Second, guests may customize packages by adding or subtracting programs. With the customized itineraries, guests choose programs from the individual program list.

To complement the structured programs at the institute, the artists-in-residence program offers guests the

Pelican Bay is a 2,104-acre planned community that incorporates a strong diversity of residential products and land uses, attracting a broad range of visitors, homeowners, and professionals. Over one-fourth of the property consists of sensitive coastal wetlands and mangrove forests set aside as a conservation area protected in perpetuity. The project includes the Philharmonic Center for the Arts; two world-class hotels, the Ritz-Carlton, Naples, and Registry Resort; beachfront access via two elevated boardwalk systems; Class A office space; and a full spectrum of residential products (single-family estates, villas, garden apartments, and mid- and high-rise apartments).

opportunity to interact with visiting professionals and noted talents in a given field. For example, a dance troupe visiting the institute might invite guests to take part in rehearsals, assist in staging performances, and provide input on choreography and design.

The Disney Institute features a variety of educational facilities and housing options. The facilities include 28 program studios, a broadcast-quality performance center, an outdoor amphitheater, a state-of-the-art cinema, a closed-circuit television station, and a closed-circuit radio station. Accommodations comprise a selection of light, airy townhouses and bungalows configured as all suites and set among pine woods, canals, and lakes. The lightly wooded, 250-acre site betrays little of its Disney and theme park connections despite its location near the Disney Village Marketplace and Pleasure Island.

Other resorts offer more modest programs. At Dewees Island, a 1,205-acre second-home community in South Carolina, two full-time professionals conduct extensive environmental education and research initiatives and provide residents with the opportunity to learn more about and play an active role in the island's stewardship. Nearby Spring Island has established a visiting artist-in-residence program. Artists in residence for several weeks give a fireside talk on their work and art each Thursday night.

Whatever the resort type, the types of programmed activities must be targeted to the market; some can be simple and down to earth. At the Ridge Tahoe, a time-share resort near Lake Tahoe, some of the most popular activities include country/western dance lessons, bingo, and cooking classes.

Operating Multiuse Resorts[2]

Large multiuse resorts can offer an extensive selection of on-premises recreational activities such as golf, skiing, tennis, watersports, etc., along with hotels and a range of residential land uses such as timeshare, condominium, and/or single-family residences. Within multiuse resorts, several factors create synergistic relationships.

• A combination of hotels, timeshares, and second homes increases the number of potential amenity users over a more substantial portion of the year.
• Hotel guests serve as potential buyers of residential real estate.
• Resorts may offer a rental program in which the owner of a residential unit elects to enter into an agreement with the hotel operator to market the unit to transient guests. Under such an agreement, the unit owner and the hotel operation split the room revenue generated by the residential unit. The arrangement offers the hotel guest the opportunity to sample residential products while the unit owner enjoys a potential return on investment. It also allows the developer to showcase various types of residential units to potential buyers.

- Golf courses necessary for resort hotel operations can be structured as equity clubs and marketed to residential unit owners to yield a significant additional source of revenue.
- Residents and guests of residents within the resort community represent a potential source of demand for such hotel services as food and beverage operations, retail goods, and recreational amenities.

These synergies can provide multiuse resorts with significant management and marketing advantages and thereby enhance the revenue stream.

At the same time, however, multiuse resort developers face many complex marketing and property management issues. Because multiuse resorts by definition include a range of owners—from timeshare owners who spend only one week a year at the property to second-home owners to year-round residents to transient guests who may return frequently or not at all—multiuse developments create their own unique universe of legal requirements, divergent property management needs, and marketing and resale programs. Moreover, large-scale multiuse resort operations require a sophisticated management system to handle the management and marketing of the homes/lots, accommodations, and numerous amenities.

Dealing with the complexities of large multiuse resorts often involves creative management structures. At Horseshoe Bay Resort, a 4,500-acre multiuse lake and golf resort near Austin, Texas, the developer set up two separate companies: one to own and operate the amenities (Lake LBJ Investment Corp.) and one to own and sell the lots (Lake LBJ Improvement Corp.). The latter company is intended to survive only until all lots are sold, whereas the Lake LBJ Investment Corp. will continue as the long-term management entity. To ensure that Horseshoe Bay remains a "pure" destination resort, the developer has stipulated that the latter company may neither participate in any way in lot sales nor encourage members or guests to purchase lots or shelter. Although the lot sales are clearly an important part of the resort, the developer's goal is to build an ongoing viable amenity operation; the amenities have been built as freestanding entities and not solely for the purpose of selling lots.

Perhaps the most management-intensive resort type is a large-scale four-season ski resort, which requires management of the various specialized tasks involved in a ski operation, including a lift operation and snowmaking (if used) as well as golf course management, tennis and swimming facility management, lot/home sales management, community association management, club management, and management of guest accommodations and various other support facilities and amenities.

Managing Competing Expectations. Given the different needs and expectations of different property owner categories in a multiuse resort, it is unusual for conflicts to arise over service levels and access to amenities. For example, a timeshare owner visiting the resort for just

Kim A. Richards
President and Chief Executive Officer
Hualalai Development Company
Kailua-Kona, Hawaii

Kim Richards joined the newly formed Hualalai Development Company (HDC) in August 1992 as president and chief executive officer. HDC is the development manager for a master-planned resort currently under construction on the island of Hawaii. The first phase of the Hualalai project includes a 250-room Four Seasons Hotel, an 18-hole Jack Nicklaus–designed golf course, and over 300 single-family residential units. In addition to his involvement with Hualalai, Richards is president and owner of the Athens Group, an Arizona-based real estate development firm specializing in the development of destination resort hotels, golf courses, and resort communities.

From 1977 to 1983, Richards was vice president and general counsel of the Estes Company. From 1983 to 1988, he was president of Estes Properties, the community development and resort properties division of the Estes Company, one of the largest privately held real estate development companies in the southwestern United States. During this period, Estes Properties was responsible for the successful acquisition, planning, and development of several large-scale master-planned communities, including Ventana Canyon in Tucson. Richards acquired Estes Properties in December 1988 and shortly thereafter renamed the company the Athens Group.

Richards received his undergraduate degree in political science and business law from Western Michigan University in 1970 and a JD from the University of Arizona College of Law in 1973.

I have often described large-scale resort development as a simultaneous equation comprised of three separate components or markets, each of which is concurrently subject to its own market cycles and variations. The three primary components are residential real estate, resort hotels, and resort/residential amenities, including golf, tennis, health, and the natural environment. Over the life of the project, each of these distinct market components must be integrated into a cohesive project concept simultaneously developed and operated and, ultimately, sold in order to maximize value and economic return. It has been my observation over the years that successful resort developers possess, out of necessity, not only the time-tested entrepreneurial skills and instincts of large-scale real estate development, but also a thorough understanding and working knowledge of the resort hotel and resort amenities business.

It is the creation of the overall resort concept and the disciplined execution of the concept over the long term that creates value, as opposed to building exactly the right hotel product or exactly the right golf course. It's how you manage and coordinate the operations of the resort components, especially the amenity package, that creates the project image and thus its perceived value in the marketplace. Resort development has evolved into much more of an entrepreneurial and operations business than it was 20 years ago when we first started developing these projects.

Generally speaking, a major resort project faces at least two down cycles during its development and sales phase. Although project timing is usually the determining factor in securing financing, it is not necessarily the critical factor in determining the development's economic success. This is due, in large part, to the fact that most large-scale resort developments have at least a projected ten-year time frame. Therefore, it is essential that a project's financing terms and structure anticipate and provide for at least one major down cycle. This is especially critical from a residential marketing strategy standpoint, from an operating hotel standpoint, and from the amenity side. You cannot predict with certainty where and when a project's returns will come from over time. To the extent possible, a resort must be structured and financed to maintain maximum flexibility in order to maximize returns during periods of opportunity in the marketplace and to mitigate against the effects of a market decline. Overall management control and structural flexibility are essential.

There are some inherent and conflicting concerns regarding the ownership and management of large-scale resort developments. As I mentioned, the management of large-scale resort development is primarily an entrepreneurial function that requires a disciplined focus on the execution and perpetuation of the project vision over the life of the project. In my view, the resort development/management team should be few in number and multifunctional in talent. On the other hand, resort development is extremely capital-intensive and thus traditionally attracts large corporate and institutional investors/owners during periods in the real estate cycle when there is an excess supply of capital. The result over the last decade, with regard to much of the resort development that has taken place, was deal structures based on unrealistic projections and ownership/management that was unwilling or incapable of adjusting to economic reality.

With regard to our general approach to a project, we incorporate a concept called "integrated resort management." It is a team approach, and a key element is the inclusion of our marketing professionals at the very inception of the project vision. The marketing concept is so fundamental to the vision of the project that it becomes the driving force of the resort, not just from the development side but also from the entitlement side. Integrated resort management requires experienced

Ventana Canyon outside Tucson, Arizona, has been lauded as a well-planned desert community that offers products for a diverse market while preserving the integrity of the desert environment.

people with multifunctional backgrounds. At Ventana Canyon, for example, the marketing and sales team was not limited to real estate professionals selling a specific product but rather included a cadre of sports, country club, and environmental professionals advocating and selling a lifestyle.

The Falls of Slick Rock Golf Course at Horseshoe Bay Resort near Austin, Texas. At Horseshoe Bay, the developer set up two companies, one to manage the amenities and one to own and sell the lots.

one week every year has needs and expectations that differ sharply from those of a year-round homeowner resident. Yet, each owner category has legitimate rights that demand the appreciation and respect of developers and resort management. The first step, notes Richard Hulbert of Hulbert Group International in Vancouver, British Columbia, is to make sure the needs of each owner are addressed individually in exactly the same way they would be in a single-purpose development. "First you have to look at the needs of each component and address those. That's critical," he says. "Once you've done that, then you have to look at ways their needs overlap and combine. But you can't do that first or you run the risk of overlooking the fact that each consumer needs something different."

Management concerns can range from discounting prices in the hotel restaurant for members to extending maid service and club membership privileges to various property owners and their guests. For any such system to work, however, it must respect each owner's rights and avoid attaching any sort of stigma to any one use, Hulbert recommends. In some instances, resorts may have to offer "separate but equal" facilities, one set for permanent residents and their guests and another for hotel guests and timeshare and fractional owners, notes Bill Byrne of the Byrne Corporation in Big Canoe, Georgia. Careful planning also can avoid most owners' rights issues, he adds, but a crucial element is proper staff training and communication. Keeping all staff members informed through staff meetings and frequent written communications helps them better market and manage the resort.

As most experts agree, anticipating and managing every detail of complex resort operations can tax even the most generously funded, most professionally managed operation. Yet, the potential rewards can more than offset the difficulties.

Marketing Multiuse Resorts. While marketing a multiuse resort involves marketing many individual compo-

nents of the resort, the marketing of the overall resort and its amenity program takes precedence. In essence, the resort must be marketed as an attractive destination for the leisure market. Marketing the amenity program is critical, as it is the attractive presentation of the amenity component that makes all the other products—homes, hotels, etc.—marketable as well. At the same time, an attractive amenity is a critical marketing tool in itself.

As for residential product, multiuse resorts can offer several marketing advantages over one-dimensional resorts. The primary advantage, says Jerry Andres, chief executive officer of Eagle Crest Partners, Ltd., the developer of Eagle Crest Resort in Redmond, Oregon, is the ability to offer product across the entire spectrum of vacation property ownership. "A mixed-use resort allows you to have a product mix from which you can sell products to a customer base for the life of their recreational needs," Andres comments. "It's similar to the GM approach in automobiles: you have entry-level products, which are timeshare properties typically, and then at the highest level you have estate homes. In between are fractionals and condos [as well as smaller single-family detached homes]."

By offering products at a variety of price points, multiuse resorts can penetrate the market much more deeply. Eagle Crest, for example, has enrolled more than 7,500 owners and has generated in excess of $100 million in business since its inception, despite the fact that its home state of Oregon is one of the nation's least populous states. "That's not possible with a single-purpose product," Andres contends. In other words, to move residents up the property ladder, management must satisfy owners' changing needs and desires. If visitors and residents are not satisfied with their accommodations and the resort's amenities and services, they will look elsewhere for their next move. Thus, a high-quality ongoing management program is also a critical marketing tool.

Marketing mixed-use resorts mimics the automobile industry in another way, Andres says, by providing a dependable mechanism for helping customers move up to higher-end models. At Eagle Crest, owners can take advantage of the company's trade-in program, which returns to them a set percentage of the purchase price of their original property when they decide to move to a more costly property. The used inventory, Andres explains, is recycled back into sales inventory, creating a constant cycle of new owners and repeat buyers moving into higher-end properties.

Residential Marketing and Sales Management

The most cost-effective markets to tap for sales of residential property in resorts are often those closest at hand—hotel guests, resort guests, and existing property owners and their acquaintances. Because the resort guest is a prospective buyer, an ongoing program geared toward a sale should be incorporated into the guest's stay (see feature box on page 212).

Major resort community destinations can benefit by combining resort and residential activities in their marketing campaigns. For example, Sun City Las Vegas offers a vacation getaway program for residents who need housing for guests. The program functions as a marketing tool to interest potential buyers looking for a retirement community. It makes available 40 villa units for three-, four-, or seven-night stays. The price includes one complimentary round of golf, complimentary use of all recreational facilities, complimentary lunch for two, and a wine and cheese party on select evenings.

Notes Charles Hewlett of Robert Charles Lesser & Co. in Chevy Chase, Maryland, "Referrals and word-of-mouth advertising play a very important role in marketing the [second-home] community. Therefore, every effort [should be] expended to ensure that the expectations of existing club members and property owners are ex-

Bordered by a dock, a 47-acre lake, and a 12-acre community park, the Information Pavilion at SilverLakes—a 2,480-acre master-planned community in Pembroke Pines, Florida—provides a strong first impression.

ceeded."[3] In fact, some recent second-home projects have developed effective marketing strategies that use little or no advertising and instead rely almost exclusively on word-of-mouth referrals. Spring Island, a high-end second-home community in South Carolina, uses no direct advertising. Sales result entirely from referrals, word-of-mouth communication, and personal letters of introduction. In addition, Spring Island has turned to public relations activities to stimulate several feature articles about the community that, in turn, have generated buyer interest. The project maintains four guest cottages for its owners/members and uses the units to bring prospects to the property.

In many cases, the marketing strategy evolves over time. At Forest Highlands, a second-home community in Flagstaff, Arizona, the developer initially used highly selective mailings to reach the targeted markets: primarily prospective second-home buyers in the Phoenix

Spring Island, a high-end second-home community near Beaufort, South Carolina, uses no direct advertising. Marketing relies entirely on referrals, word-of-mouth communication, and personal letters of introduction. Effective public relations have also been used to generate a number of feature articles about the community and the unique natural and historic features of the site that have generated buyer interest.

The role of a resort hotel in the successful marketing and sales of affiliated real estate products is extremely important and may even be termed critical. Yet, the successful sale of a resort hotel's affiliated real estate requires the clear understanding and agreement of the hotel operators regarding the use of the hotel as a magnet for real estate prospects. Some key points and programs that should be considered in the marketing effort are outlined below.

Integration and Support of Hotel Marketing Efforts

- Establish the philosophy that a hotel guest is a resort guest.
- Request the hotel to prepare a preopening marketing plan for endorsement by the resort developer/operator.
- Ensure that the resort and hotel marketing programs are coordinated and integrated wherever possible so that the combined efforts lead to success for both interests.
- Require the hotel operations to preapprove all collateral material and all preopening advertising to ensure that the materials present the hotel within the context of the entire resort community.
- Incorporate the name of the hotel into the name of the resort community, with the hotel operator's name as the prefix or suffix.
- Assign a resort sales or marketing staff member to the hotel's preopening sales offices to foster team building, close communication, and collaboration.
- Establish a budget item and process for room revenue credit subsidies to help the hotel compete for and book groups that promise to bring desirable, qualified prospects.
- Establish a resort database that allows the hotel to compile data on past hotel guests; permit the hotel to tap the database at no cost.
- Establish a concierge service that contacts hotel guests before their arrival and offers to arrange for the use of resort amenities.
- Operate a resort (not hotel) transportation service to facilitate airport transfer; the service should continue after residences are occupied and cover the residential units as well.
- Provide resort information to professional associations and corporate meeting planners.

The Conversion Process of On-Site Guests

- Even though resort guests may enjoy some familiarity with the club community and/or its real estate offerings before their arrival, they rarely begin a visit thinking about the prospect of a real estate purchase.
- The subtle exposure of the resort guest to the surrounding community and its real estate offerings is the single most important sales program to be undertaken.
- Two factors are critical to the sales process. First, the sales process should in no way compromise the resort guest's sense of privacy and relaxation. Second, the surrounding club community and its real estate should be shown to the resort guest in a noncommercial, nonthreatening, and entertaining fashion.
- Once hotel management and real estate management understand and agree on these principles, the options and methods for accomplishing them become clear.

Marketing

The resort hotel is the nucleus of the resort marketing effort. By attracting a large number of guests, the resort hotel creates an opportunity for turning guests into sales prospects. Certainly, the resort is far less likely to transform prospects into buyers if they never leave home. Thus, marketing dollars should be reasonably allocated to the promotion of the resort hotel itself.

The following ideas can enhance the on-site marketing program:

- Use registration packets and bellmen's pitches to market the overall resort and its many offerings.
- Program a button on the in-room telephones for a direct connection to the interpretive center (discussed below).
- Offer incentives to concierges who make reservations for guests to take the interpretive tour.
- Collect all guest history information and home addresses for input into the resort database.
- Develop a guest card with a place for the referring member.
- Use freestanding, tasteful signage or displays that refer interested persons to the main sales office. Place the signs in high-traffic areas such as the golf club, the beach club, and the tennis center.
- Make certain that a bottle of wine or a fruit basket is in the guest's room upon the guest's arrival. Insert a card from the resort's assigned sales representative.
- Arrange for the resort's sales representative to take the guest party on a special jeep tour of the property's special features, including the golf course. The tour may incorporate a picnic and historic site interpretation and should focus on a complete description of the resort's genius.
- Enter the guest's name on a mailing list for periodic updates on the resort.
- Encourage the inclusion of interpretive center activities in corporate and association meeting programs.
- Use resort vans or limousines for group arrivals.
- Require real estate representatives to attend preconference meetings.

Interpretive Center

- A section of the hotel can be designed as an interpretive center that also functions as a sales center. The center can be designed as a salon or living room—a friendly, beckoning space that attracts guests.
- The center should mirror the tone, texture, personality, and ambience of the larger community and the region in which it is located. It should be tasteful, nonthreatening, and hospitable.
- The center may also serve as a library for guests. It can offer historical, cultural, environmental, and anthropological exhibits and displays as well as low-key information about the club and community, thereby allowing visitors to browse in a nonthreatening atmosphere.
- The interpretive center may include a scale model of the community, low-key information about the community (mostly on easels, as in an art gallery, or out of sight in desk drawers), and a small facility for serving refreshments.
- The interpretive center should be considered another of the hotel's amenities.
- Part of the center, not readily evident to visitors, should be devoted to the sales staff's administrative office. Another part of the center should be designed as a small theater for viewing a video on the club and community.
- A suitable interior may have rugs and hardwood floors, residential-style furniture, shelves for displaying books and pottery, and storage areas for literature and sales materials.
- Well-trained, intelligent sales reception personnel should greet and welcome guests.
- The hospitality staff should qualify each entering guest and visitor to determine whether a sales representative should be called in. Thus, the sales process begins.

The Interpretive Tour

The tour can be the most important part of the entire conversion process.

- A typical tour might be a 45-minute drive through both the immediate and surrounding areas. It should orient the newly arrived guest to the amenities of the resort and provide an enlightening description of the club, the community, and its sense of place and hospitality. The tour should feature both the golf course and residential areas in a noncommercial fashion.
- Key staff of the resort, the hotel, and the amenities should recognize the tour's role in the success of the sales effort. Early on, staff should ask guests whether they have yet taken the tour. If guests have not toured the property, staff should urge them to do so.

Other suggestions for promoting the tour call for

- including tour information with the reservation confirmation material mailed to the guest before arrival;
- including tour information in the printed material given to the guest at check-in;
- requiring the hospitality staff to mention the tour at check-in;
- providing in-room material such as a small, attractive booklet outlining the principles of the resort community and a map and stylized historical/anthropological interpretive site plan;
- placing in each hotel room a card inviting the guest to take the tour the day after check-in; and
- using the hotel's in-room channel to promote the tour and provide a brief description of the community.

Hotel Staff Training

The key to successful hotel staff cooperation is establishing as early as possible a clear relationship with the hotel's general manager. The general manager must understand not only the importance of the hotel to the overall real estate sales effort but also the significance of the low-key style that governs the marketing effort.

In addition to receiving training in the attitude and style of the resort and community, staff who interact with the guests should be oriented to the community plan. Staff should also recognize the role of the guest's hotel experience in the overall marketing plan. Staff should be trained to recognize opportunities for assisting in the marketing effort.

Source: David Pearson, president, Pearson Associates, Coral Gables, Fla., 1995.

area. In addition, the strategy called for placing advertisements in golf and local/regional magazines. As the project developed, the developer organized home tours to promote the sale of finished product and to publicize local builders. Further, when new lots came onto the market, the developer offered current owners the first opportunity to "trade up." As the project matured, existing owners became an invaluable source of referrals. Highly visible golf tournaments and rankings in *Golf Digest* and *Golf* magazine also provided significant market exposure.[4]

Sales Management

A marketing director and an appropriate marketing system are essential for a successful sales program. A key member of the development team should direct the sales program in a manner consistent with program objectives. Given that resort communities typically sell a particular lifestyle, marketing personnel must accurately interpret and convey the project's strengths and appeals. To ensure that the sales staff performs responsibly, the marketing director must provide sales incentive compensation and strong sales management.

A basic decision regarding sales personnel is whether to employ an on-site staff or to contract with a realty firm. In some situations, developers may prefer their own staff, which is controlled by and accountable to the development organization. If a resort is situated in a remote location, some on-site salespeople are generally required. In smaller market areas and for smaller projects, developers should seriously consider contracting with one or more real estate firms either to serve as the sales staff or to generate referrals. In the case of an outside firm, the developer must determine that the firm is experienced in selling the particular product type to be marketed.

Even with an on-site sales staff, a developer often establishes cobrokerage arrangements with outside sales organizations that maintain contacts with likely sales prospects. Under a cobrokerage agreement, a cooperating broker who makes a sale in the developer's project receives a percentage of the brokerage commission (often half). Without this type of arrangement, brokers might not show up or fail to refer prospects to the developer's project.

If finished homes are being sold, model units can assist the sales staff in showing the product to best advantage. Even if the project is primarily oriented to lot sales, models still provide examples of the style and quality of housing planned for the community. Models are vital for sales of cluster and multifamily units in resort- and second-home communities.

The collateral materials required for an effective real estate sales operation include a sales brochure/folder that explains the total community concept; a site plan; a buyer's guide that outlines all basic project data such as areas of development, building design, floorplans, and prices; a room card that invites guests to visit the sales center or attend a social mixer and see property

products; direct-mail pieces; and all other documents used as sales tools.

Sales Organization. Within the limits of a projected sales forecast and program budget, the sales manager must decide how many people are needed on staff or retainer to market the development. Usually a development needs at least one sales manager who assumes responsibility for all phases of product sales. Obviously, sales managers require a strong knowledge of both sales techniques and the product being sold. Planning and design consultants for the project can offer valuable sales training by thoroughly explaining the rationale for the land plan and design.

The sales organization should be carefully structured from the beginning of the presales period. All members of the team should be aware of how their efforts will be supervised and evaluated and how they will be compensated. From the outset, a policy statement should clarify the respective responsibilities of the developer and the sales staff. The sales manager should establish procedures that the sales staff must follow in reporting prospects, daily and weekly activity summaries, and monthly sales productivity. By analyzing sales and traffic data, the sales manager can accurately assess sales staff productivity. One measure of staff effectiveness is a conversion ratio that indicates the number of contracts written as a percent of total traffic.

Training. An effective residential sales strategy must focus on the training and management of the sales or leasing team—the people directly responsible for closing deals. They are vital components of the marketing plan.

Specific training should be developed and delivered for each new project element so that the sales staff fully understands the targeted markets and the nature of the product offered. More specifically, the sales staff needs to understand the psychographic profile of the targeted markets. Just as traditional demographic analysis allows salespeople to group customers on the basis of age, sex, income, and family size, psychographic analysis allows the sales staff to segment the overall population into groups that share the same general outlook on life. Knowledge of what customers want as individuals allows salespeople to present a product that meets needs that customers may not even perceive.

A one-week, intensive training program for the sales staff at the beginning of the project is typical. Developers should then conduct weekly meetings, often on Friday just before the active weekend selling period. Among the topics covered in the initial training sessions and the weekly meetings are a description of the project, its benefits and conveniences, the history of the development firm, and lectures and demonstrations on proper selling techniques such as the use of displays, how to conduct tours of projects, and proper closing procedures. Salespeople also need to know how far they can go in adjusting the standard purchase contract with a customer. The weekly meetings should therefore also address such issues as nonstandard upgrades, extended closing

Terravita in Scottsdale, Arizona. First-year sales for the 823-acre project were twice that of projected sales, with more than 250 homes sold before the model was completed. More than 300 homes were sold within 17 weeks of the opening in November 1993. Home prices increased by more than $20,000 (13 percent) in the first five months of sales. Concerned that demand would exceed supply, Terravita executives scaled back advertising efforts. Pictured is the model home sales center's reception area and the front elevation of the Nimbus model.

R.B. Photographic

dates, contingency contracts, early move-in dates, the form of payment of earnest money, and other related matters.

Given resorts' reputation for aggressive and sometimes unethical sales practices (deserved or otherwise), salespeople must be fully acquainted with ethical practices and counseled against misrepresenting the development. Overzealous and/or high-pressure sales techniques, while possibly yielding higher sales over the short run, can severely tarnish the resort's image over the long run. Misrepresentation of the resort community—regarding future facilities, owners' rights, timing of development, etc.—can even lead to legal action against the developer. Thus, careful management of the sales staff is important (see feature box on page 216).

Measuring Market Acceptance

Measuring the performance of the marketing program is a critical final element in the marketing process.

While completed sales are the ultimate measure of performance, professional marketing consultants can analyze traffic by conducting "exit polls" at the property to gauge consumers' impressions of the project. They can also try to ascertain the effectiveness of each stage of the marketing effort.

Because of the value of consumer impressions, all visitors to the sales office should be asked to fill out entry cards. Potential buyers who visit the property should be surveyed on site after they have toured the models. Another option is to use the sales staff's follow-up call as an opportunity for a short survey. Prospects may also be selected at random for a more extensive telephone survey to assess their attitudes toward the resort. The opinions of prospects who ultimately buy units must also be considered. These consumers might be asked to complete a short questionnaire when they sign a sales agreement.

In addition to focusing on the units, the amenities, and the community itself, surveys should probe respondents' opinions on the major aspects of the property's marketing effort. Questions should cover all phases of the marketing effort so that consultants and developers can ascertain the effectiveness of their advertising and merchandising programs and fine-tune advertisements and other materials accordingly. Monitoring the effectiveness of marketing and sales—by evaluating traffic, absorption, and profiles of buyers against projections and corresponding budgeted expenditures—ensures that the marketing plan is an appropriate strategy for maximizing market penetration.

Monitoring does not end with the completion of a sale. Developers should learn from their successes and failures by soliciting continuous feedback and using the

The Interstate Land Sales Full Disclosure Act

The 1960s witnessed a dramatic increase in rural and recreation-related development. Throughout this period, many land developers and subdividers undertook mass marketing campaigns to sell unimproved land. Fraudulent television and radio advertising, direct-mail campaigns, and telephone solicitations deceived thousands of vulnerable and unsophisticated consumers who fell prey to land scams. As a result, Congress enacted the Interstate Land Sales and Full Disclosure Act (ILSFDA) in 1969.

The underlying aim of the ILSFDA is to reduce fraud and misrepresentation in the sale of unimproved land that involves interstate commerce. Although the act was originally aimed at curbing the fraudulent and deceptive sales techniques commonly associated with certain recreational developers, it covers a broad development spectrum and affects the sale of a large percentage of unimproved real property.

The ILSFDA requires developers to file extensive registration and disclosure documents with the U.S. Department of Housing and Urban Development's (HUD) Office of Interstate Land Sales Registration (OILSR) before using any instruments of interstate commerce (including mail and telephone services as well as transportation resources) in the sale or lease of undeveloped land. The act nevertheless provides for several exemptions. Given the financial and time requirements to complete and maintain an OILSR registration, developers typically seek exemption (discussed below).

The ILSFDA establishes two basic methods of registration and disclosure. First, developers must provide each prospective purchaser with a *property report*, which includes relevant information about the subdivision, the developer, and the developer's plan and methods of operation, thereby enabling the prospective buyer to make an informed decision. Second, developers must file a *statement of record* with the OILSR. The statement must include detailed land use and title verifications as well as the name and address of each prospective buyer. In addition to the registration and disclosure requirements, the act and its regulations contain sales practice sections that prohibit fraudulent sales activities.

As previously mentioned, the act provides for certain specific exemptions from coverage. Developers of resort-related communities commonly seek exemptions for

- the sale or lease of lots in a subdivision containing fewer than 25 lots;
- the sale or lease of improved land on which is erected a residential, commercial, or condominium unit for which a contract obligates the seller or lessor to erect such building within a two-year period;
- the sale or lease of land by any government or government agency; and/or
- the sale or lease of lots to any person who acquires such lots for the purpose of constructing residential or commercial structures.

It should be noted that timeshare unit sales are generally subject to the same guidelines under the ILSFDA as ordinary condominiums or other housing types. If the timeshare product gives its owner rights to a particular unit or any specific space, the product is considered a lot and must be registered, unless an exemption is available.

In 1979 and 1984, Congress revised several features of the ILSFDA's registration requirements and exemption guidelines. Furthermore, a 1989 amendment has provided HUD with the procedural framework to impose civil money penalties on any person who knowingly and materially violates the ILSFDA. A penalty of up to $1,000 may be imposed for each violation, with the maximum penalty for all violations by a particular party during a one-year period limited to $1 million.

Due to frequent changes in the ILSFDA, developers must regularly reevaluate their sales programs to ensure continuing compliance with the law.

results of that feedback to plan the next development phase or the next development. Feedback is a dialogue between developers and community associations, if they exist, or between developers and individual residents. To be able to correct undesirable patterns of development that do not work (or work infrequently), developers should solicit residents' opinions to learn first-hand what is wrong with a development.

Managing Rental Programs

The use of rental programs in resort residential properties serves two primary purposes. First, a rental program can be an important tool in boosting sales to second-home investors who wish to create an income stream to offset the property's debt service. Further, a rental program can be an effective marketing tool even when it turns out that buyers do not rent their units or that developers place limited emphasis on rental programs. William Bone, chair of the Sunrise Company in Palm Desert, California, notes that 50 percent of his second-home buyers intend to rent, but less than 10 percent actually do. Of the more than 10,000 homes he has built in the Palm Springs area, Bones estimates that only about 300 participate in rental programs.

Second, residential units placed in rental pools tend to be used more, increasing the resort's visitor base and occupancy level and thereby boosting revenues from income-producing amenities and other services. According to a 1995 survey conducted for Chase Manhattan's Personal Financial Service unit, 28 percent of second-home owners rent out their homes at an average of $706 per week.

The operation of rental programs, however, generally requires the continuing long-term involvement of the resort developer/manager. Rental programs work best when they are planned from the outset. They do not perform well when the residential community or the individual units have been designed without rental use in mind (for example, without provision for owner closets and a central laundry).

In addition, a rental program must be structured to pay for the high marketing and management costs it generates. Using a rental program as a sales incentive without charging fees substantial enough to offset costs is a serious mistake. As much as 50 percent of rental receipts may have to be retained to cover management costs. Moreover, the legalities of rental programs suggest that caution is in order. One caveat relates to the Securities and Exchange Commission's requirement that rental programs must be kept completely separate from real estate sales activities.

In most cases, it is in the developer's best interest to control the rental program rather than assign it to local brokers. As many projects have demonstrated, resort guests can be a great source of prospective buyers. If more than one entity is handling rentals, however, resort guests might receive different benefits and services, which can create dissension among renters and undermine their desire to purchase property.

Another benefit of in-house management is that it permits continuity in the management of various resort facilities, an important consideration for providing efficient and effective customer service. In fact, resorts with hotels often operate rental programs through the hotel operation. Even if a developer is interested in engaging outside brokers to manage rentals, it may be difficult to find a broker willing to spend enough time to do an effective job, especially during the early stages of a project. When a program is refined and has proven successful, a developer can consider the use of a local broker under appropriate terms and controls.

Two other management questions are of special importance in rental programs. First, should the resort require owners to place their units in the rental pool for a certain number of weeks per year or simply make the rental program completely discretionary? Many of the newer rental programs take the former approach, but the decision largely depends on the kind of community, the type of product, and buyer preferences. Resorts that depend on a high volume of visitors to support an income-producing amenity program (such as most ski resorts) are more likely to require owners to place their units in a rental program than resorts that use a club structure to manage amenities (such as those in Palm Springs).

Second, how does the rental program manager ensure that units are properly maintained and updated to remain marketable? Since the condition of rental units is an indication of overall resort quality, units must meet certain standards to sustain and enhance the resort's reputation. Silverado Country Club and Resort in Napa Valley, California, relies on a discretionary rental program in which improperly maintained units are excluded from the rental pool (see feature box on page 218).

Managing the Affordable Housing Issue in Resort Communities

Today, many resort communities face rapidly rising housing costs that increasingly threaten their long-term economic viability.[5] Ten to 20 years ago, a large pool of labor was always available to resort communities in the form of young baby boomers glad to take off a year or two and suffer through substandard living conditions simply to be part of the resort lifestyle. Housing affordability was not a significant issue. Today, however, both the communities and their labor forces are maturing, presenting a dilemma for the individuals who, as members of the local community and the labor pool, require suitable quarters for their young families.

More of the aging U.S. population is moving to resort communities on either a full- or part-time basis thanks to the flexibility afforded by advanced telecommunication technology and the trend toward active retirement accompanied by better health. New residents whose wealth exceeds that of existing local residents drive up the price of limited land or the existing housing stock. The result is an ever-widening gap in purchasing power between new residents—who bring high expecta-

Silverado Country Club and Resort

The Silverado Country Club and Resort, which originally opened in 1966, is now a four-star golf resort and residential community located about 55 miles northeast of San Francisco in the Napa Valley, northern California's famous "wine country." Built around a 19th-century mansion, the 1,200-acre property is located about a one-and-one-half-hour drive from the San Francisco airport and within easy access of the Bay Area.

Silverado is unique in several respects. First, it pioneered the condominium resort concept, an idea that evolved from its owner's experience in developing the first high-rise condominiums in Hawaii and the first residential condominium projects in California. Second, it is a resort without a hotel, although lodging is available through rental of the resort's housing stock. Condominium owners place their units in a rental pool on a discretionary basis. A central management company manages the rental program.

Project History
Silverado evolved into a resort from an 18-hole Robert Trent Jones–designed golf course and country club whose members held an equity interest. The mansion on the property, dating back to 1870, served as the clubhouse. The facility operated as the Silverado Country Club until 1966, when Westgate Factors purchased it for $3 million. Amfac, a related company, managed the property.

Westgate bought a property planned for 1,058 condominium and single-family units, installed utilities and roads, remodeled the mansion to serve as both a club facility and fine restaurant, constructed a new golf clubhouse, and sought to position Silverado as a national and international destination resort. Silverado began to prosper as a resort community in 1967, when small condominiums were built and sold and the original golf course was redesigned and expanded into two Robert Trent Jones–designed golf courses. The concept of privately owned condominiums as resort housing quickly took root. The early condominiums rapidly appreciated in value, with a second group of larger units built and sold in the early 1970s. In total, the period between 1967 and 1973 saw the construction of 532 units.

By the early 1970s, although Silverado was a successful land development, its positioning as a national and international resort was unsuccessful. In particular, the rental pool had failed to achieve high occupancies. It was under these conditions that Amfac management bought out Westgate. The resort continued to limp along with low occupancies until its $19.2 million sale in 1984 to Robert Meyer, a prominent California developer.

Meyer added an exclusive conference center and repositioned the property from a destination resort to a

The Silverado Country Club and Resort, which opened as a resort in 1966, is a four-star golf resort located in the Napa Valley, northern California's famous "wine country." The historic mansion on the property is now used as a clubhouse.

regional and conference resort. Once the conference center opened, occupancies rose to about 80 percent, a level that dropped somewhat during the most recent California recession. The average length of stay has remained fairly consistent at 2.5 days per visit. Units closest to the mansion and conference center achieve the strongest occupancies and command the highest room rates.

In addition to the 532 condominiums already built and sold and the 248 single-family homesites, Meyer secured authorization to develop 280 additional units. Original lot prices for the homesites ranged from $13,000 to $31,000 and, in some cases, were purchased solely to obtain membership in the golf club. By the late 1980s, resales had reached the $200,000 range. Custom-designed houses sell for $500,000 to $1 million and enhance the value of the resort condominium properties.

The most recent owner of Silverado is a Japanese businessman who purchased the resort in 1989 and constructed a new clubhouse. Amfac continues to manage the rental component.

Management and Financial Results
The rental pool is made up of about half the privately owned units, which owners contribute to the resort operation. Given that participation in the pool is discretionary, the number of rooms in the pool varies. Since Meyer's acquisition, however, the number of condominiums contributed to the rental pool has remained constant at around 280, including one-, two-, and three-bedroom cottage condominiums. A second or third bedroom can be rented independently, as the 280 condominiums can be configured into 500 rooms.

More recently developed condominium/hotel projects around the country require owners to place their units in the rental inventory for a specified number of days per year. Despite the current trend, Silverado's discretionary system has continued to perform well under Amfac's careful management. To remain in the rental program, owners must maintain their units in accordance with standards set by the management company. In fact, maintenance has emerged as an issue with the aging of the units. If owners do not make the repairs suggested by the management company, the affected unit is dropped from the rental pool. It is essential that only Class A units are offered to resort guests. Each condominium development has its own homeowners' association that maintains common areas.

Silverado's two 18-hole golf courses have always been an asset. From time to time, the resort has hosted various PGA and PGA Seniors events as well as the Anheuser Busch Classic and other events. The courses have received consistently high ratings from various golf magazines.

The country club is a nonequity club that currently counts about 650 members. The courses are semiprivate; that is, resort play is combined with membership play. In 1967, Amfac authorized "grandfather" memberships in the new country club for members of the original club who predated the Westgate takeover. Silverado is one of the first resorts not to designate one course for members and the other for resort guests; instead, members are permitted to play both courses. Management

Silverado is a resort with no hotel, but it offers lodging through the rental of its resort housing stock—individually owned condominiums that are contributed by owners on a discretionary basis to a rental pool. The number of condominiums contributed to the rental pool has been consistently around 280, including one-, two-, and three-bedroom cottage units.

designates one course for members-only play four days a week but permits members to play the other course in the morning. Most resort guests get afternoon tee times following morning meetings. Members can also get priority tee times two days in advance. Resort guests are allowed to sign up for tee times as far in advance as they make their room reservations. Unlike other resorts where conflicts between resort guests and club members have been a major problem, Silverado has successfully managed competing demands.

Silverado has been financially successful for each of its owners. While Westgate made a substantial investment in upfront site improvements, it realized a good return on its land sales program. And with resort housing part of Westgate's larger land sales program, the low occupancies did not cause the development's owners major financial distress; they did not own the rental properties in the rental pool. Silverado has been successful in part because of its phasing effort, which allowed portions of the project to be financed and sold—with accompanying capital recovery—a little at a time. The phasing also reduced risk, particularly when absorption of the condominiums was slow.

Despite its acquisition costs, Silverado also proved a success for Meyer. His addition of the conference center is what finally positioned Silverado for long-term success. The conference center has boosted revenues for both the resort facilities and the condominiums in the rental pool and drawn considerable patronage from among corporate citizens of the Bay Area. Throughout Silverado's history, the various owners have enjoyed a good return on the lot sales program. Values have continued to increase due to Silverado's amenity offerings and the growth in the Napa Valley's attractions: the winery tourist business and shopping opportunities. Silverado's golf is outstanding, and, with the Bay Area suburbs expanding toward the Napa Valley, lot sales values have continued to escalate.

In short, Silverado provides a unique example of a resort development that, even without a hotel, has maintained its financial success during a long buildout. Under Amfac's management, Silverado pioneered the concept of a discretionary owner rental pool. Silverado has also adopted innovative approaches to managing potential conflicts between its golf club members and resort guests.

tions for community and lifestyle services—and long-time local residents and employees of local businesses—who cannot afford to live where they work.

While housing affordability is not a problem unique to resort communities, one byproduct of the problem is that communities' economic potential is weakened as local residents and workers move farther and farther away from resort centers. Unlike traditional metropolitan communities and exclusive suburbs, the resort economy thrives only when businesses deliver what their market demands: innovative amenities provided in a spirit of good service. If resort area employees cannot find decent housing they can afford, the resort community can no longer sustain its economy. A shortage of affordable housing leads to disgruntled and surly employees forced to choose between long commutes and substandard local housing. Other related issues include high levels of employee absenteeism and turnover; increased operating costs for businesses, which must offer higher wages to secure the labor they need; and the potential liability faced by owners who have too few staff to comply with safety measures.

The housing affordability problem is especially evident in the Intermountain West, where, unlike many eastern communities, it is not possible to develop affordable housing in the next village over the hill. A combination of difficult topography, limited infrastructure, and large federal landholdings makes it difficult to site new development within 15 to 20 miles of employment centers. As a result, many employees in Intermountain West communities must travel up to 60 to 80 miles each way to work, often in bad weather and on treacherous roads. Long commutes to more affordable housing translate into additional impacts on idyllic communities and their larger regions. Air quality in already sensitive airsheds deteriorates rapidly as the number of vehicle trips in and out of a community increases. Social problems such as escalating crime rates, domestic violence, and substance abuse are brought on by long work days, often at low-paying jobs, made longer by commutes to and from distant housing. Consequently, communities that avoid aggressive resolution of the affordable housing issue often find themselves providing increased security and police services, more family counseling services, and higher subsidies to daycare and mass transit programs.

Causes. With resort communities positioned to grow well into the next two decades, many resort towns that have not yet had to address the affordable housing issue will likely find themselves tackling the problem before too long. Certainly, it is far more cost-effective to plan for the inevitable by creating a strategic approach to the issue than to wait until it reaches crisis proportions. Several common threads run through the housing affordability problem facing American resort communities, but recognizing and dealing with the following three matters can help resorts craft solutions before housing affordability compromises successful resort operations.

Land Costs. In resort communities, land costs represent upwards of 60 to 70 percent of total housing prices.

In other suburban or urban settings, the traditional average is 25 to 30 percent of final prices. In the end, requiring some level of affordable housing in new market-rate developments by using excess public lands or buying down land costs with subsidies from taxes or bonds is the key to achieving realistic solutions.

Construction Costs. In many communities in the Intermountain West, construction costs include a 10 to 20 percent premium to cover such considerations as remote locations, limited pools of skilled labor, and the short construction seasons experienced in some mountain areas. Ironically, one of the major factors in construction cost premiums is the overall lack of affordable housing, which results in higher costs to contractors who must pay higher subsistence charges to attract imported labor. One successful solution has been the increased reliance on prefabricated construction. It limits the requirements for skilled labor and reduces exposure to seasonal weather fluctuations.

Community Resentment. Some residents of resort communities perceive affordable housing as occasioning unwanted community growth, environmental degradation, expensive public subsidies, increased traffic, and a heavy burden on community services. In reality, a lack of affordable housing often does more than new construction to bring about undesirable effects. In addition, given current demographic trends toward growth in resort areas, the decision not to develop affordable housing will not make the problem go away; it will only exacerbate it. Instead, savvy issues management programs can help accelerate the public approval process and hold down development costs.

Solutions. Communities that have successfully addressed the affordability problem have used a complex array of programs, all of which have emerged from such approaches as public/private partnerships, land writedowns or donations, innovative construction technologies, and long-term management and affordability assurance programs. Common elements of successful programs include the following:

Deed Restrictions. At the heart of any long-term affordable housing solution are deed restrictions placed on housing units. The restrictions are limited to a specific segment of the population, usually employees (generally defined as individuals working 30 or more hours per week, nine months of the year) in either the defined community or the surrounding county or region.

Early Recognition of the Problem. Many resort communities or resort community developers view employee housing as community infrastructure and therefore just as important to the success of the resort as sewer and water service and recreational amenities. Communities need to adopt zoning and land use codes that address affordable housing needs yet minimize affordable housing's impact on the development community.

Broad Funding Strategies Adopted Early. A variety of funding strategies can help offset the costs of developing affordable housing. For example, real estate transfer taxes generate funds for affordable housing from the economic dynamic that fuels the escalation in land prices; entertainment and lodging taxes generate income from the services that create most of a community's low-paying jobs; and dedicated sales taxes generate funds to help support such programs as transit, affordable housing, daycare, and open space management.

Implementing an Affordable Housing Program. Implementation is far more difficult than simply identifying the issues and solutions. While some solutions are common from community to community and project to project, the implementation structure is unique to each situation. In the absence of a prescription for structuring successful projects, the public/private partnership can serve as a universal model for implementation.

The public/private partnership relies on a division of responsibilities. While each role can be played by separate individuals or agencies, a single agency may in some cases play two roles (i.e., public sector and developer). What makes the model unique to resort communities as opposed to traditional metropolitan areas is the strong presence of a definable user: the business owner who can become a willing partner and benefit from the development of housing that is affordable to his or her employees. In turn, the developer provides a valuable community service while gaining financial assistance from the user in the form of long-term master leases, the purchase of subordinated debt, land donations, or direct participation in the project's development and financing. At the same time, the public sector facilitates the development of housing and solves a community problem.

Once identified, the partnership can rely on a number of creative tools, as noted below, to form an affordable housing program.

Land Banking. A community that undertakes land banking can limit the need for public subsidies. Land banking calls for identifying sites for affordable housing early in the formulation of community land use planning strategies or private development proposals and then carrying the costs in market-rate units built on land not subject to banking. Nearly mature communities that have not provided adequate sites before build-out often set public subsidies equal to 50 percent of the overall project cost.

Public Lands. Some communities use public lands for affordable housing by packaging the development of affordable units with open space preservation. Combining open space preservation and affordable housing units often resolves two issues concurrently and recognizes that the competing demands of open space and growth controls sometimes fuel the affordability crisis. In certain instances, employee housing can be developed on land that is part of existing community open space or part of public utility or municipal district holdings.

Inclusionary Zoning or Market Approach. Inclusionary zoning requires a certain percentage of affordable hous-

Marolt Ranch in Aspen provides an affordable housing solution to participants in the Aspen summer music festival. The ranch is a 100-unit complex consisting of 14 buildings. It provides 300 beds in summer and 100 in winter, a main cafeteria, and a series of practice rooms. Aspen Music Associates master leases all 100 units from June through August for its students. During fall and winter, the units are rented to seasonal workers who come in to serve the tourist trade.

Photo courtesy of Design Workshop Inc.

Two communities that offer a noteworthy contrast in their approach to providing affordable housing are Aspen and Vail, Colorado.

Since its climb to fame began in the 1940s, Aspen, a small community of 7,000 residents, has always exemplified the resort community lifestyle. Originally an 1880s mining center, the town saw its rebirth as a ski attraction in the early 1930s. It grew quietly through the 1940s and developed as a resort area that combined recreation, spiritual growth, and education. The success of these ideals brought new residents whose desire to limit growth led to even more restrictive policies, including the Pitkin County growth management plan of the 1970s. This plan, one of the earliest and most comprehensive approaches to growth management, established a limit on the number of new housing units that could be constructed each year. Recognizing that capping supply would directly affect housing affordability, the town and county concurrently created the Aspen/Pitkin Housing Agency to ensure an adequate supply of affordable units for local employees.

To some, the agency stands as the best example of one community's attempt to deal with the affordable housing problem; to others, it is the worst example of government intervention and social engineering. Regardless of one's viewpoint, the agency's ability to create affordable housing is undeniable. Since its inception in the mid-1970s, the housing agency has directly or indirectly developed over 1,500 affordable rental and for-sale units.

By contrast, Vail grew out of a vision to create a new master-planned resort community. Begun in the 1960s, the resort was designed around a European village theme and built on a site that offered little more than a spectacular setting and the promise of good access. Driven more by real estate and recreation principles than by Aspen's altruism, the town has grown successfully into a full-time community of more than 3,000 residents. Its government has remained small and, by mandate of the local constituency, has shied away from the affordable housing arena. In the absence of public intervention, Vail Associates, the major employer, with over 3,500 people on its payroll, has had to take a more active role. The company currently manages more than 600 housing units either through master leasing or direct ownership and management.

Although they are two markedly different towns, Aspen and Vail face the same dilemma. Escalating land and housing values have brought about increasing housing shortages for employees. As a result, both communities are slowly becoming weekday ghost towns. They are populated only on weekends and holidays when their largely second-home residents are present. Day-to-day businesses and even volunteer organizations are finding it increasingly difficult to survive in the absence of a full-time resident population. This reality has led to different but equally successful solutions.

Few events exemplify Aspen's commitment to the arts and culture as does its summer music festival. For over 25 years, students from around the world have traveled to Aspen to study, practice, and perform with conductors and musicians of international renown. In the early years, students lived with local residents, enjoying affordable housing while contributing to the town's ambience as a music center. Residents strolled through town to the sound of young musicians practicing classical and contemporary scores.

In the early 1980s, however, many residents found the economic temptation of summer and winter rentals too much to pass up. As a result, housing became increasingly scarce for students until the only available options were located in communities 20 to 40 miles away. Music Associates of Aspen, the music festival's nonprofit sponsor, considered seeking an alternative venue that the students could more easily afford. Faced with the possibility of losing one of its most cherished institutions, the community rallied to develop Marolt Ranch.

The 100-unit complex of 14 buildings provides 300 beds in summer and 100 in winter, a main cafeteria, and a series of practice rooms. Aspen Music Associates master leases all 100 units from June through August for its students. During the fall and winter, the units are rented to seasonal workers who serve the fall and winter tourist trade. Dave Tollen, project manager with the Aspen/Pitkin County Housing Authority (APCHA), says that the project is fully leased earlier each year. For 1995, the complex was leased out by the end of September 1994.

To make the project affordable, Aspen offered several community inducements. For example, the city leases the land at minimal cost. Covenants on the remaining site provide perpetual open space surrounding the project. A combination of general obligation and revenue bonds approved by the voters provided the financing. The APCHA manages the property, which is funded through community taxes and a real estate transfer tax. Aspen's extraordinary real estate market provides almost $2 million per year to the APCHA for operations and new project development.

Another example is Lake Creek Village in Edwards, Colorado, an innovative model of affordable housing involving both a developer who brought entrepreneurial skill and knowledge to package the deal and a public agency that facilitated approvals and funding strategies.

The 270-unit project was developed by Corum Real Estate Group, Inc., of Englewood, Colorado.

As part of a new golf course community project in Edwards, Corum identified an unproductive site that had little value to the project's developer but great potential to the community for affordable housing. By optioning the property at a favorable price, Corum was able to secure the land below its market value for the development of Lake Creek Village. Working with the county, Corum helped organize a new nonprofit housing authority to develop the site into an apartment community. Under a provision of Internal Revenue Service statute 63-20, the authority issued tax-exempt bonds for the project, leading to 100 percent debt financing. Local resort operators Vail Associates, Cordillera, and Arrowhead bought junior debt issues to make the offering of unrated bonds more attractive to the capital markets. In the end, the $23 million project was issued in three tranches, with the first tranche bought by an institutional investor at 8.25 percent tax exempt. For their role in providing credit enhancements, the three resorts received housing credits applied against the county's newly enacted affordable housing requirements for resort expansion projects as well as a highly favorable 11 percent tax-exempt return.

Since opening in spring 1994, Lake Creek Village has reached 95 percent occupancy. Rates are set by the housing authority's board, which includes representatives from Corum, the three supporting resorts, and the county. Board members set rates that are affordable to community employees but ensure project viability. In the end, the project avoids direct public subsidies without compromising the price of housing.

Source: Adapted from Jim Heid, "A Strategic Approach to Affordable Housing in Resort Communities," *Urban Land*, August 1995, pp. 34–37, 81.

Twin Ridge in Aspen, Colorado, is a 25-unit affordable housing development that is targeted to working professionals. The 12 attached and 13 detached homes were sold—with deed restrictions—to long-term, middle-income area residents and employees who otherwise had limited options for real estate ownership in the local housing market.

ing units to be constructed as part of a community's overall development program. In today's programs, this share ranges from 15 to 30 percent of the total approved unit count. Developers who provide affordable units are often granted increased densities, infrastructure assistance, or accelerated approval times.

Resident Accessory Units. In some areas characterized by large second-home units, communities require the concurrent construction of caretaker or accessory units. This strategy provides the community with affordable housing at no cost and ensures that a local resident base will reside in a neighborhood of seasonal houses on a year-round basis. At the same time, the homeowner realizes a small income stream from the unit's rental and benefits from the presence of a caretaker who provides varying degrees of security and property care.

Free Market/Submarket. Several communities are experimenting with a free-market/submarket approach to affordable housing. Privately developed employee housing units sell on the open market to the highest bidder who can meet employee qualifications. Proponents of the strategy theorize that housing reaches a level of acceptable pricing based on what local employees can afford, without the need for community pricing intervention. Some communities that have recently instituted such programs, however, underestimated the pent-up demand at the time of implementation and are finding that the strategy works only if the supply of new units can keep pace with demand. Otherwise, new units are immediately bid up beyond the reach of most local employees.

Nonprofit Development Corporations. One of the most interesting programs used in some Colorado resort communities takes advantage of Internal Revenue Service statute 63-20, which allows the issuance of tax-free bonds to acquire, develop, and operate housing under an approved nonprofit housing corporation. A public authority can initiate and sponsor the nonprofit corporation's formation, with a private development entity undertaking the project for a fee and often a long-term management contract. Local users who benefit from close-in affordable housing for their employees can provide the credit enhancements necessary to make the unrated bonds attractive to the capital markets.

The discussion of affordable housing in resort communities should focus not on whether such housing is necessary but rather when it will be needed. Given the current demographic shifts projected over the next two decades, the demand for affordable housing is sure to accelerate. With foresight and the formation of creative partnerships among key players, communities can devise cost-effective housing solutions that both ensure the long-term success of their local economy and enhance their quality of life.

Timeshare Marketing and Management

Marketing and managing timeshare resorts requires specialized expertise beyond that usually associated with resort marketing and management staffs. Specifically, effective timeshare marketing depends on a well-trained sales staff capable of clearly explaining the product concept. In addition, marketing and managing timeshares demands a strong partnership with one of the interval service firms and a property management program similar to that required for a hotel.

Timeshare and Vacation Ownership Marketing

Depending on the nature of the project, many vacation ownership companies contract for outside professional assistance for some of the many tasks that timeshare marketing involves. As the vacation ownership industry grows more competitive, professional expertise

Profile and Comments: Robert J. Lowe

Robert J. Lowe
President and Chief Executive Officer
Lowe Enterprises, Inc.
Los Angeles, California

As president and chief executive officer, Robert Lowe directs the business activities of Lowe Enterprises. The firm is a multifaceted real estate company whose activities include the development of single- and multifamily properties; the development and management of commercial properties; the development and management of resorts and hotels; the development and marketing of land; the management of real estate investments for pension funds and other investors; and the general management of complex real estate problems and organizations on behalf of institutional and private investors.

In 1972, Lowe was the principal founding shareholder of the corporation that became Lowe Enterprises, Inc. Before establishing the Lowe group of companies, Lowe held various management positions in public and private corporations.

Lowe received a degree in economics from Claremont McKenna College and an MBA from the Stanford University Graduate School of Business.

The quality and focus of sales and marketing programs are as critical to the success of high-end resort development as they are to high-volume lot sales or timeshare products. But they are markedly different. In the case of the high-end development product, a developer needs to do three things. He needs to reach the market that already knows about and is coming to the existing resort. He needs to focus on the quality of what he is building because word-of-mouth advertising probably will represent the greatest source of buyers. Third, it is very important to have a captive sales force to shorten the time

period for marketing. I need salespeople who totally understand my product and whose only way of making a dollar is by selling my product. I want salespeople waking up every morning, and all they are thinking about is selling my product. While a developer needs to work with the local brokerage community, it is rare that this community will provide a lot of buyers.

Integrating hotel facilities and services within a second-home community can be advantageous to the home purchaser. Those purchasers provide an additional revenue base for the restaurants, shopping, and entertainment facilities in the hotel that typically are supported by transient hotel guests. Similarly, a developer can afford to provide better golf and tennis facilities for the second-home community if these facilities also are supported by transients.

The most critical conflicts arise at the high end of the market over both the use of the facilities and issues of public or private access. High-end purchasers are more than willing to pay the price for exclusivity. In middle-market projects, however, spreading the costs over a variety of different users is helpful. Second-home residents need to realize that a resort hotel often can allow the developer to build facilities that otherwise would not have been built if they were to be supported solely by the residents. A developer needs to decide what it is he is trying to accomplish, what is the strategy, and then be true to that strategy from the beginning. Conflicts arise from a lack of clarity or misrepresentation, perhaps unintentionally.

is evolving as a standard element of the market research and advertising effort. Marketing is especially crucial for the vacation ownership industry, which still needs to overcome the negative image created by the unsavory practices of marketers in years past.

The primary goals of vacation ownership marketing are

- to illuminate the market regarding the availability of a specific project;
- to educate the market about the nature of the time-share product in general and the specific product offered for sale;
- to provide a flow of legitimate potential buyers; and
- to rely on a talented sales team whose detailed sales strategy can maximize product exposure.[6]

Vacation ownership marketing has traditionally relied on a unique set of strategies to draw people to the project. But as vacation ownership markets and products have evolved over the past two decades, new marketing strategies and management operations have emerged. Markets have become more niche-specific, creating a new set of challenges for reaching potential buyers. Traditional vacation ownership marketing strategies such as cold calling, unsolicited direct mail, and tele-marketing are still practiced, but their effectiveness has waned. Consumers have become more cautious; it is highly unlikely that potential buyers will respond to the urgings of a person they do not know and commit thousands of dollars to a project they have not researched.

The tremendous growth of the vacation ownership industry has driven many of the marketing changes. Annual sales have increased from approximately $400 million in 1980 to over $5 billion in 1995. Today, the market is much larger and more diverse. Rapid growth, the entry of large hospitality corporations, and the maturity of large regional developers have all forged marketing innovations and techniques.

Marketing Tools. Traditional vacation ownership sales tools have often included some mix of the following:

Off-Premise Contacts (OPCs). Off-premise contacts are staffed marketing booths/stations located in a well-traveled pedestrian area (for instance, a mall, town center, hotel lobby, or fair) that invite individuals in a qualified market to visit a project. To attract people to the site, OPCs often rely on persuasive strategies such as the offer of a token gift (an answering machine or radio) or entry in a prize drawing.

Box Programs. A box program is a simple marketing station without staffing that provides information on a project. It invites potential buyers to fill out a form with their name and address and promises some type of gift in return. Box programs are also located in highly traveled pedestrian areas such as grocery stores, restaurants, and hotel lobbies. Expenses for a box program are minimal; typically, the location management assesses a modest monthly rental fee.

Off-Site Sales Center. An off-site sales center is a sales office in a location other than the timeshare property

Branded vacation ownership companies are able to reach a vast market by marketing in all of their hospitality projects. For a relatively low cost, a project such as the Marriott's Harbour Club in Hilton Head Island, South Carolina, can reach potential owners around the country through other Marriott products.

site. Unlike an OPC that directs people to the property to buy, the off-site center is intended to convince people to make a purchase without ever visiting the site. The sales center development cost is significant and sales are naturally more difficult. As the demographic breadth of vacation ownership purchasers expands, more individuals have begun purchasing vacation ownerships in sales locations away from the product. In 1980, an estimated 98 percent of sales were made on site. In 1995, however, over 20 percent of sales were made off site, and the trend is expected to grow. By 2005, vacation ownership experts predict that over 50 percent of sales will be conducted off site.[7] They believe that the increase in off-site sales is attributable to the improved image of vacation ownership and exchange policies that help maintain a consistent standard.

Sweepstakes and Gifts. Sweepstakes and gift programs, often advertised in the various media, are used commonly to draw potential clients to a project or at least to capture information that allows the client to be contacted later. Sweepstakes draw clients by offering the possibility to win a prize, such as a car. A gift program offers clients a gift such as a telephone, radio, or lawn chair simply for visiting the project. In the past, one reason for timeshares' unsavory image was the volume of illegitimate or fraudulent sweepstakes and gifts. Nonetheless, sweepstakes and gifts remain one of the most effective means of attracting potential buyers.

Smugglers' Notch, a rural Vermont timeshare resort, is targeted to families with an annual income greater than $75,000 and two children under 12 years old. To gather the greatest number of potential buyers that qualify within its niche, the resort purchases lists from magazines that market high-end children's clothing and other products.

Telemarketing. An extremely common form of marketing, telemarketing has many uses, including generating leads and prospects, qualifying people who have responded to other prospect-generation programs, making special offers to buyers and nonbuyers, and asking for referrals.[8]

Direct Mail. Direct mail is still the most common and one of the most expensive forms of advertising. It uses a large quantity of information to develop a story. Different approaches can be tested to determine which sales strategy is most effective.

The Internet and Other New Technologies. Numerous advanced technologies are creating new avenues for timeshare marketing, including the Internet and the World Wide Web, CD-ROM technology, interactive kiosks, virtual reality, and database marketing techniques.

Advertising and Promotion. A well-designed advertising campaign is essential for reaching the intended market. As compared to reliance on a single medium, a

multimedia strategy reaches a broader spectrum of purchasers. Marketing experts concur that the buyer typically needs to be reached three to six times before he or she will respond to an advertisement. The odds of a response increase if the potential buyer is exposed to advertisements from different media sources.

Marketing experts have concluded that direct mail is most effective when it follows three earlier attempts to reach the buyer via other media sources. A combination of television, travel-oriented magazines, and direct mail work well, according to Mac MacEwan, president of MacEwan & Company in Seattle.[9] Television reaches the greatest number of people faster than any other medium while selective program scheduling allows an advertisement to reach a more specific market. Radio advertising reaches a broad base and achieves its greatest impact in a news/talk format. Magazines offer a longer shelf-life readership; in fact, advertising is especially effective in travel magazines.

For certain niches, printed material produced regularly by a public relations department is another effective marketing strategy. Some timeshares have found that newsletters help sell the image of a lifestyle through photographs and current events articles. Newsletters not only set the tone for the ambience the vacation ownership resort seeks to present to purchasers (it can act as a "how to enjoy the timeshare" guide), but they also instill a sense of what the project is like for potential buyers in a more convincing medium than an advertisement.

Targeting Niches. As the vacation ownership market becomes more niche-specific, the established methods of marketing will vary. What works for one niche does not always work for another; as a result, niche marketing should take its impetus from various regional, economic, and psychodemographic considerations.

A successful niche marketing strategy must be carefully tailored in terms of both its marketing pitch and the media sources selected for use. Family-oriented timeshares, for example, require promotional materials that focus on children's activities and a family atmosphere. Smugglers' Notch, a rural Vermont timeshare, markets to families with an annual income greater than $75,000 and two kids under 12. To gather the greatest number of potential buyers who qualify within its niche, the timeshare purchases lists from magazines that market high-end children's clothing and other products. A couples vacation ownership in Aruba, in contrast, uses appropriate media to promote images of solitary couples walking along a beach at sunset, drinks at a pool bar, sunbathers, and romantic candlelight dinners.

Economic considerations play a significant role in niche marketing and the tools that support it. Potential buyers who focus on lower-priced projects respond well to box programs, OPCs, and prize incentives. For example, at Peppertree Corporation, a vacation ownership company that manages 13 reasonably priced resorts, 85 percent of the 25,000 qualified tours originated from a

"Computing," notes author and futurist Nicolas Negroponte, "is no longer about computers. It is about living." Computers have infiltrated every aspect of our personal and professional lives, and timeshare marketing is certainly no exception. An electronic revolution in timeshare marketing is changing the way marketers interact with prospects and clients. By employing a variety of digital technologies that allow vast amounts of information to be transmitted electronically, marketers can now target their audience and tailor the message with increasing precision. These technologies—including the Internet, CD-ROM, interactive kiosks, and virtual reality—favor imaginative, forward-looking marketers at the expense of those who still rely solely on more traditional methods.

One of the main advantages of computer-based technologies is that the roles of buyers and sellers are virtually reversed. Instead of having the product pushed at them, consumers select from a rich database of products that they are interested in buying.

Traditionally, timeshare marketers have relied on off-premise contacts (OPCs) that attract prospects by offering premiums to interested consumers who agree to tour a timeshare property. In addition, timeshare marketers use direct-mail campaigns to offer prospective buyers minivacations at their properties. These methods, however, are labor-intensive and costly, and they typically produce low closing rates. While electronic media are just as expensive, they hold the promise of higher closing rates by shifting the sales paradigm. Instead of feeling manipulated, consumers feel that they are in control of the sales process.

The Internet

One medium that empowers consumers is the Internet. With over 50 million users estimated worldwide, the Internet has become the hottest marketing tool of the late 20th century. It offers unprecedented opportunities for inventive marketers to reach the public with promotional information about the amenities, facilities, and services available at individual resorts as well as with specific offers such as minivacations or resales. Marketers who have mastered the nuances of the World Wide Web (the graphic section of the Internet) understand that they no longer are searching for customers—they are helping customers find *them*. The key is to exploit existing search engines such as Wahoo, Excite, Web Crawler, and Infoseek to lead prospective customers to a particular home page. An intelligent timeshare marketer makes sure that any net surfer searching for a "vacation," a "timeshare," or a "resort" finds the home page featuring that marketer's resort or resort chain. The home page of the Orange Tree Interval Ownership Resort in Scottsdale, Arizona, for instance, functions as an electronic

OPC that invites potential customers to call a toll-free telephone number to sign up for minivacations.

While the Internet has not yet fulfilled its potential as a viable commercial distribution channel, several impending changes will guarantee its success. Among those changes are

- a standard protocol for securing financial transactions on the Web. Both VISA and MasterCard have agreed to the protocol, which will allow consumers to make credit card purchases safely on the Web.
- faster access to the Internet. Today, access is slow and overcrowded, but faster computers and modems, ISDN lines, and cable modems (devices that allow high-speed data access via a typical cable television outlet) all promise an accessible, speedy Internet in the near future.
- a proliferation of intelligent agents—software entities that can search for information according to a user's needs and wants. Vacationers will soon send their intelligent buyer agents onto the Web to search for vacation bargains while marketers will use intelligent seller agents to find those buyer agents and present them with prospective deals.

In this age of information overload and overwhelming choices, marketers who employ the best navigational tools will profit most from the new electronic media.

CD-ROM Directory

Another effective technology for information searches is the CD-ROM, which can be used to market catalogs, directories, or travel planners. Like other interactive media, CD-ROMs allow users to view only what they want to see, eliminating the searching and indexing that accompanies printed publications. A good example is Interval International's CD-ROM directory, which contains a complete database of Interval's affiliated resorts. It allows members to search for resorts by geographic area, amenities, or activities, enabling them to find their perfect vacation quickly and efficiently.

Group marketing efforts are also ideally suited to CD-ROM technology. For instance, an *Interactive Guide to the Vail Valley* on CD-ROM features information and videos about several resorts in and around Vail, Colorado. By working together and sharing costs, Vail-area resorts can promote themselves in the context of the local area and its attractions. Once marketers have identified prospects who own computers, CD-ROMs will offer a cost-effective solution to the spiraling costs of printing and mailing that characterize direct-mail campaigns.

Interactive Kiosks

Interactive kiosks are gaining widespread acceptance in the travel, hospitality, and real estate industries and have numerous potential applications in the timeshare industry. Marketers can install multimedia kiosks that feature a mix of photographs, videos, virtual reality, and choice-based presentations in places frequented by a high volume of qualified prospects, including malls, hotels, and airports. Kiosks can offer a wide variety of consumer products, and marketers using kiosks can generate significant income, potentially even recouping the total cost of their kiosk investments by selling advertising to associated marketers. Timeshare marketers, for instance, might sell advertising space to restaurants or amusement parks.

At the point of sale, timeshare marketers can use touch-screen kiosks as sales tools to help their sales force. At Polo Towers in Las Vegas, for example, interactive kiosks allow prospective buyers to explore vacation options while the Disney Vacation Club uses touch-screen kiosks to explain the concept of points. Kiosks are also particularly adaptable to off-site sales environments, where they function as lead generators and database marketing lists that provide demographic and economic information. When connected to peripheral devices such as modems and printers, kiosks can be used for telemarketing or filling requests for brochures.

Virtual Reality

The technology exists today to create computerized virtual-reality (i.e., three-dimensional) walk-throughs of any physical space anywhere in the world by using photographs, videos, and specialized computer software. Although some such systems require head-tracking helmets, Quick Time Virtual Reality allows viewers with an ordinary computer and mouse to navigate a beach, a forest, a local attraction, or the interior spaces of a resort. With tours and premiums the highest-cost facets of timeshare marketing, marketers employing virtual walk-throughs can reap enormous savings by enabling prospects to tour on a remote computer and using the experience itself as a premium.

The primary advantage of virtual reality, of course, is that it takes the user where he or she is not, immediately opening immense new possibilities for off-site locations and OPCs. Now that the Internet supports virtual reality, several timeshare marketers are developing virtual walk-throughs of their resorts, the resort units, and resort amenities for prominent display on their Web home pages. The power of inviting prospective purchasers to tour a resort from the comfort of their home anywhere in the world illustrates why virtual reality has the potential to become the greatest marketing tool of the next decade.

Database Marketing and Cross Marketing

Database marketing marries sophisticated statistical techniques to modern data management technology. It helps marketers recognize the categories of prospects predisposed to purchase a particular product or service as well as the incentives and media most likely to evoke a favorable response.

Database marketing begins with profile analysis that describes one customer segment in relation to another and identifies key demographic and psychographic elements that define the customer base to which a given vacation ownership product will appeal. Then, predictive modeling defines the characteristics of an individual customer for that product, enabling marketers to focus on people with the highest propensity to purchase.

Companies are becoming increasingly aware that once they have developed their own databases, their existing customer databases are valuable to other companies offering noncompetitive products and services. This sharing of clients, known as cross marketing, can dramatically reduce the costs of acquiring customers. It can also convey a tacit endorsement that enhances the customer's predisposition to accept a second company's message.

Some timeshare developers have already gained access to extensive cross-marketing resources that are being used to explore a variety of novel ways to generate additional high-quality sales leads. The importance of cross marketing will probably grow in the years ahead as hospitality industry firms and other large companies with diverse enterprises and clientele become involved in the timeshare industry.

Other Emerging Technologies

Before the next millennium, facsimile marketing, video conferencing, and interactive television will probably become significant factors in the marketing of timeshare resorts. Progressive marketers in Japan are already using facsimile marketing to market travel and vacation bargains.

Facsimile machines are much more common in Japanese homes than in American homes, but with the advent of less costly machines and simple facsimile software, faxing could become another inexpensive alternative to direct mail. Of course, marketers must obtain the permission of potential customers before faxing offers to them. While direct mail costs the recipient nothing, customers pay for paper and toner when they receive facsimile transmissions.

Video conferencing, although prohibitively expensive at the moment, will soon be sufficiently cost-effective to realize the dreams of one-on-one marketers: face-to-face contact. The addition of miniature video cameras, microphones, and video-conferencing software will transform ordinary computers into global communicators capable of transporting users to the far reaches of the world. Even though video-conferencing technology will raise issues of privacy and security, answers will emerge so that everyone can reap the benefits of video conferencing.

Telephone, cable, and utility companies are investing heavily in interactive television. Within a few years, consumers in large urban centers in the United States will start receiving broadcast and cable television, video on demand, computer access, Internet access, and telephone access through a small box that sits atop their television set. If you can imagine sitting on your couch and flipping back and forth between a television show, the stock market, the telephone, and a timeshare exchange network's directory of resorts, you can understand the strong appeal of interactive television for investors.

A Kinder, Gentler Process

From its inception, the timeshare industry has grown through experimentation and innovation. Now technology is taking over, opening new channels for identifying, attracting, and selling to prospective clients while expanding the scale and scope of the global marketplace for vacation ownership products and associated leisure services.

This trend has the potential to generate unprecedented profitability. As with any revolution, those who adopt the new technologies first will bear the greatest risks and enjoy the greatest rewards. The biggest winners, of course, will be the timeshare consumers who experience a kinder, gentler sales process and a previously unparalleled variety of superior vacation ownership products.

Source: James Dunn, "The Impact of Technology on Timeshare Marketing," *Urban Land*, August 1996, pp. 55–57.

sweepstakes box program. All leads lived within 150 miles of the resorts.

Targeting international markets, an increasingly important option for timeshares both nationally and internationally, also requires specialized approaches. South American countries such as Chile, Brazil, Venezuela, and Colombia, for example, have responded to timeshare product offerings through direct sales and, in particular, through "off-site" purchases. International prospects are excellent clients as they tend to purchase larger units for longer periods of time. In reaction to this market change, corporations such as the Allegro Resort Corporation are becoming multilingual; some of Allegro's sales and marketing teams offer video presentations and literature in up to five different languages.[10]

Follow-Up Marketing. The marketing strategy does not end with drawing potential buyers to the vacation ownership. Follow-up marketing has become a standard tool in many marketing programs. Follow-up calls answer any questions that might have occurred to prospects after the tour. Feedback from prospective buyers also alerts developers to potential problems. Follow-up calls conducted with sincerity establish a stronger relationship of trust. Given that the goal of the product information strategy is to foster trust, sincere follow-up helps ensure that when buyers make a purchase decision, they will turn to the project they understand best and trust most.

This low-key marketing approach is perhaps best exemplified by Disney at the Disney Vacation Club. Located within Disney World in Florida, the Disney Vacation Club (DVC) capitalizes on innovative marketing techniques and in-house marketing capabilities. DVC's carefully planned marketing strategy and unparalleled location have created perhaps the most successful vacation ownership resort of its time. With a reliable flow of prospects, Disney has implemented a "soft" sales approach that diverges strongly from traditional vacation ownership sales techniques.

At the DVC, vacation club guides (the title deemphasizes the sales orientation of the sales staff) do not expect to sell a vacation ownership to the prospect immediately. Instead, potential buyers participate in a multifaceted program that informs them about current DVC issues and offerings. The program allows the guests to absorb the sales information at their own pace, reminds them of the DVC experience, and fosters a relationship that builds trust over time. The Disney name, symbolizing a high-quality vacation experience and financial strength, makes Disney's "soft" technique extremely effective. Likewise, other hospitality corporations have adopted a soft sales approach.

The Resale Issue. One of the problems that remains for timeshare marketers is the resale issue. Many of the fee-simple timeshares developed in the 1970s and 1980s have proven difficult to resell, leading to disgruntled owners and unfavorable publicity for the industry. The resale issue is less of a problem for the point system programs that offer more flexibility and do not overemphasize the real estate investment angle. Nonetheless, the negative publicity associated with resales still taints the industry. Unfortunately, while many other problematic aspects of vacation ownership have improved, resales have remained a dilemma with no clear answers.

Much of the problem stems from confusion over the ability to resell a vacation ownership interval for a profit. Historically, salespeople and buyers have considered timeshare intervals much like a real estate investment and assumed that the timeshare would appreciate. Today, industry experts concur that salespeople should educate buyers to think of vacation ownership intervals as a product that loses value over time (much like a car). Even products that hold their face value will not generate an investment return for the buyer because of the relatively high cost of selling the timeshare; in fact, sales commissions for resales run at 20 percent or more. In many states, a salesperson may be liable for selling an interval under the pretense that the interval may later sell at a greater value. Even so, many salespeople continue to lead prospective buyers to believe that their intervals will appreciate. A Ragatz Associates survey of buyers conducted in 1993 and 1994 revealed that one-fifth of buyers expect to sell their interval for a profit.

Ironically, improvements in timeshare products have compounded the resale problem. With the relatively rapid evolution of the industry, the continuing enhancement of timeshare membership strategies and products has attracted buyers to innovative vacation ownership intervals. As a result, older product types become more difficult to sell. According to Bert Blicher, chair of the resale task force for the ARDA (American Resort Development Association), the resale issue would be reduced by 75 percent if the problems with older timeshares could be eliminated.

At present, either the development company or an independent resale brokerage company usually handles resales. The timeshare management often offers a list of resale brokerage companies to help facilitate resales but remains independent of the process. For example, Outer Banks Resort Rentals in Nags Head, North Carolina, is responsible for resales for over 12 vacation ownership products in the area. The firm charges a nominal fee for advertising costs and a 17 percent commission for the sale.[11] While Outer Banks Resort Rentals resells vacation ownership intervals exclusively, most brokerage companies offer a resale service among their other services. Typically, resale brokers charge a commission between 18 and 25 percent.

Some timeshare companies have become involved in the resale process and bear the burden of conducting a resale program themselves. However, many timeshare developers view resales as an activity that undermines new unit sales momentum. In addition, understanding the related securities and antitrust laws is difficult and

Disney's Old Key West Resort, located within Walt Disney World in Orlando, Florida, exemplifies a vacation ownership concept that capitalizes on innovative marketing techniques and internal marketing capabilities. The project's carefully planned marketing and fortuitous location have resulted in one of the most successful vacation ownership resorts of its time.

requires considerable time. Along with the vested interests of the development team and the failure of selling members to align themselves, salespeople are not financially motivated to work on resales; the lower-value unit usually sells at a lower rate of commission. By contrast, salespeople typically receive 40 to 55 percent for new intervals.[12]

Nevertheless, some timeshares view the role of resales as a service to their members and an important marketing tool for new sales. Managers perceive the service as a testament of faith in the quality of the project and the level of member service—even if it hurts new interval sales. In projects that have completely sold, resale activity is easier to manage and often more successful. The Marriott Vacation Club International in Orlando, for example, operates a resale program at five of its properties where it is not selling new units.

Another strategy adopted by some vacation ownership programs is the right to buy back a resale interval. The Disney Vacation Club, for example, retains the right of first refusal and often purchases the interval because of its demand. It seems therefore that the quality of the vacation ownership product is the primary determining factor in the success of the resale process.

Timeshare and Vacation Ownership Management

The vacation ownership industry has entered a phase in its history that demands a more acute focus on management of operations. This phase began in the late 1980s during the industry's rapid expansion and maturation. With the emergence of many new products and a correspondingly more competitive market, vacation ownership developers began to realize the importance of management. Moreover, relatively new players such as major hospitality companies have inspired a new level of service in the vacation ownership industry. The increasing quality of service, together with the added flexibility offered by point systems, has resulted in more sophisticated management systems and strategies.

Dealing with Owners. Management is a particularly challenging endeavor in the vacation ownership industry. The primary reason is that owners are essentially a hybrid of renters and owners; they think like owners but act like renters. Thus, vacation ownership management is accountable for a unique set of expectations. Traditionally, common belief held that timeshares did not offer the same level of service as hotels simply because such service was not cost-effective. But with the continuing integration of hotels and vacation ownership, consumers' service expectations are increasing. Further, as the vacation ownership industry has become more saturated with alternatives, it has undergone a shift from quantity to quality. Property management has become the vacation ownership fulcrum that determines the continued success of many timeshares.

The homeowners' association/developer relationship is the key to successful management. Without proper structuring and attention, a poor relationship is likely to evolve and eventually cripple any vacation ownership

A key management and marketing problem faced by Melrose on Daufuskie Island, South Carolina, was an island location with no bridge. Melrose operates a fleet of boats to transport members from the mainland—Hilton Head Island—to Daufuskie Island. While some members enjoy the ride, others find access difficult; the access problem has hampered sales.

project. Property management typically involves the management of large homeowners' associations ranging upwards from 1,000 individual owners. At sellout, a homeowners' association board of directors, too often made up of unqualified individuals, assumes the management function only to find itself incapable of dealing with the complexity of association requirements. It is not surprising, then, that professional property management organizations have become commonplace and are better positioned to manage homeowners' association budgets and administrative issues, hospitality services at the front desk, reservations, visitors and renters, and exchanges.[13]

Management Goals. To ensure a well-managed program, vacation ownership management should strive toward achievement of at least the four following goals:

Construct a Realistic Budget. In the wake of the attention focused on construction and sales, management and budgeting frequently receive short shrift. Nonetheless, property management must develop a realistic budget. That budget must account for the fact that marketing strategies often contribute to the perception of a less expensive product by failing to anticipate necessary management costs. The result is dissatisfied owners, who in turn can make for unfavorable public relations, which leads to fewer sales and serious resale problems (perhaps the greatest problem of the timeshare industry). An unhappy owner who pays higher-than-expected maintenance fees is hardly a benefit to the development. On the other hand, artificially inflated maintenance fees deter prospective buyers. Research has confirmed that owners are willing to pay for quality if the established fees are consistent with that quality, according to Carol W. Sullivan of Creative Resort Services.[14]

Establish an ABC Strategy. An assessment, billing, and collection (ABC) policy should establish clear guidelines for the payment of maintenance assessments. The policy should specify due dates, late fees, and penalties for nonpayment. To ensure the collection of maintenance fees on a timely basis, the policy must be made explicit to owners. Part of the process of collecting assessments on a timely basis is communicating with and educating owners. Late fees and penalties such as loss of privileges must be consistently enforced to stress the importance of timely payments. Consistent enforcement leads to dramatic improvements in compliance.[15]

Communications with Owners. Perhaps the most important consideration in ensuring owner satisfaction is ongoing communications. An owners' committee that meets periodically with the management board about operations issues and costs can successfully maintain two-way channels of communication. Once the owners' committee understands the fee collection and expenditure process, committee members are usually satisfied that their investment is properly managed. They, in turn, can relay their sentiments to other owners. Educating owners about the vacation ownership business minimizes perceived industry complexities and increases owner satisfaction.

Provide State-of-the-Art Technology. The proper technology and management systems are necessary to streamline costs and communication. A management operation that functions at maximum efficiency can focus on owners' service demands.[16]

Exchange Programs. The option to exchange a timeshare for another location has dramatically changed the nature of the vacation ownership industry. Initially, consumers bought a timeshare product with the intention of returning to the same location every year (similar to a second home). Today, consumers purchase vacation ownership intervals largely to avail themselves of the additional opportunity to trade for a timeshare in another location.[17] As the timesharing industry has grown, the role of exchange companies has likewise grown and become an influential element of the industry.

Exchange programs rank timeshares according to the quality, location, and types of amenities offered. However, when a member wants to trade his or her timeshare for another location, he or she must also consider the time of year (a timeshare in Vail during Christmas might be equal to a timeshare in Hilton Head during a Fourth of July weekend.) As a result, exchange programs have helped standardize the industry, providing an incentive for developers to create a high-quality product that earns preferential trading rights. Exchange companies have also brought a reliable service to the timesharing industry, something it desperately needed during the 1970s and 1980s.

The two exchange companies that vastly dominate the industry are Resort Condominiums International (RCI) and Interval International (II). RCI is the largest exchange company, providing exchange opportunities to approximately 1.9 million member families in the world and incorporating over 2,800 affiliated resorts. In 1995, RCI sent 5 million travelers around the world, arranging for 1.4 million vacation exchanges. Typically, members pay annual dues and a small fee for an exchange to take place. Members call to learn what opportunities are available for other timeshare opportunities, as units are listed on a space-available basis (if another person wants to exchange timeshares). For more information, the *AEI Resource Manual* provides an excellent in-depth explanation of exchange programs.[18]

Hospitality/Vacation Ownership Partnerships

The entry of major hospitality companies into the vacation ownership industry has brought considerable benefits: credibility, financial capability, long-term management skills, and significant human resources. The involvement of hospitality companies has translated into a revolution in both market strategies and physical products. For example, today's timeshare units reflect a higher level of design flexibility than traditional vacation ownership products.

Gary A. Terry of Jones, Waldo, Holbrook points to the following advantages of combining timeshares with a hotel resort:

- The financial risk of a resort can be spread over a broader range of products.
- The marketing cost for the overall resort can be leveraged between various product components.
- Especially during nonpeak and off seasons, vacation ownership properties can increase a resort's overall occupancy, which, in turn, can increase operating efficiency and amenity income.[19]

The symbiosis of hotels and vacation ownership products requires a new dynamic of management whose rewards minimize operations costs and maximize profits. The benefits are immense if property management is capable of adjusting to the associated complexities. However, an unprepared and unskilled management team attempting to handle both hotel and vacation ownership operations will encounter serious problems that may degrade both products.

Higher Occupancies/Lower Operations Costs. Timeshares benefit hotel operations by increasing the overall number of guests at the resort and decreasing the dramatic swings between the high and low seasons, thus increasing the revenues from such hotel amenities as restaurants, bars, tennis courts, and golf courses. A hotel/timeshare partnership can also benefit by sharing many operations costs and thereby minimizing net management expenses. A hotel and vacation ownership partnership can, for example, use the same front desk, maintenance facilities, etc.

The Hilton Grand Vacations Club Flamingo Hilton in Las Vegas is one of a long and growing list of Hilton vacation ownership properties.

Many resorts must subsidize their amenities as necessary components of a high-quality resort experience. Timeshares, however, help ensure that more individuals use the resort amenities over a longer period of time, thereby increasing revenues and reducing the depth of subsidies. The result is decreased per room/unit operations costs for both the hotel and the timeshare.

Edwin McMullen, a leader in the vacation ownership industry and current chair of Hilton Grand Vacations, foresees a future fusion of vacation ownerships and hotels. He says that "many traditional hotel and resort developers and operators may find it imperative to include a timesharing component in conjunction with new or renewed facilities simply to afford the costs and keep occupancies at profitable levels."

Better Service. Timeshares affiliated with a hotel can offer a level of service not economically feasible in the highest-quality standalone timeshare facilities. That is, hotel service can provide the luxuries that many people want but that are not otherwise offered by traditional vacation ownership products: proximity to gourmet restaurants; concierge, valet, and porter services; communication capabilities; and highly professional front desk operations. Finally, because a hotel/timeshare combination can offer relatively stable employment with minimal layoffs during the off season (a major problem in many seasonal resorts), it can attract better-qualified employees and further enhance the quality of its services.

Marketing Advantages. Vacation ownerships associated with major hospitality corporations also have distinct advantages when it comes to marketing. The hotel can provide the timeshare with a stream of qualified buyers and inexpensive but excellent advertising opportunities. The hotel/vacation ownership partnership allows for easy step-up purchase potential from a hotel unit to a vacation ownership unit. Hotel guests are perhaps the best potential buyers because they virtually "test drive" the same amenities available to the vacation ownership properties. In addition, fully integrated hospitality companies maintain a database of frequent guests and operate frequent guest programs from which to target their marketing. With these resources, hospitality companies can undertake in-house marketing at reduced cost with increased profitability.

Another important marketing advantage offered by partnerships involves maximizing vacation point flexibility by offering additional opportunities to exchange vacation ownership points for discount travel to a resort, reduced hotel rates, and discounted amenities. Points serve as currency. Vacation ownership companies have entered into partnerships with airlines, rental car companies, and other related service businesses to enhance vacation point flexibility. Hilton, for example, operates a program that permits timeshare participants to exchange points for a stay at any Hilton at a reduced rate, the purchase of a reduced-fare ticket on Delta Airlines, or automobile rental through Alamo Rent-a-Car. The

Photo courtesy of EDSA

Hyatt's Grand Cypress Hotel in Orlando, Florida, has 750 guest rooms and 148 suites. It offers a wide range of amenities and services, including a golf academy and course, an equestrian facility, a raquet club, fitness trails, and nature trails. It is also close to Walt Disney World's Magic Kingdom and surrounding theme parks.

increased flexibility bolsters Hilton customer allegiance and provides customers with an incentive to use Hilton hospitality services as frequently as possible.

Resort Hotel Management and Operations

As with hotels in general, the management and operations of a resort hotel encompasses many issues too numerous to discuss thoroughly in this text. Entire books have been devoted to the subject; thus, this section addresses just a few of the operations issues that distinguish resort hotels from other types of hotels and give rise to unique operations and financial considerations. In particular, relative to other hotel product segments, resort hotels generally achieve substantially higher revenue levels; yet, the extensive range of facilities and related services that typify resort hotels contributes to increased operating expenses.

In general, resort hotels are complex operations that are labor- and management-intensive. They are service businesses as much as real estate. Resort developers who wish to manage their own hotel should be prepared for a challenge. In multiuse resorts where the hotel is only one element in the larger resort, an experienced hotel operator—either independent or chain-affiliated—is to be preferred.

Whatever the management approach, the multiuse resort developer should ensure the development of a strong relationship between hotel operations and operations of the other elements of the resort, especially the residential sales effort. With each hotel guest a prospective buyer of property in the resort, access to hotel guest information is critical to the sales effort (see feature box on page 212). Moreover, as already mentioned, hotel operations are increasingly involved in timeshare management and marketing, further complicating the resort hotel management and marketing program.

Resort Hotel Operations Characteristics

While resort hotels cost more to build than traditional hotels, they generate greater revenues from longer guest stays, higher occupancy and room rates, and other on-site services. Specific factors that distinguish resort hotel operations from other hotel operations include the following:

Occupancy. Traditional hotels typically cater to weekday travelers and thus face an occupancy threshold they cannot surpass without penetrating the weekend-meeting or FIT-getaway markets. Resort hotels, on the other hand, typically face strong seasonal fluctuations in occupancy. Reputable resort hotel properties can achieve occupancies of 80 percent or higher during most of their peak operating season. According to data from Smith Travel Research, occupancy rates in 1994 for full-service resort hotels stood at 69.2 percent, which was comparable to occupancy rates of 69.8 and 71.3 percent, respectively, for both full-service urban and suburban hotels.

Rates. Traditional hotels provide deep discounts on the weekends, whereas resort hotels are inclined to do just the opposite. During off seasons and shoulder seasons, resort hotels may offer rates at almost half those of the peak season, often with inducements that traditional hotels typically cannot provide. Full-service resort hotels achieve a significantly higher average rate per occupied room night than full-service urban and suburban hotels, according to Smith Travel Research. The average rate in 1994 was $104.68, substantially higher than the $93.39 and $72.55 achieved by urban and suburban full-service hotels, respectively.

Food and Drink. As a result of menu pricing, the greater number of meals captured on site, and higher occupancy per room, resort hotels can achieve much higher per capita food and beverage revenues than

Profile and Comments: Mark M. Hemmeter

Mark M. Hemmeter
President and Director
Hemmeter Enterprises, Inc.
Denver, Colorado

Mark Hemmeter is executive vice president and director of Hemmeter Enterprises, Inc., a real estate development and gaming company founded by his father, hotel and resort developer Christopher B. Hemmeter. The company currently employs about 1,500 persons and achieves annual revenues of approximately $1.7 million. It owns and operates the largest gaming company in Colorado and recently opened a $210 million riverboat gaming project in New Orleans. An affiliate, Grand Palais Enterprises, Inc., is a one-third partner in New Orleans's only land-based casino.

Before his appointment as executive vice president of Hemmeter Enterprises, Hemmeter was responsible for the implementation and management of guest amenity programs at the Westin Maui, Westin Kauai, and Hyatt Regency Waikoloa. He also served as president of the Hemmeter-owned architectural company, Hemmeter Design Group and, since 1987, has been responsible for the family investment portfolio.

Hemmeter graduated from the University of Colorado Business School in 1985.

A developer should always minimize overhead in the home office and should use local and regional outside experts, whenever possible. Our corporate office has only about 18 employees, and we don't expect it to get any bigger. Although the firm has 1,500 total employees, most of the employees are located at the operating entities.

When entering into a joint venture relationship, be sure that your partner has a common vision or goal. Also, be sure that the partner has different expertise from you. When developing and operating a project in an area outside your home base, always have a knowledgeable local partner who can specialize in government and public relations. Ninety percent of our projects now are joint ventures. When a developer is conceptualizing a project, a joint venture partner has to buy into the developer's dream or vision. Successful joint venture partners complement the developer and help round out the whole team in terms of expertise. A developer gets into trouble, however, when the joint venture partner lacks flexibility.

When forecasting market size or market demand, a developer should realize that with the appropriate product, he can create a much larger market than a standard demographic study might suggest. In short, there is both an existing, unmet demand and an induced demand. The real trick is forecasting the induced demand. When a developer is introducing a new product, such as gaming today or destination resort hotels in Hawaii in the late 1970s, trying to forecast the success of a project is hard. We have found that using standard gaming or hotel analysis produces a low estimate of demand. The analysis always underestimates the induced market. We do a demographic analysis, but a lot of our estimation of the total market is based on "gut feel" because forecasting the induced demand is so difficult.

It is becoming much more difficult, if not impossible, to build megaresorts in the 1990s. The success of several early megaresorts, particularly in Hawaii, spawned many imitators; consequently, a large oversupply of hotel rooms was developed. The subsequent drop in disposable income, particularly in southern California and Japan, affected every Hawaiian resort whether or not it was a good project. Resort areas that can, have learned the lessons of oversupply and regulate the available supply of rooms. There are some areas around the world where megaresorts still can work. It is more likely, however, that smaller projects, approximately 600 hotel rooms, will be built rather than the megaprojects of the 1990s. We believe that what will be developed in North America are more mixed-use projects that include a hotel, golf, a timeshare, a marina, shopping, and perhaps some residential. These projects are not so dependent on one segment of customer and therefore spread their risk.

■

urban or suburban commercial hotels. The Smith Travel Research data show that the average revenue from food and beverage in a full-service resort hotel in 1994 was $63 per occupied room night, as compared to $43 for a full-service urban hotel and only $31 for a full-service suburban hotel.

Retail Shops and Other Revenue Centers. Traditional hotels typically achieve limited retail sales, mainly of convenience items. Resort hotels, however, stock souvenirs, arts and crafts, and designer resort wear and logo items, all of which help their retail departments contribute to the bottom line. They also achieve revenues from the operation of a variety of other revenue centers, including golf and tennis facilities, health clubs, barber/beauty shops, and equipment rentals. The Smith Travel Research data show that the average revenue from minor operated departments, rentals, and other income in a full-service resort hotel in 1994 was $20.34

The Homestead in Hot Springs, Virginia, is owned and operated by Club Resorts, an affiliate of Club Corporation of America. Carriage rides and children's programs are just two of the many services offered to resort guests. The year-round, supervised Mountain Friends Programs—including activities such as indoor and outdoor games, nature walks, crafts, golf, swimming, and movies—are offered daily for children.

per occupied room night, as compared to $5.53 for a full-service urban hotel and $3.37 for a full-service suburban hotel.

Operating Expenses. While revenues are often higher in a resort hotel, expenses tend to be higher as well. The Smith Travel Research data reveal that higher operating expenses result not only from higher department operating expenses associated with more extensive operations—such as food, beverage, and minor operations—but also from undistributed operating expenses such as general and administrative, marketing, and property operations and maintenance. The marketing cost in 1994 for a full-service resort hotel, for example, was more than double that for a full-service suburban hotel.

Figure 5-1 highlights some operating features in greater detail.

Managing Resort Hotel Services

The management of resort hotels can differ significantly from the management of commercial hotels in two primary ways. First, resort hotels generally provide more services and are typically in the business of pampering their guests to ensure that they enjoy their stay. Second, unlike commercial hotels, resort hotels sometimes offer their services in a one-price package.

More Services. Resort hotels generally offer a wider variety of services to their guests than typical commercial hotels; many of these services are related to recreational pursuits. For example, at Marriott's Grand Hotel & Resort in Point Clear, Alabama, fishing is a popular pursuit on Pavilion Wharf, where resort staff members are available to bait hooks, clean the day's catch, and carry it to the hotel's chef, who cooks the fish to order. The staff of 500 outnumbers guests by a 2:1 ratio.

Most resort hotels also offer special children's programs. At the Innisbrook Hilton Resort in Tarpon Springs, Florida, children can enroll in the resort's Zoo Crew program, which features playground activities, games, relay races, sports clinics, arts and crafts, story sessions, pool play, miniature golf, bowling, and movies.

Service Pricing/Packaging.[25] Resort hotel operations can also differ from commercial hotel operations in the way they offer, market, and price services. For example, all-inclusive resort hotels, whose fee structure typically includes accommodations, meals, recreational activities, airport transfers, service charges, and/or gratuities at a single predetermined price, are gaining popularity in many destination resort areas. Indeed, today's vacationers are value-conscious, and their growing preference for active vacationing has boosted the popularity of all-inclusive vacation packages. Tour operators and travel agents like to promote the all-inclusive resort vacation since it is typically easier to sell. More important, the total travel package generally yields a higher commission.

The aim is to decrease seasonality, boost occupancy, and control costs. Besides finding favor with the market and typically attracting guests for longer-than-average stays, all-inclusive resorts are generally easier to operate.

figure 5-1

Full-Service Hotels—Urban, Suburban, and Resort
Statements of Operating Income and Expenses for 1994

Amounts per Occupied Room Night

	Urban	Suburban	Resort
Occupancy	69.8%	71.3%	69.2%
Average Size of Property (rooms)	431	228	407
Average Rate	$93.39	$72.55	$104.68
Revenue			
Rooms	$93.39	$72.55	$104.68
Food	30.81	22.14	45.59
Beverage	8.28	6.12	13.34
Other Food and Beverage	3.43	3.22	3.66
Telephone	4.27	2.91	2.37
Minor Operated Departments	3.14	2.00	16.07
Rentals and Other Income	2.39	1.37	4.27
Total	**$145.71**	**$110.31**	**$191.29**
Departmental Expenses			
Rooms	$25.81	$18.59	$27.47
Food and Beverage	35.49	24.88	49.94
Telephone	2.37	1.56	2.38
Other Departmental Expenses	2.49	1.75	12.41
Total	**$66.16**	**$46.78**	**$92.20**
Total Departmental Profit	**$79.55**	**$63.53**	**$99.09**
Undistributed Operating Expenses			
Administrative and General	$13.76	$10.53	$17.83
Marketing	9.72	6.51	3.31
Franchise Fee	1.17	1.45	.97
Energy	6.37	5.21	8.01
Property Operation and Maintenance	7.87	5.73	11.13
Total	**$38.89**	**$29.43**	**$51.25**
Gross Operating Profit	**$40.66**	**$34.10**	**$47.84**

Source: Smith Travel Research, *The HOST Study: Hotel Operating Statistics 1995: Report for the Year 1994* (Hendersonville, Tenn: Smith Travel Research, 1995).

The Salish Lodge in Snoqualmie, Washington, is a nonchain boutique hotel positioned as a regional retreat. The hotel is a member of the Preferred Chain of Hotels, an association of private unique and exclusive hotels that band together to promote themselves.

Dick Busher

The food and beverage operations are more controllable. Further, with minimal cash transactions occurring on site, the requirements for internal cash and accounting controls are lower.

So far, the all-inclusive concept has failed to gain a foothold on the U.S. mainland. Its most significant venue is the Caribbean, where concern for off-premises safety originally led operators to create self-contained resorts that provided for virtually all guest needs. Certain U.S. markets that are either international gateway cities or near such cities offer the greatest potential for all-inclusive resort operations. For example, as the gateway to Latin America and a city frequented by foreign travelers, Miami provides an opportunity for all-inclusive resorts targeted to the international market.

Resort Hotel Marketing

While resort hotel marketing encompasses many of the same marketing strategies used to market the overall resort, two additional factors are critical in marketing resort hotels. The first is the benefit of chain affiliation or some other type of network that provides advantages similar to those offered by a chain operation. The second is the growing importance of conference facilities as a draw for resort hotels.

Although the major national and international hotel chains were slow to enter the resort market, they are now the dominant players in large resort hotels. During the 1970s and 1980s, U.S. hotel chains such as Hilton, Sheraton, Hyatt, and Marriott identified and targeted an opportunity in the resort segment of the lodging industry. Such chains recognized that with proper facility planning, they could effectively accommodate both the individual-tourist and group segments of the market and, at the same time, reduce severe seasonal fluctuations in demand and improve overall annual occupancy. To the resort field, these major chains brought their traditional strategic advantages, including their extensive referral networks,

their marketing expertise and seasoned experience in handling groups, and their well-established image and mass appeal. In many cases, the hotel chain may not actually manage the hotel, but the chain affiliation still provides a critical marketing and positioning benefit.

While chain affiliation is an important factor in marketing resort hotels, there are niches for unaffiliated hotels as well. The Salish Lodge in Snoqualmie, Washington, for example, is a nonchain boutique hotel that has successfully created a special market position for itself. Located in the Cascade Mountains, the lodge occupies a unique site next to a lovely waterfall, which is a significant tourist attraction in its own right. The hotel's marketing strategy initially involved a regional approach that used a variety of packages to position the lodge as a special-occasion weekend retreat. As an unexpected benefit, the lodge also attracted a corporate business market that filled rooms during the week. The corporate market was so strong that the hotel doubled its meeting space just two years after the lodge's opening. Thus, the lodge established itself as a highly attractive conference hotel.

By 1993, the lodge had also tapped an international clientele as a result of the fame it earned as the setting for the television series *Twin Peaks*. In the series, the lodge was known as the Great Northern Hotel. The series aired in Japan and Europe, and the media exposure brought the lodge new business from international tour groups.

Even independent boutique hotels such as the Salish Lodge can benefit from affiliation. As a result of its newfound fame and its own elegance, the lodge was asked to join the Preferred Chain of Hotels, an association of unique and exclusive private hotels that band together to promote themselves and publish a book of preferred hotels. In a recent *Conde Nast Traveler* magazine ranking of the top 100 hotels in the world, the Salish Lodge ranked 56, up from its ranking of 84 the year before.

Community Management and Operation[21]

The development of a successful resort community obviously involves more than just a good master plan, an attractive amenity package, and desirable real estate products. The developer must recognize the need for and the synergy that can be created by a unifying management structure. That structure may include one or more government bodies, tax-exempt organizations, or community associations or perhaps some combination specifically designed to meet the needs and goals of the particular community. In selecting the most appropriate structure, it is important to understand the available options and how they might be used to maximize flexibility for the developer during both the development process and the long-term operation of the community.

A structure and program for community management is essential to the implementation and protection of the developer's master plan for the community. A carefully designed community management structure provides a mechanism for

- ensuring the preservation of common areas, including those that buffer the community and set it apart from surrounding areas;
- long-term ownership, maintenance, and operation of amenities that benefit property owners and increase the community's attractiveness to visitors and prospective property purchasers;
- fulfilling long-term and continuing obligations undertaken by the developer as a condition of obtaining development approval; and
- establishing and enforcing communitywide standards of maintenance and design.

A variety of community management structures may accomplish the above objectives; indeed, no single structure works best for all communities. In many cases, two or more structures may need to be combined to address a particular community's needs. In determining which option or combination of options is most appropriate for a given community, the developer should consider the community's particular characteristics, goals, and constraints, including

- the types of uses planned for the community and the approximate area and acreage to be devoted to each use;
- the proposed location of different land uses in relation to each other;
- the types of amenities proposed for inclusion in the community and the extent to which they benefit each of the various land uses;
- the development timetable and phasing plan;
- the extent to which the developer intends to retain long-term ownership or control of one or more components of the community;
- the nature and scope of responsibilities to be fulfilled by the governing entity or entities;
- the nature and scope of services to be provided to the various land uses that make up the community;
- the legal foundation and "tools" made available by the jurisdiction in which the community is located;
- the relationship with local government; and
- the targeted market.

The basic organizational options fall into three major categories: government bodies, nonprofit tax-exempt corporations, and community associations. These options may be varied and combined to maximize control and flexibility for the developer during the development process and to enhance community marketability.

Government Bodies

Municipal corporations and community improvement districts can both play a valuable role in the development

At Horseshoe Bay Resort near Austin, Texas, a municipal utility district was formed to issue bonds for the installation of water and sewage treatment facilities.

and operation of a resort community. As standalone entities, however, they have disadvantages that generally make them inadequate for addressing all the needs of any type of master-planned community. Therefore, they are most helpful when used in combination with other options.

Municipalities and special taxing districts generally have the power to tax and the power of eminent domain. They usually have access to public funds for various projects and services and may issue debt to finance certain activities, thereby offering a lower-cost method of financing public infrastructure and facilities than traditional, tax revenue-based means. Generally, the taxes paid by property owners are deductible, making municipal incorporation or creation of a community improvement district an attractive vehicle for undertaking many "public" functions within the community.

Government bodies are, however, subject to constitutional restraints and must operate in accordance with the demands of state and federal law, which generate additional costs for property owners. For example, government bodies cannot restrict public access to parks, streets, and other property and thus do not have the flexibility to create private amenities for the exclusive use of the community's property owners and their tenants and guests.

Perhaps the most significant factor to consider is that of control. In both a municipality and a community improvement district, most decisions rest with an elected body. Few if any decisions require a vote of the property owners, and the developer has no basis on which to retain veto power. In fact, a municipality's residents elect the governing body from the outset; thus, the developer does not enjoy even an initial period of control. From the developer's perspective, this lack of control means that there is no assurance that the municipality will accept ownership of or maintenance responsibility for the open spaces, parks, and other amenities created for the community.

Although the election provisions under enabling statutes for community improvement districts vary, the developer, as the major landowner, may be able to control the election of the district's governing board for several years. In some jurisdictions, though, the enabling statutes require the eventual election of the district's governing board by the "qualified electors" of the district, that is, those residents who are eligible and registered to vote. This requirement may exclude property owners who do not reside in the district, including the developer. In a resort or second-home recreational community with few permanent residents, the vast majority of property owners might not be represented at all.

Even if the developer resides in the community improvement district, his or her vote is equal to that of a resident who does not own property. Thus, control may be taken out of the developer's hands long before the community is built out. Therefore, the developer must carefully consider the nature of the facilities to be handled through the community improvement district and the degree to which the eventual loss of control could affect development of the overall project and the marketing of the balance of the community.

Nonprofit Tax-Exempt Organizations

A nonprofit corporation structured to meet the requirements of a civic league under Section 501(c)(4) of the Internal Revenue Service code can in part address the control issue. To qualify for tax-exempt status, the nonprofit corporation must serve "the common good and general welfare of the people of a community," which must bear a reasonable relationship to an area ordinarily identified as a government area. Thus, like a municipality, the corporation's property must be available for use and enjoyment by the general public. The corporation is not, however, required to have members; it may be guided solely by its board of directors.

The IRS code grants wide discretion in determining the mechanism for establishing the corporation's board. Thus, the developer may indefinitely control the appointment of the board and convey to the corporation such community facilities as roads, open space, wetlands, and conservation easements, which are intended to benefit the entire community. In this way, the developer can ensure that facilities are maintained at an acceptable level.

A 501(c)(4) corporation may engage in a wide variety of activities without losing its tax-exempt status. Such activities include maintenance of roadways, parkways, sidewalks, street lights, and similar infrastructure and enforcement of covenants. A declaration of covenants may give the corporation the authority to exercise architectural control over all property subject to its terms as well as the power to assess such property for a share of the corporation's expenses, among other things.

It may also be desirable to establish one or more 501(c)(3) organizations to solicit and accept tax-exempt contributions for such purposes as environmental and conservation activities, provision of low-income housing for resort employees, and educational and cultural activities such as art festivals, museums, and concerts. However, neither 501(c)(4) nor 501(c)(3) organizations can provide maintenance on private property. As a result, these entities lack the flexibility to provide certain services to property owners as well as the authority to enforce covenants, both of which may be desirable in a master-planned community. Therefore, the tax-exempt organization option is best used in combination with other options that can assure the developer maximum flexibility in the development and operation of the community.

Community Associations

A community association structure, either alone or in conjunction with the options discussed above, may provide the greatest flexibility for a resort community. Although membership in a community association extends to all property owners, the association may be established with multiple classes of membership in order to vest control in the developer for an extended development period while providing for transition to the owners at a future date.

A community association structure generally provides broad flexibility in allocating voting rights and economic burdens among property owners, allowing for the assessment of property owners in accordance with benefits received rather than strictly on the basis of property value. Moreover, a community association may own and maintain property not intended for public use. Thus, a community association is able to provide varying levels of service to property owners, maintain private amenities for the primary use and benefit of particular areas within the community, and exercise self-help to maintain private property not maintained to an acceptable level by its owner.

Community Management at Vail Village

Vail Village is generally considered the first major planned ski-oriented resort community in North America. Before the development of Vail Village in 1961, the Gore Creek Valley was undeveloped agricultural land with virtually no infrastructure improvements. Today, it boasts over 300,000 square feet of retail uses and nearly 2,000 residential units.

Vail Associates, Inc. (VAI), was the original project developer of Vail Village. VAI's vision called for a community modeled after an Alpine village. The design concept integrates a variety of European town planning principles, including narrow streets, uniform building materials, an irregular street pattern, automobile-free pedestrian zones, a mix of retail and residential uses, and prominently located public plazas. Reliance on a stringent set of codes, covenants, and restrictions allowed the developer to regulate design and development within the village.

Vail Village is considered the first major planned resort community oriented toward skiing in North America. Although most of the village is built out, redevelopment and expansion activity has continued in the 1990s.

During the initial years of operation, VAI not only provided Vail's economic base but also delivered needed municipal services (including road maintenance, utility infrastructure, and fire protection). VAI later transferred these services to the town of Vail, which incorporated in 1966. Following incorporation, the town government assumed responsibility for all municipal services, zoning administration, and subdivision/development review. The town enacted land use ordinances to ensure that future development (and redevelopment) within the village would comply with the original and existing design parameters. These ordinances actively discourage building setbacks and retail square footage limitations, establish view corridors, require first-floor retail uses in all buildings, and prohibit parking in the village core. The success of Vail Village can be largely attributed to the collaborative efforts of VAI and the town of Vail, which encouraged the evolution of the village in a manner true to the original design concepts.

While most of the village is built out, redevelopment and expansion activity has remained strong throughout the 1990s. Vail redevelopment initiatives have often involved the total demolition of structures followed by the development of top-quality residential and commercial projects. In 1991, redevelopment and remodeling of existing property in the village accounted for $7.6 million in expenditures.

VAI has continued to play an active role in supporting community initiatives and citizen programs. It was responsible for creating an organization that has evolved into the Vail Valley Foundation. A nonprofit organization, the foundation is dedicated to enhancing the local quality of life from an educational, athletic, and cultural standpoint. Examples of the foundation's programs include the 1989 World Alpine Ski Championship, the Gerald Ford Amphitheater, and the Bolshoi Ballet Academy at Vail. In an ongoing effort to support community economic development, VAI is also marketing local summer programs.

Figure 5-2 describes the relative advantages and disadvantages of various community association structures that could be used to manage a resort community. In determining which structure is the most appropriate, the developer must consider the needs and goals of the particular community.

In addition to the factors already mentioned, a resort community development should consider those aspects of community management that are unique to resort communities. How should the interests of residents be balanced against the interests of hotels and other resort operators? How will the anticipated level of absentee ownership in the resort affect the functioning of the management structure? Will the governing body be asked or want to provide special services or a menu of services to assist in the management of individual prop-

figure 5-2

Comparison of Community Association Structures

Type of Association	Advantages	Disadvantages
Single community association with parcel structure	• Simplicity; minimizes administrative burden of managing multiple associations. • Provides unifying body to maintain a communitywide standard.	• May be perception that separately incorporated parcel associations would have greater autonomy. • Subjects nonresidential owners to control of residential owners or vice versa, which can affect marketing of "subject" properties.
Single residential association with neighborhood structure and covenant to share costs on nonresidential properties	• Provides autonomy to owners of nonresidential properties by not involving them in administration of primarily residential community.	• Can be cumbersome in projects characterized by multiple nonresidential parcels and nonresidential uses geographically interspersed with residential properties. • Provides little protection for residential owners concerned about use and appearance of nonresidential properties.
Dual associations (one residential, one nonresidential) with joint committee	• Provides desired level of autonomy to residential and nonresidential owners while maintaining communitywide standards and common areas through joint committee composed of representatives of each association. • Provides for long-term developer control over communitywide standards and properties without interfering in or unnecessarily delaying the transition to owner control within each association. • Joint committee can serve as mediator or arbiter of disputes between associations; may act as managing agent on behalf of associations to reduce administrative costs for each.	• Joint committee may be perceived as an additional administrative layer, although perception can be addressed by minimizing or eliminating "membership" in entity and limiting the scope of committee powers.
Dual associations (residential and nonresidential) with covenant to share costs	• Provides desired level of autonomy to residential and nonresidential owners. • Minimizes number of entities involved in community governance as well as perception of layering.	• No single entity to establish and enforce a communitywide standard. • Provides little protection for residential owners concerned about use and appearance of nonresidential properties and vice versa.

Source: Hyatt & Stubblefield, Atlanta, Ga.

erties? What level of control will the governing body assert over traditionally public areas such as beaches? What types of "public" services such as transportation, maintenance, and security will the governing body need or wish to provide? What is the most appropriate method of paying for such services?

Once these questions are answered, the community needs to determine whether all land uses should fall under the jurisdiction of a single association or whether residential and nonresidential uses should be handled separately. Even though it may be preferable to handle the various uses separately, some mechanism should link them. That mechanism would then ensure that communitywide standards are met and maintained, that all land uses pay their fair share of expenses incurred for the maintenance of property that benefits all, and that

At Callawassie Island in South Carolina, the annual property owner association dues run $665 per year (1995) and provide for maintenance of roadways, security, architectural review, community pest control, and landscaping of common properties. Homesites range in price from $25,000 (for the smallest lots with wooded views) to $235,000 (for the larger lots with marsh/river views).

Community centers run by the community association play an important role in enhancing lifestyle and fostering a sense of community at Sun City Las Vegas.

a communication system is in place to air and resolve common issues. While a structure that relies on a single community association with jurisdiction over the entire community may ensure unity and simplicity, it should also provide various parcels with some degree of autonomy. That is, the structure should allow for the provision of varying levels of service to different parcels without the need for separately incorporated subassociations.

If the decision is made to treat residential and nonresidential uses separately, the developer should consider whether the various uses need their own association or whether a single residential association with a covenant obligating the nonresidential property owners to share certain costs incurred by the residential association might suffice. In the case of separate associations, additional issues arise with respect to relying on a cove-

The Roles and Responsibilities of the Community Association

A critical element that contributes to the success of any planned development is a governance mechanism that unifies the various community components into a single community with certain communitywide standards. Without such a mechanism, each component is autonomous and, through action or inaction, can have a significant impact on the value and desirability of the other components of the planned development. The result is that the developer's original plan for the community becomes indiscernible as the developer's control and involvement diminish over time.

A community association with jurisdiction over all property in the planned development can be a highly effective, if not the most effective, mechanism for ensuring success while preserving the developer's flexibility, minimizing liability, and maximizing marketability of the developer's product.

A community association is a mandatory membership association responsible for performing various functions within a planned real estate development. Each property owner automatically becomes a member of the community association upon acceptance of a deed to property in the development. The mandatory membership aspect of the community association sets it apart from a civic association, social or business club, or other volunteer organization. The community association has long been used in purely residential developments but is increasingly becoming the norm in mixed-use projects as well.

A community association is an appropriate mechanism for any development characterized by

- individually owned parcels of property or "units" and common features and facilities benefiting all individually owned parcels;
- common services, such as common maintenance, security, or similar services, provided to two or more parcels within the development; or
- a need or desire for regulation and enforcement of communitywide standards of maintenance, architecture, use, and conduct for the enhancement and protection of property values.

The community association, like a corporation, has a perpetual existence separate from any individual or group of individuals. Like a corporation or municipal government, it acts on behalf of its members/owners—its "citizens." It is a separate entity from the developer, governed by a set of legal documents and applicable law.

The basic governing documents of any community association are the declaration, which contains various covenants, conditions, restrictions, and easements applicable to the development, and the association's bylaws. The declaration sets forth the plan of development and ownership, the proposed method of operation, and the relative responsibilities and rights of the association and the owners of individual parcels within the development. It is a "covenant running with the land" in that it is recorded in the land records and, like the provisions of a deed, continues to govern the ownership of the property even when title changes hands. The bylaws set out the administrative procedures for the internal government and operation of the association.

A community association can own and/or maintain various property and improvements that benefit the entire community, such as stormwater drainage facilities, open space, community signage, parks and recreational facilities, and landscaping within public rights-of-way. The community association is also an ideal entity to "catch" any continuing obligations that the developer may have assumed as a condition of development approval, such as maintenance of conservation areas or parks and monitoring of traffic patterns.

Community associations have a dual role: that of a business in managing and maintaining private property and that of a government in delivering services and enforcing covenants and rules. In many developments, the association exercises architectural control over and may provide some level of maintenance for individually owned property. It often provides all or some of the utility services, common area maintenance, street lighting, refuse removal, security services, and other related "municipal" services. It may sponsor various forms of communication within the community, such as newsletters or electronic bulletin boards. It may also offer cultural, educational, and recreational programs and activities and sponsor

nant to share costs or forming a simple "joint committee" to establish the relationship between the associations, thereby eliminating the need to create a master association (which would encumber the property with another level of government).

The ultimate goal in determining the management structure for any resort community is to maximize the developer's flexibility while providing for the smooth operation of the community during and after the development period. Whether or not the developer intends to retain ownership of major components of the community for an extended period, a flexible structure that addresses the short- and long-term needs of the community is critical to the success of the development plan (see feature box on page 244).

special events such as festivals, parades, and concerts to create synergy and a sense of community.

Acting through its board of directors, the association is charged with enforcing any specific covenants and restrictions set forth in the declaration and is typically authorized to make and to enforce additional rules and regulations as well. Such restrictions and rules may include limits on land use, prohibitions on certain types of activities, restrictions designed to control architecture and aesthetics within the development, and regulations regarding use of common areas and individually owned properties.

Two powers granted to the association—the power to levy and the power to control property—reinforce the governance aspect of the association's role. These powers are usually created in the declaration and, in some cases, by statute and are enforceable through state courts.

The power to levy is, of course, the association's power to assess property owners for their pro rata share of association expenses. Clearly analogous to the municipality's power to tax, the power to levy includes the obligation of the association or its board of directors to develop a fiscal plan, assign a share of the cost of that plan to the property owners as a charge against their individual properties, and collect the assessment through lien rights and state court action in the event that the assessment is not paid as scheduled. The assessment is not equivalent to membership dues or some other discretionary charge but is in fact a proportionate share of the expenses incurred to fund the association's business and governance services.

The power to control the use and enjoyment of property through the exercise of architectural and environmental controls, use restrictions, and rule-making authority allows the association to exert tremendous influence over the bundle of rights normally enjoyed as a concomitant part of fee-simple property ownership. This relatively high degree of control is vested through and must be exercised in accordance with the recorded declaration and applicable law.

From a legal standpoint, the community association exists from the time the developer records the declaration in the land records of the jurisdiction in which the property is located. For a period of time after the sale of the first unit in the community until a large proportion (typically about 75 percent) of the property is sold, the developer usually appoints a majority of the members of the association's board of directors, thereby retaining control of the operation and management of the association. In this capacity, the developer must consider a number of important issues involving cooperation, control, and management of the project.

Rather than "being the association," the developer is in the position of either a majority stockholder in a corporation or the managing partner in an unincorporated organization. The developer in control of a community association must be concerned with the fact that he or she is a fiduciary whose duty runs to both the association and its members. Therefore, in the exercise of the right to control, the developer must at all times be sensitive to the needs of the association as well as to the interests and needs of the development entity. The failure to maintain a sense of balance or conduct the association's affairs with fairness and in good faith can subject the developer to substantial liability.

Because of the unique roles and functions filled by the association, it is important that the association begin to operate as soon as the developer sells the first parcel of property, if not before. This permits the developer and the other association members, working within the framework established by the declaration and bylaws, to develop and implement the policies and procedures necessary to ensure that the association functions smoothly and efficiently both during and after the period of developer control. A clear understanding of the community association's unique role and function, in combination with a commitment from the developer and the association's officers, directors, and members to work together for the common good within the framework of the association's governing documents, is essential to the successful self-government of the common interest community.

Source: Jo Anne P. Stubblefield, partner, Hyatt & Stubblefield, Atlanta, Ga., 1995.

Heritage Hills of Westchester is an 1,100-acre planned community of condominium homes designed as a controlled recreational adult community. It is located in Somers, New York, a rural area in Westchester County, New York City's affluent suburb to the north. It is adjacent to Fairfield County, Connecticut, another affluent suburb. Developed by Heritage Development Group, whose principal is Henry J. Paparazzo, it is the second project of its type conceived and built by the company. Heritage Hills directly undertakes all land development, construction, and sales activities.

Heritage Hills was positioned as an adult community, not a retirement community; initially, it imposed a minimum age restriction of 40 and did not permit children under 18 years. Since the community's inception, however, federal law has outlawed age restrictions such as that imposed at Heritage Hills. Nonetheless, the community has been creatively maintained as a master-planned adult condominium community that offers a lifestyle and activities for those with considerable leisure time.

Rather than just providing a golf course and club, Heritage Hills is organized around the concept of a society. That is, each owner becomes a member of the Heritage Hills Society, Ltd., at the time of unit purchase.

The homes at Heritage Hills have been developed in phases or sections averaging 100 units per section. Each section has its own board of managers responsible for the maintenance of common elements within its geographic boundaries. At buildout, Heritage Hills will claim 31 separate condominium boards of managers.

Rather than just providing a golf course and club, Heritage Hills is organized around the concept of a society. That is, each owner becomes a member of the Heritage Hills Society, Ltd., at the time of unit purchase. The society has formed and manages over 100 clubs and organizations representing many types of hobbies and social interests. It is governed and directed by the homeowners themselves to ensure that it provides the lifestyle and activities desired by the community. Neither the developer nor outside parties provide the social programming.

The society oversees maintenance of the major roads as well as operation of the uniformed security service and the recreational facilities (except golf). It operates a shuttle bus system that transports residents to the nearby New York City commuter train station and local shopping centers. Under a fee arrangement, a management/maintenance company affiliated with the developer provides snow plowing, grounds maintenance, billing, collection, and financial management services for the society and most of the condominiums.

The society owns and operates four "satellite" recreation centers scattered throughout the project. At projected buildout of 2,900 units, the project will include five swimming pools, eight tennis courts, platform tennis courts, a gymnasium, theater, auditorium, library, saunas, whirlpool, pottery studios, game room, woodworking shop, workout rooms, classrooms, etc.

The project includes 27 holes of golf designed by architect Geoffrey Cornish. The developer owns and operates the golf courses as a private country club. Residents are not automatically members of the golf club, and club membership is not restricted to residents. Yearly membership costs $2,000 to $3,000. The golf club breaks even at the current buildout of 2,000 units.

A well-run community association can be more than simply a management structure; it can often take on a life of its own and become an important social and civic amenity, especially in resort communities that include a substantial retired population. For example, at Sun City Las Vegas, the community association plays a central role in enhancing the development's lifestyle and fostering a sense of community. At present, the association operates three community centers and offers a wide variety of activities to provide residents with lifestyle options. In addition to managing the community center facilities, the community association facilitates and supports all kinds of classes, support groups, and clubs. Residents are active in over 50 recreational and social clubs, including aquacize, sewing, golf, aerobics, tennis, computer, dance, bowling, and book clubs.

The community association is supported by an annual fee of $375 per household, by golf fees and pro shop income, and by food and beverage revenues from the clubs. The annual association fee includes full use of all recreational facilities except the golf club.

Club Management and Operations[22]

In any resort and recreational community development, the recreational amenity program is typically considered the principal defining element. Since the 1970s, organizational structures for managing and operating recreational amenities in resort and recreational communities have evolved from traditional country clubs to sophisticated entities that offer a wide range of facilities and services in a variety of packages that appeal to specific market segments.

This section begins by describing four basic organizational structures for amenity programs in resort and recreational communities. Next, it outlines three alternative methods for structuring membership rights within the basic organizational structures. It concludes by reviewing general approaches for adapting the basic organizational and membership structures for use in various types of resort and recreational communities.

Market preferences constantly change and create new development opportunities. Successful resort and recreational community developers have learned to adapt the basic amenity program alternatives to these new opportunities. The organizational and membership structures used for amenity programs in the 1980s and early 1990s should therefore be viewed as building blocks for creating new types of amenity programs in the future.

In any scenario, the owner of the recreational amenities typically contracts with one or more professional management companies for day-to-day management and operations activities. A number of national, regional, and local companies can provide management and operations services to developers, clubs, and community associations.

At Callawassie Island in South Carolina, the purchase price of each club cottage homesite includes an equity club membership. The equity membership contribution includes a $24,000 golf membership and a $10,000 social membership. The club cottages range in size from 1,700 to 2,300 square feet and in price from $190,000 to $270,000 (1995 prices).

Organizational Structures

Developers of resort and recreational communities have at least four basic options for the ownership, operations, and management of a community's recreational amenities: equity clubs, right-to-use clubs, convertible club programs, and association ownership (see figure 5-3). Each of these structures represents a unique approach to members and membership rights. In addition, developers may choose to own and operate an amenity themselves, as is often the case with a ski area.

Equity Club. To create an equity club, the developer forms a nonprofit corporation to serve as an independent club entity. The developer agrees contractually to contribute the recreational facilities to the club in exchange for the club's equity memberships. Subsequently, equity memberships are sold to recoup the costs of the facilities.

Although ownership of the recreational facilities is transferred to the club entity, the developer retains the right to operate and manage the facilities until most of the residential property (or all of the equity memberships) has been sold. Continued control eliminates the developer's apprehension that the club will be operated in a way that would adversely affect the sale of the remaining real estate product or equity memberships. After the sale of the real estate product, the club becomes member-controlled as well as member-owned. At that time, equity members elect a board of directors to control and manage the club entity and its facilities.

Members in an equity club are entitled to use the club's facilities upon payment of regular dues. In addition to enjoying the right to control and use the club's facilities, equity members participate in any appreciation in the value of their memberships within the limitations imposed by federal and state securities laws. Equity members may also have an opportunity to arrange for the purchaser of their residential property to "inherit" the equity membership. (These rights may also apply with right-to-use clubs, described below.) This additional advantage may increase the value of the equity member's residential property when all club memberships are sold. Unless "inherited" memberships are available, new property owners must wait until memberships become available before they can be full participants in the amenities program.

Right-to-Use Club. With a right-to-use program, the developer retains full ownership and control of the recreational facilities. No transfer of the recreational facilities is made or contemplated in the near term. The developer sells memberships, but the memberships represent only a license to use the recreational facilities, not an ownership interest in the facilities.

Members of right-to-use clubs are generally required to make initial payments and pay annual dues commensurate with their category of membership. The devel-

figure 5-3

Comparison of Basic Options for Club Structures[1]

Features	Equity Club[2]	Right-to-Use Club[3]	Convertible Club Program[4]	Association Ownership[5]
Up-front cost charged for unlimited golf privileges	Cost of equity membership is typically the highest among program options.	Initiation fee is generally less than price of equity membership. Membership price upon conversions greater than equity membership price but generally reduced by amount of initiation fee.	Initiation fee is less than equity membership price or convertible initiation fee.	None unless annual memberships are sold; annual membership price is very low.
Gross proceeds from membership program	Less than convertible, but most certainty in collections.	Highest, but less certainty in selling memberships (obtaining dollars) at time of conversion.	Less than equity and convertible.	None unless annual memberships are sold.
Ability to obtain proceeds from mortgage on recreational facilities	Good, but reflected in price of equity membership.	Same as equity, but delayed.	No ability.	Greatest.
Initial operational cash flow	Low. Owner/equity member play supplemented by recallable non-owner/right-to-use play.	Moderate. Owner/member play supplemented by recallable nonowner member play.	Moderate. Owner/member play supplemented by recallable nonowner member play.	Low.
Sell out operational cash flow	Greatest due to equity member use frequency exceeding right-to-use member use frequency.	Comparable to equity.	Lower cash flow.	Lower cash flow.
Effect on potential buyers of real estate	Positive since buyers know the ultimate club ownership status and provide vehicle for predominantly owner-only membership.	May affect marketability to serious golfer because of uncertainty of conversion and price of membership.	May impair marketability to serious golfer because of uncertainty as to the status of program (sale of recreational facilities or conversion); however, this is less true today than in the recent past, and right-to-use is now a popular option.	Positive since buyers know the ultimate ownership of the recreational facilities.

Source: Hyatt & Stubblefield, Atlanta, Ga.

oper determines whether initial member payments will be in the form of initiation fees, initiation deposits, or a combination.

Initiation Fee Programs. Under an initiation fee program, a member who resigns from the club may forfeit the initiation fee previously paid or, in some cases, receive a full or partial refund. Any refund is conditioned on the reissuance of the membership to a new member (as is the case for equity clubs). The refund may equal any portion of the initiation fee paid by the member or a portion of the initiation fee charged for memberships at the time the resigned membership is reissued to another member. Either way, the initiation fee paid by the member is taxable income to the developer and a deductable business expense when refunded to a resigning member.

Features	Equity Club[2]	Right-to-Use Club[3]	Convertible Club Program[4]	Association Ownership[5]
Sense of community	Good sense of continuity between property ownership and membership.	Less than equity because loss of owner control and certainty over recreational facilities.	Even less than convertible because no owner control over recreational facilities.	Greatest since association owns and operates recreational facilities.
Developer flexibility in operation of club	Limited to terms of membership plan.	Tied substantially to terms of membership plan.	Greatest flexibility.	None.
Litigation risk to developer	Low.	Moderate to low depending on details of conversion disclosure.	Greatest when developer sells recreational facilities or converts.	Low.
Nonowner access to club facilities	Limited to available memberships until cap is reached.	Good until conversion, then recalled to extent necessary for owners.	Greatest.	Varies.
Refundability of upfront costs paid by users	Initiation fee: greater of purchase price or up to 80% of initiation fee upon reissuance. Initiation deposit: returned at some point in the future. Annual fee: no refund or pro rata portion; more common now than in the 1980s.	Same as equity.	Same as equity.	None.
Member liability for assessments	None before substantial sellout of memberships.	None before substantial sellout of memberships and the conversion.	None.	Property owners pay assessments to the association.

[1]Chart reflects typical structures of basic programs. Actual structure may vary and benefits may differ depending on market acceptance of the membership program.

[2]Equity. Refers to an equity membership program formed by the developer at the initial stages of development.

[3]Right to Use. Refers to a right-to-use membership program without a disclosed plan to convert to an equity membership program.

[4]Convertible. Refers to a right-to-use membership program formed with a disclosed plan by the developer (at its option) to convert the right-to-use program to an equity program.

[5]Association Ownership. Refers to an association-owned program where the developer has transferred the recreational facilities to a community association formed for the residential property within the development.

To avoid challenges that a membership with a refundable initiation fee is a security under federal and some state securities laws, developers of right-to-use clubs often limit the amount of the initiation fee that may be refunded to the greater of the amount of the initiation fee paid by the member or up to 80 percent of the initiation fee charged at the time of resignation (as is the case with equity clubs).

Initiation Deposit Programs. Under an initiation deposit program, members receive a full refund of their initiation deposit either when they resign from the club under specified, limited circumstances or on a predetermined date (usually 20 to 30 years after the date of acceptance for membership). The refund on the predetermined date must not be contingent on another party taking the resigning member's place in the club.

Given that the initiation deposit paid by members is fully refundable on a predetermined date, it may be possible to characterize the deposit as a loan to the recreational facilities owner that is not taxed as income at the time of receipt. However, several conditions must be met in order to characterize a membership deposit as a loan rather than as taxable income. Further, it is always possible that the Internal Revenue Service will issue regulations regarding the taxability of membership deposits. Therefore, it is generally prudent for developers to consult with their tax advisers before relying on the potential tax benefits of a membership deposit program.

Convertible Club Program. In a convertible club program, the developer begins with a right-to-use club but has a clearly disclosed plan to convert it to an equity club. As in a right-to-use club program, members pay a one-time initiation fee or deposit that is refundable as described above. At the time of payment, members learn when and how the conversion to an equity club will take place, including the total purchase price to be paid by the members for the recreational facilities and the additional amount, if any, required of each member of the right-to-use club to become an equity club member. Often, the initiation fee or deposit paid by members is applied to the membership purchase price when the developer converts the recreational facilities to an equity club. Convertible programs are attractive alternatives for developers who recognize that a market exists for an equity club but are uncertain as to when they will be prepared to turn the club over to the equity owners.

Association Ownership. In an association-owned amenities program, the developer transfers the recreational facilities to the homeowners' association established for the surrounding residential property. Depending on state law, the facilities may be subject to a debt in the amount of the cost of their construction. The members of the homeowners' association do not buy memberships but may pay off the debt through association assessments and use fees, if any. Additional funds can be generated through the sale of memberships (which generate annual dues) to homeowners who desire some type of preferential treatment.

An association-owned program can be designed to allow the developer to recover the cost of constructing the recreational facilities other than through the sale of real property. As a result, the return on the development as a whole may increase in that the profit on real property sales does not have to offset the construction costs of the recreational facilities. The key to an association-owned program, however, is upfront planning, especially in the areas of accounting and economic forecasting. The numbers must work with reasonable certainty so that the homeowners' association can maintain the facilities and pay off any debt while keeping assessments at an acceptable level.

Membership Structures

Within each of the basic organizational structures for the management and operation of a community's recreational amenities, developers can structure memberships in a variety of ways that both provide members with rights to use different facilities and grant different privileges for the use of major amenities, particularly golf. The method a developer selects for structuring memberships depends on market factors and the resort and recreational community's overall development concept. Recreational communities made up of primary residences typically make the amenities available in long-term membership packages that generally do not change until the member ceases to own property in the community. In contrast, recreational communities comprised of second-home owners who visit for relatively short periods typically offer memberships that allow members to make continual changes to the packages of facilities and services. The following examples of the most common structures can be adapted, modified, combined, etc., to fit a particular project.

Tiered Membership. A tiered membership structure involves several different categories of membership, each with limits on the number of available memberships, different membership prices, and varying annual dues and use rights. A person desiring a membership chooses from one of the available categories and pays the membership price associated with that category. Each membership category includes distinct privileges. For example, 30-day-advance-tee-time-reservation privileges may be available to full golf members while limited golf members may be able to reserve tee times only five days in advance. Members are able to change membership categories only by resigning from the existing membership category and applying for membership in a different category.

With a limited number of memberships in each membership category, a tiered membership structure encourages prospective members to apply for memberships with the maximum level of privileges in order to ensure that they, and possibly the purchasers of their property, will always enjoy access to the community's most desirable facilities and privileges. Consequently, tiered membership structures may create more demand for the highest level of membership than would other-

The 25,000-square-foot Broken Top Clubhouse at Broken Top in Bend, Oregon, incorporates a Frank Lloyd Wright style of design with a strong rustic and western flavor on the interior; the clubhouse serves as the heart of the Broken Top resort community.

Gary W. Fenchuk
President
East West Partners of Virginia, Inc.
Midlothian, Virginia

Gary Fenchuk is president of East West Partners of Virginia, Inc. He is the senior partner in charge of real estate development projects in Virginia, Georgia, and Florida, including Brandermill and Woodlake. Before assuming these duties in 1980, Fenchuk was the group's vice president of finance. Fenchuk's real estate career began with the Sea Pines Company, where he last served as vice president of finance. He holds an undergraduate degree from Alma College in Michigan and an MBA from the Wharton School of the University of Pennsylvania.

Our niche has been to offer a superior lifestyle without having the price go through the roof. We do it many ways. The road to success is not in doing one thing 100 percent better but in doing 100 things 1 percent better.

We attempt to buy land at a low basis in an emerging area. Some others may call it a fringe area. We look at the fundamentals and the growth that will be shifting that way in the future. It allows us to retain that affordability and keep that economic cost structure down. We do not go into the hottest area and pay the inflated prices. This destroys the formula immediately. We go into an emerging area and, through development, create value. We create such an extraordinary lifestyle that we can compete with some of our higher-priced competitors. We're basically taking the customers in the middle of the economic pyramid.

Also, we have to put in an extraordinary amenity package within a feasible, finite budget. We keep the affordability issue in front of us, and we are students of value engineering. Based on extensive market research—focus groups, surveys, etc.—we decide where we can get the most bang for the buck. This makes us superior from the customer's perspective.

We have stayed away from the large clubhouses and have concentrated on the recreational facilities themselves. Some of our competitors have employed a swimming/tennis complex within a homeowners' association, which runs up the monthly cost. It can also alienate some people who will not use the complex. We have an optional, pay-as-you-go approach. It allows us to build the facilities and price the memberships so that they can pay for themselves. We get a free amenity that's better for the consumer and is better than the competition. We run our own clubs under our club operation and don't turn them over to a homeowners' association.

We have an aggressive marketing program. We have a lower profit margin than many of our competitors who may need a higher cost margin when they sell 75 units per year and we sell 300 units a year. We can amortize our fixed costs over a greater number of units and get by with a lower profit margin per unit. That has profound ramifications on our ability to be affordable. If you can sell more, you can keep your prices lower, and if you keep your prices lower, you can sell more. There is no magic percentage as to what a profit margin should be. We liken it to the food industry. Most supermarkets are high-volume, low-profit-margin operations. A convenience store is a lower-volume, high-profit-margin operation. These are two valid strategies, but we tend to be closer to the supermarket model than the convenience store model.

We try to employ our marketing on a high-impact basis to distinguish us from the competition. We almost always generate high-volume, high-traffic events such as the Parade of Homes. Also, we have had *Southern Living* do a program with us.

We have a superior management team. East West Partners has a core team that has been with the company for 15 to 20 years. This seems to be unusual for the industry, but it has allowed us to stay ahead of the learning curve. We have been able to keep that experience in house while many competitors are not that deep in experience. All the key managers are equity players, which creates incentives for them. It has helped us retain good people, but it tends to put golden handcuffs on them as well. We have buy-sell agreements. If people leave, they have to give up all that equity in projects. We have tried to stay on site and manage projects locally; managers live in their own projects, as opposed to not living in the community.

■

wise materialize if a different membership structure were in place. The number of available golf memberships may need to be adjusted to avoid a situation whereby the golf course operates at less-than-maximum capacity even though all golf memberships have been issued.

The tiered membership structure works well in residential recreational communities where the number of available memberships reasonably equals the number of homes in the community. In fact, this relationship generally holds so long as the number of active memberships does not exceed the normally perceived maximum capacity of the recreational facilities. When restraints on capacity cannot be met, one of the other membership structures may be more appropriate.

Unitary Membership. In a unitary membership structure, all members acquire the same interest in the recreational facilities by paying the membership price. Each year, members select from a variety of dues categories, each of which represents a different set of privileges. No limits are placed on the number of members in any dues category; therefore, artificial demand is not created for any membership category. Because members can select a new set of membership privileges at the beginning of each membership year, a person who chooses the social dues category is always assured that he or she or a subsequent purchaser of his or her home will enjoy future access to the golf facilities. Any subsequent purchaser of a member's real property would not be bound by the fact that the previous owner had never chosen the golf dues category and would be free to choose from among all dues categories at the beginning of each membership year.

A unitary structure works best when the recreational facilities are clearly insufficient to satisfy all resident demands. Because artificial demand is not created for any category of membership, the members tend to select the dues category that most accurately reflects their use patterns. And since all members do not choose the same dues category, the number of members in each category typically tends to average out to acceptable levels from year to year. Imbalances can be resolved through annual adjustments to the types and prices of memberships offered.

Add-On Membership. An add-on membership structure is a combination of the tiered membership and unitary membership structures. The member begins by purchasing a basic social membership and may upgrade at any time to a membership that permits use of the golf or other facilities by paying the difference between the membership price for the higher-category membership and the member's current category of membership. In the absence of caps on any membership category, there is no artificial demand for higher categories of membership. Property owners need only purchase a membership that permits use of the desired facilities.

An add-on structure can work well when a tiered program would otherwise be suitable but the developer remains unsure about the number of golfers likely to be attracted to the community. An add-on program allows the number of members in each category to seek its own level without creating any artificial demand for any particular category of membership.

General Approaches

Most developers use the various club organizational and membership structures as building blocks and mix and match from and among them in order to satisfy the needs of a particular development project. For example, a developer may create an equity club that, in addition to offering full golf memberships to its equity members, offers right-to-use limited golf or social memberships. Alternatively, a developer may offer a tiered golf membership in a right-to-use club that homeowners can supplement on an annual basis with horse-back-riding, fitness and spa, or winter sports memberships. The important issue is to create a structure that fits the development project rather than one that fits into some definitional box.

In resort communities, property owners and hotel guests often share recreational amenities. Creating a club for residential property owners and providing hotel guests with some opportunity to use the club's facilities offers several advantages to the developer. First, the developer is able to offer higher-quality amenities to both hotel guests and club members than if separate facilities were provided for each group. Second, the developer is able to offer club members many special hotel services, such as use of the concierge, room service, and other enhancements. Third, hotel guests can add to the vibrancy of a club in its initial stages of development by ensuring use of the facilities. Finally, hotel guests are often the next purchasers of residential property. Developers can even offer purchasers of custom lots discounts on hotel accommodations so they can supervise the construction of their homes.

Developers who combine traditional clubs with hotels must, however, remain mindful of the different and sometimes conflicting needs of club members and hotel guests. Club members expect exclusivity and want to feel that they are receiving special privileges on account of their membership. Hotel guests want assurances that the desired facilities will be available during their stay. Developers can minimize the conflicts between club members and hotel guests by creating distinct use rights, reservation privileges, and programs that balance the needs of each group.

For example, at PGA National in Palm Beach Gardens, Florida, a continuing dilemma is how to provide for the needs of the resort hotel guests cost effectively, how to maintain exclusivity for the residential owners, and how to meet the needs of PGA members. One strategy lies in the project's physical plan, which is organized around a relatively self-contained resort core. By locating the pro shop and the golf clubhouse in the resort hotel, for example, the development avoided the expensive duplication of facilities. This arrangement meant, however, that two conflicting user groups often concentrated in the same area. To resolve the conflict, the resort provides a members-only lounge and other private areas.

At PGA National in Palm Beach Gardens, Florida, golf managers seek to concentrate members and guests on different golf courses—on a rotating basis—to minimize conflict.

Photo courtesy of EDSA

Other strategies at PGA National focus on management techniques, rules, and regulations intended to minimize conflict. Golf managers attempt to concentrate guests, owners, and PGA members on different courses. A rotating course is reserved each day for members. Starting times can be allocated differently to each group. Members can book slots up to a few days in advance while guests are limited to a much shorter advance booking period. Memberships and greens fees are priced differentially in favor of residential members. PGA National recently adopted a computerized system of controlling tee times for residential members, guests, and PGA members. Although the club may not be as exclusive as other projects in the area, its lower rates and premier facilities are viewed as a relative bargain. The bottom line for PGA National is that it serves the needs of all its communities—residential owners, resort guests, and PGA and other organization members—by taking a hands-on approach to meeting the diverse and ever-changing needs of its market.

Developers of club communities are continually expanding the traditional club structures, combining them with different elements such as hotels and timeshares and creating new amenity programs that meet the needs of a constantly changing market. Undoubtedly, the future will bring more combinations of club structures and membership programs that balance the needs of the diverse groups using resort amenities.

Managing Major Amenities

Many resorts manage and operate their amenities as income-producing properties either apart from or in conjunction with an association and/or club structure. This is particularly true of amenities associated with resort hotels and destination resorts that cater to a large number of hotel guests. In these situations, it is important for the resort operator to maintain access to and/

or control of the amenity to ensure that it remains available for guest use and is properly managed to enhance the resort's overall attractiveness. In some cases, such as with golf courses and tennis facilities, the amenity may be operated as both a private membership and publicly accessible amenity. In others, such as with ski facilities, the amenity is more likely to be operated strictly as an income-producing amenity with minimal club or association involvement.

General Operations Issues

Managing and maintaining income-producing amenities requires special expertise. Depending on the business plan and strategy, the task can be approached from several perspectives. For example, amenities owned either by private developers or other commercial interests must generate a profit, except when potential profits in interrelated areas justify subsidizing certain operations. While it is the objective of most resort amenity owners and operators to make money on the operation of the amenity, the amenity may in some cases operate at break even or even at a loss as a way to add value to other elements of the resort. Such a strategy can be risky, however, and should be carefully considered to minimize operating losses. In evaluating the potential for a commercial operation, the developer must undertake a thorough economic analysis of the business prospects for the amenity.

Resort owners face three choices in operating an income-producing amenity: they can operate it with their own in-house staff, they can operate it under a contract to a third-party operator, or they can turn to a third-party owner and operator.

One problem with developer-owned amenities in resort communities is that users tend to expect more than the developer can afford and therefore often pressure the developer to provide a greater array and higher level of services. An independent owner/operator, however, can deflect such pressure.

In many cases, specialized resort owners/operators that operate resort hotels also manage their properties' amenities. Club Resorts, Inc., for example, specializes in owning and managing resort hotel properties with varied amenities, especially golf. The firm owns and operates such resorts as the Homestead in Virginia, Pinehurst in North Carolina, Barton Creek in Texas, Quail Hollow Resort & Country Club in Ohio, Shanty Creek in Michigan, and Shangri-La Resort in Oklahoma. It also operates several other resorts under consulting contracts. Club Resorts has adopted a club philosophy in its resort operations that stresses the similarity between resorts and private clubs. The company is an affiliate of Club Corporation of America (CCA), which owns and operates private city, country, and athletic clubs. Each Club Resorts property strives to emulate the service standards of CCA as evidenced by the slogan, "Club Resorts. Where Every Guest Is a Member."

Specialized REITs (real estate investment trusts) have also become active players in amenity operations, especially golf courses. National Golf Properties, a REIT based in Santa Monica, California, is a major investor in golf properties. The firm's strategy is to acquire undermanaged golf properties or golf properties from undercapitalized residential or resort developers that are looking to raise cash by unloading a project's golf component. The firm then leases the course to its management affiliate, American Golf Corp.

Specialized contracted management can be particularly useful when commercial ownership or developer expertise is either unavailable or uneconomical. This strategy demands careful negotiation of a management services contract that specifies both the level of involvement and financial objectives. Good communication between owners and operators is important to ensure the proper level of management.

Maintenance budgets for amenities and natural resources must be carefully prepared, with reserves established for major repairs or rebuilding programs. A good technique is to account for costs by type of activity or facility and then review the costs periodically against the budget. Even so, objectives and operations must be kept flexible to adapt to various levels of service demand and income streams.

While resorts incorporate a broad array of amenities (see Chapter 3), four amenity types are particularly common and/or important as income-producing operations and thus require extensive and specialized management: golf, tennis, skiing, and marinas.

Managing Golf Amenities

For years, the benefits of a golf course to a real estate project so far outweighed its costs that management issues often went neglected. As both capital and operating costs have risen, however, course and club management have taken on additional importance. This trend has led to an increasingly wide range of organizational arrangements for management as well as to new techniques for operations and maintenance practices that are designed to control costs and increase the number of rounds played. Many developers have begun to view courses as potential profit centers in their own right.

A course remains largely a fixed-cost operation. If, however, a course is operated on a daily-fee basis with a marginal increase in revenue for every additional round of golf played, a golf course management system can have tremendous implications for profitability. For example, timely and effective maintenance operations can be designed to minimize down time. An efficient starting system can help reduce waiting times and maximize the number of rounds played. Controlling costs for food and beverage operations can help obviate the need to recover losses from real estate operations. In sum, the management program eases pressures to cut maintenance expenditures or to raise greens fees or rental rates.

Management Approaches. In situations where the developer or owner retains full operational control, the course should be structured for accounting purposes as a separate cost or profit center, usually with procedures to accommodate both direct and indirect expenditures. The golf operation as cost center may be separated from or combined with other club operations. Operational responsibility should rest with a club manager, a staff of golf professionals responsible for the pro shop as well as for instruction and programs, and a course superintendent. The principal advantage of the cost center arrangement is that the developer is assured of ongoing control over the operations of the club and golf course. Such control is usually valuable when it comes to convincing both lenders and real estate prospects of the project's viability. The disadvantage is that a developer, especially if his or her firm is small or inexperienced, may not have access to the kinds of superior managers needed to make the cost center arrangement work.

The Homestead in Virginia is operated by Club Resorts, Inc., which specializes in owning and managing resort hotel properties with varied amenities, especially golf. Club Resorts practices a club philosophy toward operating resorts, often stressing a similarity between resorts and private clubs.

In a trend that has become much more prevalent in recent years, the developer contracts with a full-service management firm. Contract management, premised on the notion that land development and golf course management are not necessarily compatible or complementary fields, is often best suited to less experienced developers. Proponents of contracted management, which is also sometimes called lease management, argue that it

Often a developer will contract outside with a specialized tennis management firm to manage the operation of a tennis club amenity. At Harbour Ridge in Stuart, Florida, for example, the developer retained overall management control of the Harbour Ridge Country Club, including the project's golf course, but because of the special operational characteristics of tennis, it contracted with an international tennis management club, Burwash International. The firm provides the project with a resident tennis professional who is responsible for directing all court scheduling and maintenance, instructional programs, tournaments, and pro shop operations.

enables clubs to enjoy access to a wider variety of skilled personnel. Most of the larger management organizations operate nationwide, with coordination at a regional level and specific managers assigned to each club. Individual managers are responsible both for their own clubs and for regional cooperation. This arrangement could provide an individual club, for example, with access to skilled professionals ranging from accountants and personnel managers to agronomists and turfgrass experts. The tradeoff for the developer, of course, is that a contracted arrangement inevitably involves some loss of operational control. For an established club, however, the control issue may be less important than for a club in the early development stages, when relationships between real estate and other components of a project remain critical.

Sources of Income. Golf income varies in source and magnitude based on type of course (private, public, or daily fee), location, market, and length of season. Daily-fee courses rely heavily on greens fees and, in some cases, on annual memberships. The breakdown of member-related income depends on the membership structure.

All types of courses also look to merchandise sales, lessons and tournament revenues, and rentals and fees for lockers, golf carts, and other equipment as important sources of income. Food and beverage operations or a driving range may bring in a large proportion of a club's revenue but typically also account for its principal expenses. Most developers agree that while bar operations can be highly profitable, food services almost always operate at a substantial loss.

Maintenance. By far the largest single expense item for a course—one that constantly challenges developers, club managers, and superintendents—is maintenance. Maintenance costs depend on a wide variety of factors, including the course's location, length of season, type, market, size, and purpose. The last factor is particularly important. Nearly an unlimited sum of money could theoretically be spent on a regulation course every year. Beyond some point, of course, every additional dollar spent would bring an ever-smaller increase in the course's quality. The challenge for the developer is to determine the point of diminishing return and to structure a maintenance program that makes appropriate tradeoffs and adjustments. If a course is intended to help sell real estate that carries the imprimatur of cost-is-no-object luxury, it is likely to be maintained at extremely high standards.

Maintenance costs clearly depend on region. Numerous surveys have consistently found, for example, that courses in the western states are more expensive to maintain than those in other regions. A good deal of the variation can be linked to a region's volume of natural precipitation and the length of the season. The most expensive-to-maintain courses are those in the arid West that must purchase their irrigation water. Courses in the South and the upper Midwest tend to report the lowest average maintenance costs.

Hosting tournaments, whether golf, tennis, or another event, has become a popular method to promote a project and attract thousands of potential real estate buyers. The Bausch & Lomb Women's International Tennis Finals on Amelia Island Plantation, Florida, has been an effective program for promoting the community to a wide range of potential buyers.

Programming. As the recreational and often social focus of a residential or resort community, a course can fulfill a variety of purposes that extend beyond golf itself. New residents can be introduced to the game and to a new set of friends. Juniors programs, leagues, club tournaments, and clinics all play an important role in creating a sense of community identity while ensuring efficient use of the golf amenity. Even though individual programs and activities focus on golf, they also reach outward into other parts of the community and for many residents constitute a core of activity that separates their community from any other.

Some developers, intrigued by the national visibility certain courses achieve, host major professional tournaments. While PGA tournaments, especially if nationally televised, can lend a project tremendous exposure and pay big public relations and marketing dividends, the costs to mount such an event can be extremely high. Moreover, some projects are clearly better suited than others for tournament play. Given the high expense, additional infrastructure, different course requirements, and uncertain benefits to the real estate operation, most developers should take a hard look at the economics of competitive professional events before committing their projects' resources.

Tennis Facility Management

The management issues concerning tennis facilities pertain mostly to those facilities that include some basic support features and services such as a clubhouse, pro shop, restaurant, locker rooms, a reservation system, lessons, clinics, and perhaps club leagues or tournaments. As with any major recreational amenity, ownership of tennis facilities can vary, and each form of ownership carries broad implications for management and operations. In resort projects, a developer often either retains ownership after a project is completed or sells or leases the amenities to a resort operator.

One clear trend in tennis club management, similar to that evidenced in golf course and marina management, is for developers to contract with a specialized tennis management firm. At Harbour Ridge in Stuart, Florida, for example, the developer retained overall management control of the Harbour Ridge Country Club, including the project's golf course. Because of the special operations characteristics of tennis, however, the developer signed on with an international tennis management club, Burwash International. The firm provides the project with a resident tennis professional responsible for all court scheduling and maintenance, instructional programs, tournaments, and pro shop operations.

Revenues and Expenses. Tennis club operating and overhead costs, like those of a golf course, are largely fixed. Therefore, one of the key management objectives is to maximize revenues from various membership dues and fees, which constitute the largest category of club income. Many tennis facilities may be open to both residents and outsiders and may rely on a dues and fee structure similar to that of a commercial club. Whatever the arrangement, dues and fees produce, on average, between 40 and 70 percent of total revenues. Other significant sources of revenue derive from the pro shop, food and beverage services, equipment rentals, lessons and clinics, and, in some cases, tournaments.

The aim of any dues and fee structure is to maximize use of the courts by setting up appropriate incentives geared to demand. A prospective club developer must examine the market's characteristics to establish a membership structure. What are the established patterns of play? Does strong demand exist for evening, midday, or morning play? At what time of day is demand weakest (when hourly rates should be dropped)?

Marketing and Promotion. In a national market that currently has, to an arguable degree, an oversupply of tennis clubs, effective marketing and promotion are crucial. With a residential or resort tennis facility, proper promotion and appropriate programs can help a project's overall marketing efforts by creating a sense of activity and community. Tennis players are generally not as loyal to their current clubs as golfers; they are more easily persuaded to change clubs. To entice established local tennis players to a fledgling club, however, a developer must establish the facility's credibility early on. One valuable technique may be to set up a tennis advisory board or committee composed of key members of the local tennis establishment and perhaps a well-known touring professional.

An increasingly popular method of establishing credibility is to host a tournament. Men's and women's professional circuit tournaments can be expensive to host, but they can greatly boost a project's image. Sea Pines Plantation's *Family Circle* Cup and Amelia Island Plantation's Bausch & Lomb Women's International Tennis Finals are widely known and attract thousands of potential real estate buyers to these communities. Some experts caution, however, that the costs of a major tournament may not equal the benefits.

For more localized promotions among the membership, clubs can organize a variety of tournaments, leagues, competitive ladders, and other events, usually under the direction of the tennis pro. Providing adequate access to courts and matching players by ability level are two important management considerations. Even though 70 percent of a typical club's memberships are family memberships, most players play without another family member and thus need appropriate partners.

Ski-Area Management

In a ski area, the management issues typically associated with any recreational amenity—catering to both residents and outsiders, maintaining design and appearance standards, controlling costs, and so on—are compounded by a number of other factors. In remote locations, for example, the limited availability of affordable housing for seasonal employees is often an issue. Similarly, ski-area managers experience difficulty predicting accurate expenses and revenues in the face of uncertain weather conditions. The risks inherent in the sport also pose a management challenge in the form of liability insurance issues. Moreover, ski areas must establish significant budgets for extensive marketing and promotion efforts, as they need to attract a large volume of skiers during peak seasons in order to remain profitable. For the developer, these and many other facility characteristics make an experienced team of ski-area managers essential.

Departmental Operations. Most ski areas are organized fiscally into a variety of departments or profit/cost centers. At the typical facility, about 80 percent of gross revenues are generated by seven major departments: lift, ski school, food service, bar, retail sales, rentals, and accommodations. By far, the greatest revenue source at the typical ski area is the sale of lift tickets, and the greatest expense is the operation of the ski lift. Most ski areas offer a variety of lift ticket prices for weekdays versus weekends, adults versus juniors, and so on. Food service and bar operations produce the next greatest amount of revenue at the average ski area.

Management of ski areas is complicated by the fact that weather conditions can greatly affect revenues and expenses. Pictured is Blackcomb in British Columbia.

Key cost centers requiring substantial management expertise and extensive staffs include operation of the ski lift, ski school, food and bar service, retail stores, rental shops, snowmaking, snow removal, and safety patrols. A substantial amount of equipment and facilities must be properly maintained to run these operations, further complicating the management process.

One of the big problems in managing ski areas is that they have high fixed operating expenses that make them vulnerable to big losses during years when attendance is off because of weather problems or other reasons. The common expenses that are most costly for a ski area are general and administrative, marketing, snowmaking, and insurance, in that order. The average ski area spent $1.03 million on general and administrative, $598,000 on marketing (advertising, public relations, and promotion), $359,000 on snowmaking, and $294,000 on insurance (property, liability) during the 1993–1994 ski season. During that season, the average ski area showed a profit of $937,000 on revenues of $10.68 million.[23]

Insurance and Risk Management. Insurance costs for ski operations are significant and highlight the importance of risk management in ski-area operations. Today, most ski areas maintain fairly comprehensive programs designed to mitigate the risks inherent in both the sport itself and facility operations. There are several elements of a successful risk management program: suitable training for lift operators and ski patrol members; timely and thorough maintenance and repairs, with suitable markings and warnings on nonskiable areas; ongoing safety programs with strict enforcement of rules and regulations; and careful monitoring of hazardous snow conditions, ice, avalanche potential, and so on. The National Ski Areas Association and other organizations issue a variety of publications, films, and other materials that are useful in organizing a risk management program. The nature of the sport is such that risks cannot be eliminated. Given the institutional pressures on the industry, however, ski-area operators should assign a high priority to reducing risk.

Marina Management

As with most aspects of marinas, operations and management present a range of options. One basic requirement, however, calls for a management structure and level of service that is congruent with both the physical facilities and the marina's overall purpose. An overcapitalized but undermanaged facility can quickly become a serious cost burden; maintenance costs mount as customer satisfaction and slip occupancy rents fall. Conversely, a relatively simple facility can be inefficiently overmanaged, particularly in the case of marinas intended to function primarily as loss leaders for real estate operations. As long as real estate sales remain strong, wasteful expenditures on operating costs and overhead will not be matters of deep concern. Ultimately, however, a marina will become a drain on its owner's resources, and retrenchment measures will be more traumatic than if the expenditure problem had been addressed earlier. Over time, the marina may become less attractive to patrons.

Facilities Management. Besides a marina's physical plant, one of the greatest influences on facilities management is the range and level of services offered to patrons. A full-service facility generally offers comprehensive boat services, including boat and engine sales; engine service; hull cleaning, repair, and painting; rigging repair; sailmaking and repair; storage; and yacht brokerage. Rarely, though, do in-house marina personnel provide all these services. Instead, local operations typically provide needed services on a contract basis, although the marina may handle all administrative work.

Marina services need not be limited to boat service and repair, of course. Many marinas also maintain a

fleet of boats for rental or lessons. In addition, special party boats or ski boats complete with a driver are popular and may be available. Again, independent contractors often handle these services.

It is axiomatic that a marina "offering only berths and moorings will fail."[24] For many marinas, however, the greatest management challenge is keeping slip occupancy levels high. Slip rentals, usually handled through a dock master's or harbor master's department, represent the greatest single source of marina revenues. A well-managed marina not only sets slip rental rates carefully, based on an analysis of comparable nearby facilities, but also maintains clearly defined procedures for filling slip vacancies. These procedures may include waiting lists, slip "inheritance" rules that apply when a boat is sold, or other measures.

If a marina owner is not fortunate enough to face unlimited demand for slips—as is often the case in a new facility—slip management can also serve an important marketing role. Transient slips can be valuable ways to introduce newcomers to a marina, for example. An added benefit for marinas with lodging, restaurants, fuel docks, or other amenities is that visitors tend to spend more money than full-time slip occupants; transient slips can thus provide significant revenue for other marina operations.

Customer satisfaction and profitability largely depend on the quality of marina maintenance. Adequate levels of property and equipment maintenance are essential to smooth operations. Because of their location, use, and materials, marina structures can deteriorate at a rate that accelerates with time. And the consequences of major equipment failure can be severe. Even relatively minor maintenance items, if deferred, can make a marina unpleasant or dangerous. For these reasons, even the most modest marina should implement a formal maintenance program that requires regular inspec-

Harbour Ridge in Stuart, Florida, includes three separate marina docks and 128 deepwater slips along the St. Lucie River.

tions and identifies and ensures completion of regular maintenance items, repairs, and overhauls.

Administrative Management. Developers have traditionally used waterfront amenities to enhance land values and add marketing appeal to their projects. Few developers pursue the profitability inherent in the use of the water amenity itself. In other words, many marinas are not designed, built, or operated to generate a profit. Nonetheless, specialized amenity management firms are convincing developers to reconsider the traditional relationship between marinas and real estate. As with any business, a profitable marina requires a clear articulation of goals and objectives along with the systems and tools to measure performance.

One of the most important management tools is the marina budget—or budgets, as systems for cash flow, capital outlays, and debt may be organized separately. Budgets serve as benchmarks for evaluating an operation's expected versus actual performance. They enable managers to make adjustments as necessary to narrow any gaps between objectives and actual performance. In real estate projects, a marina budget is usually subordinate to the overall project budget and phasing and capital investment plans.

Historical data on the various expected costs and revenues associated with operating a marina form the basis of the budget(s). New operations generally base their budgets on comparable operations. An integrated marina budget should be organized on a monthly basis to respond to seasonal fluctuations in revenues and expenses, staffing levels, and inventory.

Developing and implementing a budget requires a well-developed system for tracking the sources and flows of costs and revenues. Given the wide range of potential costs in marina operations, it is essential to match costs as closely as possible to corresponding revenues. The correspondence between costs and revenues should directly reflect the marina's organization. A marina that offers a full range of services is generally organized around those aspects of the operation that generate identifiable categories of revenues and that can be specifically assigned corresponding costs. These profit centers are typically isolated by function: marina management, dock master or harbor master, service, boat sales, retail sales, and food and beverage.

Renovation, Repositioning, and Revitalization

Renovation and repositioning is a fundamental activity for resort development. As mentioned earlier, the development process is iterative, and the iterative process does not stop with completion of the project. Resort management involves a constant examination of the resort in terms of what is working and what is not working and what needs to be changed to maintain or improve performance. At certain points, the examination may suggest a significant repositioning or redevelopment strategy.

While much of this book focuses on the development of new resorts, a considerable portion of the discussion is also applicable to the revitalization, renovation, and repositioning of existing resorts. In fact, much of the resort development activity taking place today in North America involves the revitalization or repositioning of existing properties. The number of resorts that exist today far exceeds the number of new resorts starting development—and the existing resorts are in need of constant renewal to maintain their competitive edge. Notes Robert J. Lowe of Lowe Enterprises, "It is far easier to build an addition onto an existing resort than it is to do a pioneering development in a new location. While there will be some pioneering developments built in the future, the vast majority of resort development—90 percent—will occur around established areas of activity."[25]

Resorts are like other forms of urban development: they typically experience cyclical periods of growth and maturation followed by periods of stagnation and decline. Both internal and external factors affect the direction, extent, and timing of these cyclical changes. Changes in access, demographics, and psychographics are the most significant factors in determining whether a given resort experiences a period of growth and maturation or a period of stagnation and decline. In addition, technological innovations along with changes in the nature of recreation and leisure are shortening the life span of many resorts and accelerating the pace of renovation.

For most resorts, renovation is a constant process; it starts the day the facility opens and continues throughout its life.[26] Ritz-Carlton's program points the way: a reserve budget covers small to moderate improvements based on regular surveys of hotel guests.

While most revitalization efforts involve physical improvements, changes to the management and operation of the resort can be equally valuable. One of the Yarmouth Group's investment funds, for example, recently bought the Cheyenne Mountain Conference Resort in Colorado Springs, Colorado, for $26.5 million and, over a 20-month period, reorganized the lodge's conference sales division, cut expenses, and identified and implemented $1 million in capital improvements, doubling the cash flow at the 216-acre, 276-room resort. The investor subsequently sold the property to Massachusetts Mutual Life Insurance Company for $45 million, an unleveraged rate of return in excess of 55 percent.[27]

The Reasons

The reasons for renovating or redeveloping a resort can vary widely depending on how well the resort is performing and the age of its physical structures.

Physical Reasons
- Repair and restore aging buildings to their original quality.
- Adapt facilities to meet changes in codes and regulations.

Ritz-Carlton has adopted a program under which reserves are set aside to cover small to moderate improvements to its hotels, based on regular surveys of hotel guests. Pictured is the Ritz-Carlton, Laguna Niguel, a 362-room luxury hotel on the southern California coast. Reminiscent of a Mediterranean villa, the four-story structure stretches along the contours of a promontory 150 feet above the Pacific.

Photo courtesy of Wimberly Allison Tong & Goo Architects/Milroy & McAleer

Photo courtesy of Wimberly Allison Tong & Goo Architects/Milroy & McAleer

- Renovate or redevelop to improve operational efficiencies.

Market Reasons
- Renovate or update to maintain appeal to existing core market.
- Reposition to appeal to a different market than that previously targeted.
- Reposition or expand to broaden market appeal, capturing a larger market spectrum.
- Reposition to focus market appeal on a narrower niche market.

The four types of renovation/repositioning effort include cosmetic renovation, minor renovations and additions, major facility renovations/repositioning, and master-planned revisions. The table below characterizes the frequency of the various types of renovations in the past and for the future.

Renovations/ Improvements	In the Past	In the Future
Cosmetic	3–5 years	ongoing
Minor	10–20 years	3–5 years
Major	25–30 years	10–20 years
Master Planned	varies	varies

While much of the discussion here focuses on physical changes, renovation and repositioning efforts may also focus on significant changes in the following: the targeted market, the property's uses, the financing strategy, the marketing strategy, and the management structures and strategies.

Cosmetic Improvements

Cosmetic renovations occur every few years throughout the life of a resort. Often, the renovations are maintenance-related—replacing worn carpets, soiled drapes, worn equipment, etc. What comes to mind most often are interior renovations of guest rooms and public spaces driven by changes in style or physical obsolescence. While fixtures and furnishings may have more life left in them physically, owners often decide to go for a fresh look. Generally, the more trendy a design, the faster it becomes obsolete. The same holds true for exterior treatments.

Three recent trends are influencing the nature of renovations. The first is the "green" movement. A recent poll revealed that 70 percent of Americans consider themselves environmentalists. Resorts that make energy-related and environmental improvements can promote that fact and market themselves as environmentally friendly. Stephen Rushmore of Hospitality Valuation Services is capitalizing on the green movement. He and his daughter just started a company called Ecotels. They

This condominium project replaced two of the early homes built in Vail Village and typifies the style and quality of redevelopment projects that have been constructed in the village in recent years.

The Homestead in Hot Springs, Virginia, one of the oldest operating resorts in the United States, provides an instructive example of how a resort can change over time. The resort traces its history to 1761 when a men's pool and bath house were constructed on the site of a natural hot spring in the mountains of Virginia; an inn was built in 1766. The property operated at this modest level until 1836, when a women's pool and bath house were added. In 1846, the inn was enlarged. Following the Civil War, the inn saw the advent of railroad service in 1891 as well as the 1892 addition of ten cottages as the hotel's West Wing. Other improvements included tennis courts, a six-hole golf course that is said to be the oldest in continuous use in the United States, and the Homestead Spa, the first of its type in America.

The entire hotel complex was destroyed by fire in 1901 and was rebuilt in brick. In 1913, the Homestead golf course was enlarged to 18 holes, and in 1924 a second 18-hole course was opened. During World War II, the U.S. Department of State commandeered the resort as an internment site for Japanese diplomats. In 1959, a ski area and skating rink were opened, and in 1963 a third golf course was completed. Conference facilities were added in 1973 as well as a swimming pool. In 1984, the property received National Historic Landmark status. Such famous personalities as Henry Ford, Thomas Edison, and John D. Rockefeller, Sr., have visited the resort. Woodrow Wilson spent part of his honeymoon at the Homestead; 13 other presidents have visited the resort as well.

During most of its history—from 1891 until 1993—the property was owned by one family-owned company, the Virginia Hot Springs Co., Inc. In 1993, Virginia Hot Springs Co. entered into a joint venture with Club Resorts, Inc., to assume full management and coownership of the Homestead, bringing the resources necessary for a loving restoration of the property. In 1999, the Dallas-based company will become sole owner of the resort.

In 1994–1995, Club Resorts invested $15 million in propertywide renovations that included updates to the Homestead Course, the Great Hall, and the Dining Room and the complete refurbishment of 86 East Wing rooms and corridors. The West and South Wing corridors have also been updated to match the East Wing. The most visible improvements include the addition of a grand staircase and new landscape treatments. The driveway's more than 50,000 brick pavers provide a more defined and attractive arrival area for guests. In addition, Club Resorts completed the restoration of the Homestead's 102-year-old spa, added a new fitness center, and restored the spring-fed pool.

The Homestead in Hot Springs, Virginia—one of the oldest operating resorts in the United States—provides an interesting example of how a resort can change over time.

Plans for 1996 called for refurbishing 100 guest rooms and all corridors in the hotel's main building, further improvements to the spa, and still more landscape upgrades. In view of its strong tradition, the Homestead will undoubtedly continue to change. And with 15,000 acres of land under its control, this historic resort can look ahead to new opportunities for development.

The Hilton Hawaiian Village is a resort hotel that had grown helter-skelter over a period of years; by the early 1980s, it was clear that the property had lost much of its luster. It was congested, offered little open space, and had failed to take advantage of its paradisal climate and oceanfront setting on a prime site in Waikiki. Sited on 20 acres and with 2,500-plus rooms, the hotel is the largest resort complex in Waikiki and occupies Waikiki's largest parcel of land.

In the words of the developer, the goal for revitalization was "a return to paradise." Plans called for reducing the resort's density and improving the image of the property to make the Hilton Hawaiian a world-class destination resort. A principal challenge was to complete the renovation without severely interrupting operations.

By incorporating water features, tropical landscaping, and a variety of textures and choices that appeal to the senses, the Hilton Hawaiian's new design created a sense of both spaciousness and activity in a villagelike environment. Despite the reality of several high-density, high-rise buildings, the plan successfully transformed the resort's central seven acres into informal, free-flowing, water-laced luxuriant tropical gardens that evoke a

sense of expansiveness, relaxation, and delight. Formerly, the area was cluttered, congested, and poorly organized.

The new master plan called for a four-phase, two-year architectural renewal that would allow the hotel to maintain ongoing operations. Specific tasks included

- demolishing, gutting, and remodeling existing structures;
- new construction (porte-cochere and entry building);
- consolidating and increasing open space, with vistas to and from the ocean;
- reorganizing and reallocating space to take advantage of views (e.g., a waterfront restaurant created from a semibasement, storage areas converted to lagoonfront function rooms);
- creating a villagelike ambience through the design of a central commons or "green space" and the incorporation of shops, restaurants, and activity spaces along newly created pathways;
- simplifying circulation in and around buildings; and
- upgrading facilities to meet the latest life safety and energy standards.

Photo courtesy of Wimberly Allison Tong & Goo Architects

At the Hilton Hawaiian Village, Waikiki, resourceful land use—resulting in fewer rooms and less building square footage—made it possible to increase open space by 20 percent (thereby improving the quality of the resort experience for people within and outside the complex) and to reposition food/beverage and retail outlets (thereby increasing their profitability).

The result was the renovation of 500,000 square feet of space and a reduction in site density by eliminating 54 rooms. User satisfaction and cost-effectiveness are evidenced by enhanced demand and a dramatic increase in occupancy rates, higher room prices, and one of the newly renovated restaurants' achievement of chainwide record-high gross income. Since the renewal, all sectors of the community have recognized and lauded the Hilton Hawaiian Village.

Increased operating revenues and higher property values are two measures of economic success that apply to the Hilton Hawaiian renovation project. In the first three years following completion of the renovation, annual revenues grew by 60 percent—from $102 million in 1987 to $164 million by the end of 1990. In addition, the developers credit the successful master plan and renovation program with doubling the value of their property in four years.

The Hilton Hawaiian Village master plan and renovation exemplifies the kind of hotel resort development that, working creatively within environmental, community, and economic constraints, achieves maximum potential without adding density or requiring additional public infrastructure. The resourceful use of land—resulting in fewer rooms and less building square footage—made it possible to increase open space by 20 percent (thereby improving the resort's aesthetic appeal for people within and outside the complex) and to reposition food and beverage and retail outlets (thereby contributing to an increase in profitability).

Improvements to the built environment included reorganizing public spaces and amenities to enhance hotel management and operations; redesigning the physical layout to open up the ocean vista and provide more landscaped open spaces; upgrading facilities to meet current building codes and requirements for safety and energy efficiency and to enhance comfort, aesthetics, and amenities; creating an elegantly informal new entry building that affords the arriving guest an expansive garden, pool, and ocean view; and installing life safety systems to ensure a high-quality and safe environment for visitors and residents and to help support the long-term viability of Waikiki as Oahu's primary resort area.

As a development project, the Hilton Hawaiian Village master plan and renovation has been an outstanding success both financially and critically. In addition to highly favorable editorial acclaim, the renovation has garnered over 30 awards, including design, engineering, landscape/environmental, and various hotel trade awards. Beyond its commercial success, the resort is also viewed as a community asset. ■

will inspect hotels in conformance with a checklist to determine their degree of ecosensitivity and then publish a directory of environmentally friendly properties.

The second trend affecting the nature of renovations in the United States is related to compliance with the Americans with Disabilities Act (ADA). The ADA is a legal issue, not a code issue, that falls under the jurisdiction of the U.S. Department of Justice, not the local building department. Given that accessibility modifications can be costly and inconvenient, it is often the threat of a lawsuit under the ADA that provides the incentive to make existing resorts accessible to the disabled. But there is also a more positive reason why these changes are being made—the chance to attract persons with disabilities. An estimated 17 percent of the U.S. population —or 43 million people—is disabled. The fact that ADA– mandated improvements can be good for business was recently illustrated on the front page of *Hotel Business*. Not only is the Embassy Suites in Lake Buena Vista filling more rooms by going well beyond what the ADA requires, but it is earning national exposure in the process.

The third trend influencing cosmetic renovations is the traveler's increasing tendency to combine business with pleasure. As resorts and hotels target the business traveler, they not only add business services but also reconfigure guest rooms to function as complete offices: more space, two telephone lines, facsimile machines, shelves, and large desks.

Minor Renovations and Improvements

A move up the renovation continuum from cosmetic improvements leads to a range of minor property renovations and additions that are generally driven by operations needs and/or changes in the marketplace. Travelers' increasing tendency to combine business and pleasure is accompanied by a related trend toward family-centered resorts that offer an expanding array of activities and facilities geared to children. Business travelers today are five times as likely to bring a child along on a trip as they were in 1985. As a result, resorts are starting to provide some innovative facilities for kids. The Grand Wailea Resort and Spa in Maui serves the intellectual and playful interests of its young guests with a 400-square-foot computer learning center. At the same time, to offset seasonal fluctuations in occupancies, many resorts are marketing group business. Not surprisingly, many renovation projects in recent years have included the addition and/or upgrading of conference and convention facilities.

Perhaps the most fascinating trend is the increasing popularity of old-fashioned romance and marriage. North America, Europe, and Asia report more than 17 million marriages each year. Weddings can dramatically boost food and beverage revenues while increasing occupancies. And then there is the honeymoon. Among first-time brides in the United States, 98 percent travel on a honeymoon. And they do not skimp. Honeymoon spending per couple has quadrupled since 1974. As a result, several resorts are adding wedding chapels,

In late 1993, South African hotelier Sol Kerzner began design work on the first-phase renovations at Atlantis on Paradise Island in the Bahamas. In May 1994, Kerzner's company, Sun International closed on the property and, over the next seven months, spent $147 million on renovations before Paradise Island's December 1994 opening.

Sun's purchase included 562 acres of land with three hotels (1,318 rooms), a golf course, and 220 acres of undeveloped land. Though new to the North American market, in 1979 Kerzner had developed Sun City, 100 miles from Johannesburg, South Africa. The program for Atlantis parallels that for Sun City and includes highly themed attractions, golf, gaming, and both four- and five-star hotels. Today, Sun City attracts 2 million visitors annually.

Kerzner had been watching the Atlantis for several years before buying it. He was aware of its financial difficulty but believed that the resort offered considerable potential. When the property went into Chapter 11, Kerzner went to the bondholders and concluded successful negotiations with the creditors rather than with the owner.

The original acquisition and a portion of the renovations were financed primarily through $125 million of equity raised from major shareholders in other ventures and an $80 million loan from the Bank of Nova Scotia. The venture was subsequently rolled into Sun International Hotels, which is listed on the New York Stock Exchange and now carries no debt.

Kerzner's vision for Atlantis took into consideration the following factors:

- The Caribbean had matured as a market, but the Bahamas, though easily accessible to North America, had been bypassed due to image problems. The Bahamas had, however, just elected a new government with reform intentions and an understanding of the importance of tourism to the economy.
- Kerzner had wanted to enter the North American market, and the Bahamas provided a good platform. Paradise Island also offered an opportunity to tie into Sun's marketing resources in Europe.
- The still-depressed U.S. real estate market, coupled with the bankruptcy of Resorts International, had depressed the value of Atlantis.

Photo courtesy of EDSA

In the redevelopment of Atlantis on Paradise Island in the Bahamas, a new marine theme was established with saltwater aquariums and freshwater ponds.

- A growing cultural shift was creating a greater demand for entertainment in all market sectors, especially in vacation environments with a family orientation.
- The Caribbean lacked a large, first-class, gaming-oriented resort with significant conference facilities.

Kerzner decided to create a resort that would appeal to a broad range of markets and feature major attractions in a tropical setting. The waterfront environment served as the stage and theme for an extensive outdoor resort amenity. The Atlantis resort showcases Bahamian marine life in the natural environment and Bahamian culture in the built environment.

The New Program
The first phase of renovations included the total make-over of the 1,147-room Atlantis resort and the 71-room Ocean Club to provide a range of high-end accommodations. The Ocean Club had been the estate of Huntington Hartford, the original developer of Paradise Island and the heir to the A&P fortune. It was converted to an elegant, small-scale Caribbean hotel. The club's classical theme is reflected in the structure's architecture and the surrounding landscape.

At Atlantis, 12 restaurants provide a wide variety of dining experiences while an upscale shopping area keeps most visitors from crossing the bridge to Nassau. A salt-water lagoon has been restored, giving the resort excellent beaches on two sides. Other attractions include an 18-hole championship golf course designed by Dick Wilson and 100,000 square feet of conference facilities.

The cornerstone of the resort, however, is entertainment. Despite its 30,000-square-foot casino, Atlantis's major component is a 14-acre waterscape that includes

- five swimming pools covering a total of 32,000 square feet;
- 40 waterfalls;
- a quarter-mile river ride;
- a waterslide;
- caves and grottoes themed with coastal rock formations;
- a 300-foot underwater viewing area and a 100-foot underwater acrylic tunnel where guests can walk among sharks, barracudas, manta rays, sea turtles, and thousands of tropical fish; and
- the world's largest outdoor open-water aquarium in six saltwater lagoons covering 120,000 square feet, holding 3.2 million gallons of water and containing more than 100 species of fish. One lagoon contains sharks and predatory fish. The aquariums require a pumping system that circulates 70,000 gallons of water per hour.

Photo courtesy of EDSA

Atlantis on Paradise Island.

The diversity of pools, marine environments, and landscaping helps keep guests on the property and encourages repeat visits.

Overall, Atlantis's site development work cost $50 million. The complex of pools, grottoes, aquariums, and landscaping provides numerous tropical stage sets for day and night activities.

Design Issues
Kerzner's hands-on enthusiasm for the project was the catalyst for the design team of Wimberly Allison Tong & Goo, responsible for the buildings, and EDSA, responsible for all site work. In addition to time constraints, the design and construction team faced other issues.

- The labor force in the area did not have experience with a project of Atlantis's magnitude. Similarly, quality control was a constant challenge.
- Some complex environmental issues in the coastal environment led to a partnership with the National Trust.
- Acquiring an adequate supply of plant material, especially coconut palms, became a problem. As a result, Sun purchased a palm nursery in Jamaica to supply a sufficient quantity of palms immune to lethal yellowing, thus ensuring the resort a lush, tropical appearance.
- To ensure continued operation of the resort, 600 rooms and one pool remained open throughout construction. Ultimately, all rooms and exterior amenities were renovated in accordance with a phased schedule.

Photo courtesy of EDSA

The square patch in the bay in this photo is the intake for water to the new saltwater aquarium. The bay was rehabilitated by building a weir to allow only incoming tides to bring in clean water from the ocean.

The environmental consultant, Applied Technology Management (ATM), was charged with restoring a polluted saltwater lagoon. With Sun's desire to showcase the marine environment, ATM designed a tidal dam that attenuated pollution from Nassau harbor as well as a groin structure that restores natural sand migration along the coast and prevents siltation. These improvements benefit both the environment and tourists. The latter enjoy a lagoon in which to swim, snorkel, and observe marine life in its natural setting.

Competitive Advantage

Recognizing the potential impact of a high-quality development on the local economy, the Bahamian government demonstrated strong support of Kerzner's efforts on Paradise Island. For example, the government granted exclusive gaming licenses to Atlantis and one other resort on New Providence Island (Nassau); no other licenses will be granted for 20 years. In addition, the government reduced the gaming tax by approximately 17 percent in proportion to the number of jobs created. During construction, Sun made every effort to employ Bahamian labor but was not restricted from importing labor if jobs could not be filled locally. Approximately 80 percent of the construction workforce was Bahamian. The government granted Sun an excise tax abatement on imported construction materials.

Kerzner has continued to nurture cooperation with the Bahamian government, participating in infrastructure improvements and islandwide planning efforts. But beyond the advantages provided by the government, he has created attractions comparable to offerings in Orlando, the nongaming powerhouse of the Florida/Caribbean resort market. In addition, the aquarium at Atlantis is competitive with municipal facilities that take advantage of lavish public subsidies.

Sun International's investment has given the company a lead over the competition. Kerzner's intention is to maintain that lead by continuing to improve on what is built and to add new attractions. Butch Kerzner, Sol Kerzner's son, commented that Sun's policy is to "keep the drama going" with new attractions as well as to rework rooms and public areas continually. For example, since major construction ended in 1994, the casino has been expanded and improved, and a second phase of construction is already on the drawing board. It includes an additional 1,200 rooms and a major expansion of the marine-based attractions. It is expected to open in mid-1998 and will most certainly raise to new heights the level of competition in the Caribbean.

Source: Adapted from William Renner, "Atlantis Redevelopment Raises the Ante," *Urban Land*, August 1996, pp. 15, 18–20.

pavilions, and other related facilities to attract the "romance" market.

Basic renovation and redesign of key resort elements is also an important consideration. Like people, resorts do not get a second chance to make a favorable first impression. Therefore, many renovation projects center around the arrival experience. Expectations are high when a guest arrives at a resort, and the property should not disappoint. Improvements to back-of-house facilities should also be considered. Many resort hotels are finding that a commitment to human resources and back-of-house renovations can contribute to a resort's ability to attract and retain employees.

In addition to building renovations, a resort's amenities require periodic evaluation and updating. Stowe Mountain Resort spent more than $40 million from 1990 to 1995—$10 million in 1995 alone—to improve the ski product and the amenities off the mountain. During the summer of 1995, it spent more than $3 million on substantial snowmaking improvements, including a 40 percent increase in air capacity, a 50 percent increase in water-pumping capacity, and 100 new snow guns. These improvements allow the resort to open twice as many trails for the Thanksgiving and Christmas holidays and to recover more quickly from adverse weather. At the Homestead in Hot Springs, Virginia, a recent key improvement called for updating the Homestead golf course (see feature box on page 263).

Major Renovations and Improvements

When a resort reaches age 25, give or take five years, it is usually time for a major renovation. At that age—especially if minor upgrades have not been undertaken on a regular basis and maintenance has been deferred—a resort is generally both functionally and physically obsolete. The need to renovate is often a question of pure survival. But it is hard to get excited about spending $10 million or $110 million on a renovation merely

to survive. The excitement comes from the opportunity to do something special. . .to breathe new life into a tired old resort, often repositioning it in the process.

Such was the case with the Catamaran Hotel on San Diego's Mission Bay. On the eve of the hotel's 29th birthday, the owners knew they had to do something. The new vision came in the form of a plan to convert the predominantly automobile-oriented motel to a guest-oriented resort hotel that is now popular with locals and visitors. The renovation program included the addition of a parking garage, five new guest room buildings, and 21,000 square feet of meeting and eating space. The Catamaran was able to continue operating throughout the renovation due to careful planning and phasing of the project.

In some cases, a new owner with new ideas will spearhead a repositioning. One example is the Kauai Marriott Resort & Beach Club. Formerly known as the Westin Kauai at Kauai Lagoons, this megaresort hotel opened in 1988 and was acquired by Marriott International in 1994. Marriott undertook an extensive $36 million renovation that involved a significant repositioning of the property, including changes to the rooms, the landscape, and the range of products offered. The original hotel consisted of 818 rooms and 29 suites. Marriott reconfigured the property into a hotel with 356 guest rooms, 190 one-bedroom suites, and 42 two-bedroom suites. The suites are now offered as vacation ownership villas known as Marriott's Kauai Beach Club; approximately 100 of the suites may be used as hotel rooms on any given night.

Marriott also sought to change the image and appeal of the hotel by redesigning the rooms, lobbies, and garden areas to be more authentically Hawaiian. The marketing materials' description of the new gardens says it all. "The metamorphosis is unmistakable at the Kauai Marriott Resort & Beach Club, where the majestic Ka Mala o Kalapaki Gardens have been meticulously trans-

At Palmas del Mar, a 2,750-acre resort community in Puerto Rico, the repositioning strategy begun in 1991 focused on the delineation of resort and residential precincts, on the concentration of tourist facilities/ activities, and on the creation of a strong Caribbean flavor.

formed into a true Hawaiian paradise. Gone are the traces of European formality and foreign fauna. In its place, a breathtaking expanse of a newly born Eden. Indigenous botanical treasures flirt with the senses."

Master Plan Improvements

In the case of megahotel and multiuse resorts, renovation and repositioning often involve rethinking the entire plan and resort concept. The effort goes far beyond the earlier examples of major renovations. In fact, the planning that goes into such a project is usually geared toward a long-term view of maximizing a return on investment.

In 1983, when Barron Hilton attended the grand opening of the newest tower on the Hilton Hawaiian Village's 20-acre property, he looked at the hodgepodge

The Kauai Marriott recently underwent a $36 million renovation and repositioning, including changes to the rooms, the landscape, and the range of products offered. The resort now offers vacation ownership suites in addition to traditional hotel rooms.

of buildings from his suite on the 35th floor and realized that there was more work to be done at his beachfront property. The idea of a master plan was born. The project involved more than a full year of planning and design and another two years of phased construction. In this case, the $100 million project—which involved demolishing buildings, consolidating utilities, moving restaurants, renovating lobbies and guest rooms, and adding extensive landscaping—was carried out while the resort continued operating (see feature box on page 264). An even larger undertaking was the reconceptualization of the Atlantis Resort and Paradise Island in the Bahamas (see feature box on page 266). (See Chapter 6 for other examples of renovation and repositioning efforts.)

A major problem with master-planned improvements in multiuse resorts involves existing property owners. Notes Wayne S. Hyatt of Hyatt & Stubblefield in Atlanta, "In dealing with restructuring a master-planned resort community, the parties are faced with special characteristics which make the process more difficult. The most significant of these characteristics includes the fact that there are people in place with direct and indirect ownership interests and that there is an independent legal entity, the community association in existence. . . . [T]he first objective is to turn the existing owners into a positive force or, at the very least, to avoid acrimony and opposition. The strategy thus must identify and reflect owner concerns in a business plan."[28]

Notes

1. J. Richard McElyea and Gregory L. Cory, "Resort Investment and Development: An Overview of an Evolving Market," *Property*, Summer 1992, pp. 3–6.

2. Adapted in part from David McCarty, "Mixed-Use Resorts: Opportunities and Challenges," *Urban Land*, August 1995, pp. 30–33, 80.

3. Personal communication with Charles Hewlett, Robert Charles Lesser & Co., June 8, 1995.

4. Ibid.

5. Adapted from Jim Heid, "A Strategic Approach to Affordable Housing in Resort Communities," *Urban Land*, August 1995, pp. 34–37, 81.

6. Arthur H. Simons and George Leposki, *ARI Resource Manual* (ARDA Education Institute, 1994), p. 28.

7. Personal communication with Edwin McMullen, chair, Hilton Grand Vacations Company, February 9, 1996.

8. Simons and Leposki, *Resource Manual*, p. 32.

9. Mac MacEwan, "Product Information Marketing: A Strategy for the Future," *RCI Perspective*, July–August 1995, pp. 4–5.

10. John Sherman, "Marketing Timeshare Worldwide," *RCI Perspective*, May–June 1995, p. 6.

11. Jane H. Lehman, "The Trouble with Selling Time-shares," *Newsday*, October 13, 1996.

12. David McCarty, "Resales: Must It Be a Win or Lose Situation," *RCI Perspective*, November–December 1994.

13. Personal communication with Edwin McMullen.

14. Carol W. Sullivan, "How Property Management Contributes to Financial Well-Being," *Developments*, April–May, 1993, pp. 11–17.

15. Ibid.

16. Paul G. Flory, "Timeshare Management: A Look at the Future," *Vacation Industry Review*, Winter 1993, pp. 11–17.

17. Eighty-two percent of individuals cited the trade-in feature as motivation for purchasing a timeshare interval. Ragatz and Associates, Inc., *Timeshare Purchasers: Who They Are, Why They Buy: 1995* (Washington, D.C.: Alliance for Timeshare Excellence, 1995).

18. Simons and Leposki, *Resource Manual*. The manual can be ordered from the ARDA Education Institute, 1220 L Street, NW, Suite 510, Washington, D.C. 20005. Telephone 202-371-6700; fax 202-289-8544.

19. Personal communication with Gary A. Terry, Jones, Waldo, Holbrook.

20. Adapted in part from M. Chase Burritt and Mark Lunt, "Lodging: A Changed Industry," *Urban Land*, August 1995, pp. 39–43, 82.

21. Wayne S. Hyatt, Hyatt & Stubblefield, Atlanta, Ga.

22. Ibid.

23. National Ski Areas Association, *1993–1994 Economic Analysis of United States Ski Areas* (Lakewood, Col.: author, 1995), p. 15.

24. Donald W. Adie, *Marinas: A Working Guide to Their Development and Design*, 3d ed. (New York: Nichols Publishing Company, 1984), p. 337.

25. Personal communication with Robert J. Lowe, president, Lowe Enterprises, 1995.

26. Adapted from Donald W.Y. Goo, "Revitalizing Resorts," paper presented at ULI Professional Development Seminar, Lake George, N.Y., June 20–21, 1994.

27. "Yarmouth Sells Colorado Resort after Doubling its Cashflow," *National Real Estate Investor*, August 1996, p. 12.

28. Wayne S. Hyatt, "Revitalizing Resort and Recreational Communities: Legal and Ownership Issues," paper presented at ULI Professional Development Seminar, Lake George, N.Y., June 20–21, 1994.

6. Case Studies

Multiuse Destination Resorts

Kiawah Island, South Carolina
A 10,000-acre multiuse destination resort on the Atlantic coast in South Carolina, featuring beaches and golf.

Beaver Creek Resort, Colorado
A 2,777-acre multiuse destination resort in the Rocky Mountains of Colorado, featuring skiing and golf.

Kapalua, Hawaii
A 1,500-acre multiuse destination resort on the island of Maui, featuring beaches and golf.

Multiuse Regional Resorts

Hidden Valley Four Seasons Resort, Pennsylvania
A 2,000-acre multiuse regional resort in the mountains of Pennsylvania, featuring skiing and golf.

The Homestead Resort, Michigan
A 514-acre multiuse regional resort on Lake Michigan, featuring beaches and skiing.

Second-Home Resort Communities

Dewees Island, South Carolina
A 1,206-acre remote second-home retreat on the Atlantic coast in South Carolina, featuring an island setting and beaches.

Forest Highlands, Arizona
A 657-acre second-home resort community in the mountains of Arizona, featuring golf.

Seaside, Florida
An 80-acre oceanfront resort town on the Gulf of Mexico in the panhandle of Florida, featuring beaches and a village-style plan.

Hotel Resorts

Boca Raton Resort & Club, Florida
A 963-room historic hotel resort on the Atlantic coast of Florida, featuring beaches and golf.

The Arizona Biltmore Hotel and Resort, Arizona
A 500-room historic hotel resort in the desert of Arizona, recently renovated and expanded, featuring golf.

Spanish Bay Resort, California
A 270-room hotel resort on the rocky central Pacific coast in California, featuring golf.

Little Nell Hotel, Colorado
A 92-room boutique resort hotel in the Rocky Mountains of Colorado, featuring skiing and Aspen town charm.

Timeshare Resorts

Disney's Old Key West Resort at Walt Disney World, Florida
A 497-unit timeshare, vacation ownership resort that is part of Walt Disney World.

Kiawah Island

Kiawah Island, South Carolina

Kiawah Island is one of the more beautiful barrier islands on the Atlantic Ocean. This 10,000-acre resort and residential community is located 21 miles south of historic Charleston, South Carolina, and is one of a necklace of barrier islands that range between North Carolina's Outer Banks and northern Florida.

The location and shape of the site provide numerous attractive features, including a long beach season, an extremely high proportion of beachfront to developable land, a wonderfully unspoiled natural environment, and proximity to Charleston, a significant tourist destination as well as a major source of potential second-home purchasers. Kiawah also has a unique east/west orientation rather than the north/south orientation typical of most U.S. coastal areas. As a result, it enjoys a steady accretion of its ten-mile-long, crescent-shaped beach.

The Site and Development Process

For most of the last 200 years, Kiawah Island was owned by the Vanderhorst family. The property played a part in both the Revolutionary and Civil Wars as well as in the War of 1812. In 1951, C.C. Royal, a South Carolina lumberman, purchased the island. During his 20-year ownership, he removed only a few specimen pines and some second-growth timber and sold beachfront parcels to a select group of individuals. Kiawah remained a small enclave until 1974, when Royal's heirs sold the island to a subsidiary of the Kuwait Investment Company, the Kiawah Island Company.

In 1974, the Kuwaiti owners engaged the Sea Pines Company, headed by the legendary Charles Fraser, to conduct land use analyses of and to create a land use plan for Kiawah. The Kuwaitis invested a great deal of money in the 16-month study, which brought together a team of environmentalists, biologists, historians, architects, and other highly qualified scientists and experts. For its time, the study earned considerable recognition as one of the most thorough land use plans ever undertaken for a resort. After all, it benefited from and was built on the lessons learned from Hilton Head, which Sea Pines had started to develop in 1956. And Hilton Head had won acclaim as one of the first and most environmentally sensitive Atlantic beach resorts.

The Kuwaiti owners invested in significant development of the property from 1974 to 1988. Specifically, they developed portions of both resort cores—West Beach Village and East Beach Village—several golf courses, and residential land. West Beach Village

opened in 1976 and contains the 150-room Kiawah Island Inn and Villas. East Beach Village, which was planned to accommodate the town center and a yet-to-be-built several-hundred-room convention hotel, opened in 1981. The first two golf courses were completed in 1976 and 1981, and residential development proceeded as the market dictated. With completion of the third golf course, the Kuwaitis ceased their major investment in Kiawah. In 1988, the existing homeowners incorporated as a town to protect their investment. At the same time, the Kuwait Investment Company sold its interest in Kiawah Island to Kiawah Resort Associates (KRA), the principals of whom were local Charleston businessmen. The purchase price was $105 million.

After initiating a series of carefully phased renovations and upgrades, KRA reached agreement with the Landmark Land Company in 1989 to assume ownership and management of Kiawah's resort amenities, which included the newly renovated Kiawah Island Inn, the three golf courses built at that time, two tennis centers, and the town center retail and conference facilities. In addition, KRA sold an oceanfront hotel site in East Beach Village and the site for the proposed Ocean Course on the island's eastern end. The total purchase price for the resort amenity package was $35 million.

To further its business and financial plan, KRA also embarked on a search to find a resort operating partner with a qualitative philosophy and image in keeping with Kiawah's standards. KRA continued its business of carefully developing the remaining acreage on the island and, in 1992, was joined in partnership by the Morgan Stanley Real Estate Fund as a substantial equity investor.

As events played out, the sale of the resort amenities—critical assets for a resort residential sales operation—proved to be an unfortunate decision in some respects. Landmark turned over development responsibilities to subsidiaries of the Oak Tree Savings Bank of New Orleans. When the savings institution subsequently failed, the Resolution Trust Corporation (RTC) stepped in as conservator, spurring Landmark to seek bankruptcy protection from its creditors in 1991. At the same time, Landmark was negotiating with a Japanese buyer for the sale of its Kiawah and other assets but ultimately could not close. After a bitter battle, the RTC wrested control of Landmark's properties—including the Kiawah resort amenities—in bankruptcy court.

In 1993, Landmark's portion of the Kiawah Island resort property was included in an RTC auction with

Kiawah Island is a 10,000-acre barrier island resort in South Carolina that, for East Coast resorts, has an unusual east/west orientation that promotes sand accretion rather than erosion. Pictured is the migrating sandbar off the island's eastern end at Stono Inlet. Sand accretion adds mass to Kiawah Island's measurements each year so that the island is actually growing.

five other luxury golf resorts. The three-hour auction drew more than 30 bidding groups that became enmeshed in layers of strategy. KRA, through its partner Morgan Stanley, sought to buy back its resort component from the RTC and thereby regain control of its important golf amenities. KSL Enterprises Group Ltd., however, outbid KRA and thereupon sold the amenities to an affiliate of the AMF Companies of Richmond, Virginia. The affiliate Virginia Investment Trusts (VIT) agreed to pay $45.1 million. VIT assumed the development restriction included in the terms of the 1989 sale to Landmark, which stipulated that VIT could not sell residential lots on its resort property and that KRA could not develop any hotels.

At $41.2 million, Kiawah sold for more than its book value at the time of sale, although the $39 million price reflected a cash discount. Federal bankruptcy court in Charleston subsequently approved the sale. The high price paid was a tribute to the quality and potential returns on the Kiawah resort property and to KRA's success in continuing a strong sales effort during a difficult period. KRA completed sales in excess of $70 million in residential real estate, even with Kiawah's major golf amenities suffering uncertain status in bankruptcy and in RTC hands.

For KRA and its partners, however, this turn of events provided continuing concern, as they still could not control the operation of key resort amenities; most important, they could not provide assurances to potential homebuyers regarding access to and pricing of the golf courses, which represented a critical component of Kiawah's value.

Since Kiawah's opening in 1976, approximately 4,000 residential properties have been sold. As of 1995, residential land sales were about 75 percent completed. Just over half of these properties have been built on, including approximately 2,500 villas, 400 cottages, and many single-family homes. No multifamily villa product has been built since 1987, and most of Kiawah's residential sales after 1987 took the form of lot sales.

Development of Kiawah Island's residential component continues, with approximately ten to 12 years of active development remaining, primarily on the island's eastern portion. About 80 to 100 homesites and new homes are developed and sold each year. Marshview properties in the northeast quadrant of the island are currently the major focus. KRA recently built the private Kiawah Island Club, featuring the River Course and a beach club. The East Beach hotel site, owned by VIT, still remains to be developed.

The Kiawah Island Club's cottages in their marshside setting. The property includes roughly 5,400 acres of highlands and 5,000 acres of marsh savannahs with maritime forest vegetation.

Master Planning and Design

The resort's planners created a plan of small, intimate communities with all amenities located within walking distance of one another. They carefully preserved the natural splendor of Kiawah's ten miles of ocean beachfront and 32 miles of marshview property, 13 miles of which front on numerous mildly salty and freshwater ponds. Kiawah encompasses roughly 5,400 acres of highlands and 5,000 acres of marsh savannahs with maritime forest vegetation. The forested areas are dominated by oaks, palmettos, and pines; a subcanopy of hickory, sweetgum, and magnolia; and an understory of redbay, sassafras, wax myrtle, and yarpon holly, many of which provide seasonal flowers. The planners relied on this natural and incredibly beautiful ecoculture to create the island's ambience and located the building sites to make Kiawah's built environment as unobtrusive as possible.

The plan's basic philosophy was to let nature have its way, with human activities "intruding" quietly and respectfully. The higher-density land uses were grouped or clustered into manageable zones on land deemed best suited to intensive use. Environmentally sensitive areas were reserved for less concentrated development or for no development at all.

Following the Sea Pines model, a key decision at the outset called for separating the resort villages from the private residential neighborhoods. While Kiawah is often thought of as primarily a resort island with lodgings, shops, golf, tennis, and the beach, resort activities are concentrated in two cores capable of accommodating the density. Together, East Beach and West Beach Villages total less than 10 percent of the island's developable acreage. The balance of Kiawah was planned as recreational areas, open spaces, and significant residential areas largely in single-family homes.

Most of Kiawah's acreage was initially planned for as many as 7,000 residential properties at full buildout for a gross density of only 1.4 units to the acre. The resort was zoned as a planned unit development (PUD) with a density cap of 7,000 units. The PUD zoning permitted flexibility in specific lot allocations and the distribution of densities. As the resort community has evolved, however, the developers have determined that only about 5,500 lots and homesites are likely to be developed and sold.

The first resort core to be developed—West Beach Village—contains the 150-room Kiawah Island Inn and Villas. It is connected to the Straw Market, where local women weave baskets and other straw products for sale. To reduce building mass, the inn was planned as four separate lodges. All rooms have private balconies with views of the ocean, dunes, or forest. The inn has easy access to three swimming pools, Marsh Point golf, the West Beach Tennis Club, shopping, and dining at four different restaurants and two bars. It includes meeting rooms for groups of up to 300.

Almost 1,400 privately owned villas and cottages are clustered around both of the resort villages. The villas

A typical pond-site home setting. The resort includes 32 miles of marsh property, 13 miles of which front on numerous mildly salty and freshwater ponds.

are multifamily condominiums ranging in size from one to four bedrooms. They are sited along the golf course fairways or on the oceanfront overlooking attractive lagoons. Owners use the villas as vacation homes and rent them by the night or week as well. The cottages are small vacation homes built on small lots. VIT manages approximately 350 of the resort villas and cottages, with check-in conveniently provided at the inn. Four independent rental companies manage another 750 villas and cottages.

East Beach Village features the 24,000-square-foot East Beach Conference Center and Town Center, which contains 15 meeting rooms and a 7,000-square-foot ballroom with a seated dinner capacity of 600. It also offers villa and cottage accommodations, the East Beach Tennis Club, the Turtle Point Golf Course, and the 21-acre Night Heron Park. The park is distinguished by large playing fields, a special play area for small children, picnic sites, a lake with a fishing dock, a 25-meter pool and recreation pavilion, an ocean access point with an observation deck, a bath house, and eating facilities. A future hotel is planned for East Beach Village.

Single-family homes account for the largest portion of Kiawah's residential development. Over 2,000 single-family homesites had been sold by the mid-1990s, with over 1,000 homes already built. Homesites range from one-quarter acre to over one acre. The Kiawah Island Architectural Review Board must approve home designs before construction. Of the homes built to date, there is a fairly even split between primary homes and second homes. Only a small number of homes are available for short-term rental. The average-

The beach at Kiawah. Conservation setbacks for oceanside homes keep the homes behind the primary dune.

size home built today is about 3,500 square feet. About 400 cottages have been constructed to date. They are detached homes on small lots clustered in areas maintained under a common homeowners' association. These two- and three-bedroom homes are located along the outer rim of Kiawah's two resort villages.

Amenities

While Kiawah's plan called for the natural beach environment to be the project's featured amenity, it also specified a variety of other recreational amenities to ensure a successful large-scale resort. These amenities largely include the five award-winning golf courses (four semiprivate, nonequity resort courses owned by VIT and one private course owned by KRA, the River Course), tennis and watersports, and leisure trails.

Marsh Point was the first golf course to open at West Beach Village (1976). Designed by Gary Player and Ron Kirby, it is of modest length: 6,203 yards from the blue tees, 5,841 yards from the white tees, and 5,055 yards from the red tees. It has an abundance of scenic marshside fairways and undulating greens well guarded by water and sandtraps. Water hazards pose a challenge on 13 holes. Most of the course plays through residential areas; fairways and greens put a premium on accuracy, not distance.

The next golf course to open was Turtle Point (1981). Located in East Beach Village, it was designed by Jack Nicklaus and has been the site of many amateur and professional tournaments. It is a championship course, the most difficult of Kiawah's courses. Its longest distance is 6,919 yards. It plays through a maritime forest for 13 holes and then explodes onto the ocean for three spectacular oceanside holes. In 1992, *Golf Digest* named Turtle Point one of the top 75 resort courses.

Completed in 1986 and allowed to mature for two years before opening in 1988, Osprey Point was designed by Tom Fazio. Perhaps the most popular course on the island, it balances playability, beauty, and challenge. Created among Kiawah's marshes and forests and around four major lakes, it includes water features on 15 holes. It, too, was named in *Golf Digest*'s 1992 list of top 75 resort courses.

The Ocean Course opened in 1991 and hosted the PGA's 1991 Ryder Cup. It won instant acclaim as Pete Dye's most exceptional layout. All 18 holes of the Ocean Course present panoramic views of the ocean; ten holes play directly along the two and one-half miles of beachfront dedicated to the course. Although the scorecard reads 7,371 yards from the tournament tees, Dye built numerous tees on each hole to allow golfers to play from as short as 4,800 yards. Upon its completion, the course was immediately named America's Best New Resort Course for 1991. It was also the youngest course ever to be named among the 100 greatest courses in the world by *Golf* magazine.

A par-72 layout stretching more than 7,000 yards from the back tees, the River Course plays along the marsh, the 30-acre Bass Pond, and the Kiawah River.

The fairway on the fourth hole of the Ocean Course, designed by Pete Dye and opened in 1991. Ten of the holes on this course play directly along the two and one-half miles of beachfront dedicated to the course.

The River Course clubhouse, overlooking the 18th green to the right. The River Course was the last of the five courses to be developed and the first course on the island to be part of a private club.

The Beach Club, designed by Robert A.M. Stern.

Designed by Tom Fazio as the centerpiece of the Kiawah Island Club, the River Course is Kiawah's fifth course and the first to become part of a private club.

In addition to golf, over 20 miles of paved trails for bicycling or jogging provide access to the beach and historic points of interest. Other features include adult-only, family, and children's pools at the Kiawah Island Inn for resort guests, a property owners-only pool in West Beach Village, the Turtle Point pool in East Beach Village, and a 25-meter pool at the Night Heron Park recreation complex. A summer recreation program for children, Kiawah Kollege features participatory beach tours led by naturalists as well as a variety of watersports and cultural activities. Nearby Bohicket Marina, although not on Kiawah, provides ready access to deep-sea fishing charters and day sailing.

Another important amenity on the island is tennis. Two separate tennis facilities were planned and built. The West Beach Tennis Club features 14 Har-Tru courts plus two lighted hard courts and a backboard. The East Beach Tennis Club has nine Har-Tru courts plus three hard courts and a zoned practice court with an automated ball machine and a retrieval system. Both clubs offer fully staffed pro shops and complete instructional facilities. The Grand Masters Pro Championship has been played at Kiawah, and the resort has consistently been rated among the top 50 tennis resorts in the United States by *Tennis* magazine.

Marketing

Kiawah's first owners made several strategic marketing decisions. First, they positioned Kiawah somewhat below Sea Pines in the resort market. They assumed that Kiawah's more moderate pricing would broaden the resort's appeal to a larger market of younger, less affluent buyers and that its greater affordability would enable it to sell despite the hard-hitting recession of the mid-1970s. The marketing strategy paid off in that Kiawah did sell well in the late 1970s and the early 1980s. However, many of its buyers tended to be the same buyers who represented the Sea Pines market and saw the value of Kiawah's lower prices.

A second strategic marketing decision called for an initial primary focus on the resort's regional market, emphasizing Kiawah's proximity to Charleston. Land sales in the early 1980s were about two-thirds regionally based. Later, however, the conference business sought out a national market while efforts to target the East Coast resort market brought in buyers from outside the immediate region.

The early villas and beach cottages began selling in 1976 for an average price of about $75,000. By 1981, the average sales price had doubled. Prices for the villas and cottages topped out in 1984 at about $200,000. During the next few years, however, they dropped back in response to the resort's lack of marketing and the dampening effect of the Tax Reform Act of 1986, which limited the benefits of investor ownership.

The average price of a residential lot of between one-quarter and one-half acre began at $20,000 in 1976. By 1980, lot prices had doubled and, by 1983, tripled. Prices dropped in the mid-1980s because of a lack of marketing and considerable uncertainty about the future of the resort and its owner. At that time, the Kuwaiti owners, in response to matters unrelated to their Kiawah project, slashed their operating budget dramatically; reduced the management staff by half; ceased capital improvements; disbanded the golf club, which was a financial liability; and cut their marketing budget from approximately $2.5 million to $250,000 annually. As a result, sales dropped precipitously between 1985 and 1988, when Kiawah Resort Associates purchased the resort. Existing property owners were so alarmed by the situation that, by 1988, they incorporated as a town.

KRA put a high priority on rebuilding Kiawah's marketing program—and sales responded accordingly. The new owner's success in wooing the Ryder Cup in 1991 provided the needed boost for sales, which extended to an international market as well. Even though Landmark filed for bankruptcy within days of the Ryder Cup, the continuing sale of residential lots was a tribute to KRA's marketing program.

By 1987, with the construction of the larger cottages, the average price of a unit had risen to close to $300,000. At that time, resales of the villas were averaging about $165,000, providing a decent return to those who had purchased before the mid-1980s. Except for the downturn in 1985 after the resort changed hands, lot prices escalated and have averaged around $200,000, reaching a high in 1992 of $245,000.

Resales have maintained their value as well. In the early 1980s, resales actually brought more than developer sales of new lots, but after the KRA acquisition, that was no longer the case. Resales still represented good equity investments for those who had bought during the 1970s and early 1980s. Even though the resort component of Kiawah was progressing through bankruptcy proceedings in the early 1990s, average prices for resales remained fairly comparable to those achieved for new product. KRA was able to compete successfully.

Average prices, however, do not tell the whole story, as oceanfront homesites are much more valuable than other lots. Fairway lots and waterview lots also command a premium. An oceanfront lot that sold in 1976 for $96,000 commands a price in the range of $1.2 million today. In addition, the size of the houses built on oceanfront homesites has increased dramatically since Kiawah's early days. Newer oceanfront houses are as large as 9,000 square feet. As a result, a current issue in siting homes is that lot widths are too narrow to accommodate expanded home sizes. Certainly, the original plan never envisioned 9,000-square-foot homes.

With development focused on the more desirable eastern end of the island, lot prices are anticipated to continue to increase and reflect Kiawah's reputation as a desirable second-home community with a long-

A typical pond villa, a popular rental unit at Kiawah.

entrenched trend of increases in value. Despite rocky times in the early 1990s with KRA's loss of control over Kiawah's amenities, KRA has witnessed a strong sales program with continuing escalation of lot values. Indeed, KRA has been satisfied with its return on investment in Kiawah. Further, its partnership with Morgan Stanley and the equity infused by a strong financial partner have enabled KRA to continue its development of the island's eastern end and to build its own golf course, the River Course, which is the centerpiece of Kiawah's first private club. The new course and club provide potential buyers with certainty regarding golf and club membership, a feature demanded in today's upscale resort communities.

Currently, Kiawah's homeowners hail from 44 states and 23 nations. The typical Kiawah owner is about 50 years old and is a business owner or corporate chief. Only about 20 percent of Kiawah's current owners are retired and either make their permanent home on Kiawah or hold a lot for future construction. Instead, most owners maintain second homes or vacation/seasonal homes on Kiawah. As the typical owner is close to preretirement age, however, Kiawah's properties will most likely become more heavily retirement-oriented in the next ten to 15 years, with a higher percentage of permanent as opposed to vacationing residents.

Lessons Learned

Kiawah's key to success has been its location and the extraordinary beauty of its beach, land, and built environment. Unlike most Atlantic beachfront, which often suffers from erosion, Kiawah's location perpendicular to the coast and unique east/west axis create a stable, accreting beach. Kiawah also enjoys a high ratio of beachfront to land, providing a maximum number of beachfront lots.

Kiawah's buyers have been drawn by the resort's extraordinary natural setting. The island's wide white sand beaches, palms, flowering plants, and live oaks draped with Spanish moss harmonize with the tasteful built environment and together have been critical to Kiawah's success as a resort community. The quality of Kiawah's golf courses and a strong location near Charleston have also contributed to the resort's financial success.

Financial success, particularly at the start of a resort's life, is highly dependent on the project's marketing approach, which demands a deep understanding of the resort's underlying demographics and psychographics. Kiawah profited from a marketing strategy that recognized and responded to the targeted market's underlying demographics.

Kiawah's initial positioning as an affordable resort, in part to deal with the recessionary market of the mid-1970s, proved to be a successful marketing strategy. Kiawah sold extraordinarily well. The resort began with a multifamily component that was affordable as well as sensitively designed to harmonize with Kiawah's unusually beautiful natural environment. The decision to build the resort and conference center in the resort's early days enabled the developers to create a critical mass and build future sales by attracting guests.

Although it seems a truism, one of the key lessons learned at Kiawah is that marketing programs and evidence of continued investment in a resort make the difference in sales. After the Kuwaiti owners ended their major marketing program and discontinued their capital improvements, sales dropped dramatically. Once KRA acquired the resort property and geared up its marketing effort, however, the sales pace accelerated.

Another important lesson to be learned at Kiawah is the significance of maintaining control of key recreational amenities that are critical to the marketability of the community. The decision to sell major golf and resort components seemed to be a good idea at the time, allowing the owner to recapitalize and successfully deal with a significant debt load. It also allowed KRA to bring in an entity with demonstrated experience in resort operations, as resort operations is a markedly different business from land development and lot sales. With the collapse of Landmark and Oak Tree Savings, however, KRA's decision became a major problem and a potential disaster for Kiawah.

Losing control of the golf courses made it more difficult to sell homes or lots—especially during the mid-1980s. The owners could give no assurances to new buyers that they could have access to a golf club and at what cost. It was a tribute to KRA's marketing strategy that the owners held on through troubled times and again achieved solid sales in the late 1980s and early 1990s. In fact, KRA provided a longer-term solution by developing its own golf course and Kiawah's first private club.

Finally, a resort with a long development time frame, spanning more than 20 years to date in Kiawah's case, needs an initial plan and zoning regime that is sufficiently flexible to address the market changes that occur over time and that promotes high-quality residential development. Kiawah's master plan and PUD zoning provided Kiawah with the tools to achieve financial success for its owners.

The Kiawah Island resort community has profited many times over from the original $1.3 million expended on its master plan by the original owners. That investment, which seemed like an extravagant sum at the time for environmental studies and land planning, provided the framework that has made the resort a success today. By the end of the 1980s, Kiawah's master plan, which sited residential areas to take advantage of the island's natural beauty and permitted the development of high-quality golf courses, had positioned Kiawah in the marketplace as an equal of Sea Pines, its forebear.

An aerial view of the island's remote eastern end.

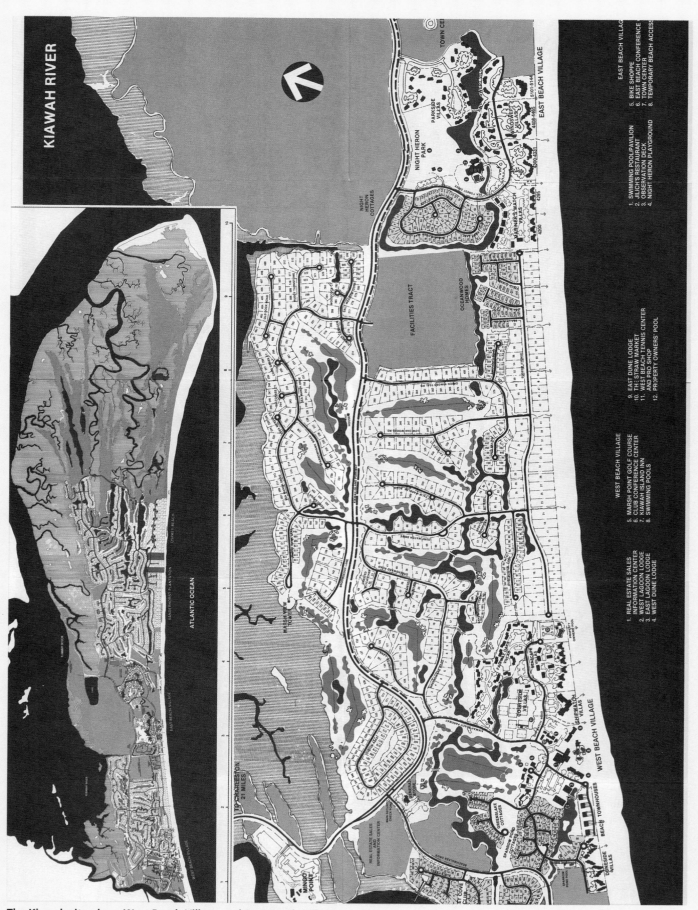

KIAWAH RIVER

KIAWAH ISLAND PLANTATION

ATLANTIC OCEAN

TOWN CENTER

NIGHT HERON COTTAGES

FACILITIES TRACT

NIGHT HERON PARK

PARKSIDE VILLAS

OCEANWOOD HOMES

EAST BEACH VILLAGE

WEST BEACH VILLAGE

WEST BEACH VILLAGE

1. REAL ESTATE SALES
   INFORMATION CENTER
2. WEST LAGOON LODGE
3. EAST LAGOON LODGE
4. WEST DUNE LODGE

5. MARSH POINT GOLF COURSE
6. KLUB CONFERENCE CENTER
7. KIAWAH ISLAND INN
8. SWIMMING POOLS

EAST BEACH VILLAGE

1. SWIMMING POOL/PAVILION
2. JILICH'S RESTAURANT
3. OBSERVATION DECK
4. NIGHT HERON PLAYGROUND

5. BIKE SHOPPE
6. EAST BEACH CONFERENCE
7. TOWN CENTER
8. TEMPORARY BEACH ACCESS

9. EAST DUNE LODGE
10. THE STRAW MARKET
11. WEST BEACH TENNIS CENTER
12. PROPERTY OWNERS' POOL

The Kiawah site plan—West Beach Village and East Beach Village.

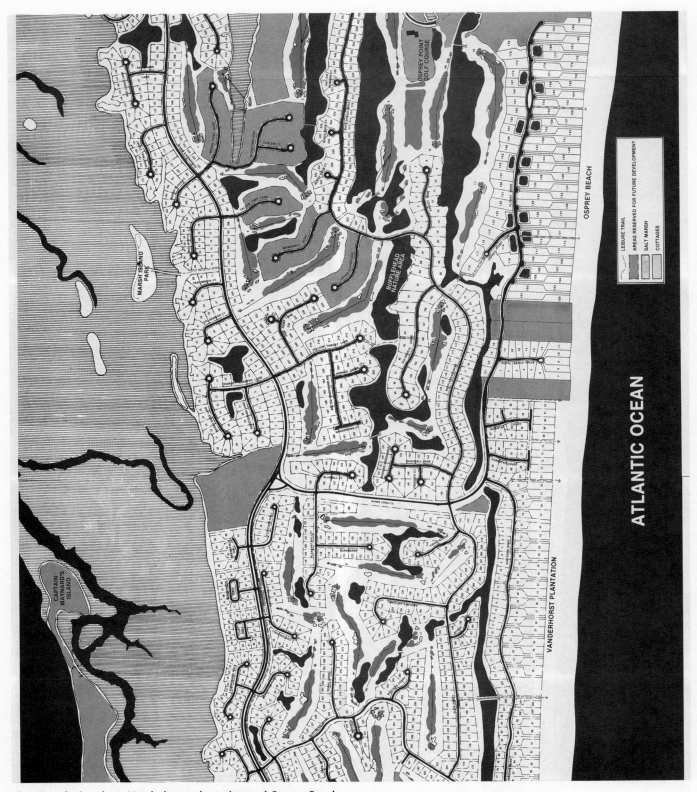

The Kiawah site plan—Vanderhorst plantation and Osprey Beach.

Project Data: Kiawah Island

Land Use Information

Island size	10,000 acres
Developable land	4,500 acres
Wetlands/undevelopable land	5,500 acres
Detached residential	5,500 lots
Number of village centers	2 (East and West Beach Villages)[1]

Amenities Information

Golf Courses

Marsh Point (1976), designed by Gary Player and Ron Kirby

Turtle Point (1981), designed by Jack Nicklaus

Osprey Point (1986), designed by Tom Fazio

The Ocean Course (1991), designed by Pete Dye

The River Course (1996), designed by Tom Fazio

Tennis Centers

East Beach Tennis Club	9 Har-Tru courts, 3 hard courts
West Beach Tennis Club	14 Har-Tru courts, 2 hard courts

Open Space Amenities

Number of ponds or lagoons	65
Miles of beach	10
Miles of leisure trails (paved)	20

Residential Unit Information

Total units planned	5,500

Multifamily Villas

Typical unit size	1–4 bedrooms
Number of units planned/built	1,100/1,000
Range of current sales prices	$100,000–$500,000

Single-Family Units

Typical lot size	20,000 square feet
Typical unit size	3,500 square feet
Number of lots planned/sold	4,400 / 2,400
Number of units planned/sold	4,400 / 1,500
Range of current lot sales prices	$195,000–$260,000
Average number of lots sold annually 1989–1993	97

Hotel Room/Conference Center Information

Number of guest rooms	150

Number of Meeting Rooms

Kiawah Island Inn in West Beach Village	10
East Beach Conference Center in East Beach Village	15

Development Schedule

1974	Site purchased/planning started by Sea Pines Company
1975	Construction started
1976	Sales started
1976	West Beach Village opened
1978	Phase I completed[2]
1981	East Beach Village opened
1988	Kuwait Investment Company sells its interest in Kiawah Island to Kiawah Resort Associates (KRA) for $105 million
1989	KRA sells ownership and management of Kiawah's resort amenities to Landmark Land Company for $35 million
1991	Oak Tree Savings of New Orleans, Landmark's primary bank creditor, fails; Resolution Trust Corporation (RTC) possesses Kiawah amenity deeds
1992	KRA joins partnership with Morgan Stanley Real Estate Fund to undertake further resort residential operations
1993	Virginia Investment Trusts (VIT) acquires Landmark's portion of Kiawah Island's property at an RTC auction for $39 million

Current Owners/Developers

Kiawah Resort Associates
P.O. Box 12001
Charleston, South Carolina 29422
803-768-3400

Virginia Investment Trusts
Richmond, Virginia

Original Developers

Kiawah Island Company
(subsidiary of Kuwait Investment Company)

Land Planners

Sea Pines Company
Hilton Head, South Carolina

EDSA
Alexandria, Virginia

Landscape Planners

Ed Pinkney & Associates
Hilton Head, South Carolina

Sandy Babcock & Associates
San Francisco, California

Notes

[1]East and West Beach Villages constitute less than 10 percent of the island's developable acreage.

[2]Phase I included West Beach Village Inn, Marsh Point Golf Course, 600 condominiums (villas), 600 lots, the West Beach Tennis Club, and the Straw Market commercial complex.

Beaver Creek Resort

Avon, Colorado

Beaver Creek, the 2,777-acre, upscale ski resort adjacent to Vail and developed by Vail Associates, has been under construction since 1978 and continues to be on the cutting edge of ski resort development. Although slow to build momentum in its early stages, the resort has steadily progressed and matured over the past two decades and is now reaching the final stages of development. Beaver Creek has set a high standard for the preservation of unique site characteristics and devised many innovative solutions to the aesthetic, ecological, and traffic-related challenges of ski resort development. It has also developed a land use plan that complements rather than competes with the natural environment.

Beaver Creek enjoys a first-class location, not only for skiing but for other leisure activities as well, and it has enthusiastically pursued the concept of a year-round resort destination. It has developed a variety of lodging types and adopted creative approaches with builders to weather the various economic cycles that have coincided with the development period. With the approval of a master plan amendment that integrates a recent acquisition, plans are underway to develop a pioneering village-to-village ski experience, a concept enjoyed by skiers in Europe but yet to be introduced in the United States.

The four-season mountain resort features numerous recreational amenities, including skiing, golf, and tennis. Currently, the resort encompasses 1,320 residential units (including 121 timeshare units), 471 hotel rooms (including a 295-room Hyatt Regency Hotel), 135,000 square feet of retail space, an 18-hole golf course, and approximately 60 trails on 1,125 acres of skiable terrain, with 11 lifts—three of which are high-speed quad chairlifts. Today, Beaver Creek has a capacity of 9,000 skiers per day. At buildout, approximately 1,600 acres of skiable terrain will accommodate a total of 11,000 skiers per day, with 15 chairlifts.

The Site and Development Process

The U.S. Forest Service targeted Beaver Creek as a ski resort site in the late 1960s. I-70 had been completed through Vail Pass and beyond, and the Eisenhower Tunnel had opened, improving access from Denver, which is 110 miles away. Beaver Creek offered a nearly perfect location, size, and orientation for a first-class ski area. Its broad north-facing slopes drop 3,350 feet to the mountain base before flattening into a gentle stream valley, with ridges affording spectacular views. The valley runs north and south with the

mountains rising to an elevation of 11,500 feet on the southern end.

Vail Associates purchased the Beaver Creek site from a sheep rancher in 1973 but had already initiated preliminary planning in 1971. Their goal was to make Beaver Creek the site of the 1976 Olympic Winter Games. Even though Coloradans voted down the Olympics site, their mandate turned out to work to Beaver Creek's long-term advantage. Without the pressure to build for an Olympics deadline, the resort could take the time to develop in a more thoughtful and environmentally sensitive manner.

In 1976, the Forest Service approved Beaver Creek's ski-area permit, subject to annual review, and the following year gave a green light to the plan. In 1978, after seven years, 52 different state and federal licenses and permits, and an estimated $7 million expended on planning and design, Beaver Creek's planned unit development (PUD) master plan gained approval.

Construction began in Beaver Creek in 1978. By the end of the 1985 season, the resort's ski facilities were about 55 percent completed, with 670 acres of trails completed. Eight chairlifts were in place, ranging from 1,200 to 6,850 linear feet. Beaver Creek was one of the first resorts to install a high-speed, detachable-quad chairlift with an hourly capacity of 2,800 skiers. The lift cut the ride time from the village to the ski areas by more than half. The older lift was relocated to open a new zone of ski terrain. The resort's skiable terrain is now approximately 70 percent completed, with 85 percent of the dwelling units built. Only a few development sites remain, and almost all are now under construction.

Beaver Creek has just completed a major revision to its original master plan to accommodate its final buildout and to integrate the plan with a recently acquired 839-acre adjacent parcel. The original master plan included an area called Upper Bachelor Gulch. Arrowhead, an adjacent resort, owned the lower portion of Bachelor Gulch. In 1993, Vail Associates acquired both Upper Bachelor Gulch and Arrowhead's existing ski areas. The revised plan will connect Arrowhead with Beaver Creek via ski trails through Forest Service property leased by Vail Associates. Bachelor Gulch, a third village between Beaver Creek and Arrowhead, will be added; its lodges will be similar to the typical national park lodges. The result will be a three-village ski area. The revised plan also addressed two other objectives: solving Beaver Creek's pedestrian access problems caused by the village's slope and elevation changes and

Beaver Creek in Avon, Colorado, is a 2,777-acre, four-season multiuse resort community in a majestic mountain setting.

energizing the village by developing new projects to provide gathering places and bring a sense of community to Beaver Creek.

A joint venture project between Vail Associates and East West Partners, called the Village Center, will complete Beaver Creek Village. The plans, with an estimated project cost of $75 million, specify a new ice rink patterned after the Sun Valley Ice Arena, along with about 20,000 square feet of retail shops, covered Alpine escalators similar to those used in European ski areas, a new transit center, and several condominium projects, including a Disney Vacation Club. The plans also call for a 500-seat performing arts center to accommodate concerts, dance performances, movies, theater, and the visual arts. Development of a portion of this project, consisting of 150 residential units and 20,000 square feet of retail space, was underway as of early 1995.

Beaver Creek's daily ski capacity at completion was originally projected at 9,000, as compared to Vail's 12,000. With the addition of Arrowhead and Bachelor Gulch, daily ski capacity is now projected at 11,000 at completion.

In addition to its ski amenities, Beaver Creek has been developed as a year-round resort. Facilities for summer activities include tennis courts, riding stables, fishing lakes, and an 18-hole golf course. The resort's four-season appeal offered financial benefits by extending the resort season and adding value to the residential property—a concept ahead of its time.

Master Planning and Design

Visitors enter the resort at the mouth of the valley. Day visitors park in surface lots near the entrance and are shuttled to the ski area about two miles up the valley. With the valley floor devoted to the golf course and limited housing development sited along the fairways and on overlooking slopes, the high-density resort core nestles between prominent open spaces. The contrast between the village cluster and the surrounding area is highlighted by the absence of large surface parking lots. Below the ski school area at the mountain base is an 18-foot truck service corridor and a 375-space parking garage. Most buildings in the resort core are multiuse structures with ground-floor retail space and accommodations above.

The mountain has 3,350 feet of vertical drop; the village is at an elevation of 8,150 feet, with the highest ski area at 11,500 feet. The master plan calls for about 50 percent of the slopes to be designed for intermediate skiers, 25 percent for beginners, and 25 percent for experienced skiers. The last area is isolated from the other slopes. Originally, the resort accommodated only a limited amount of advanced terrain, but the addition of ski areas at Grouse Mountain in 1991 remedied the situation. In addition, Beaver Creek offers 20 kilometers of groomed cross-country ski tracks at McCoy Park, reached by a chairlift from the base area. Advanced cross-country skiers can telemark their way down to the resort village.

Beaver Creek comprises 471 hotel rooms (including the 295-room Hyatt Regency in the foreground), 1,320 residential units (including 121 timeshare units), and 135,000 square feet of retail space.

The resort is a four-season operation that offers tennis, hiking, fly fishing, golf, mountain biking, hot air ballooning, horse-back riding, and concerts and festivals on the village green as key warm weather recreational activities.

David Lokey

The ski component of Beaver Creek encompasses approximately 60 trails on 1,125 acres of skiable terrain. Three of its 11 lifts are high-speed quad chairlifts. At buildout, there will be approximately 1,600 acres of skiable terrain.

Ken Redding

Jane Lidz

The Hyatt Regency Beaver Creek is a key focal point of the resort, providing 22,341 square feet of retail space and nine penthouse condominiums that were sold to individuals.

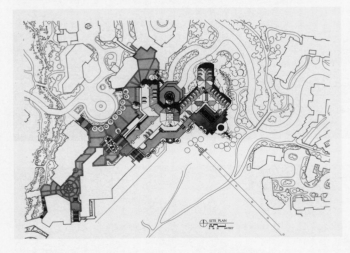

The resort's original master plan was developed as a planned unit development and included 3,223 dwelling units at gross densities ranging from one to 26 dwellings per acre. Only about 275 single-family homesites were planned and 380,000 square feet of commercial space approved for a resort core at the mountain base, where 70 percent of the units were to be sited.

Designing the 18-hole golf course in the narrow mountain valley without creating an undesirable alley effect proved difficult. The clubhouse was sited near the resort core while the holes were strung down the valley in a narrow loop. Golfers play out nine holes and back

nine holes and in the process descend and climb about 450 vertical feet. Rather than allow residential development adjacent to the fairways—a typical design solution to maximize fairway site values—the developer permitted only a small area of large-lot single-family homes to share the edge of the fairway with a heavily wooded creek bed, thereby making the houses less conspicuous. The more valuable residential lots are ski-in-ski-out lots, the equivalent of beachfront lots.

No less than 75 pages of design regulations spelled out Beaver Creek's overall design concept. The guidelines aimed to encourage architecture and outdoor spaces that, from a distance, would appear as a unified, almost indigenous mountain village characterized by simple, strong, and understated forms. The guidelines provided detailed prototypes and guidance on architecture, including roof forms, exterior wall materials and colors, fenestration, walls, and fences. The design blended the simple forms, pitched roofs, and native materials of early valley structures with an Alpine feel. The site planning and landscape design were treated in similar detail. The spatial organization, circulation, and land use patterns of the resort reinforce the Alpine village theme.

Management and Financing

Vail Associates is currently owned by the Apollo Ski Company, a Wall Street investment group. Vail Associates developed the resort community with a combination of private and metropolitan district bond financing. The bonds paid for much of the infrastruc-

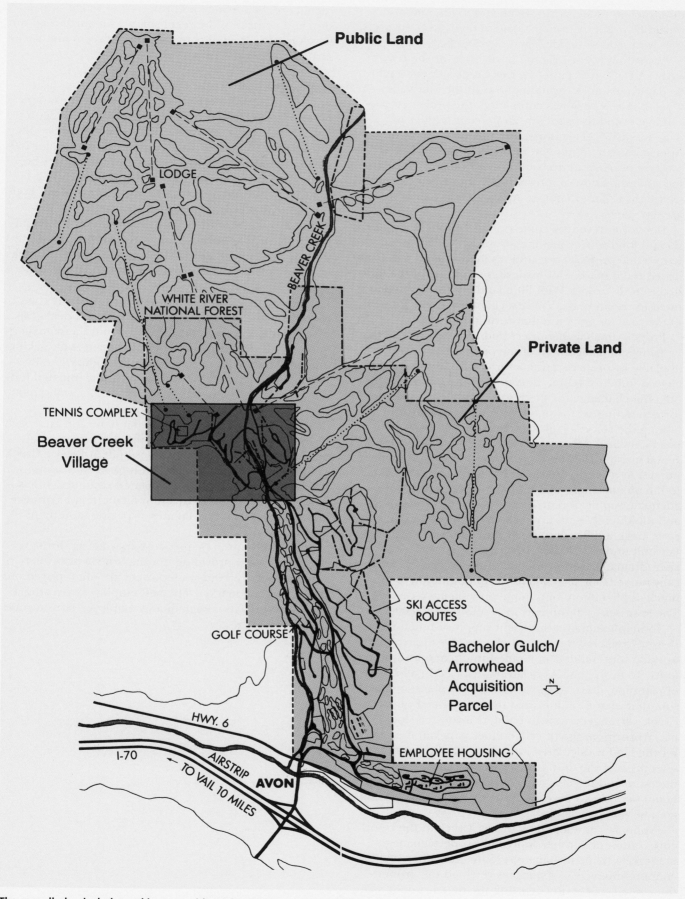

Public Land

Private Land

LODGE

BEAVER CREEK

WHITE RIVER
NATIONAL FOREST

TENNIS COMPLEX

**Beaver Creek
Village**

SKI ACCESS
ROUTES

**Bachelor Gulch/
Arrowhead
Acquisition
Parcel**

N

GOLF COURSE

EMPLOYEE HOUSING

HWY. 6

I-70

AIRSTRIP

TO VAIL 10 MILES

AVON

The overall plan includes a ski area, residential neighborhoods, and the village core.

ture, such as water, storm sewer, and roads, and are repaid by property owners through their property taxes. Lots were sold to builders and developers.

According to the original projection for the resort's early years, 75 percent of Beaver Creek's skiers would be day skiers, not overnight guests in the Vail Valley. Once Beaver Creek was completed, the projected percentage would drop to only 20 percent, similar to Aspen and Vail. This projection has been realized. Approximately 75 percent of skiers in Beaver Creek are now overnight guests in the Vail Valley, representing a combination of international, out-of-state, and overnight Colorado guests. Approximately 25 percent are day skiers.

Developer revenues come primarily from land sales, ski and food service income, property management fees, rental property reservations income, and fees from leased retail space. Vail Associates owns one of the four hotels in the resort. With little land left for development in recent years, Vail Associates has plowed much of the revenue back into improving the resort.

Property management fees and reservations income come from management of the pool of units made available by property owners for rental. Keeping a sufficient number of rental units in the pool has been an ongoing challenge for the resort. Rentals are essential for generating ski income, which is necessary for maintaining the resort's high standards. Empty beds do not produce skiers. Many owners, however, do not need rental income and therefore prefer not to rent their homes. As a result, the resort has had to pay attention to the mix of single- and multifamily units to ensure an adequate supply of rental units. While the mid-priced and multifamily units are most likely to rent, high land costs make it difficult to build these units or keep costs per unit under $400,000. In fact, property values have risen dramatically over the life of the resort. Prices typically range from $500,000 for a condominium to as much as $5 million for a home on a ski-in-ski-out lot. The lowest-priced unit currently sells for $350,000.

To help maintain a sufficient supply of rental units, Beaver Creek has implemented a creative approach to working with builders of condominium and townhouse units. To begin, Vail Associates is involved in all aspects of planning, down to the review of floorplans, to make sure that what is built is what the resort needs. Beaver Creek's arrangement with builders involves a "look-back" provision: the price a builder pays Vail Associates for the land is calculated at 15 percent of the estimated sales price of the unit. If the unit sells for more than the estimated price, which commonly occurred in boom periods, 15 percent of the excess sales price also goes to Vail Associates.

Properties developed by Beaver Creek in the resort's core represent another source of property management fees. While upstairs residential units were sold as condominiums, Vail Associates retained the ground-floor retail spaces. Recognizing the time it would take to reach the critical mass sufficient to maintain a lively retail core, Vail Associates preferred to retain ownership and control of the retail spaces, which allowed the developer the flexibility to provide the retail mix necessary to support the resort's ambience.

Lessons Learned

Beaver Creek Resort provides an excellent example of how careful and flexible initial planning can see a resort successfully through a series of economic cycles. Beaver Creek's master plan did not require a major amendment until almost 20 years into the resort's life. At this juncture, the interests of the developer, Vail Associates, needed to be balanced against those of both the Beaver Creek homeowners' association and surrounding county residents. Through careful communication, participants found solutions that preserved the initially determined density but provided Beaver Creek with the flexibility to move that density to other locations to meet the resort's goals and vision.

Beaver Creek continues its success as a resort community in part because it plows back a great deal of its revenue into improving the ski areas and the ski experience. It invests heavily in the most current snowmaking and grooming equipment and ski lift equipment. By introducing quads early, for example, it eliminated long queuing times. It also has benefited from a well-capitalized owner in the Apollo Ski Company.

Vail Associates has maintained a hands-on approach in the disposition of its residential and commercial parcels to make sure that what is built at Beaver Creek enhances the overall resort and improves its bottom line in terms of potential ski-related revenues. It has paid great attention to detail in facilitating a cohesive architectural style that creates a specific mountain ambience.

It is important to be proactive in working through the problems of providing housing for ski resort personnel in an area where employees are often priced out of the housing market. The best employees are attracted to a resort with a high-quality employee housing and amenity package.

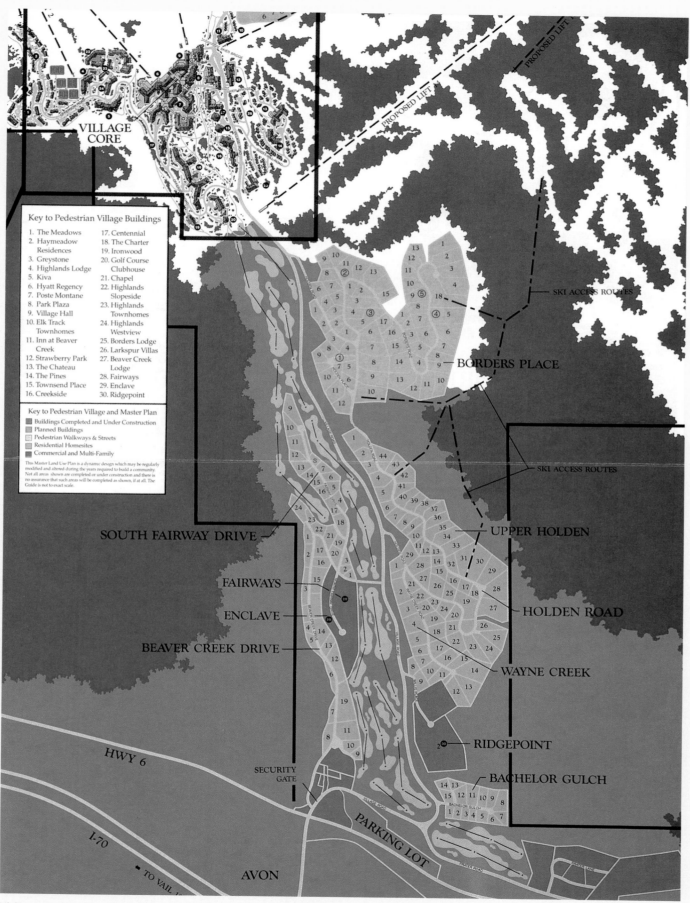

Visitors receive this orientation map, highlighting the residential lots and the golf course.

Key to Pedestrian Village Buildings

1. The Meadows
2. Haymeadow Residences
3. Greystone
4. Highlands Lodge
5. Kiva
6. Hyatt Regency
7. Poste Montane
8. Park Plaza
9. Village Hall
10. Elk Track Townhomes
11. Inn at Beaver Creek
12. Strawberry Park
13. The Chateau
14. The Pines
15. Townsend Place
16. Creekside

17. Centennial
18. The Charter
19. Ironwood
20. Golf Course Clubhouse
21. Chapel
22. Highlands Slopeside
23. Highlands Townhomes
24. Highlands Westview
25. Borders Lodge
26. Larkspur Villas
27. Beaver Creek Lodge
28. Fairways
29. Enclave
30. Ridgepoint

Key to Pedestrian Village and Master Plan

Buildings Completed and Under Construction
Planned Buildings
Pedestrian Walkways & Streets
Residential Homesites
Commercial and Multi-Family

This Master Land Use Plan is a dynamic design which may be regularly modified and altered during the years required to build a community. Not all areas shown are completed or under construction and there is no assurance that such areas will be completed as shown, if at all. The Guide is not to exact scale.

VILLAGE CORE

PROPOSED LIFT

SKI ACCESS ROUTES

BORDERS PLACE

SKI ACCESS ROUTES

SOUTH FAIRWAY DRIVE

UPPER HOLDEN

FAIRWAYS

HOLDEN ROAD

ENCLAVE

BEAVER CREEK DRIVE

WAYNE CREEK

HWY 6

RIDGEPOINT

SECURITY GATE

BACHELOR GULCH

I-70

PARKING LOT

TO VAIL

AVON

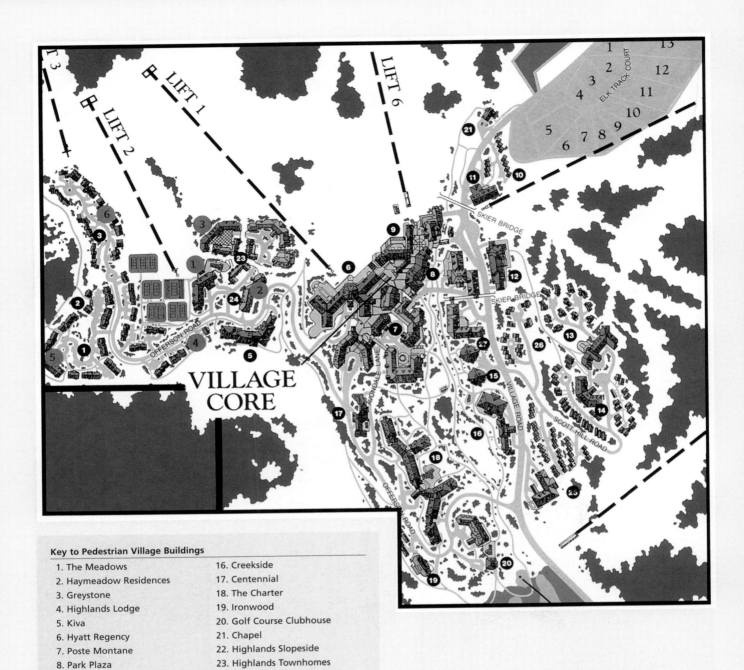

Key to Pedestrian Village Buildings

1. The Meadows
2. Haymeadow Residences
3. Greystone
4. Highlands Lodge
5. Kiva
6. Hyatt Regency
7. Poste Montane
8. Park Plaza
9. Village Hall
10. Elk Track Townhomes
11. Inn at Beaver Creek
12. Strawberry Park
13. The Chateau
14. The Pines
15. Townsend Place
16. Creekside
17. Centennial
18. The Charter
19. Ironwood
20. Golf Course Clubhouse
21. Chapel
22. Highlands Slopeside
23. Highlands Townhomes
24. Highlands Westview
25. Borders Lodge
26. Larkspur Villas
27. Beaver Creek Lodge
28. Fairways
29. Enclave
30. Ridgepoint

The Beaver Creek village core.

Project Data: Beaver Creek Resort

Land Use Information

Site area	2,777 acres
Total dwelling units allowed	3,223
Total dwelling units planned	2,083
Total dwelling units built	1,791
Gross density	0.9 dwelling units per acre
Average net density (net of golf course, open space, roads)	0.2 dwelling units per acre

Land Use Plan

	Acres	Percent of Site
Low-density residential	359	12.9%
Medium-density residential	16	0.6%
High-density residential	22	0.8%
Resort commercial	64	2.3%
Resort services	35	1.3%
Golf course	131	4.7%
Open space[1]	2,055	74.0%
Roads	95	3.4%
Total	2,777	100.0%

Residential/Hotel Unit Information

Unit Type	Units Planned/Built	Current Price Range[2]
Single-family/cluster home	204/166	$400,000–$1,600,000 per lot
Condominium/townhouse	1,187/1,033	$200–$700 per square foot
Timeshare (three properties built)	221/121	$1,000–$25,000 per interval week
Hotel rooms (four properties built)	471/471	$100–$400 per day
Total	2,083/1,791	

Development Schedule

1971	Site purchased
1973	Planning started
1977	Construction started
1978	Sales started
1978	First closing

Development Cost Information (to 1995)[3]

Site Acquisition Cost	$9,100,000

Site Improvement Costs

Water	$5,600,000
Roads/storm sewer	7,500,000
Communications	1,800,000
Fire station/equipment	800,000
Total	$15,700,000

Construction Costs

Incurred by developer	$72,400,000
Incurred by others	466,000,000
Total	$538,400,000

Ski-Area Development Costs

Trails, lifts, snowmaking	$34,800,000
Lodge (for skiers only)	8,000,000
Total	$42,800,000

Golf Course Development Costs

Construction and irrigation	$2,500,000
Clubhouse	2,300,000
Total	$4,800,000

Total Development Cost (to 1995)	$610,800,000

Developer

Vail Associates Real Estate Group
P.O. Box 959
Avon, Colorado 81620
303-845-2535

Planners

Vail Associates
Avon, Colorado

Various consultants

Notes

[1]Includes a portion of Beaver Creek Ski Mountain. This portion contains on-mountain recreational lodging facilities, mountain restaurants and picnic decks, and private club/restaurant facilities.

[2]Ranges include both off-season and high-season rates for hotel and timeshares. Ranges are large because of variety of home options.

[3]Some costs are developer estimates.

Kapalua
Maui, Hawaii

Kapalua is an upscale, self-contained, master-planned resort community set amid a 23,000-acre privately owned pineapple plantation. It is located on the scenic northwest coast of Maui, approximately a one-hour drive from Maui's main airport in Kahului and a five-minute drive from the Kapalua–West Maui Airport. It has been developed as a destination resort on 1,500 acres along three miles of shoreline, of which 3,700 feet are prime beach frontage on the Pacific Ocean, including several bays. The land consists of sloping hills and valleys, with elevations ranging from sea level to approximately 750 feet.

A primary focus of the resort has been the development of condominiums, or villas, in addition to resort hotels and single-family fee-simple homesites. The single-family owners provide the resort with the stability of long-term occupancy and add profitable land use alternatives to high-density resort hotel and commercial uses.

Kapalua stands as a model for contemporary resort development in that it is an exclusive resort whose design is highly sensitive to its surrounding natural environment. It has successfully preserved the natural contours of the land without mass grading and has taken advantage of the existing plantation roads to create the framework for a unified design, which is a harmonious blend of the site's natural beauty and the land uses necessary for the resort's success. No megahotels make exotic statements at Kapalua; instead, the hotels complement rather than compete with the ocean frontage.

Today, Kapalua includes three world-class resort properties—the Ritz-Carlton Kapalua, the Kapalua Bay Hotel and Villas, and the Kapalua Villas—as well as seven residential communities, three championship golf courses, two tennis centers, three white sand beaches, and specialty shopping. The community is about 50 percent completed.

The Site and Development Process
In the late 1800s, Kapalua was part of Honolua Ranch, an agricultural operation noted for its taro patches, coffee beans, and cattle. At the turn of the century, Maui businessman H.P. Baldwin acquired the ranch. He planted pineapple as well as a variety of other crops (macadamia, mango, aloe, corn) and hundreds of trees, including Cook and Norfolk pines. Colin Cameron, a fifth-generation descendant of Baldwin, founded the Kapalua resort. His conservation mentality led to extraordinarily sensitive environmental and site planning.

The resort is now owned and managed by the developer, Kapalua Land Company, Ltd., a subsidiary of Maui Land & Pineapple Company, Inc. The company set out to create a high-quality, self-contained, full-destination resort with a unified design and carefully planned mix of facilities targeted primarily to the free independent traveler and high-quality tour groups. Planned components included luxury hotel accommodations, attached and detached housing, golf, tennis, beach/ocean recreation, restaurants, and shops. Free, resortwide shuttle service was considered essential. The project has been developed in two major phases.

Phase I: 1964 to 1985. The first phase of the project was developed over a 21-year period, with construction and sales beginning in 1975. The resort currently consists of the following:

- Kapalua Bay Hotel and Villas, a 194-room hotel with an open-air configuration of rooms and suites as well as 100 one- and two-bedroom villas. The complex is noted for the Point, which, with its butterfly-shaped pool and dramatic ocean panoramas, is a popular site for weddings. Its amenities include private-room lanais, afternoon tea service, complimentary in-room videos, year-round children's programs, whale/ocean lectures, an exercise room, and two hours' complimentary use of watersports equipment at Kapalua Bay on a daily basis. In 1995, the developer sold the project to KBH Operations Limited Partnership.
- Condominium Villas, four separate projects totaling 488 units, including the Bay Villas, 141 one- and two-bedroom units on 16.5 acres, completed in 1977; the Golf Villas, 186 one- and two-bedroom units on 15.8 acres, completed in 1979; the Ridge Villas, 161 one- and two-bedroom units on 22 acres, completed in 1980; and the Ironwoods, 40 units in ten plantation-style buildings with four homes in each building, completed in 1980 on 9.2 acres.
- Pineapple Hill, 99 single-family, fee-simple detached homesites on 45.5 acres, first made available in 1985 and sold out by 1987.

Phase I amenities include two 18-hole golf courses designed by Arnold Palmer—the 6,600-yard Bay Course, which opened in 1975, and the 6,632-yard Village Course, which opened in 1980; the Tennis Garden, with ten courts, four of them lighted for night play, which opened in 1979; and the Kapalua Shops, a 40,000-

Kapalua is a 1,500-acre community that offers an outstanding setting for a destination resort, including an oceanfront location in Hawaii and three golf courses.

square-foot boutique shopping center adjacent to the Kapalua Bay Hotel, completed in 1979.

Phase II: 1986 to present. The second and more recent phase of development includes

- Kapalua Place, eight fee-simple, single-family home-sites in a private, gated oceanfront community on 8.9 acres. First offered in 1989, the sites sold out in one year.
- Plantation Estates, 36 fee-simple, single-family home-sites in a private, gated golf community on 108.4 acres. First offered for sale in 1990, the sites are nearly sold out.
- The 550-room Ritz-Carlton Kapalua hotel, opened in late 1992. It is owned by the Maui Land & Pineapple Company, Nissho Iwai, and the Ritz-Carlton Hotel Company and operated by Ritz-Carlton. Situated on 37 acres, the hotel is bordered by a white sand beach and the Bay Course. It features an open-air configuration of oceanfront rooms and suites, including 58 executive suites and two Ritz-Carlton suites. All guest rooms have spacious lanais. The hotel also has a 10,000-square-foot,

three-level swimming pool with a 20,000-square-foot sun deck; over 30,000 square feet of meeting space; a 165-seat theater; a private lounge serving continental breakfast, afternoon tea, cocktails, and after-dinner cordials; and five restaurants.

Phase II amenities include the Plantation Course, an 18-hole, 7,263-yard championship course designed by Bill Coore and Ben Crenshaw, which opened in 1991 and is the heart of Plantation Estates; a 33,000-square-foot clubhouse with a full-service golf shop, men's and women's locker facilities, and a restaurant, which also opened in 1991; and the Village Tennis Center, a landscaped tennis complex located on the oceanfront lawns of the Ritz-Carlton Kapalua hotel, which opened at the end of 1992 and includes ten courts, half of them lighted for night play.

Master Planning and Design

At Kapalua, developers used low-rise, low-density construction to blend with the site's natural contours. The unified design is distinctive yet appropriate to both the site and the Hawaiian islands. Rules adopted for each

The three-mile Kapalua coastline includes several bays, some rocky terrain, and 3,700 feet of prime beach frontage.

segment of the resort control design and construction as well as the selection of architects. The design and construction rules for each community are part of the declaration of covenants, conditions, and restrictions for that community.

In Pineapple Hill, for example, design standards define the general style as cascading hipped-roof forms with strong overhanging masses composed of basic earthtone colors that blend into the natural setting. Consistency of roof form and restraint in use of materials and color are central design elements. Grading is minimal, and buildings are "stair stepped" with the existing contours.

Condominiums at Pineapple Hill are developed in small clusters and sited for maximum orientation toward views. In addition to ocean views, the site offers many attractive nonocean views of the adjoining land, which is still used for pineapple farming. Forestland and watersheds provide mountain vistas as well. Careful placement of buildings ensures natural air circulation and protection from wind. The covenants and design review regulations specify continuing site planning guidelines that ensure maximum view orientation for each residence.

The design guidelines for Plantation Estates require homeowners to use informal landscaping such as cascading vines to soften retaining walls. The guidelines

also require residents to ensure that buildings and trees—except for the historic Norfolk pines—do not exceed 35 feet in height in deference to views. Homeowners may use a limited variety of plants to establish their lots' overall landscape theme, which must reinforce the character of the golf course within a transitional area between the golf course and the residences. Gulches—defined as densely vegetated land with slopes of 20 percent or greater and inaccessible without major landform adjustments—require protection; they may not be altered without the written approval of the design review committee.

The plan leaves sensitive areas undeveloped, greatly enhancing the development's environmental setting. An ancient burial ground has been preserved as well as Pu'u Kukui, an 8,661-acre rare native rainforest. Situated above Kapalua in the West Maui Mountains, the rainforest is home to three native bird species, five rare snail species, and 12 natural communities. In 1992, Colin Cameron granted the Nature Conservancy of Hawaii a permanent easement over the native forest, creating the state's largest private nature preserve. In 1978, the state declared Honolua and Mokuleia Bays marine life conservation districts and, in an effort to protect Maui's unique ocean resources, prohibited fishing in the bays.

Overlooking Kapalua Bay, the Kapalua Bay Hotel and Villas—comprising 194 hotel rooms and 100 villas—remain the centerpiece of the resort.

Located in scenic enclaves throughout the resort, Kapalua's villas are characterized by low-density development, with architectural designs created to complement the terrain.

Management and Marketing

The wide variety of Kapalua's hotel, residential, and recreational offerings has led to a complex resort operation—made up of numerous operating entities—and a detailed merchandising plan. For example, Kapalua Bay Hotel and Villas is owned and managed by the KBH Operations Limited Partnership, which acquired the property from the developer in 1985; the latter continues to own the land and leases it to the hotel. Other villa rentals are managed by the Kapalua Land Company. Their amenities include privileges at the Ritz-Carlton Kapalua hotel, including the Ritz Kids program, spa, and pool. All villas at Kapalua are individually owned.

The Kapalua Land Company owns the three golf courses, which are open to the public. The Kapalua Club, a nonequity club managed by the developer, gives priority to members and resort guests, who are allowed to book tee times in advance of other players. Golf play among members and owners accounts for only about 7 percent of golf activity and 20 percent of tennis activity. Golf play among resort guests represents about 50 percent. The balance is attributable to visitors staying off the resort and to the local community.

The Kapalua Club offers three classes of membership: resort, golf, and corporate. Resort memberships are available for purchase by resort property owners; in addition, a limited number (at present not to exceed 100) is available for nonproperty owners. Initiation fees are moderate—$500 for property owners and $1,000 for nonproperty owners. Annual dues are currently $150 for property owners, $300 for nonproperty owners. Resort privileges include beach and pool facilities with payment of equipment rental fees, complimentary tennis court fees, a year-round calendar of member activities, advance golf reservations at reduced fees, eligibility for spa memberships at the Ritz-Carlton Kapalua hotel, and discounts on the published rack rate for resort properties and on restaurant charges.

Golf memberships may be purchased by a limited number of resort property owners (at present not to exceed 100) and nonproperty owners (at present not to exceed 50). The initiation fee is currently $8,500 for property owners and $14,000 for nonproperty owners; 80 percent of the fee is refundable if a replacement member is found. Golf privileges include resort membership, complimentary greens fees at the golf courses, seven-day advance reservations at the Bay and Village Courses, ten-day advance reservations at the Plantation Course, complimentary privileges at the two practice ranges, and reduced lesson and other fees.

Kapalua provides a good example of how a new destination-resort community is by nature a long-term undertaking that requires significant resources and a

The 6,632-yard Village Course, which opened in 1980, climbs into the West Maui Mountains, 750 feet above sea level.

financial partner with staying power. Even though Kapalua had to develop most of its infrastructure, the resort has achieved financial success. In the mid-1970s, the developer had to absorb significant design, infrastructure, and carrying costs. Revenues from resort operations and lot sales did not offset expenses until Kapalua achieved reasonable maturity in the mid-1990s. Only then did the developer break even on the initial resort infrastructure.

In 1994, approximately one-third of the developer's resort operations revenues came from golf and tennis fees, one-fourth from retail sales, about 15 percent from condominium rentals, 8 percent from commercial leases, 6 percent from membership and utility company income, and 15 percent from other sources.

The hotels sold off by the developer have experienced numerous ups and downs. The Kapalua Bay Hotel and Villas opened in 1979. From then until the complex's sale in 1985, occupancy ranged from 54 percent to 68 percent, and the hotel did not operate at a profit. The property had three good years from 1986 to 1989, with occupancy rates reaching 87 percent. After 1989, however, a glut of high-end room inventory on Maui and in Hawaii in general, coupled with poor economic growth, resulted in low occupancy and losses.

Since the Ritz-Carlton Kapalua hotel opened, occupancy has averaged 58 percent. The hotel has consistently generated positive cash flow from operations before debt service. However, the cash flow has not been sufficient to cover debt service on the mortgage; the hotel is currently restructuring its debt.

Kapalua's residential component provides an additional revenue source. In the resort's early days, investors bought many of the villas and lots. Recently, however, the trend has shifted toward owner-occupancy. Oceanfront lots are the most valuable sites, with two-third-acre lots at Kapalua Place currently selling for between $2.5 million and $2.8 million. The price of golf course frontage lots varies, but Pineapple Hill's predominantly quarter-acre lots sell for approximately $450,000. Lots in Plantation Estates have been selling for about $1 million per acre, with lot sizes of two or more acres. Comparing prices among developments is difficult. Each development is unique, and lot sizes vary in keeping with Kapalua's hallmark land plan in which lots are shaped by and complement the terrain.

Lot sales and housing prices climbed until the recession of the early 1990s, when they began to fall. As of 1995, however, they had stabilized. Over the last two years, sales averages in Pineapple Hill have been up by 45 percent over original prices.

Kapalua capitalizes on its extraordinary environmental setting by providing ecovacation packages, a recent trend in the resort business. In 1993, it launched Eco Resort Shuttle Tours to highlight Kapalua's environmental and preservation efforts.

The 33,000-square-foot Plantation Clubhouse and Golf Course, overlooking the Pacific Ocean, was opened in 1991.

Lessons Learned

Kapalua provides a good example of how environmentally sensitive planning and design enforced by covenants and design review standards and procedures ultimately translates into financially rewarding investments. However, the time required for financial success can extend for several years. Kapalua Land Company was fortunate that its parent company, Maui Land & Pineapple Company, Inc., was well capitalized and had the financial staying power necessary to provide upfront planning and infrastructure years before construction could begin. It could also weather the long period before sufficient revenues enabled the resort to break even.

The resort also provides a good lesson in how important it is for self-contained destination resorts to create diverse environments that include residential components. Kapalua's residential component stabilized the resort and created additional business for resort operations. Resort components, in turn, supported and fed the marketing effort for the residential lots, helping generate a greater market for luxury housing and multimillion-dollar estates, important profit centers for the resort.

The developer's decision to undertake maximum-quality environmental planning has paid handsome dividends as reflected in the final product. Kapalua's incomparable natural features have benefited from the ongoing requirements for high-quality design. The resort's harmonious relationship with its surroundings and the company's stewardship of the land have played a large part in enhancing the value of residential real estate in Kapalua. Kapalua's developer chose a path that differs dramatically from that of Maui's other megahotels and has proven that environmentally sensitive land planning translates into unparalleled results that withstand the test of time.

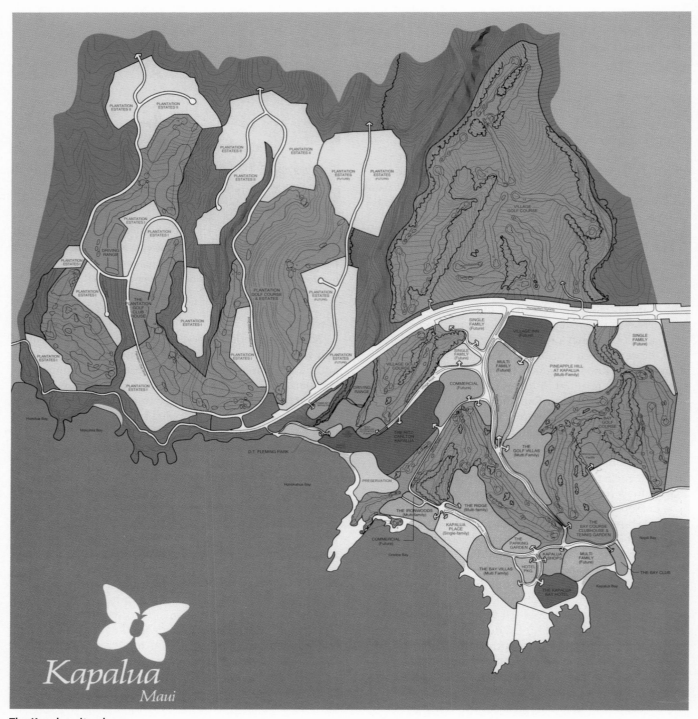

The Kapalua site plan.

Project Data: Kapalua

Land Use Plan

	Acres
Detached residential	205
Attached/multifamily residential	260
Hotel	85
Golf courses	550
Roads	50
Common open space	300
Commercial	15
Other	35
Total	1,500

Hotel Information

Number of separate hotels planned	3
Number of separate hotels completed	2
Total hotel rooms planned	1,380
Total hotel rooms completed	744
Average daily room rate	$250
Average annual occupancy rate	60%

Development Schedule

Early 1900s	Site purchased
1964	Planning started
1975	Construction started
1975	Sales started
1977	Bay Villas completed
1979	Golf Villas completed
1980	Ridge Villas completed
1980	Ironwoods completed
1987	Pineapple Hill completed
1989	Kapalua Place completed
1990	Plantation Estates I completed
1995	Percent completed (50 percent)

Developer

Kapalua Land Company, Ltd.
(subsidiary of Maui Land & Pineapple Company, Inc.)
1000 Kapalua Drive
Kapalua, Maui, Hawaii 96761
808-669-5622

Site Planner

Belt Collins and Associates
680 Ala Moana Boulevard, Suite 200
Honolulu, Hawaii 96813
808-521-5361

Residential Unit Information (1995)

Completed Areas	Acres	Lot Size (square feet)	Unit Type	Number of Units Planned/Built	Range of Sales Prices
Bay Villas	16.5	1,560	Multifamily	141/141	$370,000–$950,000
Golf Villas	15.8	1,500	Multifamily	186/186	$300,000–$460,000
Ridge Villas	22.0	1,650	Multifamily	161/161	$295,000–$460,000
Ironwoods	9.2	2,520	Multifamily	40/40	NA
Pineapple Hill	45.5	11,000	Single-family	99/99	$212,500–$430,000[1]
Kapalua Place	8.9	43,800	Single-family	8/8	NA
Plantation Estates I	22.5	113,000	Single-family	36/36	$585,000–$950,000
Total residential units				671/671	

Notes

NA = not available.

[1] Price for lots only. Homes typically sell for around $1.15 million.

Hidden Valley Four Seasons Resort

Hidden Valley, Pennsylvania

Hidden Valley Four Seasons Resort provides an early example of an accelerating trend in resort communities: a resort that offers activities for all seasons, a "lifestyle resort." It also illustrates the trend toward upgrading, expanding, and diversifying older resort facilities.

Hidden Valley was a small country inn with a weekend ski slope and a small adjacent subdivision when it was purchased in 1983 from its original owner by Kettler Brothers, Inc. (KBI), a Washington, D.C.-based builder of residential communities. Hidden Valley was well located, in their view, in the mountains of Somerset County, Pennsylvania, about 60 miles southeast of Pittsburgh.

KBI conceived of a full-fledged resort community and planned to augment the primary recreational amenity—skiing—with a range of year-round recreational activities, including golf and tennis, and a conference center to attract demand for resort rentals and recreational facilities, especially in the nonwinter months. It was a concept that has lived up to its expectations. Today, Hidden Valley is a successful year-round resort community that includes lodging, second homes, and primary homes for year-round residents.

Hidden Valley provides a good example of how smaller, older ski resorts can diversify their income stream by turning to real estate development, thereby tapping markets and revenue sources that may have gone previously overlooked. Skiing by itself is a seasonal and highly variable source of revenue. Especially in the eastern United States, where adjacent land is more likely to be privately owned, ski resort owners may have access to additional acreage that can support the transition from ski area to year-round resort and residential community.

The Site and Development Process

Hidden Valley is a resort community of approximately 2,000 acres located about an hour southeast of Pittsburgh. It is adjacent to roughly 25,000 acres of public land. Its location allows the resort to tap a multistate regional market, as it is approximately 200 miles from major urban areas in Pennsylvania, Ohio, Maryland, New York, and the District of Columbia.

Since the early 1950s, a small country inn had been operating on the site. Intrigued by the growing popularity of downhill skiing in the late 1950s, the innkeepers opened the first ski slopes and lift in 1958. A small subdivision followed and, in 1977, the first vacation townhouse project opened; the latter was constructed in part

due to the efforts of a KBI executive who had built a vacation home in the resort.

KBI acquired the property in 1983. Given the relatively low land cost, the developer formulated a plan with an unusually low gross density of about two dwelling units per acre. Together with the adjacent 25,000 acres of public land, the property's low density gives the resort a rural and isolated feel despite its proximity to Pittsburgh.

The centerpiece of KBI's strategy at Hidden Valley was the resort's transformation from a single-season recreational facility with limited real estate operations to a four-season resort and conference center with a wide variety of real estate products and recreational amenities. Specifically, KBI targeted golf as a critical amenity, with the hope of putting it on an equal footing with skiing as a marketing draw. At the same time, KBI planned to expand and improve Hidden Valley's traditional strength—skiing—to help support the development of the residential resort community. More recently, mountain biking has become a major activity at the resort.

At the outset, KBI projected that the resort, when completed, would include an 18-hole golf course, a conference center, a doubling of ski capacity, and numerous other recreational facilities that would support the approximately 3,000 housing units planned for the property. By 1989, KBI had constructed approximately 500 housing units and had completed the golf course, cross-country ski trails, and many of the recreational facilities. As of 1991, the project included 213 hotel rooms of 460 planned and 960 residential units of 3,000 planned. By 1995, approximately 1,000 units had been sold, with the resort one-third built out.

The conference center, a critical element of the four-season strategy, could handle groups of up to 200 when KBI purchased the resort. In the late 1980s, KBI expanded the center to its current configuration, which can accommodate groups of up to 400 people.

Master Planning and Design

Hidden Valley's respect for its natural setting and environment has been a strong guiding principle in its development. Rather than dramatically changing the natural beauty of the landscape to make way for homes, the developer has adapted the residential and recreational development to the setting.

The plan includes several primary sectors. A cross-country ski center, including shops and dining and several lakes and trails, is located near the entrance and

Following acquisition of the resort in 1983, the developer's central strategy at Hidden Valley has been to transform the resort from a single-season recreational facility with limited real estate operations to a four-season resort and conference center with a wide variety of real estate products and recreational amenities. Pictured is the inn and conference center area.

just off Route 31, which provides the primary access to the resort. The entrance road leads to the inn and conference center area—located adjacent to a lake on the northern side of the property—that includes the Four Seasons Inn, the conference center, a health club, swimming pool, restaurant and lounge, gift shop, and fishing and boating docks.

Farther into the site to the south is the lodge at the base of the primary ski slope. The base area features a restaurant and lounge, a cafeteria, the snowmaking headquarters, ski rentals and tickets, a ski shop, and the

ski school. Seven lifts serve 14 slopes from the base location while another crossover lift leads to three additional slopes served by one additional chairlift. Residences are located between the two slope areas.

Still farther into the site, in the southwestern sector, is the primary residential area developed to date, including a variety of townhouse and detached products, some of which are adjacent to the golf course. Residential areas completed or under development include Stonewood, South Ridge, Powder Ridge, Eagle's Ridge, the Fairways, the Highlands, Alpine Woods, and the Summit. The objective guiding the residential areas has been to develop a high-quality second-home environment by using the finest materials and providing a consistent "look" while creating a variety of unique homes that appeal to different tastes. Several small lakes are interspersed throughout the residential areas.

The golf course is widely spread out through a heavily wooded area on the southern and southeastern portions of the property. It roughly follows a double-necklace pattern, with the clubhouse located near the center of the course; a tennis club is located just to the north of the clubhouse.

As with many resort developments, the appropriate handling of domestic wastewater treatment was a concern. To treat wastewater in the most environmentally sound manner, Hidden Valley has relied on a "spray-irrigation" system. Though more expensive than traditional systems that discharge treated water into streams and rivers, the spray-irrigation system has beneficial environmental impacts on the forest ecosystem. The system's "living filter" process creates increased habitat and food

The golf course spreads widely through a heavily wooded area on the southern and southeastern portions of the property in a rough double-necklace pattern, with the golf clubhouse located near the center of the course.

supply for wildlife, encourages tree and shrub growth, and recharges groundwater with clean water by recycling water within the same aquifer.

Recreational Amenities

In the early days of KBI's development, the ski resort featured 11 slopes, which supported an estimated daily capacity of 5,000 skiers. Considering the relatively modest area of skiable terrain, the resort's lift capacity was fairly high. Four chairlifts, including a high-capacity dual-triple lift, moved skiers quickly. The total vertical drop of 511 feet was typical for the region. About half the skiable terrain was dedicated to intermediate skiers, 30 percent to beginners, and 20 percent to expert skiers.

By 1995, the resort community had almost doubled its ski capacity and now boasts 17 slopes and eight lifts that support an estimated daily capacity of 6,500 skiers. Today, intermediate terrain accounts for 35 percent of the skiable terrain, beginner terrain for another 35 percent, and expert terrain for 30 percent. The vertical drop has increased to 610 feet, expanding the number of expert trails. In addition to downhill skiing, the resort currently maintains 20 miles of cross-country ski trails linked to 20 additional miles of state trails.

A major new feature at Hidden Valley is its upgraded 18-hole championship golf course. Situated atop the resort's 3,000-foot summit, the Golf Club at Hidden Valley is designed to capture the beauty of its mountaintop setting. Golf course architect Russell Roberts designed the course along the natural fall line, taking advantage of 30-mile vistas. The par-72 course includes 6,579 sprawling yards with none of the course's narrow tree-lined fairways running parallel. The course was targeted to fill a gap between the relatively low-quality public courses nearby and the exclusive private clubs in the area. The Golf Club's amenities include a full-service pro shop, golf cart and club rental, a driving range, and putting green and chipping area as well as the Clubhouse Bar and Grill.

Since the golf course was first built in 1988–1989, it has undergone renovations, including the upgrading of tees and lengthening of some holes to make the course more challenging. The Keystone Public Golf Association, an affiliate of the United States Golf Association, gave the renovated course a new rating of 142. The Pennsylvania courses that host the U.S. Open and the Senior PGA Tour are rated at 143.

Hidden Valley has joined the recent "ecotrend" in golf course design and is now registered with the Audubon Cooperative Sanctuary System. It is currently working toward certification in several achievement categories, including environmental planning, public involvement, integrated pest management, wildlife food enhancement, wildlife cover enhancement, water conservation, and water enhancement.

The resort's other amenities are designed for both conference center guests and the residential and resort family market. The inn and conference center complex houses the Sports Club, which offers year-round indoor

The resort includes 85 acres of skiable terrain, 17 slopes, eight lifts, and a vertical drop of 610 feet.

recreation. Facilities include three racquetball courts, which can be converted to court basketball and wallyball, an indoor heated pool, a sauna and whirlpool, suntan and therapeutic massage rooms, and a video game room—along with an exercise room. Overnight guests receive complimentary use of the Sports Club, but the racquetball courts, tanning salon, massage rooms, and specialized training services require a fee. Annual memberships are sold.

Outdoor amenities, centered around the four-acre lake, are oriented toward families that own or rent at Hidden Valley. The lake is stocked seasonally with trout and bass, and canoes, paddleboats, sailboats,

kayaks, and bicycles are available. Other amenities include three heated outdoor pools, 30 miles of hiking and bicycling trails, an 18-station par course, and a playground with basketball and volleyball courts.

There are currently nine tennis courts at Hidden Valley. The tennis club, located at the summit, features six carefully maintained Har-Tru (clay) courts, two of which are lighted for night play. Tennis memberships are available; nonmembers are charged an hourly court fee. The inn and conference center courts feature three hard courts with a synthetic Decoralt surface. Resort guests enjoy complimentary use of these courts.

The resort currently provides over 1,000 residential units, a large percentage of which are townhouses like those pictured here.

Residential Products

Homebuyers may select from a variety of attached and detached home products, including slopeside homes, golf course homes, forest homes, and lakeside homes. To date, approximately 1,000 homes have been built, including condominiums, townhouses, and single-family homes.

In the late 1980s, the primary product was 1,400-square-foot townhouses, sold fully furnished and placed in a rental program managed by KBI. They sold at an average price of about $96,000 in 1987. Garden apartment condominiums and zero-lot-line, single-family homes were also popular. Housing prices ranged from about $70,000 to over $200,000 depending on the location, type, and size of the unit. Fairway lots commanded a premium as did ski-in-ski-out lots. About 800 of the 3,000 units planned were designed as fairway lots.

As of 1995, approximately 1,000 units of the 3,000 originally planned had sold. New homes sell from the $130,000s. Townhouses are still the most common housing type. Current townhouse communities such as the Summit View Condominiums located along the top of Angel's Elbow ski trail are typified by decks overlooking the ski trails. The slopeside townhomes are large four-bedroom, four-bath townhouses located next to Beginner's Bowl at the ski area. Both of these communities offer ski-in-ski-out living and start at $137,900.

Luxury single-family homes are currently selling well. Stonewood is a community of exclusive large-lot custom homes situated on dramatic mountain overlooks. The homes' fieldstone, cedar, and glass facades blend into their wooded settings. Many of these homes are selling for upwards of $300,000.

Marketing and Management

In the early days of the resort, KBI focused its marketing efforts on the Pittsburgh area, which generated about 70 percent of real estate sales. The developer also marketed both second homes and conference services to the Baltimore and Washington area as well as west to Cleveland and promoted the conference center to the New York City area. KBI's original marketing strategy turned out to be relatively right on target. Pittsburgh, as might be expected, provided the largest share of the market; Washington, D.C., was next; Cleveland, third; other Ohio areas, next; and other local Pennsylvania areas, last. The New York City area did not provide any market share.

During the initial stages of the project, the amount of upfront capital required for investment meant that Hidden Valley was not profitable, although it did generate a positive cash flow. Once major improvements were in place, however, the resort showed a dramatic turnaround in cash flow starting in 1990. With most major capital expenditures now completed, revenues and traffic have improved substantially. The sale of real estate is the single largest profit center, contributing 50 percent of the resort's total revenues. In addition, the executive conference center, ski area, and inn are important revenue producers.

KBI operates the lot and homesite sales program while Hidden Valley Resort L.P. operates the resort component. In particular, the resort company runs the conference center and the 225 homes that are, on average, contributed to the rental pool. A commission structure that permits rental owners to receive 60 percent of rental income and Hidden Valley Resort 40 percent has been in place for some time. To ensure that rental units meet Class A standards, the resort sets specifications for each unit to be met by owners and makes periodic unit inspections. By providing maintenance services, the homeowners' association also plays a role in ensuring Class A standards.

The Hidden Valley Foundation, which was the homeowners' association in place when KBI purchased the resort, is an independent entity run by its own board of directors. The foundation has enjoyed an excellent working relationship with KBI over the years and has not opposed changes planned by KBI at the resort. Membership in the sports club, golf club, and tennis association confers automatic membership in the homeowners' association.

The resort offers a variety of camps for children and hosts golf and tennis camps for adults. Kid's Kamps include the Great Outdoor Camp, Adventure Camp, and All Sports Camp, which are offered for weekly full-day or half-day sessions. In addition, the resort offers a residents' camp.

With its family focus, Hidden Valley is known for its ski school for both adults and children and offers a special Kinder Inn child care program, Kinder Ski, ski camps, and youth racing programs. Always seeking additional forms of recreation and entertainment, the resort has recently instituted old-fashioned sleigh rides in both bob-sleighs and small carriages. It also has been promoting mountain biking during the summer and in recent years has been the site of numerous mountain biking competitions, including the Annual Fat Tire Stampede.

Hidden Valley also hosts a wide range of events, many of which are held for the benefit of local charitable organizations. Some of the major events include a jazz festival, blue grass festival, and charity golf tournaments. The resort is one of the largest employers in Somerset County—with a staff of nearly 1,000—and strives to be a good corporate citizen.

The ski area is separately owned and operated by Hidden Valley Ski, Inc., an independent company that is solely responsible for the operations and maintenance of the ski area and ski facilities. In view of the liability issues involved in ski resort operations, KBI decided to turn over ski operations to a separate entity.

Lessons Learned

Hidden Valley has been relatively successful with its original four-season concept and, given current trends in lifestyles and vacation patterns, is likely to continue

its tradition of success. As more people take shorter vacations and look for activities for the whole family, four-season resorts like Hidden Valley that offer a variety of leisure activities will have great appeal to both owners and renters.

Hidden Valley has dealt fairly successfully with the issues inherent in long-term development of a resort property. It benefited at the outset from low land costs and built as demand dictated without creating excess supply. About 15 years into its life, Hidden Valley is still only one-third built out, as it has had to deal with slow sales in recessionary times, competition with resales in offering new product, and adjustment of its product mix to meet changing expectations for resort homes. It has reserved many of the better ski-in-ski-out and fairway lots for future development so that it can continue to provide both prime lots and a variety of other products over the remaining years of its buildout.

The resort has successfully broadened its market beyond its Pittsburgh base, although that city still remains Hidden Valley's major source of business. Efforts to market Hidden Valley beyond a five-hour drive-time radius, which extends to the Washington, D.C., and Cleveland areas, have not succeeded. Therefore, as it has evolved, Hidden Valley has appropriately focused on its core market and continues to upgrade its resort facilities to accommodate that market.

With 30 miles of hiking and biking trails, the resort has been promoting mountain biking to increase summer activity and has been the site for numerous mountain biking competitions in recent years, including the Annual Fat Tire Stampede.

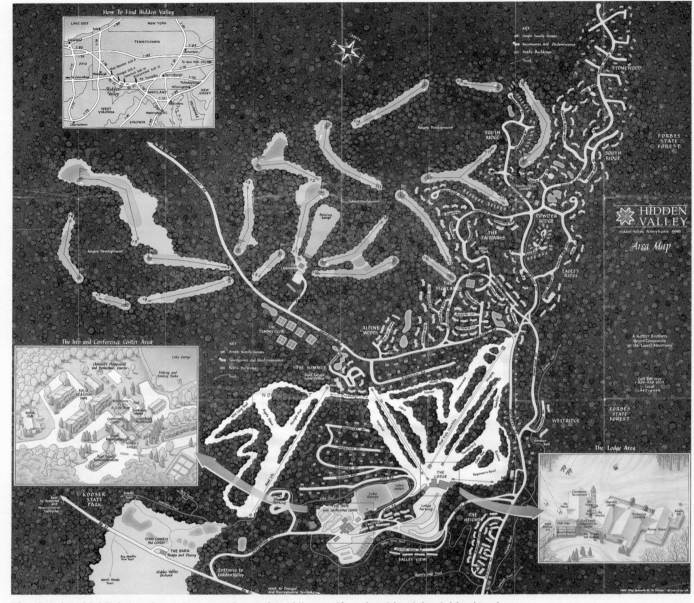

The site plan, highlighting the major areas devoted to skiing, golf, and residential neighborhoods.

Project Data: Hidden Valley Four Seasons Resort

Land Information

Site size (approximate)	2,000 acres

Residential Unit Information

Number of residential housing units planned	3,000
Number of units or lots sold (1995)	1,000

Product	Typical Prices
Single-family homes	$300,000
Townhouses	$137,900

Ski-Area Information

Skiable area	85 acres
Number of slopes	17
Number of lifts	8
Vertical drop	610 feet
Daily capacity	6,500

Hotel Information

Total hotel rooms planned	460
Total hotel rooms completed	213
Conference center	31,265 square feet

Development Schedule

1949	Site acquired by initial developer
1958	First ski run and lift developed
1977	First townhouses built
1983	Property sold to current owner
1988	Golf course started

Developer

Kettler Brothers, Inc.
One Craighead Drive
Hidden Valley, Pennsylvania 15502
814-443-6454

Resort Operator

Hidden Valley Resort L.P.
One Craighead Drive
Hidden Valley, Pennsylvania 15502
814-443-6454

Ski Operator

Hidden Valley Ski, Inc.
Hidden Valley, Pennsylvania

Site Planner

Greenhorne and O'Mara, Inc.
Fairfax, Virginia

Primary Architect

Maleady, Roy & O'Brien

Golf Course Architect

Russell Roberts
Gaithersburg, Maryland

The Homestead Resort

Glen Arbor, Michigan

The Homestead Resort, a four-season resort on Lake Michigan in Glen Arbor, Michigan, has earned a reputation as one of the highest-end resorts in the Midwest. The regional resort and second-home community is located in the northwest quarter of Michigan's lower peninsula, approximately 15 miles from Traverse City. Residents and guests enjoy 1.8 miles of beach frontage on Lake Michigan and four miles of frontage on the Crystal River, which winds its way through the adjacent Sleeping Bear Dunes National Lakeshore. The site features sandy beaches and a major sand dune between the lake and the river. The resort is unique in that it includes a ski component along with a beachfront and related amenities.

Though a four-season operation, the Homestead does not now offer golf; it is, however, seeking to build a course to strengthen its spring and fall seasons. While the resort is noted for its environmentally sound design, a major environmental battle erupted when Robert Kuras, developer of the Homestead, acquired a 267-acre tract—which included 87 acres of wetlands along the river—adjacent to the resort and proposed a golf course in 1986. As of 1995, the issue had not been resolved. The developer has not easily given up on the idea, as golf is a dominant competitive factor in the Michigan resort industry during the spring and fall, and the addition of an 18-hole golf course would solidify the Homestead's draw as a four-season resort.

Master Planning and Design

Planning for the resort began in the early 1970s. The Homestead was initially planned on 221 acres for 600 single-family and condominium units. The project is approximately 90 percent built out, with 16 single-family homes, 500 condominiums, and 29 timeshare units completed and sold as of 1995. Lot sales are 100 percent completed; only 34 custom single-family homes remain to be built on lots already sold. A total of as many as 48 additional timeshare or condominium units also remain to be developed, whereupon development on the original acreage will be completed.

Over 80 percent of the resort's units and half of its acreage have been planned for condominiums, for an average gross density of 2.7 units per acre and a maximum permitted gross density of 4.3 units per acre. The sensitively planned project blends with the site's natural amenities. It enjoys a site coverage of only 12 percent of the original 220 acres, including roads,

parking, buildings, and recreational facilities. The golf course, planned for an adjacent 267 acres but currently without necessary permits, would double the resort's acreage.

The Homestead was planned around two cores, one oriented toward the waterfront for the summer months and the other toward the ski resort for the winter months. Each core provides an activity center with commercial, food service, and recreational facilities. A system of interconnecting bicycle paths and cross-country ski trails is laced throughout the project. The trails link the various facilities and provide pedestrian, bicycle, and skier access. A jitney operated by the Homestead is intended to discourage automobile traffic but has been only moderately successful in meeting an overall planning goal of reduced reliance on private automobiles.

In establishing design parameters, the resort specifically wished to avoid a suburban appearance. The site is steeply sloped and, in some areas, characterized by as much as a 45 percent grade. Buildings are sited in conformance with the natural contours, with sites making extensive use of retaining walls and landscaped terraces. The homes have been stepped into a series of deep valleys and ridges and sited at irregular distances and angles. Residential views are oriented toward Lake Michigan and the adjacent national lakeshore. Among the newer developments is the Pinnacle Place condominiums, completed in the early 1990s on the ski hill's summit; the condominiums overlook the sand dunes and the national park. Several ski runs allow ski-in-ski-out access to Pinnacle Place.

The Homestead has successfully implemented a major tree-save program. In addition, to minimize paved areas and save as many trees as possible, the resort used boardwalks rather than paved sidewalks while deed restrictions required common driveways. Parking areas are small and heavily landscaped. Roadway widths were reduced to 22 feet and roads intentionally curved to avoid long site distances that encourage vehicle speed.

A detailed set of protective covenants requires all residential building plans to include a detailed survey, topographic map, and tree survey for submission to and approval by the Homestead's management before construction on any residential homesite. The management grants very few modifications to the basic building plans and encourages natural materials and colors. Buildings are characterized by low eave lines, steeply pitched

The Homestead Resort has 1.8 miles of beach frontage on Lake Michigan and four miles of frontage on the Crystal River, which winds its way through the adjacent Sleeping Bear Dunes National Lakeshore.

roofs, and multiple-floor elevations. Courtyards, patios, and screen fences help deemphasize scale. The project is an excellent example of environmentally sensitive design; by clustering the core facilities and housing, the plan has maintained the vast proportion of the site in its natural state.

Infrastructure, including the expensive undergrounding of utilities and the developer's provision of central water and sewer systems, was developed for the entire site. The systems were rebuilt in 1994 to reflect the state of the art in meeting environmental regulations.

Amenities

Amenities reflecting the resort's family focus include the beach, the Club (beach, racquet, and food service facilities), a small craft harbor, three swimming pools, two hydropools, five clay tennis courts, a golf academy, hiking trails, fitness trails, exercise room and sauna, daycare center with children's programs for children of resort guests, children's play areas, and downhill and cross-country skiing. The number and quality of amenities have continued to increase over the life of the resort. In 1995, for example, a golf academy was added to keep the Homestead's market position as competitive as possible.

The operation of the skiing facilities is more akin to a private club than a public resort. Ticket sales are limited to a specified number of skiers, although the resort is served by one double and two triple chairs plus a Pony for maximum lift capacity of more than 2,000 skiers per hour. Specially designed low-rise towers protect skiers from the Lake Michigan winds. A unique feature of skiing at the Homestead is the view: not mountains but rather the whitecapped breakers of Lake Michigan in the distance. The slopes rise steeply to a ridge 375 feet above the water level.

In 1986, to make the Homestead a full four-season resort and ensure its competitiveness, the developer acquired an adjacent 267-acre parcel for a golf course. The site included 87 acres of wetlands along the Crystal River and required a permit to fill 12 acres of affected wetlands. While subsequent plan revisions reduced the

fill area to 3.6 acres, Kuras worked diligently between 1986 and 1992 to demonstrate the merits of his golf course proposal. He commissioned studies of alternative sites, researched over 100 comparable projects, held 13 public workshops, commissioned 16 environmental studies, made several hundred changes to the original plan, met with regulatory agencies nearly 40 times, won a voter referendum, received approval from the state's wetlands investigator, and won 40 court decisions, including an order to issue a permit. Despite all his efforts, Kuras has not yet received permission to begin golf course construction.

The Pennsylvania Department of Natural Resources (DNR) finally issued a permit for the golf course in 1990. Both a circuit court judge and an administrative law judge reviewed the DNR's action, which then received the approval of the Pennsylvania Natural Resources Commission (the DNR's parent). The Chicago office of the U.S. Environmental Protection

In addition to hillsides and lakeshore, the site offers attractive woodlands and streams.

Agency, however, overruled the commission, citing the loss of natural wetlands and the risk of chemical runoff from the golf course into the national lakeshore and the Crystal River. Pennsylvania's governor took the fight to the EPA's headquarters, which overruled the regional EPA decision. In turn, the regional EPA took the case to court. The court ruled that EPA headquarters had no jurisdiction in the matter and pointed out that the wetlands permit decision rests with the U.S. Army Corps of Engineers. The Corps has invited the owner to begin the wetlands permit process all over again.

While golf resorts often encounter major opposition, the bizarre history of the Homestead's permit process provides an example of the potential strength of that opposition. The Friends of the Crystal River, an organization that quickly emerged after Kuras made his plans public, included members from major corporations who brought significant political clout to bear. While members of the organization wished to preserve their summer community the way it was, they fought their battle solely on environmental grounds, enlisting the support of the National Wildlife Federation, Trout Unlimited, the Michigan United Conservation Clubs, and the Sierra Club.

Management

In recognition of changing market demand, the Homestead has continued to alter its product offerings over the almost 20 years of the resort's life. The project began with the sale of single-family homes that ranged from 900-square-foot beach cottages to 2,000-square-foot four-bedroom homes on approximately half-acre lots. As land became more valuable, higher-density condominiums assumed the major product focus. In the 1980s, the Homestead embarked on a major condominium program. Units ranged from 400-square-foot efficiencies to 1,700-square-foot four-bedroom dwellings.

Dietrich Floeter

The resort includes a nine-hole, par-3 golf course and golf academy that were opened in 1995. Although an 18-hole golf course has been planned, thus far the developer has failed to obtain the necessary permits, primarily in regard to wetlands issues.

The Homestead is unusual in that it is both a beach resort and a ski resort and includes 18 acres of skiable terrain with four lifts and 14 trails.

Dietrich Floeter

Cafe Manitou on Lake Michigan is a popular resort dining and gathering place.

Dietrich Floeter

Both lot sales and construction of the additional homes proceeded slowly through the 1980s. In the mid-1990s, the resort began developing and selling detached single-family, zero-lot-line condominiums as well as custom homes on waterfront lots. The zero-lot-line condominium lots now sell for $150,000, as compared to $25,000 for the original single-family sites. In a recent offering of 21 single-family sites, nearly half of the lots sold over a remarkably short period. Waterfront lots are particularly valuable. In a project of eight waterfront homesites, lots have been selling for approximately $350,000 each and custom-built homes for at least $1 million.

The first timeshare project of 12 units began sales in 1990. Today, however, the Homestead offers 29 timeshare units in three projects that are about 65 percent sold out. The resort deeds a one-quarter interest in a condominium unit based on a rotating and preset schedule, which is generally one week per month in the off-season months and larger blocks of time (either two or four weeks) in summer. Heavy reserves are held, sufficient for replacement of 80 percent of the interior furniture, fixtures, and equipment (FFE) every five years.

The Homestead offers a rental component to accommodate those not interested in ownership. Specifically, it operates a commission-based rental management program for owners who wish to rent, with housekeeping and maintenance services provided by a year-round staff. For units to qualify for management by the resort, rental rates must honor a detailed pricing formula set by the Homestead and homes must pass a semiannual inspection. The resort's commission is 50 percent of gross rental income on the published guest rate, less amenity fees. Timeshare owners are eligible for participation in the program as well. In addition to owner rentals, the resort retains and owns 77 units for rent. About 50 percent of owners make use of the Homestead's rental program.

As the resort began to show signs of age over the years, the Homestead management had to convince owners of rental units to maintain and renovate their units in order to maintain them at contemporary Class A resort standards. The timeshare program provided one method of ensuring Class A rental units. In addition, the resort initiated an upgrade program for fee-owned units. It hired a decorator to provide four decorating schemes and to sell package upgrades from these schemes to unit owners on a cost-plus basis. The package includes management of the renovation and is particularly attractive to owners who live several hours away and do not have the time to oversee a renovation. At the same time, owners benefit from the resort's ability to buy large quantities of materials at wholesale. Further, their units become more desirable rentals. Presumably, their rental income increases with new furniture, carpets, kitchens, or baths.

The Homestead set up an overall community association and individual associations for the various residential complexes. The condominium associations manage the common areas, including any landscaping. Even for the detached single-family condominiums, which are largely built on common area, the owner is not responsible for outdoor maintenance. Instead, the condominium association is responsible for maintaining outdoor areas.

Lessons Learned

The major lesson to be learned from the Homestead's unsuccessful attempt to date to gain approval for its proposed golf course is the importance of political and community support for a project. Once a resort is established, it is likely to experience tremendous difficulties in gaining approval for even minor modifications. The Homestead's battle highlights the leverage that an established resort community with a no-growth agenda can bring to a development proposal by invoking environmental laws and regulations. At relatively little expense, existing landowners can hold up and completely derail changes to a resort, pursuing agendas that are not strictly environmental. After five years, the Friends of the Crystal River had expended about $150,000, as compared to the over $3 million in expenses incurred by the developer.

To minimize the risk of community opposition to a resort, it is crucial to incorporate into a resort's original plan the full range of amenities and expansion options that, over time, will help ensure the resort's financial health. Unfortunately, what makes a resort profitable in the long term cannot always be foreseen. In a resort such as the Homestead, which relies on natural amenities such as pristine beaches and slopes, the potential for environmental litigation is high and must be reflected in the project's budget. Similarly, a resort with a long life expectancy requires major financial staying power. The Homestead has had some difficulty weathering the financial hardships related to the lack of an 18-hole golf course and its impact on occupancies and the resort's meeting business.

While the Homestead has had its problems, it provides an outstanding example of an upscale, sensitively designed resort. It is notable for its success in blending the resort's homes into the pristine dunes and surrounding national lakeshore. It is unusual in combining major beach and skiing facilities in a single resort and thus has emerged as a major year-round resort destination for visitors from throughout the upper Midwest.

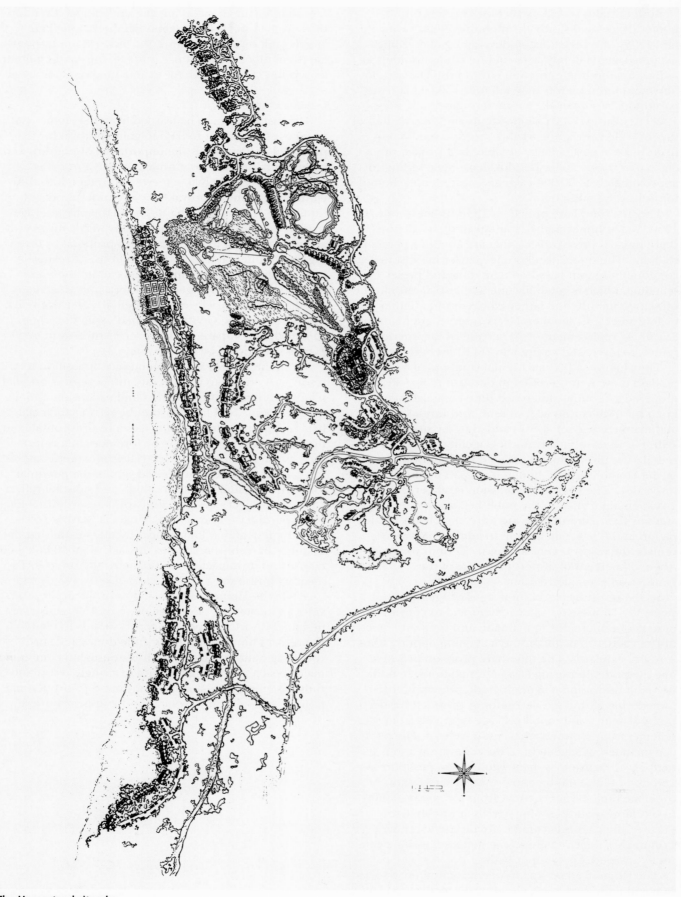

The Homestead site plan.

Project Data: The Homestead Resort

Land Use Plan

	Acres
Detached residential	59
Attached/multifamily residential 118	
Hotel	4
Roads	20
Common open space	161
Ski area	19
Golf academy	3
Proposed golf course site	130
Total	514

Residential Unit Information

Unit Type	Unit Size (square feet)	Number of Units Planned/Built
Studio	400	8/8
1 bedroom	650–800	82/72
2 bedroom	800–1,400	196/184
3 bedroom	1,200–2,400	219/190
4 bedroom	1,800 +	45/35

	Range of Current Sales Prices	Rent/Day
Studio	$40,000–$50,000	$82–$193
1 bedroom	$70,000–$115,000	$116–$344
2 bedroom	$120,000–$300,000	$161–$438
3 bedroom	$150,000–$400,000	$190–$461
4 bedroom	$250,000–$1,000,000	$296–$512

Ownership Type	Number of Units Planned/Built
Fee-simple detached homes	50/16
Condominiums	500/500

Timeshare Information

Timeshare units planned/built	77/29
Typical cost per timeshare interval unit	$80,000 per quartershare

Hotel Information

Total hotel rooms planned	129
Total hotel rooms completed	77
Average daily room rate	$130

Ski-Area Information

Vertical drop	375 feet
Skiable area	18 acres
Number of lifts	4
Number of trails	14

Development Cost Information (1995)

Site Acquisition Cost	$1,120,000 (1972–1979)

Site Improvement Costs

Water and sewer	$1,000,000
Roads	250,000
Utilities (relocation underground)	150,000
Total	$1,400,000

Amenities Costs

Tennis courts and platform tennis	$190,000
Beach club	225,000
Cross-country skiing trails	60,000
Raquet club	400,000
Total	$875,000

Development Schedule

1974	Site purchased
1974	Planning started
1974	Sales started
1974	First closing
1975	Construction started
1986	Golf course site acquired
1990	First timeshares offered for sale

Developer/Operator

Kuras Properties
Wood Ridge Road
Glen Arbor, Michigan 49636
616-334-5210

Site Planner

Guidelines
Lincoln, Massachusetts

Architect

Community Design Services
Traverse City, Michigan

Dewees Island
Dewees Island, South Carolina

Dewees Island is a private island community dedicated to the principles of environmentally responsible development. The concept and driving force behind the island's development plans is that residential development and the natural environment can coexist in harmonious balance. Dewees Island emphasizes respect for its natural setting by nesting homes within the island's abundant flora. Low-impact amenities support an outdoor lifestyle.

Located approximately 12 miles east of Charleston, South Carolina, Dewees is a 1,206-acre barrier island situated between the commercially developed Isle of Palms to the south and the Cape Romain National Wildlife Refuge to the north. It is accessible only by private boat or developer-operated ferry and offers its residents unrivaled seclusion and nature-based amenities.

The community's extensive environmental covenants and design guidelines strictly protect the island's water quality, vegetation, and wildlife habitat while providing for the development of 137 single-family residential units. No cars are permitted on Dewees. Electric carts serve as the island's primary form of transportation. Commercial activities on the island are limited to those that directly support the residents. The island's undeveloped character and environmental assets are marketed as the community's principle amenities.

Site and Development Process
Dewees Island and neighboring Capers Island were purchased in 1972 by a group of five South Carolina investors for $2.3 million. Several years later, the state of South Carolina purchased Capers Island for the purpose of creating a wildlife refuge. A 19-year period saw several unsuccessful attempts to develop Dewees Island. Significant entitlement obstacles, community opposition, and financial difficulties thwarted each development attempt.

In 1991, a joint venture partnership called the Island Preservation Partnership (IPP) formed to develop Dewees. The group consisted of the owners of Dewees Island, who provided the land, and a group of developers, who provided equity as well as development expertise. Before formation of the IPP, a large percentage of the island's phase I infrastructure had already been developed (including roads, power, water, and telephone), thereby significantly decreasing the partnership's upfront risk exposure and development costs.

Recognizing the potential ecological impacts of residential development on a fragile barrier island along with growing consumer demand for environmentally responsible development, the IPP devised an innovative master plan supported by a series of progressive environmental covenants and design guidelines. The Dewees master plan is not only a strategic planning tool but also a legal document administered by the state of South Carolina in the form of a deeded conservation easement across the entire island. The master plan/ environmental covenants limit development on the island to 150 private residences built on one- to three-acre parcels. (The IPP did not own 13 preexisting lots on the island.)

A comprehensive inventory and analysis of the island's soils, wetlands, flora, and fauna preceded development of the Dewees Island master plan. The studies indicated that all development on the island should be clustered in the most hearty of the island's ecosystems— a maritime forest located away from the island's fragile dunes, beaches, and wetlands.

The prospect of disrupting ecosystems and wildlife corridors received careful consideration throughout the planning, design, and development of Dewees. As a result, more than 65 percent of the island will remain completely undeveloped, with over 350 acres on the northeastern end of the island designated as a wildlife refuge. Development impact is designed to reach a maximum disturbance of only 5 percent of the island.

The IPP, led by its chief executive officer, John L. Knott, Jr., worked with environmental groups throughout the development process to establish open communications and collaborative decision making on several of the project's potentially controversial components (including the island's sewage treatment system). Environmental groups also played an instrumental role in supporting the regulatory approval of environmentally responsible building materials and techniques not permitted under conventional code.

Master Planning and Design
The Dewees Island architectural and environmental guidelines promote environmental responsibility, sustainability, resource efficiency, community development, and use of the local vernacular. To minimize habitat disturbance, stormwater runoff, and nonpoint source pollution, the Dewees Island guidelines strictly prohibit the development of impervious surfaces. A network of natural sand-based roads effectively transports the island's fleet of electric vehicles and preserves the island's undeveloped character. Poured con-

Dewees Island is a 1,206-acre second-home community—on a private oceanfront island—that uses environmental preservation as a guiding principle. The island can be reached by a regularly scheduled, ten-minute ferry ride.

With vast areas of Dewees left untouched by the developer, programs like this managed impoundment enhance the habitat for all forms of wildlife.

crete driveways and paths are forbidden. Instead, natural sand, pine needle mulch, and crushed oyster shells are used throughout the island. The sand-based roadways and paths have dramatically reduced the developer's infrastructure development and maintenance expenses.

In an effort to prevent the destruction of native vegetation and other natural features, a maximum of only 7,500 square feet of disturbed space is allowed on each site regardless of lot size. Disturbable area includes the footprint of the home, the driveway, pathways, porches, decks, patios, and easements. The guidelines assign high priority to such site planning considerations as tree preservation, viewshed analysis, passive solar orientation (including the path of the sun and prevailing breezes), and drainage impact.

To preserve the island's prominent tree canopy, building heights throughout the island cannot exceed

Beach access paths and bridging systems were designed to minimize environmental impact.

Design guidelines encourage home design and site orientation to maximize the use of natural breezes and lighting.

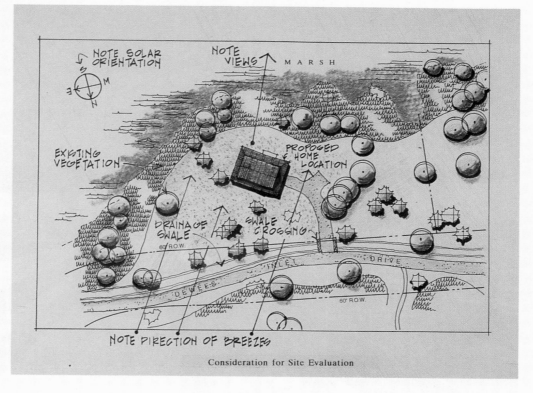

Consideration for Site Evaluation

40 feet. Home sizes on Dewees are limited to a maximum of 5,000 square feet to minimize development impact. In addition, unlike many exclusive island community developments, Dewees has no minimum residential square footage requirement and no requirement that landowners must build.

IPP staff conduct weekly inspections of construction sites to verify compliance with the building and environmental guidelines. Contractors are required to

post a $5,000 cash bond per homesite to cover potential environmental damage.

All buildings developed on Dewees are required to maintain the regional architectural character of the South Carolina Low Country. Wide overhanging eaves and porches, operable shutters, buildings on pilings, and narrow wings are design features that are not only indigenous to the Charleston region but also a direct response to the area's climate, thereby increasing energy efficiency and enhancing functionality.

Dewees has served as a model of and testing ground for resource- and energy-efficient building materials and systems. The IPP has gone to great lengths to use resource- and energy-efficient building materials and systems within community buildings and strongly encourages property owners to use the same in the construction of their homes. Among the resource-efficient design and development techniques frequently applied in island construction are passive solar ventilation/cooling, shading, daylighting, solar water heating, waste management, and water conservation.

The Dewees Island Architectural Resource Board not only administers the island's design guidelines but also compiles information on environmentally responsible building materials and systems for dissemination to designers, contractors, property owners, and others throughout the community. In fact, Dewees sponsors an annual conference on environmentally responsible building materials to educate local builders, designers, and developers. Examples of the several environmentally responsible building materials used on Dewees include Trex plastic lumber (made from recycled garbage bags,), cotton insulation, Fiberbond (made from recycled newspaper), Hardiplank siding (made from wood chips and concrete), and Hydrostop roofing. The application of these materials has proven cost-effective, highly functional, and aesthetically pleasing.

With an average development/construction cost of $110 per square foot, home construction costs on Dewees are approximately 15 percent higher than those on the local mainland. The difference is largely attributable to the island's limited access as well as to its requirements for such amenities as fire sprinkler and central security systems.

Jessica Grossman

The Dewees Island Landings Center features a ferry landing area and a community center with a post office, library, educational center, and community offices.

Community Resources/Amenities

Unlike many second-home resort communities throughout the South Carolina marketplace, Dewees will never have a golf course; instead, the community's primary recreational amenities are the island's unrivaled environmental assets, including two and three-quarters miles of beaches, a 200-acre tidal lake, a 120-acre impoundment/estuary, and a 350-acre wildlife refuge. Community facilities include traditional recreational amenities such as tennis courts and a swimming pool.

Residents can reach the island's beaches by a combination of community pathways and elevated wooden walkways, which follow the contours of the land and thus provide for a wide variety of unique entry/access point settings. Community facilities such as crabbing and fishing docks provide access to the island's saltwater marshes and tidal waterways. Boat access to Dewees is carefully controlled to protect the island's shellfish resources. While the island offers significant berthing facilities, private docks are not permitted.

The Dewees Island Landings Center will serve as the island's community center. Situated across from the ferry landing, the landing center will house the Dewees Island post office, library, educational center, and community offices. It will also be used as a central charging station for the island's fleet of electric vehicles. In addition, the developer is building a bed-and-breakfast lodging, the Hyler House, that will include hospitality suites to accommodate a small number of island visitors.

The IPP considers environmental education and research an invaluable component of the island community. Two full-time professionals conduct extensive environmental education and research initiatives and provide residents with the opportunity to learn more about and play an active role in the environmental stewardship of the island. All environmental programs will be funded in perpetuity through a 1.5 percent real estate transfer tax split equally between homebuyer and seller.

Management and Marketing

To ensure its ability to meet its long-range objectives, the IPP was formed as an equity-based development effort. The only debt on the project was a preexisting $5 million note, which the partnership assumed as part of the land contribution for a 50 percent interest in the joint venture. As of June 1995, all but $500,000 of the note had been repaid.

To date, the IPP has achieved a gross income of approximately $12 million. It has reinvested the revenues in the project until the island's infrastructure is completed (as of 1995, the remaining infrastructure expenses were estimated at $2 million).

The projected gross income for the project is $44 million. As of September 1995, 47 lots had been sold, 12 homes had been completed, two homes were under construction, and approximately seven homes were in the design/approval stage. Dewees is projected to complete its lot sales program by 1999.

The IPP successfully achieved its investment break-even point after the sale of the 40th lot. As of September 1995, the project was behind its pro forma sales pace by about 15 lots; however, higher-than-forecast lot prices have allowed Dewees to achieve net profits that exceed the pro forma by approximately 90 percent.

Dewees Island's active communication campaign markets the project as a "private oceanfront island retreat dedicated to environmental preservation." Homeowners on Dewees are often attracted to the island's family orientation, which residents view as a "legacy investment." Most owners use their Dewees residence as a second home; however, given the island's proximity to Charleston, a significant number of residents are building primary homes on the island.

Lessons Learned

Once perceived to be extremely risky within the real estate marketplace, the use of stringent development guidelines that, for example, prohibit cars, beachfront development, impervious surfaces, and houses larger than 5,000 square feet have enabled Dewees Island to realize considerable market differentiation within an increasingly competitive market. By designing and developing in an environmentally holistic and integrated fashion, the developer not only achieved environmental goals but also realized economic and competitive benefits, including more predictability in entitlements, decreased development costs for infrastructure and amenities, and higher profitability.

The IPP's creation of strategic alliances with local environmental groups proved highly valuable. Open communication and partnerships with environmental groups helped transform Dewees Island from a potentially controversial project into a national prototype.

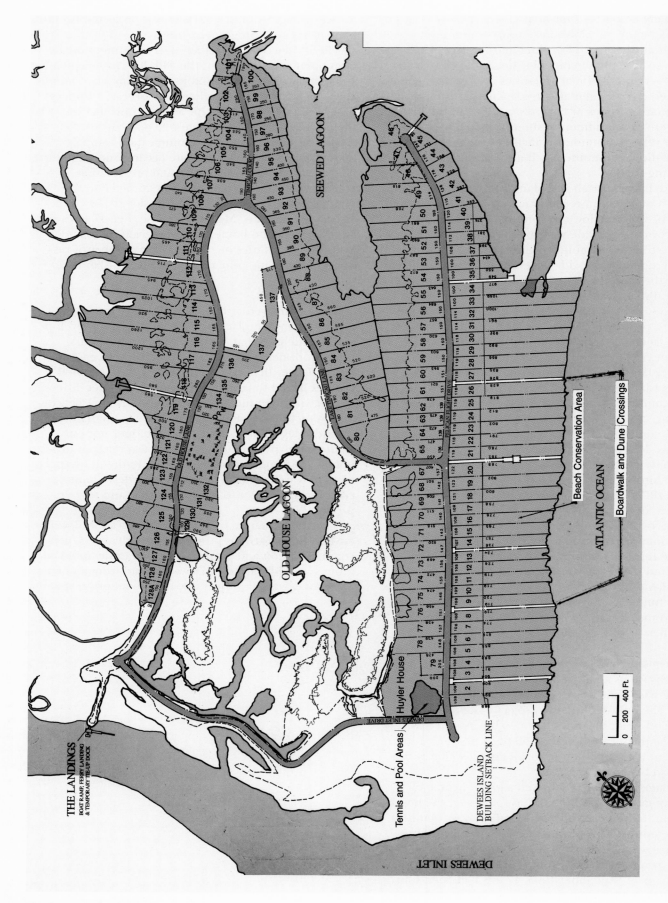

The Dewees Island site plan.

Land Use Information

Site area	1,205 acres
Total dwelling units planned	137
Total lots sold (September 1995)	47
Total dwelling units completed	12
Gross density	0.12 units per acre
Average net density	0.36 units per acre

Land Use Plan

	Acres
Detached residential	300
Open space/amenities	114
Roads	7.5
Conservation area	783.5
Total	1,205

Residential Use Information[1]

Unit Type	Number of Units Available/Sold	Range of Sale Prices
Oceanfront	48/17	$340,000–$475,000
Oceanview/bluff	12/0	Not set—Phase III
Oceanview	19/12	$200,000–$270,000
Impoundment	22/10	$175,000–$220,000
Salt marsh	36/0	$210,000–$275,000

Development Costs[2]

Site Acquisition Cost[3]

Site Improvement Costs

Island cleanup	$156,000
Wildlife management	115,000
Roads and bridges	320,000
Water and sewer system and plant	842,000
Beach access and landscaping	259,000
Boardwalks and decks	505,000
Total	$2,197,000

Community Facilities Costs

Huyler House	$610,000
Caretaker's house	215,000
Landing/nature center	220,000
Public works buildings	300,000
Recreational amenities	136,000
Total	$1,481,000

Island Management Costs

Fire, safety, ferry	$405,000
Operations and maintenance	680,000
Property owners' association and utility subsidy	1,060,000
Total	$2,145,000

Soft Costs

Architecture/engineering	$623,000
Development and administration	2,850,000
Legal	282,000
Interest	975,000
Property tax	435,000
Marketing	4,005,000
Environmental reserve	325,000
Total	$9,995,000

Total Development Cost (1995)	**$15,818,000**

Development Schedule

June 1991	Site purchased
July 1991	Planning started
November 1991	Construction started
August 1992	Sales started
August 1992	First closing
March 1993	Phase I completed
December 1996	Project completed

Developer

Island Preservation Partnership
P.O. Box 361
Dewees Island, South Carolina 29451
803-886-8783

Site Planner/Architect

Burt Hill Kosar Rittelmann Associates
1056 Thomas Jefferson Street, N.W.
Washington, D.C. 20007-3813
202-333-2711

Engineer/Surveyor

E.M. Seabrook, Engineers, Inc.
Mt. Pleasant, South Carolina

Landscape Design

Steve Goggins & Associates
Charleston, South Carolina

Brickman Group, Ltd.
Laurel, Maryland

Notes

[1] As of early 1995.

[2] Expected at buildout.

[3] The Island Preservation Partnership was formed as an equity-based development effort. Land was acquired, including a $5 million debt, in return for a 50 percent interest in the joint venture.

Forest Highlands
Flagstaff, Arizona

Forest Highlands is a 657-acre second-home and golf course community set in the pine forests of Arizona's high country near Flagstaff. The site, which is part of the Coconino National Forest, is wooded primarily with tall Ponderosa pines and studded with stands of aspen and oak that provide splashes of color in autumn. An 18-hole golf course, the focus of the community, follows the natural contours of the hilly site, in several instances running along natural watercourses on the valley floor.

The sensitive siting of Forest Highlands was not an accident; the developers of the community understood the significance and value of the woodland as a unique environment that needed to be preserved if the community were to be developed successfully. With this precept in mind, the design team sought to minimize both tree removal and the disturbance of the existing topography and vegetation. In addition, the developers provided a highly sophisticated wastewater treatment system and other utility systems to limit the community's impact on existing ecosystems. The project offers 642 single-family lots, including 515 lots at approximately one-half acre distributed around the golf course and 127 cottage lots clustered around the clubhouse near the center of the site.

As of 1995, over 382 single-family houses had been constructed on lots ranging from one-quarter to one-half acre. Amenities include an 18-hole golf course and clubhouse, a practice area, an 18-hole putting course, a swimming pool, tennis courts, and children's playground facilities.

The Site and Development Process

The 657-acre site, which lies at the 7,000-foot elevation level, is located six miles south of Flagstaff, about a two-and-one-half-hour drive from Phoenix. The site is bordered on three sides by undeveloped state, federal, and private lands and on the fourth by a 20-year-old subdivision. Topographically, the site ranges from Alpine meadows to steep ravines and offers a distant view of the 13,000-foot, snowcapped peaks of the San Francisco Mountains. The entrance to Forest Highlands is reached by a one-mile-long, two-lane road provided by the developer. The road meanders through the adjacent public domain.

Forest Highlands was conceived by the Bailey Bartlett Group, a general partnership founded in 1985 by Jim Bartlett and Dick Bailey. Before embarking on Forest Highlands, the two had worked together in developing Desert Highlands, an upscale golf community in Scottsdale, Arizona, and Singletree, a golf course community near Vail, Colorado. The Bailey Bartlett Group formed a new general partnership in 1986 expressly to develop Forest Highlands. Included were several financial partners who advanced working capital for the project until financing for land acquisition could be obtained from an Arizona bank. Subsequently, a limited partnership was formed in which a regional savings and loan institution took a 49 percent limited-partner position.

Forest Highlands adopted many of the same approaches that had worked extraordinarily well in Desert Highlands. The two projects, however, differed along one critical dimension that did not become evident until soon after land acquisition. While Desert Highlands began in the era of 20 percent interest rates in the early 1980s—just in time for lot prices to skyrocket well beyond initial projections—Forest Highlands was conceived in the boom market of the mid-1980s and was then developed and marketed all the way through the Arizona real estate recession until it was completely sold out in early 1992.

The Forest Highlands construction program was limited to road construction, development of utilities, lot subdivision, and construction of the golf course, clubhouse, and amenities. Residential construction was left to lot owners, speculative builders, and subdivision builders (for the cottages). As of 1995, approximately 314 homes had been constructed.

Master Planning and Design

The Forest Highlands site plan was developed through an intensive design "charrette," a concentrated process wherein the members of the development team—the developer, land planner/architect, golf course designer, and civil engineer—spent several days together alternately walking the site and meeting in a hotel room to work out a land plan that achieved the goals of each participant. By working together in this way, all participants quickly came to understand each other's objectives and perspectives as a prelude to resolving issues on the spot. According to Gage Davis, the project land planner, the process addressed perhaps 80 percent of the design problems in 20 percent of the usual time.

The project was designed in accordance with the particulars of the site. To preserve as much pine forest as possible, for example, the Forest Highlands Golf Course,

Forest Highlands is a 657-acre, second-home and golf course community set in the pine forests of Arizona's high country.

designed by Jay Morrish and Tom Weiskopf, was laid out along the open areas of the existing drainage courses and in other nonforested areas. As a measure of the success of the course's design, in 1991 the golf course earned a first-place Arizona and 39th-place national ranking from *Golf Digest*.

The design team rejected the "18th-hole solution" for the clubhouse and instead focused on the visibility of the clubhouse, not only the view of it as residents move through the community but also the view from it. For this reason, the designers set the clubhouse on a rise near the seventh green and toward the back of a broad, open green used as a practice area. The clubhouse veranda looks out across the "village green" to the snow-capped peaks of the San Francisco Mountains.

To keep costs in line with the marketing program, the developers reduced the clubhouse's size. The lower operating costs of a smaller clubhouse were

The 16,000-square-foot clubhouse, which overlooks pine trees and the golf practice area, also provides views of the peaks of the San Francisco Mountains.

Homes must be carefully sited within a specified "building envelope" to preserve mature trees and other natural landscape elements.

appealing to those buying into the community during the recession. Attractive siting and superlative views, however, helped offset the facility's smaller size. In addition, the clubhouse offered a unique putting green similar to a miniature golf course.

About half of the single-family residential lots border the fairways, with six parcels close to the clubhouse designated for cluster housing. These parcels, which have been sold to independent developers, were created for subdivision into somewhat smaller-lot, single-family homes called cottages.

A strict set of residential development standards preserves the forest environment. These standards were based on the concept of the building envelope as an area not exceeding 50 percent of the lot per the mutual concurrence of the lot owner and the design review committee. To preserve the lot's natural features, all land development on the lot, including the home, parking area, and landscaping, must be confined to the designated building envelope for that lot.

Within the envelope, a transitional area outside the residence or site walls accommodates landscape alterations in accordance with an approved-plant list. In the private area, which is that portion of the envelope shielded from public view, residents may create as varied a landscape as desired, provided that they do not select from plants on a prohibited-plant list. Beyond the envelope, only minimal landscaping or other changes to natural features are permissible. Other development standards govern building materials, roof types, building heights, colors, and other features to encourage "natural materials that blend and are compatible with the native landscape."

Community facilities at Forest Highlands include the golf course, the 16,000-square-foot clubhouse and adjacent practice area, an 18-hole putting course, a swimming pool, four tennis courts, a park, a playground, stocked ponds for fishing, and pedestrian walkways. A staffed security gatehouse marks the entrance to the community. Membership in the golf club comes with lot purchase; no outside memberships are sold.

Marketing

An important factor in the success of Forest Highlands was the developers' identification of both a market opportunity and a piece of property well suited to that opportunity. The question in the case of Forest Highlands was whether to develop a distinctly family-oriented second-home community or a retirement community. The decision to develop the former recognized that a fairly substantial retirement market would eventually develop on its own. Had the developers positioned the product as a retirement-oriented community, they would have missed their primary market and would never have appealed to young families, which turned out to account for about 80 percent of sales. Had the developers promoted retirement and family living equally at the same time, they would have diluted their message to the marketplace and would have been far less successful. A clear market position is critical to successful second-home development.

In addition, the developers of Forest Highlands targeted three well-defined geographic markets: prospective second-home buyers residing in the Phoenix metropolitan area, prospective second-home buyers living outside the metropolitan Phoenix area (notably, elsewhere in Arizona and in California and Nevada), and primary-home buyers in or near Flagstaff.

Initially, the developers reached the three market segments through highly selective mailings and through advertising in golf and local/regional magazines. As the project developed, the developers used home tours to promote the sale of finished product and to publicize local builders. As new lots came onto the market, current owners were given the first opportunity to trade up. Most important, as the Forest Highlands community grew and matured, the owners of the lots and homes

became invaluable sources of referrals. More recently, highly visible golf tournaments and rankings in *Golf Digest* and *Golf* magazine have provided significant marketing exposure.

Lots adjacent to the fairways typically sold for $50,000 to $75,000 more than interior lots. An exception, however, was the group of ridgeview lots that offered views of the San Francisco Mountains. These lots generally sold for at least $25,000 more than fairway lots.

The average lot price was in the range of $100,000, which was much lower than the typical $200,000 lot price at Desert Highlands. By taking a conservative position on pricing and pricing as low as possible to maximize absorption, the developers sustained lot sales through the 1990s recession. Absorption and concurrent reduction in risk, as compared to maintaining the illusory benefit of hoping to achieve a high sales price, helped the development weather the recession.

Another innovative marketing technique that worked during the recession was the creation of a lifetime membership in the golf club. Although a lot purchase was a requirement for one of 100 lifetime memberships, a buyer could pay cash for a lot and gain a membership. Even if he or she subsequently sold the lot or home, the buyer could retain the membership and was not required to sell it back to the club. For families with older children who did not qualify for family membership, they could buy lifetime memberships for additional family members.

The developer offered financing for lot purchases. The terms included a 20 percent minimum downpayment for a ten-year, fully amortizing loan at prime plus 1 percent, adjusted quarterly. In 1987, the first year of sales, 147 lot sales were closed, followed by only 118 in 1988. As the recession of the late 1980s and early 1990s hit Arizona, sales rates slowed, but the early momentum carried the project to completion in 1993. However, the lines of credit that backed the seller financing were called, requiring payment to the sav-

A gatehouse, designed in a style similar to that of the clubhouse, greets residents and visitors at the end of the mile-long entry road.

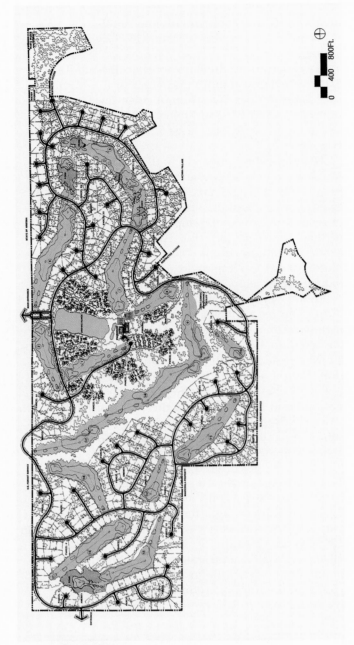

The Forest Highlands site plan.

ings and loan. The project's value was such that the financing was successfully restructured, although what little profit there was accrued primarily to the lenders.

About 65 percent of the lots have been sold to Phoenix-area residents, 20 percent to other Arizona residents, and 15 percent to out-of-state purchasers. About 10 percent of buyers purchased lots for their primary residence. Word-of-mouth referrals have been a major contributor to sales, spurred in no small part by the developers' extra attention to the details that matter to homeowners.

Lessons Learned

Forest Highlands, developed as it was during one of the worst recessions in memory, provides an excellent example of how high-quality and incomparable elements—such as the setting itself with its views of snow-capped peaks, the unique 18-hole putting green, and a highly acclaimed golf course—provided at a conservative cost can carry a project through difficult times by ensuring a reasonable sales and absorption rate. Paying attention to fundamentals and economizing—to the degree that project quality is not compromised—is also critical.

Forest Highlands also underscores the range of issues involved in turning over a club to owners. With the project developed in a soft market, the developers planned to turn the club over to homeowners free and clear no later than 1990, thereby providing some measure of security to wary buyers. By eliminating questions of fair pricing, the developers could focus on the level and kind of available reserves as well as on ongoing membership responsibilities for road construction and maintenance—before the membership would agree to accept club ownership—even at no cost.

Another significant lesson to be drawn from both the Desert Highlands and Forest Highlands experiences is that the greatest value to both the developer and the community is derived from the lowest density that can be sustained financially. After the first phase at Desert Highlands sold out, the developers reduced densities by almost half. At Forest Highlands, where the prices were half those of Desert Highlands, the developers did not enjoy the same luxury. The developers would have developed at 20 percent less density had they been able to achieve 20 percent more in price at Forest Highlands.

The charrette process of design was a successful approach to planning. A charrette can be a valuable technique for the rapid synthesis of design opportunities and constraints and the similarly rapid evolution of design solutions that incorporate the perspectives of all members of the development team.

Finally, it is perhaps better to view the golf clubhouse as a type of civic center rather than as merely a country club. Thus, the clubhouse's siting, design, and facility program should consider the needs of all constituents of the community, including children. At the same time, the clubhouse can provide a focal point for denser housing and ensure proximity to the "town center."

Project Data: Forest Highlands

Land Use Information

Site area	657 acres
Total dwelling units planned	642
Total dwelling units completed (1995)	382
Gross density	1 unit per acre
Average net density	2 units per acre (net of amenities)

Land Use Plan

	Acres
Residential lots	417
Roads	70
Golf course (including related amenities, open space)	170
Total	657

Residential Unit Information

Unit Type	Average Lot Size (square feet)	Number of Units Planned/Built	Lot Sales Price (1993)
Large lots	0.5	515/287	$70,000–$250,000
Cottage lots	0.25	127/95	$55,000–$225,000

Club Revenues and Expenses (1994)

Member dues	$1,583,000
Pro shop operations	165,000
Golf club maintenance	(589,000)
Food and beverage	(151,000)
Clubhouse administration	(355,000)
Recreation	(36,000)
Amenities maintenance	(185,000)
Security	(177,000)
Net revenues	$255,000

Development Schedule

June 1985	Planning started
January 1986	Site purchased
June 1986	Construction started
June 1986	Sales started
February 1987	First closing
March 1993	Sales completed

Development Cost Information (1993)

Site Acquisition Cost	$4,718,000

Site Improvement Costs

Excavation/grading	$3,535,000
Sewer/water/drainage	6,328,000
Paving/curbs/sidewalks	2,764,000
Landscaping/irrigation	167,000
Fees/general conditions	844,000
Telephone and electric	525,000
Wastewater treatment plant	4,151,000
Wells	1,960,000
Total	$20,274,000

Construction Costs

Golf course	$5,830,000
Clubhouse[1]	3,983,000
Other amenities[2]	956,000
Total	$10,769,000

Soft Costs

Architecture/engineering	$2,260,000
Project administration[3]	5,919,000
Marketing	8,590,000
Construction interest and fees	7,787,000
Total	$24,556,000

Total Development Cost	$60,317,000
Total Development Cost Per Lot	$92,087

Developer

Forest Highlands Group Limited Partnership/The Bailey Bartlett Group
7373 N. Scottsdale Road, Suite B-160
Scottsdale, Arizona 85253
602-948-2902

Land Planner/Clubhouse Architect

Gage Davis Associates
Scottsdale, Arizona

Golf Course Designer

Weiskopf/Morrish Golf Course Design
Scottsdale, Arizona

Notes

[1]Includes swimming pool and four tennis courts.
[2]Includes parks, signage, gatehouse, and fencing.
[3]Includes real estate taxes.

Seaside

Walton County, Florida

Seaside is a small 80-acre resort town on the Gulf of Mexico in northwest Florida, in Walton County not far from Panama City. Its original master plan called for 350 houses, 200 apartment units, and 200 hotel rooms as well as office and retail space and a small conference center. Seaside's compact village plan, innovative development standards and building code, and unifying palette of forms and materials make the town a unique second-home resort community. Its spirit is reminiscent of small-town rural America, though the community evidences a contemporary flair in its neoclassical architecture.

Seaside reflects not only the tradition of early-20th century resort communities such as Oak Bluffs on Martha's Vineyard and Mackinac Island, Michigan, but also the feel of small southern towns. It is a significant departure from the typical high-density beachfront condominiums or self-contained planned unit residential developments with cookie-cutter buildings and lot sizes. It deliberately incorporates varying lot types and home designs. Seaside's urban design and architectural code carefully spelled out the standards that would create the unifying Seaside spirit and compact village densities while encouraging a diverse group of houses, offices, shops, and workshops.

Master Planning and Design

Seaside is located on the ocean in Florida's panhandle. Immediately adjacent to the east is the village of Seagrove Beach, a collection of bungalows, small stores, and motels built since the mid-1940s. Route 30A, a county road with a 70-foot right-of-way, splits Seaside's 80-acre site and runs parallel to the beach. The beach itself is broad, with fine white sand backed by 30-foot-tall dunes covered with a variety of vegetation. Two gorges breach the dunes, allowing pedestrian access to the shoreline.

Seaside's developer—Seaside Community Development Corporation (Robert Davis, principal)—and the planning and design team of Andres Duany and Elizabeth Plater-Zyberk of Miami—along with design consultants Robert A.M. Stern of New York and Leon Krier of London, England—worked together to make Seaside a genuine town with more than just beach houses. Seaside boasts public buildings, civic spaces, apartments, offices, and retail activity at the core organized around a geometric, hierarchical system of roads and pathways that encourages walking in favor of driving. The goal was to create a lively, urban-type setting at the beach that would maximize beachfront access and ocean views.

Drawn from small-town archetypes, the project's street pattern is the plan's organizing element. The central square provides an overall community focus while a concentric street pattern responds to the topography and takes its cue from the existing grid in an adjacent beach development. Streets run north and south and terminate at the beach to afford a greater number of buildings an ocean view. A network of alleylike public pathways lined with picket fences—with numerous through-block connections—is designed to make walking more convenient than driving.

Major public facilities (town hall, church, school, and club) are sited well back from the beach to encourage activity on the site's inland portions. Along the beach is a series of small neoclassical beach pavilions, each of which belongs to the homeowners' association of the corresponding north/south street. A pair of larger, centrally located beachfront clubhouses serves residents along east/west streets. A restaurant and small retail market complement the central beachfront area. The Park—located in the northeast corner of Seaside—offers tennis courts, a croquet court, a fitness center, and other small amenities set among the trees and linked by informal footpaths.

The carefully crafted master plan spread the oceanfront value across the site. Further, instead of assuming that large upfront investments in amenities would generate marketing payoffs, the development moved slowly under the guidance of the master plan and seeded amenities throughout the development.

The heart of the Seaside master plan is a hierarchy of lot types for private buildings, which fall into eight categories. Three categories generally cover mixed-use development at various scales, three deal with residential development, and one addresses workshops. For each category, the code spells out standards for yards, porches, outbuildings, parking, and building heights. The first building types constructed were of Type VI, the "suburban section" of Seaside. Based on prototypes found throughout the South, these homes are low, freestanding residences with front porches, picket fences, and gable or shed roofs. To ensure that all homes enjoy views of the sea, the plan waives height limits for small-footprint towers. The "suburban" lots become smaller as they progress toward the town center.

In contrast, Type I lots, which define the town's large central square, were intended for ground-floor retail uses with residential occupancies above. The urban design code for Type I lots mandates buildings of up to five stories, with party walls and an arcade along the front. Parking is located at the front of the buildings.

Steven Brooke

Steven Brooke

Seaside is an 80-acre resort community that has pioneered neotraditional planning principles. Pictured is a view of Odessa Street and the street's beach pavilion. Beach pavilions punctuate the coastline at the end of each of the seven north/south streets in the community.

The honeymoon cottages along the beach, as viewed from the East Ruskin Pavilion. Seaside's building code is intended to produce simple, durable structures that reflect regional building traditions, styles, and materials.

The plan also provides for other development types such as office space with apartments in the style of the New Orleans Vieux Carré, large mansions or rooming houses that line a broad processional boulevard, and sideyard houses on small lots as in Charleston. A large-lot category allows for yet another building option.

Understandable even to nondesigners, the urban design code is presented in a one-page diagrammatic table of performance standards. With most resort devel-

opment characterized by a highly refined design concept coupled with central ownership and tight control over design and building decisions, Seaside has instead encouraged authentic diversity by delegating to others as many design decisions as possible while still holding to the dictates of the sophisticated urban design plan. Design controls, though strict, are limited to specific relevant provisions that support the overall urban design concept. To promote diversity, the code allows

The Ruskin Place Artist Colony Townhomes.

Steven Brooke

The townscape seen from the roof of the Holl Building. The plan and building code produced graceful buildings that are well adapted to the region's climate and that aged well as a result of using largely indigenous and time-tested materials.

Steven Brooke

the owner or designer to participate directly in the building design. In practice, Seaside's framework for design has produced a remarkably unified though genuinely diverse place.

A more detailed aesthetic and construction code, also easily comprehensible to the nonprofessional, governs specific building forms and materials. Design controls ensure that all development reflects the character of the area, particularly wood construction, porches and deep roof overhangs, numerous vertically proportioned windows, and above-grade floors. In fact, most of Seaside's early houses had pine floors, wood walls and ceilings, and crimped-tin roofs. Lot buyers or their designers submit building plans to the town architect (who is selected by the developer and planners) and to the construction inspector. The developer retains final approval. To preserve flexibility, any requirements can be waived for exceptional architectural merit.

By scattering small-scale amenities—such as the Park, the pavilions, pools, tennis courts, and the town square—throughout Seaside, the community created value for the surrounding lots. For example, a small

beach pavilion built at opening for $20,000 greatly increased the value of adjacent lots. A $12,000 gazebo created an early focal point for Seaside away from the beach and spurred the development of an 11-unit planned unit development, boosting lot values in the vicinity of the gazebo.

Management and Marketing

In 1980, developer Robert Davis paid $1 million for 80 acres on Florida's panhandle, about $12,000 per acre, and named the development Seaside. Davis invested a considerable amount in upfront planning, with an excellent return on investment as it turned out. He invested another $35,000 per acre in site improvements, bringing the total cost of finished lots to $50,000 per acre. Davis began to sell the lots at a deliberately slow pace in order to reduce risk. In fact, he chose not to record the master plan until he had gained several years' experience with building and marketing. The deferred recordation allowed for minor refinements in the development strategy, plan, and timing, all as prices rose accordingly.

By 1986, three of the project's six phases were underway, and 126 lots had been sold and 60 houses built. Phased development began on the eastern half of the site. Beach pavilions for each of the north/south streets were built as well as a pool and tennis court, restaurant and market, and Greek Revival post office.

From the outset, the financial results were dramatic. Lots that sold for $15,000 to $25,000 in the early 1980s would have sold for $50,000 to $75,000 if available for resale in 1986. Moreover, the early sale lots were not even prime beachfront lots; instead, they were located up to 200 yards from the beach and were as small as 1,700 square feet. For their part, beachfront lots sold at close to four times the amount of the more interior lots. Between 1982 and 1996, the town enjoyed a 25 percent annual appreciation in the price of its lots. As of 1995, all of the lots had sold, over 225 homes had been built, and the community was more than 80 percent completed. Purchasers of homesites are required to construct a cottage within two years of the date of purchase.

The national media attention generated by Seaside has helped attract buyers and visitors to the community from around the country. In 1990, *Time* magazine recognized the project as Best Design of the Decade. *U.S. News and World Report*, the *Atlantic Monthly*, and numerous newspapers have likewise featured Seaside. The May 15, 1995, issue of *Newsweek* said, "Seaside— with its cozy, narrow streets, its jumble of pastel-colored homes—is probably the most influential resort community since Versailles." With accolades such as this in the national press, it is no wonder that visitors have flocked to the community and that home/lot prices have risen dramatically.

In addition to home sales, rental occupancies have been high. Early on, about half of Seaside's owners participated in a rental program managed by a subsidiary of the development company. Combined with the town hall's small meeting space that accommodates around 100, the rental program allows Seaside to accommodate small groups.

Each owner of a lot belongs to a neighborhood association that is responsible for maintenance of private common areas and the street. Common maintenance costs for each association cover insurance; painting and repairs to the beach pavilion, gazebos, and garden structures; street landscaping; and maintenance of the street itself.

Lessons Learned

Seaside demonstrates the potential for high financial return from excellent—and innovative—design and planning. The combination of a low-density beachfront and high-density town core concept was unique for its time. Residents can enjoy an unspoiled beach environment while experiencing small-town life focused around an old-fashioned town square. Rental apartments and hotel rooms are available in the core. The north/south orientation of the town maximizes beach views. The carefully thought out road and path system provides easy access to the beach and town center.

Seaside's urban design and architectural code provided unifying neoclassical and small-town elements while providing flexibility in building styles. The strict code ensured buyers that surrounding houses would be compatible and tasteful and not block their beach views or access. The fact that the code was simple and could be easily interpreted by owners who wanted to design their own house by engaging just a builder created additional market opportunities. The variation in lot sizes and house sizes recreated the natural diversity that characterizes small towns. For example, simple cottages as well as mansions designed by famous architects line Seaside's streets.

Seaside also provides an example of how a low basis in land is pivotal to strong financial results. Seaside's acquisition cost left room for the upfront investment in planning and design that has made the community the success it is today. It also demonstrates that major upfront amenities are not critical to a strong sales program. Small amenities are equally as valuable in maximizing lot values. The creative use of amenities in areas of the development away from the beach can also assist in maximizing lot values. A master plan that makes the most of beach views and access spreads beachfront value across the development.

Seaside also provides a lesson in how urban design controls can promote diversity and good taste without resorting to traditional subdivision ordinances. The latter often contain restrictive street standards and setback requirements that result in a uniformity of lot sizes and architectural elevations and, ultimately, boring and uninspiring communities. Had Seaside not been approved before Walton County enacted a performance zoning ordinance, with which Seaside does not comply, Seaside would never have become an architectural gem.

The Seaside Post Office. The neoclassical style exhibited here is only one of a number of styles—including Georgian, Victorian, Arts and Crafts, etc.—found in Seaside.

The Town of
SEASIDE

SEASIDE, FLORIDA

MASTER PLAN AND PRICES SUBJECT TO CHANGE WITHOUT NOTICE

© 1995 BY SEASIDE COMMUNITY REALTY, INC.

Project Data: Seaside

Land Use Information

Site area	80 acres
Gross density	9 dwelling units per acre
Net density	15 dwelling units per acre

Total Dwelling Units

350 single-family homes

Approximately 300 apartments and hotel rooms

Land Use Plan

	Acres
Residential	23.6
Workshop (commercial/residential)	2.5
Retail and hotel	11.0
Beach	14.0
The Park	7.5
Plazas and parks	9.0
Streets	11.6
Meeting spaces (town hall and church)	0.8
Total	80.0

Residential Information

Lot Size (square feet)	Number
1,680	32
2,500	46
3,600	102
4,800	45
5,760	62
2,500 (beachfront)	14
5,000 (beachfront)	14
Total	315
Residences built (1996)	259

Rental Homes

Rental cottages	206
Honeymoon cottages	12
Dreamland suites	8
Motor court suites	6
25 Central Square	7
Total	239

Amenities

Tennis courts	6
Swimming pools	3
Beachfront	0.5 mile
Beach pavilions	8
Food service outlets	10
Town hall	2,000 square feet
Other	Croquet, catamaran rentals, bicycle rentals, shuffleboard, nature walks

Commercial Sales/Rent Information

Retail sales	$300–$1,630 per square foot
Office rents	$18–$20 per square foot

Development Schedule

1980	Site purchased
1981	Construction started
1982	Lot sales began
1996	Approximately 80 percent complete
2000	Estimated completion date

Developer

Seaside Community Development Corporation, Inc.

P.O. Box 4730

County Road 30A

Santa Rosa Beach, Florida 32459

904-231-2207

Town Planner

Duany & Plater-Zyberk Architects

1023 Southwest 25th Avenue

Miami, Florida 33135

305-644-1023

Design Consultants

Robert A.M. Stern

New York, New York

Leon Krier

London, England

Boca Raton Resort & Club

Boca Raton, Florida

The Boca Raton Resort & Club is a historic resort hotel and club in one of the premier resort areas of the United States, the Atlantic beaches of southern Florida known as the Gold Coast. It is not only a hotel but also a private club, and much of its bottom-line profit results from its club operations. Throughout its history, it has been a renowned resort and was one of the great society hotels of the 1930s and 1940s as well as an exclusive private country club. It has continued to operate and maintain its five-star rating throughout numerous ownerships dating back to its origins in 1926.

Over the property's history, Boca Raton's owners have implemented a strategy of ongoing renovation and new construction in order to maintain the resort's historically high standards and market position. While hotel/resort renovations have typically taken place every four to five years at Boca Raton, scheduled renovations have been carried out every year since 1983. In addition, numerous additions to both the hotel and club have been completed over time. The high standard established and maintained by the Boca Raton Resort & Club was in fact a critical factor in setting the standards for the entire Boca Raton resort area, which is now one of the most exclusive resort and recreational communities in the United States.

Early Development History

In 1926, Addison Mizner bought 17,500 acres of land in the Boca Raton area and built a hotel originally called the Cloister Inn. After his success with the wealthy of Palm Beach, who clamored for him to design their estates, Mizner began to design "the greatest resort in the world" in Boca Raton. His Cloister Inn was the most expensive 100-room hotel built at that time. It attracted royalty and the exclusive social set of the era. After opening the hotel, however, Mizner went bankrupt amid the bust of Florida's land boom. Charles Dawes, a former U.S. vice president, and his brother Rufus took over the financial chaos.

In 1928, the Dawes brothers sold the hotel to a utility magnate who invested another $8 million in an exclusive "gentlemen's club" and expanded the property to include additional rooms. The owner subsidized the perennial club deficit through the years of the Great Depression. During World War II, the U.S. government took over the hotel as an Army Air Corps trainee facility.

J. Meyer Schine, a hotel, theater, and real estate magnate and developer, purchased the property in 1946 for only $3 million and restored it to its former grandeur. He also brought convention business to the hotel. In 1956, Schine sold it to Arthur Vining Davis for $22.5 million, the largest real estate deal in Florida at the time. Davis formed the Arvida Corporation in 1958, which subsequently owned and operated the hotel until 1983. During its tenure, Arvida initiated a $14 million expansion program that included the 27-story Tower and the Golf Villa. In addition, Arvida developed a conference center to give the hotel a balanced mix of both leisure and convention business. In 1980, Arvida opened the Boca Beach Club to replace the old Cabana Club. The new club features a half-mile private beach, two swimming pools, 214 rooms, and two restaurants.

Recent Development History

In 1983, Arvida sold the property for approximately $100 million to a limited partnership led by general partner VMS Realty Corporation. The new buyers raised about $90 million in loan funds, primarily from a savings and loan and another $140 million from investors. Funds over and above the purchase price were necessary to provide debt service reserves, pay syndication fees, and provide adequate reserves for capital improvements. At that time, the hotel achieved a net operating income of only about $8 million, an amount insufficient to carry the debt service.

VMS and its management entity continued the tradition of reinvesting in and improving the hotel and club. In 1988, the Boca Raton Resort & Club acquired the Boca Country Club, approximately seven miles from the main hotel, which featured luxury homes and condominiums, a championship 18-hole golf course, tennis courts, a fitness center, and dining facilities for hotel guests, club members, and property residents. In the same year, the owners completed a major reconstruction of the original golf course. The reconstruction featured an added lake, reshaped traps, seven rebuilt holes, and new grass on greens and fairways.

In 1991, the resort and club underwent an $11 million renovation. Additional work through 1994 brought the total amount spent on refurbishment and new facilities to $60 million since 1983. The hotel's financial performance improved steadily during this time. Since 1988, every guest room in the resort has been refurbished and the 48-room concierge-level Palm Court Club has been added to the property. Meeting facilities and restaurants have been upgraded, and a

A venerable Florida resort with a long history dating back to 1926, the Boca Raton Resort & Club today includes 963 hotel rooms on 356 acres.

new fitness facility was added to the Cloister Inn. The Boca Country Club golf course was also renovated and five new tennis courts added. During the VMS ownership, Arvida retained its 40-year management contract and control of the country club, as it still owned several thousand surrounding acres of developable property.

The purchase of an Arvida condominium or home was a condition of club membership. To be sure, the resort was a superb marketing tool for selling homes. The hotel and club's longstanding reputation for luxury had created and maintained a high-end image for the Boca Raton and carried over to the development of residential communities.

The hotel's location on the Atlantic Ocean enabled the inland Boca Raton residential communities developed by Arvida to enjoy beach and marina access as a benefit of club membership in the resort, thereby creating additional real estate value. Because Arvida controlled the resort as well as thousands of acres of residential land, it was uniquely positioned sell "waterfront lots" in inland Boca Raton. Arvida developed 14,000 units in a four-golf course community in Boca West and

Boca Sound and another 1,000 second-home units eight miles west of the ocean.

During the last recession, VMS was unable to refinance the debt coming due. The savings and loan that financed the loan on the property had failed. The Resolution Trust Corporation (RTC) took control of the loan, although the debt was still a performing loan. The partnership offered to purchase the loan at par if the RTC would offer new terms, but the RTC refused. The RTC put the debt up for sale, but no buyers came forth as a result of the proxy involving VMS (the general partner) and other limited partners. The dispute cast a cloud on who legally held control and ownership of the property.

The new group that eventually replaced VMS as the general partner is the Boca Raton Management Company, led by John Temple. The new general partner refinanced the property for $150 million, worked out a settlement on the management contract with Arvida and then canceled it, and, in so doing, assumed control of the resort's destiny. Subsequently, the resort's operating revenues improved substantially.

The main entry to the resort. The resort has undergone extensive renovation in recent years, including approximately $60 million in improvements from 1983 to 1994.

The Cloister Inn at night, with the Intracoastal Waterway in the foreground.

The Resort Plan Today

The 356-acre Boca Raton Resort & Club consists of the Cloister, the Tower, the Boca Beach Club, the Golf Villas, the Boca Country Club, a convention center, two 18-hole championship golf courses, 34 tennis courts, five pools, an indoor basketball court, four indoor racquetball courts, a 25-slip marina with full fishing and boating facilities, and a half-mile private beach with watersports facilities.

The resort's original building remains an architectural jewel. The 338-room, six-level structure designed by Addison Mizner reflects Spanish-Mediterranean, Moorish, and Gothic influences. The Cloister is characterized by hidden gardens, barrel tile roofs, archways, decorative columns, finials, intricate mosaics, fountains, and beamed ceilings of ornate pecky cypress.

The luxurious Tower, with marble accents everywhere, contains 242 guest rooms and suites. The Cloisters and the Tower connect on the west side of the Intracoastal Waterway. The 214-room Boca Beach Club is located on the ocean on the east side of the resort property. It has a relaxed but elegant and airy feeling. The Golf Villas, a resort for families and serious golf groups, with 120 rooms, lies on the resort's Course.

One of the most impressive elements of the resort is its well-tended landscapes and gardens, including 60 acres of botanical gardens, a 30,000-square-foot on-site nursery, 14,000 feet of formal hedges, and many 75-foot-tall trees. This landscape, together with the complex's impressive Mediterranean architecture, gives the resort a distinctive sense of place and conveys the feeling of a rich tradition.

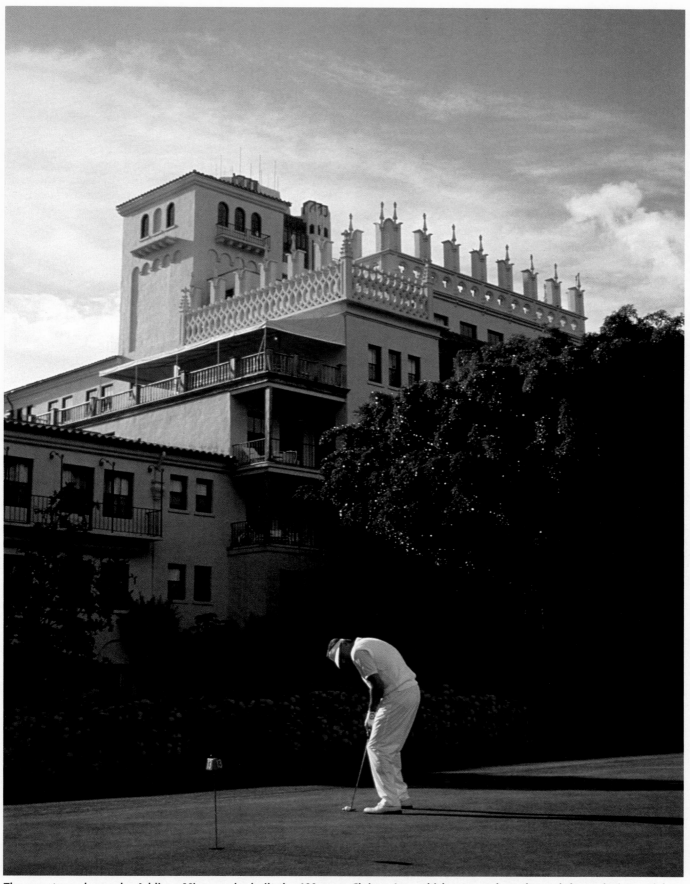

The resort was begun by Addison Mizner, who built the 100-room Cloister Inn, which attracted royalty and the exclusive social set of the era.

The Boca Beach Club, containing 214 rooms, opened in 1980 and offers the only accommodations in the resort located on the beach itself.

Two golf courses are included in the resort operation. The first is located on the grounds of the historic Cloister Inn. It was designed by architect William Flynn in 1926 and redesigned by Robert Trent Jones in 1956. The second course, as mentioned, was acquired in 1988 and is located at the Boca Country Club. It includes a 40,000-square-foot clubhouse and a tennis complex.

In addition to the approximately 963 guest rooms, the resort includes approximately 70,000 square feet of meeting facilities, which have been upgraded to reflect the state of the art. Other facilities and amenities include numerous swimming pools, three fitness clubs, nine restaurants, and several shops. The tennis facility, including 34 tennis courts, has placed the resort among the top 50 tennis resorts in the country, according to *Tennis* magazine. And the 25-slip marina offers a variety of fishing, boating, and watersports facilities and services, including deep-sea fishing charters, sailing char-

ters, luxury motor yacht cruises, power-boat rentals, cigarette boat rides, catamaran cruises, scuba diving, and Everglades tours. The marina can accommodate vessels up to 170 feet long.

Lessons Learned

The Boca Raton Resort & Club, while unique in many respects, provides an excellent example of how a resort must evolve and change over time if it is to remain economically feasible. It also demonstrates how a rich tradition can enhance a resort's standing. The Boca Raton Resort & Club has survived some lean years but stands today as a premier resort. In fact, it just recently received a five-star rating from the Mobil Travel Guide and a five-diamond rating from the American Automobile Association.

The property provides a poignant example of how resort amenities—and club memberships to these amenities—can be used as a key marketing tool for successful residential resort sales, even when residences are not directly proximate to the amenity. Several communities in the Boca Raton area have been successfully marketed in part because of their affiliation with the Boca Raton Resort & Club.

It is also clear that maintaining the first-class status of an older, established, heavily used resort requires constant reinvestment and renovation. As noted, every guest room in the resort has been refurbished since 1988. The resort owners have established a strategy based on the principle that "Renovation Never Rests," and they project that they will continue to spend $4 to $5 million annually on capital improvements and facility enhancements in coming years.

A rendering of the resort used in marketing materials.

Project Data: Boca Raton Resort & Club

Land Use Information

Site size	356 acres

Amenity Information

Golf courses	2 courses, 36 holes
Tennis courts	34
Marina slips	25
Private beach	0.5 miles
Swimming pools	5

Hotel Information

Total Hotel Rooms	**963**
The Cloister	338
Palm Court Club	49
The Tower	242
Golf Villas	120
Boca Beach Club	214

Average Daily Room Rate	**$250**
The Cloister	$200
The Tower	$275
Golf Villas	$250
Boca Beach Club	$330

Meeting Rooms	**70,000 square feet**

Renovation Costs

1983–1994	$60 million
Projected annual renovation cost	$4–$5 million

Development History

1926	Original site acquired
1926	The Cloister started
1928	First golf course built
1940	Use as housing for U.S. Army
1946	Hotel refurbished
1956	Resort acquired by Arthur Vining Davis
1969	Tower and Golf Villas started
1980	Boca Beach Club opened
1983	Resort acquired by VMS Limited Partnership
1988	Boca Country Club acquired
1991	Resort renovated again
1993	Acquired by current owner

Current Owner/Developer

Boca Raton Management Company and
Boca Raton Hotel & Club Limited Partnership
501 E. Camino Real
P.O. Box 5025
Boca Raton, Florida 33431
407-395-3000

Golf Course Architects

First 18-hole course designed by William Flynn, 1926
Redesigned by Robert Trent Jones, 1956
Second course designed by Joe Lee, 1985

Original Developer and Architect

Addison Mizner

Arizona Biltmore Hotel and Resort

Phoenix, Arizona

Originally built in 1929, the 500-room Arizona Biltmore Hotel and Resort, located in Phoenix, Arizona, is widely recognized for its architectural design and detail. Frank Lloyd Wright played a valuable role in the resort's original design and development, serving as consulting architect during the property's initial construction. Over the years, however, the property lost much of its luster, becoming physically dated and lacking the level of services and amenities required in an increasingly competitive luxury hotel and resort marketplace.

In June 1992, the principals of the Grossman Company Properties (GCP) acquired the resort for $61.5 million. To reposition the underperforming property, GCP devised a strategy that successfully combined value-added rehabilitation and refurbishment, new construction, and strengthened management and marketing. Throughout the project's repositioning and development initiatives, GCP faced the formidable challenge of preserving the property's architectural integrity while maintaining a competitive construction cost budget.

The resort occupies only 29.9 acres, but strategic building placement and view corridors, combined with extensive landscaping, make the property appear far larger and more spacious. Into this confined but extremely well-organized site, GCP built several essential improvements, including a pool complex (with food and beverage facilities and a 92-foot-long waterslide), a large conference/ballroom facility, and 78 two-bedroom resort condominium villas. In improving and enlarging the resort's facilities, the developer managed to maintain the resort's Frank Lloyd Wright character and sense of openness and elegance.

Hotel Renovation and Redevelopment

In an effort to adhere to the resort's original design, the developer/owner hired architect Vernon Swaback (a former apprentice of Frank Lloyd Wright) to supervise the three-phase rejuvenation project. Early in the development process, the design team researched the hotel's prominent history and original design concepts by studying archival photographs. As the resort is made up of several architecturally significant buildings (each designed and developed during different periods), the project's design and construction team had to learn and adapt to the different construction methodologies applied throughout the resort's phased buildout.

To decrease the exposure to risk typically associated with the hidden conditions of a renovation/rehabilitation effort, the development team avoided wall and demolition work wherever possible. It stripped away the hotel's dated fixtures and furniture, most of which had been installed during the property's earlier renovation. Throughout the rehabilitation and refurbishment of the hotel's guest rooms and common areas, the development team aimed for casual elegance with more of a residential theme than had existed in recent years. Dated hotel furnishings were replaced with fixtures designed in the Arts and Crafts idiom, creating a more integrated, elegant, and historically correct interior design theme. To meet market expectations for upscale resort accommodations, all guest bathrooms received marble detailing.

The Biltmore's central kitchen was so outdated that early in the development process the Phoenix Department of Health required GCP to renovate the facility to comply with local codes. Expanding and renovating the kitchen cost approximately $1 million more than the original pro forma projections, largely due to hidden conditions that came to light during the renovation.

The Biltmore's banquet/conference facilities were expanded in response to a predevelopment feasibility analysis indicating that an expansion of the facilities was essential to the resort's financial success. A 16,000-square-foot freestanding banquet/ballroom and conference facility that can accommodate up to 1,500 guests was completed in January 1995. The development team chose an innovative design for this facility, spending a considerably higher percentage of construction costs on technological applications (including a rear-screen projection system and a state-of-the-art lighting system) than on fixtures and furniture (that is, plush carpeting, ceiling finishes, and chandeliers). Innovative sales and marketing tools, including the production of a CD-ROM, allow prospective clientele to visualize the reception space and its wide range of applications. This new facility was built for approximately $60 per square foot.

To compete with the growing number of upscale hotel resorts within the Phoenix market, GCP added a luxurious pool complex, which includes six pools and two spas, an elegant bar and café, guest cabanas, and a waterslide. The waterslide, designed by Swaback (to attract and accommodate a younger market), was built within an architecturally prominent structure. In addition, to provide both a new amenity for hotel guests

The Arizona Biltmore, designed in part by Frank Lloyd Wright, opened in 1929 and helped establish the Phoenix area as a resort destination. The property has been completely renovated with some new additions made.

and an additional source of revenue, the developers turned a portion of the land surrounding the guest cottages into the 18-hole championship Biltmore Putting Course. The 715-yard course, designed to PGA specifications, provides an authentic golf experience for the serious golfer and an enjoyable, nonthreatening experience for the novice. Guests also enjoy access to the Arizona Biltmore Country Club and its two 18-hole golf courses—the Adobe and the Links. Other amenities and leisure activities include eight tennis courts, croquet, lawn chess, and bicycle riding through the adjacent Biltmore Estates.

Villa Development

A central component of the Arizona Biltmore's repositioning is the development of 78 for-sale second-home resort condominium villas. Constructed on 4.9 acres surrounding the resort's historic 1929 catalina pool, the villa complex comprises 18 individual structures, each housing four to six condominium units. Also designed by Swaback, the villas are two-story, stick-built structures with scored stucco exteriors resembling the resort's historic concrete block buildings. The decorative brickwork (a.k.a. Wrightian Block) found on buildings throughout the property has been incorporated throughout the newly developed villa complex. The ornate blocks

Frank Lloyd Wright was consulting architect to the original 1929 building.

The newly developed condominium villas have scored stucco exteriors that resemble the decorative concrete block buildings that are found throughout the historic resort property.

(trademarked by the developer as Biltmore Block) were reproduced cost effectively by using a light-weight—but extremely dense—molded polyurethane foam that was later painted to resemble the original decorative concrete block.

Biltmore condominium owners have the option of placing their respective units in the resort/hotel rental pool when not in use. With this in mind, the 1,626-square-foot, two-bedroom, two-bathroom condominiums were planned and designed with two separate outside entrances and a locking door to allow each unit to be divided into a one-bedroom suite and an upscale hotel room.

Built for approximately $118 per square foot, the villas cost more than originally projected. After the model units were designed, built to residential specifications, and sold, local regulatory officials required the remainder of the units to be built in compliance with commercial specifications for enhanced fire protection, including a two-hour firewall separation between units and extensive sprinkling systems.

Operation and Management

Condominium Villa Management. The condominium villa/hotel strategy created win-win opportunities for both condominium owners and GCP. By placing their condominiums in the resort's rental pool, owners can generate limited cash flow when their units are not in use. The developer was able to generate profitable yields from the initial sale of each unit and, at the same time, finance the expansion of the hotel with minimal capital investment and no future debt service obligations.

The management of the villa rental pool is relatively straightforward. Participating condominiums are pooled, with the total room revenue generated by the villas divided equally among the villa owners and the developer. Once the villa owners achieve a predetermined level of return, the developer receives approximately 65 percent of total villa revenues. This "hurdle rate" gives the hotel an added incentive to increase villa rental occupancy.

With an average sale price of $204 per square foot, all 78 villas sold between November 1994 and December 1995, 12 months sooner than expected. Approximately 80 percent of villa owners participate in the rental program, increasing the resort's room inventory by approximately 20 percent.

Resort/Hotel Management. Shortly after assuming ownership of the underperforming hotel, GCP dismissed the national hotel management corporation that had been operating the property for approximately 17 years. The typical standardization and institutional practices of a national hotel management entity ran contrary to both GCP's repositioning and management philosophies and the image of the Arizona Biltmore. Independent management and operation have proven successful for the Biltmore owners. In 1990, two years before acquisition, the property generated a $4.1 million loss before debt service and capital expenditures. In 1995, the hotel produced a positive cash flow exceeding $11 million, also before debt service and capital expenditures.

Throughout the resort's 30-month renovation and repositioning, the phased construction and refurbishment initiatives allowed the hotel to operate efficiently. No more than half of the hotel's guest rooms were removed from the rental pool, permitting the hotel to maintain reasonable occupancy rates and cash flow during all phases of rejuvenation.

The Arizona Biltmore pool complex.

The new championship 18-hole putting course is nestled among the property's guest cottages.

Lessons Learned

Meeting guest expectations while a project is under construction within a resort setting can be a challenging endeavor that requires considerable management initiative. Nevertheless, the rejuvenation period can provide valuable training for resort employees who are often forced to devise appropriate and cost-effective solutions to problems during potentially difficult times.

While the developer was able to use condominium development to increase the resort's profitability, room inventory, and future cash flow, a possible drawback to this approach is that a cadre of condominium owners may perceive that they have an interest in the resort's management and operation decisions and thereby demand a high level of property management and residential services.

By embracing the resort's unique historic and architectural assets, the developer successfully repositioned the property in a sensitive yet market-driven and cost-effective manner. By choosing to operate and manage the upscale resort independently, GCP enhanced and capitalized on the resort's distinctive attributes and historic reputation and avoided any conflicting identity that an institutional hotel management entity might bring to the resort.

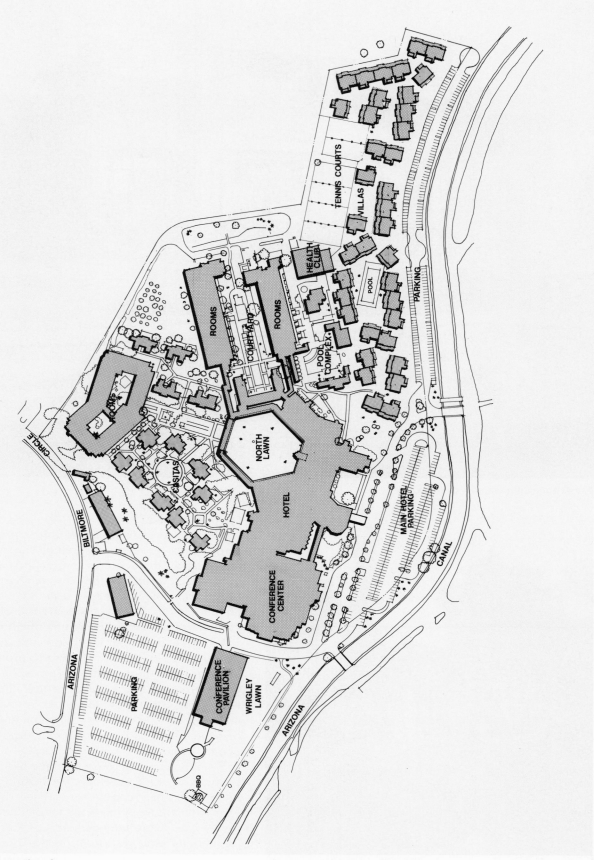

The Arizona Biltmore site plan.

Project Data: Arizona Biltmore Hotel and Resort

Land Use Plan

	Acres
Hotel	25.0
Condominium villas	4.9
Total	29.9

Hotel Information

Total hotel rooms planned	600
Total hotel rooms completed	500
Average daily room rate	$190
Average annual occupancy rate	68%

Condominium Villa Information

Condominium square footage	1,626
Number of units planned / built	78 / 40
Range of current sales prices	$289,000-$435,000[1]
Rents	$1,850
Typical price per condominium villa unit	$372,000
Units sold	78
Units under construction (1996)	38

Site Acquisition Cost

Site Acquisition Cost	$61,500,000

Hotel Renovation and Expansion Costs

Construction Costs

Room renovation and upgrade	$8,936,006
New pools, tennis, and spa facility	3,023,195
Public area and site upgrades	1,981,296
New pavilion conference facility	4,021,554
Engineering, HVAC, roofs, fire safety	3,435,484
Systems upgrades and electronic locks	760,307
Laundry expansion and upgrades	322,868
Food and beverage renovation and expansion	5,690,449

Soft Costs

Soft Costs	$4,443,138

Total renovation and expansion costs	$32,614,787

Condominium Villa Development Costs

Site Improvement Costs

Excavation/grading	$110,315
Sewer/water/drainage	173,801
Paving/curbs/sidewalks	229,715
Landscaping/irrigation	38,874
Fees/general conditions	122,578
Total	$675,283

Construction Costs

Superstructure	$4,065,205
HVAC	196,629
Electrical	220,828
Plumbing/sprinklers	13,673
Finishes	2,103,272
Graphics/specialties	20,000
Fees/general conditions	308,260
Total	$6,927,867

Soft Costs

Architecture/engineering	$93,722
Project management	74,583
Marketing	250,000
Legal/accounting	54,331
Construction interest and fees	118,688
Total	$591,324

Total Villa Development Costs (1995)	$8,194,474
Total Villa Development Costs Expected at Buildout	$16,899,684

Development/Renovation Schedule

June 1992	Hotel purchased
June 1992	Planning started
May 1993	Renovation started
November 1994	Villa sales started
November 1995	Renovation completed
December 1995	Villa sales completed

Developer

Grossman Company Properties
3101 N. Central Avenue
Phoenix, Arizona 85012
602-285-1300

Architect/Site Planner

Vernon Swaback Associates
7550 E. McDonald Drive
Scottsdale, Arizona 85250
602-991-6700

Note

[1]Plus furniture package at $45,000.

Spanish Bay Resort

Pebble Beach, California

The Spanish Bay Resort was developed by the Pebble Beach Company on the Monterey Peninsula in the 1980s to create world-class visitor accommodations and golf, tennis, and residential facilities that would complement the company's existing resort and recreational facilities at the Lodge at Pebble Beach. The two resorts are located less than five miles from both Monterey and Carmel on the famous 17-mile drive in the Del Monte Forest area of northern California.

The Spanish Bay Resort is unique in that it reused and rehabilitated a highly disturbed site containing a silica sand mine and two processing plants. Mining activities had severely modified about 80 percent of the site's terrain, leaving only small remnants of pine forest and shoreline dune habitat. The Pebble Beach Company was able to overcome substantial community concerns, achieve the company's development expectations, and meet the critical environmental planning objectives necessary for successful restoration. The company's accomplishment is especially notable for northern California, where environmental and growth concerns have run strong for several years.

The Pebble Beach Company recreated much of the original character of the dune landform and shoreline area. It improved public access to the beach and, in restoring the dunes and terrain disrupted by previous mining use, enhanced the area inhabited by endangered species and native vegetation. The company publishes an annual environmental report on these and other ongoing activities for the benefit of the community.

The Site and Development Process

The 236-acre Spanish Bay Resort clings to sloping sand dunes on a rugged sweep of coastline perched on the edge of the 5,300-acre Del Monte Forest on the Monterey Peninsula. The Del Monte Forest adjoins some of California's most appealing towns: Monterey, Carmel, and Pacific Grove. The Spanish Bay Resort site is nestled on a coastal strand along the Monterey Bay Marine Sanctuary on the Pacific Ocean.

Before 1909, the Del Monte Forest contained only a narrow dirt drive and a log cabin. The drive was a scenic carriage route for guests of the old Hotel Del Monte located in nearby Monterey while the log cabin served as a rest stop along the drive. In 1919, the Del Monte Properties Company acquired the Pebble Beach site and built the Lodge at Pebble Beach. The privately held company evolved in 1919 out of various railroad interests and remained under the control of Samuel F. B. Morse until 1969.

In 1969, the Del Monte Properties Company went public. Several ownership evolutions followed through the 1970s. In the late 1970s, the Twentieth Century Fox Company acquired Del Monte Properties. In turn, Martin Davis purchased Twentieth Century Fox and acquired control of the Del Monte Properties Company.

From the 1920s through the 1960s, silica sand mining had been the principal business activity of the Pebble Beach Company on the Spanish Bay site. In the 1970s, as its mining business wound down—and development opportunities became more favorable for this outstanding oceanfront site—the company's main business focus shifted to resort development and operation. Planning began for a new resort community that would complement the existing Pebble Beach Resort and accommodate larger groups in the same luxurious style made famous by the Lodge at Pebble Beach.

The commercial use of Spanish Bay as a resort community was originally the vision of Morse in the 1930s. In 1966, he succeeded in obtaining a commercial designation for the site in the local county general plan. Active planning for the resort began in the mid-1970s. Davis continued pursuing development of a resort community on the Spanish Bay site, ultimately bringing in partners to direct the necessary real estate development activities. Completion of the entitlement processes occurred under the ownership of the Miller-Klutznick-Davis-Gray Company (MKDG) in 1984 and construction of the inn and golf course began in 1985.

The Development Concept

Given the high-end market position already established at Pebble Beach and the high cost of developing a site that would generate considerable difficulties during the entitlement process—not to mention numerous community concerns—the Pebble Beach Company adopted the strategy that a luxury, high-end project would be the most likely candidate for both approval and financial success. The resort includes the 270-room oceanside Inn at Spanish Bay. As a luxury facility, the inn boasts deluxe accommodations that feature fireplaces. Built on 20 acres, the property is oriented to conference guests and offers 14,000 square feet of meeting and banquet space on two levels. A state-of-the-art meeting facility with an 800-seat ballroom that can be divided into three smaller sections is complemented by a 15-foot-high ceiling that accommodates displays, projection requirements and special

The Spanish Bay Resort in Pebble Beach, California, encompasses 237 acres and features a 270-room hotel and 48 condominium units, with an additional 32 units planned.

lighting effects, and an indoor/outdoor prefunction promenade. Five additional meeting rooms with capacities that range from ten to 250 are equipped with sound and teleconferencing systems.

The resort's primary amenity is the classic par-72, 18-hole, 6,820-yard Scottish links-style golf course surrounding the inn, integrally incorporated into the restored dunes landscape. The resort also plans an 80-unit project of luxury residences on 20 acres. As of 1995, more than half the units were completed with the remainder under construction. The residences, in the form of four townhouse units per building, are clustered adjacent to the 12th, 13th, 14th, and 18th holes. Units range from 3,600 to 4,200 square feet. The hotel and residences form islands in the golf course, which is laid out primarily along the ocean around the resort's perimeter.

The golf links opened in late 1987, and the golf clubhouse and inn in 1988. The first residences were sold in 1989; phase I of the residences sold out in 1990. Phase II was virtually sold out by early 1995. The final phase (phase III) is underway.

Amenities

The main amenity is the spectacular links-style golf course built on 176 acres. Three of golf's most prominent figures—U.S. Open Champion Tom Watson, former USGA President Sandy Tatum, and golf course architect Robert Trent Jones, Jr.—collaborated on the design of the Links at Spanish Bay. Attesting to the successful collaboration, *Golf Digest* named the Links at Spanish Bay Best New Resort Course shortly after its opening in 1988.

The site available to the designers was perfectly suited to links-style design: a gently rolling, windswept oceanside area typified by sand dunes. The design's Scottish influence is observable everywhere on the course. The small greens are nestled between dunes, pot bunkers hide behind grassy mounds, and fescue grasses cover tees, fairways, and greens to provide the firm playing surface characteristic of the historic Scottish links. The oceanside holes offer splendid views of the crashing Pacific. The inland holes are bordered by tall pines that vest the course with a classic look. Among the course's memorable holes are the third,

The hotel pool with the golf/fitness club in the background.

The golf/fitness club exterior, as viewed from the first tee.

which is a par-4, 425-yard hole from a dramatic elevated tee, and the 13th hole, which turns the player back toward the Pacific and into the dunes.

In addition to resort guests and homeowners, the public enjoys access to the golf course. Although several other outdoor amenities are available to resident and nonresident nongolfers, the Spanish Bay Club features both a heated pool and a first-class spa with state-of-the-art fitness equipment, massages, spa therapy treatments, and group fitness classes. As its name suggests, the Spanish Bay Tennis Pavilion offers tennis facilities. With a local membership of nearly 500, the Spanish Bay Club has also become a popular retreat for the local community.

With 30 acres of the 176 acres of golf course fronting on the ocean and beach, the public frequently uses the course for walking and nature study. Boardwalks provide access to the beach, which is the province of surfers and kayakers. The inn employs a nature concierge who assists in arranging and coordinating group or individual activities for "back to nature" experiences. A professional photographer from the Ansel Adams Gallery at the inn hosts camera walks.

The Del Monte Forest is laced with more than 25 miles of riding and hiking trails, some of which originate from Spanish Bay and some of which originate from the Pebble Beach Equestrian Center, which provides guided trail rides. Nature walks through the Samuel F. B. Morse Botanical Reserve are another option. Bicycling, kayaking, fishing, scuba diving, and whale-watching excursions can also be arranged.

Approval Process

The Spanish Bay Resort project was subjected to a complex approval process that stretched over a ten-year period. Primary opposition surfaced from environmental and no-growth groups and some local residents who had used the resort's site for seaside walks after the sili-

A public boardwalk was built to provide pedestrian access to the oceanfront over a restored dune habitat.

ca mine had ceased operation. Chief concerns related to continued access to the shoreline and its sandy beaches, setback distances between the beach and golf course, and hotel setbacks from both the beach and the 17-mile drive. The Pebble Beach Company adopted a methodical approach for slowly overcoming each expressed concern and incorporating meaningful design criteria into a comprehensive coastal development plan, which is now under development by the county board of supervisors and the California Coastal Commission. The company succeeded in obtaining the necessary approvals through perseverance, in-depth documentation of evidence on each issue, thorough and professional environmental analysis and planning, and well-maintained records of every conversation and meeting held with the community and community groups on issues of concern.

As a measure of the deliberateness of the company's approach, neither the project design nor site plan

underwent any significant change in the first five years following the grant of project approval. For example, in anticipation of citizen calls for reconstruction of the shoreline and dunes to their premining state, the company built test dunes for the purpose of applying a variety of revegetation strategies. In this way, the company could—in advance of public hearings—identify the best-performing revegetation alternatives, identify the cost implications of various alternatives, and specify the ultimately acceptable revegetation approaches.

An important first step the company took in working with the community was to identify a cadre of citizens who would serve as community representatives, thereby ensuring that dialogue would proceed on a reasonable and technical basis. The community task force that emerged from the company's efforts permitted the developer to deal primarily with relatively few representatives—rather than with an entire body of citizens. In addition, the local homeowners' association, the Del

Monte Forest Property Owners (DMFPO), established an Open Space Advisory Committee comprised of a group of respected local biologists and naturalists who had previously held leadership positions in local chapters of prominent environmental organizations. The committee successfully documented community concerns and presented and discussed alternatives that responded to these concerns, again in a climate of reasonableness.

The advisory group ultimately supported the project and concluded that the Spanish Bay plan provided environmental benefits. The county board of supervisors also recognized the project's environmental and economic benefits, especially in view of the role of tourism as a vital part of the county's economy and tax base. With the board's support and after a ten-year effort that addressed myriad concerns, the project won county approval.

Even after approval, however, some of the project's more vocal critics were not silenced. It was a testament to the documentation, negotiating skill, and diligence of the developers of Spanish Bay that no opponent ever filed a lawsuit or called for a referendum, presumably because no basis could be found to oppose the project. In the end, the public at large and local and state decision makers were won over by the merits of the project

and the strong commitment of the Pebble Beach Company to put forth all efforts necessary to implement the plan responsibly and to comply with the many conditions imposed on the project.

Master Planning and Design

The site presented several challenging planning demands, including the need to restore the terrain disrupted by past silica mining, the need to set the hotel and golf course back from the shoreline to conform to regional planning criteria, and the need to preserve and enhance remnant sand dune and forested areas. Fitting a variety of resort uses into the environment with the least disruption of public views while creating a user-friendly and operationally efficient facility was difficult at best.

While the development's impact on the shoreline was a major issue, the mining operation had left little of value to preserve—other than views and access to the shoreline. As a result, a major opportunity for shoreline restoration presented itself in the form of golf course development. Development of the links in accordance with a specific routing concept and an extensive restoration plan for the dune landforms that stretched along the golf course all helped to address restoration and

Eighty luxury residential units are planned for the property. The 3,300- to 4,200-square-foot units will range in price from $900,000 up to $2.5 million.

reclamation concerns. In particular, the dune landform restoration involved the replanting of the dunes with indigenous plants, including endangered species.

Additional concerns focused on access to the shoreline and the sandy beach. As it happened, Spanish Bay Beach was located next to Asilomar State Beach Park. Over the years, park visitors and local residents had used the beachfront as a walking route. To facilitate continued and enhanced pedestrian access, Spanish Bay agreed to build boardwalks along the shoreline with connections to the resort hotel, nearby public roads, and the state park.

The company addressed shoreline setback, visual exposure, and height limit issues by siting the hotel and residences at a location that took advantage of a change in elevation, a break in the terrain, and forest clearings previously cut for the sand processing plants. Stepped back into the dunes on the ocean side to mitigate its mass, the inn appears to be only a two-story building on the 17-mile drive side. The inn and links course were sited to cause the least disruption of public views while creating an appealing and operationally efficient facility.

In an area characterized by a severe shortage of water, the Pebble Beach Company demonstrated creativity in meeting the demand for this critical resource. In the case of golf course irrigation, the company agreed to use reclaimed water as soon as it became available and to assume a leadership role to establish a public/private partnership to bring reclaimed water to all of the golf courses of the Del Monte Forest. With the completion of a $34 million reclamation project that is financially guaranteed by the Pebble Beach Company, reclaimed water delivery to all Del Monte Forest golf courses, including the Links at Spanish Bay, began in 1994.

The Spanish Bay Resort has earned recognition for the outstanding manner in which it achieved a variety of environmental goals. Just obtaining the necessary permits to build a shoreline development on the extremely sensitive Monterey Peninsula is testament to the company's environmental responsibility. Further, local residents understand the development's public benefits. The Spanish Bay Resort opened to the public a previously industrial portion of shoreline and improved it immeasurably. The resort maximizes the scenic grandeur of its site while its sensitive design fits into and respects the shoreline.

Management and Marketing

In addition to its primary fame as a world-class golf resort, the Spanish Bay Resort is positioned as a meeting

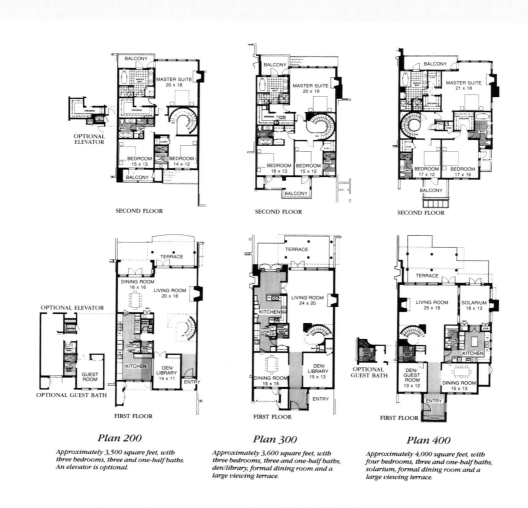

Plan 200

Approximately 3,500 square feet, with three bedrooms, three and one-half baths. An elevator is optional.

Plan 300

Approximately 3,600 square feet, with three bedrooms, three and one-half baths, den/library, formal dining room and a large viewing terrace.

Plan 400

Approximately 4,000 square feet, with four bedrooms, three and one-half baths, solarium, formal dining room and a large viewing terrace.

The golf course—named the Links at Spanish Bay—is a world-class course that benefits greatly from its proximity to and association with the world-famous Pebble Beach courses.

and conference facility. It promotes its relaxed, stress-free environment and the natural beauty of the Monterey Peninsula. The Inn at Spanish Bay is designed to provide a great deal more in leisure activities than the average resort.

Clearly, the resort's several accolades have greatly enhanced its market position. Among the accolades are *Conde Nast Traveler*'s 1993 Readers' Choice Awards, which ranked the resort number one among mainland resorts and number one worldwide. The complex also received the *Mobil Travel Guide*'s four-star award in 1994 and the American Automobile Association's four-diamond award in 1994. *Golf* magazine awarded the resort the Silver Medal Award for best golf resort in America in 1988, 1990, and 1992. The Links at Spanish Bay is ranked 24th in the 1992 list of *Golf Digest*'s greatest resort courses. In addition, *Meetings and Conventions* magazine bestowed its 1994 Gold Tee Award on the Links at Spanish Bay, which also recently became the first golf course in the state of California to achieve recognition by the New York Audubon Society for environmentally friendly design and operating policies.

Due to its exceptional quality, the Inn at Spanish Bay achieved an average annual occupancy rate of close to 85 percent in 1994 and an average daily room rate in excess of $250, both well above industry norms for resort hotels. The Inn at Spanish Bay and the Lodge at

Pebble Beach are both owned and managed by the Pebble Beach Company. The larger share of income comes from the inn as opposed to golf course operations. While both the inn and lodge are heavily patronized, the inn with its 270 rooms represents a higher-volume business. The golf course is managed as part of the inn's operations; inn guests receive priority for golf reservations.

One reason behind the development of the Spanish Bay Resort was to make the existing Pebble Beach resort more available to a wider range of business. The Lodge at Pebble Beach contained only 161 rooms, making it inadequate for larger groups. With 270 rooms, Spanish Bay's inn and conference facility was sized to accommodate large groups; even larger groups can be housed jointly at both the inn and the lodge. Business is balanced between individual and corporate customers.

In addition to the inn, the property consists of 80 luxury residential units on 20 acres. As of mid-1995, 48 of the units were completed and 46 sold. Over time, the price of the units has ranged between $900,000 and $2.5 million. The most desirable units, located on the golf course with ocean views, have sold for premiums ranging from $0.5 to $1.5 million. The value of the units depends on market conditions, site configuration, and the internal characteristics of the unit—whether an interior or end unit. The highest-priced unit to date sold for $2.5 million in 1989. Sales slowed during the recession of the early 1990s but have continued to represent a 25 percent market share of sales of comparably priced units in the Del Monte Forest area.

The cost of construction of the resort and links totaled about $140 million, which was financed by First Chicago Bank. The Pebble Beach Company's long history of successful ongoing operations and ownership of the Lodge at Pebble Beach and its strong balance sheet permitted the company to finance a high-quality, luxury project at a sufficiently deep level without cutting corners despite a tight construction budget.

Lessons Learned

The Spanish Bay Resort is a good example of how projects that depend on an inordinately lengthy entitlement process and generate considerable controversy can succeed only if the developer has the wherewithal to stay the course. In the case of the Pebble Beach Company, the developer also had the depth to hire the expertise needed to arrive at creative solutions to environmental problems while designing a functional and feasible project. At the same time, however, developing in markets in which entitlements are difficult to obtain and controversy is the norm can result in impressive returns simply because the regulatory environment keeps competition to a minimum.

The company took its environmental responsibilities seriously. It engaged experts to craft solutions to restoration and reclamation issues in ways that resulted in a first-class resort community. It sited structures and golf links in ways that permit successful operating results despite ongoing opposition. Even today, the company continues its community dialogue regarding its environmental responsibilities with the publication of an annual environmental report. Each year's report catalogs the ongoing work that is necessary to provide the solutions that the company promised at the outset.

Developing property along the coast of California is an arduous and time-consuming process. Thus, it could be argued that the Inn at Spanish Bay is a unique achievement. What gives the project its exclusive character is the site's innate beauty and dramatic qualities—which made the approval process so difficult—and the sensitive way the resort has been developed. The site's poor predevelopment condition also favored development. Considering that it took ten years to gain approval for what is without question a significant improvement in land use for the site, it is likely that resorts such as Spanish Bay will be few and far between in the next decades—at least on the coast of California.

The hotel exterior seen from across the tenth fairway.

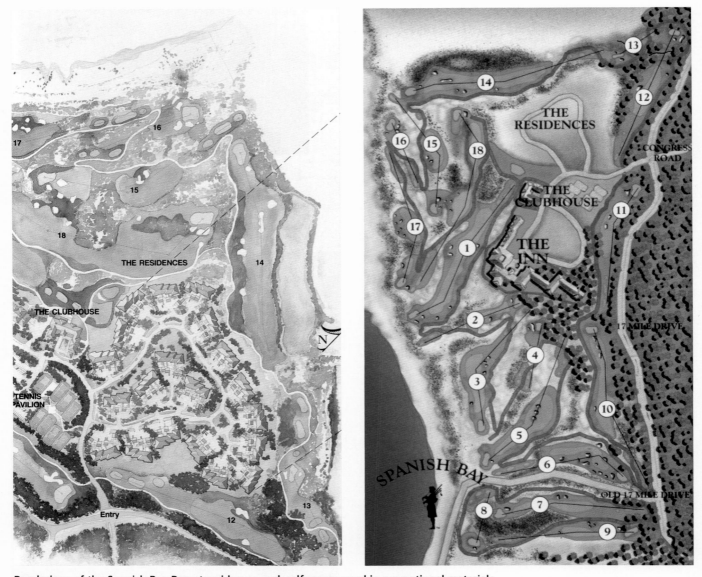

Renderings of the Spanish Bay Resort residences and golf course used in promotional materials.

Project Data: Spanish Bay Resort

Land Use Plan

	Acres
Residential	21
Hotel	20
Golf course	195
Shoreline dunes	37
Total	237

Residential Unit Information

Unit Type	Unit Size (square feet)
Condominiums—4 units/building	3,300–4,200
Plan 100, 3 bedrooms	4,200
Plan 200, 3 bedrooms	3,500
Plan 300, 3 bedrooms	3,600
Plan 400, 4 bedrooms	4,000
Number of units planned/built	80/48
Range of current sales prices	$0.5–$1.5 million

Hotel Information

The Inn at Spanish Bay	
Total hotel rooms planned	270
Total hotel rooms completed	270
Average room size	650 square feet
Conference, meeting, banquet space	14,000 square feet
Number of restaurants	2 (The Dunes, The Bay Club)
Average daily room rate	$252
Average annual occupancy rate	83.8%

Development Schedule

1919	Site purchased
1976	Planning started
1985	Construction started
1988	Hotel opened
1989	First residences sold
1995	Phase III construction started (residential units)

Developer

Pebble Beach Company
P.O. Box 1767
Pebble Beach, California 93953
408-625-8449

Golf Course Architect

Robert Trent Jones II
705 Forest Avenue
Palo Alto, California 94301
415-326-3833

Hotel Architect

Bull, Stockwell, Allen & Ripley
350 Pacific Avenue, Musto Plaza
San Francisco, California 94111
415-781-1526

Residential Architect

Esherrick, Homsey, Dodge & Davis
San Francisco, California

Landscape Architect

MPA Design
San Francisco, California

Environmental Planner and Entitlements

The Larry Seeman Company
Carmel, California

Master Builder

C.M. Peletz Company
San Francisco, California

Civil Engineers

Bestor Engineers
Monterey, California

The Little Nell Hotel

Aspen, Colorado

In the context of resort development, the Little Nell Hotel in Aspen, Colorado, is likely to be viewed as a one-of-a-kind project. It is the uniqueness of how this project was assembled and what it has achieved that helps illustrate how other unique situations can be approached.

The Little Nell Hotel incorporates two adjoining and interrelated structures—a skier services facility and a hotel. The first component, completed in 1987, was the initial portion of a 15,000-square-foot skier services facility. It functions as the base station for a gondola lift ascending Aspen Mountain and provides public conveniences, administrative space, and mechanical space that is used year round.

The completion of the Little Nell Hotel followed in 1989 and incorporated 92 guest rooms, 148 below-grade parking spaces, 3,840 square feet of conference space, 11,200 square feet of food and beverage uses, and associated athletic and administrative space. At ground level throughout the project is 12,500 square feet of independently leased retail space, including a newsstand and a variety of specialty clothing and other merchants.

Located in the center of town at the mountain's edge, the project is the primary embarkation point between the mountain and town. An open plaza is the focal point for public access at one end of the property, with a more private hotel entry anchoring the other end of the compact 1.98-acre site. An underground service corridor connects the hotel service dock to the gondola for mountaintop restaurant and other on-mountain services.

Project History and Objectives

Before its development, the site served primarily as the outrun for skiers coming off Aspen Mountain. Given its proximity to the center of Aspen, the site was generally viewed as underused and somewhat unsightly. While the Aspen Ski Company had over the years contemplated various uses for the site, it did not undertake serious planning efforts until 1985.

What stimulated the "infilling" of the site was the decision by the operator of the ski facilities to invest in a new gondola lift that would provide access to the adjoining mountain peak. Located near the center of town—and adjacent to the transit terminal that provides access to three other nearby ski mountains operated by the developer—the site was ideally positioned to evolve into the base for the new lift. The addition of the hotel allowed the site to capitalize further on the value of its mountainside location (now enhanced with the addition of the gondola) by providing adjacent parking where none had previously existed and completing the definition of the urban edge of the town fronting on the mountain base.

The developer saw that the lift/base area/hotel combination represented an important opportunity both to improve the community of Aspen and the ski mountain experience and to reinforce one of Aspen's strengths: proximity between town facilities and mountain amenities. With a heavy orientation toward pedestrian activity—Aspen features a series of successful pedestrian malls along closed streets—development of the Little Nell Hotel complex rejuvenated two long-abandoned streets, resulting in a 25 percent increase in Aspen's pedestrian space and providing a significant boost to the tax base related to the surrounding properties. The integration of the skiing facility into the town-oriented plaza linked the mountain user and town visitor experiences like never before.

The project site is zoned as a specially planned area, one of only two such sites in town. The zoning designation ensured that the site would be subject to a comprehensive and interactive review process. A less valuable site would not likely have received such a designation, nor would it likely have attracted the same level of developer investment.

The approval process took 18 months and, despite the proposal's distinction as the largest project under consideration in Aspen at the time, it moved along fairly quickly. The relatively rapid progress was the product of preliminary discussions between the developer and adjoining property owners and recognition by both public and private interests that compromise was essential to moving the proposal forward. In the end, it was the merit of the project concept that facilitated approval. In particular, the solution to achieving multiple objectives for the small site revolved around mixing uses, going underground, containing building height, relying on extensive architectural variation, and devoting extraordinary attention to design, construction, and operations details.

Development Team

The Little Nell Hotel was developed and is owned by the Aspen Ski Company, which had for many years owned the subject land as part of its base mountain lift facilities. The company's primary activity is skier-related operations at both Aspen Mountain and four other mountain complexes in the Aspen area. The Aspen Ski

The Little Nell Hotel in Aspen, Colorado, is a 92-room luxury boutique resort that incorporates retail shops, skier services, and a pedestrian plaza.

Company invests in all on-mountain improvements and leases most of the ground for its operations under a use agreement with the U.S. Forest Service. The company operates and leases out a variety of skier support facilities and owns two other lodging complexes in Aspen and nearby Snowmass.

Acting as developer, the Aspen Ski Company combined its local operations and construction experience with that of its corporate owner, the Crown family and managing partner Miller-Klutznick-Davis-Grey (MKDG). MKDG gained extensive operations and development experience with the development of the Lodge at Pebble Beach and the more recently completed Inn at Spanish Bay, also at Pebble Beach. MKDG's expertise was critical to the thinking, commitment, and approach to financing the hotel. Further, MKDG's involvement throughout the design phase ensured that the design and construction processes addressed important operating concerns. In the years following the hotel's development, MKDG ended its involvement in the project. As of early 1995, ownership of the Aspen Ski Company remained in the private hands of the Crown family.

As a leader in providing skier services, the Aspen Ski Company is fundamentally committed to the philosophy of providing high-quality services. The high-end concept for the Little Nell complex—which incorporates a range of facilities and a clublike level of skier support for the top end of its user market—dominated the company's decision to operate the hotel as a division of the parent company rather than contracting out for management services. The full-time general manager hired by the Aspen Ski Company during construction has stayed on with the property. Cottle Graybeal Yaw Architects designed the hotel while the Design Workshop provided planning services.

Hotel Design and Operations

The Little Nell Hotel is configured in a "U" shape around a natively landscaped open courtyard and outdoor heated pool area. The building combines the traditions of earlier Rocky Mountain lodges with the guest hotel features associated with the Alps. The massing, detailing, and materials harmonize with the existing textures of downtown Aspen, helping reduce the perceived size of the four-story building. This effect was achieved by creating a series of major and minor dormers along the facades and incorporating the top-floor rooms into the roof. A composite steel-frame construction technique helped reduce floor depth to a minimum.

A private courtyard for guests offers hotel dining, a swimming pool, and an outdoor spa. The courtyard is immediately adjacent to the public places and conceals the two-level parking structure. A seasonal garden is used for special events, such as food and wine festivals.

Targeting the upper end of the luxury market, the hotel facilities and services are consistent with the highest national standards. Each of the 50 standard guest rooms (640 square feet) features a gas-log fireplace and balcony or patio. The 42 premium rooms and suites offer a range of sizes and vistas. The mix of rooms has proven appropriate. Although no lock-off rooms were anticipated in the original design, some have been added since completion, affording even greater flexibility in accommodations.

The hotel's common spaces create an intimate atmosphere. The lobby is a residentially scaled living room, with the hotel bar separated to maintain the lobby's tranquillity. The main hotel dining room can seat up to 145 persons and competes for honors as offering the finest dining in Aspen. Because the facility also serves as the ski-area base, it incorporates a skier-oriented restaurant/bar that, though located in the same building, is separated from the hotel operations. After initially leasing the restaurant/bar to an outside operator, the Aspen Ski Company has taken over control of the facility to enhance its own flexibility and avoid operational conflicts.

The hotel's conference and banquet space is located on the lower level. Demand for the facilities has exceeded original projections and could easily support a facility double in size. During early project planning, a question arose as to the scale and appropriateness of conference use of the hotel. In practice, the high level of demand has eliminated any need for discounting average room rates and erased any concerns that a "conference"-type image would dominate the overall operation.

Comprehensively equipped and staffed health and workout facilities round out the in-hotel amenity offerings. The heated pool is a requisite feature and provides an attractive courtyard presence.

Concerning staffing—which is always a challenge in Aspen due to the high cost of area housing for employees—recruitment and retention at the Little Nell has benefited from a combination of the property's profile, its connection with the Aspen Ski Company, and its ability to offer genuine year-round income potential, as compared to many more seasonal competitors in Aspen or elsewhere.

Year-round hotel occupancy has run in the range of 76 percent, varying from near 100 percent in the peak winter and summer months to about 55 percent during the slower spring and fall seasons. Characteristic of broad industry trends, the Little Nell has experienced significant growth in nonski-season patronage, accentuated by the hotel's direct access to both town and mountain. Repeat business continues to grow, running at 65 percent in the 1993–1994 winter season. International business, which accounted for 10 percent of patronage in 1994, is the target of an increasing marketing effort.

The Little Nell's mountainside location and image have served the property well in earning name recognition in the facility's primary target markets, which is

Photo courtesy of Hagman Yaw Architects

The hotel's design combines traditions of earlier Rocky Mountain lodges with guest hotel features associated with the European Alps. The massing, detailing, and materials were planned to harmonize with the existing textures of downtown Aspen. The design uses a series of major and minor dormers along the facades and incorporates the rooms of the top floor into the steeply sloped roof.

especially remarkable considering the hotel's relatively young age. The facility received a five-star rating after just a year and a half of operation and has retained it ever since. Rates for standard rooms for the 1994–1995 season averaged $400 (double occupancy) during the winter months and fluctuated downwards over other periods.

Retail Space and Skier Services

Retail uses played an integral part in the original approval of the Little Nell complex and have since been an important part of the property's continuing integration within the community. The various offerings complement Aspen's thriving "destination shopping" function. As the ground-level link between town, plaza, and skier and lodging structures, the retail uses serve as physical and functional bonds. Almost all of the property's on-site retail spaces are oriented outward to the street rather than inward to the hotel, providing another example of the concerns for symbiosis of hotel and town. From the perspective of the project

Photo courtesy of Design Workshop Inc.

owner, it is critical that retailers reinforce the right tone regarding merchandise, image/style, and hours of operation.

The track record for the first five years has indicated the following:

- Smaller specialty stores perform more successfully than larger ones, reflecting local trends and befitting the hotel's one-of-a-kind image.
- Similarly, local or regional tenants meet community and guest expectations better than national operating tenants.
- Most retailers stay open seven days a week until 8:00 p.m. (in season).
- In most cases, tenants pay for their own fit-up and stocking of space.
- The Aspen Ski Company is responsible for all common area maintenance and for assessing a pro rata pass-through to tenants net of the skier-related traffic

impact; the pass-through is competitive with comparable retail space.

- For the most part, tenants have approached the landlord, although the Aspen Ski Company has courted some specific users to help round out the tenant mix.
- Net lease rates for tenants began in the range of $60 per square foot, but leases struck after the early 1990s generally exceed $110 per square foot, placing the Little Nell's retail space on par with the priciest locations in town.
- Each retailer is generally responsible for its own marketing. There is an in-room marketing brochure for the retailers, and Little Nell Hotel guests can charge purchases to their room account.
- Traffic volumes and the demand for space have resulted in efforts to relocate some Aspen Ski Company administrative offices outside the complex and to push out some perimeter walls to expand the available retail space.

The success of the shops at the Little Nell affirms that the right retailing at the right location supported by motivated landlord management can succeed year round in a resort environment.

An essential project consideration for the Aspen Ski Company was the provision of a higher and more personalized level of skier services that go well beyond space for ski storage, rentals, and uphill transportation. Apart from the obvious amenity offered by the hotel itself, the base development offers nonhotel guests a comfortable setting in which to discuss instruction and equipment or obtain lift tickets. In addition, parking is available on a seasonal basis right at the gondola base. Close-in parking is rare to nonexistent in downtown Aspen. Of the 148 parking spaces beneath the Little Nell, only 77 are required to be reserved to support the hotel. Most of the remainder may be rented on a monthly ($200 per month as of 1995) or seasonal basis.

Lessons Learned

Due to high labor costs and difficulty in transporting materials, construction costs in the Aspen area exceed national averages. Not counting land and the mechanicals for the gondola and fit-up of the retail space, construction of the Little Nell as of 1989 totaled approximately $97 per square foot and reflected significant efforts to value engineer all project components. From an accounting standpoint, construction costs could be divided between components. From a profitability standpoint, the hotel operation reportedly exceeded pro forma expectations immediately upon opening, reaching within only two years the economic stabilization needed to cover its portion of development costs.

The Aspen Ski Company generally views long-term returns against the perceived contribution of the facility to overall operations. This measure is not unlike the construction of infrastructure at a beach community or the completion of a clubhouse for golf use. Faced with the question of spinning off its hotel operations, the Aspen Ski Company decided to retain hotel operations—not because of a special fondness for hotel operations but rather because of the significance of the Little Nell to the larger mountain community.

The Little Nell also illustrates how multiple land use objectives can find common ground when both setting and purpose are compelling. In this case, the commitment of the developer to own and operate the entire facility in a manner that benefits its own much larger interests—its own recreational facilities and other community experiences—is probably the most distinguishing factor behind the Little Nell's success.

The success in marketing the property to the high-end market has helped enhance the image of all parties while underwriting a high level of annual reinvestment. The cost of maintaining the public space represents a combination of nurturing the visitor experience and maintaining positive levels of community goodwill. The level of congestion, particularly on sunny peak-season ski days, runs high but was purposefully intended.

Given the Little Nell's tight site, the potential for conflict between uses was viewed as inevitable from the outset. The result is that constant management attention is required to keep intrusion levels comfortable. (The living room lobby and adjacent bar have proved so popular that usage requires limits at times.) Finally, by retaining ownership control and sustaining a high sense of public visibility, the Aspen Ski Company has the ability to revise, update, and move the property forward. In other words, the facility can over time continue to play out its role of promoting positive visitor experiences.

The hotel has achieved high occupancies throughout the year, not just during the ski season, due to its location in the heart of Aspen.

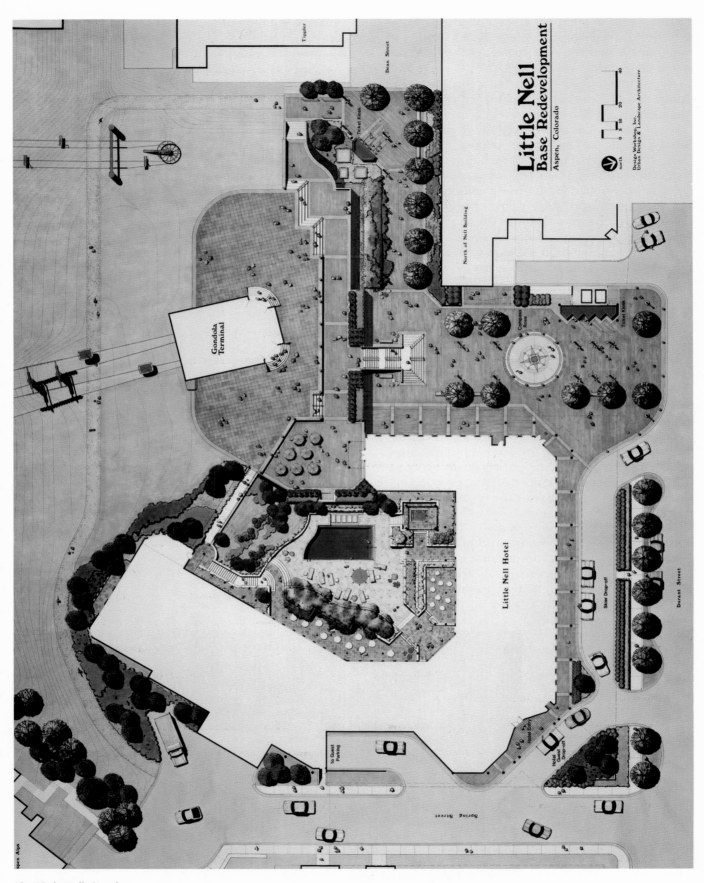

Little Nell
Base Redevelopment
Aspen, Colorado

0 5 10 20 40

north

Design Workshop, Inc.
Urban Design & Landscape Architecture

Gondola Terminal

Ticket Kiosk

Dean Street

North of Nell Building

Tipple

Compass Rose

Ticket Kiosk

Little Nell Hotel

Skier Drop-off

Durant Street

Hotel Entry

Hotel Guest Drop-off

to Guest Parking

Spring Street

Aspen Alps

The Little Nell site plan.

Hotel Information

Hotel rooms	92
Standard rooms	50 (640 square feet)
Premium rooms	42 (size varies)
Peak-season daily room rate	$400
Average annual occupancy rate	76%

Site/Building Information

Site Size	1.98 acres

Hotel Space (square feet)

Guest rooms	74,710
Public lobby	3,087
Restaurants, lounge bar (including kitchen)	11,206
Administrative	1,552
Banquet/conference	3,14
Health	2,611
Public restrooms and lockers	3,120
Service, mechanical, and support	28,545
Parking	60,686
Total	188,657

Retail Space (square feet)	12,355

Skier Services Facility (square feet)	10,934

Total Interior Space (square feet)	211,855

Development Costs

$97 per square foot (excluding land, mechanicals for skiing, and retail fit-up)

Development Schedule

1985	Planning started
November 1987	Phase I completed
November 1989	Project completed

Developer

Aspen Skiing Company
P.O. Box 1248
Aspen, Colorado 81612
303-231-9440

Site Planner

Design Workshop Inc.
Suite 200
1390 Lawrence Street
Denver, Colorado 80204
303-623-5186

Architect

Cottle Graybeal Yaw Architects, Ltd.
510 East Hyman
Suite 21
Aspen, Colorado 81611
303-925-2867

Disney's Old Key West Resort at Walt Disney World

Lake Buena Vista, Florida

After years of planning and research, the Walt Disney Company entered the timeshare market in October 1991 with the opening of the Old Key West Resort—which was originally named the Disney Vacation Club Resort. Near Orlando, Disney's Old Key West Resort is a 497-unit timeshare resort community that features a full amenity package, including a health club, tennis courts, restaurants, a lounge, and a convenience store. It is the first of several Disney Vacation Club timeshare resorts that have been developed in recent years. For a one-time purchase price and annual dues, purchasers obtain an undivided leasehold interest in the resort and are credited with an annual allotment of "vacation points." Vacation points can be used not only to reserve accommodations and to stay at the resort but also can be exchanged for a small transaction fee for accommodations at more than 200 premium national and international resorts. Unlike traditional timesharing, which has a reputation for a fair degree of inflexibility, the vacation point system provides flexibility with respect to time of year, length of stay, and size of accommodations.

Sales have been brisk, with approximately 12,000 memberships sold as of 1994; 1,500 sales were made during the first six months alone. The entry price was $12,915 in 1995, with annual dues of $566; the average price is $15,000+. Roughly 60 percent of purchasers have used financing; Disney offers five types of financing with terms ranging from one to ten years.

An important element in the Disney approach is to expand the timeshare concept from the purchase of a single timeshare unit to the purchase of a unit within a resort club. The use of the word "club" in the product's name is an important element of the program. Disney's research indicated that people want to feel a sense of belonging, exclusivity, and membership. The club breaks new ground by melding the traditional elements of a hotel, travel agency, and timeshare. By calling an 800 number, members can complete hassle-free, one-stop shopping for vacation planning and delivery, which covers everything from airline reservations to tee times. Moreover, until the end of the decade, club members are entitled to free admission to the Magic Kingdom, Epcot, and MGM Studios for the length of their stay and to discounted admissions to other Walt Disney World Resort attractions.

Development Process

In 1989, Disney executives formally recognized that hotel guests represented a potential market for the purchase of timeshare products at Walt Disney World. In evaluating the market, Disney used focus groups and quantitative research methods to develop an understanding of the needs of consumers and to gauge consumer reaction. The research identified the primary targeted market as middle- to upper-middle-income "Disneyphiles" with household income in the $60,000 to $70,000 range. Disney's unique point system, designed to respond to these consumers' expressed need for flexibility, also helps differentiate the Disney product from other timeshare products.

The 150-acre development site, located in the heart of the Walt Disney World Resort on the Lake Buena Vista Golf Course, was already under Disney ownership and planned for residential use. Disney used market studies and competitive analysis to prepare a development program and to determine site capacity on 74 developable acres. Disney then tested the feasibility of the project by using a market-sizing study, making price-value tradeoffs to determine where resources should be allocated.

Construction of phase I began in September 1990 and was completed in August 1992. Phase I consisted of Commodore House, a 15,000-square-foot sales and marketing center; Turtle Krawl, the village center; core recreational facilities, including a main swimming pool and two tennis courts; 19 residential buildings containing 197 units; and a pool complex for the first residential village. Commodore House and 50 units opened in December 1991.

Disney has subsequently constructed an additional 300 units and three more village pool complexes in two phases. In the future, Commodore House will be removed and replaced by approximately 34 additional units.

Master Planning and Design

As in its other resort products, Disney adopted a theme—in this case, turn-of-the-century Key West—and developed a story line and design details around it. The details are reflected in place and street names and interior design treatment.

The design guidelines incorporated the following key principles:

- Create the atmosphere of a casual vacation home, not a hotel room or a formal suite. Following the Key West theme, the homes are outfitted with casual rattan furniture, ceiling fans, and artwork by Key West artists. Mat flooring—as opposed to carpeting—cot-

Disney's Old Key West Resort is a 74-acre enclave of two- and three-story vacation ownership lodgings with a turn-of-the-century Key West theme. The resort features a festive boardwalk and a village of colorful clapboard-sided, tin-roofed residences. It offers a themed restaurant, two open-air bars, four on-site pools, a lighthouse sauna, and two tennis courts.

ton throw rugs, plaid sofa upholstery faded to look old, and other features all invite residents to put their feet up.

- Accentuate the theme's sense of place within the overall community design. With the entry into the resort already fixed, the same entry components that characterize Key West were transplanted to the resort, including a spine road and bridges. Parking is accommodated off the spine road at each cluster of housing units. A Key West lighthouse is a focal point. The single-loaded housing units capitalize on the existing views of Lake Buena Vista and the golf course, accentuating the site's already established sense of place. The buildings are combined in irregular outlines to echo Key West and its unplanned neighborhoods. Without sacrificing authenticity,

architectural details are kept to a minimum to reduce both initial and ongoing maintenance costs. Architectural features include stamped-aluminum rails in a Key West motif, two or three gable-end details and trellis details, picket fences, entry courtyards, and pastel colors reminiscent of Key West.

- Use the opposite rules of hotels in space planning for units and public spaces. Compared to a typical resort hotel, the resort club offers smaller, cozy public areas and larger spaces within the units. Not a single unit or room is rectangular. Rather, angled spaces lead to long views out of the units' many windows, further heightening the sense of space.
- Incorporate the theme and casual atmosphere into the marketing facilities. Commodore House includes decision rooms instead of closing rooms as well as a

The resort includes 497 units, most of which are two-bedroom units containing about 1,400 square feet.

temporary hospitality house and sales center designed for conversion into additional timeshare units when the sales program concludes. The design details follow the story line, including Victorian-style living room furniture, an aquarium at the front desk (Little Mermaid details, of course), and an intimate lobby lounge named after Papa Hemingway, with authentic artwork and objects of interest. The several activity areas for children permit adults to consider their decisions without interruptions.

Disney's designers worked hard to create a sense of community. The local gathering spot is the Turtle Krawl boardwalk, which is lined with a restaurant, snack bar, general store, game room, and community hall. Residential units are clustered in two- and three-story buildings of six to 18 units each. Considerable effort was made to ensure that all units have relatively equal views and proximity to recreational amenities.

The design of lock-off units was central to providing flexibility in the types of accommodations to be offered. The core product is a 1,395-square-foot, two-bedroom unit that can be locked off to create one-bedroom and studio units. Nearly an equal number of units is dedicated to two-bedroom units without the lock-off option.

The remaining 5 percent of the inventory consists of three-bedroom, two-story townhouses called grand villas.

Each dedicated lock-off studio contains two queen-size beds and features a wet bar, minirefrigerator, microwave oven, coffee maker, color television, and private porch. Larger units contain a king-size bed in the master suite and queen-size sleep sofa in the living room, full-size washer and dryer, television with VCR in the living room, additional televisions in each bedroom, private porch, whirlpool tub in the master bath, and fully equipped kitchen.

Sales and Marketing

With the benefit of Disney's reputation for quality, the company's large consumer base, and a new twist on an old product, Disney decided initially to market the club without any incentives or premiums. The results have been impressive: approximately one in four families that visits Commodore House decides to purchase, and 50 percent make their decision during their stay at Walt Disney World.

Disney generates interest in the club primarily by communicating with guests at the more upscale Disney World hotels. Most hotel guests receive information before arrival; on arrival, they can learn more about the club

Three-bedroom grand villa.

Two-bedroom vacation home floorplan. The second bedroom can be locked off to create a studio and a one-bedroom unit that can be used separately.

Since units are intended to be a "home away from home," they are attractively furnished in a casual, eclectic style.

from a six-minute program on the in-room channel and from information desks in hotel lobbies and theme parks. After learning quickly that many prospects wanted to find out more about the club but did not want to take time out of their vacation to visit Commodore House, Disney created a special team of salespeople who send information to and follow up with interested parties. Telesales represent 20 to 25 percent of total sales.

Complimentary transportation is available between Commodore House and anywhere in Walt Disney World. Each visit to Commodore House is tailored to a family's time frame. Once a family arrives, it generally spends 60 to 90 minutes for a full presentation. Approximately 50 to 60 families visit Commodore House each day.

A family spends all of its time during the visit with a Disney salesperson called a vacation club guide. Sales representatives are Disney employees who receive a base salary combined with incentives tied to sales volume and the quality of sales presentations. The latter is measured through customer surveys. Following the presentation, prospects are asked to evaluate their experience by either completing a survey form or answering a few questions by telephone.

The first 30 minutes of the presentation consist of an informative and entertaining ten-minute multime-

dia overview of the Walt Disney Company followed by two six-minute video introductions to the key features, benefits, and realities of the Disney Vacation Club. These presentations ensure that all guests receive consistent information yet allow maximum flexibility for adjusting the length of the visit to the interest of each guest. Next, guests are invited to tour a two-bedroom lock-off unit and a grand villa. Finally, prospects are invited to meet with the guide in a private conference room to review pricing, financing, and other details. The low-key presentation is completely open-ended, and guests are welcome to leave at any time. The presentation is also low pressure; salespeople neither offer incentives to buy nor negotiate on price.

With the summer 1996 opening of a second Disney Vacation Club Resort at the Walt Disney World Resort (Disney's BoardWalk Villas), a new and special name was given to the Disney Vacation Club at Walt Disney World, DVC's first and flagship resort. After considerable research and in-depth interviews with DVC members, Disney cast members, and other key audiences, Disney's Old Key West Resort emerged as the name that best captured the guest experience and turn-of-the-century Key West theming.

Commodore House houses the club's sales and marketing center.

Management and Operations

Disney's Old Key West Resort is managed and operated like a hotel. Currently, 40 to 45 percent of the units are rented through Disney's central reservations system. The club's operating budget looks to the day when the club is owned completely by its members and assessments for property management are made on a per point basis, with Disney contributing a subsidy to pay the assessments on the points that remain to be allocated. The average number of points owned by each member currently ranges between 250 and 260; assessments, including ad valorem taxes, average $650 to $700 per year.

The club incorporates most of the services and elements typically expected in a Disney hotel. Disney has tried to concentrate on highly valued services, eliminating those considered superfluous. It has taken several years of operation to find the proper balance.

The club offers an extensive menu of "soft programming" activities for children and families, including events centered on major holidays. Given the resort's location, however, on-site programs and activities are not as extensive as they might need to be elsewhere.

A service called Member Getaways allows club members to visit over 200 premium vacation resorts around the world for week-long stays. By reserving a week-long stay at the Disney resort and paying a small transaction fee, members can exchange that week for a week at a choice of resorts affiliated with Resort Condominiums International, Inc., the world's largest timeshare exchange company. Members can also exchange their points for stays at most Disney hotels worldwide, for stays at other selected Disney-affiliated resorts, and for Disney Adventure Vacations, including bicycle trips, cruises, and river rafting expeditions. Disney uses the RCI exchange system as wells as its own Buena Vista Trading Company Exchange System.

Lessons Learned

The point system has succeeded in creating the flexibility needed by the targeted market. Disney is in the forefront of this latest concept in timeshare development. Some unsettled issues, however, remain. For example, the sale of all units and all times would create gridlock. Disney has yet to determine the right breakpoint. It will probably still be some time before the vacation point system dominates the industry. The resale market for individual leasehold interests and points is also still in its infancy.

In future projects, Disney is planning some minor changes to the units, including downsized kitchens and reconfigured lock-off units whose second bedroom contains both a sleeper sofa and a dedicated queen-size bed when used as a studio.

Disney's sales approach has worked well for the relatively affluent purchasers attracted to the Orlando area. Sales figures show that customers appreciate the honesty and straightforwardness of the sales presentations. Sales revenues have grown in excess of 20 percent each year, and more than 25 percent of members have bought an additional interest in the club, with an average of 75 points per addition. However, it is difficult to draw too many conclusions from this success, as the Disney theme park creates a pool of potential buyers that other timeshare developments do not enjoy and cannot duplicate.

Disney's experience is once again proof that high quality and corporate credibility are major selling points in the timeshare business. The name brands in the timeshare industry, such as Disney, Marriott, and Hilton, all have strong reputations in the resort and hospitality business, a factor that has been instrumental to their success.

Finally, by emphasizing service, exclusivity, privilege, and a sense of community, the club concept is an important element of this and future timeshare developments. As with other resort developments, the hallmarks of a good timeshare development are a high-quality product, a competitive sales price, a good location, and a sense of exclusivity.

Disney's Old Key West Resort at Walt Disney World site plan.

Project Data: Disney's Old Key West Resort[1]

Land Use Information

Site area	74 acres
Total dwelling units planned	531[2]
Total dwelling units completed	497
Gross density	6.7 units per acre
Off-street parking spaces	1,113

Land Use Plan

	Acres
Buildings and common facilities	10.5
Roads and parking areas	16.5
Common open space	24.0
Other[3]	23.0
Total	74.0

Residential Unit Information

Unit Type	Floor Area (square feet)	Number of Units Planned/Completed
Two-bedroom (with lock-off studio unit)	1,395	224/212
Two-bedroom (without lock-off studio unit)	1,410	280/260
Three-bedroom (grand villa)	2,375	27/25

Commercial/Recreation Center Information

	Square Feet
Reception	3,300
Community hall	1,200
Fitness center	1,600
Restaurant/food service	4,300
General store	2,400
Game room	200
Other retail	100
Other[4]	14,900
Total	28,000

Vacation Point Information[5]

	Studio Home	1-Bedroom Vacation Home	2-Bedroom Vacation Home	3-Bedroom Grand Villa
Adventure season	17	35	47	77
Choice season	21	42	57	92
Dream season	25	50	67	112
Magic season	28	57	77	130
Premier season	38	77	105	170

Annual Operating Expenses (1994)

Ad valorem taxes	$5,683,021
Fees	55,016
Income taxes	42,096
Annual audit	22,000
Insurance	200,000
Services[6]	2,897,368
Maintenance[7]	5,501,080
Utilities	1,621,204
Legal	15,000
Management/administration	2,860,431
Reserves	2,161,639
Income (breakage, interest from ad valorem taxes)	(471,789)
Total	$20,586,967

Development Schedule

Summer 1989	Site selected
Fall 1989	Planning started
September 1990	Construction started
October 1991	Sales started
January 1992	First closing
August 1992	Phase I completed
October 1993	Phase II completed
May 1994	Phase III completed

Developer/Owner

Disney Vacation Development Company
6751 Forum Drive, Suite 220
Orlando, Florida 32821
407-827-1900

Architects

Richardson Nagy Martin
Newport Beach, California

Basenian Lagoni
Newport Beach, California

Fugleberg Koch Architects, Inc.
Winter Park, Florida

Notes

[1] Development cost not available.

[2] Approximately 34 units will be added after the marketing center is demolished.

[3] Includes bodies of water, sidewalks, and nonbuilding recreational areas.

[4] Includes administration areas, restrooms, storage, and corridors.

[5] Number of points required for a Friday or Saturday night stay; approximately 60 percent fewer points are required for stays on other nights.

[6] Includes transportation, member activities, security, and cable television.

[7] Includes housekeeping, maintenance, and building painting.

7. Trends and Outlook

Significant changes over the past 30 years have had a major influence on the pace, pattern, and character of contemporary resort and resort community development. These changes include

- improved access made possible by expanded air travel opportunities and completion of the interstate highway system;
- the widespread availability of air conditioning;
- advances in communication technology, particularly overnight delivery services, the facsimile machine, and the Internet;
- increasing affluence among the highest-income groups;
- the trend toward shorter vacations;
- the proliferation of a weekend escape mentality in many urban areas;
- the evolution of timeshares and other vacation ownership products;

- changes in the availability and use of leisure time;
- the increased popularity of golf, tennis, skiing, travel, and other recreational pursuits brought about in large part by television;
- the growth of shopping, dining, and other types of entertainment as leisure activities;
- the growth in health awareness and a corresponding increased interest in spa and soft adventure vacations;
- the increased popularity of gaming; and
- the rapid growth of the cruise industry.

While most experts agree that the demand for resort and recreational development products will continue to grow in the near future and that the market will become increasingly competitive, a wide range of factors and issues—and opinions—must be considered in assessing what the future holds for resort and recreation development.

When ULI Recreational Development Council members were recently asked to identify the most significant trends and issues for resort development over the next five years, they gave high ratings to five interrelated factors: demographics and psychographics; timesharing; gaming; international travel and tourism; and the environment. A focus group of a cross section of council members subsequently discussed the results of this survey. The fast pace of change was a constant theme in participants' remarks. As one participant noted, had the survey been conducted five years earlier, neither timesharing

Big Cedar Lodge is an 800-acre resort on Table Rock Lake near Branson, Missouri, that features a variety of recreational pursuits, including fishing, boating, golf, tennis, and equestrian activities. In addition, the many entertainment venues in Branson are only ten miles away. The resort was originally developed in the 1920s as a luxurious vacation retreat for two wealthy Missourians and subsequently converted into a guest resort in 1947. In 1987, it was acquired by Bass Pro Shops, which has been pursuing an aggressive expansion and improvement program for the property.

nor gaming would have made the list of significant trends or issues. Another participant stated that the proliferation of new options for resort and recreational activities represents a fundamental change for the industry; the range of today's alternatives is remarkable—from cruise ships to gaming to learning vacations to international resorts and on and on.

This section provides a review of a variety of issues, trends, and factors that are likely to affect the resort business over the next five years, including social trends, trends in related industries, recreational trends, and resort real estate trends. It then provides an outlook for the resort business, focusing on the prospects for the development of new resorts—both domestic and international—and the revitalization and repositioning of existing resorts.

Social Trends

Demographics and Psychographics

Over the next 20 years, the baby boom generation will likely constitute the largest potential market ever for resort real estate products, especially second homes and timeshares. Experience indicates that second-home or retirement-home purchases are most often made by individuals in their 50s and 60s—and the boomers are heading into those years. If the boomers follow the pattern, the market will be rife with prospects. Notes a 1995 *Barron's* article on the second-home market, "Boomers flooded elementary schools with kids, then they bid up the prices of primary residences, and now they're about to make second homes scarce. It's important to note, though, that the strongest surge in demand for vacation homes won't be felt in the '90s, as forecast, but will unfold over the next 10 or even 20 years."[1]

According to a 1995 survey by Opinion Research Corporation for Chase Manhattan's Personal Financial Services unit, the percentage of households that own a second home rises from 5 percent among those aged 35 to 44 years to 7 percent among those aged 45 to 54 years to 9 percent among those aged 55 to 64 years. Another study by Mediamark, a New York–based consumer research firm, finds that "the odds of owning a second home jump sometime around one's 50th birthday, with people between the ages of 45 and 54 being 33% more likely to buy. . . . By the time Americans have reached 'pre-retirement' ages, between 55 and 64, they are 65% more likely than all other adults to own a second home." If the boomers follow the pattern of their parents and 7 percent of them buy second homes, "the number of second home owners could swell by more than 40% in the next decade. And this is a group that tends to satisfy its desires quickly—bidding up prices in the process."[2]

The question that remains unanswered is, To what degree will baby boomers' resort usage and leisure-home purchasing patterns differ from previous generations? The baby boom generation differs from the pre-

Profile and Comments: James W. Mozley, Jr.

James W. Mozley, Jr.
President and Chief Executive
Molokai Ranch, Limited
Honolulu, Hawaii

James W. Mozley, Jr., is president and chief executive of Molokai Ranch, Limited, which owns 53,000 acres and leases an additional 6,000 acres on the island of Molokai in Hawaii. Molokai Ranch is being managed and developed to enhance, preserve, and protect the positive elements of the island, its people, and its heritage. Mozley is also director of Hawaii's Land Use Research Foundation.

Mozley began his career in 1973 with the Sea Pines Company, where he shared responsibility for the design and development of numerous projects, including Kiawah Island. He joined the Arvida Corporation in 1978 as a project manager for the development of luxury single-family homes, resort rental condominiums, luxury resort villas, sports facilities, and amenities at Boca West near Boca Raton, Florida.

From 1981 to 1989, he headed Mozley Company, Inc., a land planning and design firm based in Atlanta. He joined Amfac/JMB Hawaii, Inc., in 1989 and became vice president and general manager of its Maui Properties Division. In that capacity, Mozley was responsible for all planning, development, construction, real estate sales, and leasing as well as for Amfac's resort operations at Kaanapali Beach Resort and the administration of marketing efforts on behalf of the Kaanapali Beach Resort hotels and operators.

Mozley received a BS from the School of Architecture at Georgia Tech in 1973.

The foundation of Molokai Ranch and the master plan for developing our property holdings is a dedication to enhancing the island's existing attributes without tarnishing the natural beauty, unique culture, and charming heritage that sets the island apart from the rest of Hawaii. Molokai is without question the most "Hawaiian" of all the Hawaiian islands and, as such, is also the least developed both physically and economically.

The sheer size of the ranch—53,000 acres, one-third of the island—offers unmatched strength and value in attaining future development in a manner that is environmentally sympathetic yet designed for carefully sustainable growth. But even though Molokai Ranch is the island's primary economic engine, the situation we face in enhancing our land values is far more complicated than that of the typical landowner and developer.

In some of the island's communities, the ranch owns virtually everything, the land underneath, the residential and commercial structures, and the basic utilities such as water and sewer service. Further complicating this mix is the fact that Molokai is the poorest island in Hawaii, with an economy and population base highly dependent on some form of government assistance and, in many instances, additional subsidies from Molokai Ranch. Thus, the responsibility of meeting the needs of the community and creating sustainable growth without compromising the island's qualities while increasing the value of the ranch's landholdings is a daunting, complex task.

The plans for Molokai Ranch call for the nurturing of three interconnected business centers that, while generating income, will also add future value to the ranch's extensive landholdings. These three business centers—agribusiness, recreation, and land development—and the direction followed by each is a continually evolving process as regional economic trends are reassessed and related opportunities are explored. Each of these business centers, however, is designed to work in harmony with the island's natural environment and social fabric, thus enhancing, preserving, and protecting the positive features that Molokai offers. Perhaps the best example of Molokai Ranch's business philosophy is our effort to develop a low-impact, sustainable market for environmental tourism. This philosophy is rooted in the realization that people would rather come to places, than things.

As the world becomes smaller and more easily accessible, it becomes increasingly important for landowners and developers to focus on what is special about a place, especially one as beautiful and culturally diverse as the islands of Hawaii. And Molokai is still a place, an entire island setting that is as beautiful and true to its heritage as can be experienced anywhere in Hawaii.

Over the years, too many places in Hawaii have developed a sameness in appearance derived from a common—and initially successful theory—of building megaresorts, or things, for visitors to come see and experience. These megaresorts have become things, and these things have frequently come to eclipse the place where they are situated.

Along Hawaii's Kona coast and Maui's Kaanapali coastline, regardless of the varied architectural beauty and immaculate care lavished on the numerous megaresorts, the two different islands are essentially the same. And this sameness in appearance levels the playing field, not only among the Hawaiian islands, but also among other tropical destinations.

The beauty of environmental tourism, particularly for Molokai, is that it also offers opportunities to sample new technology and have people become comfortable with its application in a permanent-home setting. A "laboratory," so to speak, can be created for testing new

environmentally sensitive products, which can then be applied in community design. And if Molokai Ranch can expose someone on vacation to the benefits of an "off the grid" canvas cottage, with a self-composting toilet, and provide a little education to go with it, the experience may ultimately influence that person's decision making when considering where to buy a new home.

Similar to what Charles Fraser did at Hilton Head Island when he created a Montessori school for the employees' children, there is a more important mission than just creating an experience for the transient tourist. There is an opportunity for improving the more permanent things that we have and do, an opportunity to create environments for living.

For Molokai Ranch, our second-home market is Hawaii. Consequently, many of the "tourists" we would try to appeal to are an 18-minute flight away on Oahu, rather than a five-hour flight from the continental United States.

Only a limited number of people could be brought to Molokai, a number that is right for the island and its rural, culturally based lifestyle. We are not interested in forcing Molokai to be something it is not. With only 300,000 visitors a year now, assuredly this limit will increase, but how quickly depends on the pace at which environmental tourism and careful development are allowed to proceed.

In today's rapidly changing business climate, developers cannot afford to build communities the same way they do a McDonald's. A cookie-cutter formula for marketing homes and lifestyle changes no longer applies in a world where people are becoming increasingly interested in the history and culture of the places they live and visit.

As much as anywhere else, this is true for Molokai Ranch. We have some future real estate products that are very rural, individual ranches, not just "subdivisions on steroids," but genuine ranches with open space, unfettered views, and an independence from manufactured energies.

Thus, for Molokai Ranch, unlike the rest of Hawaii, investing in a school or health care facility will increase our land values more than building golf courses and resort condominiums.

vious generation in several ways. On the one hand, it faces rising and more formidable college tuition costs than its parents' generation; it is living in an economy where job security is a perceived problem; it is largely made up of two-income households with limited leisure time; and it is concerned about saving for a secure retirement that is threatened by projected financial strains on Social Security and Medicare once the boomers start to retire. On the other hand, baby boomers have indulged themselves and are strongly oriented toward spending discretionary dollars on entertainment and leisure travel. Moreover, the growing popularity of the timeshare product—a very affordable alternative to whole ownership—will continue to broaden second-home options for baby boomers.

How these various differences play out in the coming years remains to be seen. Contrary to general perceptions, *Barron's* reports that "it's becoming clear that Boomers are not only earning more than their parents did, but saving a higher percentage of their income. A study published in 1994 in the *Federal Reserve Bank of New York Quarterly Review*, for example, compares wealth-to-income ratios among the first wave of Boomers to the percentage of incomes that their parents had saved at the same age. Boomers are ahead with wealth averaging 2.76 times their income, as against 2.07 for their parents."[3] Moreover, boomers are positioned to inherit a tremendous amount of wealth in the coming years, and studies have shown that the purchase of a second home is often stimulated by inheritances and other large wealth transfers.

There are other psychographic changes to consider as well. James Chaffin, president of the Spring Island Company in South Carolina, believes that several important psychographic shifts are changing the resort and second-home business. He notes that a shift in values is taking place, from being status-driven to being principle-driven, from lifestyle to life experiences, from being well off to well-being, and from being wealthy to being healthy.[4]

Perhaps the most crucial change in marketing resort real estate, resort hotels, and destination resorts is the recognition of many distinct market niches, each of which can be described according to demographic and psychographic profiles. Each market niche has its own unique interests and leisure pursuits, and some of these provide new opportunities. For example, cultural, wellness, and education programs are currently assuming a higher-profile position in resorts. As Harry H. Frampton III, president of East West Partners's Western Division, puts it, if traditional resorts do not "reinvent themselves" to provide people with new options for spending their leisure time, "they are just going to get killed."

In addition, a growing recognition among resort community developers suggests that demand for second homes and high-quality resort experiences extends well below the top 5 percent of the population in terms of wealth. This rarefied group, which has accrued the largest share of economic benefits in recent years, has most often been the target of resort community developers largely as a result of the relative prestige, certainty, stability, and profit potential involved. Greater depth and variety of product within resort communities and greater attention to products that are more affordable can also be profitable and would yield societal benefits as well.

As much as 95 percent of the potential demand for resort facilities comes from the middle-income market segment, a figure that contrasts dramatically with much of the current supply of resorts and resort communities and their high-end orientation. The next decade's successful resorts will respond to the larger market segment by recasting themselves as more affordable resort accommodations that stress value. Increasingly, perceived value will be based on the quality of the overall resort experience and less on the luxury of a resort's rooms.[5] Moreover, notes Gadi Kaufmann of Robert Charles Lesser & Co. in Los Angeles, "there is a deficiency of resort products in the market that cater to families with young children, a segment that is growing currently."[6]

Communications and Technology

Moving to resort areas has become an increasingly popular option for executives and small companies as innovations in communications and computer technology make it possible to conduct business from nonurban locations.[7] This trend is likely to continue well into the next decade as the World Wide Web, telecommunication technologies, convenient air travel, and overnight delivery services become increasingly accessible and cost-effective. Presumably, the new job opportunities created in the communities where executives and small companies choose to relocate will produce a trickle-down effect, enabling others to make a living in resort destinations as well.

Technology could also lead to longer visitor stays at resorts, in the vacation tradition of the 19th and early 20th centuries. Families once habitually migrated to a resort area and stayed for a month or most of the season. The breadwinner commuted irregularly to the workplace while the rest of the family remained in the resort area. Over the next decade, the number of resort guests with two breadwinners in the family will grow. Both parties may have to attend to business occasionally, either planned or on short notice, thereby increasing the demand for video conferencing services and computers with e-mail. The vacation property that helps guests avoid the inconvenience, disruption, and additional expense of abrupt treks back home will win over vacationers more successfully than a resort where technology is not an option.[8]

In addition, the increased use of computers and the availability of software specifically designed for office management, project management, and financial analysis will continue to change the practice of resort development. As in other businesses, these new tools enable resort developers to keep their staffs small and overhead low relative to the resources that were needed before the advent of advanced technology. The result-

Desert Island in Rancho Mirage, California, is positioned not only as an island in the desert, but also as an island escape, featuring privacy and spectacular views of the surrounding mountains, as well as golf. Mid-rise units are clustered on the island, which is accessible via a bridge with security gate; the golf course is located on the surrounding land.

ing economies of time and money may encourage experienced developers to consider expanding their businesses into more affordable markets and product types.

The ability to create databases, communicate, and market via the Internet and to share information as a result of improved computer and communication technologies is likely to streamline business operations further and rationalize decision making in the resort development business. Just as other industries have benefited from a greater awareness of and ability to target markets, resort developers will be better able to anticipate and respond to market preferences in the future as databases expand and become more user-friendly.

Education

Education is increasingly viewed as a lifelong venture. Educational pursuits can be motivated by either necessity or pleasure; for many people, continuing education is both a necessity and a pleasure. Resorts are tapping into this trend in numerous ways. One way is through the conference business, which is essentially a form of continuing education for specialized groups. The conference business has been and will continue to be an important and growing sector for resorts. Another way is by offering learning vacations and educational opportunities in resort environments, an important consideration in the resort industry; today, more and more resorts and resort communities are seeking to provide a variety of learning and educational experiences as a

part of their leisure offerings. The Disney Institute is a good example.

Moreover, the opportunities for partnering with colleges and universities to combine vacations with educational experiences is an emerging area of opportunity, especially for nonurban colleges and universities. Universities have been providing summer continuing education classes and short programs for many years, and more recently retirement communities have sprouted around such university towns as Charlottesville, Virginia, the many small college towns in New England, and in many other areas. Resorts in these locations have an opportunity to tap into special educational offerings as a means to diversify the resort experience.

Eastern Michigan University (EMU), for example, has developed an off-campus education program under the name Adventures in Education. The program is built around the concept of high-quality academic experiences in beautiful settings. Among the locations used by Adventures in Education is the Treetops Sylvan Resort in Gaylord, Michigan, which has a conference center suitable for classroom activities. Course offerings range from cross-country skiing to poetry reading to interpersonal communication. Other sites for EMU's programs include Florida, Hawaii, and Colorado.

Work and Leisure

Rigid patterns of work and leisure continue to erode, both in the United States and abroad. The implications for resort development are significant. Today's vacationing family or household faces ever-increasing demands on its free time. The stress and time constraints associated with demanding professional careers and the scheduling limitations associated with dual-income households and children's school calendars have already combined to make it more difficult for many families to plan leisure time, much less make getaways and take vacations. Rather than reducing demand, however, these factors are likely to redirect it by making certain products and locations more popular than others.

In the past, most people worked a fairly inflexible five-day week and took a one- or two-week annual vacation. Today, an increasing number of people are scheduling more frequent short breaks and getaways in lieu of or in addition to an occasional longer vacation. These short breaks and getaways often occur around long holiday weekends. Longer vacations of two weeks or more are growing less common, sometimes occurring only once every two, three, or four years.

People with limited time are less likely to travel great distances to a resort. Thus, properties close to a primary market are likely to be highly competitive in the near future.[9] Successful resort management must anticipate regular guests' shorter but more frequent visits and develop programs and products that effectively tap the short-stay market. Most industry experts agree that demand for second-home purchases will continue to be strongest for weekend and getaway homes within a two-and-one-half- to three-hour drive of the purchaser's primary residence.

Population shifts, geographic expansion of urban areas, highway improvements, higher speed limits, and increased flexibility in the workplace will continue to make new locations accessible for resort development close to primary markets. A variety of real estate products, including townhouses and apartment condominiums, can meet the demand for weekend and getaway homes, but single-family detached houses or cabins will likely continue to be the most desirable real estate product for potential purchasers who can afford single-family products.

Patterns of work and leisure time are also changing in other parts of the world. In many European countries, where vacations for the entire month of August have been the tradition, annual vacations are becoming shorter and supplemented by other breaks and holidays. In many Asian countries, governments and corporations are increasing paid holidays and vacation time and reducing standard work weeks and days to encourage citizens to take more time off. Historically, cultural shifts involving work and leisure time have taken generations to take hold, but major shifts now seem to be occurring much more quickly.

People's perceptions about job security, work-related stress, and the availability of leisure time are also major factors affecting how households choose to spend their leisure time and discretionary money. Despite the debate about whether people actually have more or less leisure time than in previous generations, it is generally agreed that the increased options available for spending leisure time make most people feel that they do not have enough time to do all the things they want to do. Most people admit to living with high levels of stress and thus voice interest in leisure-time activities and experiences that will help reduce tension. In weak economic times, when job security is lowest, people are more likely to defer major discretionary expenditures such as vacation travel and purchases of resort real estate.

One of the more recent leisure trends is toward vacations spent at home, a development that does not bode well for resorts. In a national survey conducted in May 1996 by Wirthlin Worldwide, a nationwide opinion research firm, nearly half of respondents said that they were likely to use part of their annual vacation to stay at home. The "nesting" trend was especially pronounced among baby boomers, according to the survey. The growing number of primary-home recreational and golf course communities in urban areas is contributing to this trend; the desire to get away to a resort is not as strong for those who already live in a golf course or country club community that feels much like a resort.[10]

Another trend is the growing preference for shopping as a leisure-time activity, a trend that can both benefit and hinder resort development depending on how well the resort can serve shoppers' needs. In Aspen, one estimate suggests that only 50 percent of winter-time visitors ski, but 80 percent of them shop. In many other resort areas, shopping at outlets is a favorite pastime. Providing attractive shopping experiences will be an important consideration for resorts that wish to remain economically viable in the near future.

The combination of these work and leisure-time trends bodes well for resorts that are easily accessible for short stays and those whose special appeal makes them destinations of choice for longer stays.

Travel and Tourism

The travel and tourism industry is a powerhouse in the global economy, generating more than $400 billion in revenue and providing more than 10 percent of the world's income and employment.[11] In the United States alone, travel and tourism accounts for more than 6 million jobs and constitutes our nation's largest service export industry.[12]

Travel and tourism is expected to continue to grow, offering U.S. developers opportunities both at home and abroad. Domestically, foreign travelers and tourists can become a major market for hotel-room and time-sharing-unit stays as well as for second-home and retirement-home sales. Worldwide, U.S. developers are in a good position to export their expertise and undertake joint ventures in parts of the world where travel is increasing as old tensions and wars wane and national markets open up.

Resort development in the United States will continue to be influenced by travel and tourism patterns, both domestic and international. During periods such as the Gulf War, when U.S. citizens were advised to limit their travel abroad, domestic resorts prospered. But when foreign travel is on the increase, domestic resorts compete with international destinations. Inbound travel from other countries is the wild card; current trends indicate that inbound travel can be expected to continue to increase in coming years. This pattern, of course, is greatly affected by the strength of the dollar. If the dollar strengthens in coming years, it will likely have an adverse impact on tourist travel to the United States.

One of the predominant tourism trends is toward shorter but more frequent trips. According to the Travel Industry Association of America, the number of weekend trips of more than 100 miles rose from 327 million in 1985 to 604 million in 1995, an 85 percent increase. For nonweekend trips, the typical adult's main out-of-town vacation lasted only 4.6 nights in 1995, as compared to 5.9 nights in 1985.[13]

In more recent years, the tourism industry has become more integrated, allowing for higher-quality and better travel services that take the hassle out of vacation and travel planning. The interdependence of the airline industry, the cruise industry, the hotel industry, the car rental business, the travel agent business, independent tour operators, local tourism development organizations, and other segments of the travel and tourism industry has become increasingly evident in recent years. Resort developers must effectively interact with these many players if they hope to compete in the new global marketplace.

In addition, incentive travel continues to grow and consolidate as companies focus on motivating their employees, especially salespeople. Incentive travel providers will become a competitive force in the industry as they move toward owning and operating their own resort facilities, expecting to fill these accommodations with their clients' award-winning employees.[14]

Related-Industry Trends

Airline Industry

Several favorable trends in the airline industry in recent years have stimulated pleasure travel. Perhaps the most important trend for the resort business and tourism in general has been the highly competitive marketplace that has evolved, keeping airfares low and thus encouraging discretionary and leisure travel. Nonetheless, growth in the air transportation business has been modest in recent years, and the airline industry struggled during the early 1990s. The total number of air passengers rose very rapidly from 1983 to 1988, plateaued from 1989 to 1991, and has been on a strong growth curve from 1992 to 1996.[15] While industry performance has improved in recent years, the legacy of low airfares and a highly competitive environment remains. If, however, discount airlines such as Valujet continue to experience problems and the industry continues to consolidate, prices could rise in the near future and adversely affect pleasure travel.

Another important trend has been the growth of frequent flyer programs; air travelers enjoy a wide range of options for adding miles to their frequent flyer accounts, including the use of certain credit cards, long distance telephone services, car rental services, hotels, mortgages, and other services. Invariably, travelers use frequent flyer miles for discretionary travel; the programs have stimulated visits to many destination resorts. One of the underlying factors connecting frequent flyer programs to destination resorts is that most people feel they should get the most out of their free flight by flying a considerable distance, a bias that favors major destination resorts in high-quality locations over more convenient locations.

Air access is a key factor in the viability of any major resort destination, and access to more and more locations will continue to improve gradually around the world, spurring more and more international competition for travel and tourism dollars. By definition, a destination resort needs to be located near an airport that offers convenient service to major markets. The number of flights available to and from that airport, the range of available airfares, and the quality of the airport facility can all affect occupancy levels at nearby resorts. The number of airports with runway lights in the United States—one indicator of the number of locations that can be served by commercial airlines—has remained relatively flat, rising from 4,822 in 1990 to 4,842 in 1994.[16] This is not expected to change, and international locations will account for most of the airports and new flight destinations in the near future.

Even in the international arena, however, change comes slowly. Airlines are understandably reluctant to extend service to new locations until market demand is sufficiently strong. This chicken-and-egg relationship puts new resort locations at a considerable disadvantage relative to well-established locations with convenient airline service. Moreover, price wars and competition among carriers and their effect on airfares can change the dynamics of the marketplace, often placing some resort destinations at a competitive advantage over others.

There is a history of successful partnerships among the airline, car rental, travel, and hotel industries to promote travel to particular destinations. Often, these partnerships are undertaken in association with coalitions of local government, business, and economic development interests. These partnerships are likely to strengthen in the future as the travel and tourism industry becomes a more mature and integrated industry.

Cruise Industry

Many resort developers are looking closely at the cruise industry as both a competitor and a model worth emulating. As the cost of cruises has dropped, the concept—a fixed-price, all-inclusive vacation with an extensive menu of optional activities—has gained popularity. Until recently, only Club Med and a handful of other resort operators offered a fixed-price structure for land-based experiences. Others are likely to follow.

figure 7-1
Cruise Industry Annual Passenger Growth

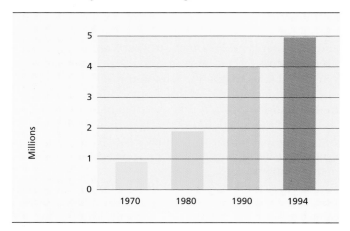

Source: *The Industry: An Overview—Marketing Edition* (New York: Cruise Lines International Association, January 1995).

Considered one of the fastest growth categories within the international leisure market, the cruise industry has experienced an annual compound growth rate of 10 percent from 1970 to 1994; between 1970 and 1974, an estimated 53 million passengers took "deepwater" cruises (two or more days). Nearly 40 percent of these passengers traveled in the years 1990 through 1994. According to the Cruise Lines International Association, by the year 2000, as many as 8 million individuals will cruise annually.[17]

Individuals 25 years or older with a household income over $20,000 (60 percent of the cruise industry's targeted population) report that they are interested in taking a cruise. Over one-third of this targeted population intends to take a cruise within the next five years. While the baby boom generation continues to be a vital consumer base for the cruise industry, demographic studies have led the industry to prospect younger, moderate-income individuals who vacation with their children.

Over the past ten years, the cruise industry has successfully responded to market and demographic trends by providing a diversified array of cruise products. To reflect the nation's changing demographic characteristics and vacation patterns, the cruise industry has implemented a wide variety of marketing initiatives, including new ship design concepts, new on-board/on-shore activities, new destinations, innovative themes, and new cruise lengths.

A large proportion of cruise passengers can be considered frequent vacationers who cruise as part of a vacation mix. Over 85 percent of passengers consider cruising an important vehicle for sampling destination areas that they may choose to revisit in the future. Nearly 50 percent of cruise passengers fully expect to return to the same geographic area/destination for another type of vacation. Thus, growth in the cruise industry does not necessarily drain dollars from land-

Profile and Comments: Peter S. Rummell

Peter S. Rummell
President/Chief Executive Officer
St. Joe Corporation
Jacksonville, Florida

Peter Rummell is president and chief executive officer of St. Joe Corporation, a large landowner and developer in Jacksonville, Florida; he assumed this position in late 1996. Previously, he served as president of Disney Design and Development Company. The comments below were made when he served in the latter position.

As president of the Disney Design and Development Company, Peter Rummell was responsible for the theme park and real estate development activities of the Walt Disney Company. The company currently encompasses several operating divisions: Walt Disney Imagineering, the group that creates and develops all Disney-themed attractions; the Disney Development Company, which manages worldwide real estate activities for the Walt Disney Company; the operations and expansion of the Disney Vacation Club, the company's new vacation product; and a division that explores new real estate ventures in various areas.

After earning an MBA from the Wharton School of the University of Pennsylvania, Rummell held management positions with the Sea Pines Company at Hilton Head, South Carolina, and Amelia Island Plantation in Florida. He then spent two years at the Ocean Reef Club in Key Largo, Florida, before joining the Arvida Corporation in 1977 as general manager and then president of the Sawgrass community near Jacksonville.

Rummell served with Arvida until 1983, when he left to become vice chair of the Rockefeller Center Management Corporation in New York City. In 1985, he rejoined Arvida as president of the Resort Communities Division and in November of that year joined the Disney Design and Development Company as president.

The world of entertainment as it meets real estate is getting a lot more interesting in terms of the opportunities out there. In the next ten years, we are going to see products that are truly new, products where you will walk in and say, "Gee, I've never really been in one of these before." Disney rejects the notion that the wiring of the world, the information superhighway so to speak, will mean that people will stay at home. People are not going to turn into couch potatoes and channel surfers.

If you mesh this notion with other trends, such as the aging of the population, the dramatic trend toward shorter vacations, and increased international access, there will be a series of new things that can happen. It's going to be an interesting confluence of technology driving a lot of things that we do but doing them in ways that we really hadn't thought about before.

The need to leave home but not go too far away is something that is real. Security and safety issues are a concern to people, more so than ten years ago. Providing interesting, safe, informative, educational environments close to home is a huge opportunity. That can range from theme park types of environments that are developed in a suburban setting, rather than a two-day drive away, to projects that are far more educational but still have the entertainment quality. I think people are less and less interested in "empty calories" entertainment. There is an interest in accomplishing something rather than passively experiencing it, and it will be a lot more fulfilling than in the past. While a certain amount of this new experience will come through a cable, other experiences will come when the consumer leaves home for a three-dimensional built environment.

Here is where there is an interesting confluence. One of the things you will find is that the worlds that are going to come into your home through a wire may be connected to a three-dimensional world that we create outside the home. There will be environments that you can explore and enjoy that will come into your home but that are reproduced in three-dimensional form in a place that you can visit. Simplistically, you could go to Disneyland by getting in your car and driving there or you could go to Disneyland on your home television by accessing a Disney channel of some kind.

Everything Disney does is developed around a theme. We make our business by creating three-dimensional environments. We are three-dimensional story tellers on the real estate side. Everything that we do, whether it is an office building, hotel, or food and beverage facility, always starts with a premise, a story of some kind. If we are building a hotel, for example, we write a story about that hotel—how it got there, why it is there, the environment it is in. By doing this, we can punch holes in the story and deal with issues that make the story concept complete. A lot of the success in creating these environments is in being consistent. And it is not about spending a lot of money as much as thinking about how to spend it.

With all of Disney's projects, there is a healthy tension between creativity and the budget. For example, before a concept emerges, we know that we have a need for X capacity, that we need to accommodate X number of people, that it would be open for Y days per year, and that we would charge Z for it. So long before a concept comes to life, we know we have X dollars to spend on a facility and can't spend any more. We are disciplined about the financial boxes we build for ourselves, and those typically are market-driven. They are done upfront so the designers always know what the constraints are.

The creative discipline is far more easily managed if it is managed within constraints.

I don't think that a budget is a constraint to creativity at all, however. I think the right way to look at it is as an integral part of the process and, if you treat it that way from the beginning, then it is not a threat, it is not a limitation, it is just something that you live with. I think one of the reasons there are such dull, boring things around the country is that people are afraid of the process. People are afraid of the creative process because they think it just means endless dollars, and they are not willing to be tough enough on themselves. They are not willing to push themselves hard enough to understand that you end up with a product that the consumer is going to be far more interested in.

There will be new paradigms, new ways of looking at real estate. Interesting things will come when you take real estate and mesh it with something else to form a hybrid. The only thing that is going to have a prayer of succeeding is something that meets an unmet market, and we think that there are some opportunities out there. Charles Fraser in the 1960s realized that people were looking for second homes and that he could build a golf course through the woods and put houses on it after he had run out of oceanfront. That was a revolutionary thought in 1965; now it just seems like falling off a log. Today we are talking about cyberspace, technology, electronics, and all sorts of other things, but the fundamental issue is the juxtaposition of these elements in some combination.

In summary, if you cannot successfully differentiate your project and create a compelling reason why, as the world gets more competitive, the risk becomes greater.

Disney's Grand Floridian Resort at Walt Disney World is tied directly to the success of Disney's theme park and entertainment business. The continued reconfiguration, growth, and innovation of the entertainment industry is simultaneously creating new competition, new expectations, and new opportunities for resort development.

based resorts; it can help promote these resorts and resort areas, leading to future growth.

Entertainment Industry

The continued reconfiguration, growth, and innovation in the entertainment industry is simultaneously creating new competition, new expectations, and new opportunities for resort development. For example, cable television, CDs, CD-ROMs, computer games, movies, the performing arts, video games, amusement and theme parks, entertainment attractions in suburban malls, and restaurants and nightclubs in urban areas all compete, to some degree, with resorts for the discretionary dollars that people spend on leisure-time pursuits. Moreover, the availability of these convenient forms of entertainment is a competitive factor in reducing an individual's or family's desire for a getaway to a resort area.

Expectations suggest that the increasing collaboration between technology and entertainment and the prospect of guests taking virtual vacations without leaving home will erode resort demand. Resort industry visionaries view the impact of technology not so much as an immediate threat but rather as an alert. Resort developers should evaluate the possibility of providing guests with computer access and entertainment facilities when those amenities suit a particular setting.[18]

To some degree, the availability of these forms of entertainment at or near one's home raises expectations that resorts will also provide state-of-the-art entertainment options. Resort hotels typically offer in-room video entertainment venues similar to what most people have in their homes—and video arcades are standard fare in amenity packages at resort hotels—but most hotels lack in-room computers and music-listening options. While clearly not for everyone, new forms of entertainment are important to a growing number of people, and developers need to keep entertainment industry trends in mind when planning for, redeveloping, or repositioning resort properties.

Large entertainment attractions also have the potential of creating increased demand for nearby resort and second-home development. For example, the casinos and live entertainment in Las Vegas, the theme parks and other attractions in Orlando, and the country music venues in Branson, Missouri, all continue to create opportunities for resort hotels, timeshare resorts, second-home communities, and multiuse resorts in surrounding areas. Synergies between traditional resort amenities—both natural and recreational—and new entertainment venues and technologies will certainly generate many other new opportunities for resort developers during the next few years.

Health Care and Wellness Industry

The link between health care and resorts goes back to early times when people visited resorts and spas in search of cures for their ailments. Today, that link is being rediscovered and strengthened as many resorts look for new ways to position themselves as destinations where people can enhance their well-being and find rest, relaxation, and rejuvenation. The link between health and resorts is visible in the provision of spa facilities and services at most upscale resort hotels; the health-related education programs now part of many vacation experiences, such as the fitness and diet programs offered by the Hilton Head Institute; and the provision of assisted-living and continuing-care facilities within resort communities.

Clearly, proximity to high-quality medical facilities will continue to be a primary concern for the growing retiree market in resort communities. Interest in preventive medicine, wellness, and fitness programs and activities in resort settings can also be expected to increase as the baby boom generation ages. In the future, new medical technology and health care practices may create additional opportunities for partnerships between the health care and resort industries.

As a result, health, wellness, and fitness facilities and programs will play a progressively important role at resorts as facilities and programs become increasingly diverse. Health spas in particular have moved toward specialized programs that differentiate them from other competitors.

Recreational Trends

Sports Participation

Research on sports participation rates reveals that the popularity of various sporting and recreational activities changes substantially over time. For resort developers, the challenge is to find ways to integrate a wide variety of activities into the resort experience, especially those that are gaining popularity. In-line skating, mountain biking, cross-country skiing, snowboarding, windsurfing, sea kayaking, and use of personal watercraft are just a few of the sports and recreational activities that have grown in importance for resorts over the past decade.

Some experts have noted the increasing popularity of individual pursuits—such as bicycling, windsurfing, in-line skating, and sea kayaking—as compared to more traditional resort activities such as tennis and golf, which typically require at least one other participant. By definition, individual pursuits can usually be undertaken more spontaneously and with less structure than organized activities. The ability to rent the necessary equipment and obtain instruction for these types of pursuits is likely to be a trend for resorts in the coming years.

According to the Sporting Goods Manufacturers Association, the most rapidly growing sports of interest to the resort community are in-line skating and mountain biking (see Figure 7-2). Many activities with the highest frequency of participation are also showing strong growth in the rate of participation. The top activity for frequent participation is fitness walking (over 16 million participants in 1994), which saw frequent participation grow by 22 percent from 1992 to 1994. Other top activities with high growth rates include freshwater fishing (over 10 million participants), which experienced a 14.6 percent increase during the same period, and running/jogging (over 9 million participants), which registered a 14.8 percent increase.

Golf

According to research by the National Golf Foundation, although golf participation has remained level for the past several years, the prospects for growth are favorable. In particular, developers and golf industry leaders will succeed in bringing more people to the game if they invest in player and facility development programs and position golf as a popular recreational activity and golf courses as environmental assets.[19]

figure 7-2

Top 20 Activities with the Largest Percentage Growth in Frequent Participation[1]

Rank / Sport	1994 (000)	1992 (000)	Percent Increase
1. In-line skating (25+ days)	6,290	2,529	148.7
5. Mountain biking (52+ days)	1,570	868	80.9
6. Cross-country skiing (15+ days)	695	389	78.7
8. Target shooting (25+ days)	3,723	2,730	36.4
10. Volleyball (25+ days)	7,517	5,564	35.1
14. Archery (25+ days)	2,255	1,718	31.3
15. Table tennis (25+ days)	3,024	2,325	30.1
16. Bicycling (touring/fitness) (100+ days)	4,996	3,929	27.2
20. Recreational vehicle camping (15+ days)	7,602	6,131	24.0

[1]In the U.S. population, six years or older. Other fast-growing activities in the top 20 but removed from the list include treadmill, cheerleading, step aerobics, stair-climbing machines, soccer, free weights, multipurpose home gyms, resistance machines, tackle football, basketball, and exercise to music. The numerous fitness and workout machines and activities on this list suggest that the use of fitness machines and facilities in general is a major area of growth that should be considered for a resort.

Source: Sporting Goods Manufacturers Association, North Palm Beach, Fla., 1995.

The Arnold Palmer Grove Course at Indian Ridge Country Club, Palm Desert, California, is one of two golf courses that enhance the setting for the approximately 1,300 homes in the community.

While the overall participation rates for golf are much lower than for some other recreational activities, such as bicycling and swimming, the important fact to keep in mind is that golf is a favored activity in the 50-to-65 age group, especially in the upper-income segment. This same group is also the prime demographic group for second-home purchase and the age group that will grow dramatically in the coming decade. The Sporting Goods Manufacturers Association released the results of a survey in 1995 showing that, among those over age 55, golf was the second most popular sport behind fitness walking as measured by frequent participation. The survey estimated that approximately 2.8 million seniors play golf 25+ days per year.[20]

Time availability affects golf and is likely to be the industry's major change agent, according to Ralph Bowden of Ralph Stewart Bowden, Inc., in Earlysville, Virginia. "With less time available, and with expanded alternative activities, people find a four- or five-hour golf game too big a time commitment. Par-3 courses are a response to this issue and are enjoying renewed popularity. The relatively short Par-3 golf game appeals to busy families and makes it possible for children to play with their parents. The briefer game is also less intimidating to the prospective golfer than is a regulation golf course."[21] Executive courses (with par 3s and 4s) are also expected to grow in popularity.

Beyond changes in the nature of golf as a pastime, recreational communities—even high-end communities —are witnessing a trend away from private, equity golf courses toward public, daily-fee courses. Developers are finding that, under the right conditions, the real estate premiums associated with frontage on and proximity to public golf courses and open space can be extremely favorable and parallel those associated with frontage on and proximity to private courses. Moreover, public courses are much easier to manage and operate efficiently. Not surprisingly, then, the trend toward public courses in second-home communities is likely to increase

as more and more developers evaluate the advantages and disadvantages of the alternatives.

Another trend that is likely to increase during the next few years is the design and operation of golf courses as environmental assets. In many situations, with proper planning and management, golf courses can actually enhance the environment, particularly where the development site can be restored or enhanced. Examples abound of golf courses that demonstrate environmental benefits. In fact, the New York Audubon Society has initiated a program that recognizes golf courses and golf course communities that meet environmental objectives.[22]

There is also a strong trend toward the professional management of golf courses. Currently, golf management companies manage between 5 and 7 percent of the total golf inventory, with about 75 such companies in the United States managing more than one golf course. More and more, experienced resort developers are establishing joint ventures with experienced golf course owners and operators. High-quality golf course management companies that are sensitive to developers' business risks and end game have much to offer resort developers in the way of capital, expertise, and value. These companies can be equity investors, purchasers, or even credit tenants whose credit rating can allow the resort developer to borrow against the lease.

Skiing and Winter Sports

Following the explosive growth in the ski industry from the late 1960s to the late 1970s, the skiing participation rate among the U.S. population has stabilized. As a result, ski areas are currently searching for strategies to survive in an increasingly competitive market. According to the National Ski Areas Association, during the 1993–1994 ski season, skier visits grew by only a modest 1.1 percent. Increased costs outstripped increased revenues, leaving the profit picture flat.[23]

This slow growth could have been even worse if not for the growing popularity of several new winter sports. According to American Sports Data, Inc., the participation rate (at least once per year) for downhill skiing increased by only 1.7 percent from 1987 to 1994. In contrast, the participation rate for snowboarding increased by 84.7 percent and for ice hockey by 14.6 percent. The participation rate for cross-country skiing posted mixed results; the at-least-once-a-year participation rate declined by 32.9 percent from 1987 to 1994, but the frequent participation rate (15+ days per year) increased by 78.7 percent from 1992 to 1994.[24]

On the whole, compared with 15 years ago, the typical skier is now older and more affluent and therefore more demanding of a higher level of services, more interested in skiing as a family experience, and less daring. The average snowboarder, on the other hand, tends to be much younger than the average skier and more daring. Snowboarding is especially popular among teenagers.

Thus, to adjust to the changing ski market, many existing ski areas are modifying their ski facilities and runs and adding special facilities and services for snow-boarding, cross-country-skiing, and ice-skating enthusiasts. Snowboarding has been especially important in recent years for many resorts. Notes Robert Kunkel of Vail Associates, Inc., of Vail, Colorado, snowboarding "has energized every segment of the sport of skiing, from retail to manufacturers to the ski school to the language of skiing."[25] Moreover, snowboarding has brought new entrants from other sports such as skateboarding and surfing; snowboarding has been instrumental in solidifying the position of ski resorts as family resorts where mom and dad ski and the kids snowboard.

Other trends in winter resort activities include snow-shoeing (on new smaller and lighter snowshoes), snow-biking (using either mountain bikes or recently developed bikes that ride on skis), and bobsled runs. Vail Mountain now offers a bobsled run that is a ride, not to mention an interesting diversion from the usual trip down the mountain.

Few if any new ski areas will be developed in the United States in the near term. In fact, the number of ski areas in the United States has fallen dramatically from approximately 1,500 in the 1960s to about 500 today. The surviving areas are generally bigger and better. This trend toward the consolidation of skiing activity at the major and established ski resorts is expected to continue. Clearly, the permitting requirements and startup costs for major new ski resorts are simply too prohibitive to generate much new development, and the viability of smaller operations is marginal.

Consolidation is also taking place among ski resort owners and operators; for example, Vail Resorts acquired several new ski resorts in 1996.

Boating and Watersports

The popularity of boating and other watersports is an important factor in assessing future demand for resort development. Boating has experienced steady growth as a recreational pursuit; the total number of recreational boats owned in the United States has risen from 11.8 million in 1980 to 16.5 million in 1993, although the growth rate in recent years has been modest. The number of boats with inboard motors (those most likely to be stored in marinas) has increased even more dramatically, rising from 1.2 million in 1980 to 2.6 million in 1993.[26]

The relative affordability of boat purchases when compared to other major recreational purchases, including second homes, makes boat ownership an economical alternative for many. With boat purchases discretionary, however, the impact of sales and luxury taxes, economic recessions, and moorage availability and fees will surely influence ownership rates in the future. Boat sales track closely with the economy; they reached a peak in 1988, fell dramatically during 1990 and 1991, and have achieved modest gains since.[27]

While boating remains popular, the participation rate (at least once a year) for many watersports has been flat or declining of late; thus, some caution is in order. From 1987 to 1994, participation in boardsailing declined by 43.9 percent, sailing by 33 percent, and water skiing by 21.7 percent. Scuba diving, on the other hand, is on the upswing, rising by 30.7 percent during the same period; both freshwater and saltwater fishing have also grown, up by 5.2 percent and 8.1 percent, respectively, during the same period. Swimming for fitness has been flat, rising by only 0.3 percent during this period.

While the participation rate for water-related sports may be down, the various activities will remain important for several resorts, especially those that are positioned to attract the experts. The popularity of several other watersports, such as sea kayaking, surfing, and the use of personal watercraft (such as jet skis and wave runners), can also play a significant role in the future of resorts. Resorts that can offer opportunities for these

The Canmore Nordic Center in Calgary, Alberta, Canada. While skiing has seen slow growth in recent years, ice skating and snowboarding have grown in popularity.

Photo courtesy of Design Workshop Inc.

and other water-based recreational pursuits will have a distinct marketing advantage for enthusiasts and novices alike.

Ecotourism and Soft Adventures

Ecotourism is one of the most widely discussed areas of ground-floor opportunity in the resort development field. While ecotourism is emerging globally, it is in short supply domestically. Nonetheless, it offers a relatively affordable resort experience that will go a long way in satisfying the increasing demand from middle-income markets both at home and abroad. Moreover, ecotourism responds to the public's heightened concern for the planet and the environment.

According to the Ecotourism Society, the industry standard-setting body, ecotourism involves responsible travel to natural areas where the environment is being conserved and the well-being of the local population is being sustained. The U.S. Travel Data Center estimates that 7 percent of U.S. travelers, or approximately 8 million people, have taken an ecotrip.

Ecotourism has gained attention as Americans continue the trend in living by principle rather than by status. Maho Bay and Harmony on St. John in the United States Virgin Islands, developed by Stanley Selengut, have been recognized for their practices of respecting the natural environment, recycling, energy conservation, and intimate interaction with the resort's native environment. These developments have also been financially successful, even as they offer the guest improved economies of scale over more intensively developed traditional resorts.

Ecotourism resorts are growing in number but are widely dispersed and most frequently located in remote areas. So far, the sheer adventure of the experience seems to outweigh the inconvenience to guests. A look at one closely watched example of an ecoresort in the making—Molokai Ranch—offers insight into this growing market trend (see feature box on page 380).[28]

The ecotourist market is best served by small boutique hotels or modest lodging facilities and service providers that can guarantee high-quality experiences without damage to the surrounding natural environment.[29] Some experts, however, have suggested that other types of resorts can also be positioned as base camps for ecotourism and adventure travel in the surrounding region.[30] Older resorts near major cities could, for example, benefit from the ecotourism trend by taking advantage of a wide range of interesting and easily accessible destinations and adventure experiences. On a large site, base camping could require the development of several smaller venues on the property to accentuate the site's different qualities. Without question, creative management is a prerequisite to the successful operation of these venues. Smaller properties might establish alliances with other venues to offer tourists a package of several experiences within the same region.

Resort communities can also incorporate opportunities for modest ecotourism and adventure travel experi-

Stanley Selengut
President
Maho Bay Camps
New York, New York

Stanley Selengut is a civil engineer specializing in resort development. He is president of Maho Bay Camps, developer and operator of Maho Bay, a 114-unit campground located within the United States Virgin Islands National Park on St. John. The environmentally responsible resort achieves a 95 percent high-season occupancy rate and is one of the most profitable businesses on St. John.

Selengut is currently developing Harmony, a research resort adjacent to the campground. Harmony is envisioned as a center for the study of sustainable resort developments. The goal of the new project is to bring together the latest ecological ideas, designs, and technologies in a vacation community that is the world's first luxury resort to operate exclusively on sun and wind power.

Selengut's varied career started in the 1950s when he created a large-volume importing company specializing in South American native crafts. His solutions to the development problems of South American villages led him to serve as a consultant to the Kennedy Administration on development projects in South America. Subsequently, he started a design consulting firm that pioneered new teaching methods and the design and manufacture of an innovative furniture and accessory system for children. A consulting assignment on low-income housing for the Rockefeller brothers led Selengut to St. John, where he faced the challenge of developing an economically viable resort facility compatible with National Park Service mandates.

Ecotourism and sustainable development are hot buzz words in the 1990s. We have been dealing with these issues for the last 18 years in our resort facility at the Virgin Islands National Park on the island of St. John. In a typical resort, all you have to do is give your customers a meaningful, comfortable vacation. In ecotourism, you not only have to provide the same for your customer but you also have to think about the well-being of the landscape that you are working with. It still has to equal profit, but it is a little more complex. In a regular resort, you can almost "cookie cutter" it and adjust the landscape to fit the resort. In ecotourism, you are working much more with your indigenous assets and choreographing the vacation experience. Essentially, you are working within the existing context as opposed to changing the context.

Sustainability is a concept that can work anywhere—conserve water and fuel, use recycled building materials, practice good recycling, use alternative energy sources. Ecotourism uses sustainability in fragile places that have some historic, natural, or cultural assets—

something that will be a specific attraction. There is a real need to maintain the integrity of that asset, that attraction.

It not only means going back to indigenous assets but also overlaying them with new techniques such as doing without fossil fuel, developing with no waste, and adopting recycling practices. Not only are we preserving the historic and natural qualities, but the customer can go back home with a few more ideas about a less consumptive lifestyle.

Ecotourism is as much selling a vacation experience in a fragile landscape as it is selling an experience of other guests experiencing that same landscape. I think we do much more show business than the traditional hotel or resort. We actually get involved in trying to orchestrate the guest experience during the course of the stay. We have a one-week minimum stay requirement. We sort of hook them for a whole week and then are responsible for making sure that there is plenty to do during that week.

What ecotourism promotes is natural reality rather than happy fantasy. Instead of an escape, it's a learning experience. I think it can be just as exciting and just as financially successful as a Disney World. An ecoresort should be a win-win situation for everyone—the local people, the staff, the customers, the environment, and the support services.

I have realized, over time, that one insensitive guest can do more damage than 100 people who are trying to help take care of a place. In terms of trying to be environmentally responsible, carrying capacity also has a direct relationship to the kind of people who are walking around. So I try to deal with people who are a little more health- and fitness-oriented, who are more activity-oriented, and who are communicative.

At this point, the concept of ecotourism seems to work in situations where guests have no ownership interest in a resort. I don't know if people would buy into a place that was run by solar and photovoltaic cells and built with recycled building materials. From a resort experience, while our occupancy is off the wall, I don't know if people are ready to live "off the grid" and have an adventure of perhaps running out of power if the weather is inclement for three or four days and they have overused the electricity. On a vacation, it really is an experience. By just making them a little apprehensive about running out of power, they are much more conscious of their energy use, and, as a result, almost no one ever does run out of power. Then they feel good about it because we give them a printout comparing their energy and water use against the norm.

Modular plans work well in an ecotourism resort because they allow more site sensitivity. You can tuck the units within the trees without much disruption to the landscape. What this also allows is the ability to build a modest number of units, get customer response, assess the environmental impact, make changes, and proceed. With Harmony, I am starting with just five units. I am building each one within different parameters—some with screened-in porches, some with open porches, some all photovoltaic, some a combination of photovoltaic and wind power, some with a propane backup, others without the backup. I'll monitor customers' responses, come up with the ideal combination, and build 30 more. It takes a tremendous arrogance to think you can prejudge the whole thing.

Since an ecotourist resort fits into the landscape, make an inventory of existing local assets, such as architecture, music, dance, food, crafts, wildlife, flora, and fauna and weave these elements into the resort's design. It is so much less expensive because it is all there for you from the start. In terms of the local community, it has evolved with a certain character, a certain image. To fight against that takes a lot more energy than to go into it and try to help the local people upgrade. Very often, not only the landscape has been degraded at one time or another but also the culture has eroded. A developer can be a real force in helping to restore the indigenous crafts, the music, and the dance. On the one hand, you are working toward an experience for your customers. On the other hand, you are working to preserve a local culture.

ences. In fact, more and more are likely to offer such opportunities as the market demands them. For example, Spring Island, a second-home community in the Low Country of South Carolina, is itself a nature preserve with its own naturalist, nature center, and extensive trail network. Owners and guests can take advantage of organized outings to observe plants and wildlife and participate in other nature-oriented programs and activities (see feature box on page 396).

Gaming

Gaming has experienced a 10 percent compound growth rate around the United States during the past ten years. And the industry continues to grow, not only in the United States but also worldwide. Resort hotels with casinos have proven to be highly profitable in many locations; in 1992, the seven casino hotels in the 250-hotel Hilton Hotel chain reportedly accounted for half of the company's revenue.[31] To appeal to the family market, casino hotels in Las Vegas and elsewhere are evolving into resort hotels that now offer a wide range of amenities.

New venues, including riverboats, Native American reservations, and cruise ships, are helping disperse casinos to locations outside Las Vegas and Atlantic City. While these new gaming centers can be a source of direct competition for resort destinations that do not offer gaming, they can also stimulate nearby resort development. Las Vegas, for example, is one of the fastest-growing locations for timeshare resorts and resort communities for retirees. It is likely that other gaming centers and even freestanding casinos will help create a critical mass of entertainment opportunities in other regions that will make resort development more feasible. Moreover, the changing face of gaming as it relates to the family market may make gaming more and more desirable as an integral part of a resort's amenities. For the near-term future, however, gaming will probably not be incorporated into most existing domestic U.S. resorts except under unique conditions. Internationally, however, gaming may well become much more common in existing resorts, especially in Asia, as the regulation of the industry is less strict in many international locations.

Resort Real Estate Trends

Hotels

In 1994, the U.S. lodging industry emerged as a changed industry following a six-year slump that resulted from overbuilding, economic recession, and cutbacks in corporate and leisure travel.[32] Most significant among the changes were the shift toward chain affiliation and brand segmentation, the appearance of new niche products, and the focus of the chains on resorts and timesharing. Similarly, a significant trend in the resort hotel market evidenced a switch from independent operations, which historically dominated the industry's resort segment, to chain affiliations. The need to increase market

presence to attract year-round business has induced many resorts to affiliate with a recognized hotel company that offers the advantages of worldwide reservations systems and sophisticated marketing networks. Hotel chain affiliation will continue to be a strategy by which owners seek to distinguish their resorts from those of competitors.

Another significant trend for resort hotels is the use of niche products designed to capture a specific market. The 1980s saw an emphasis on building large resort hotels, especially conference-oriented facilities. While such facilities will remain important, opportunities have recently expanded for smaller niche products and hotels targeted to the free independent traveler. Currently, some of the most popular niche products are all-inclusive resorts (where resort guests pay a fixed price that includes lodging, meals, and programs), golf resorts, and environmentally sensitive resorts, including those that offer ecotours or tours of nearby major natural features. Not surprisingly, then, the megaresort hotel is a product type that is not expected to see much new development over the near term. In the future, successful resort hotels will continue to position and reposition themselves as necessary to appeal to specific niche markets.

Many resort hotel developers and operators also recognize that multiuse resorts offer opportunities and efficiencies that are the product of synergistic relationships among land uses. Resort hotels linked with fee-simple or timeshare residential products are able to offer a greater variety of recreational facilities and retail facilities than resort hotels that are not linked to these products. Convention and meeting facilities and a diverse selection of food and beverage outlets can also be included to advantage. Recognizing that multiuse synergy brings with it substantial rate and price premiums as well as property value appreciation, more and more resort hotels will be developed as components of larger projects.

Finally, many resort developers believe that resort development budgets will allocate a smaller share of dollars to guest rooms than in the 1990s. Psychographic studies suggest that people are becoming more principle-oriented and less status-oriented as they move through the 1990s. This trend bodes well for the industry in some key respects and validates the practice of devoting more of the development budget to guest facilities and programs than to sleeping quarters. This shift in focus will lead to smarter spending; it points to greater returns because of lower room development costs, longer stays once guests identify their favorite activities, and increased repeat visits from loyal guests, thereby leading to reduced marketing expenses.[33]

Timesharing/Vacation Ownership

Vacation ownership is poised to become the preferred ownership choice for a substantial portion of the resort and second-home market. Its improving image and identity have benefited from a more consistent and reliable product, a commitment to ethically driven (and legally enforced) vacation ownership resorts, and the entry of major hospitality companies noted for their strength and credibility. In particular, the participation of hospitality companies will continue to have a profound influence on the industry's rapid expansion.

Consolidation will also continue as large companies acquire independent and faltering vacation ownership properties. Ed McMullen of Hilton Grand Vacations Company predicts that 95 percent of the timeshare business will become the province of major firms within ten years, as opposed to an estimate of only 5 percent today. In addition, McMullen believes that the method of timeshare sales will undergo a major transformation. Currently, 90 percent of timeshares are sold on site; McMullen believes that up to 50 percent of timeshares will be sold off site within the next ten years.[34]

In tune with the baby boomer market, vacation ownership products are adapting to a market more inter- ested in shorter vacation periods and greater flexibility. Vacation clubs (and related products) are well suited to these new demands and appear to be gaining a proportion of market share. Nonetheless, fee-simple, fixed-interval products will continue to dominate the market in terms of total units.

The design trend of the lock-off unit will become the standard among hotelier/vacation corporations. The increased flexibility offered by lock-offs has recently revolutionized the timeshare product; in fact, companies are designing alternatives to the two-unit lock-off. Hilton has recently designed a three-bedroom lock-off. The flexibility associated with larger units makes the units more marketable for corporate use and the international market, which typically travels with a larger family. The four-bedroom lock-off should become a product in the near future.[35]

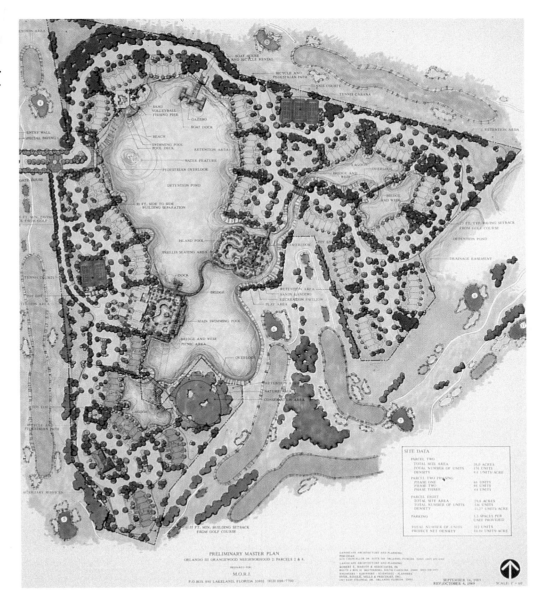

Marriott's Cypress Harbour Resort in Orlando is a 506-unit upscale vacation ownership property that surrounds a lake. It contains two-bedroom, two-bath units in mid-rise buildings, each of which contains 22 to 24 units.

Along the South Carolina coast, in an area known appropriately as the Low Country, lies a small, 3,000-acre island called Spring Island. Here, where bald eagles roost, alligators lurk, deer rove, fox squirrels play, and 300-year-old live oaks stand majestically in the subtropical forest, a unique second-home development is taking shape. Not incidentally, that development will preserve much of the island's rich history, animal habitat, and natural beauty.

The Spring Island Company, which purchased the virtually undeveloped island in 1990, is pursuing an unconventional development plan that preserves one-third of the island and calls for no more than 500 homes on the remaining two-thirds. By contrast, a previous developer had obtained approval to build 5,500 homes on the island. According to Jim Chaffin, president of the Spring Island Company, "building that many homes would have ruined the island." Spring Island's development philosophy is to protect and preserve the land's integrity, character, and beauty. The company hopes to capitalize on the growing market for environmentally sensitive development—development that harmonizes with its natural environment. "Nature is the single most important amenity of the project," stresses Chaffin.

Bounded by the Chechessee and Colleton Rivers and surrounded by more than 3,000 acres of marshes, the island features ponds, fields, abundant wildlife, and dense forests, including a 600-acre live oak forest—the largest live oak forest on the East Coast of the United States. The island lies about five miles northwest of Hilton Head and 13 miles southwest of Beaufort. It is accessible from neighboring Callawassie Island by boat or by a private bridge built and paid for by the Spring Island Company. Geologically, Spring Island is the granddaddy of the area's islands, about 30,000 years older than Hilton Head Island. Although a coastal island, it is no pancake. Its average elevation is 19 feet above sea level, with a high point of 35 feet, as compared to an average elevation of only seven to 12 feet on nearby islands. Spring Island even boasts an eight-foot waterfall, not exactly Victoria Falls but unusual in its neck of the woods.

Native Americans occupied the island until 1706, when Scotsman John Cochran was granted two 500-acre parcels. Since then, the island has remained in private hands. In the early 1800s, George Edwards established a cotton plantation on the island and built a tabby (crushed shell and mortar) home, whose ruins remain and will be preserved. Following the Civil War, the plantation deteriorated. Subsistence farming was the chief land use for a few decades. In 1895, the property was purchased for a hunting preserve. For years, affluent hunters from the North flocked to the Low Country each fall to shoot

Spring Island, South Carolina, is a 3,000-acre, low-density recreational community in the Low Country with 500 homesites. Over one-third of the island has been deeded as permanent open space to be controlled by the Spring Island Trust, an organization created to study, educate, and learn about the island. The development concept for the island strongly emphasizes and is committed to preserving the integrity of the environment.

quail, ducks, turkey, and deer. In 1995, the hunting program was moved to the mainland; hunting has ceased on the island.

Before the first lot was sited, a team of professionals (including a biologist, naturalist, forester, landscape designer, environmental scientist, and the former plantation manager) conducted a comprehensive environmental inventory of the island's wildlife, soils, vegetation, geology, and hydrology. The Spring Island Company then developed a list of wildlife species that were to be protected—eagles, quail, river otters, fox squirrels, songbirds, and wading birds—and identified, mapped, and incorporated the habitat of each species into the land management plan. The primary objectives of the plan call for providing a maximum diversity of plants and animals, ensuring that the needs of wildlife are met, and creating an aesthetically pleasing environment for recreation.

The biggest challenge was to determine how much development the island could accommodate without overburdening the ecosystem or detracting from it aesthetically. The amount would have to be at least enough to make the project feasible. "We had to determine the critical mass of homes needed to make the project economically viable," recalls Chaffin. By balancing environmental constraints against business needs, the Spring Island Company came up with a development plan that calls for 500 homes plus a par-72, 18-hole golf course. Tennis courts are also included.

To accommodate the 500 homes, 125 cottage homesites are grouped in three clusters; 300 estate homesites are located around the perimeter of the island and enjoy water views; and 75 homesites are situated adjacent to the golf course. Lots vary in size from one to ten acres and sell for an average price of $280,000. The initiation fee for an equity golf membership is $35,000, with annual dues of $3,600. The homeowners' association fee is another $1,000 per year. As of mid-1996, approximately 250 lots had sold with 26 houses completed.

Among the many environmentally sensitive design features that characterize the project are narrow unpaved roads, deep setbacks for homes along the water, and the use of native plants for landscaping. Cottage homes must be set back at least 50 feet and estate homes 100 feet from any marsh or pond. An architectural review board scrutinizes all aspects of home design, including siting, landscaping, and the alteration of natural foliage, to ensure that each proposed house meets strict environmental controls.

Perhaps the most important step was the establishment of a 1,000-acre nature preserve owned and managed by the nonprofit Spring Island Trust, an entity created by the developer. The trust will be supported by a 1.5 percent fee on the initial sale of each lot and a 1 percent transfer fee on subsequent sales. Activities in the preserve will be limited to low-impact recreation such as walking, birdwatching, fishing, and horse-back riding. An extensive trail system links each lot with a network of trails in the preserve. In fact, the island boasts more miles of trails than roads. A full-time naturalist—half of whose salary is paid by the trust and half by the developer—manages the preserve. For its environmentally sensitive land stewardship, the Spring Island Trust received the 1993 Conservation Award from the South Carolina Wildlife Federation.

Source: Adapted from David Salvesen, "Preservation through Limited Development," *Urban Land*, August 1994, pp. 66–68.

■

Moreover, the timeshare market is expected to become increasingly sophisticated. People are much more knowledgeable today about the concept of timesharing than they were 20 years ago when the concept was introduced, and the trend is expected to continue and broaden.

In general, the vacation ownership industry has proven itself a major component of the resort industry, and it shows no indications of faltering. The general market trend demonstrates increasing interest in buying timeshares. Accordingly, the industry can tap a much broader segment of the market that cannot otherwise afford a vacation property. With this growth and the improving image of the industry, timeshares will likely remain one of the fastest-growing segments of the resort and vacation industry for some time to come and become increasingly important components in existing multiuse resort properties. They offer one more way for large resorts to attract vacation visitors and create vacation property sales. In the future, many a resort that now offers resort hotels and second homes will add timeshares.

Housing and Second Homes

The overall housing industry can be expected to influence future residential resort development in several distinct but interrelated ways. For example, among the major trends in primary-home residential design and construction are increased density, increased home size, increased use of energy-efficient practices and materials, increased attention to safety and security, increased use of "smart house" technology, and increased off-site manufacturing of housing components. These trends are also influencing the design and construction of second homes.

Safety and security issues are at least as important for resort and second-home markets as for primary-home markets since resort communities have high degrees of transiency and often experience low occupancies at certain times of the year. The use of secured gates, perimeter fencing, surveillance cameras, alarm systems, and private security patrols are the typical means of addressing security concerns and, along with other measures, will likely become more and more common in resort projects.

The incorporation of "smart house" technology also has many useful applications for the second-home and resort residential markets. Given that second homes experience staggered periods of use to a greater extent than primary homes, technology for controlling a home's heating, air conditioning, lighting, security, communications, and entertainment systems provide significant convenience as well as a distinct marketing advantage. Current technology allows second-home owners to program the opening of their weekend home for their arrival so that the shutters are up, the lights are on, and the Jacuzzi is filled with hot water.

From a community planning perspective, the neo-traditional movement, sometimes known as the new

At SilverLakes in Pembroke Pines, Florida, more than 33 species of animals and birds thrive in the wetlands, including these Giant Pink Flamingos. The 2,480-acre community leaves 1,200 acres in open natural space, including 802 acres in lakes and 300 acres in replanted wetlands. The community has received the Florida Quality Development designation from the state of Florida, and the FQD has since become the foundation for SilverLakes's successful "green" marketing and positioning program.

Sanacore Photography

urbanism or traditional neighborhood design (TND), is also likely to continue to have an impact on some new resort development. The resort community of Seaside, Florida (see case study on page 334), a pioneering example of neotraditionalism, has received widespread acclaim in the popular media and has performed well in the marketplace. Several other new and influential projects either now on the drawing board or in the early stages of development have incorporated elements of the neotraditional design philosophy. These projects include Disney's new town of Celebration near Disney World in Orlando, Aspen Highlands near Aspen, and Windsor in Vero Beach, Florida. The neotraditional concept may also be useful in the renovation and revitalization of existing resort communities.

The delivery of housing in resort communities will also increasingly move toward turnkey packages that provide the lot buyer with the option of building a house without a major hassle. Resort communities with such programs, notes Gadi Kaufmann of Robert Charles Lesser & Co. in Los Angeles, will fare much better than those that offer no such services.[36]

In terms of preferred housing types, consumer tastes are likely to vary greatly from one place to the next and as the economy cycles up and down. For example, *Barron's* recently reported that "In New Hampshire . . . it's the old-fashioned single-family home that's in vogue—or at least holding value—while condos of the 'Seventies sink. In Naples, Fla., the situation is reversed: Condos

carry a certain cachet, and are appreciating 1%–15% a year, while some single-family homes—even waterfront properties on the canals leading to the Gulf—have fallen from favor."[37] These cycles will undoubtedly continue, making local market research even more crucial for the future.

Environmentally Responsible Development

Environmentally responsible development is a process of thinking about land uses and buildings to ensure that they connect to and work in harmony with the natural environment.[38] A short definition of environmentally responsible development is the production of buildings and communities that conserve resources and reduce waste through more efficient use of materials, energy, and water; that are more durable and useful; and that are designed for adaptive use or the recycling of their materials. Practicing environmentally responsible development can reduce real costs and create economic value in the form of long-term savings in energy and water consumption, recycling of building materials, increased safety, and reduced maintenance costs. If environmentally responsible development principles are successfully applied, the final benefit is the creation of a marketing advantage and increased profit margins.

The understanding of what constitutes environmentally responsible development practices is increasing among practitioners and consumers alike. As this understanding takes hold, more and more resort developers and operators will need to become committed to using environmentally responsible development practices in their projects. To a large extent, the adoption of these practices will result from enlightened self-interest. Several years ago, a poll revealed that over 70 percent of Americans think of themselves as environmentalists. In this context, it is clear that environmentally responsible development can help market a resort. In fact, to some degree, most resorts already market the quality of their natural surroundings and their sensitivity to those surroundings.

The market for resorts that incorporate environmentally responsible development practices is expected to increase as consumers become more educated about the choices available to them and demand higher and higher levels of responsibility. For resort hotels and lodging facilities, the ecotourism movement will likely play a major role in educating consumers and ensuring the credibility of resorts' claims of adherence to environmentally responsible principles. For resort real estate products in resort communities, some type of certification program designed to recognize adherence to environmentally responsible development principles will probably emerge from within the development industry.

In addition, a major opportunity for resort developers involves the restoration and enhancement of degraded natural landscapes. Degraded landscapes are easily found in many prime resort locations, often resulting from previous poor-quality development or from past agricultural, logging, or mining activities. Both the technology and scientific knowledge required to undertake restoration and enhancement are rapidly advancing, making these activities more cost-effective and likely to succeed. The encouragement of resort development and redevelopment that results in a net improvement in the quality of the surrounding natural environment can be an important part of a region's strategy to increase its appeal as a tourist and recreational destination.

The Outlook for Resorts

With growth in the resort industry highly cyclical and subject to broader economic trends, the short-term prospects will vary substantially from year to year over the next decade, although projections call for modest near-term growth. The long-term (ten to 20 years) forecast is generally favorable, largely due to the advancing age of the baby boom generation. As mentioned, earlier generations have represented strong market segments for second-home and retirement-home purchases—as well as for leisure travel—once they entered their 50s and 60s. If this pattern holds for the baby boom generation, it should bode well for the resort and second-home industry over the next ten to 20 years.

Changes in tax laws as they relate to second-home properties could, however, adversely affect the favorable forecast. Prohibitive restrictions on the deductibility of second-home mortgage interest seem much more likely in the late 1990s than in the past several decades; indeed, this likelihood has already affected market demand and the feasibility of resort development. Current law allows second-home owners to write off mortgage interest as long as the combined total of the loans on their primary and second homes does not exceed $1.1 million. Notes Ralph Bowden of Ralph Stewart Bowden, Inc., "Resort

Federal Tax Implications for Second-Home Ownership

Estimates vary, but roughly 3 to 6 percent of U.S. households own the 4 to 6 million second homes located throughout the United States and are currently entitled to several deductions on their federal income tax. For example, they can deduct their mortgage interest and property taxes in a fashion similar to that of a primary residence.

The tax benefits associated with second-home ownership have been a popular target of American tax reformers over the past several decades. By enacting the Tax Reform Act of 1969, lawmakers introduced second-home owners to "hobby loss" restrictions, which complicated and limited tax deduction provisions. Years later, the Tax Reform Act of 1976 limited the deductibility of maintenance costs and depreciation. The Tax Reform Act of 1986, which was aimed primarily at reducing tax shelter ventures, subjected second-home owners to additional limitations, which included restrictions on the deduction of mortgage interest as well as severe limits on the deduction of passive losses. The 1986 law prohibited the deduction of personal interest, which generally included interest on a second-home mortgage; however, the regulation contains an exception for second homes that are considered a "qualified residence."

To be considered a "qualified residence," a second home must be occupied by its owners for more than 14 days or for 10 percent of the rental days for a particular year. By fulfilling the 14 day/10 percent criterion, second-home owners can treat all or a portion of the interest expense on a qualified residence as a fully deductible expense. Property taxes for "qualified residences" are deductible as well. Deduction of normal business expenses, such as maintenance and depreciation, are limited to properties held for rental. If the second home is held exclusively as a rental property, these items are generally deductible. If, however, the second home is also used by the owner for personal use, the deductibility of expenses from the property (including depreciation) is limited to the percent of time that the home is used by the owner as compared to the amount of time that the home is rented.

According to the American Resort Development Association (ARDA), timeshare interests share many of the common tax benefits associated with conventional second-home ownership. If a timeshare unit (including a timeshare of less than two weeks) is not rented by the owner to others during the tax year, the owner can elect to treat the timeshare unit as a second residence and deduct mortgage interest on the unit. In the rare case that a timeshare owner both uses the property personally and rents it to others during the tax year, numerous stipulations can reduce or eliminate the tax benefits of a timeshare interest. For instance, the 14 day/10 percent criterion would have to be met by the owner in order to deduct the mortgage interest attributable to the owner's personal use of the timeshare.

Further changes to tax laws as they relate to second homes are difficult to predict, but the mere specter of loss of deductibility is a significant problem for the industry. Thus, careful monitoring of developments in this area is critical to keep tabs on which direction the wind is blowing.

■

investors in the 1990s are a different breed from those of the 1970s. The lack of investment tax incentives and the lurking threats by lawmakers that they will eliminate the second-home mortgage interest deduction has turned many an investor into a resort owner. Investment-oriented owners are more involved, more educated, and more sophisticated than nonowner investors in their selection of a resort product."[39] However, the Chase survey referred to earlier found that 59 percent of responding second-home owners paid all cash,[40] suggesting that the effect of changes to the tax laws may not be as severe as feared.

The reality of the situation is that leisure travel and resort real estate purchases are and always will be discretionary purchases; there can therefore never be complete certainty about future markets. But the travel and tourism business is among the largest industries in the world, and as the global economy becomes more global each day, there is little doubt that travel and tourism will continue to play a strong and growing role in the worldwide economy. Nonetheless, the prospects for resort development and operation, both new and existing, will vary considerably depending on location and type of resort. In short, new destination resort development is expected to be strongest internationally. In the United States, the emphasis will be on regional resorts, second-home communities, timeshares, and the expansion, redevelopment, and repositioning of existing resorts and resort areas.

The Prospects for New Resorts in the United States

In general, opportunities for new destination and large multiuse resort projects in the United States seem to be more limited today than in recent decades. The reasons are fourfold: principally more stringent environmental regulations, increased costs of development, greater competition from established projects, and the lack of prime sites that have not already been developed. "Ideal resort locations in the United States and Europe are increasingly rare," notes Ralph Bowden of Ralph Stewart Bowden, Inc. "The development of new resorts in pristine areas faces unprecedented regulatory obstacles that drive up costs, preventing the resort from appealing to the broad middle-income market and forcing it to focus on the smaller, higher-income target market."[41]

Most resort developers believe that it is unlikely that many new pioneering large-scale destination resort projects (such as Sea Pines Plantation, Beaver Creek, or Pebble Beach) will be successfully initiated in the United States for many years to come. "In the near future," notes Harry Frampton III of East West Partners in Beaver Creek, Colorado, "we are not likely to see developed what I call new 'resort cities.' By that, I mean areas where pioneering resorts were started many years earlier and which now have had many resorts built around them. Hilton Head, the Vail Valley, and the Scottsdale area come to mind. These core areas are likely to be where the action is in the next five to ten years. It is unlikely that developers will be pioneering whole new areas

because the rules of the game have changed dramatically. What may be developed are small- to medium-sized developments on the periphery of these existing resort areas."[42]

Domestic resort development activity is expected to be focused primarily in established resort areas, with three types of development expected to predominate: timeshare projects and hotel/timeshare combinations; moderately sized second-home communities; and modestly sized resort hotels targeted to the free independent traveler, including families.

In terms of location, much of the development activity will take place around existing regional resorts near major urban areas and within the many existing multiuse resort properties that have not yet been fully built out. Some new opportunities will emerge as highways are improved, speed limits raised, and metropolitan areas extend farther and farther into surrounding areas.

Strong locations in the United States for retirement-home development are likely to continue to be already well-established retirement areas as well as other areas that are within an easy drive of major metropolitan areas. Only 10 percent of retired people choose to move away from their existing primary home, and, for many, the move turns out to be temporary—for periods of ten years or less. Good opportunities therefore seem to exist for year-round and seasonal retirement homes in areas close to major metropolitan areas. Locations near high-quality health care facilities and educational or cultural institutions will have a distinct advantage.

One region that is expected to draw second-home and retirement-home buyers to more remote locations is the Mountain West. The Melrose Company and Club Corporation of America, for example, have recently initiated a new 974-acre second-home and retirement community in Carbondale, Colorado, called Aspen Glen. The community is located well outside—31 miles—the established resort communities of Aspen and Snowmass. Several other projects are also underway nearby, including Cordillera, Cotton Ranch, and Country Club of the Rockies. Other similar projects such as Las Campaas are under development near Santa Fe and are under consideration for the outlying areas around Park City and Deer Valley in Utah.[43] These new developments are not only fairly remote from major urban areas but also well beyond established resort areas, thereby pioneering new and relatively less expensive locations.

The Prospects for New International Resorts

The new international tourism and leisure environment is changing from old travel patterns to new travel patterns. The new travel patterns, notes Richard McElyea of Economics Research Associates in San Francisco, reflect changes in consumer behavior, shifting economic strengths, the opening of source markets, access to new destinations, and political realignments. In addition, world tourism has changed significantly in response to a shift in travel patterns: from an east/west

The spa at Palm Hills Golf Resort and Spa at Itoman City, Okinawa, Japan. Perched on a hill overlooking Itoman City and the ocean, this inland resort includes a hotel, an 18-hole golf course, and a golf clubhouse. Also planned are a botanical garden, resident homesites, and an additional nine holes of golf.

Robert Miller— Photo courtesy of Wimberly Allison Tong & Goo Architects

The 300-hectare An-Nasriyyah Village in Saudi Arabia is envisioned as a master-planned, self-contained, leisure village oriented to the waters of Half Moon Bay. Major plan components include private single-family homesites, rental housing compounds, a marina village, recreational facilities, a commercial center, and support facilities. The recommended master plan shows a total of 1,115 homes.

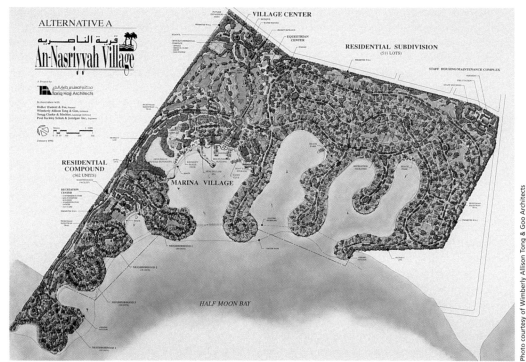

Photo courtesy of Wimberly Allison Tong & Goo Architects

to north/south orientation in Asia, North America, and Europe and from Atlantic dominance to Pacific dominance. Moreover, McElyea believes that emerging destinations will shortly dominate established destinations. New destinations provide the traveler with greater choice at lower market cost when compared to established destinations. An example is Mexico. The California market is shifting to Mexico and away from Hawaii.[44]

Several factors favor international resort development, but the primary one is the tremendous growth in many developing countries around the world. These countries are in a position today both to finance new resort development and to attract international and domestic tourists to new resort locations and properties. The world is more accessible for tourism than ever before, and nearly every country in the world is now in the tourism

Center Parcs: The European Innovator of Short-Break Holiday Vacation Villages

The Center Parcs Company has become one of the leading European corporations specializing in the development and operation of short-stay resort villages. Over the past 27 years, Center Parcs, a division of the British brewing and leisure company Scottish & Newcastle, has developed 13 holiday villages throughout Europe, including the Netherlands, Belgium, Britain, France, and Germany. The company's design, development, and marketing strategies are largely based on the premise that the general public's vacation and leisure time has shrunk and will continue to decrease significantly. Consequently, Center Parcs focuses its resort development efforts on providing "short-break" vacation accommodations close to major metropolitan population centers. Center Parcs's villages have become the European standard in short-term holiday resorts.

With an average size of 400 acres, Center Parcs's villages successfully integrate villa accommodations with an extensive array of indoor and outdoor recreational amenities. The focus of each Center Parcs village is the "Subtropical Swimming Paradise," a transparent covered dome that houses a selection of water activities within an indoor landscaped environment. Temperature within the Subtropical Swimming Paradise is a constant 84 degrees Fahrenheit. The domed tropical setting is detailed with specially quarried and polished natural rocks as well as with tropical trees, plants, and flowers. The amenity offers a selection of water activities, including Jacuzzis, saunas, children's pools, a wave pool, and river slides and rides. The indoor leisure pool enables Center Parcs's clientele to participate in a wide variety of recreational options regardless of weather. The Subtropical Swimming Paradise has proven to be an invaluable amenity in northern Europe and the United Kingdom. In fact, Center Parcs often markets its resort villages as "a holiday experience the weather cannot spoil."

In addition to the swimming paradise, all Center Parcs villages incorporate a wide variety of recreational facilities, including tennis, squash, sailing, golf, and fitness. By providing ample facilities and programs that cater to children of all ages, Center Parcs is an attractive resort setting for families.

Center Parcs resort villages are made up of an average of 600 villas built in small clusters and dispersed across the site. Villas range from one to four bedrooms and contain spacious living areas and well-equipped kitchens. An integral component of the Center Parcs formula is the inclusion of a variety of restaurants, retail establishments, and supermarket facilities within a European village setting. Such facilities have proven to be an invaluable source of cash flow, accounting for approximately 40 percent of Center Parcs's total revenues.

Environmental responsibility is a major element of the Center Parcs development and operations philosophy. The criteria used for site selection during the planning and construction of a village ensure minimum disruption to the indigenous surroundings. The layout of the village's central features and villas harmonizes with the natural surroundings and preserves ecological resources. Sophisticated environmental restoration and landscaping techniques protect and enhance existing vegetation. It is not uncommon for a Center Parcs environmental plan to include the planting of 500,000 trees and shrubs. The creation of streams, lakes, and waterways is an integral Center Parcs design component. The movement of water throughout these systems is carefully planned and controlled. The introduction of appropriate aquatic vegetation attracts native wildlife. In keeping with its stringent environmental policies, Center Parcs places strict limits on automobile access throughout its resort villages. Bicycles, which are rented to guests upon arrival, are the primary source of transportation within the village.

Despite the economic recession that troubled Europe throughout much of the 1990s, Center Parcs has continued to achieve annual occupancy rates above 90 percent. In 1994, over 3 million guests stayed at Center Parcs's 13 villages. In Holland, as much as 10 percent of the total population visits a Center Parcs resort each year.

■

business. Even countries with minimum resort infrastructure can tap into the new ecotourism trends by providing nature-based experiences and adventures that attract visitors.

Much of the new destination resort development activity is likely to be concentrated in Asian countries, particularly in Malaysia, Indonesia, and Vietnam. Latin America is likely to emerge as another active area, especially Brazil and Argentina, but smaller countries such as Costa Rica are also attracting tourists and retirees from the United States. Prospects for major new resorts favor Mexico over the United States, as more prime sites are still available in Mexico. Further, Mexico offers a hospitable climate and is well positioned to capture both U.S. tourists and the growing number of international tourists, especially from South America and Europe. The Caribbean will also continue to be a strong area for resorts; Cuba, if and when its politics and economy open, could become a major area for new development in the next several decades.

Worldwide, U.S. developers are in a good position to export their expertise and undertake joint ventures in parts of the world where travel is increasing as old tensions give way and markets open up. Many architectural and land planning firms are already heavily involved in international work.

One important consideration for U.S. developers and other real estate professionals undertaking resort development in other parts of the world is the need to make every effort to preserve and reflect the cultural integrity of the subject area. Given that most international travelers seek out unique and authentic cultural experiences, it makes good economic sense for developers to respond to the cultural integrity of the area. Other benefits include fostering constructive connections with the local people and the local economy. In the past, many resorts have mistakenly transplanted customs and architectural styles from one culture to another in an effort to appeal to the presumed preferences of a homogeneous international clientele. Such approaches have often proven unwise.

Overseas opportunities must be tempered by the risks inherent in conducting business abroad. For example, such external and unpredictable factors as economic and political conditions, climatic and weather events, and natural disasters often affect global travel and tourism patterns. Further, the realities of doing business in developing countries typically means significant delays and uncertainties throughout the course of any real estate development project. The best advice is to involve local experts as members of the project team whenever possible.

The Prospects for Repositioning Existing Resorts in the United States

In the continental United States, major opportunities abound for the expansion, redevelopment, or repositioning of many existing resorts. In fact, existing resorts control many of the prime resort locations.

The redevelopment and repositioning trend is pertinent to nearly all resort property types. For resort hotel properties, the cost of acquisition and redevelopment is typically less than the cost of new construction, particularly when the market is oversupplied and properties can often be purchased for cents on the dollar. Moreover, the unique character of existing properties combined with the benefit of being located in a convenient and established location often makes redevelopment and repositioning of existing resort hotel properties considerably more advantageous than new construction.

Destination resorts in the United States are likely to undergo redevelopment as international competition grows. With the worldwide increase in travel and tourism, foreign visitation and direct competition from resorts in other countries will exert new pressures on existing domestic resorts. In addition, improved access will continue to open up new regions of the world to resort development, in some cases adversely affecting the viability of established resort locations. Thus, to remain competitive, established destination resorts will need constant revitalization and repositioning. And, as the pattern of change quickens, revitalization and repositioning efforts will often need to be undertaken collaboratively by a consortium of resorts within a region to ensure success.

Regional resorts are likely to be redeveloped because of the strong demand among time-pressed households for convenient and affordable resort experiences. In many cases, these resorts are older properties that need to be both preserved and modernized.

Repositioning is also necessary to adapt to changing recreational patterns. The increasing popularity of golf has changed the land plan of many a resort that previously did not offer golf. More recently, the advent of mountain biking, in-line skating, snowboarding, and other recreational pursuits has led resort operators to modify facilities and recreational areas to accommodate these new activities.

Redevelopment may even involve the replacement of existing resort residential units with newer homes. At Amelia Island Plantation in Florida, for example, resort units built over 20 years ago are being demolished and replaced with products that better address the contemporary demands of the marketplace.[45]

In many cases, the redevelopment or repositioning effort may lead to the transformation of a resort into a multiuse resort property. Diversification of real estate and recreational offerings at existing resorts is a major trend that is likely to continue. The addition of timeshares and second homes to resort hotel properties, of resort hotels to second-home communities, and of recreational amenities to all of the above will expand the options available to visitors at many existing resorts in the coming years.

In general, revitalization and repositioning offers strong economic advantages when compared to new development. The track record for new resorts in the United States—especially large-scale ventures—has not always been impressive, and thus there is a strong tendency today for resort developers to focus on acquiring and/or repositioning existing resorts as the most prudent and profitable strategy. Many significant resort properties have been resold several times throughout their active life, often while in severe distress when the selling price was substantially less than the replacement cost. When such properties become available, opportunities exist for savvy investors to obtain a resort property and turn it around for a substantial return. The redevelopment approach seems especially prudent in the mid-1990s, when resorts developed in the late 1980s and early 1990s are being bought for as little as 40 cents on the dollar.

The physical form and legal structure of existing resorts and resort real estate products are certain to continue to evolve in response to changing market demand and other factors. Therefore, it is more important than ever to maintain a competitive edge in today's resort business environment. To remain competitive in the future, however, resort developers and operators will need to monitor closely changing market demand as well as the offerings of both competing resorts and competing forms of recreation and entertainment.

Resorts are by definition interesting and "attractive" places and, in the future, to maintain that attractive quality, astute resort developers and operators must continue to reinvent, redefine, and adapt their properties in an effort to satisfy the needs and desires of the various market segments they serve in a highly competitive domestic and international resort marketplace.

Notes

1. Maggie Mahar, "Eden for Sale: By the Year 2000, demand for second homes should rise sharply," *Barron's*, July 3, 1995, p. 23.
2. Ibid.
3. Ibid.
4. James Chaffin, Presentation entitled "Resort Communities 2010," ULI Fall Meeting, Philadelphia, Penn., October 31–November 4, 1995.
5. Ralph Bowden, "Redefining Resorts," *Urban Land*, August 1995, pp. 25–29, 78–79.
6. Gadi Kaufmann, Presentation entitled "Resort Communities 2010," ULI Fall Meeting, Philadelphia, Penn., October 31–November 4, 1995.
7. Christopher B. Leinberger, "Flexecutives: Redefining the American Dream," *Urban Land*, August 1994, p. 51–54.
8. Bowden, "Redefining Resorts," pp. 25–29.
9. Ibid.
10. Peter Finn, "Getting Away from It All, at Home," *Washington Post*, August 26, 1996, pp. A1, A4.
11. The White House Conference on Travel and Tourism, Advertising Supplement to the *Washington Post*, October 30, 1995.
12. Ibid.
13. Finn, "Getting Away."
14. Bowden, "Redefining Resorts."
15. Air Transport Association of America.
16. U.S. Federal Aviation Administration.
17. *The Industry: An Overview. Marketing Edition* (New York: Cruise Lines International Association, January 1995).
18. Bowden, "Redefining Resorts."
19. Libby Howland, "The Business of Golf," *Urban Land*, August 1994, pp. 45–50, 75–77.
20. Sporting Goods Manufacturers Association, Press release. North Palm Beach, Fla., May 17, 1995.
21. Bowden, "Redefining Resorts."
22. More information about golf and the environment is available from the Golf Course Superintendents Association of America, the USGA Green Section; the American Society of Golf Course Architects; and the National Golf Foundation.
23. National Ski Areas Association, *1993–1994 Economic Analysis of United States Ski Areas* (Lakewood, Col.: author, September 1995), p. 1.
24. Sporting Goods Manufacturers Association, Press release. North Palm Beach, Fla., May 25, 1995.
25. Robert Kunkel, Presentation entitled "The New Sports, Ecotourism, and Their Effect on Resort Real Estate Development," ULI Fall Meeting, Philadelphia, Penn., October 31–November 4, 1995.
26. National Marine Manufacturers Association, as cited in the *Statistical Abstract of the United States 1995*.
27. National Sporting Goods Association, as cited in the *Statistical Abstract of the United States 1995*.
28. Bowden, "Redefining Resorts."
29. J. Richard McElyea, "Hot Amenities in Resorts," *Urban Land*, August 1994, p. 24.
30. Michael S. Rubin and Robert Gorman, "Reinventing Leisure," *Urban Land*, February 1993, pp. 26–32.
31. Thomas Farrell, Hilton Hotel Corporation, speech at ULI Fall Meeting, Los Angeles, Calif., October 24, 1992.
32. M. Chase Burritt and Mark Lunt, "Lodging: A Changed Industry," *Urban Land*, August 1995, pp. 39–43, 82–83.
33. Bowden, "Redefining Resorts."
34. Ed McMullen, Presentation entitled "Resort Communities 2010," ULI Fall Meeting, Philadelphia, Penn., October 31–November 4, 1995.
35. "The Sky's the Limit in Product Development," *Developments*, October 1995, p. 11.
36. Kaufmann, "Resort Communities."
37. Mahar, "Eden for Sale."
38. George Burton Brewster, "A Better Way to Build," *Urban Land*, June 1995, pp. 30–35.
39. Bowden, "Redefining Resorts."
40. Mahar, "Eden for Sale."
41. Bowden, "Redefining Resorts."
42. Personal communication with Harry H. Frampton III, president, East West Partners–Western Division, 1995.
43. Harlan C. Clifford, "High in Colorado Rockies, a Golf-Housing Complex," *New York Times*, August 18, 1996, section 9, p. 7.
44. Personal communication with J. Richard McElyea, Economics Research Associates, 1993.
45. Bowden, "Redefining Resorts."

Index

Index

Note: Italicized page numbers refer to picture and figure captions. Bold page numbers refer to "Profile and Comments."

Casino resorts, 7, 26, **66**, 169, 175–80, 388, 394. *See also specific resort*
Casper, Billy, 52, 80, *80*
Catamaran Hotel (California), 269
Caudle, Theron L. "Pete," 15
Celebration (Florida), 398
Center Parcs Company, 402
Chaffin, James J., Jr., 38, **46**, 382, 396
Chaffin/Light Associates, **46**, **78–79**, *79*
Chamonix, France, 173
Charles E. Fraser Company. *See* Fraser, Charles E.
Charleston, South Carolina, 112
Chase Manhattan Personal Financial Services, 217, 380, 400
Chautauqua (New York), 20
Cheyenne Mountain Conference Resort (Colorado), 260
Chickering, Robert, 87
Circus-Circus Enterprises, 65, 180
Clean Water Act, 113, 127
Cloister (Georgia), 23
Cloister Inn (Florida), 23, 340, 341, 342, *342, 343,* 344
Clowdus, W. Michael, 127–29
Club Corporation of America (CCA), *236,* 254, 400
Club Hotel (France), 28
Club Med, 385
Club Newport (Florida), 197–98
Club Resorts, Inc., *236,* 254, *255,* 263
ClubCorp, 22
Clubhouses, *124,* 125, 147, 160–61, *160. See also specific resort*
Clubs, 153–54, 217, 247–50, *247, 248–49,* **252,** 253–54, *255. See also specific resort or club*
Clustered development, 88–89, *94,* 116–17
Coastal resorts. *See* Waterfront resorts
Coeur d'Alene Resort (Idaho), 173
Coffin, Howard, 23
Colorado: casinos in, 175. *See also* Aspen, Colorado; Vail, Colorado; *specific resort*
Commercial facilities: feasibility analysis for, 77–78, *77,* 79, 90, *101;* and marinas, 143; and market analysis, 61, 64, 67–69; mix of, 172, 173; operations/management of, 236; and outlet centers, 170; planning and design of, 79, 143, 151, 170–75, *171, 174;* principles for success for, 172–74; and technology, 173–74; trends and outlook for, 384. *See also specific resort or type of resort*
Commodore House (Florida), 370, 371–72, 373, *374*
Community associations, 34–35, 49, 217, 231, 239, 240–45, *242,* 247, 250, **252.** *See also specific resort*
Competing expectations: management of, 208, 210, 219, **224,** 253–54
Concept planning, 130–33
Condominiums, 26, **57, 66;** and feasibility analysis, 74; legal issues concerning, 216; pioneering of resort concept for, 218–19; planning and design of, 186, 187; and second homes, 48–49; trends and outlook for, 384, 398
Coney Island (New York), 20

Conference resorts, 294, 394. *See also specific resort*
El Conquistador (Puerto Rico), *188*
Construction, 34, 220; financing for, 103, 107–9
Consultants, 4, 29–30, 214, 215
Convertible club programs, 250
Coore, Bill, 297
Copa, Roberto, 170
Cordillera (Colorado), *34, 163,* 223, 400
Cornish, Geoffrey, 246
Corum Real Estate Group, Inc., 223
Cory, Gregory L., 205
Coto de Caza (California), 165
Cottle, John, 113
Cottle Graybeal Yaw Architects, 113, 363
Cotton Ranch (Colorado), 400
Country Club of the Rockies (Colorado), 400
Courtside Village at Racquet Park (Florida), 165
Crawford-Welch, Simon, 60
Creative Resort Services, 232
Crocker, Charles, 19
Crown family, 363
Cruise industry, 385–86, *386,* 388, 394
Cruise Lines International Association, 386
Cultural activities, 6, 7, 169–70, *169,* 403. *See also specific resort*
Cunningham, Tallman, Pennington, *204*

■
Daufuskie Island, South Carolina, *130, 138,* 139
Davis, Arthur Vining, 340
Davis, Martin, 352
Davis, Robert, 113, 334, 356
Dawes, Charles and Rufus, 340
Deed restrictions, 220, *223*
Deer Valley Resort (Utah), 26, *72,* 170, 196
Deering Bay (Florida), *35, 134*
Del Monte Forest (California), 352, 354, 355–56, 357, 359
Del Monte Hotel (California), 19, 20, 352
Del Monte Properties Company, 19, 352
Del Webb (Arizona), **16**
Del Webb Corporation, 52–53, 80
Demographic data, 38–41, **43,** 44, 214, 228, 260; and trends and outlook, 379, 380, 382, 386
Desert Highlands (Arizona), **120,** 121–22, 123–25, *123, 124,* **132,** 328, 331, 332
Desert Inn (Nevada), 24
Desert Island, California, *383*
Desert Mountain (Arizona), **120**
Desert resorts, 121–22. *See also specific resort*
Desert Springs Marriott (California), *9,* **32,** 63
Design Workshop, Inc., 363
Destination resorts, **33, 62,** 136–37; case studies about, 274–303; characteristics of, 4–5; and feasibility analysis, 82–83; hotel resorts as, 8, 236; mountain/ski resorts as, 6; multi-use, 274–303; ocean resorts as, 6; operations/ management of, 203, 254; repositioning of, 403; and site selection, 82–83; trends and outlook for, 385, 400, 402, 403. *See also specific resort or location*

Developers: characteristics of, **46;** defining business of, 78; dreams/visions of, **132, 235;** as general contractors, 34; homeowners' relationship with, 231; and operations/ management, 201; role and functions of, 4, 27– 30, 73, 201; training of, **17, 79.** *See also specific person, corporation, resort, or topic*
Development program, **16–17,** 27–30, 34–35, 71–81, **209.** *See also specific step*
Development team, 27–30, *30,* **43,** 214, 403
Dewees Island (South Carolina), 12, 114, 119, 138, 139, 207; case study about, 320–27; pictures of, *119, 206, 321, 322, 323, 324, 325;* project data about, *327*
Dewey Beach, Delaware, 167
Diamondhead Corporation, 22
Discount packages, 62–63
Disney, 58, **62,** 374; Fraser's comments about, **17;** and timeshares, 26, **29;** tourist villages of, 174–75
Disney, Walt, 23
Disney Adventure Vacations, 374
Disney Design and Development Company, **386–87**
Disney Development Company, 190, **386**
Disney Institute (Florida), 206–7, 383
Disney Vacation Club (DVC), *10, 29,* 196–97, *196,* 198, 228, 229, 288, 370, 373, 374–75, **386.** *See also specific resort*
Disney World (Florida), 6, 83, 138, 169, 190, *191,* 229, *234, 388,* 398. *See also* Disney's Old Key West Resort at Walt Disney World (Florida)
Disneyland, 23
Disney's Dolphin Hotel (Florida), 9–10, 190
Disney's Grand Floridian Resort (Florida), *191, 388*
Disney's Hilton Head Island Resort (South Carolina), *29*
Disney's Old Key West Resort at Walt Disney World (Florida), *68, 174, 196, 230,* 370–77, *371, 372, 373, 376, 377*
Disney's Swan Hotel (Florida), 9–10, 190
Disney's Vero Beach Resort (Florida), *196*
Divide (Colorado), 118, *118*
Dorado Beach (Puerto Rico), 25
Duany, Andres, 113, 334

■
Eager, William R., 136, 137
Eagle Crest Partners, Ltd., 210–11
Eagle Crest Resort (Oregon), 210–11
East West Partners, 107, *252,* 288, 382, 400
Eastern Michigan University (EMU), 383
Eastlake Country Club (California), **32**
Ecclestone, E. Llwyd, 158
Economics Research Associates, 75, 87, 205, 400
Ecotels, 262, 265
Ecotourism, 392, **392–93,** 394, 398, 403
Ecotourism Society, 392
Educational and activity programming, 205–7, *206,* 383
Embassy Suites (Florida), 265
English Turn Golf & Country Club (Louisiana), *162*
English Turn Tennis Center (Louisiana), *162*

National Sporting Goods Association, 41, 162
Natural-attraction resorts, 6, 23. *See also specific resort*
Nature-based recreation, 168–69
Negroponte, Nicolas, 227
"Nesting" trend, 384
New Horizon Kids' Quest, 179
New Seabury (Massachusetts), 25
New York-New York (Nevada), 180
Newport, Rhode Island, 20, 22
Niche marketing strategies, 226, 229
Nicklaus, Jack, *120*, 123, *123*, 125, **208**, 278
Nippon Landic, 108
Nonprofit development corporations, 223–24
Nonprofit tax-exempt corporations, 239, 240
Northstar at Tahoe (California), 25

■

Occupancy: of hotel resorts, 234; and time-share-hotel partnerships, 232–33
Ocean City, Maryland, 26, 119
Ocean Club (Bahamas), 267
Ocean Grove, New Jersey, 20
Ocean resorts. *See* Waterfront resorts; *specific resort*
Off-premise contacts (OPCs), 225, 226, 228, 229, 395
Office of Interstate Land Sales Registration (OILSR), 24, 216
Old Faithful Lodge (Yellowstone National Park), 23
Olmsted, Frederick Law, 22
Omni Classic Resort, 21
Open space, 168–69
Operations/management: of amenities, 201, 202, 217, **224**, 254–60; comments about, **62**, **208–9**, **224**, **235**; of competing expecta-tions, 208, 210, 219, **224**, 253–54; contract-ed, 255, 256, 257, 259; developer's role in, 201; and educational and activity program-ming, 205–7, *206*; and environmental issues, *205*, *206*, *207*; and feasibility analysis, 76, 81, 89–90, *96*; and financing, 106; general issues in, 201–8, 210–11; and golf, 89–90, 202, *202*, 208; and image/reputation of resorts, 202, 203, **209**; and joint ventures, 76, *76*; and overview of development program, 34–35; of rental programs, 217, 218– 19, *219*, 230–31; and second home, 48, 49; special problems in, **209**; specialized, 35, 201; team approach to, **209**; and technology, 232; and timeshare-hotel partnerships, 232. *See also* Community associations; Marketing; *specific resort or type of resort*
Opinion Research Corporation, 380
Orange Tree Resort (Arizona), 198, 227
Orlando, Florida, 83, 388. *See also specific resort*
Outer Banks Resort Rentals, 230
Ownership: fee-simple, 195, 395; fixed-interval, 195, 395; key characteristics of, *195*; key fac-tors affecting success of, *198*; and operations/management, 231–32; pros and cons of point-based, *197*; right-to-use, 195; of time-shares, 194–99, *197*, 231–32; and UCIOA, 129. *See also* Community associations

■

Pacific Grove (California), 20
Pacific Improvement Company, 19
Packaged vacations, **66**, 236
Paepcke, Walter, 24
Palm Beach, Florida, 22–23. *See also specific resort*
Palm Beach Gardens, Florida, *126*, 127. *See also* PGA National
Palm Beach Polo and Country Club (Florida), 25, 26, *165*, 166
Palm Court Club (Florida), 340
Palm Hills Golf Resort and Spa (Japan), *401*
Palm Springs, California, 54. *See also specific resort*
Palm Valley Country Club (California), **32**
Palmas del Mar (Puerto Rico), **16**, 25–26, **46**, *269*
Palmetto Dunes (South Carolina), 144
Paparazzo, Henry J., 246
Paris Casino Resort (Nevada), 180
Park Creek (Utah), 151
Parking, 137, 151–52, 187–88
Partnerships: with hospitality companies, 232–34
Partnerships. *See* Joint ventures
Patio houses, 183, 185
Pebble Beach, California, 6, 19, 400. *See also specific resort*
Pebble Beach Company, 19, 26, 352, 355, 356, 357, 358, 359
Pebble Beach Equestrian Center (California), 354
Pebble Beach Resort (California), 67, *67*, 143
Pelican Bay (Florida): amenities at, 143, 169–70, *169*; commercial facilities at, *14*, 77, *171*; and history of resorts, 25; housing at, *14*; as multiuse resort, *14*; operations/management of, *207*; planning and design of, 114, 116, *116*, 119, 121, 143, 169–70, *169*, *171*, 190
The Peninsula (North Carolina), *13*
Peppertree Corporation, 226, 229
Permanent financing, 103
Permar, Diana, 44
PGA of America, 106
PGA National (Florida): financing of, 106–7, *106*; master plan for, *159*; operations/man-agement of, 253, *254*; planning and design of, 114, 116, *117*, *126*, 127, 157, 158–59, *158*, *159*, 162, 189; sites for, *106*, 189; tennis facilities at, 162
PGA National Venture, Ltd., 106
PGA West (California), 26, **32**
Phasing and timing of development, 79–81, **209**
Philharmonic Center for the Arts (Florida), *169*, 170
Phoenician Resort (Arizona), 168
Pine Mountain (Georgia), 168, 170
Pinehurst Resort and Country Club (North Carolina), 20, 22, *22*, 112, 157, *157*, *162*, 254
Piper Dunes (Florida), 188
Pirate's Cove (North Carolina), *142*
Planned community district (PCD), *126*, 127
Planned unit development (PUD), *25*, 116–17, *126*, 127, 277, 282, 286, 290

Planning and design: of amenities, 161–65, 167–68, *167*, 169–80, *169*; and approval process, 134, *142*; of commercial facilities, 143, 151, 170–75, *171*, 174–75; and concept planning, 130–33; of desert resorts, 121–22; of entertainment facilities, 172–75; and en-vironmental issues, 113–14, *118*, 119, *119*, *142*, 154, 155, 189; and final planning, 135, 137; and financing, 103; of golf courses, 121, *123*, 143, 152–61, *153*, *154*, 155–57, *156*, *157*; of housing, 180–88, *182*, *183*, *184*, *186*, *187*; of infrastructure, 137–43, *141*; of mari-nas, 143–47, *146*; of mountain sites, 117–18; and positioning, 114, 116–17, 190; and pre-liminary planning, 133–35; and regulatory issues, 126–29, 192; of sites, 111–14, 116–19, 121–22, 181–82; and technology, 150, 173–74; of transportation, 136–39, *136*, *138*, *139*, *140*; of utilities, 137, 139–41, 143; of water-front sites, 119, 121, 143–47, *146*. *See also* Master plan; *specific resort*
Plater-Zyberk, Elizabeth, 113, 334
Player, Gary, 278
Pocono Manor (Pennsylvania), 22
Polo Towers (Nevada), 228
Ponce de Leon (Florida), 20
Port de Plaisance (St. Martin), *147*
Positioning: Anderson's comments about, **120**; and feasibility analysis, *47*; of hotel resorts, 190, 394; and operations and man-agement, 260–71; and planning and design issues, 114, 116–17, 190; trends and outlook for, 388, 400, 403–4
Preferred Chain of Hotels, 238, *238*
Preliminary planning, 133–35
Preretirement buyers, 51, 54
Presales planning, 202, 203
The Preserve (Delaware), 82, *83*, 182–83, *183*
Presidential Place (Florida), **57**
Pricing, **33**, **133**
Primadonna Resorts, 180
Primary homes, 54, **57**, **120**, 157, 168, 250, 384, 397
Princeville Resort (Hawaii), 169
Professional Golfers Association of America (PGA), 158, 159, 347
Project managers: developers as, 28
Promotion, 202, 203, 226, 257–58
Psychographics, 38–41, **43**, 44, 214, 228, 260; and trends and outlook, 379, 380, 382, 394
Public lands, 150–51, 221
Public policy, 126
Public relations, 15, 202, 203, 211, *211*, 257
Public sector: role of, 4
Puerto Rico, 126. *See also specific resort*
Puerto Rico Tourism Company, 104
Puget Western, Inc., 192, 194

■

Quail Hollow Resort & Country Club (Ohio), 254
Quail Lodge Resort & Golf Club (California), 168, 189
Quebec, Canada, 172
Quick Time Virtual Reality, 228

Ventana Canyon Resort (Arizona), *121*, 122, 190, **208**, *209*, **209**
Ventana Inn (California), 9, 140
Vero Beach Resort (Florida), *10*
Vic Braden Tennis College, 165
Victoria (Nevada), 180
Vintage Club (California), 122
Virginia Hot Springs Co., Inc., 263
Virginia Investment Trusts (VIT), 275, 278
Virtual reality, 227, 228
VMS Realty Corporation, 340, 341

■

Wachesaw Plantation (South Carolina), *113, 160*
Wade, John, 15
Waikoloa, Hawaii, 25
Wailea Four Seasons Resort Hotel (Hawaii), *36*, 113, *115*, 116, 138, *140*, 190
Wakena Resort (Hawaii), 190
Walt Disney Company, **57**, 370, 373, **386**
Walt Disney hotel resorts: 9–10
Walt Disney Imagineering, **386**
Warren, E. Burgess, 21
Washington (state), 126. *See also specific resort*
Wastewater, 140–41, *141*, 143
Water provisions, 140
Waterfront resorts: characteristics of, 5–6; as destination resorts, 6; hotel resorts as, 189, 190; housing for, 188; planning and design of, 119, 121, 143–47, 188. *See also specific resort*
Watersports, 391–92. *See also specific sport*
Wesleyan Grove Retreat (Massachusetts), 20
Westgate Factors, 218, 219
Westin: and timeshares, 29
Westin Kauai at Kauai Lagoons (Hawaii), 269
Westin Maui (Hawaii), 162
Westin Rio Mar Beach Resort and Country Club (Puerto Rico), 104–5, *104*
Wheeler, Jerome B., 20
Whistler (British Columbia), *152*, 172, 173–74
White Sulphur Springs (West Virginia), 20
Whitetail Ski Resort and Mountain Biking Center (Pennsylvania), 148
Wholesale markets, 61, 62–63
Wilberly Allison Tong & Goo, 267
Williamsburg, Virginia, *5*, 6–7, *7*
Willowbend Corporation, 104, 105
Wilson, Dick, 267
Wilson Miller Capital Corporation, **42**
Windsor (Florida), *50*, *131*, 398
Winter sports, 390–91. *See also specific sport*
Wintergreen (Virginia), 8, **46**, *151*
Wirthlin Worldwide, 384
Wit's End Guest Ranch and Resort (Colorado), 166–67
Wolgin, Norman, 21
Women's Tennis Association (WTA), 162
Woodlake, **252**
Woodrun Place (Colorado), *70*
Woodstock Inn and Resort (Vermont), 112

Work and leisure, 383–84
Workouts, 109
World Wide Web, 205, 226, 227, 382–83
Wright, Frank Lloyd, 23, 346, *347*, *348*

■

Xeriscaping, 122

■

Yarmouth Group, 260

■

Zmistowsky, William, 124, *124*, 125